INTRODUCTION TO
ENGINEERING
TECHNOLOGY
BMET · CET · EET

Taken from:

Starting Out with Programming Logic & Design
by Tony Gaddis

Digital Fundamentals, Ninth Edition
by Thomas L. Floyd

Electronics Fundamentals, Sixth Edition
by Thomas L. Floyd

Principles of Electric Circuits, Conventional Current Version, Eighth Edition
by Thomas L. Floyd

Custom Publishing

New York   Boston   San Francisco
London   Toronto   Sydney   Tokyo   Singapore   Madrid
Mexico City   Munich   Paris   Cape Town   Hong Kong   Montreal

Cover Art: Courtesy of EyeWire/Getty Images.

Taken from:

Starting Out with Programming Logic & Design
by Tony Gaddis
Copyright © 2008 by Pearson Education, Inc.
Published by Addison-Wesley
Boston, Massachusetts 02116

Digital Fundamentals, Ninth Edition
by Thomas L. Floyd
Copyright © 2006, 2003, 2000, 1997, 1994, 1990, 1986, 1982, 1977 by Pearson Education, Inc.
Published by Prentice Hall
Upper Saddle River, New Jersey 07458

Electronics Fundamentals: Circuits, Devices, and Applications, Sixth Edition
by Thomas L. Floyd
Copyright © 2004, 2001, 1998, 1995, 1991, 1987 by Pearson Education, Inc.
Published by Prentice Hall

Principles of Electric Circuits, Conventional Current Version, Eighth Edition
by Thomas L. Floyd
Copyright © 2007, 2003, 2000, 1997, 1993, 1989, 1985, 1981 by Pearson Education, Inc.
Published by Prentice Hall

Printed in the United States of America

10 9 8 7 6 5 4 3

2008360474

KW

Pearson
Custom Publishing
is a division of

www.personhighered.com

ISBN 10: 0-536-36718-3
ISBN 13: 978-0-536-36718-1

Contents

Preface

Introduction to Engineering Technology—BMET, CET, and EET

Introduction to Engineering Technology presents engineering technology students with selected introductory material explaining digital and analog circuits, as well as computer programming basics. This customized text, tailored for DeVry University students, combines material taken from three separate textbooks authored by Thomas Floyd and Tony Gaddis.

The custom text covers fundamental principles and applications for basic electric circuits as presented by Floyd. The DC chapters cover basic electrical concepts and material up to and including series and parallel circuits. The digital electronic chapters cover basic information on combinational digital circuitry, from Boolean algebra through simple digital circuit design. The material from these two segments serves as a valuable resource for a beginning engineering technology students as they progress into their electronics fundamentals courses.

The third segment of the text covers programming concepts presented by Gaddis. The material includes logic development methodologies used in programming courses in an easy to understand manner. This segment of the text prepares the beginning students for their upcoming programming courses.

DeVry University welcomes you into your chosen program in engineering technology. Your field of study can lead to an exciting career upon graduation. Congratulations on making the decision to study engineering technology!

1

COMPONENTS, QUANTITIES, AND UNITS

INTRODUCTION

The topics in this chapter present a basic introduction to the field of electronics. An overview of electrical and electronic components and instruments gives you a preview of the types of things you will study throughout this book.

You must be familiar with the units used in electronics and know how to express electrical quantities in various ways using metric prefixes. Scientific notation and engineering notation are indispensable tools whether you use a computer, a calculator, or do computations the old-fashioned way.

CHAPTER OBJECTIVES

- Recognize some common electrical components and measuring instruments
- State basic electrical and magnetic quantities and their units
- Use scientific notation (powers of ten) to express quantities
- Use engineering notation and metric prefixes to express large and small quantities
- Convert from one metric-prefixed unit to another

CHAPTER OUTLINE

KEY TERMS

- Resistor
- Capacitor
- Inductor
- Transformer
- DC power supply
- Function generator
- Digital multimeter
- Oscilloscope
- Scientific notation
- Power of ten
- Exponent
- Engineering notation
- Metric prefix

WWW. VISIT THE COMPANION WEBSITE

Study aids for this chapter are available at
http://www.prenhall.com/floyd

1-1 ELECTRICAL COMPONENTS AND MEASURING INSTRUMENTS

A thorough background in dc and ac circuit fundamentals provides the foundation for understanding electronic devices and circuits. In this book, you will study many types of electrical components and measuring instruments. A preview of the basic types of electrical and electronic components and instruments that you will be studying in detail in this and in other courses is provided in this section.

After completing this section, you should be able to

- **Recognize some common electrical components and measuring instruments**
- State the basic purpose of a resistor
- State the basic purpose of a capacitor
- State the basic purpose of an inductor
- State the basic purpose of a transformer
- List some basic types of electronic measuring instruments

Resistors

Resistors* resist, or limit, electrical current in a circuit. Several common types of resistors are shown in Figure 1–1 through Figure 1–4.

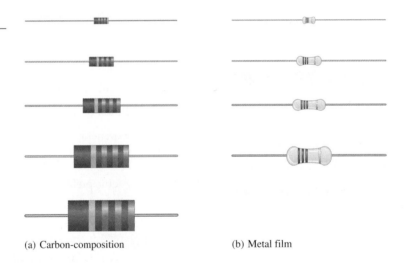

(a) Carbon-composition (b) Metal film

(a) Metal film chip resistor (b) Chip resistor array (c) Resistor network (simm) (d) Resistor network (surface mount)

▲ **FIGURE 1–2**

Chip resistor and resistor networks.

---

* The bold terms in color are key terms and are also defined at the end of the chapter.

(a) Axial-lead wirewound

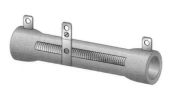

(b) Adjustable wirewound

(c) Radial-lead for PC board insertion

(d) Surface m

▲ **FIGURE 1–3**

Common types of power resistors.

(a) Lead mounted

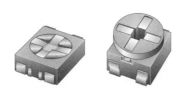

(b) Surface mounted

◀ **FIGURE 1–4**

Common types of variable resistors.

Capacitors

Capacitors store electrical charge and are used to block dc and pass ac. Figure 1–5 and Figure 1–6 show several typical capacitors. Electrolytic capacitors have plus and minus or other markings, indicating that they are polarized.

Inductors

Inductors, also known as *coils,* are used to store energy in an electromagnetic field; they serve many useful functions in an electrical circuit. Figure 1–7 shows several typical inductors.

Transformers

Transformers are used to couple ac voltages from one point in a circuit to another, or to increase or decrease the ac voltage. Several types of transformers are shown in Figure 1–8.

Semiconductor Devices

Several varieties of diodes, transistors, and integrated circuits are shown in Figure 1–9. A wide selection of packages are used for semiconductor devices, depending on the function and the power requirements.

▷ **FIGURE 1–5**

Common types of fixed capacitors.

(a) Electrolytic, axial-lead, and surface mount

(b) Ceramic, axial-lead, and surface mount

(c) Film, axial-lead, and chip

▷ **FIGURE 1–6**

Typical variable capacitors.

▷ **FIGURE 1–7**

Some fixed and variable inductors.

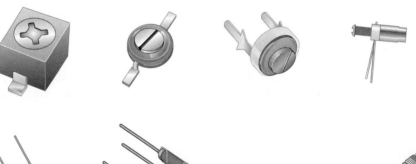

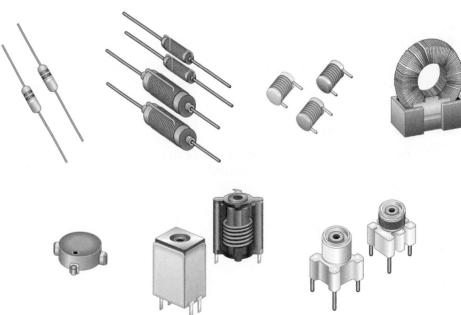

▲ FIGURE 1–8

Typical transformers.

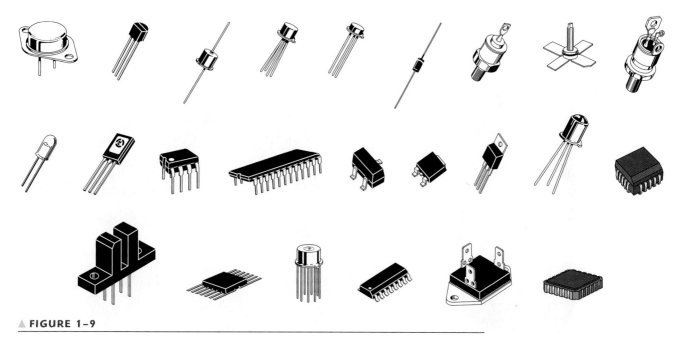

▲ FIGURE 1–9

An assortment of semiconductor devices.

Electronic Instruments

Figure 1–10 shows four basic electronic instruments found on the typical laboratory work-bench and which will be discussed throughout the book. These instruments include the **dc power supply** for providing current and voltage to power electronic circuits, the **function generator** for providing electronic signals, the **digital multimeter** (DMM) with its voltmeter, ammeter, and ohmmeter functions for measuring voltage, current, and resistance, respectively, and the **oscilloscope** for observing and measuring ac voltages.

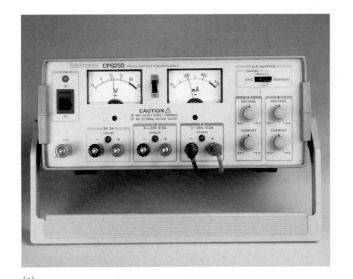

(a)

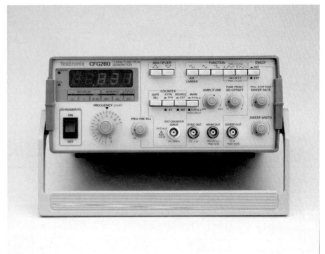

(b)

(c)

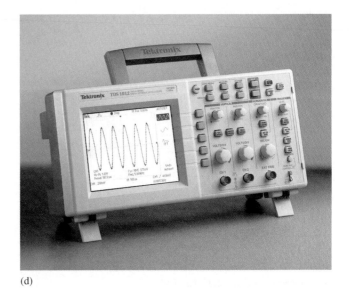

(d)

▲ FIGURE 1–10

Typical instruments. (a) DC power supply; (b) Function generator; (c) Digital multimeter; (Photography courtesy of B&K Precision Corp.) (d) Digital storage oscilloscope. ((a), (b), and (d) Copyright © Tektronix, Inc. Reproduced with permission.)

1–2 ELECTRICAL AND MAGNETIC UNITS

In electronics, you must deal with measurable quantities. For example, you must be able to express how many volts are measured at a certain test point in a circuit, how much current there is through a conductor, or how much power a certain amplifier delivers. In this section, you are introduced to the units and symbols for most of the electrical and magnetic quantities that are used throughout the book. Definitions of these and other quantities are presented as they are needed in later chapters.

After completing this section, you should be able to

■ **State basic electrical and magnetic quantities and their units**

■ Specify the symbol for each quantity

■ Specify the symbol for each unit

Letter symbols are used in electronics to represent both quantities and their units. One symbol is used to represent the name of the quantity, and another is used to represent the unit of measurement of that quantity. For example, *P* stands for *power,* and *W* stands for *watt,* which is the unit of power. Table 1–1 lists the most important electrical quantities, along with their SI units and symbols. These will be used throughout the text. The term *SI* is the French abbreviation for *International System (SystËme International* in French). Table 1–2 lists the magnetic quantities with their SI units and symbols.

QUANTITY	SYMBOL	UNIT	SYMBOL
capacitance	*C*	farad	F
charge	*Q*	coulomb	C
conductance	*G*	siemens	S
current	*I*	ampere	A
energy	*W*	joule	J
frequency	*f*	hertz	Hz
impedance	*Z*	ohm	Ω
inductance	*L*	henry	H
power	*P*	watt	W
reactance	*X*	ohm	Ω
resistance	*R*	ohm	Ω
voltage	*V*	volt	V

◀ TABLE 1–1

Electrical quantities and their corresponding units with SI symbols.

QUANTITY	SYMBOL	UNIT	SYMBOL
flux density	*B*	tesla	T
magnetic flux	*ϕ*	weber	Wb
magnetizing force	*H*	ampere-turns/meter	At/m
magnetomotive force	F_m	ampere-turn	At
permeability	*μ*	webers/ampere-turns-meter	Wb/Atm
reluctance	*ℛ*	ampere-turns/weber	At/Wb

◀ TABLE 1–2

Magnetic quantities and their corresponding units with SI symbols.

1–3   SCIENTIFIC NOTATION

In the electrical and electronics fields, you will find both very small and very large quantities. For example, electrical current can range from hundreds of amperes in power applications to a few thousandths or millionths of an ampere in many electronic circuits. For resistive quantities, a wire may have less than one ohm of resistance whereas resistance values of several million ohms are common in circuit applications. This range of values is typical of many other electrical quantities also.

After completing this section, you should be able to

■ **Use scientific notation (powers of ten) to express quantities**

■ Express any number using a power of ten

■ Do calculations with powers of ten

Scientific notation provides a convenient method for expressing large and small numbers and for performing calculations involving such numbers. In scientific notation, a quantity is expressed as a product of a number between 1 and 10 (one digit to the left of the decimal point) and a power of ten. For example, the quantity 150,000 is expressed in scientific notation as 1.5×10^5, and the quantity 0.00022 is expressed as $2.2\ 3 \times 10^{-4}$.

Powers of Ten

Table 1–3 lists some powers of ten, both positive and negative, and the corresponding decimal numbers. The **power of ten** is expressed as an *exponent* of the *base* 10 in each case.

$$\underset{\text{Base}}{\searrow}\ 10^{\underset{\text{Exponent}}{\swarrow} x}$$

The **exponent** indicates the number of places that the decimal point is moved to the right or left to produce the decimal number. If the power of ten is positive, move the decimal point to the right to get the equivalent decimal number. As an example, for an exponent of 4,

$$10^4 = 1 \times 10^4 = 1.0000. = 10,000.$$

If the power of ten is negative, move the decimal point to the left to get the equivalent decimal number. As an example, for an exponent of

$$10^{-4} = 1 \times 10^{-4} = .0001. = 0.0001$$

The negative exponent does not make a number negative; it simply moves the decimal point to the left.

▶ **TABLE 1–3**

Some positive and negative powers of ten.

$10^6 = 1,000,000$	$10^{-6} = 0.000001$
$10^5 = 100,000$	$10^{-5} = 0.00001$
$10^4 = 10,000$	$10^{-4} = 0.0001$
$10^3 = 1,000$	$10^{-3} = 0.001$
$10^2 = 100$	$10^{-2} = 0.01$
$10^1 = 10$	$10^{-1} = 0.1$
$10^0 = 1$	

EXAMPLE 1–1

Express each number in scientific notation:

(a) 200   (b) 5000   (c) 85,000   (d) 3,000,000

Solution   In each case, move the decimal point an appropriate number of places to the left to determine the positive power of ten.

(a) $200 = 2 \times 10^2$ (b) $5000 = 5 \times 10^3$

(c) $85,000 = 8.5 \times 10^4$ (d) $3,000,000 = 3 \times 10^6$

Related Problem   Express 750,000,000 in scientific notation.

EXAMPLE 1–2

Express each number in scientific notation:

(a) 0.2　　(b) 0.005　　(c) 0.00063　　(d) 0.000015

Solution　In each case, move the decimal point an appropriate number of places to the right to determine the negative power of ten.

(a) $0.2 = 2 \times 10^{-1}$　　　　(b) $0.005 = 5 \times 10^{-3}$

(c) $0.00063 = 6.3 \times 10^{-4}$　　(d) $0.000015 = 1.5 \times 10^{-5}$

Related Problem　Express 0.00000093 in scientific notation.

EXAMPLE 1–3

Express each of the following numbers as a normal decimal number:

(a) 1×10^5　　(b) 2×10^3　　(c) 3.2×10^{-2}　　(d) 2.5×10^{-6}

Solution　Move the decimal point to the right or left a number of places indicated by the positive or the negative power of ten respectively.

(a) $1 \times 10^5 = 100,000$　　　(b) $2 \times 10^3 = 2000$

(c) $3.2 \times 10^{-2} = 0.032$　　(d) $2.5 \times 10^{-6} = 0.0000025$

Related Problem　Express 8.2×10^8 as a normal decimal number.

Calculations Using Powers of Ten

The advantage of scientific notation is in addition, subtraction, multiplication, and division of very small or very large numbers.

Addition　The steps for adding numbers in powers of ten are as follows:

1. Express the numbers to be added in the same power of ten.
2. Add the numbers without their powers of ten to get the sum.
3. Bring down the common power of ten, which is the power of ten of the sum.

EXAMPLE 1–4

Add 2×10^6 and 5×10^7 and express the result in scientific notation.

Solution
1. Express both numbers in the same power of ten: $(2 \times 10^6) + (50 \times 10^6)$
2. Add $2 + 50 = 52$.
3. Bring down the common power of ten (10^6) and the sum is $52 \times 10^6 = 5.2 \times 10^7$.

Related Problem　Add 4.1×10^3 and 7.9×10^2.

Subtraction   The steps for subtracting numbers in powers of ten are as follows:

1. Express the numbers to be subtracted in the same power of ten.

2. Subtract the numbers without their powers of ten to get the difference.

3. Bring down the common power of ten, which is the power of ten of the difference.

EXAMPLE 1–5

Subtract 2.5×10^{-12} from 7.5×10^{-11} and express the result in scientific notation.

Solution   1. Express each number in the same power of ten:
$(7.5 \times 10^{-11}) - (0.25 \times 10^{-11})$

2. Subtract $7.5 - 0.25 = 7.25$.

3. Bring down the common power of ten (10^{-11}) and the difference is
7.25×10^{-11}.

Related Problem   Subtract 3.5×10^{-6} from 2.2×10^{-5}.

Multiplication   The steps for multiplying numbers in powers of ten are as follows:

1. Multiply the numbers directly without their powers of ten.

2. Add the powers of ten algebraically (the powers do not have to be the same).

EXAMPLE 1–6

Multiply 5×10^{12} by 3×10^{-6} and express the result in scientific notation.

Solution   Multiply the numbers, and algebraically add the powers.

$$(5 \times 10^{12})(3 \times 10^{-6}) = 15 \times 10^{12+(-6)} = 15 \times 10^{6} = \mathbf{1.5 \times 10^{7}}$$

Related Problem   Multiply 1.2×10^{3} by 4×10^{2}.

Division   The steps for dividing numbers in powers of ten are as follows:

1. Divide the numbers directly without their powers of ten.

2. Subtract the power of ten in the denominator from the power of ten in the numerator (the powers do not have to be the same).

EXAMPLE 1–7

Divide 5.0×10^{8} by 2.5×10^{3} and express the result in scientific notation.

Solution   The division problem is written with a numerator and denominator.

$$\frac{5.0 \times 10^{8}}{2.5 \times 10^{3}}$$

Divide the numbers and subtract 3 from 8.

$$\frac{5.0 \times 10^8}{2.5 \times 10^3} = 2 \times 10^{8-3} = \mathbf{2 \times 10^5}$$

Related Problem   Divide 8×10^{-6} by 2×10^{-10}.

Scientific Notation on a Calculator

Throughout this textbook, the calculator examples are based on the TI-86 calculator. Other calculators are similar but may differ in some functions.

Entering a Number in Scientific Notation   There are two ways to enter a number in scientific notation.

1. *Mode screen*   Select **Sci** on the Mode screen. When you enter a number, it is automatically converted to scientific notation.

2. *EE key*   Enter the number with one digit to the left of the decimal point, press EE, and enter the power of ten. This method requires that the power of ten be determined before entering the number.

EXAMPLE 1–8

Enter the number 23,560 using the Sci mode.

Solution   Call up the Mode screen with the following key sequence and use the right arrow key to select **Sci:**

Exit the Mode screen: [EXIT]

Enter the number: [2] [3] [5] [6] [0]

Press [ENTER]

    23560
        2.356e4

    Scientific notation

Related Problem   Use the Sci mode to enter the number 150,968 in scientific notation.

EXAMPLE 1–9

Enter 23,560 (same number as in Example 1–8) in scientific notation using the EE key.

Solution   Move the decimal point four places to the left so that it comes after the digit 2. This results in the number expressed in scientific notation as

$$2.3560 \times 10^4$$

Enter this number on your calculator as follows:

[2] [.] [3] [5] [6] [0] [EE] [4]   2.3560E4

Related Problem   Enter the number 573,946 using the EE key.

1–4   ENGINEERING NOTATION AND METRIC PREFIXES

Engineering notation is a specialized form of scientific notation. It is used widely in technical fields to express large and small quantities. In electronics, engineering notation is used to express values of voltage, current, power, resistance, capacitance, inductance, and time, to name a few. Metric prefixes are used in conjunction with engineering notation as a "shorthand" for the certain powers of ten that are used.

After completing this section, you should be able to

- **Use engineering notation and metric prefixes to express large and small quantities**
- List the metric prefixes
- Change a power of ten in engineering notation to a metric prefix
- Use metric prefixes to express electrical quantities
- Enter numbers in engineering notation into your calculator
- Convert one metric prefix to another

Engineering Notation

Engineering notation is similar to scientific notation. However, in **engineering notation** a number can have from one to three digits to the left of the decimal point and the power-of-ten exponent must be a multiple of three. For example, the number 33,000 expressed in engineering notation is 33×10^3. In scientific notation, it is expressed as 3.3×10^4. As another example, the number 0.045 is expressed in engineering notation as 45×10^{-3}. In scientific notation, it is expressed as 4.5×10^{-2}.

EXAMPLE 1–10

Express the following numbers in engineering notation:

(a) 82,000

(b) 243,000

(c) 1,956,000

Solution   In engineering notation,

(a) 82,000 is expressed as $\mathbf{82 \times 10^3}$.

(b) 243,000 is expressed as $\mathbf{243 \times 10^3}$.

(c) 1,956,319 is expressed as $\mathbf{1.956 \times 10^6}$.

Related Problem   Express 36,000,000,000 in engineering notation.

EXAMPLE 1–11

Convert each of the following numbers to engineering notation:

(a) 0.0022   (b) 0.000000047   (c) 0.00033

Solution In engineering notation,

(a) 0.0022 is expressed as $\mathbf{2.2 \times 10^{-3}}$.   (b) 0.000000047 is expressed as $\mathbf{47 \times 10^{-9}}$.

(c) 0.00033 is expressed as $\mathbf{330 \times 10^{-6}}$.

Related Problem Express 0.0000000000056 in engineering notation.

Metric Prefixes

Metric prefixes are symbols that represent each of the most commonly used powers of ten in engineering notation. These metric prefixes are listed in Table 1–4 with their designations.

METRIC PREFIX	SYMBOL	POWER OF TEN	VALUE
pico	p	10^{-12}	one-trillionth
nano	n	10^{-9}	one-billionth
micro	μ	10^{-6}	one-millionth
milli	m	10^{-3}	one-thousandth
kilo	k	10^{3}	one thousand
mega	M	10^{6}	one million
giga	G	10^{9}	one billion
tera	T	10^{12}	one trillion

◄ **TABLE 1–4**

Metric prefixes with their symbols and corresponding powers of ten and values.

A metric prefix is used to replace the power of ten in a number that is expressed in engineering notation. Metric prefixes are used only with numbers that have a unit of measure, such as volts, amperes, and ohms, and are placed preceding the unit symbol. For example, 0.025 amperes can be expressed as 25×10^{-3} A. This quantity is expressed using a metric prefix as 25 mA, which is read 25 milliamps. Note that the metric prefix *milli* has replaced 10^{-3}. As another example, 100,000,000 ohms can be expressed as 100×10^{6} Ω. This quantity is expressed using a metric prefix as 100 MΩ, which is read 100 megohms. The metric prefix *mega* has replaced 10^{6}.

EXAMPLE 1–12

Express each quantity using an appropriate metric prefix:

(a) 50,000 V   (b) 25,000,000 Ω   (c) 0.000036 A

Solution (a) $50{,}000 \text{ V} = 50 \times 10^{3} \text{ V} = \mathbf{50 \text{ kV}}$ (b) $25{,}000{,}000 \text{ } \Omega = 25 \times 10^{6} \text{ } \Omega = \mathbf{25 \text{ M}\Omega}$

(c) $0.000036 \text{ A} = 36 \times 10^{-6} \text{ A} = \mathbf{36 \text{ } \mu\text{A}}$

Related Problem Express each quantity using appropriate metric prefixes:

(a) 56,000,000 Ω   (b) 0.000470 A

Engineering Notation on a Calculator

As previously mentioned, the calculator examples in this textbook are based on the TI-86 calculator. Other calculators are similar but may differ in some functions.

Entering a Number in Engineering Notation   There are two ways to enter a number in engineering notation, similar to the methods for scientific notation.

1. *Mode screen*   Select **Eng** on the Mode screen. When you enter a number, it is automatically converted to engineering notation.

2. *EE key*   Enter the number with one, two, or three digits to the left of the decimal point, press EE, and enter the power of ten that is a multiple of three. This method requires that the appropriate power of ten be determined before entering the number.

EXAMPLE 1–13

Enter the number 75,200 using the Eng mode.

Solution   Call up the Mode screen with the following key sequence and use the right arrow key to select **Eng:**

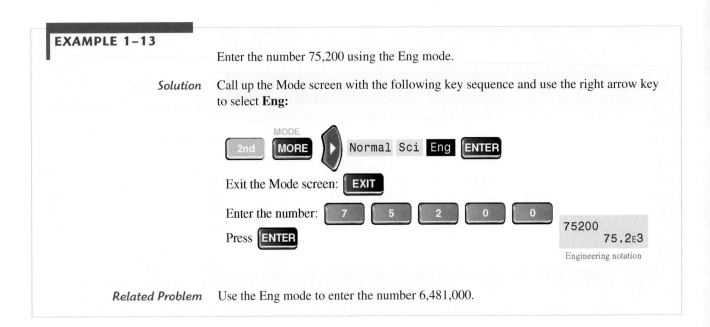

Related Problem   Use the Eng mode to enter the number 6,481,000.

EXAMPLE 1–14

Enter 51,200,000 in engineering notation using the EE key.

Solution   Move the decimal point six places to the left so that it comes after the digit 1. This results in the number expressed in engineering notation as

$$51.2 \times 10^6$$

Enter this number on your calculator as follows:

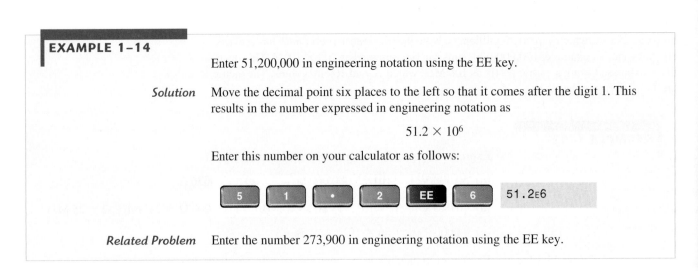

Related Problem   Enter the number 273,900 in engineering notation using the EE key.

1–5   METRIC UNIT CONVERSIONS

It is often necessary or convenient to convert a quantity from one metric-prefixed unit to another, such as from milliamperes (mA) to microamperes (μA). A metric prefix conversion is accomplished by moving the decimal point in the number an appropriate number of places to the left or to the right, depending on the particular conversion.

After completing this section, you should be able to

■ **Convert from one metric-prefixed unit to another**

■ Convert between milli, micro, nano, and pico

■ Convert between kilo and mega

The following basic rules apply to metric unit conversions:

1. When converting from a larger unit to a smaller unit, move the decimal point to the right.

2. When converting from a smaller unit to a larger unit, move the decimal point to the left.

3. Determine the number of places that the decimal point is moved by finding the difference in the powers of ten of the units being converted.

For example, when converting from milliamperes (mA) to microamperes (μA), move the decimal point three places to the right because there is a three-place difference between the two units (mA is 10^{-3} A and μA is 10^{-6} A). The following examples illustrate a few conversions.

EXAMPLE 1–15

Convert 0.15 milliampere (0.15 mA) to microamperes (μA).

Solution   Move the decimal point three places to the right.

$$0.15 \text{ mA} = 0.15 \times 10^{-3} \text{ A} = 150 \times 10^{-6} \text{ A} = \mathbf{150\,\mu A}$$

Related Problem   Convert 1 mA to microamperes.

EXAMPLE 1–16

Convert 4500 microvolts (4500 μV) to millivolts (mV).

Solution   Move the decimal point three places to the left.

$$4500 \text{ μV} = 4500 \times 10^{-6} \text{ V} = 4.5 \times 10^{-3} \text{ V} = \mathbf{4.5\,mV}$$

Related Problem   Convert 1000 μV to millivolts.

EXAMPLE 1–17

Convert 5000 nanoamperes (5000 nA) to microamperes (μA).

Solution   Move the decimal point three places to the left.

$$5000 \text{ nA} = 5000 \times 10^{-9} \text{ A} = 5 \times 10^{-6} \text{ A} = \mathbf{5\,\mu A}$$

Related Problem   Convert 893 nA to microamperes.

EXAMPLE 1–18

Convert 47,000 picofarads (47,000 pF) to microfarads (μF).

Solution   Move the decimal point six places to the left.

$$47,000 \text{ pF} = 47,000 \times 10^{-12} \text{ F} = 0.047 \times 10^{-6} \text{ F} = \mathbf{0.047\,\mu F}$$

Related Problem   Convert 0.0022 μF to picofarads.

EXAMPLE 1–19

Convert 0.00022 microfarad (0.00022 μF) to picofarads (pF).

Solution   Move the decimal point six places to the right.

$$0.00022\,\mu\text{F} = 0.00022 \times 10^{-6} \text{ F} = 220 \times 10^{-12} \text{ F} = \mathbf{220\ pF}$$

Related Problem   Convert 10,000 pF to microfarads.

EXAMPLE 1–20

Convert 1800 kilohms (1800 kΩ) to megohms (MΩ).

Solution   Move the decimal point three places to the left.

$$1800 \text{ k}\Omega = 1800 \times 10^{3} \,\Omega = 1.8 \times 10^{6} \,\Omega = \mathbf{1.8\ M\Omega}$$

Related Problem   Convert 2.2 kΩ to megohms.

When adding (or subtracting) quantities with different metric prefixes, first convert one of the quantities to the same prefix as the other quantity.

EXAMPLE 1–21

Add 15 mA and 8000 μA and express the result in milliamperes.

Solution   Convert 8000 μA to 8 mA and add.

$$15 \text{ mA} + 8000\,\mu\text{A} = 15 \text{ mA} + 8 \text{ mA} = \mathbf{23\ mA}$$

Related Problem   Add 2873 mA to 10,000 μA.

SUMMARY

- Resistors limit electrical current.
- Capacitors store electrical charge.
- Inductors store energy in their electromagnetic field.
- Inductors are also known as *coils*.
- Transformers magnetically couple ac voltages.
- Semiconductor devices include diodes, transistors, and integrated circuits.
- Power supplies provide current and voltage.
- The voltmeter function on a DMM is used to measure voltage.
- The ammeter function on a DMM is used to measure current.
- The ohmmeter function on a DMM is used to measure resistance.
- A multimeter includes a voltmeter, ammeter, and ohmmeter combined into one instrument.
- Scientific notation is a method for expressing very large and very small numbers as a number between one and ten (one digit to left of decimal point) times a power of ten.
- Engineering notation is a form of scientific notation in which quantities are expressed with one, two, or three digits to the left of the decimal point times a power of ten that is a multiple of three.
- Metric prefixes are symbols used to represent powers of ten that are multiples of three.

KEY TERMS

Capacitor An electrical device consisting of two conductive plates separated by an insulating material and possessing the property of capacitance.

DC power supply An electronic instrument that produces voltage, current, and power from the ac power line or batteries in a form suitable for use in powering electronic equipment.

Digital multimeter (DMM) An electronic instrument that combines meters for the measurement of voltage, current, and resistance.

Engineering notation A system for representing any number as a one-, two-, or three-digit number times a power of ten with an exponent that is a multiple of 3.

Exponent The number to which a base number is raised.

Function generator An electronic instrument that produces electrical signals in the form of sine waves, triangular waves, and pulses.

Inductor An electrical device formed by a wire wound in a coil around a core having the property of inductance and the capability to store energy in its electromagnetic field; also known as a coil or, in some applications, a choke.

Metric prefix A symbol that is used to replace the power of ten in numbers expressed in engineering notation.

Oscilloscope A measurement instrument that displays signal waveforms on a screen.

Power of ten A numerical representation consisting of a base of 10 and an exponent; the number 10 raised to a power.

Resistor An electrical component designed specifically to provide resistance.

Scientific notation A system for representing any number as a number between 1 and 10 times an appropriate power of ten.

Transformer A device formed by two or more windings that are magnetically coupled to each other and provide a transfer of power electromagnetically from one winding to another.

Answers are at the end of the chapter.

1. Which of the following is not an electrical quantity?
   (a) current   (b) voltage   (c) time   (d) power

2. The unit of current is
   (a) volt   (b) watt   (c) ampere   (d) joule

3. The unit of voltage is
   (a) ohm   (b) watt   (c) volt   (d) farad

4. The unit of resistance is
   (a) ampere   (b) henry   (c) hertz   (d) ohm

5. Hertz is the unit of
   (a) power   (b) inductance   (c) frequency   (d) time

6. 15,000 W is the same as
   (a) 15 mW   (b) 15 kW   (c) 15 MW   (d) 15 μW

7. The quantity 4.7×10^3 is the same as
   (a) 470   (b) 4700   (c) 47,000   (d) 0.0047

8. The quantity 56×10^{-3} is the same as
   (a) 0.056   (b) 0.560   (c) 560   (d) 56,000

9. The number 3,300,000 can be expressed in engineering notation as
   (a) 3300×10^3 (b) 3.3×10^{-6} (c) 3.3×10^6 (d) either answer (a) or (c)

10. Ten milliamperes can be expressed as
    (a) 10 MA   (b) 10 μA   (c) 10 kA   (d) 10 mA

11. Five thousand volts can be expressed as
    (a) 5000 V   (b) 5 MV   (c) 5 kV   (d) either answer (a) or (c)

12. Twenty million ohms can be expressed as
    (a) 20 mΩ (b) 20 MW   (c) 20 MΩ (d) 20 $\mu\Omega$

PROBLEMS

SECTION 1–3   Scientific Notation

1. Express each of the following numbers in scientific notation:
   (a) 3000   (b) 75,000   (c) 2,000,000

2. Express each fractional number in scientific notation:
   (a) 1/500   (b) 1/2000   (c) 1/5,000,000

3. Express each of the following numbers in scientific notation:
   (a) 8400   (b) 99,000   (c) 0.2×10^6

4. Express each of the following numbers in scientific notation:
   (a) 0.0002   (b) 0.6   (c) 7.8×10^{-2}

5. Express each of the following numbers in scientific notation:
   (a) 32×10^3 (b) 6800×10^{-6} (c) 870×10^8

6. Express each of the following as a regular decimal number:
   (a) 2×10^5 (b) 5.4×10^{-9} (c) 1.0×10^1

7. Express each of the following as a regular decimal number:
   (a) 2.5×10^{-6} (b) 5.0×10^2 (c) 3.9×10^{-1}

8. Express each number in regular decimal form:
   (a) 4.5×10^{-6} (b) 8×10^{-9} (c) 4.0×10^{-12}

9. Add the following numbers:

   (a) $(9.2 \times 10^6) + (3.4 \times 10^7)$ (b) $(5 \times 10^3) + (8.5 \times 10^{-1})$

   (c) $(5.6 \times 10^{-8}) + (4.6 \times 10^{-9})$

10. Perform the following subtractions:

    (a) $(3.2 \times 10^{12}) - (1.1 \times 10^{12})$ (b) $(2.6 \times 10^8) - (1.3 \times 10^7)$

    (c) $(1.5 \times 10^{-12}) - (8 \times 10^{-13})$

11. Perform the following multiplications:

    (a) $(5 \times 10^3)(4 \times 10^5)$ (b) $(1.2 \times 10^{12})(3 \times 10^2)$

    (c) $(2.2 \times 10^{-9})(7 \times 10^{-6})$

12. Divide the following:

    (a) $(1.0 \times 10^3) \div (2.5 \times 10^2)$ (b) $(2.5 \times 10^{-6}) \div (5.0 \times 10^{-8})$

    (c) $(4.2 \times 10^8) \div (2 \times 10^{-5})$

SECTION 1–4   **Engineering Notation and Metric Prefixes**

13. Express each of the following numbers in engineering notation:

    (a) 89,000   (b) 450,000   (c) 12,040,000,000,000

14. Express each number in engineering notation:

    (a) 2.35×10^5 (b) 7.32×10^7 (c) 1.333×10^9

15. Express each number in engineering notation:

    (a) 0.000345   (b) 0.025   (c) 0.00000000129

16. Express each number in engineering notation:

    (a) 9.81×10^{-3} (b) 4.82×10^{-4} (c) 4.38×10^{-7}

17. Add the following numbers and express each result in engineering notation:

    (a) $(2.5 \times 10^{-3}) + (4.6 \times 10^{-3})$ (b) $(68 \times 10^6) + (33 \times 10^6)$

    (c) $(1.25 \times 10^6) + (250 \times 10^3)$

18. Multiply the following numbers and express each result in engineering notation:

    (a) $(32 \times 10^{-3})(56 \times 10^3)$ (b) $(1.2 \times 10^{-6})(1.2 \times 10^{-6})$

    (c) $100(55 \times 10^{-3})$

19. Divide the following numbers and express each result in engineering notation:

    (a) $50 \div (2.2 \times 10^3)$ (b) $(5 \times 10^3) \div (25 \times 10^{-6})$

    (c) $560 \times 10^3 \div (660 \times 10^3)$

20. Express each number in Problem 13 in ohms using a metric prefix.

21. Express each number in Problem 15 in amperes using a metric prefix.

22. Express each of the following as a quantity having a metric prefix:

    (a) 31×10^{-3} A   (b) 5.5×10^3 V   (c) 20×10^{-12} F

23. Express the following using metric prefixes:

    (a) 3×10^{-6} F   (b) 3.3×10^6 Ω   (c) 350×10^{-9} A

24. Express the following using metric prefixes:

    (a) 2.5×10^{-12} A   (b) 8×10^9 Hz   (c) 4.7×10^3 Ω

25. Express each quantity by converting the metric prefix to a power-of-10:

    (a) 7.5 pA   (b) 3.3 GHz   (c) 280 nW

26. Express each quantity in engineering notation:

    (a) 5 μA   (b) 43 mV   (c) 275 kΩ   (d) 10 MW

SECTION 1–5 **Metric Unit Conversions**

27. Perform the indicated conversions:

    (a) 5 mA to microamperes   **(b)** 3200 μW to milliwatts

    (c) 5000 kV to megavolts   **(d)** 10 MW to kilowatts

28. Determine the following:

    (a) The number of microamperes in 1 milliampere

    (b) The number of millivolts in 0.05 kilovolt

    (c) The number of megohms in 0.02 kilohm

    (d) The number of kilowatts in 155 milliwatts

29. Add the following quantities:

    (a) 50 mA + 680 μA   **(b)** 120 kΩ + 2.2 MΩ **(c)** 0.02 μF + 3300 pF

30. Do the following operations:

    (a) 10 kΩ ÷ (2.2 kΩ + 10 kΩ)   **(b)** 250 mV ÷ 50 μV   **(c)** 1 MW ÷ 2 kW

SELF-TEST

1. (c)	**2.** (c)	**3.** (c)	**4.** (d)	**5.** (c)	**6.** (b)
7. (b)	**8.** (a)	**9.** (d)	**10.** (d)	**11.** (d)	**12.** (c)

2

VOLTAGE, CURRENT, AND RESISTANCE

INTRODUCTION

The three basic electrical quantities presented in this chapter are voltage, current, and resistance. No matter what type of electrical or electronic equipment you may work with, these quantities will always be of primary importance.

To help you understand voltage, current, and resistance, the basic structure of the atom is discussed and the concept of charge is introduced. The basic electric circuit is studied, along with techniques for measuring voltage, current, and resistance.

CHAPTER OBJECTIVES

- Describe the basic structure of an atom
- Explain the concept of electrical charge
- Define *voltage* and discuss its characteristics
- Define *current* and discuss its characteristics
- Define *resistance* and discuss its characteristics
- Describe a basic electric circuit
- Make basic circuit measurements
- Recognize electrical hazards and practice proper safety procedures

CHAPTER OUTLINE

KEY TERMS

- Atom
- Electron
- Free electron
- Conductor
- Semiconductor
- Insulator
- Charge
- Coulomb (C)
- Voltage
- Volt (V)
- Sine wave
- Cycle
- Period (t)
- Frequency
- Hertz
- Amplitude
- Oscillator
- Function generator
- Instantaneous value
- Peak value
- Peak-to-peak value
- Current
- Ampere (A)
- Resistance
- Ohm (Ω)
- Conductance
- Siemens (S)
- Resistor
- Potentiometer
- Rheostat
- Circuit
- Load
- Schematic
- Closed circuit
- Open circuit
- Switch
- Fuse
- Circuit breaker
- AWG
- Ground
- Voltmeter
- Ammeter
- Ohmmeter
- Electrical shock

WWW.   VISIT THE COMPANION WEBSITE
Study aids for this chapter are available at
http://www.prenhall.com/floyd

2–1 ATOMS

All matter is made of atoms; and all atoms are made of electrons, protons, and neutrons. In this section, you will learn about the structure of an atom, electron orbits and shells, valence electrons, ions, and types of materials used in electronics. Semiconductive material such as silicon or germanium is important because the configuration of certain electrons in an atom is the key factor in determining how a given material conducts electric current.

After completing this section, you should be able to

■ **Describe the basic structure of an atom**

■ Define *nucleus, proton, neutron,* and *electron*

■ Define *atomic number*

■ Define *shell*

■ Explain what a valence electron is

■ Describe ionization

■ Explain what a free electron is

■ Define *conductor, semiconductor,* and *insulator*

 An **atom** is the smallest particle of an **element** that retains the characteristics of that element. Each of the known 109 elements has atoms that are different from the atoms of all other elements. This gives each element a unique atomic structure. According to the classic Bohr model, an atom is visualized as having a planetary type of structure that consists of a central nucleus surrounded by orbiting electrons, as illustrated in Figure 2–1. The **nucleus** consists of positively charged particles called **protons** and uncharged particles called **neutrons.** The basic particles of negative charge are called **electrons.**

Each type of atom has a certain number of electrons and protons that distinguishes it from the atoms of all other elements. For example, the simplest atom is that of hydrogen, which has one proton and one electron, as pictured in Figure 2–2(a). As another example, the helium atom, shown in Figure 2–2(b), has two protons and two neutrons in the nucleus and two electrons orbiting the nucleus.

▶ **FIGURE 2–1**

The Bohr model of an atom showing electrons in orbits around the nucleus. The "tails" on the electrons indicate they are moving.

● Electron ● Proton ● Neutron

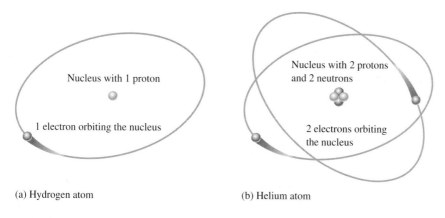

Nucleus with 1 proton

1 electron orbiting the nucleus

Nucleus with 2 protons and 2 neutrons

2 electrons orbiting the nucleus

(a) Hydrogen atom

(b) Helium atom

Atomic Number

All elements are arranged in the periodic table of the elements in order according to their **atomic number.** The atomic number equals the number of protons in the nucleus. For example, hydrogen has an atomic number of 1 and helium has an atomic number of 2. In their normal (or neutral) state, all atoms of a given element have the same number of electrons as protons; the positive charges cancel the negative charges, and the atom has a net charge of zero, making it electrically balanced.

Electron Shells and Orbits

Electrons orbit the nucleus of an atom at certain distances from the nucleus. Electrons near the nucleus have less energy than those in more distant orbits. It is known that only discrete (separate and distinct) values of electron energies exist within atomic structures. Therefore, electrons must orbit only at discrete distances from the nucleus.

Energy Levels   Each discrete distance (orbit) from the nucleus corresponds to a certain energy level. In an atom, the orbits are grouped into energy bands known as **shells.** A given atom has a fixed number of shells. Each shell has a fixed maximum number of electrons at permissible energy levels (orbits). The differences in energy levels within a shell are much smaller than the difference in energy between shells. The shells are designated 1, 2, 3, and so on, with 1 being closest to the nucleus. This energy band concept is illustrated in Figure 2–3, which shows the 1st shell with one energy level and the 2nd shell with two en-

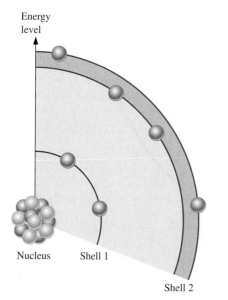

Energy level

Nucleus   Shell 1

Shell 2

◀ FIGURE 2–3

Energy levels increase as the distance from the nucleus increases.

ergy levels. Additional shells may exist in other types of atoms, depending on the element.

The number of electrons in each shell follows a predictable pattern according to the formula, $2N^2$, where N is the number of the shell. The first shell of any atom can have up to 2 electrons, the second shell up to 8 electrons, the third shell up to 18 electrons, and the fourth shell up to 32 electrons.

Valence Electrons

Electrons that are in orbits farther from the nucleus have higher energy and are less tightly bound to the atom than those closer to the nucleus. This is because the force of attraction between the positively charged nucleus and the negatively charged electron decreases with increasing distance from the nucleus. Electrons with the highest energy levels exist in the outermost shell of an atom and are relatively loosely bound to the atom. This outermost shell is known as the **valence** shell, and electrons in this shell are called **valence electrons.** These valence electrons contribute to chemical reactions and bonding within the structure of a material, and they determine a material's electrical properties.

Ionization

When an atom absorbs energy from a heat source or from light, for example, the energy levels of the electrons are raised. The valence electrons possess more energy and are more loosely bound to the atom than inner electrons, so they can easily jump to higher orbits within the valence shell when external energy is absorbed.

If a valence electron acquires a sufficient amount of energy, it can actually escape from the outer shell and the atom's influence. The departure of a valence electron leaves a previously neutral atom with an excess of positive charge (more protons than electrons). The process of losing a valence electron is known as **ionization,** and the resulting positively charged atom is called a *positive ion.* For example, the chemical symbol for hydrogen is H. When a neutral hydrogen atom loses its valence electron and becomes a positive ion, it is designated H^+. The escaped valence electron is called a **free electron.** When a free electron loses energy and falls into the outer shell of a neutral hydrogen atom, the atom becomes negatively charged (more electrons than protons) and is called a *negative ion,* designated H^-.

The Copper Atom

Because copper is the most commonly used metal in **electrical** applications, let's examine its atomic structure. The copper atom has 29 electrons that orbit the nucleus in four shells, as shown in Figure 2–4. Notice that the fourth or outermost shell, the valence shell, has only

▶ **FIGURE 2–4**

The copper atom.

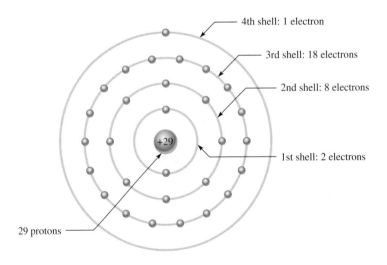

4th shell: 1 electron
3rd shell: 18 electrons
2nd shell: 8 electrons
1st shell: 2 electrons
29 protons

1 valence electron. When the valence electron in the outer shell of the copper atom gains sufficient thermal energy, it can break away from the parent atom and become a free electron. In a piece of copper at room temperature, a "sea" of these free electrons is present. These electrons are not bound to a given atom but are free to move in the copper material. Free electrons make copper an excellent conductor and make electrical current possible.

Categories of Materials

Three categories of materials are used in electronics: conductors, semiconductors, and insulators.

Conductors   **Conductors** are materials that readily allow current. They have a large number of free electrons and are characterized by one to three valence electrons in their structure. Most metals are good conductors. Silver is the best conductor, and copper is next. Copper is the most widely used conductive material because it is less expensive than silver. Copper wire is commonly used as a conductor in electric circuits.

Semiconductors   **Semiconductors** are classed below the conductors in their ability to carry current because they have fewer free electrons than do conductors. Semiconductors have four valence electrons in their atomic structures. However, because of their unique characteristics, certain semiconductor materials are the basis for modern **electronic** devices such as the diode, transistor, and integrated circuit. Silicon and germanium are common semiconductive materials.

Insulators   Insulating materials are poor conductors of electric current. In fact, **insulators** are used to prevent current where it is not wanted. Compared to conductive materials, insulators have very few free electrons and are characterized by more than four valence electrons in their atomic structures.

2–2   ELECTRICAL CHARGE

As you learned in the last section, the two types of **charge** are the positive charge and the negative charge. The electron is the smallest particle that exhibits negative electrical charge. When an excess of electrons exists in a material, there is a net negative electrical charge. When a deficiency of electrons exists, there is a net positive electrical charge.

After completing this section, you should be able to

- **Explain the concept of electrical charge**

- Name the unit of charge

- Name the types of charge

- Describe the forces between charges

- Determine the amount of charge on a given number of electrons

The charge of an electron and that of a proton are equal in magnitude. Electrical charge, which is a fundamental characteristic of electrons and protons, is symbolized by Q. Static electricity is the presence of a net positive or negative charge in a material. Everyone has

experienced the effects of static electricity from time to time, for example, when attempting to touch a metal surface or another person or when the clothes in a dryer cling together.

Materials with charges of opposite polarity are attracted to each other; materials with charges of the same polarity are repelled, as indicated symbolically in Figure 2–5. A force acts between charges, as evidenced by the attraction or repulsion. This force, called an *electric field*, consists of invisible lines of force as represented in Figure 2–6.

(a) Uncharged: no force (b) Opposite charges attract (c) Like positive charges repel (d) Like negative charges repel

▲ **FIGURE 2–5**

Attraction and repulsion of electrical charges.

▶ **FIGURE 2–6**

Electric field between oppositely charged surfaces.

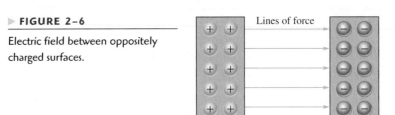

Lines of force

Coulomb: The Unit of Charge

Electrical charge is measured in **coulombs**, symbolized by C.

One coulomb is the total charge possessed by 6.25×10^{18} electrons.

A single electron has a charge of 1.6×10^{-19} C. The total charge Q, expressed in coulombs, for a given number of electrons is found by the following formula:

Equation 2–1

$$Q = \frac{\text{number of electrons}}{6.25 \times 10^{18} \text{ electrons/C}}$$

Positive and Negative Charge

Consider a neutral atom—that is, one that has the same number of electrons and protons and thus has no net charge. If a valence electron is pulled away from the atom by the application of energy, the atom is left with a net positive charge (more protons than electrons) and becomes a positive ion. If an atom acquires an extra electron in its outer shell, it has a net negative charge and becomes a negative ion.

The amount of energy required to free a valence electron is related to the number of electrons in the outer shell. An atom can have up to eight valence electrons. The more complete the outer shell, the more stable the atom and thus the more energy is required to release an electron. Figure 2–7 illustrates the creation of a positive ion and a negative ion when a hydrogen atom gives up its single valence electron to a chloride atom, forming gaseous hydrogen chloride (HCl). When the gaseous HCl is dissolved in water, hydrochloric acid is formed.

Hydrogen atom
(1 proton, 1 electron)

Chloride atom
(17 protons, 17 electrons)

(a) The neutral hydrogen atom has a single valence
electron.

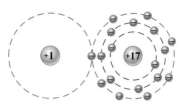

(b) The atoms combine by sharing the
valence electron to form gaseous
hydrogen chloride (HCl).

◄ FIGURE 2-7

Example of the formation of positive
and negative ions.

Positive hydrogen ion
(1 proton, no electrons)

Negative chloride ion
(17 protons, 18 electrons)

(c) When dissolved in water, hydrogen chloride gas separates into positive hydrogen ions
and negative chloride ions. The chloride atom retains the electron given up by the
hydrogen atom, forming both positive and negative ions in the same solution.

EXAMPLE 2-1

How many coulombs of charge do 93.8×10^{16} electrons represent?

Solution

$$Q = \frac{\text{number of electrons}}{6.25 \times 10^{18} \text{ electrons/C}} = \frac{93.8 \times 10^{16} \text{ electrons}}{6.25 \times 10^{18} \text{ electrons/C}} = 15 \times 10^{-2} \text{ C} = \textbf{0.15 C}$$

*Related Problem** How many electrons does it take to have 3 C of charge?

2-3 VOLTAGE

As you have seen, a force of attraction exists between a positive and a negative charge.
A certain amount of energy must be exerted in the form of work to overcome the force
and move the charges a given distance apart. All opposite charges possess a certain
potential energy because of the separation between them. The difference in potential
energy of the charges is the potential difference or **voltage.** Voltage is the driving force
in electric circuits and is what establishes current.

After completing this section, you should be able to

■ **Define *voltage* and discuss its characteristics**

■ State the formula for voltage

■ Name and define the unit of voltage

■ Describe the basic sources of voltage

Voltage (*V*) is defined as energy (*W*) per unit of charge (*Q*) and is expressed as

Equation 2–2

$$V = \frac{W}{Q}$$

where *W* is expressed in **joules** (J) and *Q* is in coulombs (C).

As a simple analogy, you can think of voltage as corresponding to the pressure difference created by a pump that causes the water to flow through a pipe in a water system.

Volt: The Unit of Voltage

The unit of voltage is the **volt,** symbolized by V.

One volt is the potential difference (voltage) between two points when one joule of energy is used to move one coulomb of charge from one point to the other.

EXAMPLE 2–2

If 50 J of energy are available for every 10 C of charge, what is the voltage?

Solution

$$V = \frac{W}{Q} = \frac{50 \text{ J}}{10 \text{ C}} = \textbf{5 V}$$

Related Problem How much energy is used to move 50 C from one point in a circuit to another when the voltage between the two points is 12 V?

BIOGRAPHY

Alessandro Volta 1745–1827

Volta, an Italian, invented a device to generate static electricity and he discovered methane gas. Volta investigated reactions between dissimilar metals and developed the first battery in 1800. Electrical potential, more commonly known as voltage, is named in his honor as is the unit of voltage, the volt. (Photo credit: Giovita Garavaglia, courtesy AIP Emilio Segrè Visual Archives, Landé Collection.)

Sources of Voltage

Batteries A voltage source is a source of electrical potential energy or *electromotive force,* more commonly known as voltage. A **battery** is a type of voltage source that converts chemical energy into electrical energy. A battery consists of one or more electrochemical cells that are electrically connected. A cell consists of four basic components: a positive electrode, a negative electrode, electrolyte, and a porous separator. The *positive electrode* has a deficiency of electrons due to chemical reaction, the *negative electrode* has a surplus of electrons due to chemical reaction, the *electrolyte* provides a mechanism for charge flow between positive and negative electrodes, and the *separator* electrically isolates the positive and negative electrodes. A basic diagram of a battery cell is shown in Figure 2–8.

▶ **FIGURE 2–8**

Diagram of a battery cell.

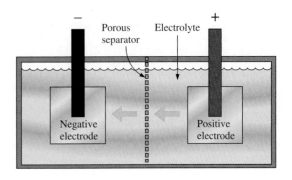

The voltage of a battery cell is determined by the materials used in it. The chemical reaction at each of the electrodes produces a fixed potential at each electrode. For example, in a lead-acid cell, a potential of -1.685 V is produced at the positive electrode and a potential of $+0.365$ V is produced at the negative electrode. This means that the voltage between two electrodes of a cell is 2.05 V, which is the standard lead-acid electrode potential. Factors such as acid concentration will affect this value to some degree so that the typical voltage of a commercial lead-acid cell is 2.15 V. The voltage of any battery cell depends on the cell chemistry. Nickel-cadmium cells are about 1.2 Vand lithium cells can be as high as almost 4 V.

Although the voltage of a battery cell is fixed by its chemistry, the capacity is variable and depends on the quantity of materials in the cell. Essentially, the *capacity* of a cell is the number of electrons that can be obtained from it and is measured by the amount of current (defined in Section 2–4) that can be supplied over time.

Batteries normally consist of multiple cells that are electrically connected together internally. The way that the cells are connected and the type of cells determine the voltage and capacity of the battery. If the positive electrode of one cell is connected to the negative electrode of the next and so on, as illustrated in Figure 2–9(a) the battery voltage is the sum of the individual cell voltages. This is called a series connection. To increase battery capacity, the positive electrodes of several cells are connected together and all the negative electrodes are connected together, as illustrated in Figure 2–9(b). This is called a parallel connection. Also, by using larger cells, which have a greater quantity of material, the ability to supply current can be increased but the voltage is not affected.

▶ **FIGURE 2–9**

Cells connected to form batteries.

(a) Series-connected battery   (b) Parallel-connected battery

Batteries are divided into two major classes, primary and secondary. Primary batteries are used once and discarded because their chemical reactions are irreversible. Secondary batteries can be recharged and reused many times because they are characterized by reversible chemical reactions.

Common Types of Batteries   There are many types, shapes, and sizes of batteries. Some of the sizes that you are most familiar with are AAA, AA, C, D, and 9 V, as shown in Figure 2–10. There is also a less common size called AAAA, which is smaller than the AAA.

▶ **FIGURE 2–10**

Sizes of common batteries.

In addition to these common sizes, there are many other physical configurations for various applications from hearing aids to lanterns. Batteries for hearing aids, watches, and other miniature applications are usually in a flat round configuration and are often called button batteries or coin batteries. Large multicell batteries are used in lanterns and industrial applications and, of course, there is the familiar automotive battery.

In addition to the many sizes and shapes, batteries are usually classified according to their chemical makeup as follows. Each of these classifications are typically available in several physical configurations.

- *Alkaline-MnO2.* This is a primary battery that is commonly used in palm-type computers, photographic equipment, toys, radios, and recorders.

- *Lithium-MnO2.* This is a primary battery that is commonly used in photographic and electronic equipment, smoke alarms, personal organizers, memory backup, and communications equipment.

- *Zinc air.* This is a primary battery that is commonly used in hearing aids, medical monitoring instruments, pagers, and other frequency-use applications.

- *Silver oxide.* This is a primary battery that is commonly used in hearing aids, watches, photographic equipment, and electronics requiring high-capacity batteries.

- *Nickel-metal hydride.* This is a secondary (rechargable) battery that is commonly used in portable computers, cell phones, camcorders, and other portable consumer electronics.

- *Lead-acid.* This is a secondary (rechargable) battery that is commonly used in automotive, marine, and other similar applications.

Solar Cells   The operation of solar cells is based on the photovoltaic effect, which is the process whereby light energy is converted directly into electrical energy. A basic solar cell consists of two layers of different types of semiconductive materials joined together to form a junction. When one layer is exposed to light, many electrons acquire enough energy to break away from their parent atoms and cross the junction. This process forms negative ions on one side of the junction and positive ions on the other, and thus a potential difference (voltage) is developed. Figure 2–11 shows the construction of a basic solar cell.

▶ **FIGURE 2–11**

Construction of a basic solar cell.

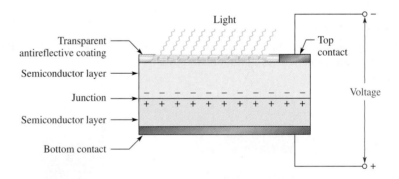

Generator   Electrical **generators** convert mechanical energy into electrical energy using a principle called *electromagnetic induction.* A conductor is rotated through a magnetic field, and a voltage is produced across the conductor. A typical generator is pictured in Figure 2–12.

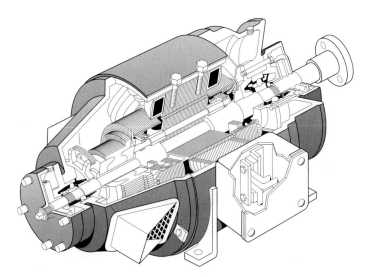

Cutaway view of a dc generator.

The Electronic Power Supply   Electronic power supplies do not produce electrical energy from some other form of energy. They simply convert the ac voltage from the wall outlet to a constant (dc) voltage that is available across two terminals, as indicated in Figure 2–13(a). Typical commercial power supplies are shown in Figure 2–13(b) on the next page.

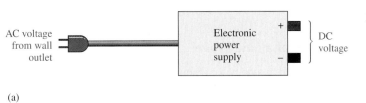

(a)

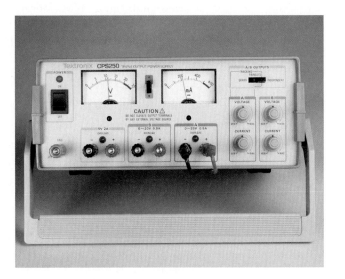

(b)

▲ FIGURE 2–13(b)

Electronic power supplies. (Copyright © Tektronix, Inc. Reproduced by permission.)

2–4   THE SINUSOIDAL WAVEFORM

▲ **FIGURE 2–14**

Symbol for a sinusoidal voltage source.

Sinusoidal voltages are produced by two types of sources: rotating electrical machines (ac generators) or electronic oscillator circuits, which are used in instruments commonly known as electronic signal generators. Figure 2–14 shows the symbol used to represent either source of sinusoidal voltage.

Figure 2–15 is a graph showing the general shape of a **sine wave**, which can be either an alternating current or an alternating voltage. Voltage (or current) is displayed on the vertical axis and time (*t*) is displayed on the horizontal axis. Notice how the voltage (or current) varies with time. Starting at zero, the voltage (or current) increases to a positive maximum (peak), returns to zero, and then increases to a negative maximum (peak) before returning again to zero, thus completing one full cycle.

▶ **FIGURE 2–15**

Graph of one cycle of a sine wave.

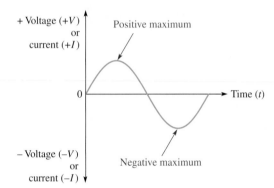

Polarity of a Sine Wave

As mentioned, a sine wave changes polarity at its zero value; that is, it alternates between positive and negative values. When a sinusoidal voltage source (V_s) is applied to a resistive circuit, as in Figure 2–16, an alternating sinusoidal current results. When the voltage changes polarity, the current correspondingly changes direction as indicated.

During the positive alternation of the applied voltage V_s, the current is in the direction shown in Figure 2–16(a). During a negative alternation of the applied voltage, the current is in the opposite direction, as shown in Figure 2–16(b). The combined positive and negative alternations make up one **cycle** of a sine wave.

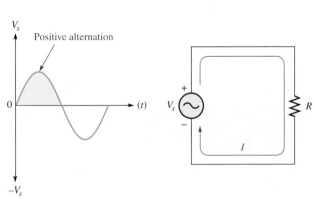

(a) During a positive alternation of voltage, current is in the direction shown.

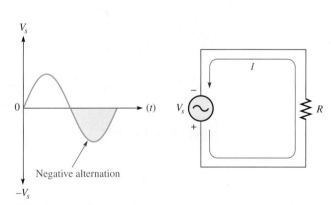

(b) During a negative alternation of voltage, current reverses direction, as shown.

▲ **FIGURE 2–16**

Alternating current and voltage.

Period of a Sine Wave

A sine wave varies with time (t) in a definable manner.

The time required for a sine wave to complete one full cycle is called the period (T).

Figure 2–17(a) illustrates the period of a sine wave. Typically, a sine wave continues to repeat itself in identical cycles, as shown in Figure 2–17(b). Since all cycles of a repetitive sine wave are the same, the period is always a fixed value for a given sine wave. The period of a sine wave can be measured from a zero crossing to the next corresponding zero crossing, as indicated in Figure 2–17(a). The period can also be measured from any peak in a given cycle to the corresponding peak in the next cycle.

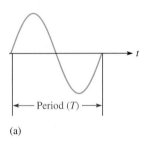

(a)

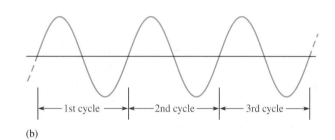

(b)

◀ **FIGURE 2–17**

The period of a sine wave is the same for each cycle.

EXAMPLE 2–3

What is the period of the sine wave in Figure 2–18?

▶ **FIGURE 2–18**

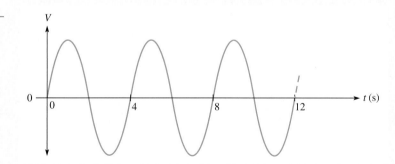

Solution   As shown in Figure 2–18, it takes four seconds (4 s) to complete each cycle. Therefore, the period is 4 s.

$$T = 4\,\text{s}$$

Related Problem   What is the period if the sine wave goes through five cycles in 12 s?

EXAMPLE 2–4

Show three possible ways to measure the period of the sine wave in Figure 2–19. How many cycles are shown?

▶ **FIGURE 2–19**

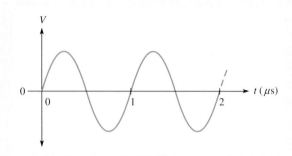

Solution **Method 1:** The period can be measured from one zero crossing to the corresponding zero crossing in the next cycle (the slope must be the same at the corresponding zero crossings).

Method 2: The period can be measured from the positive peak in one cycle to the positive peak in the next cycle.

Method 3: The period can be measured from the negative peak in one cycle to the negative peak in the next cycle.

These measurements are indicated in Figure 2–20, where **two cycles of the sine wave** are shown. Keep in mind that you obtain the same value for the period no matter which corresponding points on the waveform you use.

▶ **FIGURE 2–20**

Measurement of the period of a sine wave.

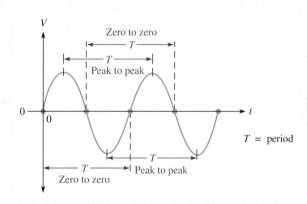

Related Problem If a positive peak occurs at 1 ms and the next positive peak occurs at 2.5 ms, what is the period?

Frequency of a Sine Wave

Frequency (f) is the number of cycles that a sine wave completes in one second.

The more cycles completed in one second, the higher the frequency. Frequency (f) is measured in units of hertz. One **hertz (Hz)** is equivalent to one cycle per second; 60 Hz is 60 cycles per second, for example. Figure 2–21 shows two sine waves. The sine wave in part (a) completes two full cycles in one second. The one in part (b) completes four cycles in one second. Therefore, the sine wave in part (b) has twice the frequency of the one in part (a).

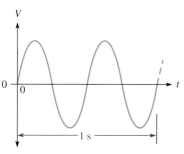

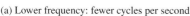

(a) Lower frequency: fewer cycles per second   (b) Higher frequency: more cycles per second

▲ **FIGURE 2–21**

Illustration of frequency.

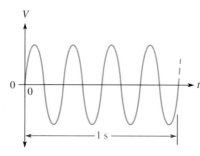
Relationship of Frequency and Period

The formulas for the relationship between frequency (f) and period (T) are as follows:

$$f = \frac{1}{T}$$

Equation 2–3

$$T = \frac{1}{f}$$

Equation 2–4

There is a reciprocal relationship between f and T. Knowing one, you can calculate the other with the x^{-1} or $1/x$ key on your calculator. This inverse relationship makes sense because a sine wave with a longer period goes through fewer cycles in one second than one with a shorter period.

EXAMPLE 2–5

Which sine wave in Figure 2–22 has a higher frequency? Determine the frequency and the period of both waveforms.

▶ **FIGURE 2–22**

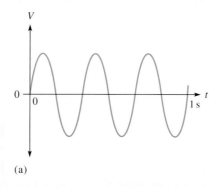

(a)

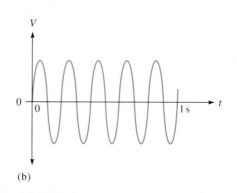

(b)

Solution   The sine wave in Figure 2–22(b) has the higher frequency because it completes more cycles in 1 s than does the sine wave in part (a).

In Figure 2–22(a), three cycles are completed in 1 s; therefore,

$$f = \textbf{3 Hz}$$

One cycle takes 0.333 s (one-third second), so the period is

$$T = 0.333 \text{ s} = \textbf{333 ms}$$

In Figure 2–22(b), five cycles are completed in 1 s; therefore,

$$f = \textbf{5 Hz}$$

One cycle takes 0.2 s (one-fifth second), so the period is

$$T = 0.2 \text{ s} = \textbf{200 ms}$$

Related Problem   If the time between negative peaks of a given sine wave is 50 μs, what is the frequency?

EXAMPLE 2–6

The period of a certain sine wave is 10 ms. What is the frequency?

Solution   Use Equation 2–1.

$$f = \frac{1}{T} = \frac{1}{10 \text{ ms}} = \frac{1}{10 \times 10^{-3} \text{ s}} = \textbf{100 Hz}$$

Related Problem   A certain sine wave goes through four cycles in 20 ms. What is the frequency?

EXAMPLE 2–7

The frequency of a sine wave is 60 Hz. What is the period?

Solution   Use Equation 2–2.

$$T = \frac{1}{f} = \frac{1}{60 \text{ Hz}} = \textbf{16.7 ms}$$

Related Problem   If $T = 15$ μs, what is f?

2–5   SINUSOIDAL VOLTAGE SOURCES

An AC Generator

Figure 2–23 shows a greatly simplified ac **generator** consisting of a single loop of wire in a permanent magnetic field. Notice that each end of the wire loop is connected to a separate solid conductive ring called a *slip ring*. A mechanical drive, such as a motor, turns the shaft to which the wire loop is connected. As the wire loop rotates in the magnetic field between the north and south poles, the slip rings also rotate and rub against the brushes that connect the loop to an external load.

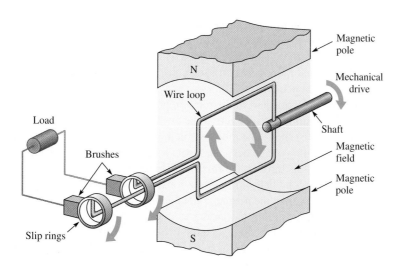

A simplified ac generator.

Magnetic pole

Mechanical drive

Shaft

Magnetic field

Magnetic pole

Wire loop

Load

Brushes

Slip rings

N

S

When a conductor moves through a magnetic field, a voltage is induced. Figure 2–24 illustrates how a sinusoidal voltage is produced by the basic ac generator as the wire loop rotates. An oscilloscope is used to display the voltage waveform.

To begin, Figure 2–24(a) shows the wire loop rotating through the first quarter of a revolution. It goes from an instantaneous horizontal position, where the induced voltage is zero, to an instantaneous vertical position, where the induced voltage is maximum. At the horizontal position, the loop is instantaneously moving parallel with the flux lines, which

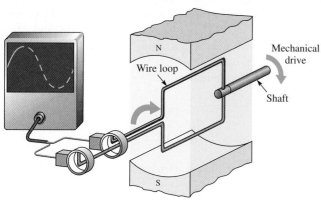

(a) First quarter-cycle (positive alternation)

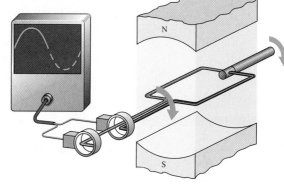

(b) Second quarter-cycle (positive alternation)

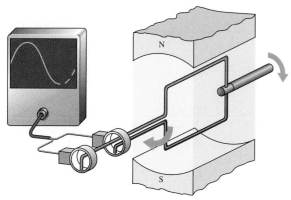

(c) Third quarter-cycle (negative alternation)

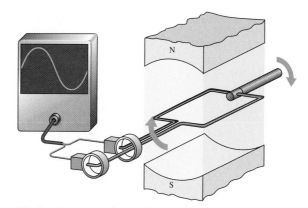

(d) Fourth quarter-cycle (negative alternation)

▲ FIGURE 2–24

One revolution of the wire loop generates one cycle of the sinusoidal voltage.

exist between the north (N) and south (S) poles of the magnet. Thus, no lines are being cut and the voltage is zero. As the wire loop rotates through the first quarter-cycle, it cuts through the flux lines at an increasing rate until it is instantaneously moving perpendicular to the flux lines at the vertical position and cutting through them at a maximum rate. Thus, the induced voltage increases from zero to a peak during the quarter-cycle. As shown on the display in part (a), this part of the rotation produces the first quarter of the sine wave cycle as the voltage builds up from zero to its positive maximum.

Figure 2–24(b) shows the loop completing the first half of a revolution. During this part of the rotation, the voltage decreases from its positive maximum back to zero as the rate at which the loop cuts through the flux lines decreases.

During the second half of the revolution, illustrated in Figures 2–24(c) and 2–24(d), the loop is cutting through the magnetic field in the opposite direction, so the voltage produced has a polarity opposite to that produced during the first half of the revolution. After one complete revolution of the loop, one full cycle of the sinusoidal voltage has been produced. As the wire loop continues to rotate, repetitive cycles of the sine wave are generated.

Frequency   You have seen that one revolution of the conductor through the magnetic field in the basic ac generator (also called an *alternator*) produces one cycle of induced sinusoidal voltage. It is obvious that the rate at which the conductor is rotated determines the time for completion of one cycle. For example, if the conductor completes 60 revolutions in one second (rps), the period of the resulting sine wave is 1/60 s, corresponding to a frequency of 60 Hz. Thus, the faster the conductor rotates, the higher the resulting frequency of the induced voltage, as illustrated in Figure 2–25.

Another way of achieving a higher frequency is to increase the number of magnetic poles. In the previous discussion, two magnetic poles were used to illustrate the ac generator principle. During one revolution, the conductor passes under a north pole and a south pole, thus producing one cycle of a sine wave. When four magnetic poles are used instead of two, as shown in Figure 2–26, one cycle is generated during one-half a revolution. This doubles the frequency for the same rate of rotation.

An expression for frequency in terms of the number of pole pairs and the number of revolutions per second (rps) is as follows:

Equation 2–5 $f = \text{(number of pole pairs)(rps)}$

EXAMPLE 2–8

A four-pole generator has a rotation speed of 100 rps. Determine the frequency of the output voltage.

Solution $f = \text{(number of pole pairs)(rps)} = 2(100 \text{ rps}) = \textbf{200 Hz}$

Related Problem   If the frequency of the output of a four-pole generator is 60 Hz, what is the rps?

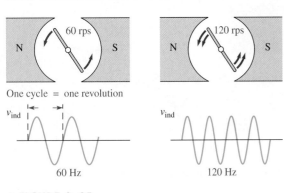

▲ FIGURE 2–25

Frequency is directly proportional to the rate of rotation of the wire loop in an ac generator.

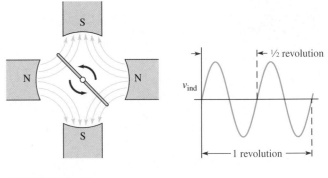

▲ FIGURE 2–26

Four poles achieve a higher frequency than two for the same rps.

Voltage Amplitude Recall from Faraday's law that the voltage induced in a conductor depends on the number of turns (*N*), and the rate of change with respect to the magnetic field. Therefore, when the speed of rotation of the conductor is increased, not only the frequency of the induced voltage increases—so also does the **amplitude**, which is its maximum value. Since the frequency value normally is fixed, the most practical method of increasing the amount of induced voltage is to increase the number of wire loops.

Electronic Signal Generators

The signal generator is an instrument that electronically produces sine waves for use in testing or controlling electronic circuits and systems. There are a variety of signal generators, ranging from special-purpose instruments that produce only one type of waveform in a limited frequency range, to programmable instruments that produce a wide range of frequencies and a variety of waveforms. All signal generators consist basically of an **oscillator**, which is an electronic circuit that produces repetitive waves. All generators have controls for adjusting the amplitude and frequency.

Function Generators and Arbitrary Waveform Generators A **function generator** is an instrument that produces more than one type of waveform. It provides pulse waveforms as well as sine waves and triangular waves. A typical function generator is shown in Figure 2–27(a).

An arbitrary waveform generator can be used to generate standard signals like sine waves, triangular waves, and pulses as well as signals with various shapes and characteristics. Waveforms can be defined by mathematical or graphical input. A typical arbitrary waveform generator is shown in Figure 2–27(b).

(a) Examples of function generators

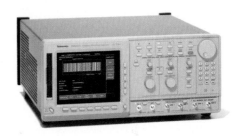

(b) A typical arbitrary waveform generator

▲ **FIGURE 2–27**

Typical signal generators. Copyright © Tektronix, Inc. Reproduced by permission.

2–6 SINUSOIDAL VOLTAGE AND CURRENT VALUES

Instantaneous Value

Figure 2–28 illustrates that at any point in time on a sine wave, the voltage (or current) has an **instantaneous value**. This instantaneous value is different at different points along the curve. Instantaneous values are positive during the positive alternation and negative during the negative alternation. Instantaneous values of voltage and current are symbolized by lowercase *v* and *i*, respectively. The curve in part (a) shows voltage only, but it applies equally for current when the *v*'s are replaced with *i*'s. An example of instantaneous values is shown in part (b) where the instantaneous voltage is 3.1 V at 1 μs, 7.07 V at 2.5 μs, 10 V at 5 μs, 0 V at 10 μs, −3.1 V at 11 μs, and so on.

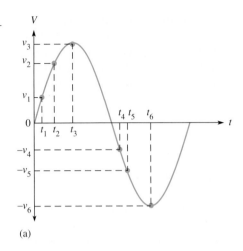
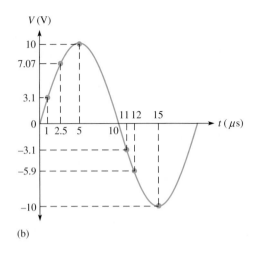

(a)   (b)

Peak Value

The **peak value** of a sine wave is the value of voltage (or current) at the positive or the negative maximum (peak) with respect to zero. Since the positive and negative peak values are equal in **magnitude**, a sine wave is characterized by a single peak value. This is illustrated in Figure 2–29. For a given sine wave, the peak value is constant and is represented by V_p or I_p.

▶ FIGURE 2–29

Peak values.

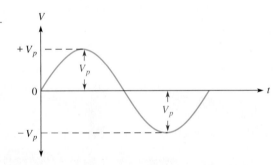

Peak-to-Peak Value

The **peak-to-peak value** of a sine wave, as shown in Figure 2–30, is the voltage or current from the positive peak to the negative peak. It is always twice the peak value as expressed in the following equations. Peak-to-peak voltage or current values are represented by V_{pp} or I_{pp}.

Equation 2–6

$$V_{pp} = 2V_p$$

Equation 2–7

$$I_{pp} = 2I_p$$

▶ FIGURE 2–30

Peak-to-peak value.

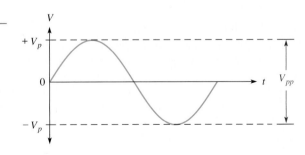

2–7 CURRENT

Voltage provides energy to electrons that allows them to move through a circuit. This movement of electrons is the current, which results in work being done in an electric circuit.

After completing this section, you should be able to

- **Define *current* and discuss its characteristics**
- Explain the movement of electrons
- State the formula for current
- Name and define the unit of current

As you have learned, free electrons are available in all conductive and semiconductive materials. These electrons drift randomly in all directions, from atom to atom, within the structure of the material, as indicated in Figure 2–31.

▶ **FIGURE 2–31**

Random motion of free electrons in a material.

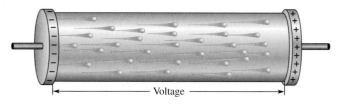

Randomly drifting free electron

Now, if a voltage is placed across a conductive or semiconductive material, one end becomes positive and the other negative, as indicated in Figure 2–32. The repulsive force produced by the negative voltage at the left end causes the free electrons (negative charges) to move toward the right. The attractive force produced by the positive voltage at the right end pulls the free electrons to the right. The result is a net movement of the free electrons from the negative end of the material to the positive end, as shown in Figure 2–32.

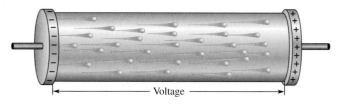

Voltage

⬛ **FIGURE 2–32**

Electrons flow from negative to positive when a voltage is applied across a conductive or semiconductive material.

BIOGRAPHY

André Marie Ampère 1775–1836

In 1820 Ampère, a Frenchman, developed a theory of electricity and magnetism that was fundamental for 19th century developments in the field. He was the first to build an instrument to measure charge flow (current). The unit of electrical current is named in his honor. (Photo credit: AIP Emilio Segrè Visual Archives.)

The movement of the free electrons from the negative end of a material to the positive end is the electrical **current**, symbolized by *I*.

Electrical current is the rate of flow of charge.

Current in a conductive material is measured by the number of electrons (amount of charge, *Q*) that flow past a point in a unit of time.

$$I = \frac{Q}{t}$$

Equation 2–8

where I is current in amperes, Q is the charge of the electrons in coulombs, and t is the time in seconds.

As a simple analogy, you can think of current as corresponding to water flowing through a pipe in a water system when pressure (corresponding to voltage) is applied by a pump (corresponding to a voltage source). *Voltage causes current.*

Ampere: The Unit of Current

Current is measured in a unit called the **ampere** or *amp* for short, symbolized by A.

One ampere (1 A) is the amount of current that exists when a number of electrons having a total charge of one coulomb (1 C) move through a given cross-sectional area in one second (1 s).

See Figure 2–33. Remember, one coulomb is the charge carried by 6.25×10^{18} electrons.

▶ **FIGURE 2–33**

Illustration of 1 A of current (1 C/s) in a material.

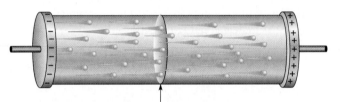

When a number of electrons having 1 coulomb of charge pass through this cross-sectional area in 1 second, there is 1 ampere of current.

EXAMPLE 2–9

Ten coulombs of charge flow past a given point in a wire in 2 s. What is the current in amperes?

Solution
$$I = \frac{Q}{t} = \frac{10 \text{ C}}{2 \text{ s}} = \textbf{5 A}$$

Related Problem If there are 8 A of direct current through the filament of a light bulb, how many coulombs have moved through the filament in 1.5 s?

2–8   RESISTANCE

When there is current in a material, the free electrons move through the material and occasionally collide with atoms. These collisions cause the electrons to lose some of their energy, and thus their movement is restricted. The more collisions, the more the flow of electrons is restricted. This restriction varies and is determined by the type of material. The property of a material that restricts the flow of electrons is called **resistance**, designated with an R.

After completing this section, you should be able to

■ **Define *resistance* and discuss its characteristics**

■ Name and define the unit of resistance

■ Describe the basic types of resistors

■ Determine resistance value by color code or labeling

Resistance is the opposition to current.

The schematic symbol for resistance is shown in Figure 2–34.

When there is current through any material that has resistance, heat is produced by the collisions of electrons and atoms. Therefore, wire, which typically has a very small resistance, can become warm or even hot when there is sufficient current through it.

As a simple analogy, you can think of a resistor as corresponding to a partially open valve in a closed water system that restricts the amount of water flowing through a pipe. If the valve is opened more (corresponding to less resistance), the water flow (corresponding to current) increases. If the valve is closed a little (corresponding to more resistance), the water flow (corresponding to current) decreases.

R

▲ **FIGURE 2–34**

Resistance/resistor symbol.

Ohm: The Unit of Resistance

Resistance, R, is expressed in the unit of **ohms** and is symbolized by the Greek letter omega (Ω).

One ohm (1 Ω) of resistance exists when there is one ampere (1 A) of current in a material with one volt (1 V) applied across the material.

Conductance   The reciprocal of resistance is **conductance**, symbolized by G. It is a measure of the ease with which current is established. The formula is

$$G = \frac{1}{R}$$

Equation 2–9

The unit of conductance is the **siemens**, symbolized by S. For example, the conductance of a 22 kΩ resistor is $G = 1/22$ k$\Omega = 45.5$ μS. Occasionally, the obsolete unit of *mho* is still used for conductance.

Resistors

Components that are specifically designed to have a certain amount of resistance are called **resistors.** The principal applications of resistors are to limit current, divide voltage, and, in certain cases, generate heat. Although different types of resistors come in many shapes and sizes, they can all be placed in one of two main categories: fixed or variable.

Fixed Resistors   Fixed resistors are available with a large selection of resistance values that are set during manufacturing and cannot be changed easily. Fixed resistors are constructed using various methods and materials. Figure 2–35 shows several common types.

One common fixed resistor is the carbon-composition type, which is made with a mixture of finely ground carbon, insulating filler, and a resin binder. The ratio of carbon to insulating filler sets the resistance value. The mixture is formed into rods which are cut into short lengths, and lead connections are made. The entire resistor is then encapsulated in an insulated coating for protection. Figure 2–36(a) shows the construction of a typical carbon-composition resistor.

The chip resistor is another type of fixed resistor and is in the category of SMT (surface-mount technology) components. It has the advantage of a very small size for compact assemblies. Figure 2–36(b) shows the construction of a chip resistor.

Other types of fixed resistors include carbon film, metal film, metal-oxide film, and wirewound. In film resistors, a resistive material is deposited evenly onto a high-grade ceramic rod. The resistive film may be carbon (carbon film) or nickel chromium (metal film). In these types of resistors, the desired resistance value is obtained by removing part of the resistive material in a helical pattern along the rod using a spiraling technique, as shown in Figure 2–37(a). Very close **tolerance** can be achieved with this method. Film resistors are also available in the form of resistor networks, as shown in Figure 2–37(b).

BIOGRAPHY

Georg Simon Ohm

1787–1854

Ohm was born in Bavaria and struggled for years to gain recognition for his work in formulating the relationship of current, voltage, and resistance. This mathematical relationship is known today as Ohm's law and the unit of resistance is named in his honor. (Photo credit: Library of Congress, LC-USZ62-40943.)

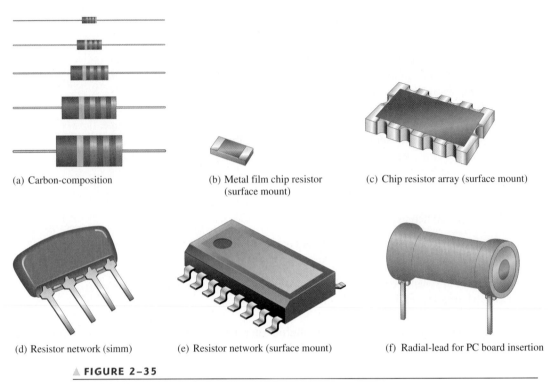

(a) Carbon-composition

(b) Metal film chip resistor (surface mount)

(c) Chip resistor array (surface mount)

(d) Resistor network (simm)

(e) Resistor network (surface mount)

(f) Radial-lead for PC board insertion

▲ FIGURE 2–35

Typical fixed resistors.

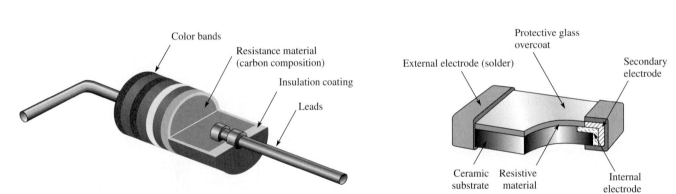

(a) Cutaway view of a carbon-composition resistor

(b) Cutaway view of a tiny surface-mount chip resistor

▲ FIGURE 2–36

Two types of fixed resistors (not to scale).

Wirewound resistors are constructed with resistive wire wound around an insulating rod and then sealed. Normally, wirewound resistors are used because of their relatively high power ratings. Since they are constructed with a coil of wire, wirewound resistors have significant inductance and are not used at higher frequencies. Some typical wirewound resistors are shown in Figure 2–38.

Resistor Color Codes   Some types of fixed resistors with value tolerances of 5% or 10% are color coded with four bands to indicate the resistance value and the tolerance. This color-code band system is shown in Figure 2–39, and the **color code** is listed in Table 2–1. The bands are always located closer to one end.

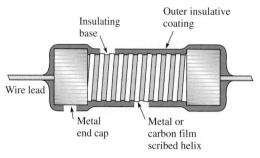

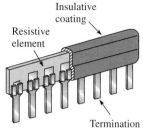

(a) Film resistor showing spiraling technique

(b) Resistor network

▲ **FIGURE 2–37**

Construction views of typical film resistors.

The 4-band color code is read as follows:

1. Start with the band closest to one end of the resistor. The first band is the first digit of the resistance value. If it is not clear which is the banded end, start from the end that does not begin with a gold or silver band.

2. The second band is the second digit of the resistance value.

3. The third band is the number of zeros following the second digit, or the *multiplier.*

4. The fourth band indicates the percent tolerance and is usually gold or silver. If there is no fourth band, the tolerance is ±20%.

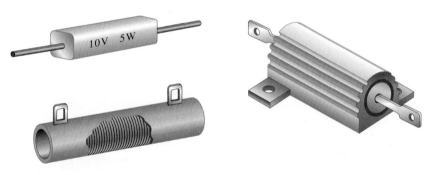

◀ **FIGURE 2–38**

Typical wirewound power resistors.

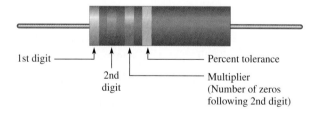

1st digit ── 2nd digit ── Multiplier (Number of zeros following 2nd digit) ── Percent tolerance

◀ **FIGURE 2–39**

Color-code bands on a 4-band resistor.

For example, a 5% tolerance means that the *actual* resistance value is within ±5% of the color-coded value. Thus, a 100 Ω resistor with a tolerance of ±5% can have an acceptable range of values from a minimum of 95 Ω to a maximum of 105 Ω.

As indicated in the table, for resistance values less than 10 Ω, the third band is either gold or silver. Gold in the third band represents a multiplier of 0.1, and silver represents 0.01. For example, a color code of red, violet, gold, and silver represents 2.7 Ω with a tolerance of ±10%.

▶ **TABLE 2–1**

Resistor 4-band color code.

	Digit	Color
Resistance value, first three bands: First band—1st digit Second band—2nd digit *Third band—multiplier (number of zeros following the 2nd digit)	0	Black
	1	Brown
	2	Red
	3	Orange
	4	Yellow
	5	Green
	6	Blue
	7	Violet
	8	Gray
	9	White
Fourth band—tolerance	±5%	Gold
	±10%	Silver
	±20%	No band

* For resistance values less than 10 Ω, the third band is either gold or silver. Gold is for a multiplier of 0.1 and silver is for a multiplier of 0.01.

EXAMPLE 2–10

Find the resistance values in ohms and the percent tolerance for each of the color-coded resistors shown in Figure 2–40.

▶ **FIGURE 2–40**

(a)   (b)   (c)

Solution **(a)** First band is red = 2, second band is violet = 7, third band is orange = 3 zeros, fourth band is silver = ±10% tolerance.

$$R = 27{,}000 \ \Omega \pm 10\%$$

(b) First band is brown = 1, second band is black = 0, third band is brown = 1 zero, fourth band is silver = ±10% tolerance.

$$R = 100 \ \Omega \pm 10\%$$

(c) First band is green = 5, second band is blue = 6, third band is green = 5 zeros, fourth band is gold = ±5% tolerance.

$$R = 5{,}600{,}000 \ \Omega \pm 5\%$$

Related Problem A certain resistor has a yellow first band, a violet second band, a red third band, and a gold fourth band. Determine the value in ohms and its percent tolerance.

Five-Band Color Code Certain precision resistors with tolerances of 2%, 1%, or less are generally color coded with five bands, as shown in Figure 2–41. Begin at the band closest to one end. The first band is the first digit of the resistance value, the second band is the second digit, the third band is the third digit, the fourth band is the multiplier (number of zeros after the third digit), and the fifth band indicates the tolerance. Table 2–2 shows the 5-band color code.

Resistor Reliability Band An extra band on some color-coded resistors indicates the resistor's reliability in percent of failures per 1000 hours (1000 h) of use. The reliability color code is listed in Table 2–3. For example, a brown fifth band on a 4-band color-coded resis-

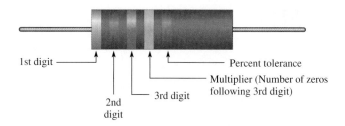

1st digit
2nd digit
3rd digit
Multiplier (Number of zeros following 3rd digit)
Percent tolerance

◀ FIGURE 2–41

Color-code bands on a 5-band resistor.

	DIGIT	COLOR
Resistance value, first three bands:	0	Black
	1	Brown
	2	Red
First band—1st digit	3	Orange
Second band—2nd digit	4	Yellow
Third band—3rd digit	5	Green
Fourth band—multiplier	6	Blue
(number of zeros following 3rd digit)	7	Violet
	8	Gray
	9	White
Fourth band—multiplier	0.1	Gold
	0.01	Silver
	±2%	Red
	±1%	Brown
Fifth band—tolerance	±0.5%	Green
	±0.25%	Blue
	±0.1%	Violet

◀ TABLE 2–2

Resistor 5-band color code.

COLOR	FAILURES DURING 1000 h OF OPERATION
Brown	1.0%
Red	0.1%
Orange	0.01%
Yellow	0.001%

◀ TABLE 2–3

Reliability color code.

tor means that if a group of like resistors is operated under standard conditions for 1000 h, 1% of the resistors in that group will fail.

Resistors, as well as other components, should be operated substantially below their rated values to enhance their reliability.

EXAMPLE 2–11

Find the resistance value in ohms and the percent tolerance for each of the color-coded resistors shown in Figure 2–42.

▶ **FIGURE 2–42**

(a)   (b)   (c)

Solution **(a)** First band is red = 2, second band is violet = 7, third band is black = 0, fourth band is gold = ×0.1, fifth band is red = ±2% tolerance.

$$R = 270 \times 0.1 = \mathbf{27\ \Omega \pm 2\%}$$

(b) First band is yellow = 4, second band is black = 0, third band is red = 2, fourth band is black = 0, fifth band is brown = ±1% tolerance.

$$R = \mathbf{402\ \Omega \pm 1\%}$$

(c) First band is orange = 3, second band is orange = 3, third band is red = 2, fourth band is orange = 3, fifth band is green = ±0.5% tolerance.

$$R = \mathbf{332{,}000\ \Omega \pm 0.5\%}$$

Related Problem A certain resistor has a yellow first band, a violet second band, a green third band, a gold fourth band, and a red fifth band. Determine its value in ohms and its percent tolerance.

Resistor Label Codes

Not all types of resistors are color coded. Many, including surface-mount resistors, use typographical marking to indicate the resistance value and tolerance. These label codes consist of either all numbers (numeric) or a combination of numbers and letters (alphanumeric). In some cases when the body of the resistor is large enough, the entire resistance value and tolerance are stamped on it in standard form. For example, a 33,000 Ω resistor may be labeled as 33 kΩ.

Numeric Labeling   This type of marking uses three digits to indicate the resistance value, as shown in Figure 2–43 using a specific example. The first two digits give the first two digits of the resistance value, and the third digit gives the multiplier or number of zeros that follow the first two digits. This code is limited to values of 10 Ω or greater.

▶ **FIGURE 2–43**

Example of three-digit labeling for a resistor.

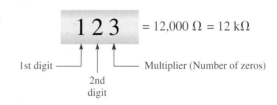

= 12,000 Ω = 12 kΩ

1st digit ⎯⎯⎯⎯⎯⎯⎯⎯⎯⎯ Multiplier (Number of zeros)

2nd digit

Alphanumeric Labeling   Another common type of marking is a three- or four-character label that uses both digits and letters. This type of label typically consists of only three digits or two or three digits and one of the letters R, K, or M. The letter is used to indicate the multiplier, and the position of the letter indicates the decimal point placement. The letter R indicates a multiplier of 1 (no zeros after the digits), the K indicates a multiplier of 1000 (3 zeros after the digits), and the M indicates a multiplier of 1,000,000 (6 zeros after the digits). In this format, values from 100 to 999 consist of three digits and no letter to represent the three digits in the resistance value. Figure 2–44 shows three examples of this type of resistor label.

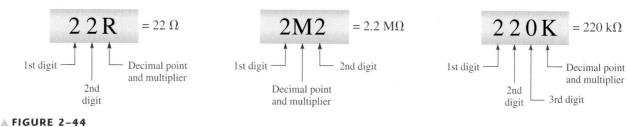

▲ **FIGURE 2–44**

Examples of the alphanumeric resistor label.

EXAMPLE 2–12

Interpret the following alphanumeric resistor labels:

(a) 470   (b) 5R6   (c) 68K   (d) 10M   (e) 3M3

Solution   (a) 470 = **470 Ω**   (b) 5R6 = **5.6 Ω**   (c) 68K = **68 kΩ**

(d) 10M = **10 MΩ**   (e) 3M3 = **3.3 MΩ**

Related Problem   What is the resistance indicated by 1K25?

One system of labels for resistance tolerance values uses the letters F, G, and J as follows:

F = ±1%   G = ±2%   J = ±5%

For example, 620F indicates a 620 Ω resistor with a tolerance of ± 1%, 4R6G is a 4.6 Ω ± 2% resistor, and 56KJ is a 56 kΩ ± 5% resistor.

Variable Resistors   Variable resistors are designed so that their resistance values can be changed easily with a manual or an automatic adjustment.

Two basic uses for variable resistors are to divide voltage and to control current. The variable resistor used to divide voltage is called a **potentiometer**. The variable resistor used to control current is called a **rheostat**. Schematic symbols for these types are shown in Figure 2–45. The potentiometer is a three-terminal device, as indicated in part (a). Terminals 1 and 2 have a fixed resistance between them, which is the total resistance. Terminal 3 is connected to a moving contact (**wiper**). You can vary the resistance between 3 and 1 or between 3 and 2 by moving the contact.

Figure 2–45(b) shows the rheostat as a two-terminal variable resistor. Part (c) shows how you can use a potentiometer as a rheostat by connecting terminal 3 to either terminal 1 or terminal 2. Parts (b) and (c) are equivalent symbols. Part (d) shows a simplified construction diagram of a potentiometer. Some typical potentiometers are pictured in Figure 2–46.

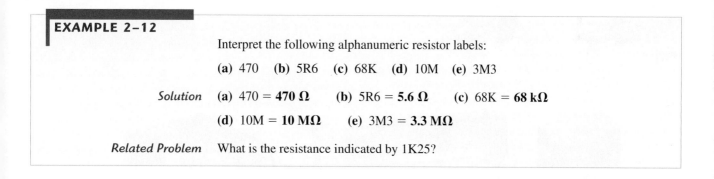

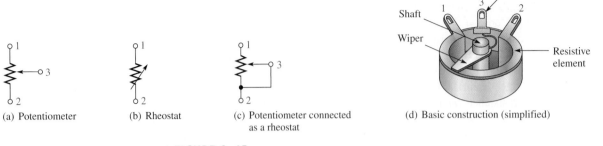

(a) Potentiometer (b) Rheostat (c) Potentiometer connected as a rheostat (d) Basic construction (simplified)

▲ FIGURE 2–45

Potentiometer and rheostat symbols and basic construction of one type of potentiometer.

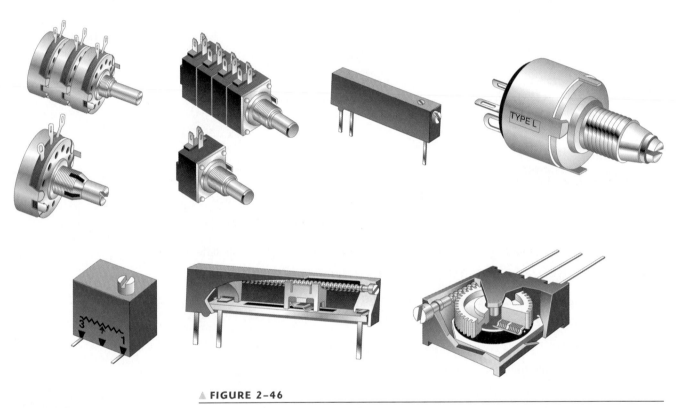

▲ FIGURE 2–46

Typical potentiometers and two construction views.

Potentiometers and rheostats can be classified as linear or tapered, as shown in Figure 2–47, where a potentiometer with a total resistance of 100 Ω is used as an example. As shown in part (a), in a linear potentiometer, the resistance between either terminal and the moving contact varies linearly with the position of the moving contact. For example, one-half of a turn results in one-half the total resistance. Three-quarters of a turn results in three-quarters of the total resistance between the moving contact and one terminal, or one-quarter of the total resistance between the other terminal and the moving contact.

In a **tapered** potentiometer, the resistance varies nonlinearly with the position of the moving contact, so that one-half of a turn does not necessarily result in one-half the total resistance. This concept is illustrated in Figure 2–30(b), where the nonlinear values are arbitrary. The potentiometer is used as a voltage-control device. When a fixed voltage is applied across the end terminals, a variable voltage is obtained at the wiper contact with respect to either end terminal. The rheostat is used as a current-control device; the current can be changed by changing the wiper position.

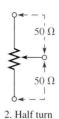 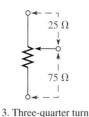 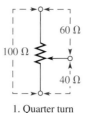 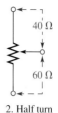 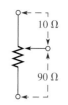

1. Quarter turn   2. Half turn   3. Three-quarter turn   1. Quarter turn   2. Half turn   3. Three-quarter turn

(a) Linear   (b) Tapered (nonlinear)

▲ **FIGURE 2–47**

Examples of (a) linear and (b) tapered potentiometers.

Two Types of Automatically Variable Resistors   A **thermistor** is a type of variable resistor that is temperature-sensitive. When its temperature coefficient is negative, the resistance changes inversely with temperature. When its temperature coefficient is positive, the resistance changes directly with temperature.

The resistance of a **photoconductive cell** changes with a change in light intensity. This cell also has a negative temperature coefficient, which means that resistance decreases with increasing temperature. Symbols for both of these devices are shown in Figure 2–48.

▶ **FIGURE 2–48**

Symbols for resistive devices with sensitivities to temperature and light.

(a) Thermistor   (b) Photoconductive cell

2–9 THE ELECTRIC CIRCUIT

A basic electric circuit is an arrangement of physical components that use voltage, current, and resistance to perform some useful function.

After completing this section, you should be able to

■ **Describe a basic electric circuit**

■ Relate a schematic to a physical circuit

■ Define *open circuit* and *closed circuit*

■ Describe various types of protective devices

■ Describe various types of switches

■ Explain how wire sizes are related to gauge numbers

■ Define *ground*

Basically, an electric **circuit** consists of a voltage source, a load, and a path for current between the source and the load. The **load** is a device on which work is done by the current through it. Figure 2–49 shows an example of a simple electric circuit: a battery connected to a lamp with two conductors (wires). The battery is the voltage source, the lamp is the load on the battery because it draws current from the battery, and the two wires provide the current path from the negative terminal of the battery to the lamp and back to the positive terminal of the battery, as indicated by the red arrows. There is current through the filament of the lamp (which has a resistance), causing it to become hot enough to emit visible light. Current through the battery is produced by chemical action.

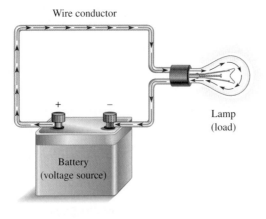

Wire conductor

▲ FIGURE 2-49

A simple electric circuit.

▲ FIGURE 2-50

Schematic for the circuit in Figure 2-49.

In many practical cases, one terminal of the battery is connected to a ground point. For example, in automobiles, the negative battery terminal is generally connected to the metal chassis of the car. The chassis is the ground for the automobile electrical system and provides a current path for the circuit. The concept of *ground* is covered later in this chapter.

The Electric Circuit Schematic

 An electric circuit can be represented by a **schematic**, a diagram that shows the interconnection of components, using standard symbols for each element, as shown in Figure 2–50 for the simple circuit in Figure 2–49. A schematic shows, in an organized manner, how the various components in a given circuit are interconnected so that the operation of the circuit can be determined.

Closed and Open Circuits

 The simple circuit in Figure 2–49 illustrates a **closed circuit**—that is, a circuit in which the current has a complete path. An **open circuit** is a circuit in which the current path is broken so that there is no current. An open circuit is considered to have infinite resistance (infinite means immeasurably large).

 Switches **Switches** are commonly used for controlling the opening or closing of circuits by either mechanical or electronic means. For example, a switch is used to turn a lamp on or off, as illustrated in Figure 2–51. Each circuit pictorial is shown with its associated

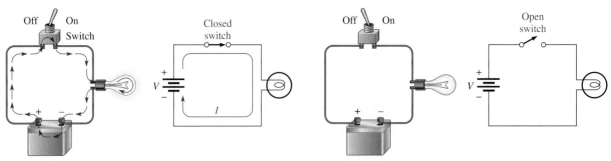

(a) There is current in a *closed* circuit because there is a complete current path (switch is ON or in the *closed* position). Current is almost always indicated by a red arrow in this text.

(b) There is no current in an *open* circuit because the path is broken (switch is OFF or in the *open* position).

▲ FIGURE 2-51

Illustration of closed and open circuits using an SPST switch for control.

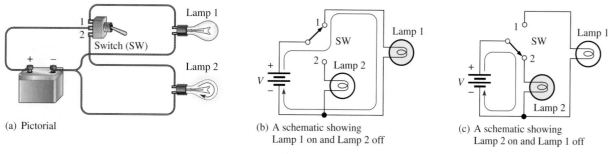

(a) Pictorial

(b) A schematic showing
Lamp 1 on and Lamp 2 off

(c) A schematic showing
Lamp 2 on and Lamp 1 off

▲ **FIGURE 2–52**

An example of an SPDT switch controlling two lamps.

schematic. The type of switch indicated is a *single-pole–single-throw* (SPST) toggle switch. The term *pole* refers to the movable arm in a switch, and the term *throw* indicates the number of contacts that are affected (either opened or closed) by a single switch action (a single movement of a pole).

Figure 2–52 shows a somewhat more complicated circuit using a *single-pole– double-throw* (SPDT) type of switch to control the current to two different lamps. When one lamp is on, the other is off, and vice versa, as illustrated by the two schematics that represent each of the switch positions.

In addition to the SPST and the SPDT switches (symbols are shown in Figure 2–53(a) and (b)), the following other types of switches are also important:

■ *Double-pole–single-throw (DPST)*. The DPST switch permits simultaneous opening or closing of two sets of contacts. The symbol is shown in Figure 2–53(c). The dashed line indicates that the contact arms are mechanically linked so that both move with a single switch action.

■ *Double-pole–double-throw (DPDT)*. The DPDT switch provides connection from one set of contacts to either of two other sets. The schematic symbol is shown in Figure 2–53(d).

■ *Push button (PB)*. In the normally open push-button switch (NOPB), shown in Figure 2–53(e), connection is made between two contacts when the button is depressed, and connection is broken when the button is released. In the normally closed push-button switch (NCPB), shown in Figure 2–53(f), connection between the two contacts is broken when the button is depressed.

■ *Rotary*. In a rotary switch, a knob is turned to make a connection between one contact and any one of several others. A symbol for a simple six-position rotary switch is shown in Figure 2–53(g).

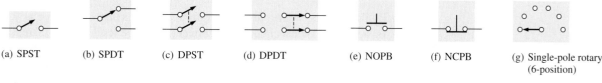

(a) SPST   (b) SPDT   (c) DPST   (d) DPDT   (e) NOPB   (f) NCPB   (g) Single-pole rotary
(6-position)

▲ **FIGURE 2–53**

Switch symbols.

Figure 2–54 shows several varieties of switches, and Figure 2–55 shows a construction view of a typical toggle switch.

Protective Devices   **Fuses** and **circuit breakers** are placed in the current path and are used to deliberately create an open circuit when the current exceeds a specified number of amperes due to a malfunction or other abnormal condition in a circuit. For example, a fuse or circuit breaker with a 20 A rating will open a circuit when the current exceeds 20 A.

▶ **FIGURE 2–54**

Typical mechanical switches.

Toggle switch   Rocker switch   PC mounted push-button switches

Push-button switches   Rotary switches

DIP switches

▶ **FIGURE 2–55**

Construction view of a typical toggle switch.

The basic difference between a fuse and a circuit breaker is that when a fuse is "blown," it must be replaced; but when a circuit breaker opens, it can be reset and reused repeatedly. Both of these devices protect against damage to a circuit due to excess current or prevent a hazardous condition created by the overheating of wires and other components when the current is too great. Because fuses cut off excess current more quickly than circuit breakers, fuses are used whenever delicate electronic equipment needs to be protected. Several typical fuses and circuit breakers, along with their schematic symbols, are shown in Figure 2–56.

Wires

Wires are the most common form of conductive material used in electrical applications. They vary in diameter size and are arranged according to standard gauge numbers, called **AWG** (American Wire Gauge) sizes. As the gauge number increases, the wire diameter de-

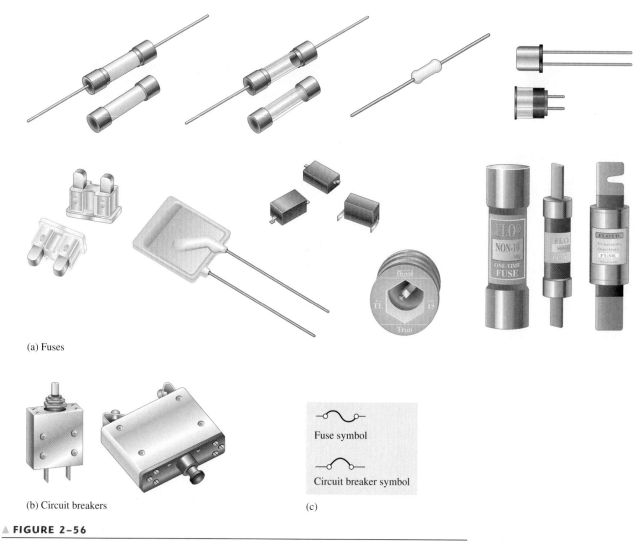

(a) Fuses

(b) Circuit breakers

Fuse symbol

Circuit breaker symbol

(c)

▲ FIGURE 2–56

Typical fuses and circuit breakers and their symbols.

creases. The size of a wire is also specified in terms of its cross-sectional area, as illustrated in Figure 2–57. The unit of cross-sectional area is the **circular mil,** abbreviated CM. One circular mil is the area of a wire with a diameter of 0.001 inch (0.001 in., or 1 mil). You can find the cross-sectional area in circular mils by expressing the diameter in thousandths of an inch (mils) and squaring it, as follows:

$$A = d2$$

Equation 2–10

where A is the cross-sectional area in circular mils and d is the diameter in mils. Table 2–4 lists the AWG sizes with their corresponding cross-sectional area and resistance in ohms per 1000 ft at 20°C.

▶ FIGURE 2–57

Cross-sectional area of a wire.

d

Cross-sectional area, A

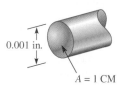

0.001 in.

$A = 1$ CM

▼ **TABLE 2–4**

American Wire Gauge (AWG) sizes and resistances for solid round copper.

AWG #	AREA (CM)	RESISTANCE (Ω/1000 FT AT 20°C)	AWG #	AREA (CM)	RESISTANCE (Ω/1000 FT AT 20°C)
0000	211,600	0.0490	19	1,288.1	8.051
000	167,810	0.0618	20	1,021.5	10.15
00	133,080	0.0780	21	810.10	12.80
0	105,530	0.0983	22	642.40	16.14
1	83,694	0.1240	23	509.45	20.36
2	66,373	0.1563	24	404.01	25.67
3	52,634	0.1970	25	320.40	32.37
4	41,742	0.2485	26	254.10	40.81
5	33,102	0.3133	27	201.50	51.47
6	26,250	0.3951	28	159.79	64.90
7	20,816	0.4982	29	126.72	81.83
8	16,509	0.6282	30	100.50	103.2
9	13,094	0.7921	31	79.70	130.1
10	10,381	0.9989	32	63.21	164.1
11	8,234.0	1.260	33	50.13	206.9
12	6,529.0	1.588	34	39.75	260.9
13	5,178.4	2.003	35	31.52	329.0
14	4,106.8	2.525	36	25.00	414.8
15	3,256.7	3.184	37	19.83	523.1
16	2,582.9	4.016	38	15.72	659.6
17	2,048.2	5.064	39	12.47	831.8
18	1,624.3	6.385	40	9.89	1049.0

EXAMPLE 2–13

What is the cross-sectional area of a wire with a diameter of 0.005 inch?

Solution

$$d = 0.005 \text{ in.} = 5 \text{ mils}$$

$$A = d^2 = (5 \text{ mils})^2 = \textbf{25 CM}$$

Related Problem What is the cross-sectional area of a 0.0201 in. diameter wire? What is the AWG # for this wire from Table 2–4?

Wire Resistance

Although copper wire conducts current extremely well, it still has some resistance, as do all conductors. The resistance of a wire depends on three physical characteristics: (a) type of material, (b) length of wire, and (c) cross-sectional area. In addition, temperature can also affect the resistance.

Each type of conductive material has a characteristic called its *resistivity,* which is represented by the Greek letter rho (ρ). For each material, ρ is a constant value at a given temperature. The formula for the resistance of a wire of length l and cross-sectional area A is

$$R = \frac{\rho l}{A}$$

Equation 2–11

This formula shows that resistance increases with an increase in resistivity and length and decreases with an increase in cross-sectional area. For resistance to be calculated in ohms, the length must be in feet (ft), the cross-sectional area in circular mils (CM), and the resistivity in CM-Ω/ft.

EXAMPLE 2–14

Find the resistance of a 100 ft length of copper wire with a cross-sectional area of 810.1 CM. The resistivity of copper is 10.37 CM-Ω/ft at 20°C.

Solution

$$R = \frac{\rho l}{A} = \frac{(10.37 \text{ CM-}\Omega/\text{ft})(100 \text{ ft})}{810.1 \text{ CM}} = \mathbf{1.280 \ \Omega}$$

Related Problem   Determine the resistance of a 1000 ft length of #22 AWG copper wire.

As mentioned, Table 2–4 lists the resistance of the various standard wire sizes in ohms per 1000 ft at 20°C. For example, a 1000 ft length of 14-gauge copper wire has a resistance of 2.525 Ω. A 1000 ft length of 22-gauge wire has a resistance of 16.14 Ω. For a given length, the smaller-gauge wire has more resistance. Thus, for a given voltage, larger-gauge wires can carry more current than smaller ones.

Ground

The term **ground** comes from the method used in ac power distribution where one side of the power line is neutralized by connecting it to a metal rod driven into the ground. This method of grounding is called *earth ground.*

In electrical and electronic systems, the metal chassis that houses the assembly or a large conductive area on a printed circuit board is used as the electrical reference point and is called *chassis ground* or **circuit ground.** Circuit ground may or may not be connected to earth ground. For example, the negative terminal of the battery and one side of all the electrical circuits in most cars are connected to the metal body chassis, which is isolated from earth ground by the tires.

Ground is the reference point in electric circuits and has a voltage of 0 V with respect to other points in the circuit. All of the ground points in a circuit are *electrically* the same and are therefore common points. Two ground symbols are shown in Figure 2–58. The symbol in part (a) is commonly used in schematic drawings to represent a reference ground, but the one in part (b) is also sometimes used. The symbol in part (a) will be used throughout this textbook.

Figure 2–59 illustrates a simple circuit with ground connections. The current is from the negative terminal of the 12 V source, through the wire to the lamp, through the lamp, and back to the positive terminal of the source through the common ground connection. Ground provides a return path for the current back to the source because all of the ground points are electrically the same point and provide a zero resistance (ideally) current path. The voltage at the top of the circuit is −12 V with respect to ground. You can think of all the ground points in a circuit as being connected together by a conductor.

(a)   (b)

▲ FIGURE 2–58

Symbols for ground.

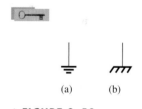

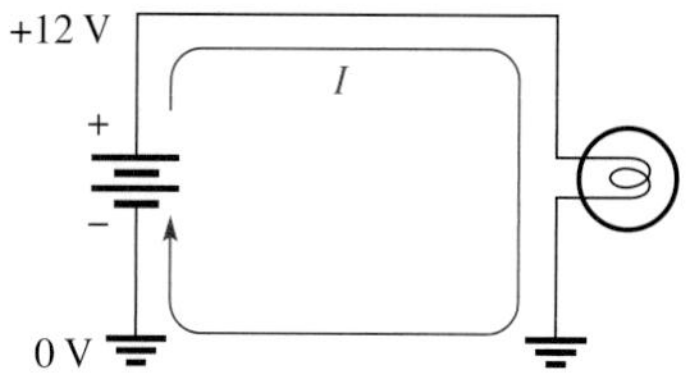

▲ FIGURE 2–59

A simple circuit with ground connections.

2–10 BASIC CIRCUIT MEASUREMENTS

In electronics technology, you cannot function without knowing how to measure voltage, current, and resistance.

After completing this section, you should be able to

■ **Make basic circuit measurements**

■ Properly measure voltage in a circuit

■ Properly measure current in a circuit

■ Properly measure resistance

■ Set up and read basic meters

Voltage, current, and resistance measurements are commonly required in electronics work. The instrument used to measure voltage is a **voltmeter**, the instrument used to measure current is an **ammeter**, and the instrument used to measure resistance is an **ohmmeter.** Commonly, all three instruments are combined into a single instrument known as a **multimeter,** in which you can choose the specific quantity to measure by selecting the appropriate function with a switch.

Typical portable multimeters are shown in Figure 2–60. Part (a) shows an analog meter with a needle pointer, and part (b) shows a digital multimeter (DMM), which provides a digital readout of the measured quantity. Many digital multimeters also include a bar graph display.

Meter Symbols

Throughout this book, certain symbols will be used in circuits to represent meters, as shown in Figure 2–61. You may see any of four types of symbols for voltmeters, ammeters, and ohmmeters, depending on which symbol most effectively conveys the information required. The digital meter symbol is used when specific values are to be indicated in a circuit. The

▶ **FIGURE 2–60**

Typical portable multimeters. (Photography courtesy of B&K Precision Corp.)

(a)

(b)

(a) Digital

(b) Analog bar graph

(c) Analog needle

(d) Generic

◀ FIGURE 2–61

Examples of meter symbols used in this book. Each of the symbols can be used to represent either an ammeter (A), a voltmeter (V), or an ohmmeter (Ω).

bar graph meter symbol and sometimes the needle meter symbol are used to illustrate the operation of a circuit when *relative* measurements or changes in quantities, rather than specific values, need to be depicted. A changing quantity may be indicated by an arrow in the display showing an increase or decrease. The generic symbol is used to indicate placement of meters in a circuit when no values or value changes need to be shown.

Measuring Current

Figure 2–62 illustrates how to measure current with an ammeter. Part (a) shows a simple circuit in which the current through a resistor is to be measured. Connect an ammeter in the current path by first opening the circuit, as shown in part (b). Then insert the meter as shown in part (c). Such a connection is a *series* connection. The polarity of the meter must be such that the current is in at the negative terminal and out at the positive terminal.

Measuring Voltage

To measure voltage, connect a voltmeter across the component for which the voltage is to be found. Such a connection is a *parallel* connection. The negative terminal of the meter

SAFETY POINT

Never wear rings or any type of metallic jewelry while working on a circuit. These items may accidentally come in contact with the circuit, causing shock and/or damage to the circuit.

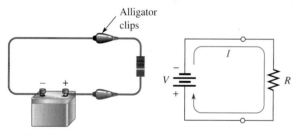
(a) Circuit in which the current is to be measured

(b) Open the circuit either between the resistor and the positive terminal or between the resistor and the negative terminal of source.

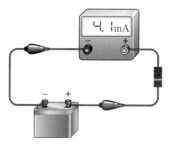

(c) Install the ammeter in the current path with polarity as shown (negative to negative, positive to positive).

▲ **FIGURE 2–62**

Example of an ammeter connection to measure current in a simple circuit.

Example of a voltmeter connection to measure voltage in a simple circuit.

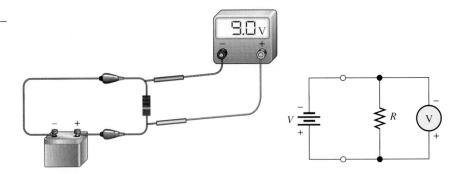

must be connected to the negative side of the circuit, and the positive terminal of the meter must be connected to the positive side of the circuit. Figure 2–63 shows a voltmeter connected to measure the voltage across the resistor.

Measuring Resistance

To measure resistance, connect an ohmmeter across the resistor. *The resistor must first be removed or disconnected from the circuit.* This procedure is shown in Figure 2–64.

Digital Multimeters (DMMs)

DMMs are the most widely used type of electronic measuring instrument. Generally, DMMs provide more functions, better accuracy, greater ease of reading, and greater reliability than do analog meters, which are covered next. Analog meters have at least one advantage over DMMs, however. They can track short-term variations and trends in a measured quantity that many DMMs are too slow to respond to. Typical DMMs are shown in Figure 2–65. Many DMMs are autoranging types in which the proper range is automatically selected by internal circuitry.

DMM Functions   The basic functions found on most DMMs are

- Ohms

- DC voltage and current

- AC voltage and current

Example of using an ohmmeter to measure resistance.

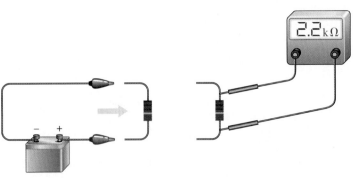

(a) Disconnect the resistor from the
     circuit to avoid damage to the meter
     and/or incorrect measurement.

(b) Measure the resistance.
     (Polarity is not important.)

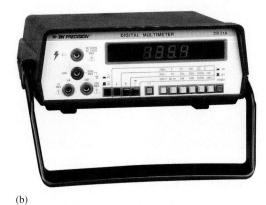

(a)   (b)

◀ FIGURE 2–65

Typical digital multimeters (DMMs).
(Photography courtesy of B&K
Precision Corp.)

Some DMMs provide additional functions such as analog bar graph displays, transistor or diode tests, power measurement, and decibel measurement for audio amplifier tests.

DMM Displays   DMMs are available with either LCD (liquid-crystal display) or LED (light-emitting diode) readouts. The LCD is the most commonly used readout in battery-powered instruments because it requires only very small amounts of current. A typical battery-powered DMM with an LCD readout operates on a 9 V battery that will last from a few hundred hours to 2000 hours and more. The disadvantages of LCD readouts are that (a) they are difficult or impossible to see in low-light conditions and (b) they are relatively slow to respond to measurement changes. LEDs, on the other hand, can be seen in the dark and respond quickly to changes in measured values. LED displays require much more current than LCD displays; and, therefore, battery life is shortened when LEDs are used in portable equipment.

Both LCD and LED DMM displays are in a seven-segment format. Each digit in the display consists of seven separate segments, as shown in Figure 2–66(a). Each of the ten decimal digits is formed by the activation of appropriate segments, as illustrated in Figure 2–66(b). In addition to the seven segments, there is also a decimal point.

Resolution   The **resolution** of a DMM is the smallest increment of a quantity that the DMM can measure. The smaller the increment, the better the resolution. One factor that determines the resolution of a meter is the number of digits in the display.

Because many DMMs have 3½ digits in their display, we will use this case for illustration. A 3½-digit multimeter has three digit positions that can indicate from 0 through 9, and one digit position that can indicate only a value of 1. This latter digit, called the *halfdigit,* is always the most significant digit in the display. For example, suppose that a DMM is reading 0.999 V, as shown in Figure 2–67(a). If the voltage increases by 0.001 V to 1 V, the dis-

(a)   (b)

◀ FIGURE 2–66

Seven-segment display.

(a) Resolution: 0.001 V   (b) Resolution: 0.001 V   (c) Resolution: 0.001 V   (d) Resolution: 0.01 V

▲ FIGURE 2–67

A 3½-digit DMM illustrates how the resolution changes with the number of digits in use.

play correctly shows 1.000 V, as shown in part (b). The "1" is the half-digit. Thus, with 3½ digits, a variation of 0.001 V, which is the resolution, can be observed.

Now, suppose that the voltage increases to 1.999 V. This value is indicated on the meter as shown in Figure 2–67(c). If the voltage increases by 0.001 V to 2 V, the half-digit cannot display the "2," so the display shows 2.00. The half-digit is blanked and only three digits are active, as indicated in part (d). With only three digits active, the resolution is 0.01 V rather than 0.001 V as it is with 3½ active digits. The resolution remains 0.01 V up to 19.99 V. The resolution goes to 0.1 V for readings of 20.0 V to 199.9 V.At 200 V, the resolution goes to 1 V, and so on.

The resolution capability of a DMM is also determined by the internal circuitry and the rate at which the measured quantity is sampled. DMMs with displays of 4½ through 8½ digits are also available.

Accuracy   The accuracy is the degree to which a measured value represents the true or accepted value of a quantity. The accuracy of a DMM is established strictly by its internal circuitry and calibration. For typical meters, accuracies range from 0.01% to 0.5%, with some precision laboratory-grade meters going to 0.002%.

Reading Analog Multimeters

Functions   The face of a typical analog needle-type multimeter is represented in Figure 2–68. This particular instrument can be used to measure both direct current (dc) and alternating current (ac) quantities as well as resistance values. It has four selectable functions: dc volts (DC VOLTS), dc milliamperes (DC mA), ac volts (AC VOLTS), and OHMS. Many analog multimeters are similar to this one, although range selections and scales may vary.

Ranges   Within each function there are several ranges, as indicated by the brackets around the selector switch. For example, the DC VOLTS function has 0.3 V, 3 V, 12 V, 60 V, 300 V, and 600 V ranges. Thus, dc voltages from 0.3 V full-scale to 600 V full-scale can be measured. On the DC mA function, direct currents from 0.06 mA full-scale to 120 mA full-scale

▶ **FIGURE 2–68**

▶ **FIGURE 2–68**

A typical analog multimeter.

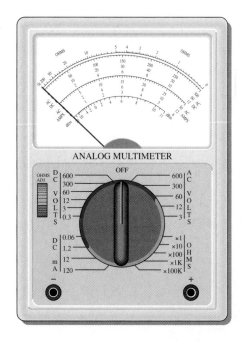

can be measured. On the ohm scale, the range settings are ×1, ×10, ×100, ×1000, and ×100,000.

The Ohm Scale   Ohms are read on the top scale of the meter. This scale is nonlinear; that is, the values represented by each division (large or small) vary as you go across the scale. In Figure 2–68, notice how the scale becomes more compressed as you go from right to left.

To read the actual value in ohms, multiply the number on the scale as indicated by the pointer by the factor selected by the switch. For example, when the switch is set at ×100 and the pointer is at 20, the reading is 20 × 100 = 2000 Ω.

As another example, assume that the switch is at ×10 and the pointer is at the seventh small division between the 1 and 2 marks, indicating 17 Ω (1.7 × 10). Now, if the meter remains connected to the same resistance and the switch setting is changed to ×1, the pointer will move to the second small division between the 15 and 20 marks. This, of course, is also a 17 Ω reading, illustrating that a given resistance value can often be read at more than one switch setting. However, the meter should be *zeroed* each time the range is changed by touching the leads together and adjusting the needle.

The AC-DC Scales   The second, third, and fourth scales from the top (labeled "AC" and "DC") are used in conjunction with the DC VOLTS, DC mA and AC VOLTS functions. The upper ac-dc scale ends at the 300 mark and is used with range settings such as 0.3, 3, and 300. For example, when the switch is at 3 on the DC VOLTS function, the 300 scale has a full-scale value of 3 V. At the range setting of 300, the full-scale value is 300 V, and so on.

The middle ac-dc scale ends at 60. This scale is used in conjunction with range settings such as 0.06, 60, and 600. For example, when the switch is at 60 on the DC VOLTS function, the full-scale value is 60 V.

The lower ac-dc scale ends at 12 and is used in conjunction with switch settings such as 1.2, 12, and 120. The remaining scales are for ac current and for decibels.

HANDS ON TIP

When you are using a multimeter, such as the analog multimeter illustrated in Figure 2–68, where you manually select the voltage and current ranges, it is good practice to always set the multimeter on the maximum range before you measure an unknown voltage or current. You can then reduce the range until you get an acceptable reading.

EXAMPLE 2–15

In Figure 2–69, determine the quantity (voltage, current, or resistance) that is being measured and its value.

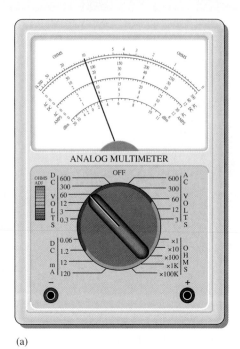

(a)

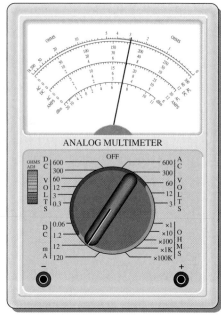

(b)

(c)

▲ **FIGURE 2–69**

Solution **(a)** The switch in Figure 2–69(a) is set on the DC VOLTS function and the 60 V range. The reading taken from the middle dc scale is 18 V.

(b) The switch in Figure 2–69(b) is set on the DC mA function and the 12 mA range. The reading taken from the lower dc scale is 7.2 mA.

(c) The switch in Figure 2–69(c) is set on the ohm (OHMS) function and the ×1000 range. The reading taken from the ohm scale (top scale) is 6.5 kΩ.

Related Problem In Figure 2–69(c) the switch is moved to the ×100 setting. Assuming that the same resistance is being measured, what will the needle do?

SUMMARY

- An atom is the smallest particle of an element that retains the characteristics of that element.
- The electron is the basic particle of negative electrical charge.
- The proton is the basic particle of positive charge.
- An ion is an atom that has gained or lost an electron and is no longer neutral.
- When electrons in the outer orbit of an atom (valence electrons) break away, they become free electrons.
- Free electrons make current possible.
- Like charges repel each other, and opposite charges attract each other.
- Voltage must be applied to a circuit before there can be current.
- Resistance limits the current.
- Basically, an electric circuit consists of a source, a load, and a current path.
- An open circuit is one in which the current path is broken.
- A closed circuit is one which has a complete current path.
- An ammeter is connected in line (series) with the current path to measure current.
- A voltmeter is connected across (parallel) the current path to measure voltage.
- An ohmmeter is connected across a resistor to measure resistance. The resistor must be disconnected from the circuit.
- Figure 2–70 shows the electrical symbols introduced in this chapter.
- One coulomb is the charge on 6.25×10^{18} electrons.
- One volt is the potential difference (voltage) between two points when one joule of energy is used to move one coulomb of charge from one point to the other.

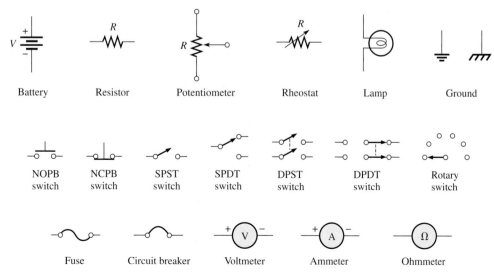

| Battery | Resistor | Potentiometer | Rheostat | Lamp | Ground |

| NOPB switch | NCPB switch | SPST switch | SPDT switch | DPST switch | DPDT switch | Rotary switch |

| Fuse | Circuit breaker | Voltmeter | Ammeter | Ohmmeter |

▲ **FIGURE 2–70**

- One ampere is the amount of current that exists when one coulomb of charge moves through a given cross-sectional area of a material in one second.
- One ohm is the resistance when there is one ampere of current in a material with one volt applied across the material.

KEY TERMS

Ammeter An electrical instrument used to measure current.

Ampere (A) The unit of electrical current.

Atom The smallest particle of an element possessing the unique characteristics of that element.

AWG (American Wire Gauge) A standardization based on wire diameter.

Charge An electrical property of matter that exists because of an excess or a deficiency of electrons. Charge can be either positive or negative.

Circuit An interconnection of electrical components designed to produce a desired result. A basic circuit consists of a source, a load, and an interconnecting current path.

Circuit breaker A resettable protective device used for interrupting excessive current in an electric circuit.

Closed circuit A circuit with a complete current path.

Conductance The ability of a circuit to allow current. The unit is the siemens (S).

Conductor A material in which electric current is easily established. An example is copper.

Coulomb (C) The unit of electrical charge; the total charge possessed by 6.25×10^{18} electrons.

Current The rate of flow of charge (electrons).

Current source A device that produces a constant current for a varying load.

DMM Digital multimeter; an electronic instrument that combines meters for measurement of voltage, current, and resistance.

Electrical shock The physical sensation resulting from electrical current through the body.

Electron The basic particle of electrical charge in matter. The electron possesses negative charge.

Free electron A valence electron that has broken away from its parent atom and is free to move from atom to atom within the atomic structure of a material.

Fuse A protective device that burns open when there is excessive current in a circuit.

Ground The common or reference point in a circuit.

Insulator A material that does not allow current under normal conditions.

Load An element (resistor or other component) connected across the output terminals of a circuit that draws current from the circuit and upon which work is done.

Multimeter An instrument that measures voltage, current, and resistance.

Ohm (Ω) The unit of resistance.

Ohmmeter An instrument for measuring resistance.

Open circuit A circuit in which there is not a complete current path.

Potentiometer A three-terminal variable resistor.

Resistance Opposition to current. The unit is the ohm (Ω).

Resistor An electrical component designed specifically to provide resistance.

Rheostat A two-terminal variable resistor.

Schematic A symbolized diagram of an electrical or electronic circuit.

Semiconductor A material that has a conductance value between that of a conductor and an insulator. Silicon and germanium are examples.

Siemens (S) The unit of conductance.

Switch An electrical or electronic device for opening and closing a current path.

Volt (V) The unit of voltage or electromotive force.

Voltage The amount of energy per charge available to move electrons from one point to another in an electric circuit.

Voltage source A device that produces a constant voltage for a varying load.

Voltmeter An instrument used to measure voltage.

FORMULAS

$$2\text{--}1 \qquad Q = \frac{\text{number of electrons}}{6.25 \times 10^{18} \text{ electrons/C}} \qquad \text{Charge}$$

$$2\text{--}2 \qquad V = \frac{W}{Q}$$

Voltage in volts equals energy in joules divided by charge in coulombs.

$$2\text{--}3 \qquad I = \frac{Q}{t}$$

Current in amperes equals charge in coulombs divided by time in seconds.

$$2\text{--}4 \qquad G = \frac{1}{R}$$

Conductance in siemens is the reciprocal of resistance in ohms.

$$2\text{--}5 \qquad A = d^2$$

Cross-sectional area in circular mils equals the diameter in mils squared.

$$2\text{--}6 \qquad R = \frac{\rho l}{A}$$

Resistance is resistivity in CM Ω/ft times length in feet divided by cross-sectional area in circular mils.

SELF-TEST

Answers are at the end of the chapter.

1. A neutral atom with an atomic number of three has how many electrons?

    (a) 1   (b) 3   (c) none   (d) depends on the type of atom

2. Electron orbits are called

    (a) shells   (b) nuclei   (c) waves   (d) valences

3. Materials in which there is no current when voltage is applied are called

    (a) filters   (b) conductors   (c) insulators   (d) semiconductors

4. When placed close together, a positively charged material and a negatively charged material will

    (a) repel   (b) become neutral   (c) attract   (d) exchange charges

5. The charge on a single electron is

    (a) 6.25×10^{-18} C   (b) 1.6×10^{-19} C   (c) 1.6×10^{-19} J   (d) 3.14×10^{-6} C

6. *Potential difference* is another term for

    (a) energy   (b) voltage   (c) distance of an electron from the nucleus   (d) charge

7. The unit of energy is the

    (a) watt   (b) coulomb   (c) joule   (d) volt

8. Which one of the following is not a type of energy source?

    (a) battery   (b) solar cell   (c) generator   (d) potentiometer

9. Which one of the following is not a possible condition in an electric circuit?

    (a) voltage and no current   (b) current and no voltage

    (c) voltage and current   (d) no voltage and no current

10. Electrical current is defined as

    (a) free electrons

    (b) the rate of flow of free electrons

    (c) the energy required to move electrons

    (d) the charge on free electrons

11. There is no current in a circuit when

    (a) a switch is closed   (b) a switch is open   (c) there is no voltage

    (d) answers (a) and (c)   (e) answers (b) and (c)

12. The primary purpose of a resistor is to

    (a) increase current   **(b)** limit current

    (c) produce heat   **(d)** resist current change

13. Potentiometers and rheostats are types of

    (a) voltage sources   **(b)** variable resistors

    (c) fixed resistors   **(d)** circuit breakers

14. The current in a given circuit is not to exceed 22 A. Which value of fuse is best?

    (a) 10 A   **(b)** 25 A   **(c)** 20 A   **(d)** a fuse is not necessary

PROBLEMS

More difficult problems are indicated by an asterisk (*).

SECTION 2–2   Electrical Charge

1. What is the charge in coulombs of the nucleus of a copper atom?

2. What is the charge in coulombs of the nucleus of a chlorine atom?

3. How many coulombs of charge do 50×10^{31} electrons possess?

4. How many electrons does it take to make 80 μC (microcoulombs) of charge?

SECTION 2–3 & 2-4   Voltage, Current, and Resistance

5. Determine the voltage in each of the following cases:

    (a) 10 J/C   **(b)** 5 J/2 C   **(c)** 100 J/25 C

6. Five hundred joules of energy are used to move 100 C of charge through a resistor. What is the voltage across the resistor?

7. What is the voltage of a battery that uses 800 J of energy to move 40 C of charge through a resistor?

8. How much energy does a 12 V battery use to move 2.5 C through a circuit?

9. If a resistor with a current of 2 A through it converts 1000 J of electrical energy into heat energy in 15 s, what is the voltage across the resistor?

10. Determine the current in each of the following cases:

    (a) 75 C in 1 s   **(b)** 10 C in 0.5 s   **(c)** 5 C in 2 s

11. Six-tenths coulomb passes a point in 3 s. What is the current in amperes?

12. How long does it take 10 C to flow past a point if the current is 5 A?

13. How many coulombs pass a point in 0.1 s when the current is 1.5 A?

14. 5.74×10^{17} electrons flow through a wire in 250 ms. What is the current in amperes?

SECTION 2–5   Resistors

15. Determine the resistance values and tolerance for the following 4-band resistors:

    (a) red, violet, orange, gold   **(b)** brown, gray, red, silver

16. Find the minimum and the maximum resistance within the tolerance limits for each resistor in Problem 21.

17. Determine the color bands for each of the following 4-band, 5% values: 330 Ω, 2.2 kΩ, 56 kΩ, 100 kΩ, and 39 kΩ.

18. Determine the resistance and tolerance of each of the following 4-band resistors:

    (a) brown, black, black, gold

    (b) green, brown, green, silver

    (c) blue, gray, black, gold

19. Determine the color bands for each of the following 4-band resistors. Assume each has a 5% tolerance.

    (a) 0.47 Ω **(b)** 270 kΩ **(c)** 5.1 MΩ

20. Determine the resistance and tolerance of each of the following 5-band resistors:

    (a) red, gray, violet, red, brown

    (b) blue, black, yellow, gold, brown

    (c) white, orange, brown, brown, brown

21. Determine the color bands for each of the following 5-band resistors. Assume each has a 1% tolerance.

    (a) 14.7 kΩ   **(b)** 39.2 Ω   **(c)** 9.76 kΩ

22. The adjustable contact of a linear potentiometer is set at the mechanical center of its adjustment. If the total resistance is 1000 Ω, what is the resistance between each end terminal and the adjustable contact?

23. What resistance is indicated by 4K7?

24. Determine the resistance and tolerance of each resistor labeled as follows:

    (a) 4R7J   **(b)** 5602M   **(c)** 1501F

SECTION 2–6   The Electric Circuit

25. Trace the current path in Figure 2–71(a) with the switch in position 2.

26. With the switch in either position, redraw the circuit in Figure 2–71(d) with a fuse connected to protect the circuit against excessive current.

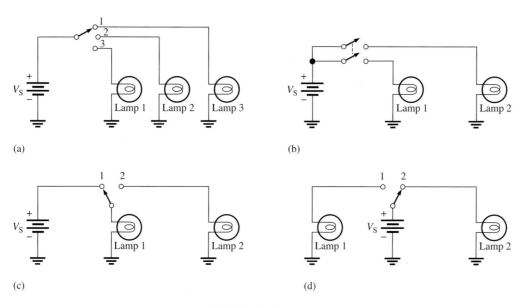

(a)   (b)

(c)   (d)

▲ **FIGURE 2–71**

27. There is only one circuit in Figure 2–71 in which it is possible to have all lamps on at the same time. Determine which circuit it is.

28. Through which resistor in Figure 2–72 is there always current, regardless of the position of the switches?

▶ **FIGURE 2–72**

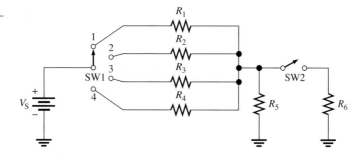

*29. Devise a switch arrangement whereby two voltage sources (V_{S1} and V_{S2}) can be connected simultaneously to either of two resistors (R_1 and R_2) as follows:

$$V_{S1} \text{ connected to } R_1 \text{ and } V_{S2} \text{ connected to } R_2$$

or V_{S1} connected to R_2 and V_{S2} connected to R_1

30. The different sections of a stereo system are represented by the blocks in Figure 2–73. Show how a single switch can be used to connect the phonograph, the CD (compact disk) player, the tape deck, the AM tuner, or the FM tuner to the amplifier by a single knob control. Only one section can be connected to the amplifier at any time.

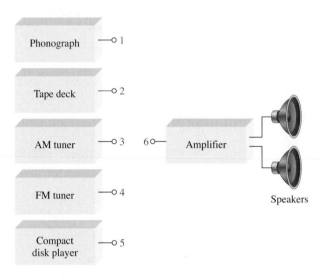

▲ FIGURE 2–73

SECTION 2–8   Basic Circuit Measurements

31. Show the placement of an ammeter and a voltmeter to measure the current and the source voltage in Figure 2–74.

▶ FIGURE 2–74

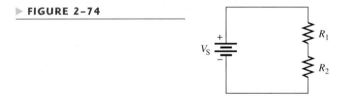

32. Explain how you would measure the resistance of R_2 in Figure 2–74.

33. In Figure 2–75, how much voltage does each meter indicate when the switch is in position 1? In position 2?

▶ FIGURE 2–75

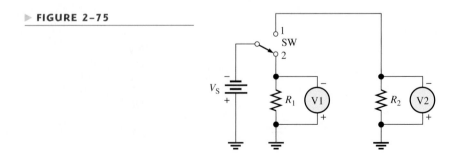

34. In Figure 2–75, indicate how to connect an ammeter to measure the current from the voltage source regardless of the switch position.

35. In Figure 2–72, show the proper placement of ammeters to measure the current through each resistor and the current out of the battery.

36. Show the proper placement of voltmeters to measure the voltage across each resistor in Figure 2–72.

37. What is the voltage reading of the meter in Figure 2–76?

▶ **FIGURE 2–76**

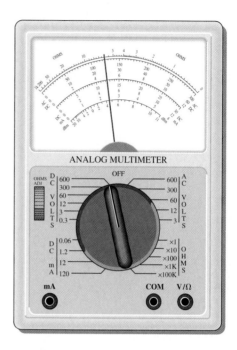

38. How much resistance is the ohmmeter in Figure 2–77 measuring?

▶ **FIGURE 2–77**

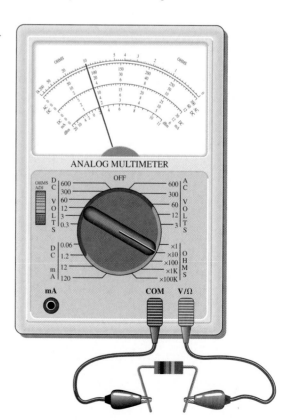

39. Determine the resistance indicated by each of the following ohmmeter readings and range settings:

    (a) pointer at 2, range setting at ×10

    (b) pointer at 15, range setting at ×100,000

    (c) pointer at 45, range setting at ×100

40. What is the maximum resolution of a $4\frac{1}{2}$-digit DMM?

41. Indicate how you would connect the multimeter in Figure 2–77 to the circuit in Figure 2–78 to measure each of the following quantities. In each case indicate the appropriate function and range.

    (a) I_1 **(b)** V_1 **(c)** R_1

▶ **FIGURE 2–78**

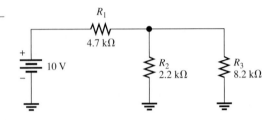

SELF-TEST

1. (b)	**2.** (a)	**3.** (c)	**4.** (c)	**5.** (b)	**6.** (b)	**7.** (c)	**8.** (d)
9. (b)	**10.** (b)	**11.** (e)	**12.** (b)	**13.** (b)	**14.** (c)		

3

OHM'S LAW, ENERGY, AND POWER

INTRODUCTION

Georg Simon Ohm (1787–1854) experimentally found that voltage, current, and resistance are all related in a specific way. This basic relationship, known as *Ohm's law,* is one of the most fundamental and important laws in the fields of electricity and electronics. In this chapter, Ohm's law is examined, and its use in practical circuit applications is discussed and demonstrated by numerous examples.

In addition to Ohm's law, the concepts and definitions of energy and power in electric circuits are introduced and the Watt's law power formulas are given.

CHAPTER OBJECTIVES

- Explain Ohm's law
- Use Ohm's law to determine voltage, current, or resistance
- Define *energy* and *power*
- Calculate power in a circuit
- Properly select resistors based on power consideration
- Explain energy conversion and voltage drop
- Discuss power supplies and their characteristics
- Describe a basic approach to troubleshooting

CHAPTER OUTLINE

KEY TERMS

- Ohm's law
- Linear
- Energy
- Power
- Joule (J)
- Watt (W)
- Kilowatt-hour (kWh)
- Watt's law
- Power rating
- Voltage drop
- Ampere-hour rating
- Efficiency
- Troubleshooting
- Half-splitting

WWW.   VISIT THE COMPANION WEBSITE

Study aids for this chapter are available at
http://www.prenhall.com/floyd

3–1 OHM'S LAW

Ohm's law describes mathematically how voltage, current, and resistance in a circuit are related. Ohm's law can be written in three equivalent forms; the formula you use depends on the quantity you need to determine. In this section, you will learn each of these forms.

After completing this section, you should be able to

- **Explain Ohm's law**
- Describe how voltage (*V*), current (*I*), and resistance (*R*) are related
- Express *I* as a function of *V* and *R*
- Express *V* as a function of *I* and *R*
- Express *R* as a function of *V* and *I*

Ohm determined experimentally that *if the voltage across a resistor is increased, the current through the resistor will increase;* and, likewise, *if the voltage is decreased, the current will decrease.* For example, if the voltage is doubled, the current will double. If the voltage is halved, the current will also be halved. This relationship is illustrated in Figure 3–1, with relative meter indications of voltage and current.

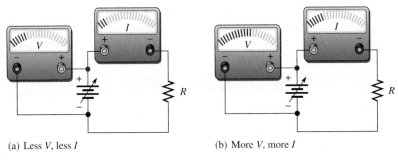

(a) Less *V*, less *I*   (b) More *V*, more *I*

▲ **FIGURE 3–1**

Effect on the current of changing the voltage with the resistance at a constant value.

Ohm's law also shows that *if the voltage is kept constant, less resistance results in more current, and more resistance results in less current.* For example, if the resistance is halved, the current doubles. If the resistance is doubled, the current is halved. This concept is illustrated by the meter indications in Figure 3–2, where the resistance is increased and the voltage is held constant.

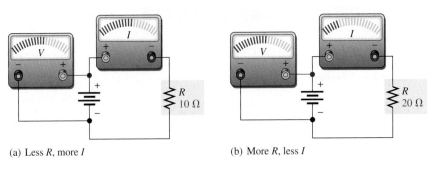

(a) Less *R*, more *I*   (b) More *R*, less *I*

▲ **FIGURE 3–2**

Effect on the current of changing the resistance with the voltage at a constant value.

Formula for Current

Ohm's law can be stated as follows:

$$I = \frac{V}{R}$$

Equation 3–1

This formula describes the relationship illustrated by the action in the circuits of Figures 3–1 and 3–2.

For a constant resistance, if the voltage applied to a circuit is increased, the current will increase; and if the voltage is decreased, the current will decrease.

$$I = \frac{V}{R} \qquad\qquad I = \frac{V}{R} \qquad\qquad R \text{ constant}$$

Increase V, I increases   Decrease V, I decreases

For a constant voltage, if the resistance in a circuit is increased, the current will decrease; and if the resistance is decreased, the current will increase.

$$I = \frac{V}{R} \qquad\qquad I = \frac{V}{R} \qquad\qquad V \text{ constant}$$

Increase R, I decreases   Decrease R, I increases

Using Equation 3–1, you can calculate the current in amperes if you know the values of voltage in volts and resistance in ohms.

EXAMPLE 3–1

Using the Ohm's law formula in Equation 3–1, verify that the current through a 10 Ω resistor increases when the voltage is increased from 5 V to 20 V.

Solution   The following calculations show that the current increases from 0.5 A to 2 A. The calculator sequence for each calculation is also shown, based on the TI-86 set in the ENG mode.

For $V = 5$ V,

$$I = \frac{V}{R} = \frac{5 \text{ V}}{10 \text{ Ω}} = \textbf{0.5 A}$$

For $V = 20$ V,

$$I = \frac{V}{R} = \frac{20 \text{ V}}{10 \text{ Ω}} = \textbf{2 A}$$

5/10
    500E‑3
20/10
    2E0

Related Problem   Show that the current decreases when the resistance is increased from 5 Ω to 20 Ω and the voltage is a constant 10 V.

Formula for Voltage

Ohm's law can also be stated another equivalent way. By multiplying both sides of - Equation 3–1 by R and transposing terms, you obtain an equivalent form of Ohm's law, as follows:

Equation 3–2

$$V = IR$$

With this formula, you can calculate voltage in volts if you know the current in amperes and resistance in ohms.

EXAMPLE 3–2

Use the Ohm's law formula in Equation 3–2 to calculate the voltage across a 100 Ω resistor when the current is 2 A.

Solution

$$V = IR = (2 \text{ A})(100 \text{ Ω}) = \mathbf{200 \text{ V}}$$

Related Problem Find the voltage across a 1.0 kΩ resistor when the current is 1 mA.

Formula for Resistance

There is a third equivalent way to state Ohm's law. By dividing both sides of Equation 3–2 by I and transposing terms, you obtain the following formula:

Equation 3–3

$$R = \frac{V}{I}$$

This form of Ohm's law is used to determine resistance in ohms if you know the values of voltage in volts and current in amperes.

Remember, the three formulas—Equations 3–1, 3–2, and 3–3—are all equivalent. They are simply three different ways of expressing Ohm's law.

EXAMPLE 3–3

Use the Ohm's law formula in Equation 3–3 to calculate the resistance in a circuit when the voltage is 12 V and the current is 0.5 A.

Solution

$$R = \frac{V}{I} = \frac{12 \text{ V}}{0.5 \text{ A}} = \mathbf{24 \text{ Ω}}$$

Related Problem Find the resistance when the voltage is 9 V and the current is 10 mA.

The Linear Relationship of Current and Voltage

In resistive circuits, current and voltage are linearly proportional. **Linear** means that if one is increased or decreased by a certain percentage, the other will increase or decrease by the same percentage, assuming that the resistance is constant in value. For example, if the voltage across a resistor is tripled, the current will triple. If the voltage is reduced by half, the current will decrease by half.

EXAMPLE 3–4

Show that if the voltage in the circuit of Figure 3–3 is increased to three times its present value, the current will triple in value.

▶ **FIGURE 3–3**

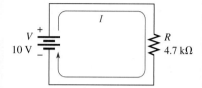

Solution With 10 V, the current is

$$I = \frac{V}{R} = \frac{10\text{ V}}{4.7\text{ k}\Omega} = \textbf{2.13 mA}$$

If the voltage is increased to 30 V, the current will be

$$I = \frac{V}{R} = \frac{30\text{ V}}{4.7\text{ k}\Omega} = \textbf{6.38 mA}$$

The current went from 2.13 mA to 6.38 mA when the voltage was tripled to 30 V.

Related Problem If the voltage in Figure 3–3 is quadrupled, will the current also quadruple?

A Graph of Current Versus Voltage

Let's take a constant value of resistance, for example, 10 Ω, and calculate the current for several values of voltage ranging from 10 V to 100 V in the circuit in Figure 3–4(a). The current values obtained are shown in Figure 3–4(b). The graph of the *I* values versus the *V* values is shown in Figure 3–4(c). Note that it is a straight line graph. This graph shows that a change in voltage results in a linearly proportional change in current. No matter what value *R* is, assuming that *R* is constant, the graph of *I* versus *V* will always be a straight line.

▼ **FIGURE 3–4**

Graph of current versus voltage for the circuit in part (a).

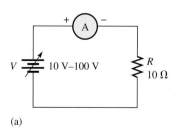

(a)

V	I
10 V	1 A
20 V	2 A
30 V	3 A
40 V	4 A
50 V	5 A
60 V	6 A
70 V	7 A
80 V	8 A
90 V	9 A
100 V	10 A

$$I = \frac{V}{10\ \Omega}$$

(b)

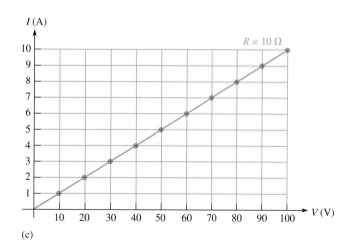

(c)

A Graphic Aid for Ohm's Law

You may find the graphic aid in Figure 3–5 helpful for applying Ohm's law. It is a way to remember the formulas.

▶ FIGURE 3–5

A graphic aid for the Ohm's law formulas.

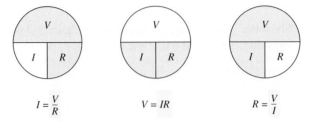

$$I = \frac{V}{R} \qquad\qquad V = IR \qquad\qquad R = \frac{V}{I}$$

3–2 APPLICATION OF OHM'S LAW

This section provides examples of the application of Ohm's law for calculating voltage, current, and resistance in electric circuits. You will also see how to use quantities expressed with metric prefixes in circuit calculations.

After completing this section, you should be able to

■ **Use Ohm's law to determine voltage, current, or resistance**

■ Use Ohm's law to find current when you know voltage and resistance

■ Use Ohm's law to find voltage when you know current and resistance

■ Use Ohm's law to find resistance when you know voltage and current

■ Use quantities with metric prefixes

Determining *I* When You Know *V* and *R*

In these examples you will learn to determine current values when you know the values of voltage and resistance. In these problems, the formula $I = V/R$ is used. In order to get current in amperes, you must express the value of V in volts and the value of R in ohms.

EXAMPLE 3–5

How many amperes of current are in the circuit of Figure 3–6?

▶ FIGURE 3–6

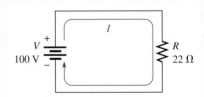

Solution Use the formula $I = V/R$, and substitute 100 V for V and 22 Ω for R.

$$I = \frac{V}{R} = \frac{100\,\text{V}}{22\,\Omega} = \textbf{4.55 A}$$

Related Problem If R is changed to 33 Ω in Figure 3–6, what is the current?

Use Multisim file E03-03 to verify the calculated results in this example and your calculation for the related problem.

In electronics, resistance values of thousands or millions of ohms are common. As you learned in Chapter 1, large values of resistance are indicated by the metric system prefixes *kilo* (k) and *mega* (M). Thus, thousands of ohms are expressed in kilohms (kΩ), and millions of ohms are expressed in megohms (MΩ). The following examples illustrate how to use kilohms and megohms when you use Ohm's law to calculate current.

EXAMPLE 3–6

Calculate the current in milliamperes for the circuit of Figure 3–7.

▶ **FIGURE 3–7**

V = 50 V, R = 1.0 kΩ, I

Solution Remember that 1.0 kΩ is the same as 1.0×10^3 Ω. Use the formula $I = V/R$ and substitute 50 V for V and 1.0×10^3 Ω for R.

$$I = \frac{V_S}{R} = \frac{50 \text{ V}}{1.0 \text{ k}\Omega} = \frac{50 \text{ V}}{1.0 \times 10^3 \, \Omega} = 50 \times 10^{-3} \text{ A} = \mathbf{50 \text{ mA}}$$

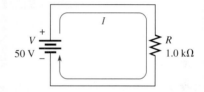

5   0   ÷   1   EE   3   ENTER   50/1E3
50E⁻3

Related Problem If the resistance in Figure 3–7 is increased to 10 kΩ, what is the current?

In Example 3–6, the current is expressed as 50 mA. Thus, *when volts (V) are divided by kilohms (kΩ), the current is in milliamperes (mA)*.

When volts (V) are divided by megohms (MΩ), the current is in microamperes (μA), as Example 3–7 illustrates.

EXAMPLE 3–7

Determine the amount of current in microamperes for the circuit of Figure 3–8.

▶ **FIGURE 3–8**

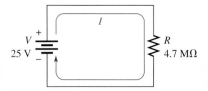

Solution   Recall that 4.7 MΩ equals 4.7×10^6 Ω. Use the formula $I = V/R$ and substitute 25 V for V and 4.7×10^6 Ω for R.

$$I = \frac{V_S}{R} = \frac{25 \text{ V}}{4.7 \text{ M}\Omega} = \frac{25 \text{ V}}{4.7 \times 10^6 \text{ }\Omega} = 5.32 \times 10^{-6} \text{ A} = \mathbf{5.32 \ \mu A}$$

```
25/4.7E6
       5.31914893617E‾6
```

Related Problem   If the resistance in Figure 3–8 is decreased to 1.0 MΩ, what is the current?

Small voltages, usually less than 50 V, are common in electronic circuits. Occasionally, however, large voltages are encountered. For example, the high-voltage supply in a television receiver is around 20,000 V (20 kV). Transmission voltages generated by the power companies may be as high as 345,000 V (345 kV).

EXAMPLE 3–8

How much current in microamperes is there through a 100 MΩ resistor when 50 kV are applied across it?

Solution   Divide 50 kV by 100 MΩ to get the current. Substitute 50×10^3 V for 50 kV and 100×10^6 Ω for 100 MΩ in the formula for current. V_R is the voltage across the resistor.

$$I = \frac{V_R}{R} = \frac{50 \text{ kV}}{100 \text{ M}\Omega} = \frac{50 \times 10^3 \text{ V}}{100 \times 10^6 \text{ }\Omega} = 0.5 \times 10^{-3} \text{ A} = 500 \times 10^{-6} = \mathbf{500 \ \mu A}$$

```
50E3/100E6
       500E‾6
```

Related Problem   How much current is there through 10 MΩ when 2 kV are applied?

Determining *V* When You Know *I* and *R*

In these examples you will see how to determine voltage values when you know the current and resistance using the formula $V = IR$. To obtain voltage in volts, you must express the value of I in amperes and the value of R in ohms.

EXAMPLE 3–9

In the circuit of Figure 3–9, how much voltage is needed to produce 5 A of current?

▶ **FIGURE 3–9**

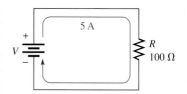

Solution   Substitute 5 A for I and 100 Ω for R into the formula $V = IR$.

$$V_S = IR = (5 \text{ A})(100 \text{ Ω}) = \textbf{500 V}$$

Thus, 500 V are required to produce 5 A of current through a 100 Ω resistor.

Related Problem   How much voltage is required to produce 8 A in the circuit of Figure 3–9?

EXAMPLE 3–10

How much voltage will be measured across the resistor in Figure 3–10?

▶ **FIGURE 3–10**

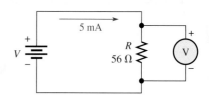

Solution   Note that 5 mA equals 5×10^{-3} A. Substitute the values for I and R into the formula $V = IR$.

$$V_R = IR = (5 \text{ mA})(50 \text{ Ω}) = (5 \times 10^{-3} \text{ A})(50 \text{ Ω}) = \textbf{250 mV}$$

When milliamperes are multiplied by ohms, the result is millivolts.

5   EE   (–)   3   ×   5   0   ENTER   5ᴇ⁻3 ✳50
                                                    250ᴇ⁻3

Related Problem   Change the resistor in Figure 3–10 to 22 Ω and determine the voltage required to produce 10 mA.

EXAMPLE 3–11

The circuit in Figure 3–11 has a current of 10 mA. What is the source voltage?

▶ FIGURE 3–11

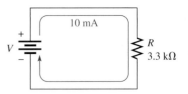

Solution Note that 10 mA equals 10×10^{-3} A and that 3.3 kΩ equals 3.3×10^3 Ω. Substitute these values into the formula $V = IR$.

$$V_S = IR = (10 \text{ mA})(3.3 \text{ k}\Omega) = (10 \times 10^{-3} \text{ A})(3.3 \times 10^3 \text{ }\Omega) = \textbf{33 V}$$

When milliamperes and kilohms are multiplied, the result is volts.

10E⁻3∗3.3E3
33E0

Related Problem What is the voltage in Figure 3–11 if the current is 5 mA?

Determining *R* When You Know *V* and *I*

In these examples you will see how to determine resistance values when you know the voltage and current using the formula $R = V/I$. To find resistance in ohms, you must express the value of *V* in volts and the value of *I* in amperes.

EXAMPLE 3–12

In the circuit of Figure 3–12 how much resistance is needed to draw 3 A of current from the battery?

▶ FIGURE 3–12

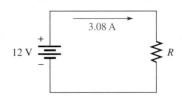

Solution Substitute 12 V for *V* and 3 A for *I* into the formula $R = V/I$.

$$R = \frac{V_S}{I} = \frac{12 \text{ V}}{3 \text{ A}} = \textbf{4 }\Omega$$

Related Problem How much resistance is required to draw 3 mA from the battery in Figure 3–12?

EXAMPLE 3–13

The ammeter in Figure 3–13 indicates 5 mA of current and the voltmeter reads 150 V. What is the value of R?

▶ **FIGURE 3–13**

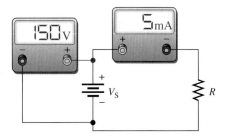

Solution   Note that 5 mA equals 5×10^{-3} A. Substitute the voltage and current values into the formula $R = V/I$.

$$R = \frac{V_S}{I} = \frac{150 \text{ V}}{5 \text{ mA}} = \frac{150 \text{ V}}{5 \times 10^{-3} \text{ A}} = 30 \times 10^3 \text{ } \Omega = \textbf{30 k}\boldsymbol{\Omega}$$

Thus, if volts are divided by milliamperes, the resistance will be in kilohms.

Related Problem   Determine the value of R if $V_S = 50$ V and $I = 500$ mA in Figure 3–13.

3–3   ENERGY AND POWER

When there is current through a resistance, electrical energy is converted to heat or other form of energy, such as light. A common example of this is a light bulb that becomes too hot to touch. The current through the filament that produces light also produces unwanted heat because the filament has resistance. Power is a measure of how fast energy is being used; electrical components must be able to dissipate a certain amount of energy in a given period of time.

After completing this section, you should be able to

■ **Define energy and power**

■ Express power in terms of energy

■ State the unit of power

■ State the common units of energy

■ Perform energy and power calculations

BIOGRAPHY

James Prescott Joule 1818–1889

Joule, a British physicist, is known for his research in electricity and thermodynamics. He formulated the relationship that states that the amount of heat energy produced by an electrical current in a conductor is proportional to the conductor's resistance and the time. The unit of energy is named in his honor. (Photo credit: Library of Congress.)

■ **Energy is the ability to do work.**

■ **Power is the rate at which energy is used.**

In other words, power, symbolized by P, is a certain amount of energy, symbolized by W, used in a certain length of time (t), expressed as follows:

$$P = \frac{W}{t}$$

Equation 3–4

Energy is measured in **joules (J),** time is measured in seconds (s), and power is measured in watts (W). Note that an italic W is used to represent energy in the form of work and a nonitalic W is used for watts, the unit of power.

Energy in joules divided by time in seconds gives power in watts. For example, if 50 J of energy are used in 2 s, the power is 50 J/2 s = 25 W. By definition,

One watt is the amount of power when one joule of energy is used in one second.

Thus, the number of joules used in 1 s is always equal to the number of watts. For example, if 75 J are used in 1 s, the power is $P = W/t = 75$ J/1 s = 75 W.

EXAMPLE 3–14

An amount of energy equal to 100 J is used in 5 s. What is the power in watts?

Solution

$$P = \frac{\text{energy}}{\text{time}} = \frac{W}{t} = \frac{100 \text{ J}}{5 \text{ s}} = \textbf{20 W}$$

Related Problem   If 100 W of power occurs for 30 s, how much energy in joules is used?

Amounts of power much less than one watt are common in certain areas of electronics. As with small current and voltage values, metric prefixes are used to designate small amounts of power. Thus, milliwatts (mW) and microwatts (μW) are commonly found in some applications.

In the electrical utilities field, kilowatts (kW) and megawatts (MW) are common units. Radio and television stations also use large amounts of power to transmit signals. Electric motors are commonly rated in horsepower (hp) where 1 hp = 746 W.

EXAMPLE 3–15

Express the following powers using appropriate metric prefixes:

(a) 0.045 W   (b) 0.000012 W

(c) 3500 W   (d) 10,000,000 W

Solution   (a) $0.045 \text{ W} = 45 \times 10^{-3} \text{ W} = \textbf{45 mW}$

(b) $0.000012 \text{ W} = 12 \times 10^{-6} \text{ W} = \textbf{12 } \boldsymbol{\mu}\textbf{W}$

(c) $3500 \text{ W} = 3.5 \times 10^{3} \text{ W} = \textbf{3.5 kW}$

(d) $10,000,000 \text{ W} = 10 \times 10^{6} \text{ W} = \textbf{10 MW}$

Related Problem   Express the following amounts of power in watts without metric prefixes:

(a) 1 mW   (b) 1800 μW   (c) 3 MW   (d) 10 kW

The Kilowatt-hour (kWh) Unit of Energy

Since power is the rate at which energy is used, power utilized over a period of time represents energy consumption. If you multiply power in watts and time in seconds, you have energy in joules, symbolized by W.

Equation 3–5

$$W = Pt$$

The joule has been defined as the unit of energy. However, there is another way to express energy. Since power is expressed in watts and time can be expressed in hours, a unit of energy called the kilowatt-hour (kWh) can be used.

When you pay your electric bill, you are charged on the basis of the amount of energy you use. Because power companies deal in huge amounts of energy, the most practical unit is the **kilowatt-hour.** *You use a kilowatt-hour of energy when you use the equivalent of 1000 W of power for 1 h.* For example, a 100 W light bulb burning for 10 h uses 1 kWh of energy.

$$W = Pt = (100 \text{ W})(10 \text{ h}) = 1000 \text{ Wh} = 1 \text{ kWh}$$

EXAMPLE 3–16

Determine the number of kilowatt-hours (kWh) for each of the following energy consumptions:

(a) 1400 W for 1 hr   **(b)** 2500 W for 2 h   **(c)** 100,000 W for 5 h

Solution   **(a)** 1400 W = 1.4 kW
$$W = Pt = (1.4 \text{ kW})(1 \text{ h}) = \mathbf{1.4\,kWh}$$

(b) 2500 W = 2.5 kW
Energy = (2.5 kW)(2 h) = **5 kWh**

(c) 100,000 W = 100 kW
Energy = (100 kW)(5 h) = **500 kWh**

Related Problem   How many kilowatt-hours of energy are used by a 250 W light bulb burning for 8 h?

Table 3–1 lists the typical power rating in watts for several household appliances. You can determine the maximum kWh for various appliances by using the power rating in Table 3–1 converted to kilowatts times the number of hours it is used.

**James Watt
1736–1819**
Watt was a Scottish inventer and was well known for his improvements to the steam engine, which made it practical for industrial use. Watt patented several inventions, including the rotary engine. The unit of power is named in his honor. (Photo credit: Library of Congress.)

▶ **TABLE 3–1**

APPLIANCE	POWER RATING (WATTS)
Air conditioner	860
Blow dryer	1300
Clock	2
Clothes dryer	4800
Dishwasher	1200
Heater	1322
Microwave oven	800
Range	12,200
Refrigerator	1800
Television	250
Washing machine	400
Water heater	2500

EXAMPLE 3–17

During a typical 24-hour period, you use the following appliances for the specified lengths of time:

air conditioner: 15 hours   microwave oven: 15 minutes

blow dryer: 10 minutes   refrigerator: 12 hours

clock: 24 hours   television: 2 hours

clothes dryer: 1 hour   water heater: 8 hours

dishwasher: 45 minutes

Determine the total kilowatt-hours and the electric bill for the time period. The rate is 10 cents per kilowatt-hour.

Solution   Determine the kWh for each appliance used by converting the watts in Table 3–1 to kilowatts and multiplying by the time in hours:

air conditioner: 0.860 kW × 15 h = 12.9 kWh

blow dryer: 1.3 kW × 0.167 h = 0.217 kWh

clock: 0.002 kW × 24 h = 0.048 kWh

clothes dryer: 4.8 kW × 1 h = 4.8 kWh

dishwasher: 1.2 kW × 0.75 h = 0.9 kWh

microwave: 0.8 kW × 0.25 h = 0.2 kWh

refrigerator: 1.8 kW × 12 h = 21.6 kWh

television: 0.25 kW × 2 h = 0.5 kWh

water heater: 2.5 kW × 8 h = 20 kWh

Now, add up all the kilowatt-hours to get the total energy for the 24-hour period.

Total energy = (12.9 + 0.217 + 0.048 + 4.8 + 0.9 + 0.2 + 21.6 + 0.5 + 20) kWh
= **61.165 kWh**

At 10 cents/kilowatt-hour, the cost of energy to run the appliances for the 24-hour period is

Energy cost = 61.165 kWh × 0.1 $/kWh = **$6.12**

Related Problem   In addition to the appliances, suppose you used two 100 W light bulbs for 2 hours and one 75 W bulb for 3 hours. Calculate your cost for the 24-hour period for both appliances and lights.

SUMMARY

- Voltage and current are linearly proportional.
- Ohm's law gives the relationship of voltage, current, and resistance.
- Current is directly proportional to voltage.
- Current is inversely proportional to resistance.
- A kilohm (kΩ) is one thousand ohms.
- A megohm (MΩ) is one million ohms.
- A microampere (μA) is one-millionth of an ampere.

- A milliampere (mA) is one-thousandth of an ampere.
- Use $I = V/R$ to calculate current.
- Use $V = IR$ to calculate voltage.
- Use $R = V/I$ to calculate resistance.
- One watt equals one joule per second.
- Watt is the unit of power, and joule is the unit of energy.
- The power rating of a resistor determines the maximum power that it can handle safely.
- Resistors with a larger physical size can dissipate more power in the form of heat than smaller ones.
- A resistor should have a power rating as high or higher than the maximum power that it is expected to handle in the circuit.
- Power rating is not related to resistance value.
- A resistor usually opens when it overheats and fails.
- Energy is equal to power multiplied by time.
- The kilowatt-hour is a unit of energy.
- An example of one kilowatt-hour is one thousand watts used for one hour.
- The formula wheel in Figure 3–14 gives the Ohm's law and Watt's law relationships.

▶ **FIGURE 3–14**

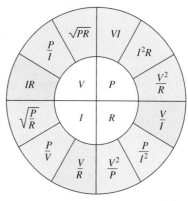

☐ Ohm's law
☐ Watt's law

KEY TERMS

Efficiency The ratio of the output power to the input power of a circuit, expressed as a percent.

Energy The ability to do work. The unit is the joule (J).

Joule (J) The unit of energy.

Kilowatt-hour (kWh) A common unit of energy used mainly by utility companies.

Linear Characterized by a straight-line relationship.

Ohm's law A law stating that current is directly proportional to voltage and inversely proportional to resistance.

Power The rate of energy usage.

Power rating The maximum amount of power that a resistor can dissipate without being damaged by excessive heat buildup.

Troubleshooting A systematic process of isolating, identifying, and correcting a fault in a circuit or system.

Voltage drop The difference in the voltage at two points due to energy conversion.

Watt (W) The unit of power. One watt is the power when 1 J of energy is used in 1 s.

Watt's law A law that states the relationships of power to current, voltage, and resistance.

FORMULAS

3–1	$I = \dfrac{V}{R}$	Ohm's law for current
3–2	$V = IR$	Ohm's law for voltage
3–3	$R = \dfrac{V}{I}$	Ohm's law for resistance
3–4	$P = \dfrac{W}{t}$	Power equals energy divided by time.
3–5	$W = Pt$	Energy equals power multiplied by time.

SELF-TEST

Answers are at the end of the chapter.

1. Ohm's law states that
   (a) current equals voltage times resistance
   (b) voltage equals current times resistance
   (c) resistance equals current divided by voltage
   (d) voltage equals current squared times resistance

2. When the voltage across a resistor is doubled, the current will
   (a) triple   (b) halve   (c) double   (d) not change

3. When 10 V are applied across a 20 Ω resistor, the current is
   (a) 10 A   (b) 0.5 A   (c) 200 A   (d) 2 A

4. When there are 10 mA of current through 1.0 kΩ resistor, the voltage across the resistor is
   (a) 100 V   (b) 0.1 V   (c) 10 kV   (d) 10 V

5. If 20 V are applied across a resistor and there are 6.06 mA of current, the resistance is
   (a) 3.3 kΩ (b) 33 kΩ (c) 330 kΩ (d) 3.03 kΩ

6. A current of 250 μA through a 4.7 kΩ resistor produces a voltage drop of
   (a) 53.2 V   (b) 1.18 mV   (c) 18.8 V   (d) 1.18 V

7. A resistance of 2.2 MΩ is connected across a 1 kV source. The resulting current is approximately
   (a) 2.2 mA   (b) 0.455 mA   (c) 45.5 μA   (d) 0.455 A

8. How much resistance is required to limit the current from a 10 V battery to 1 mA?
   (a) 100 Ω (b) 1.0 kΩ (c) 10 Ω (d) 10 kΩ

9. An electric heater draws 2.5 A from a 110 V source. The resistance of the heating element is
   (a) 275 Ω (b) 22.7 mΩ (c) 44 Ω (d) 440 Ω

10. The current through a flashlight bulb is 20 mA and the total battery voltage is 4.5 V. The resistance of the bulb is
   (a) 90 Ω (b) 225 Ω (c) 4.44 Ω (d) 45 Ω

CIRCUIT DYNAMICS QUIZ

Answers are at the end of the chapter.

1. If the current through a fixed resistor goes from 10 mA to 12 mA, the voltage across the resistor
   (a) increases   (b) decreases   (c) stays the same

2. If the voltage across a fixed resistor goes from 10 V to 7 V, the current through the resistor
   (a) increases   (b) decreases   (c) stays the same

3. A variable resistor has 5 V across it. If you reduce the resistance, the current through it
   (a) increases   (b) decreases   (c) stays the same

4. If the voltage across a resistor increases from 5 V to 10 V and the current increases from 1 mA to 2 mA, the resistance
   (a) increases   (b) decreases   (c) stays the same

Refer to Figure 3–13.

5. If the voltmeter reading changes to 175 V, the ammeter reading
   (a) increases   (b) decreases   (c) stays the same

6. If R is changed to a larger value and the voltmeter reading stays at 150 V, the current
   (a) increases   (b) decreases   (c) stays the same

7. If the resistor is removed from the circuit leaving an open, the ammeter reading
   (a) increases   (b) decreases   (c) stays the same

8. If the resistor is removed from the circuit leaving an open, the voltmeter reading
   (a) increases   (b) decreases   (c) stays the same

PROBLEMS

More difficult problems are indicated by an asterisk (*).

SECTION 3–1   Ohm's Law

1. In a circuit consisting of a voltage source and a resistor, describe what happens to the current when
   (a) the voltage is tripled
   (b) the voltage is reduced by 75%
   (c) the resistance is doubled
   (d) the resistance is reduced by 35%
   (e) the voltage is doubled and the resistance is cut in half
   (f) the voltage is doubled and the resistance is doubled

2. State the formula used to find I when the values of V and R are known.

3. State the formula used to find V when the values of I and R are known.

4. State the formula used to find R when the values of V and I are known.

5. A variable voltage source is connected to the circuit of Figure 3–15. Start at 0 V and increase the voltage in 10 V steps up to 100 V. Determine the current at each voltage point, and plot a graph of V versus I. Is the graph a straight line? What does the graph indicate?

▶ **FIGURE 3–15**

Variable V 100 Ω

6. In a certain circuit, $I = 5$ mA when $V = 1$ V. Determine the current for each of the following voltages in the same circuit:
   (a) $V = 1.5$ V   (b) $V = 2$ V   (c) $V = 3$ V
   (d) $V = 4$ V   (e) $V = 10$ V

7. Figure 3–16 is a graph of current versus voltage for three resistance values. Determine R_1, R_2, and R_3.

▶ **FIGURE 3–16**

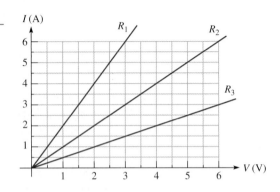

8. Plot the current-voltage relationship for a four-band resistor with the color code gray, red, red, gold.

9. Plot the current-voltage relationship for a five-band resistor with the color code brown, green, gray, brown, red.

10. Which circuit in Figure 3–17 has the most current? The least current?

▶ **FIGURE 3–17**

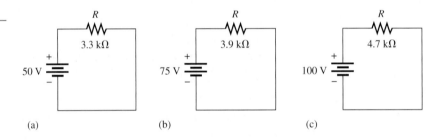

(a)   (b)   (c)

*11. You are measuring the current in a circuit that is operated on a 10 V battery. The ammeter reads 50 mA. Later, you notice that the current has dropped to 30 mA. Eliminating the possibility of a resistance change, you must conclude that the voltage has changed. How much has the voltage of the battery changed, and what is its new value?

*12. If you wish to increase the amount of current in a resistor from 100 mA to 150 mA by changing the 20 V source, by how many volts should you change the source? To what new value should you set it?

13. Plot a graph of current versus voltage for voltage values ranging from 10 V to 100 V in 10 V steps for each of the following resistance values:

(a) 1.0 Ω   (b) 5.0 Ω   (c) 20 Ω   (d) 100 Ω

14. Does the graph in Problem 13 indicate a linear relationship between voltage and current? Explain.

SECTION 3–2   Application of Ohm's Law

15. Determine the current in each case:

(a) $V = 5$ V, $R = 1.0$ Ω   (b) $V = 15$ V, $R = 10$ Ω

(c) $V = 50$ V, $R = 100$ Ω   (d) $V = 30$ V, $R = 15$ kΩ

(e) $V = 250$ V, $R = 5.6$ MΩ

16. Determine the current in each case:

(a) $V = 9$ V, $R = 2.7$ kΩ   (b) $V = 5.5$ V, $R = 10$ kΩ

(c) $V = 40$ V, $R = 68$ kΩ   (d) $V = 1$ kV, $R = 2.2$ kΩ

(e) $V = 66$ kV, $R = 10$ MΩ

17. A 10 Ω resistor is connected across a 12 V battery. What is the current through the resistor?

18. A certain resistor has the following color code: orange, orange, red, gold. Determine the maximum and minimum currents you should expect to measure when a 12 V source is connected across the resistor.

19. A 4-band resistor is connected across the terminals of a 25 V source. Determine the current in the resistor if the color code is yellow, violet, orange, silver.

20. A 5-band resistor is connected across a 12 V source. Determine the current if the color code is orange, violet, yellow, gold, brown.

21. If the voltage in Problem 20 is doubled, will a 0.5 A fuse blow? Explain your answer.

*22. The potentiometer connected as a rheostat in Figure 3–18 is used to control the current to a heating element. When the rheostat is adjusted to a value of 8 Ω or less, the heating element can burn out. What is the rated value of the fuse needed to protect the circuit if the voltage across the heating element at the point of maximum current is 100 V and the voltage across the rheostat is the difference between the heating element voltage and the source voltage?

▶ **FIGURE 3–18**

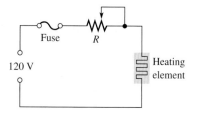

23. Calculate the voltage for each value of I and R:

  (**a**) $I = 2$ A, $R = 18$ Ω   (**b**) $I = 5$ A, $R = 56$ Ω

  (**c**) $I = 2.5$ A, $R = 680$ Ω   (**d**) $I = 0.6$ A, $R = 47$ Ω

  (**e**) $I = 0.1$ A, $R = 560$ Ω

24. Calculate the voltage for each value of I and R:

  (**a**) $I = 1$ mA, $R = 10$ Ω   (**b**) $I = 50$ mA, $R = 33$ Ω

  (**c**) $I = 3$ A, $R = 5.6$ kΩ   (**d**) $I = 1.6$ mA, $R = 2.2$ kΩ

  (**e**) $I = 250$ μA, $R = 1.0$ kΩ   (**f**) $I = 500$ mA, $R = 1.5$ MΩ

  (**g**) $I = 850$ μA, $R = 10$ MΩ   (**h**) $I = 75$ μA, $R = 47$ Ω

25. Three amperes of current are measured through a 27 Ω resistor connected across a voltage source. How much voltage does the source produce?

26. Assign a voltage value to each source in the circuits of Figure 3–19 to obtain the indicated amounts of current.

▶ **FIGURE 3–19**

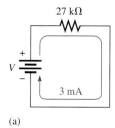

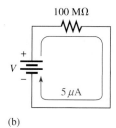

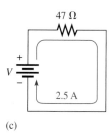

  (a)   (b)   (c)

*27. A 6 V source is connected to a 100 Ω resistor by two 12 ft lengths of 18 gauge copper wire. The total resistance is the resistance of both wires added to the 100 Ω resistor. Determine the following:

  (**a**) Current

  (**b**) Resistor voltage drop

  (**c**) Voltage drop across each length of wire

28. Calculate the resistance of a rheostat for each value of V and I:

(a) $V = 10$ V, $I = 2$ A   (b) $V = 90$ V, $I = 45$ A

(c) $V = 50$ V, $I = 5$ A   (d) $V = 5.5$ V, $I = 10$ A

(e) $V = 150$ V, $I = 0.5$ A

29. Calculate the resistance of a rheostat for each set of V and I values:

(a) $V = 10$ kV, $I = 5$ A   (b) $V = 7$ V, $I = 2$ mA

(c) $V = 500$ V, $I = 250$ mA   (d) $V = 50$ V, $I = 500$ μA

(e) $V = 1$ kV, $I = 1$ mA

30. Six volts are applied across a resistor. A current of 2 mA is measured. What is the value of the resistor?

31. The filament of a lamp in the circuit of Figure 3–20(a) has a certain amount of resistance, represented by an equivalent resistance in Figure 3–20(b). If the lamp operates with 120 V and 0.8 A of current, what is the resistance of its filament when it is on?

▶ FIGURE 3–20

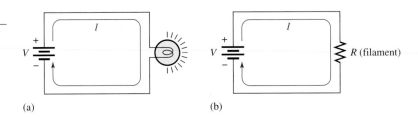

(a)   (b)

32. A certain electrical device has an unknown resistance. You have available a 12 V battery and an ammeter. How would you determine the value of the unknown resistance? Draw the necessary circuit connections.

33. By varying the rheostat (variable resistor) in the circuit of Figure 3–21, you can change the amount of current. The setting of the rheostat is such that the current is 750 mA. What is the resistance value of this setting? To adjust the current to 1 A, to what resistance value must you set the rheostat? What is the problem with this circuit?

▶ FIGURE 3–21

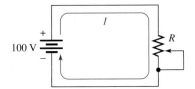

*34. A 120 V lamp-dimming circuit is controlled by a rheostat and protected from excessive current by a 2 A fuse. To what minimum resistance value can the rheostat be set without blowing the fuse? Assume a lamp resistance of 15 Ω.

35. Repeat Problem 34 for a 110 V circuit and a 1 A fuse.

SELF-TEST

1. (b)   2. (c)   3. (b)   4. (d)   5. (a)   6. (d)   7. (b)   8. (d)

9. (c)   10. (b)

4

SERIES CIRCUITS

INTRODUCTION

Resistive circuits can be of two basic forms: series or parallel. In this chapter we discuss series circuits. In this chapter you will see how Ohm's law is used in series circuits; and you will study another important law, Kirchhoff's voltage law. Also, several important applications of series circuits are presented.

CHAPTER OBJECTIVES

- Identify a series circuit
- Determine the current in a series circuit
- Determine total series resistance
- Apply Ohm's law in series circuits
- Determine the total effect of voltage sources in series
- Apply Kirchhoff's voltage law
- Use a series circuit as a voltage divider
- Determine power in a series circuit
- Determine and identify ground in a circuit
- Troubleshoot series circuits

KEY TERMS

- Series
- Series-aiding
- Series-opposing
- Circuit ground
- Kirchhoff's voltage law
- Voltage divider
- Open
- Short

WWW. VISIT THE COMPANION WEBSITE

Study aids for this chapter are available at
http://www.prenhall.com/floyd

4–1 RESISTORS IN SERIES

 When connected in **series,** resistors form a "string" in which there is only one path for current.

After completing this section, you should be able to

■ **Identify a series circuit**

■ Translate a physical arrangement of resistors into a schematic

Figure 4–1(a) shows two resistors connected in series between point A and point B. Part (b) shows three resistors in series, and part (c) shows four in series. Of course, there can be any number of resistors in series.

▶ **FIGURE 4–1**

Resistors in series.

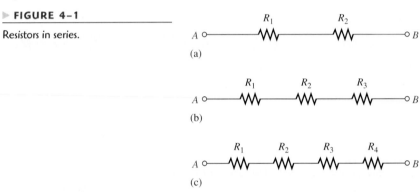

When a voltage source is connected between point A and point B, the only way for electrons to get from one point to the other in any of the connections of Figure 4–1 is to go through each of the resistors. A series circuit is identified as follows:

A series circuit provides only one path for current between two points so that the current is the same through each series resistor.

Identifying Series Circuits

In an actual circuit diagram, a series circuit may not always be as easy to identify as those in Figure 4–1. For example, Figure 4–2 shows series resistors drawn in other ways with a voltage applied. Remember, if there is only one current path between two points, the resistors between those two points are in series, no matter how they appear in a diagram.

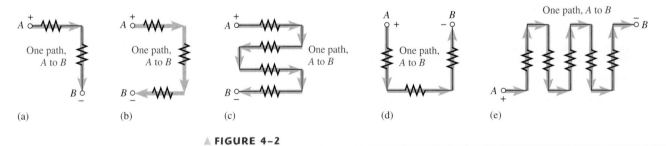

▲ **FIGURE 4–2**

Some examples of series connections of resistors. Notice that the current must be the same at all points because the current has only one path.

EXAMPLE 4–1

Five resistors are positioned on a circuit board as shown in Figure 4–3. Wire them together in series so that, starting from the negative (−) terminal, R_1 is first, R_2 is second, R_3 is third, and so on. Draw a schematic showing this connection.

▶ FIGURE 4–3

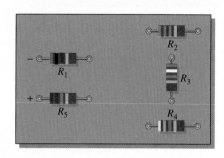

Solution   The wires are connected as shown in Figure 4–4(a), which is the assembly diagram. The schematic is shown in Figure 4–4(b). Note that the schematic does not necessarily show the actual physical arrangement of the resistors as does the assembly diagram. The schematic shows how components are connected electrically; the assembly diagram shows how components are arranged and interconnected physically.

▶ FIGURE 4–4

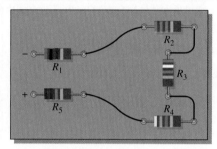

(a) Assembly diagram

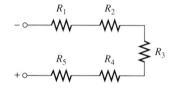

(b) Schematic

Related Problem   (a) Show how you would rewire the circuit board in Figure 4–4(a) so that all the odd-number resistors come first followed by the even-numbered ones.

(b) Determine the value of each resistor.

EXAMPLE 4–2

Describe how the resistors on the printed circuit (PC) board in Figure 4–5 are related electrically. Determine the resistance value of each resistor.

▶ FIGURE 4–5

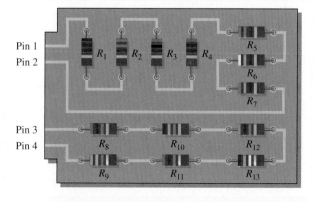

Solution   Resistors R_1 through R_7 are in series with each other. This series combination is connected between pins 1 and 2 on the PC board.

Resistors R_8 through R_{13} are in series with each other. This series combination is connected between pins 3 and 4 on the PC board.

The values of the resistors are $R_1 = 2.2$ kΩ, $R_2 = 3.3$ kΩ, $R_3 = 1.0$ kΩ, $R_4 = 1.2$ kΩ, $R_5 = 3.3$ kΩ, $R_6 = 4.7$ kΩ, $R_7 = 5.6$ kΩ, $R_8 = 12$ kΩ, $R_9 = 68$ kΩ, $R_{10} = 27$ kΩ, $R_{11} = 12$ kΩ, $R_{12} = 82$ kΩ, and $R_{13} = 270$ kΩ.

Related Problem   How is the circuit in Figure 4–5 changed when pin 2 and pin 3 are connected?

4–2   CURRENT IN A SERIES CIRCUIT

The current is the same through all points in a series circuit. The current through each resistor in a series circuit is the same as the current through all the other resistors that are in series with it.

After completing this section, you should be able to

■ **Determine the current in a series circuit**

■ Show that the current is the same at all points in a series circuit

Figure 4–6 shows three resistors connected in series to a voltage source. *At any point in this circuit, the current into that point must equal the current out of that point,* as illustrated by the current directional arrows. Notice also that the current out of each of the resistors must equal the current in because there is no place where part of the current can branch off and go somewhere else. Therefore, the current in each section of the circuit is the same as the current in all other sections. It has only one path going from the negative ($-$) side of the source to the positive ($+$) side.

In Figure 4–7, the battery supplies 1 A of current to the series resistors. There is one ampere of current out of the battery's negative terminal. As shown, one ampere of current is measured at several points in the series circuit.

▶ **FIGURE 4–6**

Current entering any point in a series circuit is the same as the current leaving that point.

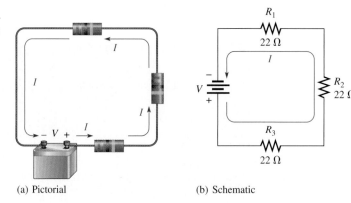

(a) Pictorial   (b) Schematic

(a) Pictorial   (b) Schematic

4–3   TOTAL SERIES RESISTANCE

The total resistance of a series circuit is equal to the sum of the resistances of each individual resistor.

After completing this section, you should be able to

■ **Determine total series resistance**

■ Explain why resistance values add when resistors are connected in series

■ Apply the series resistance formula

Series Resistor Values Add

When resistors are connected in series, the resistor values add because each resistor offers opposition to the current in direct proportion to its resistance. A greater number of resistors connected in series creates more opposition to current. More opposition to current implies a higher value of resistance. Thus, for every resistor that is added in series, the total resistance increases.

Figure 4–8 illustrates how series resistances add together to increase the total resistance. Part (a) has a single 10 Ω resistor. Part (b) shows another 10 Ω resistor connected in series with the first one, making a total resistance of 20 Ω. If a third 10 Ω resistor is connected in series with the first two, as shown in part (c), the total resistance becomes 30 Ω.

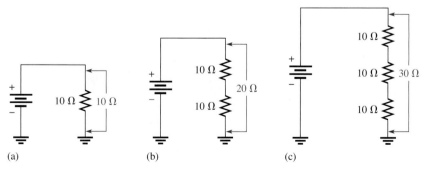

(a)   (b)   (c)

▲ FIGURE 4–8

Total resistance increases with each additional series resistor. The ground symbol used here was introduced in Section 2–6.

Series Resistance Formula

For any number of individual resistors connected in series, the total resistance is the sum of each of the individual values.

$$R_T = R_1 + R_2 + R_3 + \cdots + R_n$$

Equation 4–1

where R_T is the total resistance and R_n is the last resistor in the series string (n can be any positive integer equal to the number of resistors in series). For example, if there are four resistors in series ($n = 4$), the total resistance formula is

$$R_T = R_1 + R_2 + R_3 + R_4$$

If there are six resistors in series ($n = 6$), the total resistance formula is

$$R_T = R_1 + R_2 + R_3 + R_4 + R_5 + R_6$$

To illustrate the calculation of total series resistance, let's determine R_T of the circuit of Figure 4–12, where V_S is the source voltage. This circuit has five resistors in series. To find the total resistance, simply add the values.

$$R_T = 56\ \Omega + 100\ \Omega + 27\ \Omega + 10\ \Omega + 47\ \Omega = 240\ \Omega$$

Note in Figure 4–9 that the order in which the resistances are added does not matter. Also, you can physically change the positions of the resistors in the circuit without affecting the total resistance or the current.

▶ **FIGURE 4–9**

Example of five resistors in series. V_S stands for source voltage.

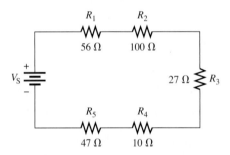

EXAMPLE 4–3

Connect the resistors on the protoboard in Figure 4–10 in series, and determine the total resistance, R_T.

▶ **FIGURE 4–10**

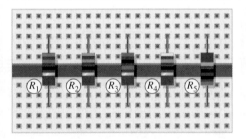

Solution   The resistors are connected as shown in Figure 4–11. Find the total resistance by adding all the values.

$$R_T = R_1 + R_2 + R_3 + R_4 + R_5 = 33\ \Omega + 68\ \Omega + 100\ \Omega + 47\ \Omega + 10\ \Omega = \mathbf{258\ \Omega}$$

▶ **FIGURE 4-11**

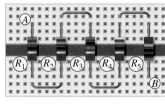

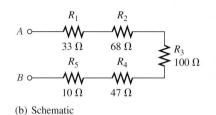

(a) Circuit assembly   (b) Schematic

Related Problem   Determine the total resistance in Figure 4–11(a) if the positions of R_2 and R_4 are interchanged.

EXAMPLE 4-4

What is the total resistance (R_T) in the circuit of Figure 4–12?

▶ **FIGURE 4-12**

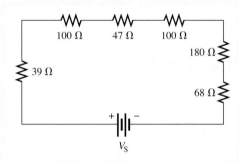

Solution   Sum all the values.

$$R_T = 39\ \Omega + 100\ \Omega + 47\ \Omega + 100\ \Omega + 180\ \Omega + 68\ \Omega = \mathbf{534\ \Omega}$$

Related Problem   What is the total resistance for the following series resistors: 1.0 kΩ, 2.2 kΩ, 3.3 kΩ, and 5.6 kΩ?

EXAMPLE 4-5

Determine the value of R_4 in the circuit of Figure 4–13.

Solution   From the ohmmeter reading, $R_T = 146$ kΩ.

$$R_T = R_1 + R_2 + R_3 + R_4$$

Solving for R_4 yields

$$R_4 = R_T - (R_1 + R_2 + R_3) = 146\ \text{k}\Omega - (10\ \text{k}\Omega + 33\ \text{k}\Omega + 47\ \text{k}\Omega) = \mathbf{56\ k\Omega}$$

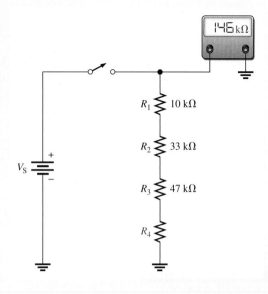

Related Problem   Determine the value of R_4 in Figure 4–13 if the ohmmeter reading is 112 kΩ.

Equal-Value Series Resistors

When a circuit has more than one resistor of the same value in series, there is a shortcut method to obtain the total resistance: Simply multiply the resistance value of the resistors having the same value by the number of equal-value resistors that are in series. This method is essentially the same as adding the values. For example, five 100 Ω resistors in series have an R_T of 5(100 Ω) = 500 Ω. In general, the formula is expressed as

Equation 4–2

$$R_T = nR$$

where n is the number of equal-value resistors and R is the resistance value.

EXAMPLE 4–6

Find the R_T of eight 22 Ω resistors in series.

Solution   Find R_T by adding the values.

$$R_T = 22\ \Omega + 22\ \Omega + 22\ \Omega + 22\ \Omega + 22\ \Omega + 22\ \Omega + 22\ \Omega + 22\ \Omega = \mathbf{176\ \Omega}$$

However, it is much easier to multiply.

$$R_T = 8(22\ \Omega) = \mathbf{176\ \Omega}$$

Related Problem   Find R_T for three 1.0 kΩ and two 680 Ω resistors in series.

4–4   OHM'S LAW IN SERIES CIRCUITS

The application of Ohm's law and the basic concepts of series circuits are presented in several examples.

After completing this section, you should be able to

■ **Apply Ohm's law in series circuits**

■ Find the current in a series circuit

■ Find the voltage across each resistor in series

Here are several key points to remember when you analyze series circuits.

1. Current through one of the series resistors is the same as the current through each of the other resistors and is the total current.

2. If you know the total voltage and the total resistance, you can determine the total current by using

$$I_T = \frac{V_T}{R_T}$$

3. If you know the voltage drop across one of the series resistors, you can determine the current by using

$$I = \frac{V_R}{R}$$

4. If you know the total current, you can find the voltage drop across any of the series resistors by using

$$V_R = I_T R$$

5. The polarity of a voltage drop across a resistor is positive at the end of the resistor that is closest to the positive terminal of the voltage source.

6. The resistor current is in a direction from the negative end of the resistor to the positive end.

7. An open in a series circuit prevents current; and, therefore, there is zero voltage drop across each series resistor. The total voltage appears across the points between which there is an open.

Now let's look at several examples that involve using Ohm's law.

EXAMPLE 4–7

Find the current in the circuit of Figure 4–14.

▶ **FIGURE 4–14**

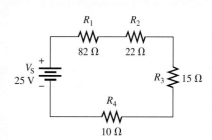

Solution   The current is determined by the source voltage V_S and the total resistance R_T. First, calculate the total resistance.

$$R_T = R_1 + R_2 + R_3 + R_4 = 82\ \Omega + 22\ \Omega + 15\ \Omega + 10\ \Omega = 129\ \Omega$$

Next, use Ohm's law to calculate the current.

$$I = \frac{V_S}{R_T} = \frac{25\ \text{V}}{129\ \Omega} = 0.194\ \text{A} = \mathbf{194\ mA}$$

where V_S is the total voltage and I is the total current. Remember, the same current exists at all points in the circuit. Thus, each resistor has 194 mA through it.

Related Problem   What is the current in the circuit of Figure 4–14 if R_4 is changed to 100 Ω?

Use Multisim file E05-07 to verify the calculated results in this example and to confirm your calculation for the related problem.

EXAMPLE 4–8

The current in the circuit of Figure 4–15 is 1 mA. For this amount of current, what must the source voltage V_S be?

▶ **FIGURE 4–15**

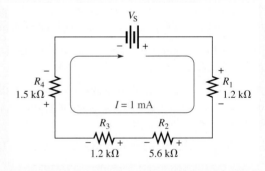

Solution   In order to calculate V_S, first determine R_T.

$$R_T = 1.2\ \text{k}\Omega + 5.6\ \text{k}\Omega + 1.2\ \text{k}\Omega + 1.5\ \text{k}\Omega = 9.5\ \text{k}\Omega$$

Now use Ohm's law to get V_S.

$$V_S = IR_T = (1\ \text{mA})(9.5\ \text{k}\Omega) = \mathbf{9.5\ V}$$

Related Problem   If the 5.6 kΩ resistor is changed to 3.9 kΩ, what value of V_S is necessary to keep the current at 1 mA?

EXAMPLE 4–9

Calculate the voltage across each resistor in Figure 4–16, and find the value of V_S. To what maximum value can V_S be raised if the current is to be limited to 5 mA?

▶ **FIGURE 4–16**

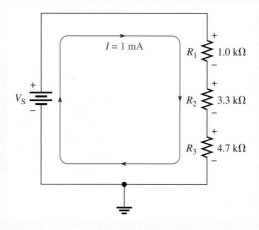

Solution By Ohm's law, the voltage across each resistor is equal to its resistance multiplied by the current through it. Use the Ohm's law formula $V = IR$ to determine the voltage across each of the resistors. Keep in mind that there is the same current through each series resistor. The voltage across R_1 (designated V_1) is

$$V_1 = IR_1 = (1 \text{ mA})(1.0 \text{ k}\Omega) = \mathbf{1 \text{ V}}$$

The voltage across R_2 is

$$V_2 = IR_2 = (1 \text{ mA})(3.3 \text{ k}\Omega) = \mathbf{3.3 \text{ V}}$$

The voltage across R_3 is

$$V_3 = IR_3 = (1 \text{ mA})(4.7 \text{ k}\Omega) = \mathbf{4.7 \text{ V}}$$

To find the value of V_S, first determine R_T.

$$R_T = 1.0 \text{ k}\Omega + 3.3 \text{ k}\Omega + 4.7 \text{ k}\Omega = 9 \text{ k}\Omega$$

The source voltage V_S is equal to the current times the total resistance.

$$V_S = IR_T = (1 \text{ mA})(9 \text{ k}\Omega) = \mathbf{9 \text{ V}}$$

Notice that if you add the voltage drops of the resistors, they total 9 V, which is the same as the source voltage.

V_S can be increased to a value where $I = 5$ mA. Calculate the maximum value of V_S as follows:

$$V_{S(max)} = IR_T = (5 \text{ mA})(9 \text{ k}\Omega) = \mathbf{45 \text{ V}}$$

Related Problem Repeat the calculations for V_1, V_2, V_3, V_S, and $V_{S(max)}$ if $R_3 = 2.2$ kΩ and I is maintained at 1 mA.

Use Multisim file E05-09 to verify the calculated results in this example and to confirm your calculations for the related problem.

EXAMPLE 4–10

Some resistors are not color coded with bands but have the values stamped on the resistor body. When the portion of the circuit board shown in Figure 4–17 was assembled, someone mounted the resistors with the labels turned down, and there is no documentation showing the resistor values. Assume that a voltmeter, ammeter, and power supply are available, but no ohmmeter. Without removing the resistors from the board, use Ohm's law to determine the resistance of each one.

▶ **FIGURE 4–17**

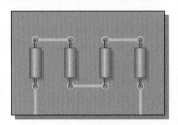

Solution The resistors are all in series, so the current is the same through each one. Measure the current by connecting a 12 V source (arbitrary value) and an ammeter as shown in Figure 4–18. Measure the voltage across each resistor by placing the voltmeter across the first resistor (R_1). Then repeat this measurement for the other three resistors. For illustration, the voltage values indicated are assumed to be the measured values.

▶ **FIGURE 4–18**

The voltages measured across each resistor are indicated beside the resistor.

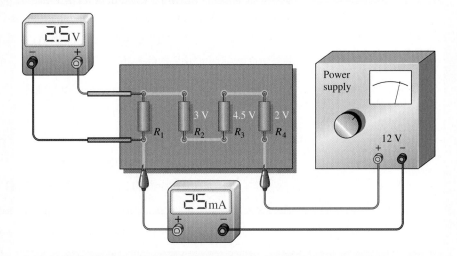

Determine the resistance of each resistor by substituting the measured values of current and voltage into the Ohm's law formula.

$$R_1 = \frac{V_1}{I} = \frac{2.5 \text{ V}}{25 \text{ mA}} = 100 \text{ } \Omega$$

$$R_2 = \frac{V_2}{I} = \frac{3 \text{ V}}{25 \text{ mA}} = 120 \text{ } \Omega$$

$$R_3 = \frac{V_3}{I} = \frac{4.5 \text{ V}}{25 \text{ mA}} = 180 \text{ } \Omega$$

$$R_4 = \frac{V_4}{I} = \frac{2 \text{ V}}{25 \text{ mA}} = 80 \text{ } \Omega$$

The calculator sequence and display for R_1 are

| 2 | . | 5 | ÷ | 2 | 5 | EE | (–) | 3 | ENTER |

```
2.5/25E-3
        100E0
```

Related Problem   If R_2 is open, what voltage is measured across each resistor?

4–5   CIRCUIT GROUND

Voltage is relative. That is, the voltage at one point in a circuit is always measured relative to another point. For example, if we say that there are +100 V at a certain point in a circuit, we mean that the point is 100 V more positive than some reference point in the circuit. This reference point in a circuit is usually the ground point.

After completing this section, you should be able to

■ **Determine and identify ground in a circuit**

■ Measure voltage with respect to ground

■ Define the term *circuit ground*

The concept of *ground* was introduced in Chapter 2. In most electronic equipment, a large conductive area on a printed circuit board or the metal chassis that houses the assembly is used as the common or reference point, called the **circuit ground** or *chassis ground,* as illustrated in Figure 4–19.

Ground has a potential of zero volts (0 V) with respect to all other points in the circuit that are referenced to it, as illustrated in Figure 4–20. In part (a), the negative side of the

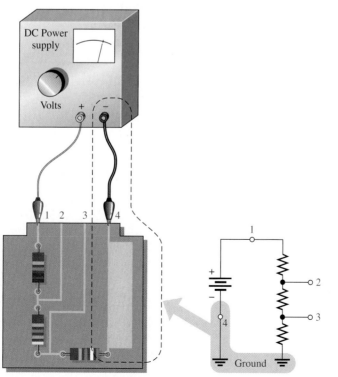

▲ **FIGURE 4–19**

Simple illustration of circuit ground.

▶ FIGURE 4–20

Examples of negative and positive grounds. Multiple ground symbols actually represent the same electrical point, so you can think of them as being connected together.

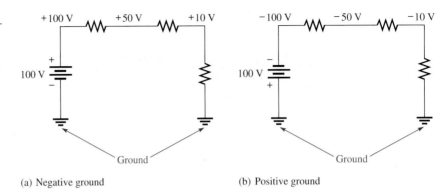

(a) Negative ground   (b) Positive ground

source is grounded, and all voltages indicated are positive with respect to ground. In part (b), the positive side of the source is grounded. The voltages at all other points are therefore negative with respect to ground.

Measuring Voltages with Respect to Ground

When voltages are measured with respect to ground in a circuit, one meter lead is connected to the circuit ground and the other to the point at which the voltage is to be measured. In a negative-ground circuit, the negative meter terminal is connected to the circuit ground. The positive terminal of the voltmeter is then connected to the positive voltage point. Measurement of positive voltage is illustrated in Figure 4–21, where the meter reads the voltage at point A with respect to ground.

For a circuit with a positive ground, the positive analog voltmeter lead is connected to ground, and the negative lead is connected to the negative voltage point, as indicated in Figure 4–22. Here the meter reads the voltage at point A with respect to ground. When using a digital voltmeter, you can connect it either way because a digital meter can display both positive and negative voltages.

▶ FIGURE 4–21

Measuring a voltage with respect to negative ground.

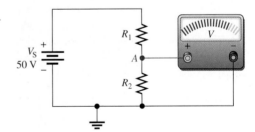

▶ FIGURE 4–22

Measuring a voltage with respect to positive ground.

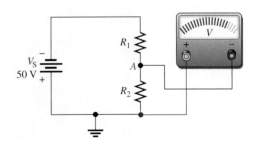

When voltages must be measured at several points in a circuit, the ground lead can be clipped to ground at one point in the circuit and left there. The other lead is then moved from point to point as the voltages are measured. This method is illustrated in Figure 4–23 and in equivalent schematic form in Figure 4–24.

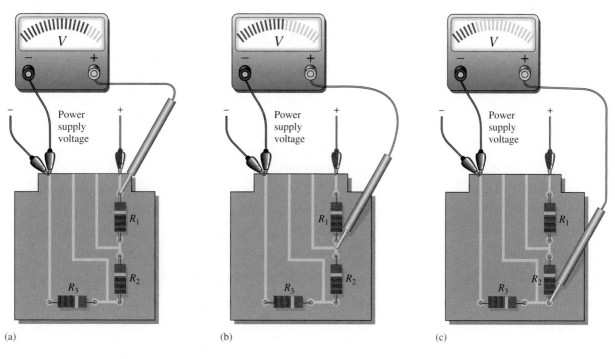

▲ FIGURE 4–23

Measuring voltages at several points in a circuit with respect to ground.

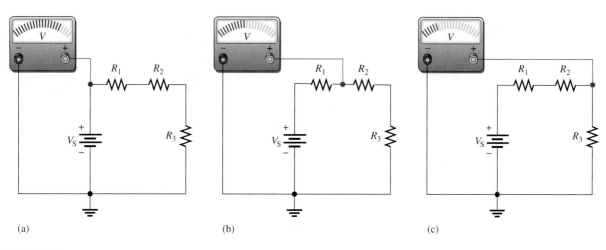

▲ FIGURE 4–24

Equivalent schematics for Figure 4–23.

Measuring Voltage across an Ungrounded Resistor

Voltage can normally be measured across a resistor, as shown in Figure 4–25, even though neither side of the resistor is connected to circuit ground.

Another method can be used, as illustrated in Figure 4–26. The voltages on each side of the resistor (R_2) are measured with respect to ground. The difference of these two measurements is the voltage drop across the resistor.

▶ **FIGURE 4–25**

Measuring voltage directly across a resistor.

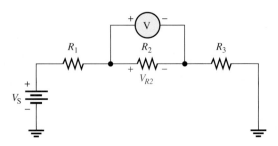

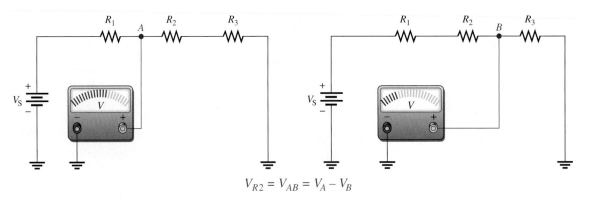

$$V_{R2} = V_{AB} = V_A - V_B$$

▲ **FIGURE 4–26**

Measuring voltage across R_2 with two separate measurements to ground.

EXAMPLE 4–11

Determine the voltages at each of the indicated points in each circuit of Figure 4–27. Since each of the four resistors has the same value, 25 V are dropped across each one.

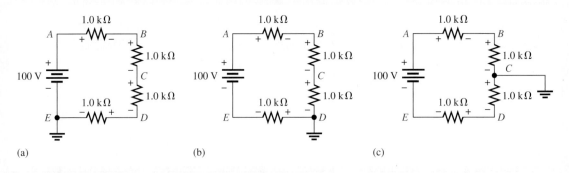

(a)   (b)   (c)

▲ **FIGURE 4–27**

Solution For the circuit in Figure 4–27(a), the voltage polarities are as shown. Point E is ground. Single-letter subscripts denote voltage at a point with respect to ground. The voltages with respect to ground are as follows:

$$V_E = 0 \text{ V}, \quad V_D = +25 \text{ V}, \quad V_C = +50 \text{ V}, \quad V_B = +75 \text{ V}, \quad V_A = +100 \text{ V}$$

For the circuit in Figure 4–27(b), the voltage polarities are as shown. Point D is ground. The voltages with respect to ground are as follows:

$$V_E = -25 \text{ V}, \quad V_D = 0 \text{ V}, \quad V_C = +25 \text{ V}, \quad V_B = +50 \text{ V}, \quad V_A = +75 \text{ V}$$

For the circuit in Figure 4–27(c), the voltage polarities are as shown. Point C is ground. The voltages with respect to ground are as follows:

$$V_E = -50 \text{ V}, \quad V_D = -25 \text{ V}, \quad V_C = 0 \text{ V}, \quad V_B = +25 \text{ V}, \quad V_A = +50 \text{ V}$$

Related Problem If the ground is moved to point A in Figure 4–27(a), what are the voltages at each of the other points with respect to ground?

4–6 KIRCHHOFF'S VOLTAGE LAW

Kirchhoff's voltage law is a fundamental circuit law that states that the algebraic sum of all the voltages around a single closed path is zero or, in other words, the sum of the voltage drops equals the total source voltage.

After completing this section, you should be able to

■ **Apply Kirchhoff's voltage law**

  ■ State Kirchhoff's voltage law

  ■ Determine the source voltage by adding the voltage drops

  ■ Determine an unknown voltage drop

In an electric circuit, the voltages across the resistors (voltage drops) *always* have polarities opposite to the source voltage polarity. For example, in Figure 4–28, follow a clockwise loop around the circuit. Note that the source polarity is minus-to-plus and each voltage drop is plus-to-minus. The voltage drops across resistors are designated as V_1, V_2, and so on.

▶ **FIGURE 4–28**

Illustration of voltage polarities in a closed-loop circuit.

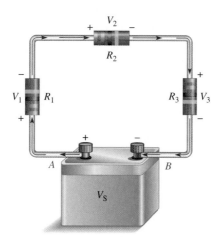

In Figure 4–28, the current is out of the positive side of the source and through the resistors as the arrows indicate. The current is into the positive side of each resistor and out the negative side. The drop in energy level across a resistor creates a potential difference, or voltage drop, with a plus-to-minus polarity in the direction of the current.

The voltage from point A to point B in the circuit of Figure 4–28 is the source voltage, V_S. Also, the voltage from A to B is the sum of the series resistor voltage drops. Therefore, the source voltage is equal to the sum of the three voltage drops, as stated by **Kirchhoff's voltage law.**

The sum of all the voltage drops around a single closed path in a circuit is equal to the total source voltage in that loop.

The general concept of Kirchhoff's voltage law is illustrated in Figure 4–29 and expressed by Equation 4–3.

Equation 4–3

$$V_S = V_1 + V_2 + V_3 + \cdots + V_n$$

where the subscript n represents the number of voltage drops.

▶ **FIGURE 4–29**

Sum of n voltage drops equals the source voltage.

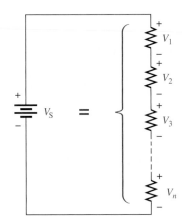

If all the voltage drops around a closed path are added and then this total is subtracted from the source voltage, the result is zero. This result occurs because the sum of the voltage drops always equals the source voltage.

The algebraic sum of all the voltages (both source and drops) around a single closed path is zero.

Therefore, another way of expressing Kirchhoff's voltage law in equation form is

Equation 4–4

$$V_S - V_1 - V_2 - V_3 - \cdots - V_n = 0$$

You can verify Kirchhoff's voltage law by connecting a circuit and measuring each resistor voltage and the source voltage as illustrated in Figure 4–30. When the resistor voltages are added together, their sum will equal the source voltage. Any number of resistors can be added.

The three examples that follow use Kirchhoff's voltage law to solve circuit problems.

Illustration of an experimental verification of Kirchhoff's voltage law.

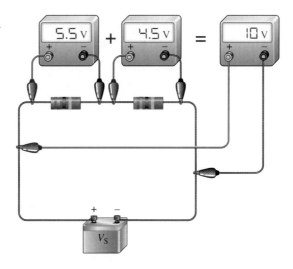

EXAMPLE 4–12

Determine the source voltage V_S in Figure 4–31 where the two voltage drops are given. There is no voltage drop across the fuse.

▶ FIGURE 4–31

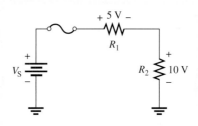

Solution By Kirchhoff's voltage law, (Eq. 4–3), the source voltage (applied voltage) must equal the sum of the voltage drops. Adding the voltage drops gives the value of the source voltage.

$$V_S = 5 \text{ V} + 10 \text{ V} = \textbf{15 V}$$

Related Problem If V_S is increased to 30 V, determine the two voltage drops. What is the voltage across each component (including the fuse) if the fuse is blown?

EXAMPLE 4–13

Determine the unknown voltage drop, V_3, in Figure 4–32.

▶ FIGURE 4–32

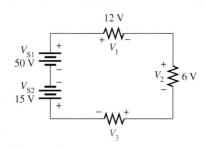

Solution By Kirchhoff's voltage law (Eq. 4–4), the algebraic sum of all the voltages around the circuit is zero. The value of each voltage drop except V_3 is known. Substitute these values into the equation.

$$-V_{S2} + V_{S1} - V_1 - V_2 - V_3 = 0$$
$$-15\ \text{V} + 50\ \text{V} - 12\ \text{V} - 6\ \text{V} - V_3 = 0\ \text{V}$$

Next, combine the known values, transpose 17 V to the right side of the equation, and cancel the minus signs.

$$17\ \text{V} - V_3 = 0\ \text{V}$$
$$-V_3 = -17\ \text{V}$$
$$V_3 = \textbf{17 V}$$

The voltage drop across R_3 is 17 V, and its polarity is as shown in Figure 4–32.

Related Problem Determine V_3 if the polarity of V_{S2} is reversed in Figure 4–32.

EXAMPLE 4–14

Find the value of R_4 in Figure 4–33.

▶ **FIGURE 4–33**

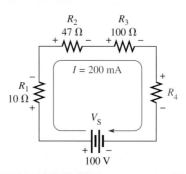

Solution In this problem you will use both Ohm's law and Kirchhoff's voltage law.
First, use Ohm's law to find the voltage drop across each of the known resistors.

$$V_1 = IR_1 = (200\ \text{mA})(10\ \Omega) = 2.0\ \text{V}$$
$$V_2 = IR_2 = (200\ \text{mA})(47\ \Omega) = 9.4\ \text{V}$$
$$V_3 = IR_3 = (200\ \text{mA})(100\ \Omega) = 20\ \text{V}$$

Next, use Kirchhoff's voltage law to find V_4, the voltage drop across the unknown resistor.

$$V_S - V_1 - V_2 - V_3 - V_4 = 0\ \text{V}$$
$$100\ \text{V} - 2.0\ \text{V} - 9.4\ \text{V} - 20\ \text{V} - V_4 = 0\ \text{V}$$
$$68.6\ \text{V} - V_4 = 0\ \text{V}$$
$$V_4 = 68.6\ \text{V}$$

Now that you know V_4, use Ohm's law to calculate R_4.

$$R_4 = \frac{V_4}{I} = \frac{68.6\ \text{V}}{200\ \text{mA}} = \textbf{343 }\boldsymbol{\Omega}$$

This is most likely a 330 Ω resistor because 343 Ω is within a standard tolerance range ($+5\%$) of 330 Ω.

Related Problem   Determine R_4 in Figure 4–33 for V_S = 150 V and I = 200 mA.

Use Multisim file E05-15 to verify the calculated results in the example and to confirm your calculation for the related problem.

4–7   VOLTAGE DIVIDERS

A series circuit acts as a voltage divider. The voltage divider is an important application of series circuits.

After completing this section, you should be able to

▪ **Use a series circuit as a voltage divider**

  ▪ Apply the voltage-divider formula

  ▪ Use a potentiometer as an adjustable voltage divider

  ▪ Describe some voltage-divider applications

A circuit consisting of a series string of resistors connected to a voltage source acts as a **voltage divider**. Figure 4–34 shows a circuit with two resistors in series, although there can be any number. There are two voltage drops across the resistors: one across R_1 and one across R_2. These voltage drops are V_1 and V_2, respectively, as indicated in the schematic. Since each resistor has the same current, the voltage drops are proportional to the resistance values. For example, if the value of R_2 is twice that of R_1, then the value of V_2 is twice that of V_1.

The total voltage drop around a single closed path divides among the series resistors in amounts directly proportional to the resistance values. For example, in Figure 4–34, if V_S is 10 V, R_1 is 50 Ω, and R_2 is 100 Ω, then V_1 is one-third the total voltage, or 3.33 V, because R_1 is one-third the total resistance of 150 Ω. Likewise, V_2 is two-thirds V_S, or 6.67 V.

▶ **FIGURE 4–34**

Two-resistor voltage divider.

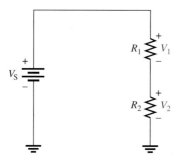

Voltage-Divider Formula

With a few calculations, you can develop a formula for determining how the voltages divide among series resistors. Assume a circuit with n resistors in series as shown in Figure 4–35, where n can be any number.

Let V_x represent the voltage drop across any one of the resistors and R_x represent the number of a particular resistor or combination of resistors. By Ohm's law, you can express the voltage drop across R_x as follows:

$$V_x = IR_x$$

▶ **FIGURE 4–35**

Generalized voltage divider with *n* resistors.

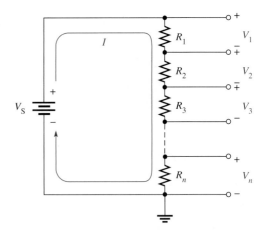

The current through the circuit is equal to the source voltage divided by the total resistance $(I = V_S/R_T)$. In the circuit of Figure 4–35, the total resistance is $R_1 + R_2 + R_3 + \cdots + R_n$. By substitution of V_S/R_T for I in the expression for V_x,

$$V_x = \left(\frac{V_S}{R_T}\right)R_x$$

Rearranging the terms you get

Equation 4–5

$$V_x = \left(\frac{R_x}{R_T}\right)V_S$$

Equation 4–5 is the general voltage-divider formula, which can be stated as follows:

The voltage drop across any resistor or combination of resistors in a series circuit is equal to the ratio of that resistance value to the total resistance, multiplied by the source voltage.

EXAMPLE 4–15

Determine V_1 (the voltage across R_1) and V_2 (the voltage across R_2) in the voltage divider in Figure 4–36.

▶ **FIGURE 4–36**

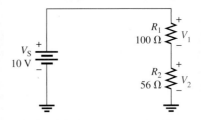

Solution To determine V_1, use the voltage-divider formula, $V_x = (R_x/R_T)V_S$, where $x = 1$. The total resistance is

$$R_T = R_1 + R_2 = 100\ \Omega + 56\ \Omega = 156\ \Omega$$

R_1 is 100 Ω and V_S is 10 V. Substitute these values into the voltage-divider formula.

$$V_1 = \left(\frac{R_1}{R_T}\right)V_S = \left(\frac{100\ \Omega}{156\ \Omega}\right)10\ V = \mathbf{6.41\ V}$$

There are two ways to find the value of V_2: Kirchhoff's voltage law or the voltage-divider formula. If you use Kirchhoff's voltage law ($V_S = V_1 + V_2$), substitute the values for V_S and V_1 as follows:

$$V_2 = V_S - V_1 = 10 \text{ V} - 6.41 \text{ V} = \textbf{3.59 V}$$

To determine V_2, use the voltage-divider formula where $x = 2$.

$$V_2 = \left(\frac{R_2}{R_T}\right)V_S = \left(\frac{56 \text{ }\Omega}{156 \text{ }\Omega}\right)10 \text{ V} = \textbf{3.59 V}$$

Related Problem   Find the voltages across R_1 and R_2 in Figure 4–36 if R_2 is changed to 180 Ω.

> Use Multisim file E05-16 to verify the calculated results in this example and to confirm your calculations for the related problem.

EXAMPLE 4–16

Calculate the voltage drop across each resistor in the voltage divider of Figure 4–37.

▶ **FIGURE 4–37**

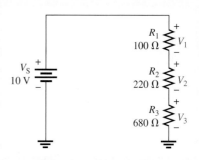

Solution   Look at the circuit for a moment and consider the following: The total resistance is 1000 Ω. Ten percent of the total voltage is across R_1 because it is 10% of the total resistance (100 Ω is 10% of 1000 Ω). Likewise, 22% of the total voltage is dropped across R_2 because it is 22% of the total resistance (220 Ω is 22% of 1000 Ω). Finally, R_3 drops 68% of the total voltage because 680 Ω is 68% of 1000 Ω.

Because of the convenient values in this problem, it is easy to figure the voltages mentally. ($V_1 = 0.10 \times 10 \text{ V} = 1 \text{ V}$, $V_2 = 0.22 \times 10 \text{ V} = 2.2 \text{ V}$, and $V_3 = 0.68 \times 10 \text{ V} = 6.8 \text{ V}$). Such is not always the case, but sometimes a little thinking will produce a result more efficiently and eliminate some calculating. This is also a good way to estimate what your results should be so that you will recognize an unreasonable answer as a result of a calculation error.

Although you have already reasoned through this problem, the calculations will verify your results.

$$V_1 = \left(\frac{R_1}{R_T}\right)V_S = \left(\frac{100 \text{ }\Omega}{1000 \text{ }\Omega}\right)10 \text{ V} = \textbf{1 V}$$

$$V_2 = \left(\frac{R_2}{R_T}\right)V_S = \left(\frac{220 \text{ }\Omega}{1000 \text{ }\Omega}\right)10 \text{ V} = \textbf{2.2 V}$$

$$V_3 = \left(\frac{R_3}{R_T}\right)V_S = \left(\frac{680 \text{ }\Omega}{1000 \text{ }\Omega}\right)10 \text{ V} = \textbf{6.8 V}$$

Notice that the sum of the voltage drops is equal to the source voltage, in accordance with Kirchhoff's voltage law. This check is a good way to verify your results.

Related Problem If R_1 and R_2 in Figure 4–37 are changed to 680 Ω, what are the voltage drops?

Use Multisim file E05-17 to verify the calculated results in this example and to confirm your calculations for the related problem.

EXAMPLE 4–17

Determine the voltages between the following points in the voltage divider of Figure 4–38:

(a) *A* to *B*   (b) *A* to *C*   (c) *B* to *C*   (d) *B* to *D*   (e) *C* to *D*

▶ **FIGURE 4–38**

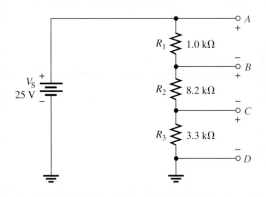

Solution First, determine R_T.

$$R_T = R_1 + R_2 + R_3 = 1.0 \text{ k}\Omega + 8.2 \text{ k}\Omega + 3.3 \text{ k}\Omega = 12.5 \text{ k}\Omega$$

Next, apply the voltage-divider formula to obtain each required voltage.

(a) The voltage *A* to *B* is the voltage drop across R_1.

$$V_{AB} = \left(\frac{R_1}{R_T}\right)V_S = \left(\frac{1.0 \text{ k}\Omega}{12.5 \text{ k}\Omega}\right)25 \text{ V} = \textbf{2 V}$$

(b) The voltage from *A* to *C* is the combined voltage drop across both R_1 and R_2. In this case, R_x in the general formula given in Equation 4–5 is $R_1 + R_2$.

$$V_{AC} = \left(\frac{R_1 + R_2}{R_T}\right)V_S = \left(\frac{9.2 \text{ k}\Omega}{12.5 \text{ k}\Omega}\right)25 \text{ V} = \textbf{18.4 V}$$

(c) The voltage from *B* to *C* is the voltage drop across R_2.

$$V_{BC} = \left(\frac{R_2}{R_T}\right)V_S = \left(\frac{8.2 \text{ k}\Omega}{12.5 \text{ k}\Omega}\right)25 \text{ V} = \textbf{16.4 V}$$

(d) The voltage from *B* to *D* is the combined voltage drop across both R_2 and R_3. In this case, R_x in the general formula is $R_2 + R_3$.

$$V_{BD} = \left(\frac{R_2 + R_3}{R_T}\right)V_S = \left(\frac{11.5 \text{ k}\Omega}{12.5 \text{ k}\Omega}\right)25 \text{ V} = \textbf{23 V}$$

(e) Finally, the voltage from *C* to *D* is the voltage drop across R_3.

$$V_{CD} = \left(\frac{R_3}{R_T}\right)V_S = \left(\frac{3.3 \text{ k}\Omega}{12.5 \text{ k}\Omega}\right)25 \text{ V} = \textbf{6.6 V}$$

If you connect this voltage divider, you can verify each of the calculated voltages by connecting a voltmeter between the appropriate points in each case.

Related Problem   Determine each of the previously calculated voltages if V_S is doubled.

Use Multisim file E05-18 to verify the calculated results in this example and to confirm your calculations for the related problem.

A Potentiometer as an Adjustable Voltage Divider

Recall from Chapter 2 that a potentiometer is a variable resistor with three terminals. A potentiometer connected to a voltage source is shown in Figure 4–39(a) with the schematic shown in part (b). Notice that the two end terminals are labeled 1 and 2. The adjustable terminal or wiper is labeled 3. The potentiometer functions as a voltage divider, which can be illustrated by separating the total resistance into two parts, as shown in Figure 4–39(c). The resistance between terminal 1 and terminal 3 (R_{13}) is one part, and the resistance between terminal 3 and terminal 2 (R_{32}) is the other part. So this potentiometer is equivalent to a two-resistor voltage divider that can be manually adjusted.

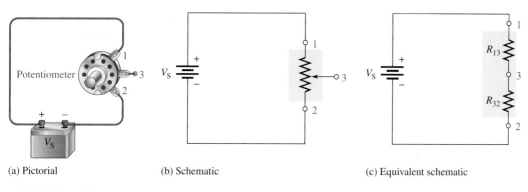

(a) Pictorial   (b) Schematic   (c) Equivalent schematic

▲ **FIGURE 4–39**

The potentiometer used as a voltage divider.

Figure 4–40 shows what happens when the wiper contact (3) is moved. In part (a), the wiper is exactly centered, making the two resistances equal. If you measure the voltage across terminals 3 to 2 as indicated by the voltmeter symbol, you have one-half of the total source voltage. When the wiper is moved up, as in part (b), the resistance between termi-

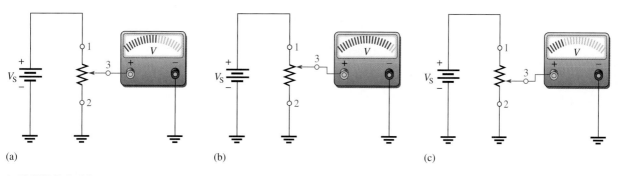

(a)   (b)   (c)

▲ **FIGURE 4–40**

Adjusting the voltage divider.

nals 3 and 2 increases, and the voltage across it increases proportionally. When the wiper is moved down, as in part (c), the resistance between terminals 3 and 2 decreases, and the voltage decreases proportionally.

Applications

The volume control of radio or TV receivers is a common application of a potentiometer used as a voltage divider. Since the loudness of the sound is dependent on the amount of voltage associated with the audio signal, you can increase or decrease the volume by adjusting the potentiometer, that is, by turning the knob of the volume control on the set. The block diagram in Figure 4–41 shows how a potentiometer can be used for volume control in a typical receiver.

▶ **FIGURE 4–41**

A variable voltage divider used for volume control in a radio receiver.

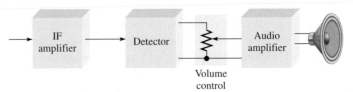

Another application of a voltage divider is illustrated in Figure 4–42, which depicts a potentiometer voltage divider as a level sensor in a liquid storage tank. As shown in part (a), the float moves up as the tank is filled and moves down as the tank empties. The float is mechanically linked to the wiper arm of a potentiometer, as shown in part (b). The output voltage varies proportionally with the position of the wiper arm. As the liquid in the tank decreases, the sensor output voltage also decreases. The output voltage goes to the indicator circuitry, which controls a digital readout to show the amount of liquid in the tank. The schematic of this system is shown in part (c).

Still another application for voltage dividers is in setting the dc operating voltage (bias) in transistor amplifiers. Figure 4–43 shows a voltage divider used for this purpose. You will study transistor amplifiers and biasing in a later course, so it is important that you understand the basics of voltage dividers at this point.

These examples are only three out of many possible applications of voltage dividers.

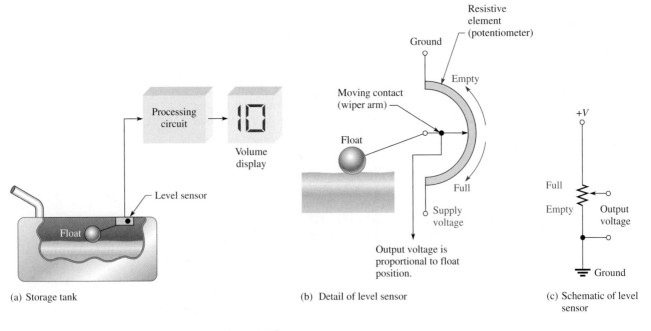

(a) Storage tank

(b) Detail of level sensor

(c) Schematic of level sensor

▲ **FIGURE 4–42**

A potentiometer voltage divider used in a level sensor.

The voltage divider used as a bias circuit for a transistor amplifier, where the voltage at the base of the transistor is determined by the voltage divider as $V_{base} = (R_2/(R_1 + R_2))V_S$.

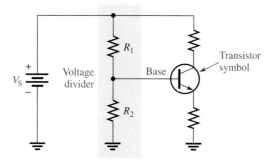

SUMMARY

- The current is the same at all points in a series circuit.
- The total series resistance is the sum of all resistors in the series circuit.
- The total resistance between any two points in a series circuit is equal to the sum of all resistors connected in series between those two points.
- If all of the resistors in a series circuit are of equal value, the total resistance is the number of resistors multiplied by the resistance value of one resistor.
- Voltage sources in series add algebraically.
- Kirchhoff's voltage law: The sum of the voltage drops equals the total source voltage, or equivalently, the algebraic sum of all the voltages around a closed path is zero.
- The voltage drops in a circuit are always opposite in polarity to the total source voltage.
- Current is out of the negative side of a source and into the positive side.
- Current is into the negative side of each resistor and out of the positive side.
- A voltage divider is a series arrangement of resistors.
- A voltage divider is so named because the voltage drop across any resistor in the series circuit is divided down from the total voltage by an amount proportional to that resistance value in relation to the total resistance.
- A potentiometer can be used as an adjustable voltage divider.
- All voltages in a circuit are referenced to ground unless otherwise specified.
- Ground is zero volts with respect to all points referenced to it in the circuit.
- *Negative ground* is the term used when the negative side of the source is grounded.
- *Positive ground* is the term used when the positive side of the source is grounded.
- The voltage across an open series component equals the source voltage.
- The voltage across a shorted series component is 0 V.

KEY TERMS

Circuit ground A method of grounding whereby the metal chassis that houses the assembly or a large conductive area on a printed circuit board is used as the common or reference point; also called *chassis ground.*

Kirchhoff's voltage law A law stating that (1) the sum of the voltage drops around a closed path equals the source voltage or (2) the algebraic sum of all the voltages (drops and source) around a closed path is zero.

Open A circuit condition in which the current path is interrupted.

Series In an electric circuit, a relationship of components in which the components are connected such that they provide a single current path between two points.

Series-aiding An arrangement of two or more series voltage sources with polarities in the same direction.

Series-opposing An arrangement of two series voltage sources with polarities in the opposite direction.

Short A circuit condition in which there is a zero or abnormally low resistance path between two points: usually an inadvertent condition.

Voltage divider A circuit consisting of series resistors across which one or more output voltages are taken.

FORMULAS

4–1	$R_T = R_1 + R_2 + R_3 + \cdots + R_n$	Total resistance of n resistors in series
4–2	$R_T = nR$	Total resistance of n equal-value resistors in series
4–3	$V_S = V_1 + V_2 + V_3 + \cdots + V_n$	Kirchhoff's voltage law
4–4	$V_S - V_1 - V_2 - V_3 - \cdots - V_n = 0$	Kirchhoff's voltage law stated another way
4–5	$V_x = \left(\dfrac{R_x}{R_T}\right)V_S$	Voltage-divider formula

SELF-TEST

Answers are at the end of the chapter.

1. Five equal-value resistors are connected in series and there is a current of 2 mA into the first resistor. The amount of current out of the second resistor is

   (a) equal to 2 mA   (b) less than 2 mA   (c) greater than 2 mA

2. To measure the current out of the third resistor in a circuit consisting of four series resistors, an ammeter can be placed

   (a) between the third and fourth resistors   (b) between the second and third resistors

   (c) at the positive terminal of the source   (d) at any point in the circuit

3. When a third resistor is connected in series with two series resistors, the total resistance

   (a) remains the same   (b) increases

   (c) decreases   (d) increases by one-third

4. When one of four series resistors is removed from a circuit and the circuit reconnected, the current

   (a) decreases by the amount of current through the removed resistor

   (b) decreases by one-fourth

   (c) quadruples

   (d) increases

5. A series circuit consists of three resistors with values of 100 Ω, 220 Ω, and 330 Ω. The total resistance is

   (a) less than 100 Ω   (b) the average of the values   (c) 550 Ω   (d) 650 Ω

6. A 9 V battery is connected across a series combination of 68 Ω, 33 Ω, 100 Ω, and 47 Ω resistors. The amount of current is

   (a) 36.3 mA   (b) 27.6 A   (c) 22.3 mA   (d) 363 mA

7. While putting four 1.5 V batteries in a flashlight, you accidentally put one of them in backward. The voltage across the bulb will be

   (a) 6 V   (b) 3 V   (c) 4.5 V   (d) 0 V

8. If you measure all the voltage drops and the source voltage in a series circuit and add them together, taking into consideration the polarities, you will get a result equal to

   (a) the source voltage   (b) the total of the voltage drops

   (c) zero   (d) the total of the source voltage and the voltage drops

9. There are six resistors in a given series circuit and each resistor has 5 V dropped across it. The source voltage is

(a) 5 V   (b) 30 V

(c) dependent on the resistor values   (d) dependent on the current

10. A series circuit consists of a 4.7 kΩ, a 5.6 kΩ, and a 10 kΩ resistor. The resistor that has the most voltage across it is

(a) the 4.7 kΩ   (b) the 5.6 kΩ

(c) the 10 kΩ   (d) impossible to determine from the given information

11. Which of the following series combinations dissipates the most power when connected across a 100 V source?

(a) One 100 Ω resistor   (b) Two 100 Ω resistors

(c) Three 100 Ω resistors   (d) Four 100 Ω resistors

12. The total power in a certain circuit is 1 W. Each of the five equal-value series resistors making up the circuit dissipates

(a) 1 W   (b) 5 W   (c) 0.5 W   (d) 0.2 W

13. When you connect an ammeter in a series-resistive circuit and turn on the source voltage, the meter reads zero. You should check for

(a) a broken wire   (b) a shorted resistor

(c) an open resistor   (d) answers (a) and (c)

14. While checking out a series-resistive circuit, you find that the current is higher than it should be. You should look for

(a) an open circuit   (b) a short   (c) a low resistor value   (d) answers (b) and (c)

PROBLEMS

More difficult problems are indicated by an asterisk (*).

SECTION 4–1   Resistors in Series

1. Connect each set of resistors in Figure 4–44 in series between points *A* and *B*.

▶ **FIGURE 4–44**

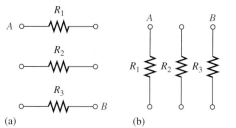 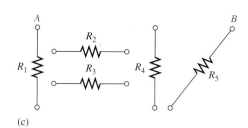

(a)   (b)   (c)

2. Determine which resistors in Figure 4–45 are in series. Show how to interconnect the pins to put all the resistors in series.

▶ **FIGURE 4–45**

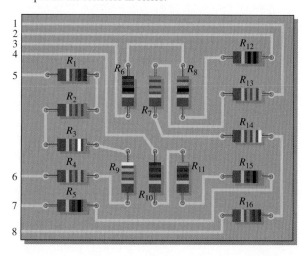

3. Determine the nominal resistance between pins 1and 8 in the circuit board in Figure 4–45.

4. Determine the nominal resistance between pins 2 and 3 in the circuit board in Figure 4–45.

5. On the double-sided PC board in Figure 4–46, identify each group of series resistors. Note that many of the interconnections feed through the board from the top side to the bottom side.

▶ **FIGURE 4–46**

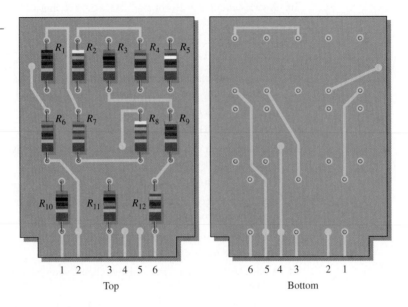

Top   Bottom

SECTION 4–2   Current in a Series Circuit

6. What is the current through each resistor in a series circuit if the total voltage is 12 V and the total resistance is 120 Ω?

7. The current from the source in Figure 4–47 is 5 mA. How much current does each milliamme-ter in the circuit indicate?

▶ **FIGURE 4–47**

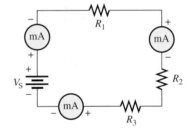

8. Show how to connect a voltage source and an ammeter to the PC board in Figure 4–45 to measure the current in R_1. Which other resistor currents are measured by this setup?

*9. Using 1.5 V batteries, a switch, and three lamps, devise a circuit to apply 4.5 V across either one lamp, two lamps in series, or three lamps in series with a single-control switch. Draw the schematic.

SECTION 4–3   Total Series Resistance

10. The following resistors (one each) are connected in a series circuit: 1.0 Ω, 2.2 Ω, 5.6 Ω, 12 Ω, and 22 Ω. Determine the total resistance.

11. Find the total resistance of each of the following groups of series resistors:

   (a) 560 Ω and 1000 Ω   (b) 47 Ω and 56 Ω

   (c) 1.5 kΩ, 2.2 kΩ, and 10 kΩ   (d) 1.0 MΩ, 470 kΩ, 1.0 kΩ, 2.2 MΩ

12. Calculate R_T for each circuit of Figure 4–48.

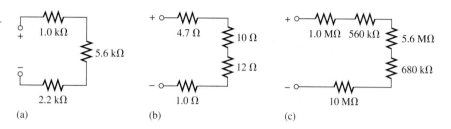

▶ **FIGURE 4–48**

(a)   (b)   (c)

13. What is the total resistance of twelve 5.6 kΩ resistors in series?

14. Six 56 Ω resistors, eight 100 Ω resistors, and two 22 Ω resistors are all connected in series. What is the total resistance?

15. If the total resistance in Figure 4–49 is 17.4 kΩ, what is the value of R_5?

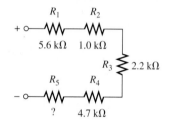

▶ **FIGURE 4–49**

*16. You have the following resistor values available to you in the lab in unlimited quantities: 10 Ω, 100 Ω, 470 Ω, 560 Ω, 680 Ω, 1.0 kΩ, 2.2 kΩ, and 5.6 kΩ. All of the other standard values are out of stock. A project that you are working on requires an 18 kΩ resistance. What combinations of the available values would you use in series to achieve this total resistance?

17. Find the total resistance in Figure 4–48 if all three circuits are connected in series.

18. What is the total resistance from A to B for each switch position in Figure 4–50?

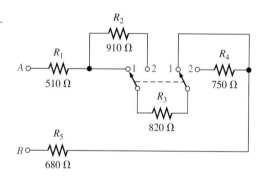

▶ **FIGURE 4–50**

SECTION 4–4 Ohm's Law in Series Circuits

19. What is the current in each circuit of Figure 4–51?

20. Determine the voltage drop across each resistor in Figure 4–51.

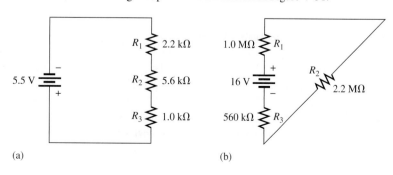

▶ **FIGURE 4–51**

(a)   (b)

21. Three 470 Ω resistors are connected in series with a 48 V source.

   (a) What is the current is in the circuit?

   (b) What is the voltage across each resistor?

   (c) What is the minimum power rating of the resistors?

22. Four equal-value resistors are in series with a 5 V battery, and 2.23 mA are measured. What is the value of each resistor?

23. What is the value of each resistor in Figure 4–52?

24. Determine V_{R1}, R_2, and R_3 in Figure 4–53.

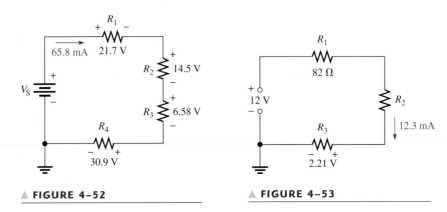

▲ FIGURE 4–52   ▲ FIGURE 4–53

25. For the circuit in Figure 4–54 the meter reads 7.84 mA when the switch is in position A.

   (a) What is the resistance of R_4?

   (b) What should be the meter reading for switch positions B, C, and D?

   (c) Will a ¼ A fuse blow in any position of the switch?

26. Determine the current measured by the meter in Figure 4–55 for each position of the ganged switch.

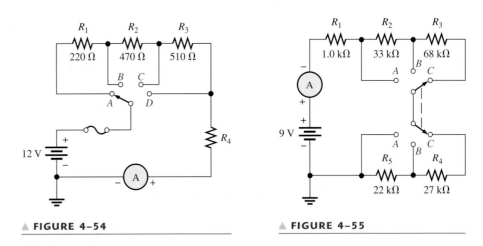

▲ FIGURE 4–54   ▲ FIGURE 4–55

SECTION 4–5 **Kirchhoff's Voltage Law**

27. The following voltage drops are measured across three resistors in series: 5.5 V, 8.2 V, and 12.3 V. What is the value of the source voltage to which these resistors are connected?

28. Five resistors are in series with a 20 V source. The voltage drops across four of the resistors are 1.5 V, 5.5 V, 3 V, and 6 V. How much voltage is dropped across the fifth resistor?

29. Determine the unspecified voltage drop(s) in each circuit of Figure 4–56. Show how to connect a voltmeter to measure each unknown voltage drop.

▷ **FIGURE 4–56**

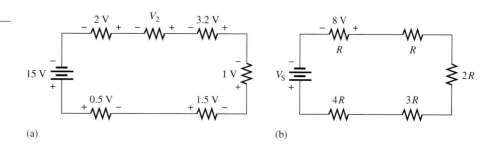

(a)   (b)

30. In the circuit of Figure 4–57, determine the resistance of R_4.

31. Find R_1, R_2, and R_3 in Figure 4–58.

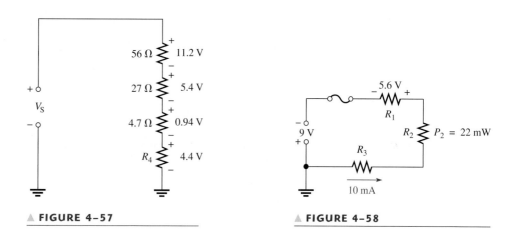

▲ **FIGURE 4–57**   ▲ **FIGURE 4–58**

32. Determine the voltage across R_5 for each position of the switch in Figure 4–59. The current in each position is as follows: A, 3.35 mA; B, 3.73 mA; C, 4.50 mA; D, 6.00 mA.

33. Using the result of Problem 35, determine the voltage across each resistor in Figure 4–59 for each switch position.

▷ **FIGURE 4–59**

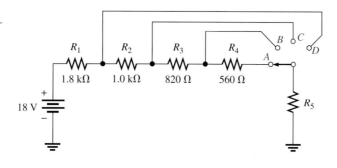

SECTION 4–7   Voltage Dividers

*34. The total resistance of a circuit is 560 Ω. What percentage of the total voltage appears across a 27 Ω resistor that makes up part of the total series resistance?

▶ FIGURE 4–60

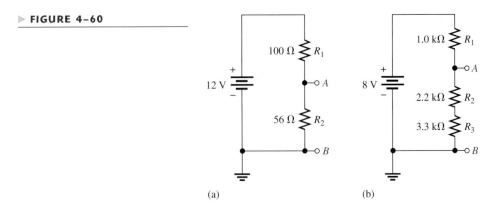

(a)   (b)

35. Determine the voltage between points *A* and *B* in each voltage divider of Figure 4–60.

36. Determine the voltage with respect to ground for output *A*, *B*, and *C* in Figure 4–61(a).

37. Determine the minimum and maximum voltage from the voltage divider in Figure 4–61(b).

*38. What is the voltage across each resistor in Figure 4–62? *R* is the lowest-value resistor, and all others are multiples of that value as indicated.

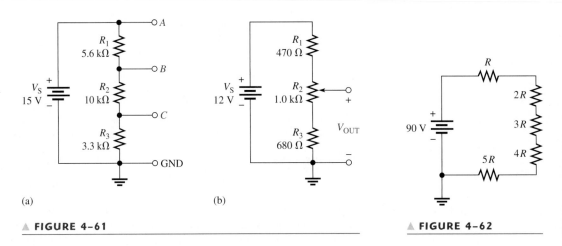

(a)   (b)

▲ FIGURE 4–61   ▲ FIGURE 4–62

39. Determine the voltage at each point in Figure 4–63 with respect to the negative side of the battery.

40. If there are 10 V across R_1 in Figure 4–63, what is the voltage across each of the other resistors?

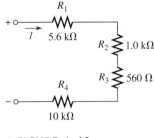

▲ FIGURE 4–63

5

PARALLEL CIRCUITS

INTRODUCTION

In Chapter 4, you learned about series circuits and how to apply Ohm's law and Kirchhoff's voltage law. You also saw how a series circuit can be used as a voltage divider to obtain several specified voltages from a single source voltage. The effects of opens and shorts in series circuits were also examined.

In this chapter, you will see how Ohm's law is used in parallel circuits; and you will learn Kirchhoff's current law. Also, several applications of parallel circuits, including automotive lighting, residential wiring, and the internal wiring of analog ammeters are presented. You will learn how to determine total parallel resistance and how to troubleshoot for open resistors.

When resistors are connected in parallel and a voltage is applied across the parallel circuit, each resistor provides a separate path for current. The total resistance of a parallel circuit is reduced as more resistors are connected in parallel. The voltage across each of the parallel resistors is equal to the voltage applied across the entire parallel circuit.

CHAPTER OUTLINE

KEY TERMS

- Branch
- Parallel
- Kirchhoff's current law
- Node
- Current divider

CHAPTER OBJECTIVES

- Identify a parallel resistive circuit
- Determine the voltage across each parallel branch
- Apply Kirchhoff's current law
- Determine total parallel resistance
- Apply Ohm's law in a parallel circuit
- Determine the total effect of current sources in parallel
- Use a parallel circuit as a current divider

WWW. VISIT THE COMPANION WEBSITE

Study aids for this chapter are available at
http://www.prenhall.com/floyd

5–1   RESISTORS IN PARALLEL

When two or more resistors are individually connected between two separate points, they are in parallel with each other. A parallel circuit provides more than one path for current.

After completing this section, you should be able to

■ **Identify a parallel resistive circuit**

  ■ Translate a physical arrangement of parallel resistors into a schematic

Each current path is called a **branch**, and a **parallel** circuit is one that has more than one branch. Two resistors connected in parallel are shown in Figure 5–1(a). As shown in part (b), the current out of the source (I_T) divides when it gets to point A. I_1 goes through R_1 and I_2 goes through R_2. If additional resistors are connected in parallel with the first two, more current paths are provided between point A and point B, as shown in Figure 5–1(c). All points along the top shown in blue are electrically the same as point A, and all points along the bottom shown in green are electrically the same as point B.

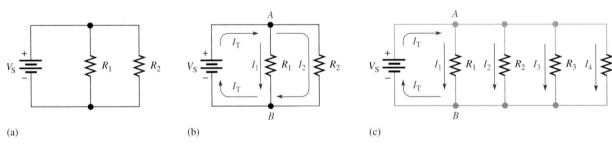

(a)   (b)   (c)

▲ **FIGURE 5–1**

Resistors in parallel.

In Figure 5–1, it is obvious that the resistors are connected in parallel. Often, in actual circuit diagrams, the parallel relationship is not as clear. It is important that you learn to recognize parallel circuits regardless of how they may be drawn.

A rule for identifying parallel circuits is as follows:

If there is more than one current path (branch) between two separate points and if the voltage between those two points also appears across each of the branches, then there is a parallel circuit between those two points.

Figure 5–2 shows parallel resistors drawn in different ways between two separate points labeled A and B. Notice that in each case, the current has two paths going from A to B, and

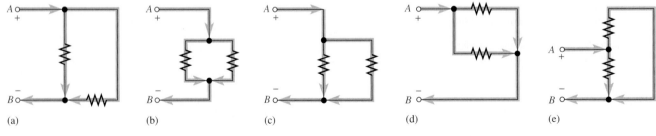

(a)   (b)   (c)   (d)   (e)

▲ **FIGURE 5–2**

Examples of circuits with two parallel paths.

the voltage across each branch is the same. Although these examples show only two parallel paths, there can be any number of resistors in parallel.

EXAMPLE 5–1

Five resistors are positioned on a protoboard as shown in Figure 5–3. Show the wiring required to connect all of the resistors in parallel between A and B. Draw a schematic and label each of the resistors with its value.

▶ FIGURE 5–3

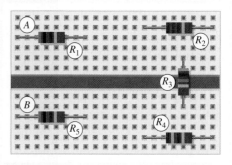

Solution Wires are connected as shown in the assembly diagram of Figure 5–4(a). The schematic is shown in Figure 5–4(b). Again, note that the schematic does not necessarily have to show the actual physical arrangement of the resistors. The schematic shows how components are connected electrically.

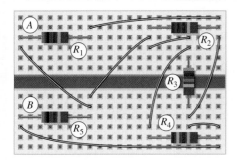

(a) Assembly wiring diagram

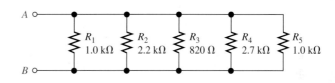

(b) Schematic

▲ FIGURE 5–4

Related Problem How would the circuit have to be rewired if R_2 is removed?

EXAMPLE 5–2

Determine the parallel groupings in Figure 5–5 and the value of each resistor.

▶ **FIGURE 5–5**

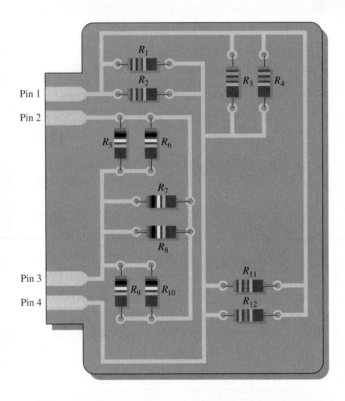

Solution Resistors R_1 through R_4 and R_{11} and R_{12} are all in parallel. This parallel combination is connected to pins 1 and 4. Each resistor in this group is 56 kΩ.

Resistors R_5 through R_{10} are all in parallel. This combination is connected to pins 2 and 3. Each resistor in this group is 100 kΩ.

Related Problem How would you connect all of the resistors in Figure 5–5 in parallel?

5–2 VOLTAGE IN A PARALLEL CIRCUIT

The voltage across any given branch of a parallel circuit is equal to the voltage across each of the other branches in parallel. As you know, each current path in a parallel circuit is called a branch.

After completing this section, you should be able to

■ **Determine the voltage across each parallel branch**

　■ Explain why the voltage is the same across all parallel resistors

To illustrate voltage in a parallel circuit, let's examine Figure 5–6(a). Points *A*, *B*, *C*, and *D* along the left side of the parallel circuit are electrically the same point because the voltage is the same along this line. You can think of all of these points as being connected by a single wire to the negative terminal of the battery. The points *E*, *F*, *G*, and *H* along the right side of the circuit are all at a voltage equal to that of the positive terminal of the source. Thus, voltage across each parallel resistor is the same, and each is equal to the source voltage. Note that the parallel circuit in Figure 5–6 resembles a ladder.

Figure 5–6(b) is the same circuit as in part (a), drawn in a slightly different way. Here the left side of each resistor is connected to a single point, which is the negative battery terminal. The right side of each resistor is connected to a single point, which is the positive battery terminal. The resistors are still all in parallel across the source.

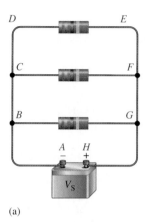

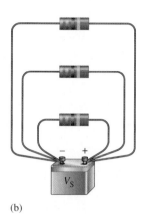

(a) (b)

In Figure 5–7, a 12 V battery is connected across three parallel resistors. When the voltage is measured across the battery and then across each of the resistors, the readings are the same. As you can see, the same voltage appears across each branch in a parallel circuit.

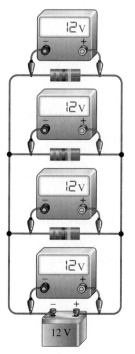

(a) Pictorial

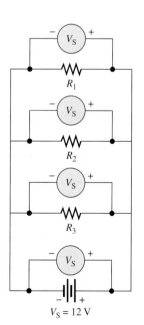

$V_S = 12 \text{ V}$

(b) Schematic

EXAMPLE 5–3

Determine the voltage across each resistor in Figure 5–8.

FIGURE 5–8

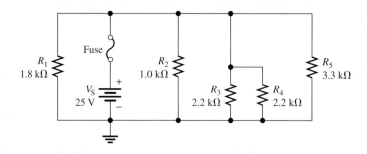

Solution The five resistors are in parallel, so the voltage across each one is equal to the applied source voltage. There is no voltage across the fuse. The voltage across the resistors is

$$V_1 = V_2 = V_3 = V_4 = V_5 = V_S = 25 \text{ V}$$

Related Problem If R_4 is removed from the circuit, what is the voltage across R_3?

Use Multisim file E06-03 to verify the calculated results in this example and to confirm your calculation for the related problem.

5–3   KIRCHHOFF'S CURRENT LAW

Kirchhoff's voltage law deals with voltages in a single closed path. Kirchhoff's current law applies to currents in multiple paths.

After completing this section, you should be able to

■ **Apply Kirchhoff's current law**

  ■ State Kirchhoff's current law

  ■ Define *node*

  ■ Determine the total current by adding the branch currents

  ■ Determine an unknown branch current

Kirchhoff's current law, often abbreviated KCL, can be stated as follows:

The sum of the currents into a node (total current in) is equal to the sum of the currents out of that node (total current out).

A **node** is any point or junction in a circuit where two or more components are connected. In a parallel circuit, a node or junction is a point where the parallel branches come together. For example, in the circuit of Figure 5–9, point *A* is one node and point *B* is another. Let's start at the positive terminal of the source and follow the current. The total current I_T from the source is *into* node *A*. At this point, the current splits up among the three branches as indicated. Each of the three branch currents (I_1, I_2, and I_3) is *out of* node *A*. Kirchhoff's current law says that the total current into node *A* is equal to the total current out of node *A*; that is,

$$I_T = I_1 + I_2 + I_3$$

Now, following the currents in Figure 5–9 through the three branches, you see that they come back together at node B. Currents I_1, I_2, and I_3 are into node B, and I_T is out of node B. Kirchhoff's current law formula at node B is therefore the same as at node A.

$$I_T = I_1 + I_2 + I_3$$

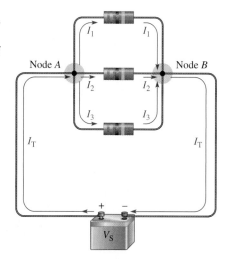

▶ **FIGURE 5–9**

Kirchhoff's current law: The current into a node equals the current out of that node.

Figure 5–10 shows a generalized circuit node where a number of branches are connected at a point in a circuit. Currents $I_{IN(1)}$ through $I_{IN(n)}$ are into the node (n can be any number). Currents $I_{OUT(1)}$ through $I_{OUT(m)}$ are out of the node (m can be any number, but not necessarily equal to n). By Kirchhoff's current law, the sum of the currents into a node must equal the sum of the currents out of the node. With reference to Figure 5–10, a general formula for Kirchhoff's current law is

$$I_{IN(1)} + I_{IN(2)} + \cdots + I_{IN(n)} = I_{OUT(1)} + I_{OUT(2)} + \cdots + I_{OUT(m)}$$

Equation 5–1

If all the terms on the right side of Equation 5–1 are brought over to the left side, their signs change to negative, and a zero is left on the right side as follows:

$$I_{IN(1)} + I_{IN(2)} + \cdots + I_{IN(n)} - I_{OUT(1)} - I_{OUT(2)} - \cdots - I_{OUT(m)} = 0$$

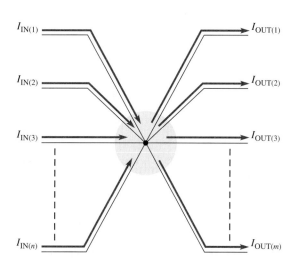

$$I_{IN(1)} + I_{IN(2)} + I_{IN(3)} + \cdots + I_{IN(n)} = I_{OUT(1)} + I_{OUT(2)} + I_{OUT(3)} + \cdots I_{OUT(m)}$$

◀ **FIGURE 5–10**

Generalized circuit node illustrating Kirchhoff's current law.

Based on this last equation, Kirchhoff's current law can also be stated in this way:

The algebraic sum of all the currents entering and leaving a node is equal to zero.

You can verify Kirchhoff's current law by connecting a circuit and measuring each branch current and the total current from the source, as illustrated in Figure 5–11. When the branch currents are added together, their sum will equal the total current. This rule applies for any number of branches.

The following three examples illustrate use of Kirchhoff's current law.

▶ **FIGURE 5–11**

An illustration of Kirchhoff's current law.

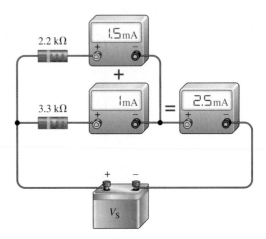

EXAMPLE 5–4

The branch currents are shown in the circuit of Figure 5–12. Determine the total current entering node A and the total current leaving node B.

▶ **FIGURE 5–12**

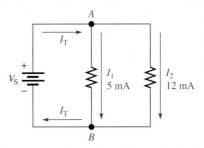

Solution   The total current out of node A is the sum of the two branch currents. So the total current into node A is

$$I_T = I_1 + I_2 = 5 \text{ mA} + 12 \text{ mA} = \mathbf{17 \ mA}$$

The total current entering node B is the sum of the two branch currents. So the total current out of node B is

$$I_T = I_1 + I_2 = 5 \text{ mA} + 12 \text{ mA} = \mathbf{17 \ mA}$$

Note that this equation can be equivalently expressed as $I_T - I_1 - I_2 = 0$.

Related Problem   If a third branch is added to the circuit in Figure 5–12 and its current is 3 mA, what is the total current into node A and out of node B?

EXAMPLE 5–5

Determine the current I_2 through R_2 in Figure 5–13.

▶ FIGURE 5–13

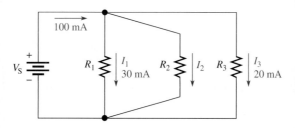

Solution The total current into the junction of the three branches is $I_T = I_1 + I_2 + I_3$. From Figure 5–13, you know the total current and the branch currents through R_1 and R_3. Solve for I_2 as follows:

$$I_2 = I_T - I_1 - I_3 = 100 \text{ mA} - 30 \text{ mA} - 20 \text{ mA} = \textbf{50 mA}$$

Related Problem Determine I_T and I_2 if a fourth branch is added to the circuit in Figure 5–13 and it has 12 mA through it.

EXAMPLE 5–6

Use Kirchhoff's current law to find the current measured by ammeters A3 and A5 in Figure 5–14.

▶ FIGURE 5–14

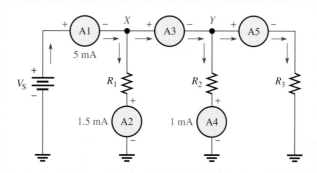

Solution The total current into node X is 5 mA. Two currents are out of node X: 1.5 mA through resistor R_1 and the current through A3. Kirchhoff's current law applied at node X gives

$$5 \text{ mA} = 1.5 \text{ mA} + I_{A3}$$

Solving for I_{A3} yields

$$I_{A3} = 5 \text{ mA} - 1.5 \text{ mA} = \textbf{3.5 mA}$$

The total current into node Y is $I_{A3} = 3.5$ mA. Two currents are out of node Y: 1 mA through resistor R_2 and the current through A5 and R_3. Kirchhoff's current law applied at node Y gives

$$3.5 \text{ mA} = 1 \text{ mA} + I_{A5}$$

Solving for I_{A5} yields

$$I_{A5} = 3.5 \text{ mA} - 1 \text{ mA} = \textbf{2.5 mA}$$

Related Problem   How much current will an ammeter measure when it is placed in the circuit right below R_3 in Figure 5–14? Below the negative battery terminal?

5–4   TOTAL PARALLEL RESISTANCE

When resistors are connected in parallel, the total resistance of the circuit decreases. The total resistance of a parallel circuit is always less than the value of the smallest resistor. For example, if a 10 Ω resistor and a 100 Ω resistor are connected in parallel, the total resistance is less than 10 Ω.

After completing this section, you should be able to

■ **Determine total parallel resistance**

  ■ Explain why resistance decreases as resistors are connected in parallel

  ■ Apply the parallel-resistance formula

As you know, when resistors are connected in parallel, the current has more than one path. The number of current paths is equal to the number of parallel branches.

In Figure 5–15(a), there is only one current path because it is a series circuit. There is a certain amount of current, I_1, through R_1. If resistor R_2 is connected in parallel with R_1, as shown in Figure 5–15(b), there is an additional amount of current, I_2, through R_2. The total current from the source has increased with the addition of the parallel resistor. Assuming that the source voltage is constant, an increase in the total current from the source means that the total resistance has decreased, in accordance with Ohm's law. Additional resistors connected in parallel will further reduce the resistance and increase the total current.

▷ **FIGURE 5–15**

Addition of resistors in parallel reduces total resistance and increases total current.

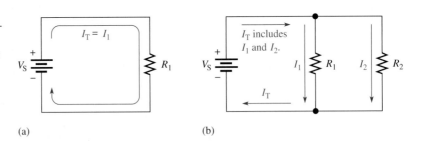

(a)   (b)

Formula for Total Parallel Resistance

The circuit in Figure 5–16 shows a general case of n resistors in parallel (n can be any number). From Kirchhoff's current law, the equation for current is

$$I_T = I_1 + I_2 + I_3 + \cdots + I_n$$

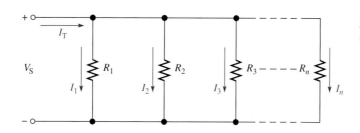

Since V_S is the voltage across each of the parallel resistors, by Ohm's law, $I_1 = V_S/R_1$, $I_2 = V_S/R_2$, and so on. By substitution into the equation for current,

$$\frac{V_S}{R_T} = \frac{V_S}{R_1} + \frac{V_S}{R_2} + \frac{V_S}{R_3} + \cdots + \frac{V_S}{R_n}$$

The term V_S can be factored out of the right side of the equation and canceled with V_S on the left side, leaving only the resistance terms.

$$\frac{1}{R_T} = \frac{1}{R_1} + \frac{1}{R_2} + \frac{1}{R_3} + \cdots + \frac{1}{R_n}$$

Recall that the reciprocal of resistance ($1/R$) is called *conductance,* which is symbolized by G. The unit of conductance is the siemens (S). The equation for $1/R_T$ can be expressed in terms of conductance as

$$G_T = G_1 + G_2 + G_3 + \cdots + G_n$$

Solve for R_T by taking the reciprocal of (that is, by inverting) both sides of the equation for $1/R_T$.

$$R_T = \frac{1}{\left(\dfrac{1}{R_1}\right) + \left(\dfrac{1}{R_2}\right) + \left(\dfrac{1}{R_3}\right) + \cdots + \left(\dfrac{1}{R_n}\right)}$$

Equation 5-2

Equation 5–2 shows that to find the total parallel resistance, add all the $1/R$ (or conductance, G) terms and then take the reciprocal of the sum.

$$R_T = \frac{1}{G_T}$$

EXAMPLE 5-7

Calculate the total parallel resistance between points A and B of the circuit in Figure 5–17.

▶ FIGURE 5-17

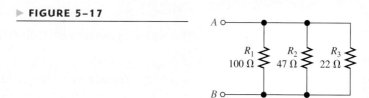

R_1 $100\ \Omega$ R_2 $47\ \Omega$ R_3 $22\ \Omega$

Solution   Use Equation 5–2 to calculate the total parallel resistance when you know the individual resistances. First, find the conductance, which is the reciprocal of the resistance, of each of the three resistors.

$$G_1 = \frac{1}{R_1} = \frac{1}{100\ \Omega} = 10\ \text{mS}$$

$$G_2 = \frac{1}{R_2} = \frac{1}{47\ \Omega} = 21.3\ \text{mS}$$

$$G_3 = \frac{1}{R_3} = \frac{1}{22\ \Omega} = 45.5\ \text{mS}$$

Next, calculate R_T by adding G_1, G_2, and G_3 and taking the reciprocal of the sum.

$$R_T = \frac{1}{G_T} = \frac{1}{10\ \text{mS} + 21.3\ \text{mS} + 45.5\ \text{mS}} = \frac{1}{76.8\ \text{mS}} = \mathbf{13.0\ \Omega}$$

For a quick accuracy check, notice that the value of R_T (13.0 Ω) is smaller than the smallest value in parallel, which is R_3 (22 Ω), as it should be.

Related Problem   If a 33 Ω resistor is connected in parallel in Figure 5–17, what is the new value of R_T?

Calculator Tip

The parallel-resistance formula is easily solved on a calculator using Equation 5–2. The general procedure is to enter the value of R_1 and then take its reciprocal by pressing the x^{-1} key. (The reciprocal is a secondary function on some calculators.) Next press the + key; then enter the value of R_2 and take its reciprocal using the x^{-1} key and press the + key. Repeat this procedure until all of the resistor values have been entered; then press ENTER. The final step is to press the x^{-1} key and the ENTER key to get R_T. The total parallel resistance is now on the display. The display format may vary, depending on the particular calculator. For example, the steps required for a typical calculator solution of Example 5–7 are as follows:

1. Enter 100. Display shows 100.

2. Press x^{-1} (or 2nd then x^{-1}). Display shows 100^{-1}.

3. Press +. Display shows 100^{-1} +.

4. Enter 47. Display shows 100^{-1} + 47.

5. Press x^{-1} (or 2nd then x^{-1}). Display shows $100^{-1} + 47^{-1}$.

6. Press +. Display shows $100^{-1} + 47^{-1}$ +.

7. Enter 22. Display shows $100^{-1} + 47^{-1} + 22$.

8. Press x^{-1} (or 2nd then x^{-1}). Display shows $100^{-1} + 47^{-1} + 22^{-1}$.

9. Press ENTER. Display shows a result of 76.7311411992E^{-3}.

10. Press x^{-1} (or 2nd then x^{-1}) and then ENTER. Display shows a result of 13.0325182758E0.

The number displayed in Step 10 is the total resistance in ohms. Round it to 13.0 Ω.

The Case of Two Resistors in Parallel

Equation 5–2 is a general formula for finding the total resistance for any number of resistors in parallel. The combination of two resistors in parallel occurs commonly in practice. Also, any number of resistors in parallel can be broken down into pairs as an alternate way to find the R_T. Based on Equation 5–2, the formula for the total resistance of two resistors in parallel is

$$R_T = \cfrac{1}{\left(\cfrac{1}{R_1}\right) + \left(\cfrac{1}{R_2}\right)}$$

Combining the terms in the denominator yields

$$R_T = \cfrac{1}{\left(\cfrac{R_1 + R_2}{R_1 R_2}\right)}$$

which can be rewritten as follows:

$$R_T = \frac{R_1 R_2}{R_1 + R_2}$$

Equation 5–3

Equation 5–3 states

The total resistance for two resistors in parallel is equal to the product of the two resistors divided by the sum of the two resistors.

This equation is sometimes referred to as the "product over the sum" formula.

EXAMPLE 5–8

Calculate the total resistance connected to the voltage source of the circuit in Figure 5–18.

▶ **FIGURE 5–18**

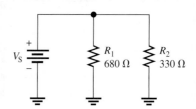

Solution   Use Equation 5–3.

$$R_T = \frac{R_1 R_2}{R_1 + R_2} = \frac{(680\ \Omega)(330\ \Omega)}{680\ \Omega + 330\ \Omega} = \frac{224{,}400\ \Omega^2}{1010\ \Omega} = \mathbf{222\ \Omega}$$

Related Problem   Determine R_T if a 220 Ω replaces R_1 in Figure 5–18.

The Case of Equal-Value Resistors in Parallel

Another special case of parallel circuits is the parallel connection of several resistors each having the same resistance value. There is a shortcut method of calculating R_T when this case occurs.

If several resistors in parallel have the same resistance, they can be assigned the same symbol R. For example, $R_1 = R_2 = R_3 = \cdots = R_n = R$. Starting with Equation 5–2, you can develop a special formula for finding R_T.

$$R_T = \cfrac{1}{\left(\cfrac{1}{R}\right) + \left(\cfrac{1}{R}\right) + \left(\cfrac{1}{R}\right) + \cdots + \left(\cfrac{1}{R}\right)}$$

Notice that in the denominator, the same term, $1/R$, is added n times (n is the number of equal-value resistors in parallel). Therefore, the formula can be written as

$$R_T = \frac{1}{n/R}$$

or

Equation 5–4
$$R_T = \frac{R}{n}$$

Equation 5–4 says that when any number of resistors (n), all having the same resistance (R), are connected in parallel, R_T is equal to the resistance divided by the number of resistors in parallel.

EXAMPLE 5–9

Four 8 Ω speakers are connected in parallel to the output of an amplifier. What is the total resistance across the output of the amplifier?

Solution   There are four 8 Ω resistors in parallel. Use Equation 5–4 as follows:

$$R_T = \frac{R}{n} = \frac{8\ \Omega}{4} = \mathbf{2\ \Omega}$$

Related Problem   If two of the speakers are removed, what is the resistance across the output?

Determining an Unknown Parallel Resistor

Sometimes you need to determine the values of resistors that are to be combined to produce a desired total resistance. For example, you use two parallel resistors to obtain a known total resistance. If you know or arbitrarily choose one resistor value, then you can calculate the second resistor value using Equation 5–3 for two parallel resistors. The formula for determining the value of an unknown resistor R_x is developed as follows:

$$\frac{1}{R_T} = \frac{1}{R_A} + \frac{1}{R_x}$$

$$\frac{1}{R_x} = \frac{1}{R_T} - \frac{1}{R_A}$$

$$\frac{1}{R_x} = \frac{R_A - R_T}{R_A R_T}$$

Equation 5–5
$$R_x = \frac{R_A R_T}{R_A - R_T}$$

where R_x is the unknown resistor and R_A is the known or selected value.

EXAMPLE 5–10

Suppose that you wish to obtain a resistance as close to 150 Ω as possible by combining two resistors in parallel. There is a 330 Ω resistor available. What other value do you need?

Solution $R_T = 150\ \Omega$ and $R_A = 330\ \Omega$. Therefore,

$$R_x = \frac{R_A R_T}{R_A - R_T} = \frac{(330\ \Omega)(150\ \Omega)}{330\ \Omega - 150\ \Omega} = 275\ \Omega$$

The closest standard value is **270 Ω**.

Related Problem   If you need to obtain a total resistance of 130 Ω, what value can you add in parallel to the parallel combination of 330 Ω and 270 Ω? First find the value of 330 Ω and 270 Ω in parallel and treat that value as a single resistor.

Notation for Parallel Resistors

Sometimes, for convenience, parallel resistors are designated by two parallel vertical marks. For example, R_1 in parallel with R_2 can be written as $R_1 \parallel R_2$. Also, when several resistors are in parallel with each other, this notation can be used. For example,

$$R_1 \parallel R_2 \parallel R_3 \parallel R_4 \parallel R_5$$

indicates that R_1 through R_5 are all in parallel.

This notation is also used with resistance values. For example,

$$10 \text{ k}\Omega \parallel 5 \text{ k}\Omega$$

means that a 10 kΩ resistor is in parallel with a 5 kΩ resistor.

5–5   APPLICATION OF OHM'S LAW

Ohm's law can be applied to parallel circuit analysis.

After completing this section, you should be able to

▪ **Apply Ohm's law in a parallel circuit**

  ▪ Find the total current in a parallel circuit

  ▪ Find each branch current in a parallel circuit

  ▪ Find the voltage across a parallel circuit

  ▪ Find the resistance of a parallel circuit

The following examples illustrate how to apply Ohm's law to determine the total current, branch currents, voltage, and resistance in parallel circuits.

EXAMPLE 5–11

Find the total current produced by the battery in Figure 5–19.

▶ **FIGURE 5–19**

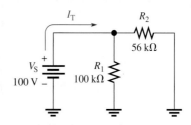

Solution The battery "sees" a total parallel resistance that determines the amount of current that it generates. First, calculate R_T.

$$R_T = \frac{R_1 R_2}{R_1 + R_2} = \frac{(100 \text{ k}\Omega)(56 \text{ k}\Omega)}{100 \text{ k}\Omega + 56 \text{ k}\Omega} = \frac{5600 \text{ k}\Omega^2}{156 \text{ k}\Omega} = 35.9 \text{ k}\Omega$$

The battery voltage is 100 V. Use Ohm's law to find I_T.

$$I_T = \frac{V_S}{R_T} = \frac{100 \text{ V}}{35.9 \text{ k}\Omega} = \textbf{2.79 mA}$$

Related Problem What is I_T in Figure 5–19 if R_2 is changed to 120 kΩ? What is the current through R_1?

Use Multisim file E06-11 to verify the calculated results in this example and to confirm your calculation for the related problem.

EXAMPLE 5–12

Determine the current through each resistor in the parallel circuit of Figure 5–20.

▶ **FIGURE 5–20**

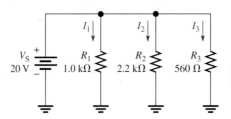

Solution The voltage across each resistor (branch) is equal to the source voltage. That is, the voltage across R_1 is 20 V, the voltage across R_2 is 20 V, and the voltage across R_3 is 20 V. The current through each resistor is determined as follows:

$$I_1 = \frac{V_S}{R_1} = \frac{20 \text{ V}}{1.0 \text{ k}\Omega} = \textbf{20 mA}$$

$$I_2 = \frac{V_S}{R_2} = \frac{20 \text{ V}}{2.2 \text{ k}\Omega} = \textbf{9.09 mA}$$

$$I_3 = \frac{V_S}{R_3} = \frac{20 \text{ V}}{560 \text{ }\Omega} = \textbf{35.7 mA}$$

Related Problem If an additional resistor of 910 Ω is connected in parallel to the circuit in Figure 5–20, determine all of the branch currents.

Use Multisim file E06-12 to verify the calculated results in this example and to confirm your calculations for the related problem.

EXAMPLE 5–13

Find the voltage V_S across the parallel circuit in Figure 5–21.

▶ FIGURE 5–21

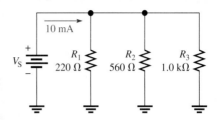

Solution The total current into the parallel circuit is 10 mA. If you know the total resistance, then you can apply Ohm's law to get the voltage. The total resistance is

$$R_T = \frac{1}{G_1 + G_2 + G_3}$$

$$= \frac{1}{\left(\dfrac{1}{R_1}\right) + \left(\dfrac{1}{R_2}\right) + \left(\dfrac{1}{R_3}\right)}$$

$$= \frac{1}{\left(\dfrac{1}{220\ \Omega}\right) + \left(\dfrac{1}{560\ \Omega}\right) + \left(\dfrac{1}{1.0\ k\Omega}\right)}$$

$$= \frac{1}{4.55\ mS + 1.79\ mS + 1\ mS} = \frac{1}{7.34\ mS} = 136\ \Omega$$

Therefore, the source voltage is

$$V_S = I_T R_T = (10\ mA)(136\ \Omega) = \mathbf{1.36\ V}$$

Related Problem Find the voltage if R_3 is decreased to 680 Ω in Figure 5–21 and I_T is 10 mA.

Use Multisim file E06-13 to verify the calculated results in this example and to confirm your calculation for the related problem.

EXAMPLE 5–14

The circuit board in Figure 5–22 has three resistors in parallel. The values of two of the resistors are known from the color bands, but the top resistor is not clearly marked (maybe the bands are worn off from handling). Determine the value of the unknown resistor R_1 using only an ammeter and a dc power supply.

▶ FIGURE 5–22

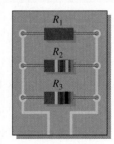

Solution   If you can determine the total resistance of the three resistors in parallel, then you can use the parallel-resistance formula to calculate the unknown resistance. You can use Ohm's law to find the total resistance if voltage and total current are known.

In Figure 5–23, a 12 V source (arbitrary value) is connected across the resistors, and the total current is measured. Using these measured values, find the total resistance.

$$R_T = \frac{V}{I_T} = \frac{12 \text{ V}}{24.1 \text{ mA}} = 498 \ \Omega$$

▶ **FIGURE 5–23**

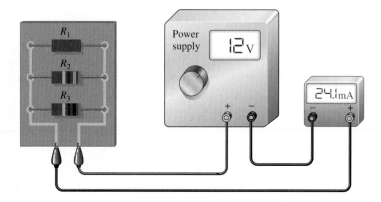

Find the unknown resistance as follows:

$$\frac{1}{R_T} = \frac{1}{R_1} + \frac{1}{R_2} + \frac{1}{R_3}$$

$$\frac{1}{R_1} = \frac{1}{R_T} - \frac{1}{R_2} - \frac{1}{R_3} = \frac{1}{498 \ \Omega} - \frac{1}{1.8 \text{ k}\Omega} - \frac{1}{1.0 \text{ k}\Omega} = 453 \ \mu\text{S}$$

$$R_1 = \frac{1}{453 \ \mu\text{S}} = \textbf{2.21 k}\boldsymbol{\Omega}$$

Related Problem   Explain how to determine the value of R_1 using an ohmmeter and without removing R_1 from the circuit.

5–6   CURRENT SOURCES IN PARALLEL

As you learned in Chapter 2, a current source is a type of energy source that provides a constant current to a load even if the resistance of that load changes. A transistor can be used as a current source; therefore, current sources are important in electronic circuits. Although the study of transistors is beyond the scope of this book, you should understand how current sources act in parallel.

After completing this section, you should be able to

■ **Determine the total effect of current sources in parallel**

  ■ Determine the total current from parallel sources having the same direction

  ■ Determine the total current from parallel sources having opposite directions

In general, the total current produced by current sources in parallel is equal to the algebraic sum of the individual current sources. The algebraic sum means that you must consider the direction of current when you combine the sources in parallel. For example, in Figure 5–24(a), the three current sources in parallel provide current in the same direction (into node A). So the total current into node A is

$$I_T = 1 \text{ A} + 2 \text{ A} + 2 \text{ A} = 5 \text{ A}$$

In Figure 5–24(b), the 1 A source provides current in a direction opposite to the other two. The total current into node A in this case is

$$I_T = 2 \text{ A} + 2 \text{ A} - 1 \text{ A} = 3 \text{ A}$$

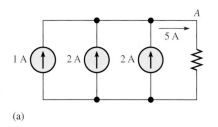

(a)

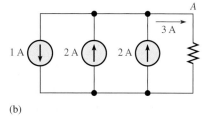

(b)

◀ FIGURE 5–24

EXAMPLE 5–15

Determine the current through R_L in Figure 5–25.

▶ FIGURE 5–25

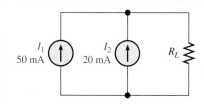

Solution   The two current sources are in the same direction; so the current through R_L is

$$I_{R_L} = I_1 + I_2 = 50 \text{ mA} + 20 \text{ mA} = \textbf{70 mA}$$

Related Problem   Determine the current through R_L if the direction of I_2 is reversed.

5–7   CURRENT DIVIDERS

A parallel circuit acts as a current divider because the current entering the junction of parallel branches "divides" up into several individual branch currents.

After completing this section, you should be able to

■ **Use a parallel circuit as a current divider**

  ■ Apply the current-divider formula

  ■ Determine an unknown branch current

In a parallel circuit, the total current into the junction of the parallel branches divides among the branches. Thus, a parallel circuit acts as a **current divider**. This current-divider principle is illustrated in Figure 5–26 for a two-branch parallel circuit in which part of the total current I_T goes through R_1 and part through R_2.

▶ **FIGURE 5–26**

Total current divides between the two branches.

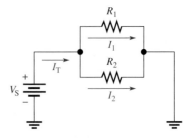

Since the same voltage is across each of the resistors in parallel, the branch currents are inversely proportional to the values of the resistors. For example, if the value of R_2 is twice that of R_1, then the value of I_2 is one-half that of I_1. In other words,

The total current divides among parallel resistors into currents with values inversely proportional to the resistance values.

The branches with higher resistance have less current, and the branches with lower resistance have more current, in accordance with Ohm's law. If all the branches have the same resistance, the branch currents are all equal.

Figure 5–27 shows specific values to demonstrate how the currents divide according to the branch resistances. Notice that in this case the resistance of the upper branch is one-tenth the resistance of the lower branch, but the upper branch current is ten times the lower branch current.

▶ **FIGURE 5–27**

The branch with the lower resistance has more current, and the branch with the higher resistance has less current.

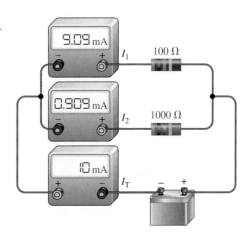

Current-Divider Formula

You can develop a formula for determining how currents divide among any number of parallel resistors as shown in Figure 5–28, where n is the total number of resistors.

▶ **FIGURE 5–28**

A parallel circuit with n branches.

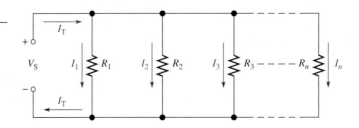

The current through any one of the parallel resistors is I_x, where x represents the number of a particular resistor (1, 2, 3, and so on). By Ohm's law, you can express the current through any one of the resistors in Figure 5–28 as follows:

$$I_x = \frac{V_S}{R_x}$$

The source voltage, V_S, appears across each of the parallel resistors, and R_x represents any one of the parallel resistors. The total source voltage, V_S, is equal to the total current times the total parallel resistance.

$$V_S = I_T R_T$$

Substituting $I_T R_T$ for V_S in the expression for I_x results in

$$I_x = \frac{I_T R_T}{R_x}$$

Rearranging terms yields

$$I_x = \left(\frac{R_T}{R_x}\right) I_T$$

Equation 5–6

where $x = 1, 2, 3$, etc.

Equation 5–6 is the general current-divider formula and applies to a parallel circuit with any number of branches.

The current (I_x) through any branch equals the total parallel resistance (R_T) divided by the resistance (R_x) of that branch, and then multiplied by the total current (I_T) into the junction of parallel branches.

EXAMPLE 5–16

Determine the current through each resistor in the circuit of Figure 5–29.

▶ **FIGURE 5–29**

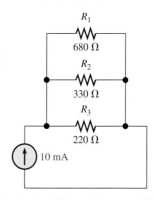

Solution   First calculate the total parallel resistance.

$$R_T = \frac{1}{\left(\dfrac{1}{R_1}\right) + \left(\dfrac{1}{R_2}\right) + \left(\dfrac{1}{R_3}\right)} = \frac{1}{\left(\dfrac{1}{680\ \Omega}\right) + \left(\dfrac{1}{330\ \Omega}\right) + \left(\dfrac{1}{220\ \Omega}\right)} = 111\ \Omega$$

The total current is 10 mA. Use Equation 5–6 to calculate each branch current.

$$I_1 = \left(\frac{R_T}{R_1}\right)I_T = \left(\frac{111\ \Omega}{680\ \Omega}\right)10\ \text{mA} = \mathbf{1.63\ mA}$$

$$I_2 = \left(\frac{R_T}{R_2}\right)I_T = \left(\frac{111\ \Omega}{330\ \Omega}\right)10\ \text{mA} = \mathbf{3.36\ mA}$$

$$I_3 = \left(\frac{R_T}{R_3}\right)I_T = \left(\frac{111\ \Omega}{220\ \Omega}\right)10\ \text{mA} = \mathbf{5.05\ mA}$$

Related Problem Determine the current through each resistor in Figure 5–29 if R_3 is removed.

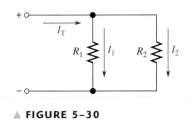

▲ **FIGURE 5–30**

Current-Divider Formulas for Two Branches Two parallel resistors are common in practical circuits, as shown in Figure 5–30. As you know from Equation 5–3,

$$R_T = \frac{R_1 R_2}{R_1 + R_2}$$

Using the general current-divider formula in Equation 5–6, the formulas for I_1 and I_2 can be written as follows:

$$I_1 = \left(\frac{R_T}{R_1}\right)I_T \quad \text{and} \quad I_2 = \left(\frac{R_T}{R_2}\right)I_T$$

Substituting $R_1 R_2/(R_1 + R_2)$ for R_T and canceling terms result in

$$I_1 = \frac{\left(\dfrac{R_1 R_2}{R_1 + R_2}\right)}{R_1}I_T \quad \text{and} \quad I_2 = \frac{\left(\dfrac{R_1 R_2}{R_1 + R_2}\right)}{R_2}I_T$$

Therefore, the current-divider formulas for the special case of two branches are

Equation 5–7

$$I_1 = \left(\frac{R_2}{R_1 + R_2}\right)I_T$$

Equation 5–8

$$I_2 = \left(\frac{R_1}{R_1 + R_2}\right)I_T$$

Note that in Equations 5–7 and 5–8, the current in one of the branches is equal to the opposite branch resistance divided by the sum of the two resistors, all multiplied by the total current. In all applications of the current-divider equations, you must know the total current into the parallel branches.

EXAMPLE 5–17

Find I_1 and I_2 in Figure 5–31.

▶ **FIGURE 5–31**

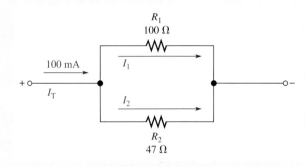

Solution   Use Equation 5–7 to determine I_1.

$$I_1 = \left(\frac{R_2}{R_1 + R_2}\right)I_T = \left(\frac{47\ \Omega}{147\ \Omega}\right)100\ \text{mA} = \textbf{32.0 mA}$$

Use Equation 5–8 to determine I_2.

$$I_2 = \left(\frac{R_1}{R_1 + R_2}\right)I_T = \left(\frac{100\ \Omega}{147\ \Omega}\right)100\ \text{mA} = \textbf{68.0 mA}$$

Related Problem   If $R_1 = 56\ \Omega$, and $R_2 = 82\ \Omega$ in Figure 5–31 and I_T stays the same, what will each branch current be?

SUMMARY

- Resistors in parallel are connected between two points (nodes).
- A parallel combination has more than one path for current.
- The total parallel resistance is less than the lowest-value resistor.
- The voltages across all branches of a parallel circuit are the same.
- Current sources in parallel add algebraically.
- Kirchhoff's current law: The sum of the currents into a junction (total current in) equals the sum of the currents out of the junction (total current out).
- The algebraic sum of all the currents entering and leaving a junction is equal to zero.
- A parallel circuit is a current divider, so called because the total current entering the junction of parallel branches divides up into each of the branches.
- If all of the branches of a parallel circuit have equal resistance, the currents through all of the branches are equal.
- The total power in a parallel-resistive circuit is the sum of all of the individual powers of the resistors making up the parallel circuit.
- The total power for a parallel circuit can be calculated with the power formulas using values of total current, total resistance, or total voltage.
- If one of the branches of a parallel circuit opens, the total resistance increases, and therefore the total current decreases.
- If a branch of a parallel circuit opens, there is no change in current through the remaining branches.

KEY TERMS

These key terms are also in the end-of-book glossary.

Branch   One current path in a parallel circuit.

Current divider   A parallel circuit in which the currents divide inversely proportional to the parallel branch resistances.

Kirchhoff's current law   A circuit law stating that the total current into a node equals the total current out of the node. Equivalently, the algebraic sum of all the currents entering and leaving a node is zero.

Node   A point in a circuit at which two or more components are connected; also known as a *junction*.

Parallel   The relationship in electric circuits in which two or more current paths are connected between two separate nodes.

FORMULAS

$$5\text{–}1 \qquad I_{IN(1)} + I_{IN(2)} + \cdots + I_{IN(N)}$$
$$= I_{OUT(1)} + I_{OUT(2)} + \cdots + I_{OUT(m)}$$

Kirchhoff's current law

$$5\text{–}2 \qquad R_T = \cfrac{1}{\left(\dfrac{1}{R_1}\right) + \left(\dfrac{1}{R_2}\right) + \left(\dfrac{1}{R_3}\right) + \cdots + \left(\dfrac{1}{R_n}\right)}$$

Total parallel resistance

$$5\text{–}3 \qquad R_T = \frac{R_1 R_2}{R_1 + R_2}$$

Special case for two resistors in parallel

$$5\text{–}4 \qquad R_T = \frac{R}{n}$$

Special case for n equal-value resistors in parallel

$$5\text{–}5 \qquad R_x = \frac{R_A R_T}{R_A - R_T}$$

Unknown parallel resistor

$$5\text{–}6 \qquad I_x = \left(\frac{R_T}{R_x}\right) I_T$$

General current-divider formula

$$5\text{–}7 \qquad I_1 = \left(\frac{R_2}{R_1 + R_2}\right) I_T$$

Two-branch current-divider formula

$$5\text{–}8 \qquad I_2 = \left(\frac{R_1}{R_1 + R_2}\right) I_T$$

Two-branch current-divider formula

SELF-TEST

Answers are at the end of the chapter.

1. In a parallel circuit, each resistor has
   (a) the same current   (b) the same voltage
   (c) the same power   (d) all of the above

2. When a $1.2\ \text{k}\Omega$ resistor and a $100\ \Omega$ resistor are connected in parallel, the total resistance is
   (a) greater than $1.2\ \text{k}\Omega$
   (b) greater than $100\ \Omega$ but less than $1.2\ \text{k}\Omega$
   (c) less than $100\ \Omega$ but greater than $90\ \Omega$
   (d) less than $90\ \Omega$

3. A $330\ \Omega$ resistor, a $270\ \Omega$ resistor, and a $68\ \Omega$ resistor are all in parallel. The total resistance is approximately
   (a) $668\ \Omega$ (b) $47\ \Omega$ (c) $68\ \Omega$ (d) $22\ \Omega$

4. Eight resistors are in parallel. The two lowest-value resistors are both $1.0\ \text{k}\Omega$. The total resistance
   (a) is less than $8\ \text{k}\Omega$ (b) is greater than $1.0\ \text{k}\Omega$
   (c) is less than $1.0\ \text{k}\Omega$ (d) is less than $500\ \Omega$

5. When an additional resistor is connected across an existing parallel circuit, the total resistance
   (a) decreases   (b) increases
   (c) remains the same   (d) increases by the value of the added resistor

6. If one of the resistors in a parallel circuit is removed, the total resistance
   (a) decreases by the value of the removed resistor   (b) remains the same
   (c) increases   (d) doubles

7. One current into a junction is 500 mA and the other current into the same junction is 300 mA. The total current out of the junction is
   (a) 200 mA   (b) unknown   (c) 800 mA   (d) the larger of the two

8. The following resistors are in parallel across a voltage source: 390 Ω, 560 Ω, and 820 Ω. The resistor with the least current is

   (a) 390 Ω   (b) 560 Ω

   (c) 820 Ω   (d) impossible to determine without knowing the voltage

9. A sudden decrease in the total current into a parallel circuit may indicate

   (a) a short   (b) an open resistor

   (c) a drop in source voltage   (d) either (b) or (c)

10. In a four-branch parallel circuit, there are 10 mA of current in each branch. If one of the branches opens, the current in each of the other three branches is

    (a) 13.3 mA   (b) 10 mA   (c) 0 A   (d) 30 mA

11. In a certain three-branch parallel circuit, R_1 has 10 mA through it, R_2 has 15 mA through it, and R_3 has 20 mA through it. After measuring a total current of 35 mA, you can say that

    (a) R_1 is open   (b) R_2 is open
    (c) R_3 is open   (d) the circuit is operating properly

12. If there are a total of 100 mA into a parallel circuit consisting of three branches and two of the branch currents are 40 mA and 20 mA, the third branch current is

    (a) 60 mA   (b) 20 mA   (c) 160 mA   (d) 40 mA

13. A complete short develops across one of five parallel resistors on a PC board. The most likely result is

    (a) the shorted resistor will burn out

    (b) one or more of the other resistors will burn out

    (c) the fuse in the power supply will blow

    (d) the resistance values will be altered

PROBLEMS

More difficult problems are indicated by an asterisk (*).

SECTION 5–1   Resistors in Parallel

1. Show how to connect the resistors in Figure 5–32(a) in parallel across the battery.

2. Determine whether or not all the resistors in Figure 5–32(b) are connected in parallel on the printed circuit (PC) board.

▶ FIGURE 5–32

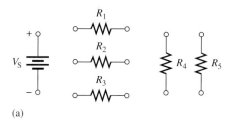

(a)

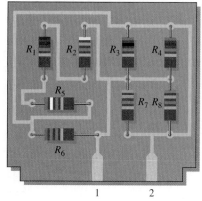

(b)

*3. Identify which groups of resistors are in parallel on the double-sided PC board in Figure 5–33.

▶ FIGURE 5–33

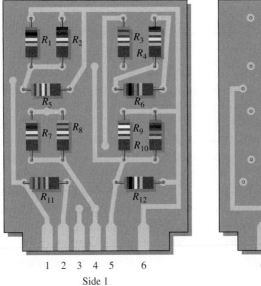
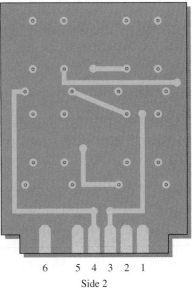

1 2 3 4 5   6
Side 1

6   5 4 3 2 1
Side 2

SECTION 5–2 Voltage in a Parallel Circuit

4. What is the voltage across and the current through each parallel resistor if the total voltage is 12 V and the total resistance is 550 Ω? There are four resistors, all of equal value.

5. The source voltage in Figure 5–34 is 100 V. How much voltage does each of the meters read?

▶ FIGURE 5–34

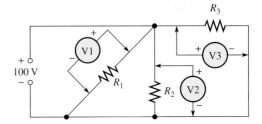

6. What is the total resistance of the circuit as seen from the voltage source for each position of the switch in Figure 5–35?

7. What is the voltage across each resistor in Figure 5–35 for each switch position?

8. What is the total current from the voltage source in Figure 5–35 for each switch position?

▶ FIGURE 5–35

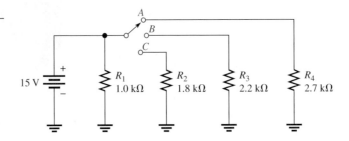

SECTION 5–3   Kirchhoff's Current Law

9. The following currents are measured in the same direction in a three-branch parallel circuit: 250 mA, 300 mA, and 800 mA. What is the value of the current into the junction of these three branches?

10. There is a total of 500 mA of current into five parallel resistors. The currents through four of the resistors are 50 mA, 150 mA, 25 mA, and 100 mA. What is the current through the fifth resistor?

11. In the circuit of Figure 5–36, determine the resistance R_2, R_3, and R_4.

▶ FIGURE 5–36

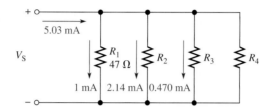

*12. The electrical circuit in a room has a ceiling lamp that draws 1.25 A and four wall outlets. Two table lamps that each draw 0.833 A are plugged into two outlets, and an electric heater that draws 10 A is connected to the third outlet. When all of these items are in use, how much current is in the main line serving the room? If the main line is protected by a 15 A circuit breaker, how much current can be drawn from the fourth outlet? Draw a schematic of this wiring.

*13. The total resistance of a parallel circuit is 25 Ω. What is the current through a 220 Ω resistor that makes up part of the parallel circuit if the total current is 100 mA?

SECTION 5–4   Total Parallel Resistance

14. The following resistors are connected in parallel: 1.0 MΩ, 2.2 MΩ, 5.6 MΩ, 12 MΩ, and 22 MΩ. Determine the total resistance.

15. Find the total resistance for each of the following groups of parallel resistors:
    (a) 560 Ω and 1000 Ω   (b) 47 Ω and 56 Ω
    (c) 1.5 kΩ, 2.2 kΩ, 10 kΩ   (d) 1.0 MΩ, 470 kΩ, 1.0 kΩ, 2.7 MΩ

16. Calculate R_T for each circuit in Figure 5–37.

▶ FIGURE 5–37

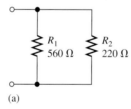

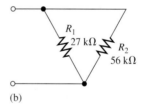

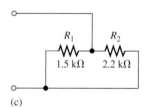

(a)   (b)   (c)

17. What is the total resistance of twelve 6.8 kΩ resistors in parallel?

18. Five 470 Ω, ten 1000 Ω, and two 100 Ω resistors are all connected in parallel. What is the total resistance for each of the three groupings?

19. Find the total resistance for the entire parallel circuit in Problem 18.

20. If the total resistance in Figure 5–38 is 389.2 Ω, what is the value of R_2?

▶ FIGURE 5–38

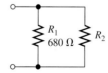

21. What is the total resistance between point A and ground in Figure 5–39 for the following conditions?

(a) SW1 and SW2 open   (b) SW1 closed, SW2 open

(c) SW1 open, SW2 closed   (d) SW1 and SW2 closed

▶ FIGURE 5–39

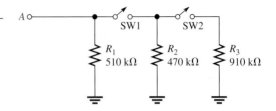

SECTION 5–5   Application of Ohm's Law

22. What is the total current in each circuit of Figure 5–40?

▶ FIGURE 5–40

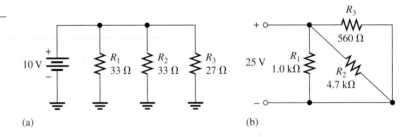

(a)   (b)

23. Three 33 Ω resistors are connected in parallel with a 110 V source. What is the current from the source?

24. Four equal-value resistors are connected in parallel. Five volts are applied across the parallel circuit, and 1.11 mA are measured from the source. What is the value of each resistor?

25. Many types of decorative lights are connected in parallel. If a set of lights is connected to a 110 V source and the filament of each bulb has a hot resistance of 2.2 kΩ, what is the current through each bulb? Why is it better to have these bulbs in parallel rather than in series?

26. Find the values of the unspecified labeled quantities in each circuit of Figure 5–41.

▶ FIGURE 5–41

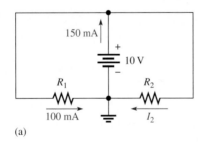

(a)

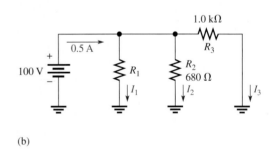

(b)

27. To what minimum value can the 100 Ω rheostat in Figure 5–42 be adjusted before the 0.5 A fuse blows?

▶ FIGURE 5–42

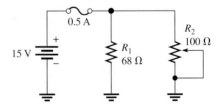

28. Determine the total current from the source and the current through each resistor for each switch position in Figure 5–43.

▶ **FIGURE 5–43**

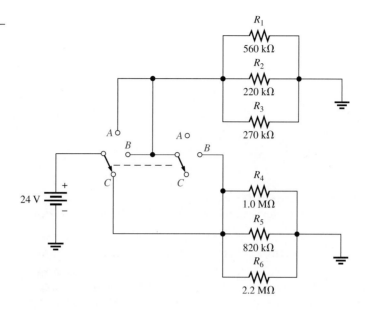

29. Find the values of the unspecified quantities in Figure 5–44.

▶ **FIGURE 5–44**

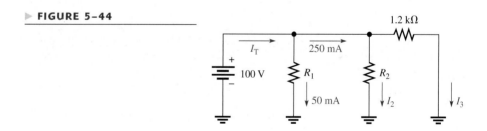

SECTION 5–6 Current Sources in Parallel
30. Determine the current through R_L in each circuit in Figure 5–45.

▶ **FIGURE 5–45**

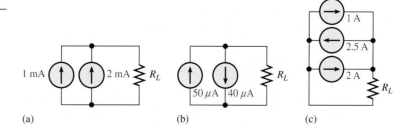

(a)   (b)   (c)

31. Find the current through the resistor for each position of the ganged switch in Figure 5–46.

▶ FIGURE 5–46

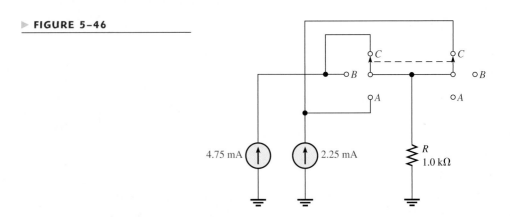

SECTION 5–7 Current Dividers

32. How much branch current should each meter in Figure 5–47 indicate?

▶ FIGURE 5–47

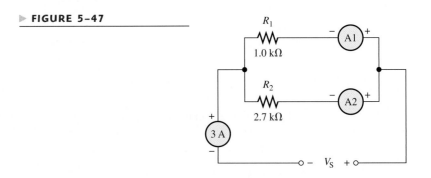

33. Determine the current in each branch of the current dividers of Figure 5–48.

▶ FIGURE 5–48

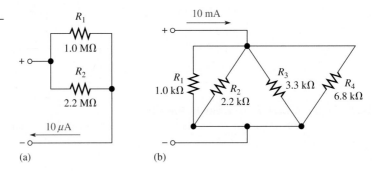

(a)   (b)

34. What is the current through each resistor in Figure 5–49? R is the lowest-value resistor, and all others are multiples of that value as indicated.

▶ FIGURE 5–49

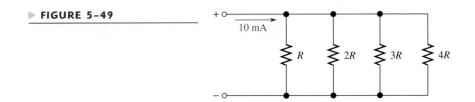

35. Determine all of the resistor values in Figure 5–50. $R_T = 773 \, \Omega$.

▶ FIGURE 5–50

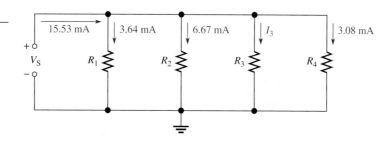

*36. Special shunt resistors designed to drop 50 mV in high current-measuring applications are available from manufacturers. A 50 mV, 10 kΩ full-scale voltmeter is connected across the shunt to make the measurement.

   (a) What value of shunt resistance is required to use a 50 mV meter in a 50 A measurement application?

   (b) How much current is through the meter?

SELF-TEST

1. (b)   2. (c)   3. (b)   4. (d)   5. (a)   6. (c)   7. (c)   8. (c)

9. (d)   10. (b)   11. (a)   12. (d)   13. (c)   14. (b)

6

DIGITAL CONCEPTS

INTRODUCTION

The term *digital* is derived from the way computers perform operations, by counting digits. For many years, applications of digital electronics were confined to computer systems. Today, digital technology is applied in a wide range of areas in addition to computers. Such applications as television, communications systems, radar, navigation and guidance systems, military systems, medical instrumentation, industrial process control, and consumer electronics use digital techniques. Over the years digital technology has progressed from vacuum-tube circuits to discrete transistors to complex integrated circuits, some of which contain millions of transistors.

This chapter introduces you to digital electronics and provides a broad overview of many important concepts, components, and tools.

CHAPTER OBJECTIVES

- Explain the basic differences between digital and analog quantities

- Show how voltage levels are used to represent digital quantities

- Describe various parameters of a pulse waveform such as rise time, fall time, pulse width, frequency, period, and duty cycle

- Explain the basic logic operations of NOT, AND, and OR

- Describe the logic functions of the comparator, adder, code converter, encoder, decoder, multiplexer, demultiplexer, counter, and register

- Identify fixed-function digital integrated circuits according to their complexity and the type of circuit packaging

- Identify pin numbers on integrated circuit packages

- Describe programmable logic, discuss the various types, and describe how PLDs are programmed

- Recognize various instruments and understand how they are used in measurement and troubleshooting digital circuits and systems

- Show how a complete digital system is formed by combining the basic functions in a practical application

KEY TERMS

Key terms are in order of appearance in the chapter.

- Analog
- Digital
- Binary
- Bit
- Pulse
- Clock
- Timing diagram
- Data
- Serial
- Parallel
- Logic
- Input

- Output
- Gate
- NOT
- Inverter
- AND
- OR
- Integrated circuit (IC)
- SPLD
- CPLD
- FPGA
- Compiler
- Troubleshooting

WWW. VISIT THE COMPANION WEBSITE
Study aids for this chapter are available at
http://www.prenhall.com/floyd

6–1 DIGITAL AND ANALOG QUANTITIES

Electronic circuits can be divided into two broad categories, digital and analog. Digital electronics involves quantities with discrete values, and analog electronics involves quantities with continuous values. Although you will be studying digital fundamentals in this book, you should also know something about analog because many applications require both; and interfacing between analog and digital is important.

After completing this section, you should be able to

- Define *analog*
- Define *digital*
- Explain the difference between digital and analog quantities
- State the advantages of digital over analog
- Give examples of how digital and analog quantities are used in electronics

An **analog*** quantity is one having continuous values. A **digital** quantity is one having a discrete set of values. Most things that can be measured quantitatively occur in nature in analog form. For example, the air temperature changes over a continuous range of values. During a given day, the temperature does not go from, say, 70° to 71° instantaneously; it takes on all the infinite values in between. If you graphed the temperature on a typical summer day, you would have a smooth, continuous curve similar to the curve in Figure 6–1. Other examples of analog quantities are time, pressure, distance, and sound.

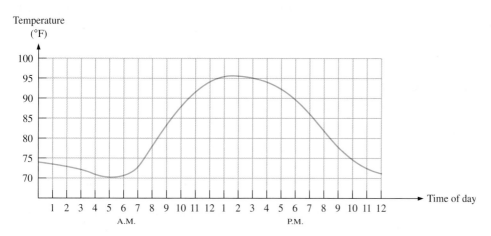

◀ **FIGURE 6–1**

Graph of an analog quantity (temperature versus time).

Rather than graphing the temperature on a continuous basis, suppose you just take a temperature reading every hour. Now you have sampled values representing the temperature at discrete points in time (every hour) over a 24-hour period, as indicated in Figure 6–2. You have effectively converted an analog quantity to a form that can now be digitized by representing each sampled value by a digital code. It is important to realize that Figure 6–2 itself is not the digital representation of the analog quantity.

The Digital Advantage   Digital representation has certain advantages over analog representation in electronics applications. For one thing, digital data can be processed and transmitted more efficiently and reliably than analog data. Also, digital data has a great

---

*The blue bold terms are key terms and are included in a Key Term glossary at the end of each chapter.

▶ **FIGURE 6–2**

Sampled–value representation (quantization) of the analog quantity in Figure 6–1. Each value represented by a dot can be digitized by representing it as a digital code that consists of a series of 1s and 0s.

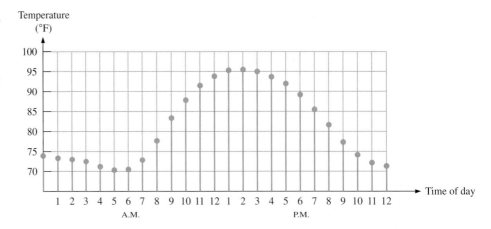

advantage when storage is necessary. For example, music when converted to digital form can be stored more compactly and reproduced with greater accuracy and clarity than is possible when it is in analog form. Noise (unwanted voltage fluctuations) does not affect digital data nearly as much as it does analog signals.

An Analog Electronic System

A public address system, used to amplify sound so that it can be heard by a large audience, is one simple example of an application of analog electronics. The basic diagram in Figure 6–3 illustrates that sound waves, which are analog in nature, are picked up by a microphone and converted to a small analog voltage called the audio signal. This voltage varies continuously as the volume and frequency of the sound changes and is applied to the input of a linear amplifier. The output of the amplifier, which is an increased reproduction of input voltage, goes to the speaker(s). The speaker changes the amplified audio signal back to sound waves that have a much greater volume than the original sound waves picked up by the microphone.

A System Using Digital and Analog Methods

The compact disk (CD) player is an example of a system in which both digital and analog circuits are used. The simplified block diagram in Figure 6–4 illustrates the basic principle. Music in digital form is stored on the compact disk. A laser diode optical system picks up the digital data from the rotating disk and transfers it to the **digital-to-analog converter (DAC).** The DAC changes the digital data into an analog signal that is an electrical reproduction of the original music. This signal is amplified and sent to the speaker for you to enjoy. When the music was originally recorded on the CD, a process, essentially the reverse of the one described here, using an **analog-to-digital converter (ADC)** was used.

▶ **FIGURE 6–3**

A basic audio public address system.

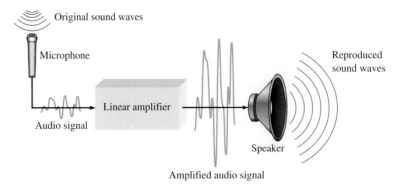

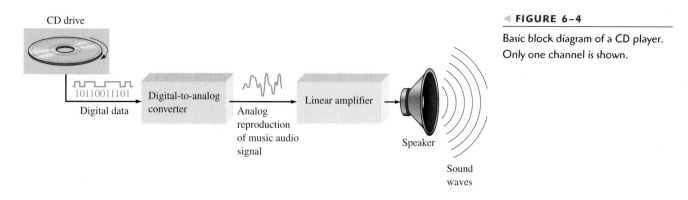

▲ **FIGURE 6-4**

Basic block diagram of a CD player. Only one channel is shown.

6-2 BINARY DIGITS, LOGIC LEVELS, AND DIGITAL WAVEFORMS

Digital electronics involves circuits and systems in which there are only two possible states. These states are represented by two different voltage levels: A HIGH and a LOW. The two states can also be represented by current levels, bits and bumps on a CD or DVD, etc. In digital systems such as computers, combinations of the two states, called *codes,* are used to represent numbers, symbols, alphabetic characters, and other types of information. The two-state number system is called *binary,* and its two digits are 0 and 1. A binary digit is called a *bit.*

After completing this section, you should be able to

- Define *binary*

- Define *bit*

- Name the bits in a binary system

- Explain how voltage levels are used to represent bits

- Explain how voltage levels are interpreted by a digital circuit

- Describe the general characteristics of a pulse

- Determine the amplitude, rise time, fall time, and width of a pulse

- Identify and describe the characteristics of a digital waveform

- Determine the amplitude, period, frequency, and duty cycle of a digital waveform

- Explain what a timing diagram is and state its purpose

- Explain serial and parallel data transfer and state the advantage and disadvantage of each

Binary Digits

Each of the two digits in the **binary** system, 1 and 0, is called a **bit,** which is a contraction of the words *binary digit.* In digital circuits, two different voltage levels are used to represent the two bits. Generally, 1 is represented by the higher voltage, which we will refer to as a HIGH, and a 0 is represented by the lower voltage level, which we will refer to as a LOW. This is called **positive logic** and will be used throughout the book.

HIGH = 1   and   LOW = 0

Another system in which a 1 is represented by a LOW and a 0 is represented by a HIGH is called *negative logic.*

Groups of bits (combinations of 1s and 0s), called *codes,* are used to represent numbers, letters, symbols, instructions, and anything else required in a given application.

Logic Levels

The voltages used to represent a 1 and a 0 are called *logic levels*. Ideally, one voltage level represents a HIGH and another voltage level represents a LOW. In a practical digital circuit, however, a HIGH can be any voltage between a specified minimum value and a specified maximum value. Likewise, a LOW can be any voltage between a specified minimum and a specified maximum. There can be no overlap between the accepted range of HIGH levels and the accepted range of LOW levels.

Figure 6–5 illustrates the general range of LOWs and HIGHs for a digital circuit. The variable $V_{H(max)}$ represents the maximum HIGH voltage value, and $V_{H(min)}$ represents the minimum HIGH voltage value. The maximum LOW voltage value is represented by $V_{L(max)}$, and the minimum LOW voltage value is represented by $V_{L(min)}$. The voltage values between $V_{L(max)}$ and $V_{H(min)}$ are unacceptable for proper operation. A voltage in the unallowed range can appear as either a HIGH or a LOW to a given circuit and is therefore not an acceptable value. For example, the HIGH values for a certain type of digital circuit called CMOS may range from 2 V to 3.3 V and the LOW values may range from 0 V to 0.8 V. So, for example, if a voltage of 2.5 V is applied, the circuit will accept it as a HIGH or binary 1. If a voltage of 0.5 V is applied, the circuit will accept it as a LOW or binary 0. For this type of circuit, voltages between 0.8 V and 2 V are unacceptable.

▷ **FIGURE 6–5**

Logic level ranges of voltage for a digital circuit.

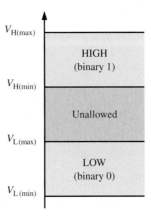

Digital Waveforms

Digital waveforms consist of voltage levels that are changing back and forth between the HIGH and LOW levels or states. Figure 6–6(a) shows that a single positive-going **pulse** is generated when the voltage (or current) goes from its normally LOW level to its HIGH level and then back to its LOW level. The negative-going pulse in Figure 6–6(b) is generated when the voltage goes from its normally HIGH level to its LOW level and back to its HIGH level. A digital waveform is made up of a series of pulses.

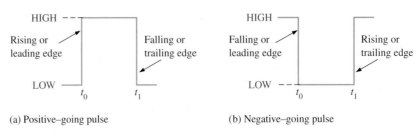

(a) Positive–going pulse   (b) Negative–going pulse

▲ **FIGURE 6–6**

Ideal pulses.

The Pulse   As indicated in Figure 6–6, a pulse has two edges: a **leading edge** that occurs first at time t_0 and a **trailing edge** that occurs last at time t_1. For a positive-going pulse, the leading edge is a rising edge, and the trailing edge is a falling edge. The pulses in Figure 6–6 are ideal because the rising and falling edges are assumed to change in zero time (instantaneously). In practice, these transitions never occur instantaneously, although for most digital work you can assume ideal pulses.

Figure 6–7 shows a nonideal pulse. In reality, all pulses exhibit some or all of these characteristics. The overshoot and ringing are sometimes produced by stray inductive and capacitive effects. The droop can be caused by stray capacitive and circuit resistance, forming an *RC* circuit with a low time constant.

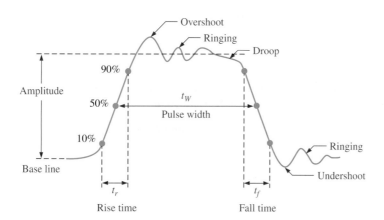

The time required for a pulse to go from its LOW level to its HIGH level is called the **rise time** (t_r), and the time required for the transition from the HIGH level to the LOW level is called the **fall time** (t_f). In practice, it is common to measure rise time from 10% of the pulse **amplitude** (height from baseline) to 90% of the pulse amplitude and to measure the fall time from 90% to 10% of the pulse amplitude, as indicated in Figure 6–7. The bottom 10% and the top 10% of the pulse are not included in the rise and fall times because of the nonlinearities in the waveform in these areas. The **pulse width** (t_W) is a measure of the duration of the pulse and is often defined as the time interval between the 50% points on the rising and falling edges, as indicated in Figure 6–7.

Waveform Characteristics   Most waveforms encountered in digital systems are composed of a series of pulses, sometimes called *pulse trains,* and can be classified as either periodic or nonperiodic. A **periodic** pulse waveform is one that repeats itself at a fixed interval, called a **period** *(T).* The **frequency** *(f)* is the rate at which it repeats itself and is measured in hertz (Hz). A nonperiodic pulse waveform, of course, does not repeat itself at fixed intervals and may be composed of pulses of randomly differing pulse widths and/or randomly differing time intervals between the pulses. An example of each type is shown in Figure 6–8.

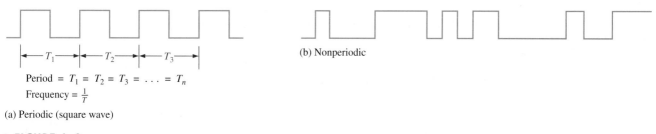

(b) Nonperiodic

Period $= T_1 = T_2 = T_3 = \ldots = T_n$
Frequency $= \frac{1}{T}$

(a) Periodic (square wave)

▲ **FIGURE 6–8**

Examples of digital waveforms.

The frequency (f) of a pulse (digital) waveform is the reciprocal of the period. The relationship between frequency and period is expressed as follows:

Equation 6–1

$$f = \frac{1}{T}$$

Equation 6–2

$$T = \frac{1}{f}$$

An important characteristic of a periodic digital waveform is its **duty cycle,** which is the ratio of the pulse width (tW) to the period (T). It can be expressed as a percentage.

Equation 6–3

$$\text{Duty cycle} = \left(\frac{t_W}{T}\right)100\%$$

EXAMPLE 6–1

A portion of a periodic digital waveform is shown in Figure 6–9. The measurements are in milliseconds. Determine the following:

(a) period   (b) frequency   (c) duty cycle

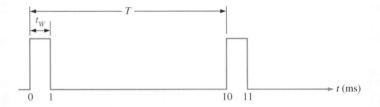

▲ **FIGURE 6–9**

Solution   (a) The period is measured from the edge of one pulse to the corresponding edge of the next pulse. In this case T is measured from leading edge to leading edge, as indicated. T equals **10 ms.**

(b) $f = \dfrac{1}{T} = \dfrac{1}{10\ ms} = $ **100 Hz**

(c) Duty cycle $= \left(\dfrac{t_W}{T}\right)100 = \left(\dfrac{1\ ms}{10\ ms}\right)100\% = $ **10%**

Related Problem   A periodic digital waveform has a pulse width of 25 μs and a period of 150 μs. Determine the frequency and the duty cycle.

COMPUTER NOTE

The speed at which a computer can operate depends on the type of microprocessor used in the system. The speed specification, for example 3.5 GHz, of a computer is the maximum clock frequency at which the microprocessor can run.

A Digital Waveform Carries Binary Information

Binary information that is handled by digital systems appears as waveforms that represent sequences of bits. When the waveform is HIGH, a binary 1 is present; when the waveform is LOW, a binary 0 is present. Each bit in a sequence occupies a defined time interval called a **bit time.**

The Clock   In digital systems, all waveforms are synchronized with a basic timing waveform called the **clock.** The clock is a periodic waveform in which each interval between pulses (the period) equals the time for one bit.

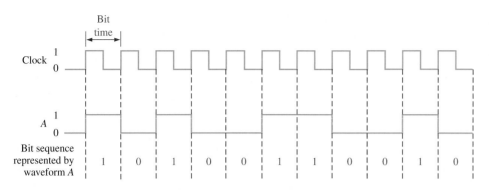

Example of a clock waveform synchronized with a waveform representation of a sequence of bits.

An example of a clock waveform is shown in Figure 6–10. Notice that, in this case, each change in level of waveform A occurs at the leading edge of the clock waveform. In other cases, level changes occur at the trailing edge of the clock. During each bit time of the clock, waveform A is either HIGH or LOW. These HIGHs and LOWs represent a sequence of bits as indicated. A group of several bits can be used as a piece of binary information, such as a number or a letter. The clock waveform itself does not carry information.

Timing Diagrams A **timing diagram** is a graph of digital waveforms showing the actual time relationship of two or more waveforms and how each waveform changes in relation to the others. By looking at a timing diagram, you can determine the states (HIGH or LOW) of all the waveforms at any specified point in time and the exact time that a waveform changes state relative to the other waveforms. Figure 6–11 is an example of a timing diagram made up of four waveforms. From this timing diagram you can see, for example, that the three waveforms A, B, and C are HIGH only during bit time 7 and they all change back LOW at the end of bit time 7 (shaded area).

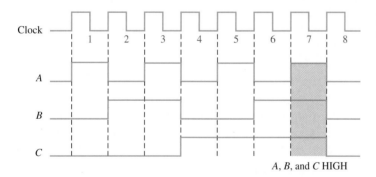

Example of a timing diagram.

Data Transfer

Data refers to groups of bits that convey some type of information. Binary data, which are represented by digital waveforms, must be transferred from one circuit to another within a digital system or from one system to another in order to accomplish a given purpose. For example, numbers stored in binary form in the memory of a computer must be transferred to the computer's central processing unit in order to be added. The sum of the addition must then be transferred to a monitor for display and/or transferred back to the memory. In computer systems, as illustrated in Figure 6–12, binary data are transferred in two ways: serial and parallel.

When bits are transferred in **serial** form from one point to another, they are sent one bit at a time along a single line, as illustrated in Figure 6–12(a) for the case of a computer-to-modem transfer. During the time interval from t_0 to t_1, the first bit is transferred. During the time interval from t_1 to t_2, the second bit is transferred, and so on. To transfer eight bits in a series, it takes eight time intervals.

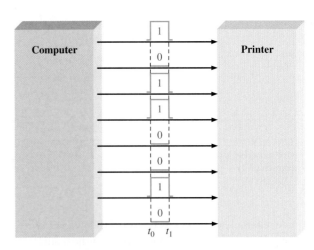

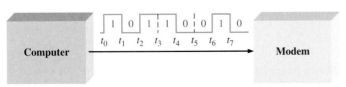

(a) Serial transfer of 8 bits of binary data from computer to modem. Interval t_0 to t_1 is first.

(b) Parallel transfer of 8 bits of binary data from computer to printer. The beginning time is t_0.

▲ **FIGURE 6–12**

Illustration of serial and parallel transfer of binary data. Only the data lines are shown.

When bits are transferred in **parallel** form, all the bits in a group are sent out on separate lines at the same time. There is one line for each bit, as shown in Figure 6–12(b) for the example of eight bits being transferred from a computer to a printer. To transfer eight bits in parallel, it takes one time interval compared to eight time intervals for the serial transfer.

To summarize, an advantage of serial transfer of binary data is that a minimum of only one line is required. In parallel transfer, a number of lines equal to the number of bits to be transferred at one time is required. A disadvantage of serial transfer is that it takes longer to transfer a given number of bits than with parallel transfer. For example, if one bit can be transferred in 1 ms, then it takes 8 ms to serially transfer eight bits but only 1 μs to parallel transfer eight bits. A disadvantage of parallel transfer is that it takes more lines than serial transfer.

EXAMPLE 6–2

(a) Determine the total time required to serially transfer the eight bits contained in waveform A of Figure 6–13, and indicate the sequence of bits. The left-most bit is the first to be transferred. The 100 kHz clock is used as reference.

(b) What is the total time to transfer the same eight bits in parallel?

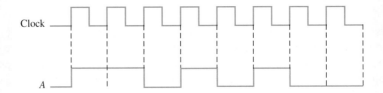

▲ **FIGURE 6–13**

Solution   (a) Since the frequency of the clock is 100 kHz, the period is

$$T = \frac{1}{f} = \frac{1}{100 \text{ kHz}} = 10 \ \mu s$$

It takes 10 μs to transfer each bit in the waveform. The total transfer time for 8 bits is

$$8 \times 10 \, \mu s = \mathbf{80 \, \mu s}$$

To determine the sequence of bits, examine the waveform in Figure 6–13 during each bit time. If waveform *A* is HIGH during the bit time, a 1 is transferred. If waveform *A* is LOW during the bit time, a 0 is transferred. The bit sequence is illustrated in Figure 6–14. The left-most bit is the first to be transferred.

▲ **FIGURE 6–14**

(b) A parallel transfer would take **10 μs** for all eight bits.

Related Problem   If binary data are transferred at the rate of 10 million bits per second (10 Mbits/s), how long will it take to parallel transfer 16 bits on 16 lines? How long will it take to serially transfer 16 bits?

6–3   BASIC LOGIC OPERATIONS

In its basic form, logic is the realm of human reasoning that tells you a certain proposition (declarative statement) is true if certain conditions are true. Propositions can be classified as true or false. Many situations and processes that you encounter in your daily life can be expressed in the form of propositional, or logic, functions. Since such functions are true/false or yes/no statements, digital circuits with their two-state characteristics are applicable.

After completing this section, you should be able to

■ List three basic logic operations

■ Define the NOT operation

■ Define the AND operation

■ Define the OR operation

Several propositions, when combined, form propositional, or logic, functions. For example, the propositional statement "The light is on" will be true if "The bulb is not burned out" is true and if "The switch is on" is true. Therefore, this logical statement can be made: *The light is on only if the bulb is not burned out and the switch is on.* In this example the first statement is true only if the last two statements are true. The first statement ("The light is on") is then the basic proposition, and the other two statements are the conditions on which the proposition depends.

In the 1850s, the Irish logician and mathematician George Boole developed a mathematical system for formulating logic statements with symbols so that problems can be written and solved in a manner similar to ordinary algebra. Boolean algebra, as it is known today, is applied in the design and analysis of digital systems and will be covered in detail in Chapter 9.

The term **logic** is applied to digital circuits used to implement logic functions. Several kinds of digital logic **circuits** are the basic elements that form the building blocks for such complex digital systems as the computer. We will now look at these elements and discuss their functions in a very general way. Later chapters will cover these circuits in detail.

FIGURE 6–15

The basic logic operations and symbols.

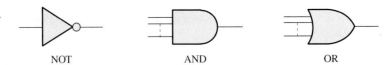

NOT
AND
OR

Three basic logic operations (NOT, AND, and OR) are indicated by standard distinctive shape symbols in Figure 6–15. Other standard symbols for these logic operations will be introduced in Chapter 8. The lines connected to each symbol are the **inputs** and **outputs.** The inputs are on the left of each symbol and the output is on the right. A circuit that performs a specified logic operation (AND, OR) is called a logic **gate.** AND and OR gates can have any number of inputs, as indicated by the dashes in the figure.

In logic operations, the true/false conditions mentioned earlier are represented by a HIGH (true) and a LOW (false). Each of the three basic logic operations produces a unique response to a given set of conditions.

NOT

The **NOT** operation changes one logic level to the opposite logic level, as indicated in Figure 6–16. When the input is HIGH (1), the output is LOW (0). When the input is LOW, the output is HIGH. In either case, the output is *not* the same as the input. The NOT operation is implemented by a logic circuit known as an **inverter.**

FIGURE 6–16

The NOT operation.

HIGH (1)
LOW (0)
LOW (0)
HIGH (1)

AND

The **AND** operation produces a HIGH output only when all the inputs are HIGH, as indicated in Figure 6–17 for the case of two inputs. When one input is HIGH *and* the other input is HIGH, the output is HIGH. When any or all inputs are LOW, the output is LOW. The AND operation is implemented by a logic circuit known as an *AND gate.*

FIGURE 6–17

The AND operation.

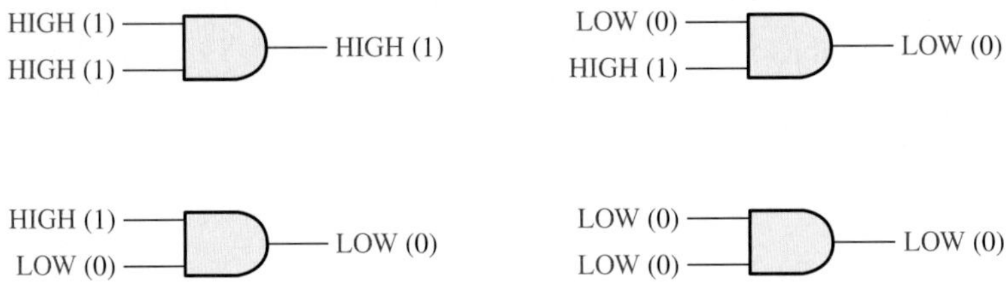

HIGH (1)
HIGH (1)
HIGH (1)
LOW (0)
HIGH (1)
LOW (0)
HIGH (1)
LOW (0)
LOW (0)
LOW (0)
LOW (0)
LOW (0)

OR

The **OR** operation produces a HIGH output when one or more inputs are HIGH, as indicated in Figure 6–18 for the case of two inputs. When one input is HIGH *or* the other input is HIGH *or* both inputs are HIGH, the output is HIGH. When both inputs are LOW, the output is LOW. The OR operation is implemented by a logic circuit known as an *OR gate.*

FIGURE 6–18

The OR operation.

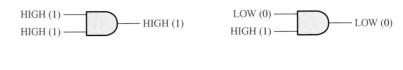

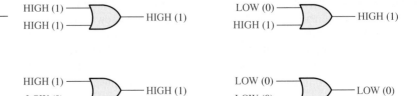

HIGH (1)
HIGH (1)
HIGH (1)
LOW (0)
HIGH (1)
HIGH (1)
HIGH (1)
LOW (0)
HIGH (1)
LOW (0)
LOW (0)
LOW (0)

6-4   OVERVIEW OF BASIC LOGIC FUNCTIONS

The three basic logic elements AND, OR, and NOT can be combined to form more complex logic circuits that perform many useful operations and that are used to build complete digital systems. Some of the common logic functions are comparison, arithmetic, code conversion, encoding, decoding, data selection, storage, and counting. This section provides a general overview of these important functions so that you can begin to see how they form the building blocks of digital systems such as computers. Each of the basic logic functions will be covered in detail in later chapters.

After completing this section, you should be able to

- Identify nine basic types of logic functions
- Describe a basic magnitude comparator
- List the four arithmetic functions
- Describe a basic adder
- Describe a basic encoder
- Describe a basic decoder
- Define multiplexing and demultiplexing
- State how data storage is accomplished
- Describe the function of a basic counter

The Comparison Function

Magnitude comparison is performed by a logic circuit called a **comparator.** A comparator compares two quantities and indicates whether or not they are equal. For example, suppose you have two numbers and wish to know if they are equal or not equal and, if not equal, which is greater. The comparison function is represented in Figure 6–19. One number in binary form (represented by logic levels) is applied to input A, and the other number in binary form (represented by logic levels) is applied to input B. The outputs indicate the relationship of the two numbers by producing a HIGH level on the proper output line. Suppose that a binary representation of the number 2 is applied to input A and a binary representation of the number 5 is applied to input B. (We discuss the binary representation of numbers and symbols in Chapter 7.) A HIGH level will appear on the $A < B$ (A is less than B) output, indicating the relationship between the two numbers (2 is less than 5). The wide arrows represent a group of parallel lines on which the bits are transferred.

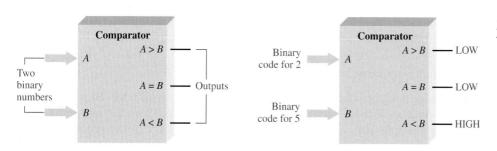

(a) Basic magnitude comparator

(b) Example: A is less than B ($2 < 5$) as indicated by the HIGH output ($A < B$)

◀ **FIGURE 6-19**

The comparison function.

FIGURE 6–20

The addition function.

The Arithmetic Functions

Addition Addition is performed by a logic circuit called an **adder.** An adder adds two binary numbers (on inputs A and B with a carry input C_{in}) and generates a sum (Σ) and a carry output (C_{out}), as shown in Figure 6–20(a). Figure 6–20(b) illustrates the addition of 3 and 9. You know that the sum is 12; the adder indicates this result by producing 2 on the sum output and 1 on the carry output. Assume that the carry input in this example is 0.

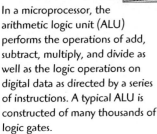

COMPUTER NOTE

In a microprocessor, the arithmetic logic unit (ALU) performs the operations of add, subtract, multiply, and divide as well as the logic operations on digital data as directed by a series of instructions. A typical ALU is constructed of many thousands of logic gates.

Subtraction Subtraction is also performed by a logic circuit. A **subtracter** requires three inputs: the two numbers that are to be subtracted and a borrow input. The two outputs are the difference and the borrow output. When, for instance, 5 is subtracted from 8 with no borrow input, the difference is 3 with no borrow output. You will see in Chapter 7 how subtraction can actually be performed by an adder because subtraction is simply a special case of addition.

Multiplication Multiplication is performed by a logic circuit called a *multiplier.* Numbers are always multiplied two at a time, so two inputs are required. The output of the multiplier is the product. Because multiplication is simply a series of additions with shifts in the positions of the partial products, it can be performed by using an adder in conjunction with other circuits.

Division Division can be performed with a series of subtractions, comparisons, and shifts, and thus it can also be done using an adder in conjunction with other circuits. Two inputs to the divider are required, and the outputs generated are the quotient and the remainder.

The Code Conversion Function

A **code** is a set of bits arranged in a unique pattern and used to represent specified information. A code converter changes one form of coded information into another coded form. Examples are conversion between binary and other codes such as the binary coded decimal (BCD) and the Gray code. Various types of codes are covered in Chapter 7.

The Encoding Function

The encoding function is performed by a logic circuit called an **encoder.** The encoder converts information, such as a decimal number or an alphabetic character, into some coded form. For example, one certain type of encoder converts each of the decimal digits, 0 through 9, to a binary code. A HIGH level on the input corresponding to a specific decimal digit produces logic levels that represent the proper binary code on the output lines.

Figure 6–21 is a simple illustration of an encoder used to convert (encode) a calculator keystroke into a binary code that can be processed by the calculator circuits.

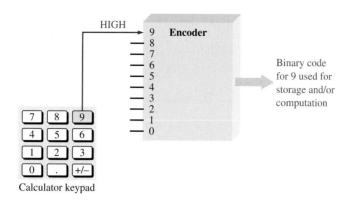

◀ FIGURE 6–21

An encoder used to encode a calculator keystroke into a binary code for storage or for calculation.

The Decoding Function

The decoding function is performed by a logic circuit called a **decoder.** The decoder converts coded information, such as a binary number, into a noncoded form, such as a decimal form. For example, one particular type of decoder converts a 4-bit binary code into the appropriate decimal digit.

Figure 6–22 is a simple illustration of one type of decoder that is used to activate a 7-segment display. Each of the seven segments of the display is connected to an output line from the decoder. When a particular binary code appears on the decoder inputs, the appropriate output lines are activated and light the proper segments to display the decimal digit corresponding to the binary code.

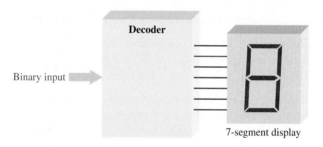

◀ FIGURE 6–22

A decoder used to convert a special binary code into a 7-segment decimal readout.

The Data Selection Function

Two types of circuits that select data are the multiplexer and the demultiplexer. The **multiplexer,** or mux for short, is a logic circuit that switches digital data from several input lines onto a single output line in a specified time sequence. Functionally, a multiplexer can be represented by an electronic switch operation that sequentially connects each of the input lines to the output line. The **demultiplexer** (demux) is a logic circuit that switches digital data from one input line to several output lines in a specified time sequence. Essentially, the demux is a mux in reverse.

Multiplexing and demultiplexing are used when data from several sources are to be transmitted over one line to a distant location and redistributed to several destinations. Figure 6–23 illustrates this type of application where digital data from three sources are sent out along a single line to three terminals at another location.

In Figure 6–23, data from input A are connected to the output line during time interval Δt_1 and transmitted to the demultiplexer that connects them to output D. Then, during interval Δt_2, the multiplexer switches to input B and the demultiplexer switches to output E. During interval Δt_3, the multiplexer switches to input C and the demultiplexer switches to output F.

To summarize, during the first time interval, input A data go to output D. During the second time interval, input B data go to output E. During the third time interval, input C data go to output F. After this, the sequence repeats. Because the time is divided up among several sources and destinations where each has its turn to send and receive data, this process is called *time division multiplexing* (TDM).

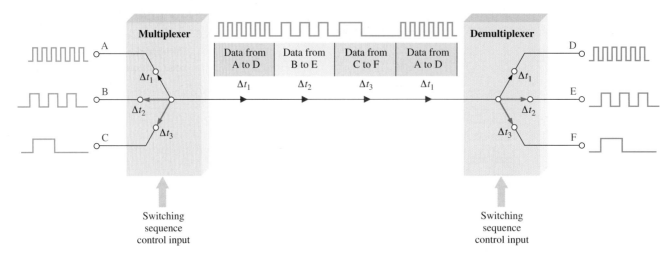

Illustration of a basic multiplexing/demultiplexing application.

The Storage Function

COMPUTER NOTE

The internal computer memories, RAM and ROM, as well as the smaller caches are semiconductor memories. The registers in a microprocessor are constructed of semiconductor flip-flops. Magnetic disk memories are used in the internal hard drive, the floppy drive, and for the CD-ROM.

Storage is a function that is required in most digital systems, and its purpose is to retain binary data for a period of time. Some storage devices are used for short-term storage and some are used for long-term storage. A storage device can "memorize" a bit or a group of bits and retain the information as long as necessary. Common types of storage devices are flip-flops, registers, semiconductor memories, magnetic disks, magnetic tape, and optical disks (CDs).

Flip-flops A **flip-flop** is a bistable (two stable states) logic circuit that can store only one bit at a time, either a 1 or a 0. The output of a flip-flop indicates which bit it is storing. A HIGH output indicates that a 1 is stored and a LOW output indicates that a 0 is stored.

Registers A **register** is formed by combining several flip-flops so that groups of bits can be stored. For example, an 8-bit register is constructed from eight flip-flops. In addition to storing bits, registers can be used to shift the bits from one position to another within the register or out of the register to another circuit; therefore, these devices are known as *shift registers*.

The two basic types of shift registers are serial and parallel. The bits are stored in a serial shift register one at a time, as illustrated in Figure 6–24. A good analogy to the serial shift register is loading passengers onto a bus single file through the door. They also exit the bus single file.

▶ **FIGURE 6–24**

Example of the operation of a 4-bit serial shift register. Each block represents one storage "cell" or flip-flop.

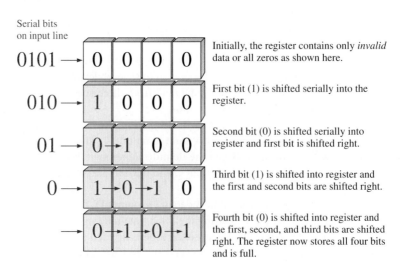

Serial bits on input line

Initially, the register contains only *invalid* data or all zeros as shown here.

First bit (1) is shifted serially into the register.

Second bit (0) is shifted serially into register and first bit is shifted right.

Third bit (1) is shifted into register and the first and second bits are shifted right.

Fourth bit (0) is shifted into register and the first, second, and third bits are shifted right. The register now stores all four bits and is full.

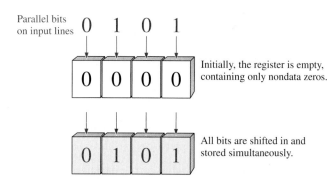

Example of the operation of a 4-bit parallel shift register.

The bits are stored in a parallel register simultaneously from parallel lines, as shown in Figure 6–25. For this case, a good analogy is loading passengers on a roller coaster where they enter all of the cars in parallel.

Semiconductor Memories   Semiconductor memories are devices typically used for storing large numbers of bits. In one type of memory, called the *read-only memory* or ROM, the binary data are permanently or semipermanently stored and cannot be readily changed. In the *random-access memory* or RAM, the binary data are temporarily stored and can be easily changed.

Magnetic Memories   Magnetic disk memories are used for mass storage of binary data. Examples are the so-called floppy disks used in computers and the computer's internal hard disk. Magneto-optical disks use laser beams to store and retrieve data. Magnetic tape is still used in memory applications and for backing up data from other storage devices.

The Counting Function

The counting function is important in digital systems. There are many types of digital **counters,** but their basic purpose is to count events represented by changing levels or pulses. To count, the counter must "remember" the present number so that it can go to the next proper number in sequence. Therefore, storage capability is an important characteristic of all counters, and flip-flops are generally used to implement them. Figure 6–26 illustrates the basic idea of counter operation.

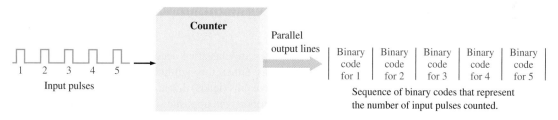

▲ FIGURE 6–26

Illustration of basic counter operation.

6–5   FIXED-FUNCTION INTEGRATED CIRCUITS

All the logic elements and functions that have been discussed are generally available in integrated circuit (IC) form. Digital systems have incorporated ICs for many years because of their small size, high reliability, low cost, and low power consumption. It is important to be able to recognize the IC packages and to know how the pin connections are numbered, as well as to be familiar with the way in which circuit complexities and circuit technologies determine the various IC classifications.

After completing this section, you should be able to

- Recognize the difference between through-hole devices and surface-mount fixed-function devices

- Identify dual in-line packages (DIP)

- Identify small-outline integrated circuit packages (SOIC)

- Identify plastic leaded chip carrier packages (PLCC)

- Identify leadless ceramic chip carrier packages (LCCC)

- Determine pin numbers on various types of IC packages

- Explain the complexity classifications for fixed-function ICs

   A monolithic **integrated circuit (IC)** is an electronic circuit that is constructed entirely on a single small chip of silicon. All the components that make up the circuit—transistors, diodes, resistors, and capacitors—are an integral part of that single chip. Fixed-function logic and programmable logic are two broad categories of digital ICs. In fixed-function logic, the logic functions are set by the manufacturer and cannot be altered.

Figure 6–27 shows a cutaway view of one type of fixed-function IC package with the circuit chip shown within the package. Points on the chip are connected to the package pins to allow input and output connections to the outside world.

▶ **FIGURE 6–27**

Cutaway view of one type of fixed-function IC package showing the chip mounted inside, with connections to input and output pins.

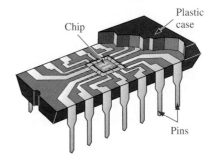

IC Packages

Integrated circuit (IC) packages are classified according to the way they are mounted on printed circuit (PC) boards as either through-hole mounted or surface mounted. The through-hole type packages have pins (leads) that are inserted through holes in the PC board and can be soldered to conductors on the opposite side. The most common type of through-hole package is the dual in-line package (**DIP**) shown in Figure 6–28(a).

▶ **FIGURE 6–28**

Examples of through-hole and surface-mounted devices. The DIP is larger than the SOIC with the same number of leads. This particular DIP is approximately 0.785 in. long, and the SOIC is approximately 0.385 in. long.

(a) Dual in-line package (DIP)

(b) Small-outline IC (SOIC)

Another type of IC package uses surface-mount technology (**SMT**). Surface mounting is a space-saving alternative to through-hole mounting. The holes through the PC board are

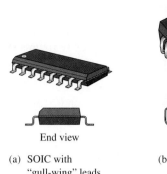

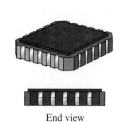

End view   End view   End view

(a) SOIC with   (b) PLCC with   (c) LCCC with no leads
    "gull-wing" leads   J-type leads   (contacts are
                                                 part of case)

◀ FIGURE 6–29

Examples of SMT package
configurations.

unnecessary for SMT. The pins of surface-mounted packages are soldered directly to conductors on one side of the board, leaving the other side free for additional circuits. Also, for a circuit with the same number of pins, a surface-mounted package is much smaller than a dual in-line package because the pins are placed closer together. An example of a surface-mounted package is the small-outline integrated circuit (SOIC) shown in Figure 6–28(b). Three common types of SMT packages are the **SOIC** (small-outline IC), the **PLCC** (plastic leaded chip carrier), and the **LCCC** (leadless ceramic chip carrier). These types of packages are available in various sizes depending on the number of leads (more leads are required for more complex circuits). Examples of each type are shown in Figure 6–29. As you can see, the leads of the SOIC are formed into a "gull-wing" shape. The leads of the PLCC are turned under the package in a J-type shape. Instead of leads, the LCCC has metal contacts molded into its ceramic body. Other variations of SMT packages include **SSOP** (shrink small-outline package), **TSSOP** (thin shrink small-outline package), and **TVSOP** (thin very small-outline package).

Pin Numbering

All IC packages have a standard format for numbering the pins (leads). The dual in-line packages (DIPs) and the small-outline IC packages (SOICs) have the numbering arrangement illustrated in Figure 6–30(a) for a 16-pin package. Looking at the top of the package, pin 1 is indicated by an identifier that can be either a small dot, a notch, or a beveled edge. The dot is always next to pin 1. Also, with the notch oriented upward, pin 1 is always the top left pin, as indicated. Starting with pin 1, the pin numbers increase as you go down, then across and up. The highest pin number is always to the right of the notch or opposite the dot.

The PLCC and LCCC packages have leads arranged on all four sides. Pin 1 is indicated by a dot or other index mark and is located at the center of one set of leads. The pin numbers increase going counterclockwise as viewed from the top of the package. The highest pin number is always to the right of pin 1. Figure 6–30(b) illustrates this format for a 20-pin PLCC package.

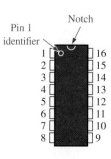
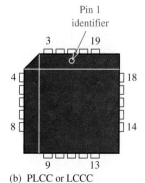

(a) DIP or SOIC   (b) PLCC or LCCC

◀ FIGURE 6–30

Pin numbering for two standard
types of IC packages. Top views are
shown.

Complexity Classifications for Fixed-Function ICs

Fixed-function digital ICs are classified according to their complexity. They are listed here from the least complex to the most complex. The complexity figures stated here for SSI, MSI, LSI, VLSI, and ULSI are generally accepted, but definitions may vary from one source to another.

- **Small-scale integration (SSI)** describes fixed-function ICs that have up to ten equivalent gate circuits on a single chip, and they include basic gates and flipflops.

- **Medium-scale integration (MSI)** describes integrated circuits that have from 10 to 100 equivalent gates on a chip. They include logic functions such as encoders, decoders, counters, registers, multiplexers, arithmetic circuits, small memories, and others.

- **Large-scale integration (LSI)** is a classification of ICs with complexities of from more than 100 to 10,000 equivalent gates per chip, including memories.

- **Very large-scale integration (VLSI)** describes integrated circuits with complexities of from more than 10,000 to 100,000 equivalent gates per chip.

- **Ultra large-scale integration (ULSI)** describes very large memories, larger **micro-processors,** and larger single-chip computers. Complexities of more than 100,000 equivalent gates per chip are classified as ULSI.

Integrated Circuit Technologies

The types of transistors with which all integrated circuits are implemented are either MOS-FETs (metal-oxide semiconductor field-effect transistors) or bipolar junction transistors. A circuit technology that uses MOSFETs is CMOS (complementary MOS). A type of fixed-function digital circuit technology that uses bipolar junction transistors is TTL (transistor-transistor logic). BiCMOS uses a combination of both CMOS and TTL.

All gates and other functions can be implemented with either type of circuit technology. SSI and MSI circuits are generally available in both CMOS and TTL. LSI, VLSI, and ULSI are generally implemented with CMOS or NMOS because it requires less area on a chip and consumes less power. There is more on these integrated technologies in Chapter 8.

Handling Precautions for CMOS   Because of their particular structure, CMOS devices are very sensitive to static charge and can be damaged by electrostatic discharge (ESD) if not handled properly. The following precautions should be taken when you work with CMOS devices:

- CMOS devices should be shipped and stored in conductive foam.

- All instruments and metal benches used in testing should be connected to earth ground.

- The handler's wrist should be connected to earth ground with a length of wire and high-value series resistor.

- Do not remove a CMOS device (or any device for that matter) from a circuit while the dc power is on.

- Do not connect ac or signal voltages to a CMOS device while the dc power supply is off.

6–6   TEST AND MEASUREMENT INSTRUMENTS

Troubleshooting is the process of systematically isolating, identifying, and correcting a fault in a circuit or system. A variety of instruments are available for use in troubleshooting and testing. Some common types of instruments are introduced and discussed in this section.

After completing this section, you should be able to

- Distinguish between an analog and a digital oscilloscope
- Recognize common oscilloscope controls
- Determine amplitude, period, frequency, and duty cycle of a pulse waveform with an oscilloscope
- Discuss the logic analyzer and some common formats
- Describe the purpose of the dc power supply, function generator, and digital multimeter (DMM)

The Oscilloscope

The oscilloscope (scope for short) is one of the most widely used instruments for general testing and troubleshooting. The scope is basically a graph-displaying device that traces the graph of a measured electrical signal on its screen. In most applications, the graph shows how signals change over time. The vertical axis of the display screen represents voltage, and the horizontal axis represents time. Amplitude, period, and frequency of a signal can be measured using the oscilloscope. Also, the pulse width, duty cycle, rise time, and fall time of a pulse waveform can be determined. Most scopes can display at least two signals on the screen at one time, enabling their time relationship to be observed. A typical oscilloscope is shown in Figure 6–31.

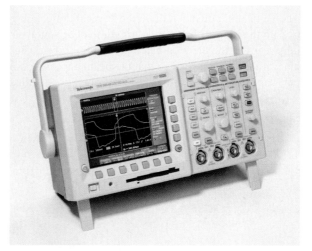

◀ **FIGURE 6–31**

A typical dual-channel oscilloscope. Used with permission from Tektronix, Inc.

Two basic types of oscilloscopes, analog and digital, can be used to view digital waveforms. As shown in Figure 6–32(a), the analog scope works by applying the measured waveform directly to control the up and down motion of the electron beam in the cathode-ray tube (CRT) as it sweeps across the display screen. As a result, the beam traces out the waveform pattern on the screen. As shown in Figure 6–32(b), the digital scope converts the measured waveform to digital information by a sampling process in an analog-to-digital converter (ADC). The digital information is then used to reconstruct the waveform on the screen.

The digital scope is more widely used than the analog scope. However, either type can be used in many applications, each has characteristics that make it more suitable for certain

Comparison of analog and digital oscilloscopes.

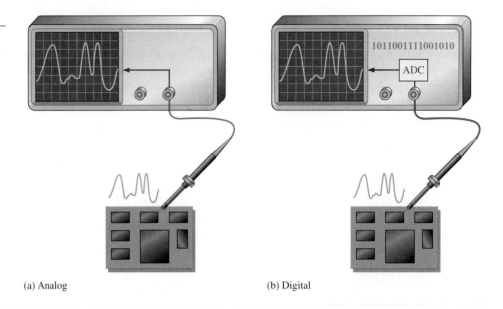

(a) Analog   (b) Digital

situations. An analog scope displays waveforms as they occur in "real time." Digital scopes are useful for measuring transient pulses that may occur randomly or only once. Also, because information about the measured waveform can be stored in a digital scope, it may be viewed at some later time, printed out, or thoroughly analyzed by a computer or other means.

Basic Operation of Analog Oscilloscopes   To measure a voltage, a **probe** must be connected from the scope to the point in a circuit at which the voltage is present. Generally, a × 10 probe is used that reduces (attenuates) the signal amplitude by ten. The signal goes through the probe into the vertical circuits where it is either further attenuated or amplified, depending on the actual amplitude and on where you set the vertical control of the scope. The vertical circuits then drive the vertical deflection plates of the CRT. Also, the signal goes to the trigger circuits that trigger the horizontal circuits to initiate repetitive horizontal sweeps of the electron beam across the screen using a sawtooth waveform. There are many sweeps per second so that the beam appears to form a solid line across the screen in the shape of the waveform. This basic operation is illustrated in Figure 6–33.

Block diagram of an analog oscilloscope.

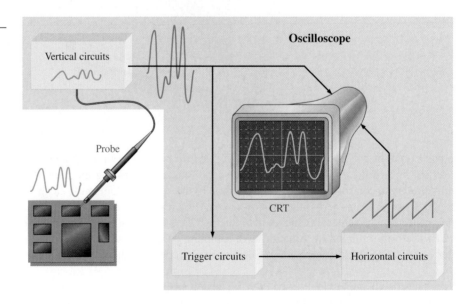

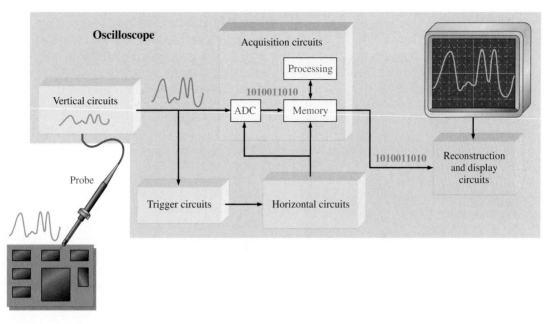

Block diagram of a digital oscilloscope.

Basic Operation of Digital Oscilloscopes   Some parts of a digital scope are similar to the analog scope. However, the digital scope is more complex than an analog scope and typically has an LCD screen rather than a CRT. Rather than displaying a waveform as it occurs, the digital scope first acquires the measured analog waveform and converts it to a digital format using an analog-to-digital converter (ADC). The digital data is stored and processed. The data then goes to the reconstruction and display circuits for display in its original analog form. Figure 6–34 shows a basic block diagram for a digital oscilloscope.

Oscilloscope Controls   A front panel view of a typical dual-channel oscilloscope is shown in Figure 6–35. Instruments vary depending on model and manufacturer, but most have certain common features. For example, the two vertical sections contain a Position control, a channel menu button, and a V/div control. The horizontal section contains a sec/div control.

Some of the main oscilloscope controls are now discussed. Refer to the user manual for complete details of your particular scope.

Vertical Controls   In the vertical section of the scope in Figure 6–35, there are identical controls for each of the two channels (CH1 and CH2). The Position control lets you move a displayed waveform up or down vertically on the screen. The Menu button provides for the selection of several items that appear on the screen, such as the coupling modes (ac, dc, or ground), coarse or fine adjustment for the V/div, probe attenuation, and other parameters. The V/div control adjusts the number of volts represented by each vertical division on the screen. The V/div setting for each channel is displayed on the bottom of the screen. The Math Menu button provides a selection of operations that can be performed on the input waveforms, such as subtraction, addition, or inversion.

Horizontal Controls   In the horizontal section, the controls apply to both channels. The Position control lets you move a displayed waveform left or right horizontally on the screen. The Menu button provides for the selection of several items that appear on the screen such as the main time base, expanded view of a portion of a waveform, and other parameters. The sec/div control adjusts the time represented by each horizontal division or main time base. The sec/div setting is displayed at the bottom of the screen.

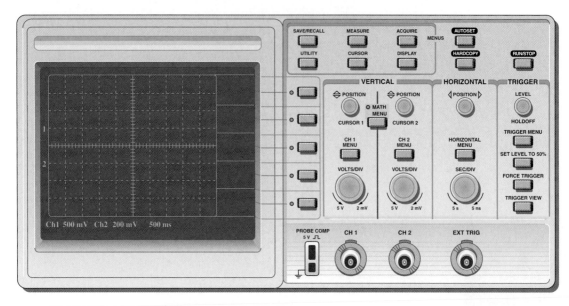

▲ **FIGURE 6–35**

A typical dual-channel oscilloscope. Numbers below the screen indicate the values for each division on the vertical (voltage) and horizontal (time) scales and can be varied using the vertical and horizontal controls on the scope.

Trigger Controls   In the Trigger control section, the Level control determines the point on the triggering waveform where triggering occurs to initiate the sweep to display input waveforms. The Menu button provides for the selection of several items that appear on the screen, including edge or slope triggering, trigger source, trigger mode, and other parameters. There is also an input for an external trigger signal.

Triggering stabilizes a waveform on the screen or properly triggers on a pulse that occurs only one time or randomly. Also, it allows you to observe time delays between two waveforms. Figure 6–36 compares a triggered to an untriggered signal. The untriggered signal tends to drift across the screen, producing what appears to be multiple waveforms.

▶ **FIGURE 6–36**

Comparison of an untriggered and a triggered waveform on an oscilloscope.

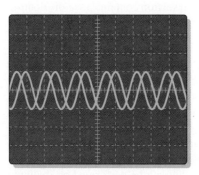

(a) Untriggered waveform display

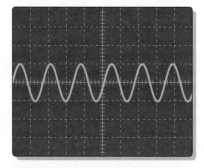

(b) Triggered waveform display

Coupling a Signal into the Scope   Coupling is the method used to connect a signal voltage to be measured into the oscilloscope. DC and AC coupling are usually selected from the Vertical menu on a scope. DC coupling allows a waveform including its dc component to be displayed. AC coupling blocks the dc component of a signal so that you see the waveform centered at 0 V. The Ground mode allows you to connect the channel input to ground

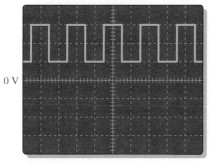

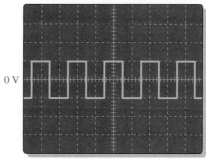

(a) DC coupled waveform

(b) AC coupled waveform

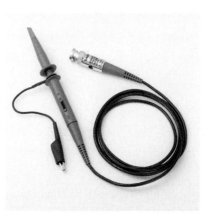

◀ FIGURE 6–38

An oscilloscope voltage probe. Used with permission from Tektronix, Inc.

to see where the 0 V reference is on the screen. Figure 6–37 illustrates the result of DC and AC coupling using a pulse waveform that has a dc component.

The voltage probe, shown in Figure 6–38, is essential for connecting a signal to the scope. Since all instruments tend to affect the circuit being measured due to loading, most scope probes provide a high series resistance to minimize loading effects. Probes that have a series resistance ten times larger than the input resistance of the scope are called ×10 probes. Probes with no series resistance are called ×1 probes. The oscilloscope adjusts its calibration for the attenuation of the type of probe being used. For most measurements, the ×10 probe should be used. However, if you are measuring very small signals, a ×1 may be the best choice.

The probe has an adjustment that allows you to compensate for the input capacitance of the scope. Most scopes have a probe compensation output that provides a calibrated square wave for probe compensation. Before making a measurement, you should make sure that the probe is properly compensated to eliminate any distortion introduced. Typically, there is a screw or other means of adjusting compensation on a probe. Figure 6–39 shows scope

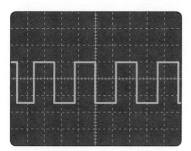

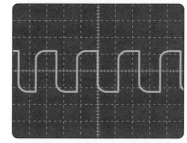

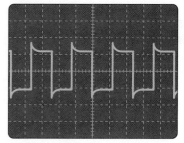

Properly compensated

Undercompensated

Overcompensated

▲ FIGURE 6–39

Probe compensation conditions.

waveforms for three probe conditions: properly compensated, undercompensated, and overcompensated. If the waveform appears either over- or undercompensated, adjust the probe until the properly compensated square wave is achieved.

EXAMPLE 6–3

Based on the readouts, determine the amplitude and the period of the pulse waveform on the screen of a digital oscilloscope as shown in Figure 6–40. Also, calculate the frequency.

▶ **FIGURE 6–40**

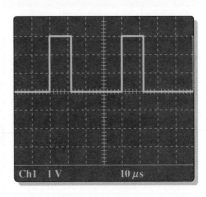

Ch1 1 V   10 μs

Solution   The V/div setting is 1 V. The pulses are three divisions high. Since each division represents 1 V, the pulse amplitude is

$$\text{Amplitude} = (3 \text{ div})(1 \text{ V/div}) = \textbf{3 V}$$

The sec/div setting is 10 μs. A full cycle of the waveform (from beginning of one pulse to the beginning of the next) covers four divisions; therefore, the period is

$$\text{Period} = (4 \text{ div})(10 \text{ μs/div}) = \textbf{40 μs}$$

The frequency is calculated as

$$f = \frac{1}{T} = \frac{1}{40 \text{ μs}} = \textbf{25 kHz}$$

Related Problem   For a V/div setting of 4 V and sec/div setting of 2 ms, determine the amplitude and period of the pulse shown on the screen in Figure 6–40.

SUMMARY

- An analog quantity has continuous values.
- A digital quantity has a discrete set of values.
- A binary digit is called a bit.
- A pulse is characterized by rise time, fall time, pulse width, and amplitude.
- The frequency of a periodic waveform is the reciprocal of the period. The formulas relating frequency and period are

$$f = \frac{1}{T} \text{ and } T = \frac{1}{f}$$

■ The duty cycle of a pulse waveform is the ratio of the pulse width to the period, expressed by the following formula as a percentage:

$$\text{Duty cycle} = \left(\frac{t_W}{T}\right)100\%$$

■ A timing diagram is an arrangement of two or more waveforms showing their relationship with respect to time.

■ Three basic logic operations are NOT, AND, and OR. The standard symbols for these are given in Figure 6–41.

▶ **FIGURE 6–41**

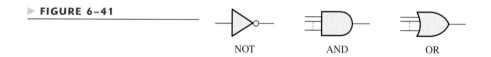

NOT   AND   OR

■ The basic logic functions are comparison, arithmetic, code conversion, decoding, encoding, data selection, storage, and counting.

■ The two broad physical categories of IC packages are through-hole mounted and surface mounted.

■ The categories of ICs in terms of circuit complexity are SSI (small-scale integration), MSI (medium-scale integration), LSI, VLSI, and ULSI (large-scale, very large-scale, and ultra largescale integration).

■ Common instruments used in testing and troubleshooting digital circuits are the oscilloscope, logic analyzer, waveform generator, function generator, dc power supply, digital multimeter, logic probe, and logic pulser.

KEY TERMS

Analog Being continuous or having continuous values.

AND A basic logic operation in which a true (HIGH) output occurs only when all the input conditions are true (HIGH).

Binary Having two values or states; describes a number system that has a base of two and utilizes 1 and 0 as its digits.

Bit A binary digit, which can be either a 1 or a 0.

Clock The basic timing signal in a digital system; a periodic waveform in which each interval between pulses equals the time for one bit.

Compiler A program that controls the design flow process and translates source code into object code in a format that can be logically tested or downloaded to a target device.

CPLD A complex programmable logic device that consists basically of multiple SPLD arrays with programmable interconnections.

Data Information in numeric, alphabetic, or other form.

Digital Related to digits or discrete quantities; having a set of discrete values.

FPGA Field programmable gate array.

Gate A logic circuit that performs a specified logic operation such as AND or OR.

Input The signal or line going into a circuit.

Integrated circuit (IC) A type of circuit in which all of the components are integrated on a single chip of semiconductive material of extremely small size.

Inverter A NOT circuit; a circuit that changes a HIGH to a LOW or vice versa.

Logic In digital electronics, the decision-making capability of gate circuits, in which a HIGH represents a true statement and a LOW represents a false one.

NOT A basic logic operation that performs inversions.

OR A basic logic operation in which a true (HIGH) output occurs when one or more of the input conditions are true (HIGH).

Output The signal or line coming out of a circuit.

Parallel In digital systems, data occurring simultaneously on several lines; the transfer or processing of several bits simultaneously.

Pulse A sudden change from one level to another, followed after a time, called the pulse width, by a sudden change back to the original level.

Serial Having one element following another, as in a serial transfer of bits; occurring in sequence rather than simultaneously.

SPLD Simple programmable logic device.

Timing diagram A graph of digital waveforms showing the time relationship of two or more waveforms.

Troubleshooting The technique or process of systematically identifying, isolating, and correcting a fault in a circuit or system.

SELF-TEST

Answers are at the end of the chapter.

1. A quantity having continuous values is
   (a) a digital quantity   (b) an analog quantity
   (c) a binary quantity   (d) a natural quantity

2. The term *bit* means
   (a) a small amount of data   (b) a 1 or a 0
   (c) binary digit   (d) both answers (b) and (c)

3. The time interval on the leading edge of a pulse between 10% and 90% of the amplitude is the
   (a) rise time   (b) fall time   (c) pulse width   (d) period

4. A pulse in a certain waveform occurs every 10 ms. The frequency is
   (a) 1 kHz   (b) 1 Hz   (c) 100 Hz   (d) 10 Hz

5. In a certain digital waveform, the period is twice the pulse width. The duty cycle is
   (a) 100%   (b) 200%   (c) 50%

6. An inverter
   (a) performs the NOT operation   (b) changes a HIGH to a LOW
   (c) changes a LOW to a HIGH   (d) does all of the above

7. The output of an AND gate is HIGH when
   (a) any input is HIGH   (b) all inputs are HIGH
   (c) no inputs are HIGH   (d) both answers (a) and (b)

8. The output of an OR gate is HIGH when
   (a) any input is HIGH   (b) all inputs are HIGH
   (c) no inputs are HIGH   (d) both answers (a) and (b)

9. The device used to convert a binary number to a 7-segment display format is the
   (a) multiplexer   (b) encoder   (c) decoder   (d) register

10. An example of a data storage device is
    (a) the logic gate   (b) the flip-flop   (c) the comparator
    (d) the register   (e) both answers (b) and (d)

11. A fixed-function IC package containing four AND gates is an example of
    (a) MSI   (b) SMT   (c) SOIC   (d) SSI

12. An LSI device has a circuit complexity of from
    (a) 10 to 100 equivalent gates   (b) more than 100 to 10,000 equivalent gates
    (c) 2000 to 5000 equivalent gates   (d) more than 10,000 to 100,000 equivalent gates

PROBLEMS

SECTION 6–1 **Digital and Analog Quantities**

1. Name two advantages of digital data as compared to analog data.

2. Name an analog quantity other than temperature and sound.

SECTION 6–2 **Binary Digits, Logic Levels, and Digital Waveforms**

3. Define the sequence of bits (1s and 0s) represented by each of the following sequences of levels:

   (a) HIGH, HIGH, LOW, HIGH, LOW, LOW, LOW, HIGH

   (b) LOW, LOW, LOW, HIGH, LOW, HIGH, LOW, HIGH, LOW

4. List the sequence of levels (HIGH and LOW) that represent each of the following bit sequences:

   (a) 1 0 1 1 1 0 1   **(b)** 1 1 1 0 1 0 0 1

5. For the pulse shown in Figure 6–42, graphically determine the following:

   (a) rise time   **(b)** fall time   **(c)** pulse width   **(d)** amplitude

▶ **FIGURE 6–42**

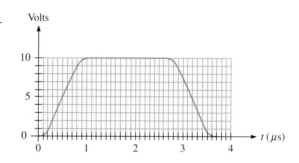

6. Determine the period of the digital waveform in Figure 6–43.

7. What is the frequency of the waveform in Figure 6–43?

8. Is the pulse waveform in Figure 6–43 periodic or nonperiodic?

9. Determine the duty cycle of the waveform in Figure 6–43.

▶ **FIGURE 6–43**

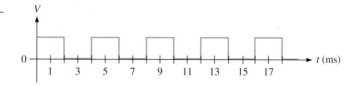

10. Determine the bit sequence represented by the waveform in Figure 6–44. A bit time is 1 μs in this case.

11. What is the total serial transfer time for the eight bits in Figure 6–44? What is the total parallel transfer time?

▶ **FIGURE 6–44**

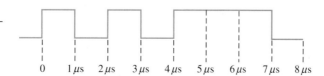

SECTION 6–3 Basic Logic Operations

12. A logic circuit requires HIGHs on all its inputs to make the output HIGH. What type of logic circuit is it?

13. A basic 2-input logic circuit has a HIGH on one input and a LOW on the other input, and the output is LOW. Identify the circuit.

14. A basic 2-input logic circuit has a HIGH on one input and a LOW on the other input, and the output is HIGH. What type of logic circuit is it?

SECTION 6–4 Overview of Basic Logic Functions

15. Name the logic function of each block in Figure 6–45 based on your observation of the inputs and outputs.

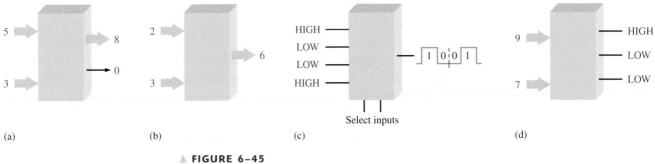

(a)   (b)   (c)   (d)

Select inputs

▲ **FIGURE 6–45**

16. A pulse waveform with a frequency of 10 kHz is applied to the input of a counter. During 100 ms, how many pulses are counted?

17. Consider a register that can store eight bits. Assume that it has been reset so that it contains zeros in all positions. If you transfer four alternating bits (0101) serially into the register, beginning with a 1 and shifting to the right, what will the total content of the register be as soon as the fourth bit is stored?

SECTION 6–5 Fixed-Function Integrated Circuits

18. A fixed-function digital IC chip has a complexity of 200 equivalent gates. How is it classified?

19. Explain the main difference between the DIP and SMT packages.

20. Label the pin numbers on the packages in Figure 6–46. Top views are shown.

▶ **FIGURE 6–46**

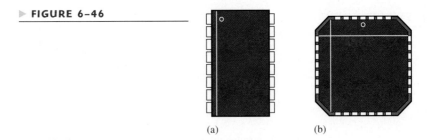

(a)   (b)

SECTION 6–6 Test and Measurement Instruments

21. A pulse is displayed on the screen of an oscilloscope, and you measure the base line as 1 V and the top of the pulse as 8 V. What is the amplitude?

22. A logic probe is applied to a contact point on an IC that is operating in a system. The lamp on the probe flashes repeatedly. What does this indicate?

SELF-TEST

1. (b)   **2.** (d)   **3.** (a)   **4.** (c)   **5.** (c)   **6.** (d)   **7.** (b)   **8.** (d)

9. (c)   **10.** (e)   **11.** (d)   **12.** (d)

7

NUMBER SYSTEMS, OPERATIONS, AND CODES

INTRODUCTION

The binary number system and digital codes are fundamental to computers and to digital electronics in general. In this chapter, the binary number system and its relationship to other number systems such as decimal, hexadecimal, and octal is presented. Arithmetic operations with binary numbers are covered to provide a basis for understanding how computers and many other types of digital systems work. Also, digital codes such as binary coded decimal (BCD), the Gray code, and the ASCII are covered. The parity method for detecting errors in codes is introduced and a method for correcting errors is described. The tutorials on the use of the calculator in certain operations are based on the TI-86 graphics calculator and the TI-36X calculator. The procedures shown may vary on other types.

CHAPTER OBJECTIVES

- Review the decimal number system

- Count in the binary number system

- Convert from decimal to binary and from binary to decimal

- Apply arithmetic operations to binary numbers

- Determine the 1's and 2's complements of a binary number

- Express signed binary numbers in sign-magnitude, 1's complement, 2's complement, and floating-point format

- Carry out arithmetic operations with signed binary numbers

- Convert between the binary and hexadecimal number systems

- Add numbers in hexadecimal form

- Convert between the binary and octal number systems

- Express decimal numbers in binary coded decimal (BCD) form

- Add BCD numbers

- Convert between the binary system and the Gray code

- Interpret the American Standard Code for Information Interchange (ASCII)

- Explain how to detect and correct code errors

CHAPTER OUTLINE

KEY TERMS

- LSB
- MSB
- Byte
- Floating-point number
- Hexadecimal
- Octal
- BCD
- Alphanumeric
- ASCII
- Parity
- Hamming code

WWW. VISIT THE COMPANION WEBSITE

Study aids for this chapter are available at
http://www.prenhall.com/floyd

7–1 DECIMAL NUMBERS

You are familiar with the decimal number system because you use decimal numbers every day. Although decimal numbers are commonplace, their weighted structure is often not understood. In this section, the structure of decimal numbers is reviewed. This review will help you more easily understand the structure of the binary number system, which is important in computers and digital electronics.

After completing this section, you should be able to

▪ Explain why the decimal number system is a weighted system

▪ Explain how powers of ten are used in the decimal system

▪ Determine the weight of each digit in a decimal number

The decimal number system has ten digits.

In the **decimal** number system each of the ten digits, 0 through 9, represents a certain quantity. As you know, the ten symbols (**digits**) do not limit you to expressing only ten different quantities because you use the various digits in appropriate positions within a number to indicate the magnitude of the quantity. You can express quantities up through nine before running out of digits; if you wish to express a quantity greater than nine, you use two or more digits, and the position of each digit within the number tells you the magnitude it represents. If, for example, you wish to express the quantity twenty-three, you use (by their respective positions in the number) the digit 2 to represent the quantity twenty and the digit 3 to represent the quantity three, as illustrated below.

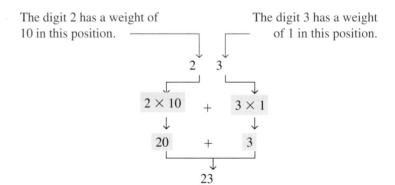

The decimal number system has a base of 10.

The position of each digit in a decimal number indicates the magnitude of the quantity represented and can be assigned a **weight.** The weights for whole numbers are positive powers of ten that increase from right to left, beginning with $10^0 = 1$.

$$\ldots 10^5 \; 10^4 \; 10^3 \; 10^2 \; 10^1 \; 10^0$$

For fractional numbers, the weights are negative powers of ten that decrease from left to right beginning with 10^{-1}.

The value of a digit is determined by its position in the number.

$$10^2 \; 10^1 \; 10^0.10^{-1} \; 10^{-2} \; 10^{-3}\ldots$$
$$\uparrow\!\!\text{——— Decimal point}$$

The value of a decimal number is the sum of the digits after each digit has been multiplied by its weight, as Examples 7–1 and 7–2 illustrate.

EXAMPLE 7–1

Express the decimal number 47 as a sum of the values of each digit.

Solution The digit 4 has a weight of 10, which is 10^1, as indicated by its position. The digit 7 has a weight of 1, which is 10^0, as indicated by its position.

$$47 = (4 \times 10^1) + (7 \times 10^0)$$
$$= (4 \times 10) + (7 \times 1) = \mathbf{40 + 7}$$

Related Problem* Determine the value of each digit in 939.

EXAMPLE 7–2

Express the decimal number 568.23 as a sum of the values of each digit.

Solution The whole number digit 5 has a weight of 100, which is 10^2, the digit 6 has a weight of 10, which is 10^1, the digit 8 has a weight of 1, which is 10^0, the fractional digit 2 has a weight of 0.1, which is 10^{-1}, and the fractional digit 3 has a weight of 0.01, which is 10^{-2}.

$$568.23 = (5 \times 10^2) + (6 \times 10^1) + (8 \times 10^0) + (2 \times 10^{-1}) + (3 \times 10^{-2})$$
$$= (5 \times 100) + (6 \times 10) + (8 \times 1) + (2 \times 0.1) + (3 \times 0.01)$$
$$= 500 + 60 + 8 + 0.2 + 0.03$$

Related Problem Determine the value of each digit in 67.924.

CALCULATOR TUTORIAL

Powers of Ten

Example Find the value of 10^3.

$$10^x$$

TI-86 Step 1. [2nd] [LOG]

Step 2. [3]

Step 3. [ENTER]

| 10 ^ 3 |
| 1000 |

TI-36X Step 1. [1] [0] [y^x]

Step 2. [3] [=]

| 1000 |

7–2 BINARY NUMBERS

The binary number system is another way to represent quantities. It is less complicated than the decimal system because it has only two digits. The decimal system with its ten digits is a base-ten system; the binary system with its two digits is a base-two system. The two binary digits (bits) are 1 and 0. The position of a 1 or 0 in a binary number indicates its weight, or value within the number, just as the position of a decimal digit determines the value of that digit. The weights in a binary number are based on powers of two.

After completing this section, you should be able to

■ Count in binary

■ Determine the largest decimal number that can be represented by a given number of bits

■ Convert a binary number to a decimal number

Counting in Binary

The binary number system has two digits (bits).

To learn to count in the binary system, first look at how you count in the decimal system. You start at zero and count up to nine before you run out of digits. You then start another digit position (to the left) and continue counting 10 through 99. At this point you have exhausted all two-digit combinations, so a third digit position is needed to count from 100 through 999.

A comparable situation occurs when you count in binary, except that you have only two digits, called *bits*. Begin counting: 0, 1. At this point you have used both digits, so include another digit position and continue: 10, 11. You have now exhausted all combinations of two digits, so a third position is required. With three digit positions you can continue to count: 100, 101, 110, and 111. Now you need a fourth digit position to continue, and so on. A binary count of zero through fifteen is shown in Table 7–1. Notice the patterns with which the 1s and 0s alternate in each column.

The binary number system has a base of 2.

▶ TABLE 7–1

DECIMAL NUMBER	BINARY NUMBER			
0	0	0	0	0
1	0	0	0	1
2	0	0	1	0
3	0	0	1	1
4	0	1	0	0
5	0	1	0	1
6	0	1	1	0
7	0	1	1	1
8	1	0	0	0
9	1	0	0	1
10	1	0	1	0
11	1	0	1	1
12	1	1	0	0
13	1	1	0	1
14	1	1	1	0
15	1	1	1	1

As you have seen in Table 7–1, four bits are required to count from zero to 15. In general, with n bits you can count up to a number equal to $2^n - 1$.

The value of a bit is determined by its position in the number.

Largest decimal number $= 2^n - 1$

For example, with five bits ($n = 5$) you can count from zero to thirty-one.

$2^5 - 1 = 32 - 1 = 31$

With six bits ($n = 6$) you can count from zero to sixty-three.

$2^6 - 1 = 64 - 1 = 63$

A table of powers of two is given in the Appendix.

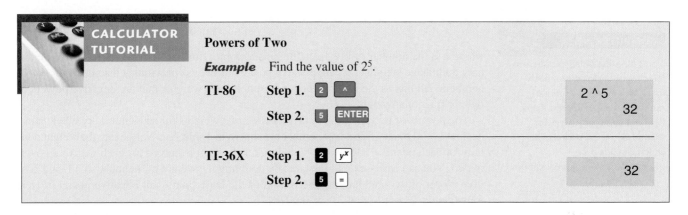

CALCULATOR TUTORIAL

Powers of Two

Example Find the value of 2^5.

TI-86   Step 1. [2] [^]   2 ^ 5

         Step 2. [5] [ENTER]   32

TI-36X   Step 1. [2] [y^x]

         Step 2. [5] [=]   32

An Application

Learning to count in binary will help you to basically understand how digital circuits can be used to count events. This can be anything from counting items on an assembly line to counting operations in a computer. Let's take a simple example of counting tennis balls going into a box from a conveyor belt. Assume that nine balls are to go into each box.

The counter in Figure 7–1 counts the pulses from a sensor that detects the passing of a ball and produces a sequence of logic levels (digital waveforms) on each of its four parallel outputs. Each set of logic levels represents a 4-bit binary number (HIGH = 1 and LOW = 0), as indicated. As the decoder receives these waveforms, it decodes each set of four bits and converts it to the corresponding decimal number in the 7-segment display. When the counter gets to the binary state of 1001, it has counted nine tennis balls, the display shows decimal 9, and a new box is moved under the conveyor. Then the counter goes back to its zero state (0000), and the process starts over. (The number 9 was used only in the interest of single-digit simplicity.)

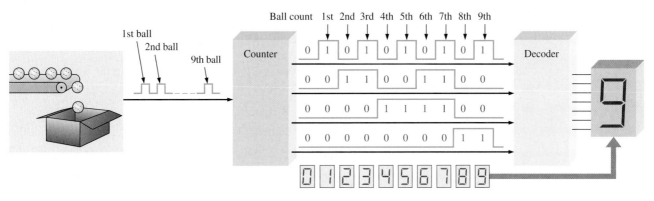

▲ **FIGURE 7–1**

Illustration of a simple binary counting application.

The Weighting Structure of Binary Numbers

The weight or value of a bit increases from right to left in a binary number.

A binary number is a weighted number. The right-most bit is the **LSB** (least significant bit) in a binary whole number and has a weight of $2^0 = 1$. The weights increase from right to left by a power of two for each bit. The left-most bit is the **MSB** (most significant bit); its weight depends on the size of the binary number.

Fractional numbers can also be represented in binary by placing bits to the right of the binary point, just as fractional decimal digits are placed to the right of the decimal point. The left-most bit is the MSB in a binary fractional number and has a weight of $2^{-1} = 0.5$. The fractional weights decrease from left to right by a negative power of two for each bit. The weight structure of a binary number is

$$2^{n-1}. \ . \ . \ 2^3 \, 2^2 \, 2^1 \, 2^0 . \, 2^{-1} \, 2^{-2} \ . \ . \ . \, 2^{-n}$$
$$\uparrow \text{—— Binary point}$$

where n is the number of bits from the binary point. Thus, all the bits to the left of the binary point have weights that are positive powers of two, as previously discussed for whole numbers. All bits to the right of the binary point have weights that are negative powers of two, or fractional weights.

The powers of two and their equivalent decimal weights for an 8-bit binary whole number and a 6-bit binary fractional number are shown in Table 7–2. Notice that the weight doubles for each positive power of two and that the weight is halved for each negative power of two. You can easily extend the table by doubling the weight of the most significant positive power of two and halving the weight of the least significant negative power of two; for example, $2^9 = 512$ and $2^{-7} = 0.0078125$.

▼ **TABLE 7–2**

Binary weights.

POSITIVE POWERS OF TWO (WHOLE NUMBERS)									NEGATIVE POWERS OF TWO (FRACTIONAL NUMBER)					
2^8	2^7	2^6	2^5	2^4	2^3	2^2	2^1	2^0	2^{-1}	2^{-2}	2^{-3}	2^{-4}	2^{-5}	2^{-6}
256	128	64	32	16	8	4	2	1	1/2	1/4	1/8	1/16	1/32	1/64
									0.5	0.25	0.125	0.0625	0.03125	0.015625

Binary-to-Decimal Conversion

Add the weights of all 1s in a binary number to get the decimal value.

The decimal value of any binary number can be found by adding the weights of all bits that are 1 and discarding the weights of all bits that are 0.

EXAMPLE 7–3

Convert the binary whole number 1101101 to decimal.

Solution   Determine the weight of each bit that is a 1, and then find the sum of the weights to get the decimal number.

$$\text{Weight: } 2^6 \, 2^5 \, 2^4 \, 2^3 \, 2^2 \, 2^1 \, 2^0$$
$$\text{Binary number: } 1 \ 1 \ 0 \ 1 \ 1 \ 0 \ 1$$
$$1101101 = 2^6 + 2^5 + 2^3 + 2^2 + 2^0$$
$$= 64 + 32 + 8 + 4 + 1 = \textbf{109}$$

Related Problem   Convert the binary number 10010001 to decimal.

EXAMPLE 7–4

Convert the fractional binary number 0.1011 to decimal.

Solution Determine the weight of each bit that is a 1, and then sum the weights to get the decimal fraction.

$$
\begin{array}{ccccc}
\text{Weight:} & 2^{-1} & 2^{-2} & 2^{-3} & 2^{-4} \\
\text{Binary number:} \ 0.\ 1 & & 0 & 1 & 1
\end{array}
$$

$$0.1011 = 2^{-1} + 2^{-3} + 2^{-4}$$
$$= 0.5 + 0.125 + 0.0625 = \mathbf{0.6875}$$

Related Problem Convert the binary number 10.111 to decimal.

7–3 BINARY ARITHMETIC

Binary arithmetic is essential in all digital computers and in many other types of digital systems. To understand digital systems, you must know the basics of binary addition, subtraction, multiplication, and division. This section provides an introduction that will be expanded in later sections.

After completing this section, you should be able to

- Add binary numbers
- Subtract binary numbers
- Multiply binary numbers
- Divide binary numbers

Binary Addition

The four basic rules for adding binary digits (bits) are as follows:

Remember, in binary $1 + 1 = 10$, not 2.

$0 + 0 = 0$	Sum of 0 with a carry of 0
$0 + 1 = 1$	Sum of 1 with a carry of 0
$1 + 0 = 1$	Sum of 1 with a carry of 0
$1 + 1 = 10$	Sum of 0 with a carry of 1

Notice that the first three rules result in a single bit and in the fourth rule the addition of two 1s yields a binary two (10). When binary numbers are added, the last condition creates a sum of 0 in a given column and a carry of 1 over to the next column to the left, as illustrated in the following addition of $11 + 1$:

$$
\begin{array}{ccc}
\text{Carry} & \text{Carry} & \\
1 \leftarrow & 1 \leftarrow & \\
0 & 1 & 1 \\
+\ 0 & 0 & 1 \\
\hline
1 & 0 & 0
\end{array}
$$

In the right column, $1 + 1 = 0$ with a carry of 1 to the next column to the left. In the middle column, $1 + 1 + 0 = 0$ with a carry of 1 to the next column to the left. In the left column, $1 + 0 + 0 = 1$.

When there is a carry of 1, you have a situation in which three bits are being added (a bit in each of the two numbers and a carry bit). This situation is illustrated as follows:

Carry bits ⌐→

$$1 + 0 + 0 = 01 \qquad \text{Sum of 1 with a carry of 0}$$
$$1 + 1 + 0 = 10 \qquad \text{Sum of 0 with a carry of 1}$$
$$1 + 0 + 1 = 10 \qquad \text{Sum of 0 with a carry of 1}$$
$$1 + 1 + 1 = 11 \qquad \text{Sum of 1 with a carry of 1}$$

EXAMPLE 7–5

Add the following binary numbers:

(a) $11 + 11$ (b) $100 + 10$ (c) $111 + 11$ (d) $110 + 100$

Solution   The equivalent decimal addition is also shown for reference.

(a)			(b)			(c)			(d)		
	11	3		100	4		111	7		110	6
	+11	+3		+10	+2		+11	+3		+100	+4
	110	6		**110**	6		**1010**	10		**1010**	10

Related Problem   Add 1111 and 1100.

Binary Subtraction

Remember in binary $10 - 1 = 1$, not 9.

The four basic rules for subtracting bits are as follows:

$$0 - 0 = 0$$
$$1 - 1 = 0$$
$$1 - 0 = 1$$
$$10 - 1 = 1 \qquad 0 - 1 \text{ with a borrow of 1}$$

When subtracting numbers, you sometimes have to borrow from the next column to the left. A borrow is required in binary only when you try to subtract a 1 from a 0. In this case, when a 1 is borrowed from the next column to the left, a 10 is created in the column being subtracted, and the last of the four basic rules just listed must be applied. Examples 7–6 and 7–7 illustrate binary subtraction; the equivalent decimal subtractions are also shown.

EXAMPLE 7–6

Perform the following binary subtractions:

(a) $11 - 01$ (b) $11 - 10$

Solution

(a)			(b)		
	11	3		11	3
	− 01	− 1		− 10	− 2
	10	2		**01**	1

No borrows were required in this example. The binary number 01 is the same as 1.

Related Problem   Subtract 100 from 111.

EXAMPLE 7–7

Subtract 011 from 101.

Solution

$$\begin{array}{cc} 101 & 5 \\ -011 & -3 \\ \hline \mathbf{010} & 2 \end{array}$$

Let's examine exactly what was done to subtract the two binary numbers since a borrow is required. Begin with the right column.

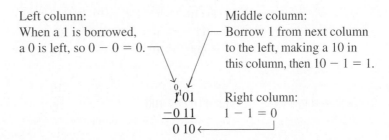

Left column:
When a 1 is borrowed,
a 0 is left, so $0 - 0 = 0$.

Middle column:
Borrow 1 from next column
to the left, making a 10 in
this column, then $10 - 1 = 1$.

$$\begin{array}{c} \overset{0}{\cancel{1}}01 \\ -0\,11 \\ \hline 0\,10 \end{array}$$

Right column:
$1 - 1 = 0$

Related Problem Subtract 101 from 110.

Binary Multiplication

The four basic rules for multiplying bits are as follows:

$$0 \times 0 = 0$$
$$0 \times 1 = 0$$
$$1 \times 0 = 0$$
$$1 \times 1 = 1$$

Binary multiplication of two bits is the same as multiplication of the decimal digits 0 and 1.

Multiplication is performed with binary numbers in the same manner as with decimal numbers. It involves forming partial products, shifting each successive partial product left one place, and then adding all the partial products. Example 7–8 illustrates the procedure; the equivalent decimal multiplications are shown for reference.

EXAMPLE 7–8

Perform the following binary multiplications:

(a) 11×11 **(b)** 101×111

Solution **(a)**

$$\begin{array}{cc} 11 & 3 \\ \times 11 & \times 3 \\ \hline \text{Partial} \left\{ \begin{array}{c} 11 \\ +11 \end{array} \right. & 9 \\ \hline \text{products} \quad \mathbf{1001} \end{array}$$

(b)

$$\begin{array}{cc} 111 & 7 \\ \times 101 & \times 5 \\ \hline \text{Partial} \left\{ \begin{array}{c} 111 \\ 000 \\ +111 \end{array} \right. & 35 \\ \hline \text{products} \quad \mathbf{100011} \end{array}$$

Related Problem Multiply 1101×1010.

A calculator can be used to perform arithmetic operations with binary numbers as long as the capacity of the calculator is not exceeded.

Binary Division

Division in binary follows the same procedure as division in decimal, as Example 7–9 illustrates. The equivalent decimal divisions are also given.

EXAMPLE 7–9

Perform the following binary divisions:

(a) $110 \div 11$ (b) $110 \div 10$

Solution

(a)
$$
\begin{array}{r} 10 \\ 11\overline{)110} \\ 11 \\ \hline 000 \end{array}
\qquad
\begin{array}{r} 2 \\ 3\overline{)6} \\ 6 \\ \hline 0 \end{array}
$$

(b)
$$
\begin{array}{r} 11 \\ 10\overline{)110} \\ 10 \\ \hline 10 \\ 10 \\ \hline 00 \end{array}
\qquad
\begin{array}{r} 3 \\ 2\overline{)6} \\ 6 \\ \hline 0 \end{array}
$$

Related Problem   Divide 1100 by 100.

7–4   1'S AND 2'S COMPLEMENTS OF BINARY NUMBERS

The 1's complement and the 2's complement of a binary number are important because they permit the representation of negative numbers. The method of 2's complement arithmetic is commonly used in computers to handle negative numbers.

After completing this section, you should be able to

■ Convert a binary number to its 1's complement

■ Convert a binary number to its 2's complement using either of two methods

Finding the 1's Complement

Change each bit in a number to get the 1's complement.

The 1's **complement** of a binary number is found by changing all 1s to 0s and all 0s to 1s, as illustrated below:

$$
\begin{array}{c}
1\ 0\ 1\ 1\ 0\ 0\ 1\ 0 \qquad \text{Binary number} \\
\downarrow \downarrow \downarrow \downarrow \downarrow \downarrow \downarrow \downarrow \\
0\ 1\ 0\ 0\ 1\ 1\ 0\ 1 \qquad \text{1's complement}
\end{array}
$$

The simplest way to obtain the 1's complement of a binary number with a digital circuit is to use parallel inverters (NOT circuits), as shown in Figure 7–2 for an 8-bit binary number.

▶ **FIGURE 7–2**

Example of inverters used to obtain the 1's complement of a binary number.

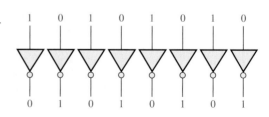

Finding the 2's Complement

The 2's complement of a binary number is found by adding 1 to the LSB of the 1's complement.

Add 1 to the 1's complement to get the 2's complement.

2's complement = (1's complement) + 1

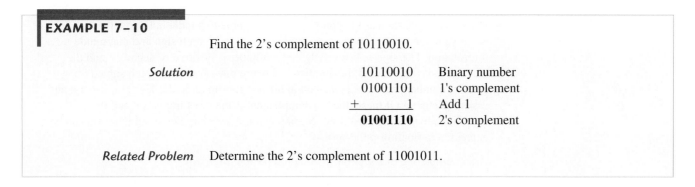

EXAMPLE 7–10

Find the 2's complement of 10110010.

Solution

```
  10110010    Binary number
  01001101    1's complement
+        1    Add 1
  01001110    2's complement
```

Related Problem Determine the 2's complement of 11001011.

An alternative method of finding the 2's complement of a binary number is as follows:

1. Start at the right with the LSB and write the bits as they are up to and including the first 1.

2. Take the 1's complements of the remaining bits.

Change all bits to the left of the least significant 1 to get 2's complement.

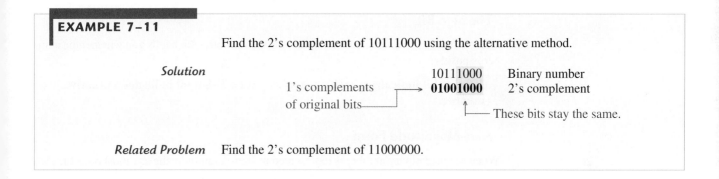

EXAMPLE 7–11

Find the 2's complement of 10111000 using the alternative method.

Solution

1's complements of original bits ⟶
10111000 Binary number
01001000 2's complement
These bits stay the same.

Related Problem Find the 2's complement of 11000000.

The 2's complement of a negative binary number can be realized using inverters and an adder, as indicated in Figure 7–3. This illustrates how an 8-bit number can be converted to its 2's complement by first inverting each bit (taking the 1's complement) and then adding 1 to the 1's complement with an adder circuit.

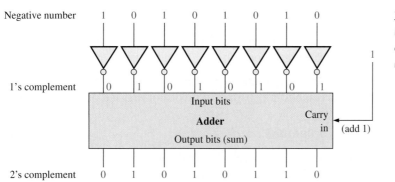

◀ **FIGURE 7–3**

Example of obtaining the 2's complement of a negative binary number.

To convert from a 1's or 2's complement back to the true (uncomplemented) binary form, use the same two procedures described previously. To go from the 1's complement back to true binary, reverse all the bits. To go from the 2's complement form back to true binary, take the 1's complement of the 2's complement number and add 1 to the least significant bit.

7–5   SIGNED NUMBERS

Digital systems, such as the computer, must be able to handle both positive and negative numbers. A signed binary number consists of both sign and magnitude information. The sign indicates whether a number is positive or negative, and the magnitude is the value of the number. There are three forms in which signed integer (whole) numbers can be represented in binary: sign-magnitude, 1's complement, and 2's complement. Of these, the 2's complement is the most important and the sign-magnitude is the least used. Noninteger and very large or small numbers can be expressed in floating-point format.

After completing this section, you should be able to

- Express positive and negative numbers in sign-magnitude
- Express positive and negative numbers in 1's complement
- Express positive and negative numbers in 2's complement
- Determine the decimal value of signed binary numbers
- Express a binary number in floating-point format

The Sign Bit

The left-most bit in a signed binary number is the **sign bit,** which tells you whether the number is positive or negative.

A 0 sign bit indicates a positive number, and a 1 sign bit indicates a negative number.

Sign-Magnitude Form

When a signed binary number is represented in sign-magnitude, the left-most bit is the sign bit and the remaining bits are the magnitude bits. The magnitude bits are in true (uncomplemented) binary for both positive and negative numbers. For example, the decimal number $+25$ is expressed as an 8-bit signed binary number using the sign-magnitude form as

$$0001\,1001$$

Sign bit ⎯↑   ↑⎯ Magnitude bits

The decimal number -25 is expressed as

10011001

Notice that the only difference between $+25$ and $+25$ is the sign bit because the magnitude bits are in true binary for both positive and negative numbers.

In the sign-magnitude form, a negative number has the same magnitude bits as the corresponding positive number but the sign bit is a 1 rather than a zero.

1's Complement Form

Positive numbers in 1's complement form are represented the same way as the positive sign-magnitude numbers. Negative numbers, however, are the 1's complements of the corresponding positive numbers. For example, using eight bits, the decimal number -25 is expressed as the 1's complement of $+25$ (00011001) as

11100110

In the 1's complement form, a negative number is the 1's complement of the corresponding positive number.

2's Complement Form

Positive numbers in 2's complement form are represented the same way as in the signmagnitude and 1's complement forms. Negative numbers are the 2's complements of the corresponding positive numbers. Again, using eight bits, let's take decimal number -25 and express it as the 2's complement of $+25$ (00011001).

11100111

In the 2's complement form, a negative number is the 2's complement of the corresponding positive number.

EXAMPLE 7–12

Express the decimal number -39 as an 8-bit number in the sign-magnitude, 1's complement, and 2's complement forms.

Solution First, write the 8-bit number for $+39$.

00100111

In the *sign-magnitude form*, -39 is produced by changing the sign bit to a 1 and leaving the magnitude bits as they are. The number is

10100111

In the *1's complement form*, -39 is produced by taking the 1's complement of $+39$ (00100111).

11011000

In the *2's complement form*, -39 is produced by taking the 2's complement of $+39$ (00100111) as follows:

$$
\begin{array}{ll}
11011000 & \text{1's complement} \\
\underline{+\quad 1} & \\
\mathbf{11011001} & \text{2's complement}
\end{array}
$$

Related Problem Express $+19$ and -19 in sign-magnitude, 1's complement, and 2's complement.

The Decimal Value of Signed Numbers

Sign-magnitude Decimal values of positive and negative numbers in the sign-magnitude form are determined by summing the weights in all the magnitude bit positions where there are 1s and ignoring those positions where there are zeros. The sign is determined by examination of the sign bit.

EXAMPLE 7–13

Determine the decimal value of this signed binary number expressed in sign-magnitude: 10010101.

Solution   The seven magnitude bits and their powers-of-two weights are as follows:

$$2^6 \quad 2^5 \quad 2^4 \quad 2^3 \quad 2^2 \quad 2^1 \quad 2^0$$
$$0 \quad\; 0 \quad\; 1 \quad\; 0 \quad\; 1 \quad\; 0 \quad\; 1$$

Summing the weights where there are 1s,

$$16 + 4 + 1 = 21$$

The sign bit is 1; therefore, the decimal number is **−21.**

Related Problem   Determine the decimal value of the sign-magnitude number 01110111.

1's Complement   Decimal values of positive numbers in the 1's complement form are determined by summing the weights in all bit positions where there are 1s and ignoring those positions where there are zeros. Decimal values of negative numbers are determined by assigning a negative value to the weight of the sign bit, summing all the weights where there are 1s, and adding 1 to the result.

EXAMPLE 7–14

Determine the decimal values of the signed binary numbers expressed in 1's complement:

(a) 00010111   **(b)** 11101000

Solution   **(a)** The bits and their powers-of-two weights for the positive number are as follows:

$$-2^7 \quad 2^6 \quad 2^5 \quad 2^4 \quad 2^3 \quad 2^2 \quad 2^1 \quad 2^0$$
$$0 \quad\;\; 0 \quad\; 0 \quad\; 1 \quad\; 0 \quad\; 1 \quad\; 1 \quad\; 1$$

Summing the weights where there are 1s,

$$16 + 4 + 2 + 1 = \textbf{+23}$$

(b) The bits and their powers-of-two weights for the negative number are as follows. Notice that the negative sign bit has a weight of -2^7 or -128.

$$-2^7 \quad 2^6 \quad 2^5 \quad 2^4 \quad 2^3 \quad 2^2 \quad 2^1 \quad 2^0$$
$$1 \quad\;\; 1 \quad\; 1 \quad\; 0 \quad\; 1 \quad\; 0 \quad\; 0 \quad\; 0$$

Summing the weights where there are 1s,

$$-128 + 64 + 32 + 8 = -24$$

Adding 1 to the result, the final decimal number is

$$-24 + 1 = \textbf{−23}$$

Related Problem   Determine the decimal value of the 1's complement number 11101011.

2's Complement   Decimal values of positive and negative numbers in the 2's complement form are determined by summing the weights in all bit positions where there are 1s and ignoring those positions where there are zeros. The weight of the sign bit in a negative number is given a negative value.

EXAMPLE 7–15

Determine the decimal values of the signed binary numbers expressed in 2's complement:

(a) 01010110   **(b)** 10101010

Solution   **(a)** The bits and their powers-of-two weights for the positive number are as follows:

$$-2^7 \quad 2^6 \quad 2^5 \quad 2^4 \quad 2^3 \quad 2^2 \quad 2^1 \quad 2^0$$
$$0 \quad\ \ 1 \quad\ \ 0 \quad\ \ 1 \quad\ \ 0 \quad\ \ 1 \quad\ \ 1 \quad\ \ 0$$

Summing the weights where there are 1s,

$$64 + 16 + 4 + 2 = \mathbf{+86}$$

(b) The bits and their powers-of-two weights for the negative number are as follows. Notice that the negative sign bit has a weight of $-2^7 = -128$.

$$-2^7 \quad 2^6 \quad 2^5 \quad 2^4 \quad 2^3 \quad 2^2 \quad 2^1 \quad 2^0$$
$$1 \quad\ \ 0 \quad\ \ 1 \quad\ \ 0 \quad\ \ 1 \quad\ \ 0 \quad\ \ 1 \quad\ \ 0$$

Summing the weights where there are 1s,

$$-128 + 32 + 8 + 2 = \mathbf{-86}$$

Related Problem   Determine the decimal value of the 2's complement number 11010111.

From these examples, you can see why the 2's complement form is preferred for representing signed integer numbers: To convert to decimal, it simply requires a summation of weights regardless of whether the number is positive or negative. The 1's complement system requires adding 1 to the summation of weights for negative numbers but not for positive numbers. Also, the 1's complement form is generally not used because two representations of zero (00000000 or 11111111) are possible.

Range of Signed Integer Numbers That Can Be Represented

We have used 8-bit numbers for illustration because the 8-bit grouping is common in most computers and has been given the special name **byte.** With one byte or eight bits, you can represent 256 different numbers. With two bytes or sixteen bits, you can represent 65,536 different numbers. With four bytes or 32 bits, you can represent 4.295×10^9 different numbers. The formula for finding the number of different combinations of n bits is

Total combinations $= 2^n$

For 2's complement signed numbers, the range of values for n-bit numbers is

Range $= -(2^{n-1})$ to $+(2^{n-1} - 1)$

The range of magnitude of a binary number depends on the number of bits (n).

where in each case there is one sign bit and $n - 1$ magnitude bits. For example, with four bits you can represent numbers in 2's complement ranging from $-(2^3) = -8$ to $2^3 - 1 = +7$. Similarly, with eight bits you can go from -128 to $+127$, with sixteen bits you can go from $-32,768$ to $+32,767$, and so on.

Floating-Point Numbers

To represent very large **integer** (whole) numbers, many bits are required. There is also a problem when numbers with both integer and fractional parts, such as 23.5618, need to be represented. The floating-point number system, based on scientific notation, is capable of representing very large and very small numbers without an increase in the number of bits and also for representing numbers that have both integer and fractional components.

A **floating-point number** (also known as a *real number*) consists of two parts plus a sign. The **mantissa** is the part of a floating-point number that represents the magnitude of the number. The **exponent** is the part of a floating-point number that represents the number of places that the decimal point (or binary point) is to be moved.

A decimal example will be helpful in understanding the basic concept of floating-point numbers. Let's consider a decimal number which, in integer form, is 241,506,800. The mantissa is .2415068 and the exponent is 9. When the integer is expressed as a floatingpoint number, it is normalized by moving the decimal point to the left of all the digits so that the mantissa is a fractional number and the exponent is the power of ten. The floatingpoint number is written as

$$0.2415068 \times 10^9$$

For binary floating-point numbers, the format is defined by ANSI/IEEE Standard 754-1985 in three forms: *single-precision, double-precision,* and *extended-precision.* These all have the same basic formats except for the number of bits. Single-precision floating-point numbers have 32 bits, double-precision numbers have 64 bits, and extended-precision numbers have 80 bits. We will restrict our discussion to the single-precision floating-point format.

Single-Precision Floating-Point Binary Numbers   In the standard format for a single-precision binary number, the sign bit (S) is the left-most bit, the exponent (E) includes the next eight bits, and the mantissa or fractional part (F) includes the remaining 23 bits, as shown next.

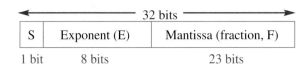

←	32 bits	→
S	Exponent (E)	Mantissa (fraction, F)
1 bit	8 bits	23 bits

In the mantissa or fractional part, the binary point is understood to be to the left of the 23 bits. Effectively, there are 24 bits in the mantissa because in any binary number the left-most (most significant) bit is always a 1. Therefore, this 1 is understood to be there although it does not occupy an actual bit position.

The eight bits in the exponent represent a *biased exponent,* which is obtained by adding 127 to the actual exponent. The purpose of the bias is to allow very large or very small numbers without requiring a separate sign bit for the exponents. The biased exponent allows a range of actual exponent values from -126 to $+128$.

To illustrate how a binary number is expressed in floating-point format, let's use 1011010010001 as an example. First, it can be expressed as 1 plus a fractional binary number by moving the binary point 12 places to the left and then multiplying by the appropriate power of two.

$$1011010010001 = 1.011010010001 \times 2^{12}$$

Assuming that this is a positive number, the sign bit (S) is 0. The exponent, 12, is expressed as a biased exponent by adding it to 127 (12 + 127 = 139). The biased exponent (E) is expressed as the binary number 10001011. The mantissa is the fractional part (F) of the binary number, .011010010001. Because there is always a 1 to the left of the binary point in the power-of-two expression, it is not included in the mantissa. The complete floating-point number is

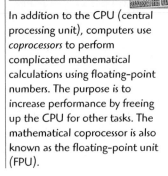

S	E	F
0	10001011	01101001000100000000000

Next, let's see how to evaluate a binary number that is already in floating-point format. The general approach to determining the value of a floating-point number is expressed by the following formula:

$$\text{Number} = (-1)^S (1 + F)(2^{E-127})$$

To illustrate, let's consider the following floating-point binary number:

S	E	F
1	10010001	10001110001000000000000

The sign bit is 1. The biased exponent is $10010001 = 145$. Applying the formula, we get

$$\text{Number} = (-1)^1 (1.10001110001)(2^{145-127})$$
$$= (-1)(1.10001110001)(2^{18}) = -1100011100010000000$$

This floating-point binary number is equivalent to $-407,688$ in decimal. Since the exponent can be any number between -126 and $+128$, extremely large and small numbers can be expressed. A 32-bit floating-point number can replace a binary integer number having 129 bits. Because the exponent determines the position of the binary point, numbers containing both integer and fractional parts can be represented.

There are two exceptions to the format for floating-point numbers: The number 0.0 is represented by all 0s, and infinity is represented by all 1s in the exponent and all 0s in the mantissa.

EXAMPLE 7–16

Convert the decimal number 3.248×10^4 to a single-precision floating-point binary number.

Solution Convert the decimal number to binary.

$$3.248 \times 10^4 = 32480 = 111111011100000_2 = 1.11111011100000 \times 2^{14}$$

The MSB will not occupy a bit position because it is always a 1. Therefore, the mantissa is the fractional 23-bit binary number 11111011100000000000000 and the biased exponent is

$$14 + 127 = 141 = 10001101_2$$

The complete floating-point number is

0	10001101	11111011100000000000000

Related Problem Determine the binary value of the following floating-point binary number:

0 10011000 10000100010100110000000

7-6 ARITHMETIC OPERATIONS WITH SIGNED NUMBERS

In the last section, you learned how signed numbers are represented in three different forms. In this section, you will learn how signed numbers are added, subtracted, multiplied, and divided. Because the 2's complement form for representing signed numbers is the most widely used in computers and microprocessor-based systems, the coverage in this section is limited to 2's complement arithmetic. The processes covered can be extended to the other forms if necessary.

After completing this section, you should be able to

- Add signed binary numbers
- Explain how computers add strings of numbers
- Define *overflow*
- Subtract signed binary numbers
- Multiply signed binary numbers using the direct addition method
- Multiply signed binary numbers using the partial products method
- Divide signed binary numbers

Addition

The two numbers in an addition are the **addend** and the **augend.** The result is the **sum.** There are four cases that can occur when two signed binary numbers are added.

1. Both numbers positive
2. Positive number with magnitude larger than negative number
3. Negative number with magnitude larger than positive number
4. Both numbers negative

Let's take one case at a time using 8-bit signed numbers as examples. The equivalent decimal numbers are shown for reference.

Addition of two positive numbers yields a positive number.

Both numbers positive:

$$
\begin{array}{rr}
00000111 & 7 \\
+\ 00000100 & +\ 4 \\
\hline
00001011 & 11
\end{array}
$$

The sum is positive and is therefore in true (uncomplemented) binary.

Addition of a positive number and a smaller negative number yields a positive number.

Positive number with magnitude larger than negative number:

$$
\begin{array}{rr}
00001111 & 15 \\
+\ 11111010 & +\ -6 \\
\end{array}
$$

Discard carry $\longrightarrow$ 1 00001001   9

The final carry bit is discarded. The sum is positive and therefore in true (uncomplemented) binary.

Addition of a positive number and a larger negative number or two negative numbers yields a negative number in 2's complement.

Negative number with magnitude larger than positive number:

$$
\begin{array}{rr}
00010000 & 16 \\
+\ 11101000 & +\ -24 \\
\hline
11111000 & -8
\end{array}
$$

The sum is negative and therefore in 2's complement form.

Both numbers negative:

$$
\begin{array}{rr}
11111011 & -5 \\
+\ 11110111 & +\ -9 \\
\hline
\text{Discard carry} \longrightarrow \boxed{1}\ 11110010 & -14
\end{array}
$$

The final carry bit is discarded. The sum is negative and therefore in 2's complement form.

In a computer, the negative numbers are stored in 2's complement form so, as you can see, the addition process is very simple: *Add the two numbers and discard any final carry bit.*

Overflow Condition When two numbers are added and the number of bits required to represent the sum exceeds the number of bits in the two numbers, an **overflow** results as indicated by an incorrect sign bit. An overflow can occur only when both numbers are positive or both numbers are negative. The following 8-bit example will illustrate this condition.

$$
\begin{array}{rr}
01111101 & 125 \\
+\ 00111010 & +\ 58 \\
\hline
10110111 & 183
\end{array}
$$

Sign incorrect ⎯⎯⎯⎯⎯⎯⎯⎯
Magnitude incorrect ⎯⎯⎯⎯⎯⎯⎯

In this example the sum of 183 requires eight magnitude bits. Since there are seven magnitude bits in the numbers (one bit is the sign), there is a carry into the sign bit which produces the overflow indication.

Numbers Are Added Two at a Time Now let's look at the addition of a string of numbers, added two at a time. This can be accomplished by adding the first two numbers, then adding the third number to the sum of the first two, then adding the fourth number to this result, and so on. This is how computers add strings of numbers. The addition of numbers taken two at a time is illustrated in Example 7–17.

EXAMPLE 7–17

Add the signed numbers: 01000100, 00011011, 00001110, and 00010010.

Solution The equivalent decimal additions are given for reference.

$$
\begin{array}{rll}
68 & 01000100 & \\
+\ 27 & +\ 00011011 & \text{Add 1st two numbers} \\
\hline
95 & 01011111 & \text{1st sum} \\
+\ 14 & +\ 00001110 & \text{Add 3rd number} \\
\hline
109 & 01101101 & \text{2nd sum} \\
+\ 18 & +\ 00010010 & \text{Add 4th number} \\
\hline
127 & \mathbf{01111111} & \text{Final sum}
\end{array}
$$

Related Problem Add 00110011, 10111111, and 01100011. These are signed numbers.

Subtraction

Subtraction is a special case of addition. For example, subtracting +6 (the **subtrahend**) from +9 (the **minuend**) is equivalent to adding −6 to +9. Basically, *the subtraction operation changes the sign of the subtrahend and adds it to the minuend.* The result of a subtraction is called the **difference.**

Subtraction is addition with the sign of the subtrahend changed.

The sign of a positive or negative binary number is changed by taking its 2's complement.

For example, when you take the 2's complement of the positive number 00000100 (+4), you get 11111100, which is −4 as the following sum-of-weights evaluation shows:

$$-128 + 64 + 32 + 16 + 8 + 4 = -4$$

As another example, when you take the 2's complement of the negative number 11101101 (−19), you get 00010011, which is +19 as the following sum-of-weights evaluation shows:

$$16 + 2 + 1 = 19$$

Since subtraction is simply an addition with the sign of the subtrahend changed, the process is stated as follows:

To subtract two signed numbers, take the 2's complement of the subtrahend and add. Discard any final carry bit.

Example 7–18 illustrates the subtraction process.

EXAMPLE 7–18

Perform each of the following subtractions of the signed numbers:

(a) 00001000 − 00000011

(b) 00001100 − 11110111

(c) 11100111 − 00010011

(d) 10001000 − 11100010

Solution Like in other examples, the equivalent decimal subtractions are given for reference.

(a) In this case, $8 - 3 = 8 + (-3) = 5$.

00001000	Minuend (+8)
+ 11111101	2's complement of subtrahend (−3)
Discard carry ⟶ **1 00000101**	Difference (+5)

(b) In this case, $12 - (-9) = 12 + 9 = 21$.

00001100	Minuend (+12)
+ 00001001	2's complement of subtrahend (+9)
00010101	Difference (+21)

(c) In this case, $-25 - (+19) = -25 + (-19) = -44$.

11100111	Minuend (−25)
+ 11101101	2's complement of subtrahend (−19)
Discard carry ⟶ **1 11010100**	Difference (−44)

(d) In this case, $-120 - (-30) = -120 + 30 = -90$.

10001000	Minuend (−120)
+ 00011110	2's complement of subtrahend (+30)
10100110	Difference (−90)

Related Problem Subtract 01000111 from 01011000.

Multiplication

The numbers in a multiplication are the **multiplicand**, the **multiplier**, and the **product**. These are illustrated in the following decimal multiplication:

8	Multiplicand
× 3	Multiplier
24	Product

Multiplication is equivalent to adding a number to itself a number of times equal to the multiplier.

The multiplication operation in most computers is accomplished using addition. As you have already seen, subtraction is done with an adder; now let's see how multiplication is done.

Direct addition and *partial products* are two basic methods for performing multiplication using addition. In the direct addition method, you add the multiplicand a number of times equal to the multiplier. In the previous decimal example (3 × 8), three multiplicands are added: 8 + 8 + 8 = 24. The disadvantage of this approach is that it becomes very lengthy if the multiplier is a large number. For example, to multiply 75 × 350, you must add 350 to itself 75 times. Incidentally, this is why the term *times* is used to mean multiply.

When two binary numbers are multiplied, both numbers must be in true (uncomplemented) form. The direct addition method is illustrated in Example 7–19 adding two binary numbers at a time.

EXAMPLE 7–19

Multiply the signed binary numbers: 01001101 (multiplicand) and 00000100 (multiplier) using the direct addition method.

Solution Since both numbers are positive, they are in true form, and the product will be positive. The decimal value of the multiplier is 4, so the multiplicand is added to itself four times as follows:

01001101	1st time
+ 01001101	2nd time
10011010	Partial sum
+ 01001101	3rd time
11100111	Partial sum
+ 01001101	4th time
100110100	Product

Since the sign bit of the multiplicand is 0, it has no effect on the outcome. All of the bits in the product are magnitude bits.

Related Problem Multiply 01100001 by 00000110 using the direct addition method.

The partial products method is perhaps the more common one because it reflects the way you multiply longhand. The multiplicand is multiplied by each multiplier digit beginning with the least significant digit. The result of the multiplication of the multiplicand by a multiplier digit is called a *partial product*. Each successive partial product is moved (shifted) one place to the left and when all the partial products have been produced, they are added to get the final product. Here is a decimal example.

239	Multiplicand
× 123	Multiplier
717	1st partial product (3 × 239)
478	2nd partial product (2 × 239)
+ 239	3rd partial product (1 × 239)
29,397	Final product

The sign of the product of a multiplication depends on the signs of the multiplicand and the multiplier according to the following two rules:

■ **If the signs are the same, the product is positive.**

■ **If the signs are different, the product is negative.**

The basic steps in the partial products method of binary multiplication are as follows:

Step 1. Determine if the signs of the multiplicand and multiplier are the same or different. This determines what the sign of the product will be.

Step 2. Change any negative number to true (uncomplemented) form. Because most computers store negative numbers in 2's complement, a 2's complement operation is required to get the negative number into true form.

Step 3. Starting with the least significant multiplier bit, generate the partial products. When the multiplier bit is 1, the partial product is the same as the multiplicand. When the multiplier bit is 0, the partial product is zero. Shift each successive partial product one bit to the left.

Step 4. Add each successive partial product to the sum of the previous partial products to get the final product.

Step 5. If the sign bit that was determined in step 1 is negative, take the 2's complement of the product. If positive, leave the product in true form. Attach the sign bit to the product.

EXAMPLE 7–20

Multiply the signed binary numbers: 01010011 (multiplicand) and 11000101 (multiplier).

Solution **Step 1:** The sign bit of the multiplicand is 0 and the sign bit of the multiplier is 1. The sign bit of the product will be 1 (negative).

Step 2: Take the 2's complement of the multiplier to put it in true form.

$$11000101 \longrightarrow 00111011$$

Steps 3 and 4: The multiplication proceeds as follows. Notice that only the magnitude bits are used in these steps.

1010011	Multiplicand
× 0111011	Multiplier
1010011	1st partial product
+ 1010011	2nd partial product
11111001	Sum of 1st and 2nd
+ 0000000	3rd partial product
011111001	Sum
+ 1010011	4th partial product
1110010001	Sum
+ 1010011	5th partial product
100011000001	Sum
+ 1010011	6th partial product
1001100100001	Sum
+ 0000000	7th partial product
1001100100001	Final product

Step 5: Since the sign of the product is a 1 as determined in step 1, take the 2's complement of the product.

$$1001100100001 \longrightarrow 0110011011111$$

Attach the sign bit

$$\longrightarrow \mathbf{1\ 0110011011111}$$

Related Problem Verify the multiplication is correct by converting to decimal numbers and performing the multiplication.

Division

The numbers in a division are the **dividend,** the **divisor,** and the **quotient.** These are illustrated in the following standard division format.

$$\frac{\text{dividend}}{\text{divisor}} = \text{quotient}$$

The division operation in computers is accomplished using subtraction. Since subtraction is done with an adder, division can also be accomplished with an adder.

The result of a division is called the *quotient;* the quotient is the number of times that the divisor will go into the dividend. This means that the divisor can be subtracted from the dividend a number of times equal to the quotient, as illustrated by dividing 21 by 7.

21	Dividend
− 7	1st subtraction of divisor
14	1st partial remainder
− 7	2nd subtraction of divisor
7	2nd partial remainder
− 7	3rd subtraction of divisor
0	Zero remainder

In this simple example, the divisor was subtracted from the dividend three times before a remainder of zero was obtained. Therefore, the quotient is 3.

The sign of the quotient depends on the signs of the dividend and the divisor according to the following two rules:

- **If the signs are the same, the quotient is positive.**
- **If the signs are different, the quotient is negative.**

When two binary numbers are divided, both numbers must be in true (uncomplemented) form. The basic steps in a division process are as follows:

Step 1. Determine if the signs of the dividend and divisor are the same or different. This determines what the sign of the quotient will be. Initialize the quotient to zero.

Step 2. Subtract the divisor from the dividend using 2's complement addition to get the first partial remainder and add 1 to the quotient. If this partial remainder is positive, go to step 3. If the partial remainder is zero or negative, the division is complete.

Step 3. Subtract the divisor from the partial remainder and add 1 to the quotient. If the result is positive, repeat for the next partial remainder. If the result is zero or negative, the division is complete.

Continue to subtract the divisor from the dividend and the partial remainders until there is a zero or a negative result. Count the number of times that the divisor is subtracted and you have the quotient. Example 7–21 illustrates these steps using 8-bit signed binary numbers.

EXAMPLE 7–21

Divide 01100100 by 00011001.

Solution **Step 1:** The signs of both numbers are positive, so the quotient will be positive. The quotient is initially zero: 00000000.

Step 2: Subtract the divisor from the dividend using 2's complement addition (remember that final carries are discarded).

01100100	Dividend
+ 11100111	2's complement of divisor
01001011	Positive 1st partial remainder

Add 1 to quotient: 00000000 + 00000001 = 00000001.

Step 3: Subtract the divisor from the 1st partial remainder using 2's complement addition.

01001011	1st partial remainder
+ 11100111	2's complement of divisor
00110010	Positive 2nd partial remainder

Step 4: Subtract the divisor from the 2nd partial remainder using 2's complement addition.

00110010	2nd partial remainder
+ 11100111	2's complement of divisor
00011001	Positive 3rd partial remainder

Add 1 to quotient: 00000010 + 00000001 = 00000011.

Step 5: Subtract the divisor from the 3rd partial remainder using 2's complement addition.

00011001	3rd partial remainder
+ 11100111	2's complement of divisor
00000000	Zero remainder

Add 1 to quotient: 00000011 + 00000001 = **00000100** (final quotient). The process is complete.

Related Problem   Verify that the process is correct by converting to decimal numbers and performing the division.

7–7   HEXADECIMAL NUMBERS

The hexadecimal number system has sixteen characters; it is used primarily as a compact way of displaying or writing binary numbers because it is very easy to convert between binary and hexadecimal. As you are probably aware, long binary numbers are difficult to read and write because it is easy to drop or transpose a bit. Since computers and microprocessors understand only 1s and 0s, it is necessary to use these digits when you program in "machine language." Imagine writing a sixteen bit instruction for a microprocessor system in 1s and 0s. It is much more efficient to use hexadecimal or octal; octal numbers are covered in Section 7–8. Hexadecimal is widely used in computer and microprocessor applications.

After completing this section, you should be able to

- List the hexadecimal characters
- Count in hexadecimal
- Convert from binary to hexadecimal
- Convert from hexadecimal to binary
- Convert from hexadecimal to decimal
- Convert from decimal to hexadecimal
- Add hexadecimal numbers
- Determine the 2's complement of a hexadecimal number
- Subtract hexadecimal numbers

The **hexadecimal** number system has a base of sixteen; that is, it is composed of 16 **numeric** and alphabetic **characters.** Most digital systems process binary data in groups that are multiples of four bits, making the hexadecimal number very convenient because each hexadecimal digit represents a 4-bit binary number (as listed in Table 7–3).

The hexadecimal number system consists of digits 0–9 and letters A–F.

◄ TABLE 7–3

DECIMAL	BINARY	HEXADECIMAL
0	0000	0
1	0001	1
2	0010	2
3	0011	3
4	0100	4
5	0101	5
6	0110	6
7	0111	7
8	1000	8
9	1001	9
10	1010	A
11	1011	B
12	1100	C
13	1101	D
14	1110	E
15	1111	F

Ten numeric digits and six alphabetic characters make up the hexadecimal number system. The use of letters A, B, C, D, E, and F to represent numbers may seem strange at first, but keep in mind that any number system is only a set of sequential symbols. If you understand what quantities these symbols represent, then the form of the symbols themselves is less important once you get accustomed to using them. We will use the subscript 16 to designate hexadecimal numbers to avoid confusion with decimal numbers. Sometimes you may see an "h" following a hexadecimal number.

Counting in Hexadecimal

How do you count in hexadecimal once you get to F? Simply start over with another column and continue as follows:

10, 11, 12, 13, 14, 15, 16, 17, 18, 19, 1A, 1B, 1C, 1D, 1E, 1F, 20, 21, 22, 23, 24, 25, 26, 27, 28, 29, 2A, 2B, 2C, 2D, 2E, 2F, 30, 31, . . .

With two hexadecimal digits, you can count up to FF_{16}, which is decimal 255. To count beyond this, three hexadecimal digits are needed. For instance, 100_{16} is decimal 256, 101_{16} is decimal 257, and so forth. The maximum 3-digit hexadecimal number is FFF_{16}, or decimal 4095. The maximum 4-digit hexadecimal number is $FFFF_{16}$, which is decimal 65,535.

COMPUTER NOTE

With computer memories in the gigabyte (GB) range, specifying a memory address in binary is quite cumbersome. For example, it takes 32 bits to specify an address in a 4 GB memory. It is much easier to express a 32-bit code using 8 hexadecimal digits.

Binary-to-Hexadecimal Conversion

Converting a binary number to hexadecimal is a straightforward procedure. Simply break the binary number into 4-bit groups, starting at the right-most bit and replace each 4-bit group with the equivalent hexadecimal symbol.

EXAMPLE 7–22

Convert the following binary numbers to hexadecimal:

(a) 1100101001010111   (b) 111111000101101001

Solution   (a) $\underline{1100}\ \underline{1010}\ \underline{0101}\ \underline{0111}$
                              C   A   5   7 = **CA57**$_{16}$

(b) $\underline{0011}\ \underline{1111}\ \underline{0001}\ \underline{0110}\ \underline{1001}$
                              3   F   1   6   9 = **3F169**$_{16}$

Two zeros have been added in part (b) to complete a 4-bit group at the left.

Related Problem   Convert the binary number 1001111011110011100 to hexadecimal.

Hexadecimal-to-Binary Conversion

Hexadecimal is a convenient way to represent binary numbers.

To convert from a hexadecimal number to a binary number, reverse the process and replace each hexadecimal symbol with the appropriate four bits.

EXAMPLE 7–23

Determine the binary numbers for the following hexadecimal numbers:

(a) 10A4$_{16}$ (b) CF8E$_{16}$ (c) 9742$_{16}$

Solution   (a) 1   0   A   4   (b) C   F   8   E   (c) 9   7   4   2

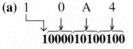
1000010100100

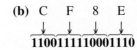
1100111110001110

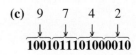
1001011101000010

In part (a), the MSB is understood to have three zeros preceding it, thus forming a 4-bit group.

Related Problem   Convert the hexadecimal number 6BD3 to binary.

Conversion between hexadecimal and binary is direct and easy.

It should be clear that it is much easier to deal with a hexadecimal number than with the equivalent binary number. Since conversion is so easy, the hexadecimal system is widely used for representing binary numbers in programming, printouts, and displays.

Hexadecimal-to-Decimal Conversion

One way to find the decimal equivalent of a hexadecimal number is to first convert the hexadecimal number to binary and then convert from binary to decimal.

EXAMPLE 7–24

Convert the following hexadecimal numbers to decimal:

(a) 1C$_{16}$ (b) A85$_{16}$

Solution   Remember, convert the hexadecimal number to binary first, then to decimal.

(a) 1   C

$\overline{0001\ 1100} = 2^4 + 2^3 + 2^2 = 16 + 8 + 4 = \mathbf{28}_{10}$

(b) A   8   5
$$\underbrace{101010000101} = 2^{11} + 2^9 + 2^7 + 2^2 + 2^0 = 2048 + 512 + 128 + 4 + 1 = \mathbf{2693}_{10}$$

Related Problem   Convert the hexadecimal number 6BD to decimal.

Another way to convert a hexadecimal number to its decimal equivalent is to multiply the decimal value of each hexadecimal digit by its weight and then take the sum of these products. The weights of a hexadecimal number are increasing powers of 16 (from right to left). For a 4-digit hexadecimal number, the weights are

16^3	16^2	16^1	16^0
4096	256	16	1

EXAMPLE 7–25

Convert the following hexadecimal numbers to decimal:

(a) $E5_{16}$ **(b)** $B2F8_{16}$

Solution   A through F represent decimal numbers 10 through 15, respectively.

(a) $E5_{16} = (E \times 16) + (5 \times 1) = (14 \times 16) + (5 \times 1) = 224 + 5 = \mathbf{229}_{10}$

(b) $B2F8_{16} = (B \times 4096) + (2 \times 256) + (F \times 16) + (8 \times 1)$
$$= (11 \times 4096) + (2 \times 256) + (15 \times 16) + (8 \times 1)$$
$$= \quad 45{,}056 \quad + \quad 512 \quad + \quad 240 \quad + \quad 8 = \mathbf{45{,}816}_{10}$$

Related Problem   Convert $60A_{16}$ to decimal.

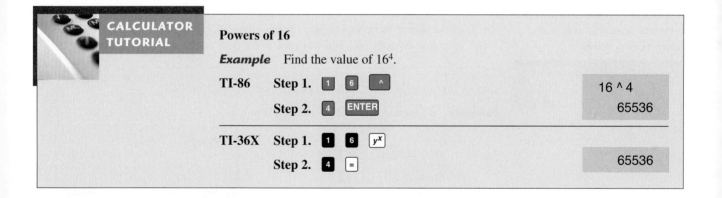

CALCULATOR TUTORIAL

Powers of 16

Example   Find the value of 16^4.

TI-86   **Step 1.** [1] [6] [^]   16 ^ 4

Step 2. [4] [ENTER]   65536

TI-36X   **Step 1.** [1] [6] [y^x]

Step 2. [4] [=]   65536

Decimal-to-Hexadecimal Conversion

Repeated division of a decimal number by 16 will produce the equivalent hexadecimal number, formed by the remainders of the divisions. The first remainder produced is the least significant digit (LSD). Each successive division by 16 yields a remainder that becomes a digit in the equivalent hexadecimal number. This procedure is similar to repeated division by 2 for decimal-to-binary conversion that was covered in Section 7–3. Example 7–26 illustrates the procedure. Note that when a quotient has a fractional part, the fractional part is multiplied by the divisor to get the remainder.

EXAMPLE 7–26

Convert the decimal number 650 to hexadecimal by repeated division by 16.

Solution

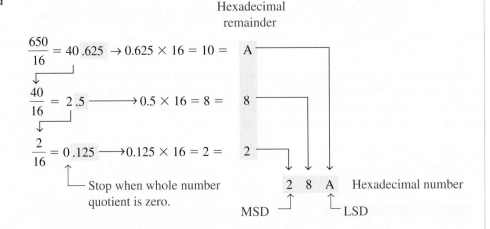

Hexadecimal remainder

$$\frac{650}{16} = 40\ .625 \rightarrow 0.625 \times 16 = 10 = \quad A$$

$$\frac{40}{16} = 2\ .5 \longrightarrow 0.5 \times 16 = 8 = \quad 8$$

$$\frac{2}{16} = 0\ .125 \longrightarrow 0.125 \times 16 = 2 = \quad 2$$

— Stop when whole number quotient is zero.

2 8 A   Hexadecimal number

MSD ↑   ↑ LSD

Related Problem   Convert decimal 2591 to hexadecimal.

Hexadecimal Addition

Addition can be done directly with hexadecimal numbers by remembering that the hexadecimal digits 0 through 9 are equivalent to decimal digits 0 through 9 and that hexadecimal digits A through F are equivalent to decimal numbers 10 through 15. When adding two hexadecimal numbers, use the following rules. (Decimal numbers are indicated by a subscript 10.)

1. In any given column of an addition problem, think of the two hexadecimal digits in terms of their decimal values. For instance, $5_{16} = 5_{10}$ and $C_{16} = 12_{10}$.

2. If the sum of these two digits is 15_{10} or less, bring down the corresponding hexadecimal digit.

A calculator can be used to perform arithmetic operations with hexadecimal numbers.

3. If the sum of these two digits is greater than 15_{10}, bring down the amount of the sum that exceeds 16_{10} and carry a 1 to the next column.

CALCULATOR TUTORIAL

Conversion of a Decimal Number to a Hexadecimal Number

Example   Convert decimal 650 to hexadecimal.

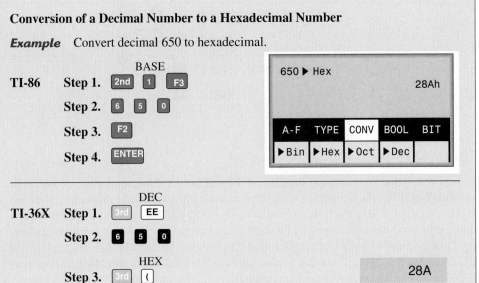

BASE

TI-86   **Step 1.** [2nd] [1] [F3]

Step 2. [6] [5] [0]

Step 3. [F2]

Step 4. [ENTER]

650 ▶ Hex

28Ah

A-F	TYPE	CONV	BOOL	BIT
▶Bin	▶Hex	▶Oct	▶Dec	

DEC

TI-36X   **Step 1.** [3rd] [EE]

Step 2. [6] [5] [0]

HEX

Step 3. [3rd] [(]

28A

EXAMPLE 7–27

Add the following hexadecimal numbers:

(a) $23_{16} + 16_{16}$ (b) $58_{16} + 22_{16}$ (c) $2B_{16} + 84_{16}$ (d) $DF_{16} + AC_{16}$

Solution   (a) 23_{16} right column: $3_{16} + 6_{16} = 3_{10} + 6_{10} = 9_{10} = 9_{16}$
             $\underline{+16_{16}}$ left column: $2_{16} + 1_{16} = 2_{10} + 1_{10} = 3_{10} = 3_{16}$
             $\mathbf{39}_{16}$

          (b) 58_{16} right column: $8_{16} + 2_{16} = 8_{10} + 2_{10} = 10_{10} = A_{16}$
             $\underline{+22_{16}}$ left column: $5_{16} + 2_{16} = 5_{10} + 2_{10} = 7_{10} = 7_{16}$
             $\mathbf{7A}_{16}$

          (c) $2B_{16}$ right column: $B_{16} + 4_{16} = 11_{10} + 4_{10} = 15_{10} = F_{16}$
             $\underline{+84_{16}}$ left column: $2_{16} + 8_{16} = 2_{10} + 8_{10} = 10_{10} = A_{16}$
             $\mathbf{AF}_{16}$

          (d) DF_{16} right column: $F_{16} + C_{16} = 15_{10} + 12_{10} = 27_{10}$
             $\underline{+AC_{16}}$ $27_{10} - 16_{10} = 11_{10} = B_{16}$ with a 1 carry
             $\mathbf{18B}_{16}$ left column: $D_{16} + A_{16} + 1_{16} = 13_{10} + 10_{10} + 1_{10} = 24_{10}$
                                    $24_{10} - 16_{10} = 8_{10} = 8_{16}$ with a 1 carry

Related Problem   Add $4C_{16}$ and $3A_{16}$.

Hexadecimal Subtraction

As you have learned, the 2's complement allows you to subtract by adding binary numbers. Since a hexadecimal number can be used to represent a binary number, it can also be used to represent the 2's complement of a binary number.

There are three ways to get the 2's complement of a hexadecimal number. Method 1 is the most common and easiest to use. Methods 2 and 3 are alternate methods.

Method 1.   Convert the hexadecimal number to binary. Take the 2's complement of the binary number. Convert the result to hexadecimal. This is illustrated in Figure 7–4.

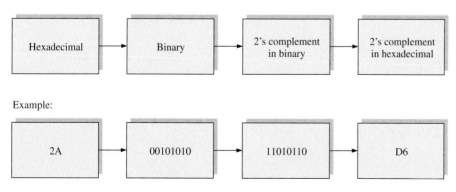

▲ **FIGURE 7–4**

Getting the 2's complement of a hexadecimal number, Method 1.

Method 2. Subtract the hexadecimal number from the maximum hexadecimal number and add 1. This is illustrated in Figure 7–5.

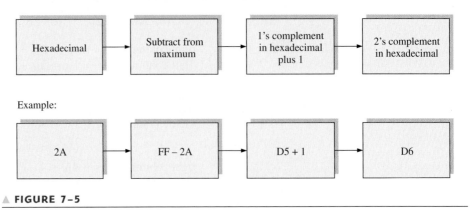

▲ **FIGURE 7–5**

Getting the 2's complement of a hexadecimal number, Method 2.

Method 3. Write the sequence of single hexadecimal digits. Write the sequence in reverse below the forward sequence. The 1's complement of each hex digit is the digit directly below it. Add 1 to the resulting number to get the 2's complement. This is illustrated in Figure 7–6.

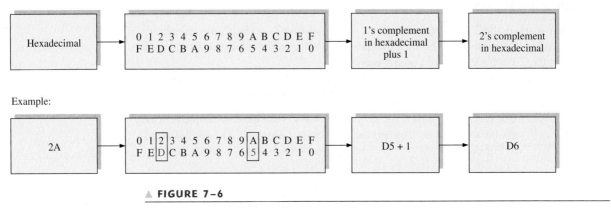

▲ **FIGURE 7–6**

Getting the 2's complement of a hexadecimal number, Method 3.

EXAMPLE 7–28

Subtract the following hexadecimal numbers:

(a) $84_{16} - 2A_{16}$ (b) $C3_{16} - 0B_{16}$

Solution   (a) $2A_{16} = 00101010$

$$\text{2's complement of } 2A_{16} = 11010110 = D6_{16} \quad \text{(using Method 1)}$$

$$
\begin{array}{r}
84_{16} \\
+ \; D6_{16} \quad \text{Add} \\
\hline
\cancel{1}5A_{16} \quad \text{Drop carry, as in 2's complement addition}
\end{array}
$$

The difference is **$5A_{16}$**.

(b) $0B_{16} = 00001011$

$$\text{2's complement of } 0B_{16} = 11110101 = F5_{16} \quad \text{(using Method 1)}$$

$$
\begin{array}{r}
C3_{16} \\
+ \; F5_{16} \quad \text{Add} \\
\hline
\cancel{1}B8_{16} \quad \text{Drop carry}
\end{array}
$$

The difference is **$B8_{16}$**.

Related Problem Subtract 173_{16} from BCD_{16}.

7–8 BINARY CODED DECIMAL (BCD)

Binary coded decimal (BCD) is a way to express each of the decimal digits with a binary code. There are only ten code groups in the BCD system, so it is very easy to convert between decimal and BCD. Because we like to read and write in decimal, the BCD code provides an excellent interface to binary systems. Examples of such interfaces are keypad inputs and digital readouts.

After completing this section, you should be able to

■ Convert each decimal digit to BCD

■ Express decimal numbers in BCD

■ Convert from BCD to decimal

■ Add BCD numbers

The 8421 Code

The 8421 code is a type of **BCD** (binary coded decimal) code. Binary coded decimal means that each decimal digit, 0 through 9, is represented by a binary code of four bits. The designation 8421 indicates the binary weights of the four bits (2^3, 2^2, 2^1, 2^0). The ease of conversion between 8421 code numbers and the familiar decimal numbers is the main advantage of this code. All you have to remember are the ten binary combinations that represent the ten decimal digits as shown in Table 7–4. The 8421 code is the predominant BCD code, and when we refer to BCD, we always mean the 8421 code unless otherwise stated.

In BCD, 4 bits represent each decimal digit.

◄ **TABLE 7–4**

Decimal/BCD conversion.

DECIMAL DIGIT	0	1	2	3	4	5	6	7	8	9
BCD	0000	0001	0010	0011	0100	0101	0110	0111	1000	1001

Invalid Codes You should realize that, with four bits, sixteen numbers (0000 through 1111) can be represented but that, in the 8421 code, only ten of these are used. The six code combinations that are not used—1010, 1011, 1100, 1101, 1110, and 1111—are invalid in the 8421 BCD code.

To express any decimal number in BCD, simply replace each decimal digit with the appropriate 4-bit code, as shown by Example 7–29.

EXAMPLE 7–29

Convert each of the following decimal numbers to BCD:

(a) 35   (b) 98   (c) 170   (d) 2469

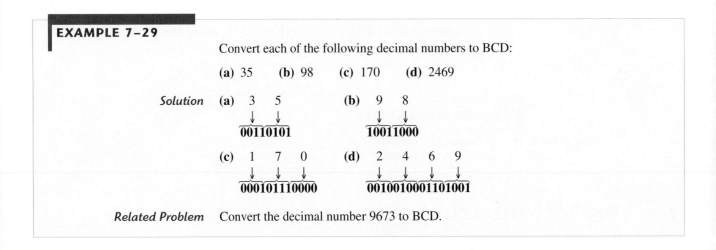

Solution

(a) 3 5
00110101

(b) 9 8
10011000

(c) 1 7 0
000101110000

(d) 2 4 6 9
0010010001101001

Related Problem Convert the decimal number 9673 to BCD.

It is equally easy to determine a decimal number from a BCD number. Start at the rightmost bit and break the code into groups of four bits. Then write the decimal digit represented by each 4-bit group.

EXAMPLE 7–30

Convert each of the following BCD codes to decimal:

(a) 10000110   (b) 001101010001   (c) 1001010001110000

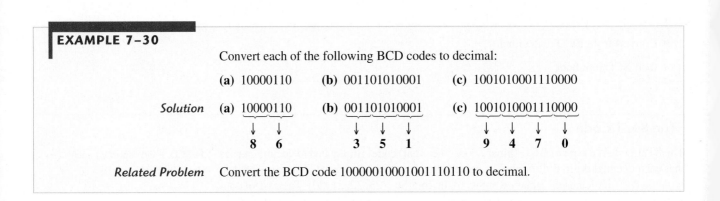

Solution

(a) 10000110
8 6

(b) 001101010001
3 5 1

(c) 1001010001110000
9 4 7 0

Related Problem Convert the BCD code 10000010001001110110 to decimal.

BCD Addition

BCD is a numerical code and can be used in arithmetic operations. Addition is the most important operation because the other three operations (subtraction, multiplication, and division) can be accomplished by the use of addition. Here is how to add two BCD numbers:

Step 1. Add the two BCD numbers, using the rules for binary addition in Section 7–3.

Step 2. If a 4-bit sum is equal to or less than 9, it is a valid BCD number.

Step 3. If a 4-bit sum is greater than 9, or if a carry out of the 4-bit group is generated, it is an invalid result. Add 6 (0110) to the 4-bit sum in order to skip the six invalid states and return the code to 8421. If a carry results when 6 is added, simply add the carry to the next 4-bit group.

Example 7–31 illustrates BCD additions in which the sum in each 4-bit column is equal to or less than 9, and the 4-bit sums are therefore valid BCD numbers. Example 7–32 illustrates the procedure in the case of invalid sums (greater than 9 or a carry).

EXAMPLE 7–31

Add the following BCD numbers:

(a) 0011 + 0100
(b) 00100011 + 00010101
(c) 10000110 + 00010011
(d) 010001010000 + 010000010111

Solution The decimal number additions are shown for comparison.

```
(a)   0011        3         (b)   0010  0011        23
    + 0100      + 4             + 0001  0101      + 15
     0111        7               0011  1000        38

(c)   1000  0110       86        (d)   0100  0101  0000       450
    + 0001  0011      + 13           + 0100  0001  0111     + 417
     1001  1001        99            1000  0110  0111       867
```

Note that in each case the sum in any 4-bit column does not exceed 9, and the results are valid BCD numbers.

Related Problem Add the BCD numbers: 1001000001000011 + 0000100100100101.

EXAMPLE 7–32

Add the following BCD numbers

(a) 1001 + 0100
(b) 1001 + 1001
(c) 00010110 + 00010101
(d) 01100111 + 01010011

Solution The decimal number additions are shown for comparison.

```
(a)        1001                                    9
         + 0100                                   +4
           1101      Invalid BCD number (>9)      13
         + 0110      Add 6
   0001    0011      Valid BCD number
     ↓       ↓
     1       3
```

(b)
```
        1001                          9
      + 1001                        + 9
   1    0010    Invalid because of carry    18
      + 0110    Add 6
 0001   1000    Valid BCD number
   ↓      ↓
   1      8
```

(c)
```
  0001    0110                              16
+ 0001    0101                            + 15
  0010    1011    Right group is invalid (>9),    31
                  left group is valid.
        + 0110    Add 6 to invalid code. Add
                    carry, 0001, to next group.
  0011    0001    Valid BCD number
    ↓       ↓
    3       1
```

(d)
```
        0110    0111                          67
      + 0101    0011                        + 53
        1011    1010    Both groups are invalid (>9)    120
      + 0110  + 0110    Add 6 to both groups
 0001   0010    0000    Valid BCD number
   ↓      ↓       ↓
   1      2       0
```

Related Problem Add the BCD numbers: 01001000 + 00110100.

7–9 DIGITAL CODES

Many specialized codes are used in digital systems. You have just learned about the BCD code; now let's look at a few others. Some codes are strictly numeric, like BCD, and others are alphanumeric; that is, they are used to represent numbers, letters, symbols, and instructions. The codes introduced in this section are the Gray code and the ASCII code.

After completing this section, you should be able to

- Explain the advantage of the Gray code
- Convert between Gray code and binary
- Use the ASCII code

The Gray Code

The single bit change characteristic of the Gray code minimizes the chance for error.

The **Gray code** is unweighted and is not an arithmetic code; that is, there are no specific weights assigned to the bit positions. The important feature of the Gray code is that *it exhibits only a single bit change from one code word to the next in sequence.* This property is important in many applications, such as shaft position encoders, where error susceptibility increases with the number of bit changes between adjacent numbers in a sequence.

Table 7–5 is a listing of the 4-bit Gray code for decimal numbers 0 through 15. Binary numbers are shown in the table for reference. Like binary numbers, *the Gray code can have*

DECIMAL	BINARY	GRAY CODE	DECIMAL	BINARY	GRAY CODE
0	0000	0000	8	1000	1100
1	0001	0001	9	1001	1101
2	0010	0011	10	1010	1111
3	0011	0010	11	1011	1110
4	0100	0110	12	1100	1010
5	0101	0111	13	1101	1011
6	0110	0101	14	1110	1001
7	0111	0100	15	1111	1000

any number of bits. Notice the single-bit change between successive Gray code words. For instance, in going from decimal 3 to decimal 4, the Gray code changes from 0010 to 0110, while the binary code changes from 0011 to 0100, a change of three bits. The only bit change is in the third bit from the right in the Gray code; the others remain the same.

Binary-to-Gray Code Conversion   Conversion between binary code and Gray code is sometimes useful. The following rules explain how to convert from a binary number to a Gray code word:

1. The most significant bit (left-most) in the Gray code is the same as the corresponding MSB in the binary number.

2. Going from left to right, add each adjacent pair of binary code bits to get the next Gray code bit. Discard carries.

For example, the conversion of the binary number 10110 to Gray code is as follows:

$$1 \; - + \rightarrow 0 \; - + \rightarrow 1 \; - + \rightarrow 1 \; - + \rightarrow 0 \qquad \text{Binary}$$
$$\downarrow \qquad \downarrow \qquad \downarrow \qquad \downarrow \qquad \downarrow$$
$$1 \qquad 1 \qquad 1 \qquad 0 \qquad 1 \qquad \text{Gray}$$

The Gray code is 11101.

Gray-to-Binary Conversion   To convert from Gray code to binary, use a similar method; however, there are some differences. The following rules apply:

1. The most significant bit (left-most) in the binary code is the same as the corresponding bit in the Gray code.

2. Add each binary code bit generated to the Gray code bit in the next adjacent position. Discard carries.

For example, the conversion of the Gray code word 11011 to binary is as follows:

$$1 \qquad 1 \qquad 0 \qquad 1 \qquad 1 \qquad \text{Gray}$$
$$\downarrow + \nearrow \; \downarrow + \nearrow \; \downarrow + \nearrow \; \downarrow + \nearrow \; \downarrow$$
$$1 \qquad 0 \qquad 0 \qquad 1 \qquad 0 \qquad \text{Binary}$$

The binary number is 10010.

EXAMPLE 7–33

(a) Convert the binary number 11000110 to Gray code.

(b) Convert the Gray code 10101111 to binary.

Solution   (a) Binary to Gray code:

$$1 \quad 1 \quad 0 \quad 0 \quad 0 \quad 1 \quad 1 \quad 0$$
$$\downarrow \quad \downarrow \quad \downarrow \quad \downarrow \quad \downarrow \quad \downarrow \quad \downarrow \quad \downarrow$$
$$1 \quad 0 \quad 1 \quad 0 \quad 0 \quad 1 \quad 0 \quad 1$$

(b) Gray code to binary:

$$1 \quad 0 \quad 1 \quad 0 \quad 1 \quad 1 \quad 1 \quad 1$$
$$1 \quad 1 \quad 0 \quad 0 \quad 1 \quad 0 \quad 1 \quad 0$$

Related Problem   (a) Convert binary 101101 to Gray code.   (b) Convert Gray code 100111 to binary.

An Application

A simplified diagram of a 3-bit shaft position encoder mechanism is shown in Figure 7–7. Basically, there are three concentric conductive rings that are segmented into eight sectors. The more sectors there are, the more accurately the position can be represented, but we are using only eight for purposes of illustration. Each sector of each ring is fixed at either a high-level or a low-level voltage to represent 1s and 0s. A 1 is indicated by a color sector and a 0 by a white sector. As the rings rotate with the shaft, they make contact with a brush arrangement that is in a fixed position and to which output lines are connected. As the shaft rotates counterclockwise through 360°, the eight sectors move past the three brushes producing a 3-bit binary output that indicates the shaft position.

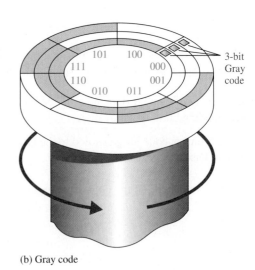

(a) Binary   (b) Gray code

▲ **FIGURE 7–7**

A simplified illustration of how the Gray code solves the error problem in shaft position encoders.

In Figure 7–7(a), the sectors are arranged in a straight binary pattern, so that the brushes go from 000 to 001 to 010 to 011, and so on. When the brushes are on color sectors, they output a 1 and when on white sectors, they output a 0. If one brush is slightly ahead of the others during the transition from one sector to the next, an erroneous output can occur. Consider what happens when the brushes are on the 111 sector and about to enter the 000 sector. If the MSB brush is slightly ahead, the position would be incorrectly indicated by a transitional 011 instead of a 111 or a 000. In this type of application, it is virtually impossible to maintain precise mechanical alignment of all the brushes; therefore, some error will always occur at many of the transitions between sectors.

The Gray code is used to eliminate the error problem which is inherent in the binary code. As shown in Figure 7–7(b), the Gray code assures that only one bit will change between adjacent sectors. This means that even though the brushes may not be in precise alignment, there will never be a transitional error. For example, let's again consider what happens when the brushes are on the 111 sector and about to move into the next sector, 101. The only two possible outputs during the transition are 111 and 101, no matter how the brushes are aligned. A similar situation occurs at the transitions between each of the other sectors.

Alphanumeric Codes

In order to communicate, you need not only numbers, but also letters and other symbols. In the strictest sense, **alphanumeric** codes are codes that represent numbers and alphabetic characters (letters). Most such codes, however, also represent other characters such as symbols and various instructions necessary for conveying information.

At a minimum, an alphanumeric code must represent 10 decimal digits and 26 letters of the alphabet, for a total of 36 items. This number requires six bits in each code combination because five bits are insufficient ($2^5 = 32$). There are 64 total combinations of six bits, so there are 28 unused code combinations. Obviously, in many applications, symbols other than just numbers and letters are necessary to communicate completely. You need spaces, periods, colons, semicolons, question marks, etc. You also need instructions to tell the receiving system what to do with the information. With codes that are six bits long, you can handle decimal numbers, the alphabet, and 28 other symbols. This should give you an idea of the requirements for a basic alphanumeric code. The ASCII is the most common alphanumeric code and is covered next.

ASCII

ASCII is the abbreviation for American Standard Code for Information Interchange. Pronounced "askee," ASCII is a universally accepted alphanumeric code used in most computers and other electronic equipment. Most computer keyboards are standardized with the ASCII. When you enter a letter, a number, or control command, the corresponding ASCII code goes into the computer.

ASCII has 128 characters and symbols represented by a 7-bit binary code. Actually, ASCII can be considered an 8-bit code with the MSB always 0. This 8-bit code is 00 through 7F in hexadecimal. The first thirty-two ASCII characters are nongraphic commands that are never printed or displayed and are used only for control purposes. Examples of the control characters are "null," "line feed," "start of text," and "escape." The other characters are graphic symbols that can be printed or displayed and include the letters of the alphabet (lowercase and uppercase), the ten decimal digits, punctuation signs and other commonly used symbols.

Table 7–6 is a listing of the ASCII code showing the decimal, hexadecimal, and binary representations for each character and symbol. The left section of the table lists the names of the 32 control characters (00 through 1F hexadecimal). The graphic symbols are listed in the rest of the table (20 through 7F hexadecimal).

COMPUTER NOTE

A computer keyboard has a dedicated microprocessor that constantly scans keyboard circuits to detect when a key has been pressed and released. A unique scan code is produced by computer software representing that particular key. The scan code is then converted to an alphanumeric code (ASCII) for use by the computer.

▼ TABLE 7-6

American Standard Code for Information Interchange (ASCII).

CONTROL CHARACTERS				GRAPHIC SYMBOLS											
NAME	DEC	BINARY	HEX	SYMBOL	DEC	BINARY	HEX	SYMBOL	DEC	BINARY	HEX	SYMBOL	DEC	BINARY	HEX
NUL	0	0000000	00	space	32	0100000	20	@	64	1000000	40	`	96	1100000	60
SOH	1	0000001	01	!	33	0100001	21	A	65	1000001	41	a	97	1100001	61
STX	2	0000010	02	"	34	0100010	22	B	66	1000010	42	b	98	1100010	62
ETX	3	0000011	03	#	35	0100011	23	C	67	1000011	43	c	99	1100011	63
EOT	4	0000100	04	$	36	0100100	24	D	68	1000100	44	d	100	1100100	64
ENQ	5	0000101	05	%	37	0100101	25	E	69	1000101	45	e	101	1100101	65
ACK	6	0000110	06	&	38	0100110	26	F	70	1000110	46	f	102	1100110	66
BEL	7	0000111	07	'	39	0100111	27	G	71	1000111	47	g	103	1100111	67
BS	8	0001000	08	(	40	0101000	28	H	72	1001000	48	h	104	1101000	68
HT	9	0001001	09	)	41	0101001	29	I	73	1001001	49	i	105	1101001	69
LF	10	0001010	0A	*	42	0101010	2A	J	74	1001010	4A	j	106	1101010	6A
VT	11	0001011	0B	+	43	0101011	2B	K	75	1001011	4B	k	107	1101011	6B
FF	12	0001100	0C	,	44	0101100	2C	L	76	1001100	4C	l	108	1101100	6C
CR	13	0001101	0D	-	45	0101101	2D	M	77	1001101	4D	m	109	1101101	6D
SO	14	0001110	0E	.	46	0101110	2E	N	78	1001110	4E	n	110	1101110	6E
SI	15	0001111	0F	/	47	0101111	2F	O	79	1001111	4F	o	111	1101111	6F
DLE	16	0010000	10	0	48	0110000	30	P	80	1010000	50	p	112	1110000	70
DC1	17	0010001	11	1	49	0110001	31	Q	81	1010001	51	q	113	1110001	71
DC2	18	0010010	12	2	50	0110010	32	R	82	1010010	52	r	114	1110010	72
DC3	19	0010011	13	3	51	0110011	33	S	83	1010011	53	s	115	1110011	73
DC4	20	0010100	14	4	52	0110100	34	T	84	1010100	54	t	116	1110100	74
NAK	21	0010101	15	5	53	0110101	35	U	85	1010101	55	u	117	1110101	75
SYN	22	0010110	16	6	54	0110110	36	V	86	1010110	56	v	118	1110110	76
ETB	23	0010111	17	7	55	0110111	37	W	87	1010111	57	w	119	1110111	77
CAN	24	0011000	18	8	56	0111000	38	X	88	1011000	58	x	120	1111000	78
EM	25	0011001	19	9	57	0111001	39	Y	89	1011001	59	y	121	1111001	79
SUB	26	0011010	1A	:	58	0111010	3A	Z	90	1011010	5A	z	122	1111010	7A
ESC	27	0011011	1B	;	59	0111011	3B	[	91	1011011	5B	{	123	1111011	7B
FS	28	0011100	1C	<	60	0111100	3C	\	92	1011100	5C			124	1111100	7C
GS	29	0011101	1D	=	61	0111101	3D	]	93	1011101	5D	}	125	1111101	7D
RS	30	0011110	1E	>	62	0111110	3E	^	94	1011110	5E	~	126	1111110	7E
US	31	0011111	1F	?	63	0111111	3F	_	95	1011111	5F	Del	127	1111111	7F

EXAMPLE 7-34

Determine the binary ASCII codes that are entered from the computer's keyboard when the following BASIC program statement is typed in. Also express each code in hexadecimal.

20 PRINT "A=";X

Solution   The ASCII code for each symbol is found in Table 7–7.

Symbol	Binary	Hexadecimal
2	0110010	32_{16}
0	0110000	30_{16}
Space	0100000	20_{16}
P	1010000	50_{16}
R	1010010	52_{16}
I	1001001	49_{16}
N	1001110	$4E_{16}$
T	1010100	54_{16}
Space	0100000	20_{16}
"	0100010	22_{16}
A	1000001	41_{16}
=	0111101	$3D_{16}$
"	0100010	22_{16}
;	0111011	$3B_{16}$
X	1011000	58_{16}

Related Problem   Determine the sequence of ASCII codes required for the following program statement and express them in hexadecimal:

80 INPUT Y

The ASCII Control Characters   The first thirty-two codes in the ASCII table (Table 7–6) represent the control characters. These are used to allow devices such as a computer and printer to communicate with each other when passing information and data. Table 7–7 lists the control characters and the control key function that allows them to be entered directly from an ASCII keyboard by pressing the control key (CTRL) and the corresponding symbol. A brief description of each control character is also given.

Extended ASCII Characters

In addition to the 128 standard ASCII characters, there are an additional 128 characters that were adopted by IBM for use in their PCs (personal computers). Because of the popularity of the PC, these particular extended ASCII characters are also used in applications other than PCs and have become essentially an unofficial standard.

The extended ASCII characters are represented by an 8-bit code series from hexadecimal 80 to hexadecimal FF.

▶ **TABLE 7-7**

ASCII control characters.

NAME	DECIMAL	HEX	KEY	DESCRIPTION
NUL	0	00	CTRL @	null character
SOH	1	01	CTRL A	start of header
STX	2	02	CTRL B	start of text
ETX	3	03	CTRL C	end of text
EOT	4	04	CTRL D	end of transmission
ENQ	5	05	CTRL E	enquire
ACK	6	06	CTRL F	acknowledge
BEL	7	07	CTRL G	bell
BS	8	08	CTRL H	backspace
HT	9	09	CTRL I	horizontal tab
LF	10	0A	CTRL J	line feed
VT	11	0B	CTRL K	vertical tab
FF	12	0C	CTRL L	form feed (new page)
CR	13	0D	CTRL M	carriage return
SO	14	0E	CTRL N	shift out
SI	15	0F	CTRL O	shift in
DLE	16	10	CTRL P	data link escape
DC1	17	11	CTRL Q	device control 1
DC2	18	12	CTRL R	device control 2
DC3	19	13	CTRL S	device control 3
DC4	20	14	CTRL T	device control 4
NAK	21	15	CTRL U	negative acknowledge
SYN	22	16	CTRL V	synchronize
ETB	23	17	CTRL W	end of transmission block
CAN	24	18	CTRL X	cancel
EM	25	19	CTRL Y	end of medium
SUB	26	1A	CTRL Z	substitute
ESC	27	1B	CTRL [	escape
FS	28	1C	CTRL /	file separator
GS	29	1D	CTRL]	group separator
RS	30	1E	CTRL ^	record separator
US	31	1F	CTRL _	unit separator

The extended ASCII contains characters in the following general categories:

1. Foreign (non-English) alphabetic characters

2. Foreign currency symbols

3. Greek letters

4. Mathematical symbols

5. Drawing characters

6. Bar graphing characters

7. Shading characters

Table 7–8 is a list of the extended ASCII character set with the decimal and hexadecimal representations.

▼ **TABLE 7–8**

Extended ASCII characters.

SYMBOL	DEC	HEX	SYMBOL	DEC	HEX	SYMBOL	DEC	HEX	SYMBOL	DEC	HEX
Ç	128	80	á	160	A0	∟	192	C0	α	224	E0
ü	129	81	í	161	A1	⊥	193	C1	β	225	E1
é	130	82	ó	162	A2	⊤	194	C2	Γ	226	E2
â	131	83	ú	163	A3	├	195	C3	π	227	E3
ä	132	84	ñ	164	A4	─	196	C4	Σ	228	E4
à	133	85	Ñ	165	A5	┼	197	C5	σ	229	E5
å	134	86	ª	166	A6	╞	198	C6	μ	230	E6
ç	135	87	º	167	A7	╟	199	C7	τ	231	E7
ê	136	88	¿	168	A8	╚	200	C8	Φ	232	E8
ë	137	89	⌐	169	A9	╔	201	C9	Θ	233	E9
è	138	8A	¬	170	AA	╩	202	CA	Ω	234	EA
ï	139	8B	½	171	AB	╦	203	CB	δ	235	EB
î	140	8C	¼	172	AC	╠	204	CC	∞	236	EC
ì	141	8D	¡	173	AD	═	205	CD	φ	237	ED
Ä	142	8E	«	174	AE	╬	206	CE	ε	238	EE
Å	143	8F	»	175	AF	╧	207	CF	∩	239	EF
É	144	90	░	176	B0	╨	208	D0	≡	240	F0
æ	145	91	▒	177	B1	╤	209	D1	±	241	F1
Æ	146	92	▓	178	B2	╥	210	D2	≥	242	F2
ô	147	93	│	179	B3	╙	211	D3	≤	243	F3
ö	148	94	┤	180	B4	╘	212	D4	⌠	244	F4
ò	149	95	╡	181	B5	╒	213	D5	⌡	245	F5
û	150	96	╢	182	B6	╓	214	D6	÷	246	F6
ù	151	97	╖	183	B7	╫	215	D7	≈	247	F7
ÿ	152	98	╕	184	B8	╪	216	D8	°	248	F8
Ö	153	99	╣	185	B9	┘	217	D9	•	249	F9
Ü	154	9A	║	186	BA	┌	218	DA	·	250	FA
¢	155	9B	╗	187	BB	█	219	DB	√	251	FB
£	156	9C	╝	188	BC	▄	220	DC	η	252	FC
¥	157	9D	╜	189	BD	▌	221	DD	²	253	FD
Pτ	158	9E	╛	190	BE	▐	222	DE	■	254	FE
ƒ	159	9F	┐	191	BF	▀	223	DF	□	255	FF

SUMMARY

- A binary number is a weighted number in which the weight of each whole number digit is a positive power of two and the weight of each fractional digit is a negative power of two. The whole number weights increase from right to left—from least significant digit to most significant.
- A binary number can be converted to a decimal number by summing the decimal values of the weights of all the 1s in the binary number.

- The basic rules for binary addition are as follows:

  $$0 + 0 = 0$$
  $$0 + 1 = 1$$
  $$1 + 0 = 1$$
  $$1 + 1 = 10$$

- The basic rules for binary subtraction are as follows:

  $$0 - 0 = 0$$
  $$1 - 1 = 0$$
  $$1 - 0 = 1$$
  $$10 - 1 = 1$$

- The 1's complement of a binary number is derived by changing 1s to 0s and 0s to 1s.
- The 2's complement of a binary number can be derived by adding 1 to the 1's complement.
- Binary subtraction can be accomplished with addition by using the 1's or 2's complement method.
- A positive binary number is represented by a 0 sign bit.
- A negative binary number is represented by a 1 sign bit.
- For arithmetic operations, negative binary numbers are represented in 1's complement or 2's complement form.
- In an addition operation, an overflow is possible when both numbers are positive or when both numbers are negative. An incorrect sign bit in the sum indicates the occurrence of an overflow.
- The hexadecimal number system consists of 16 digits and characters, 0 through 9 followed by A through F.
- One hexadecimal digit represents a 4-bit binary number, and its primary usefulness is in simplifying bit patterns and making them easier to read.
- A decimal number can be converted to hexadecimal by the repeated division-by-16 method.
- A decimal number is converted to BCD by replacing each decimal digit with the appropriate 4-bit binary code.
- The ASCII is a 7-bit alphanumeric code that is widely used in computer systems for input and output of information.

KEY TERMS

Alphanumeric Consisting of numerals, letters, and other characters.

ASCII American Standard Code for Information Interchange; the most widely used alphanumeric code.

BCD Binary coded decimal; a digital code in which each of the decimal digits, 0 through 9, is represented by a group of four bits.

Byte A group of eight bits.

Hexadecimal Describes a number system with a base of 16.

LSB Least significant bit; the right-most bit in a binary whole number or code.

MSB Most significant bit; the left-most bit in a binary whole number or code.

Answers are at the end of the chapter.

1. $2 \times 10^1 + 8 \times 10^0$ is equal to
   (a) 10   (b) 280   (c) 2.8   (d) 28
2. The binary number 1101 is equal to the decimal number
   (a) 13   (b) 49   (c) 11   (d) 3
3. The binary number 11011101 is equal to the decimal number
   (a) 121   (b) 221   (c) 441   (d) 256
4. The decimal number 17 is equal to the binary number
   (a) 10010   (b) 11000   (c) 10001   (d) 01001
5. The decimal number 175 is equal to the binary number
   (a) 11001111   (b) 10101110   (c) 10101111   (d) 11101111
6. The sum of 11010 + 01111 equals
   (a) 101001   (b) 101010   (c) 110101   (d) 101000
7. The difference of 110 − 010 equals
   (a) 001   (b) 010   (c) 101   (d) 100
8. The 1's complement of 10111001 is
   (a) 01000111   (b) 01000110   (c) 11000110   (d) 10101010
9. The 2's complement of 11001000 is
   (a) 00110111   (b) 00110001   (c) 01001000   (d) 00111000
10. The decimal number +122 is expressed in the 2's complement form as
    (a) 01111010   (b) 11111010   (c) 01000101   (d) 10000101
11. The decimal number −34 is expressed in the 2's complement form as
    (a) 01011110   (b) 10100010   (c) 11011110   (d) 01011101
12. A single-precision floating-point binary number has a total of
    (a) 8 bits   (b) 16 bits   (c) 24 bits   (d) 32 bits
13. In the 2's complement form, the binary number 10010011 is equal to the decimal number
    (a) −19   (b) +109   (c) +91   (d) −109
14. The binary number 100011010100011010111 can be written in hexadecimal as
    (a) $AD467_{16}$ (b) $8C46F_{16}$ (c) $8D46F_{16}$ (d) $AE46F_{16}$
15. The binary number for $F7A9_{16}$ is
    (a) 1111011110101001   (b) 1110111110101001
    (c) 1111111010110001   (d) 1111011010101001
16. The BCD number for decimal 473 is
    (a) 111011010   (b) 110001110011   (c) 010001110011   (d) 010011110011

PROBLEMS

SECTION 7–1 Decimal Numbers

1. What is the weight of the digit 6 in each of the following decimal numbers?
   (a) 1386   (b) 54,692   (c) 671,920
2. Express each of the following decimal numbers as a power of ten:
   (a) 10   (b) 100   (c) 10,000   (d) 1,000,000
3. Give the value of each digit in the following decimal numbers:
   (a) 471   (b) 9356   (c) 125,000
4. How high can you count with four decimal digits?

SECTION 7-2   **Binary Numbers**

5. Convert the following binary numbers to decimal:

   (a) 11   **(b)** 100   **(c)** 111   **(d)** 1000

   (e) 1001   **(f)** 1100   **(g)** 1011   **(h)** 1111

6. Convert the following binary numbers to decimal:

   (a) 1110   **(b)** 1010   **(c)** 11100   **(d)** 10000

   (e) 10101   **(f)** 11101   **(g)** 10111   **(h)** 11111

7. Convert each binary number to decimal:

   (a) 110011.11   **(b)** 101010.01   **(c)** 1000001.111

   (d) 1111000.101   **(e)** 1011100.10101   **(f)** 1110001.0001

   (g) 1011010.1010   **(h)** 1111111.11111

8. What is the highest decimal number that can be represented by each of the following numbers of binary digits (bits)?

   (a) two   **(b)** three   **(c)** four   **(d)** five   **(e)** six

   (f) seven   **(g)** eight   **(h)** nine   **(i)** ten   **(j)** eleven

9. How many bits are required to represent the following decimal numbers?

   (a) 17   **(b)** 35   **(c)** 49   **(d)** 68

   (e) 81   **(f)** 114   **(g)** 132   **(h)** 205

10. Generate the binary sequence for each decimal sequence:

    (a) 0 through 7   **(b)** 8 through 15   **(c)** 16 through 31

    (d) 32 through 63   **(e)** 64 through 75

SECTION 7-3   **Binary Arithmetic**

11. Add the binary numbers:

    (a) 11 + 01   **(b)** 10 + 10   **(c)** 101 + 11

    (d) 111 + 110   **(e)** 1001 + 101   **(f)** 1101 + 1011

12. Use direct subtraction on the following binary numbers:

    (a) 11 − 1   **(b)** 101 − 100   **(c)** 110 − 101

    (d) 1110 − 11   **(e)** 1100 − 1001   **(f)** 11010 − 10111

13. Perform the following binary multiplications:

    (a) 11 × 11   **(b)** 100 × 10   **(c)** 111 × 101

    (d) 1001 × 110   **(e)** 1101 × 1101   **(f)** 1110 × 1101

14. Divide the binary numbers as indicated:

    (a) 100 ÷ 10   **(b)** 1001 ÷ 11   **(c)** 1100 ÷ 100

SECTION 7-4   **1's and 2's Complements of Binary Numbers**

15. Determine the 1's complement of each binary number:

    (a) 101   **(b)** 110   **(c)** 1010

    (d) 11010111   **(e)** 1110101   **(f)** 00001

16. Determine the 2's complement of each binary number using either method:

    (a) 10   **(b)** 111   **(c)** 1001   **(d)** 1101

    (e) 11100   **(f)** 10011   **(g)** 10110000   **(h)** 00111101

SECTION 7-5   **Signed Numbers**

17. Express each decimal number in binary as an 8-bit sign-magnitude number:

    (a) +29   **(b)** −85   **(c)** +100   **(d)** −123

18. Express each decimal number as an 8-bit number in the 1's complement form:

    (a) −34   **(b)** +57   **(c)** −99   **(d)** +115

19. Express each decimal number as an 8-bit number in the 2's complement form:

    (a) $+12$ **(b)** -68 **(c)** $+101$ **(d)** -125

20. Determine the decimal value of each signed binary number in the sign-magnitude form:

    (a) 10011001   **(b)** 01110100   **(c)** 10111111

21. Determine the decimal value of each signed binary number in the 1's complement form:

    (a) 10011001   **(b)** 01110100   **(c)** 10111111

22. Determine the decimal value of each signed binary number in the 2's complement form:

    (a) 10011001   **(b)** 01110100   **(c)** 10111111

23. Express each of the following sign-magnitude binary numbers in single-precision floating-point format:

    (a) 0111110000101011   **(b)** 100110000011000

24. Determine the values of the following single-precision floating-point numbers:

    (a) 1 10000001 01001001110001000000000

    (b) 0 11001100 10000111110100100000000

SECTION 7–6   **Arithmetic Operations with Signed Numbers**

25. Convert each pair of decimal numbers to binary and add using the 2's complement form:

    (a) 33 and 15   **(b)** 56 and -27 **(c)** -46 and 25   **(d)** -110 and -84

26. Perform each addition in the 2's complement form:

    (a) 00010110 + 00110011   **(b)** 01110000 + 10101111

27. Perform each addition in the 2's complement form:

    (a) 10001100 + 00111001   **(b)** 11011001 + 11100111

28. Perform each subtraction in the 2's complement form:

    (a) 00110011 − 00010000   **(b)** 01100101 − 11101000

29. Multiply 01101010 by 11110001 in the 2's complement form.

30. Divide 01000100 by 00011001 in the 2's complement form.

SECTION 7–7   **Hexadecimal Numbers**

31. Convert each hexadecimal number to binary:

    (a) 38_{16} **(b)** 59_{16} **(c)** $A14_{16}$ **(d)** $5C8_{16}$

    (e) 4100_{16} **(f)** $FB17_{16}$ **(g)** $8A9D_{16}$

32. Convert each binary number to hexadecimal:

    (a) 1110   **(b)** 10   **(c)** 10111

    (d) 10100110   **(e)** 1111110000   **(f)** 100110000010

33. Convert each hexadecimal number to decimal:

    (a) 23_{16} **(b)** 92_{16} **(c)** $1A_{16}$ **(d)** $8D_{16}$

    (e) $F3_{16}$ **(f)** EB_{16} **(g)** $5C2_{16}$ **(h)** 700_{16}

34. Convert each decimal number to hexadecimal:

    (a) 8   **(b)** 14   **(c)** 33   **(d)** 52

    (e) 284   **(f)** 2890   **(g)** 4019   **(h)** 6500

35. Perform the following additions:

    (a) $37_{16} + 29_{16}$ **(b)** $A0_{16} + 6B_{16}$ **(c)** $FF_{16} + BB_{16}$

36. Perform the following subtractions:

    (a) $51_{16} - 40_{16}$ **(b)** $C8_{16} - 3A_{16}$ **(c)** $FD_{16} - 88_{16}$

SECTION 7–8 **Binary Coded Decimal (BCD)**

37. Convert each of the following decimal numbers to 8421 BCD:

    (a) 10   (b) 13   (c) 18   (d) 21   (e) 25   (f) 36

    (g) 44   (h) 57   (i) 69   (j) 98   (k) 125   (l) 156

38. Convert each of the decimal numbers in Problem 45 to straight binary, and compare the number of bits required with that required for BCD.

39. Convert the following decimal numbers to BCD:

    (a) 104   (b) 128   (c) 132   (d) 150   (e) 186

    (f) 210   (g) 359   (h) 547   (i) 1051

40. Convert each of the BCD numbers to decimal:

    (a) 0001   (b) 0110   (c) 1001

    (d) 00011000   (e) 00011001   (f) 00110010

    (g) 01000101   (h) 10011000   (i) 100001110000

41. Convert each of the BCD numbers to decimal:

    (a) 10000000   (b) 001000110111

    (c) 001101000110   (d) 010000100001

    (e) 011101010100   (f) 100000000000

    (g) 100101111000   (h) 0001011010000011

    (i) 1001000000011000   (j) 0110011001100111

42. Add the following BCD numbers:

    (a) 0010 + 0001   (b) 0101 + 0011

    (c) 0111 + 0010   (d) 1000 + 0001

    (e) 00011000 + 00010001   (f) 01100100 + 00110011

    (g) 01000000 + 01000111   (h) 10000101 + 00010011

43. Add the following BCD numbers:

    (a) 1000 + 0110   (b) 0111 + 0101

    (c) 1001 + 1000   (d) 1001 + 0111

    (e) 00100101 + 00100111   (f) 01010001 + 01011000

    (g) 10011000 + 10010111   (h) 010101100001 + 011100001000

44. Convert each pair of decimal numbers to BCD, and add as indicated:

    (a) 4 + 3   (b) 5 + 2   (c) 6 + 4   (d) 17 + 12

    (e) 28 + 23   (f) 65 + 58   (g) 113 + 101   (h) 295 + 157

SECTION 7–9 **Digital Codes**

45. In a certain application a 4-bit binary sequence cycles from 1111 to 0000 periodically. There are four bit changes, and because of circuit delays, these changes may not occur at the same instant. For example, if the LSB changes first, the number will appear as 1110 during the transition from 1111 to 0000 and may be misinterpreted by the system. Illustrate how the Gray code avoids this problem.

46. Convert each binary number to Gray code:

    (a) 11011   (b) 1001010   (c) 1111011101110

47. Convert each Gray code to binary:

    (a) 1010   (b) 00010   (c) 11000010001

48. Convert each of the following decimal numbers to ASCII. Refer to Table 7–7.

    (a) 1   (b) 3   (c) 6   (d) 10   (e) 18

    (f) 29   (g) 56   (h) 75   (i) 107

49. Determine each ASCII character. Refer to Table 7–7.

    (a) 0011000   **(b)** 1001010   **(c)** 0111101

    (d) 0100011   **(e)** 0111110   **(f)** 1000010

50. Decode the following ASCII coded message:

    1001000 1100101 1101100 1101100 1101111 0101110
    0100000 1001000 1101111 1110111 0100000 1100001
    1110010 1100101 0100000 1111001 1101111 1110101
    0111111

51. Write the message in Problem 58 in hexadecimal.

52. Convert the following computer program statement to ASCII:

    30 INPUT A, B

ANSWERS

SELF-TEST

1. (d)   **2.** (a)   **3.** (b)   **4.** (c)   **5.** (c)   **6.** (a)   **7.** (d)   **8.** (b)

9. (d)   **10.** (a)   **11.** (c)   **12.** (d)   **13.** (d)   **14.** (c)   **15.** (a)   **16.** (c)

8

LOGIC GATES

INTRODUCTION

The emphasis in this chapter is on the operation, application, and troubleshooting of logic gates. The relationship of input and output waveforms of a gate using timing diagrams is thoroughly covered.

Logic symbols used to represent the logic gates are in accordance with ANSI/IEEE Standard 91-1984. This standard has been adopted by private industry and the military for use in internal documentation as well as published literature.

Both programmable logic and fixed-function logic are discussed in this chapter. Because integrated circuits (ICs) are used in all applications, the logic function of a device is generally of greater importance to the technician or technologist than the details of the component-level circuit operation within the IC package. Therefore, detailed coverage of the devices at the component level can be treated as an optional topic.

CHAPTER OBJECTIVES

■ Describe the operation of the inverter, the AND gate, and the OR gate

■ Describe the operation of the NAND gate and the NOR gate

■ Express the operation of NOT, AND, OR, NAND, and NOR gates with Boolean algebra

■ Describe the operation of the exclusive-OR and exclusive-NOR gates

■ Recognize and use both the distinctive shape logic gate symbols and the rectangular outline logic gate symbols of ANSI/IEEE Standard 91-1984

■ Construct timing diagrams showing the proper time relationships of inputs and outputs for the various logic gates

■ Discuss the basic concepts of programmable logic

■ Make basic comparisons between the major IC technologies—CMOS and TTL

■ Explain how the different series within the CMOS and TTL families differ from each other

■ Define *propagation delay time, power dissipation, speed-power product,* and *fan-out* in relation to logic gates

■ List specific fixed-function integrated circuit devices that contain the various logic gates

■ Use each logic gate in simple applications

■ Troubleshoot logic gates for opens and shorts by using the oscilloscope

CHAPTER OUTLINE

KEY TERMS

- Inverter
- Truth table
- Timing diagram
- Boolean algebra
- Complement
- AND gate
- Enable
- OR gate
- NAND gate
- NOR gate
- Exclusive-OR gate
- Exclusive-NOR gate
- AND array
- Fuse
- Antifuse
- EPROM
- EEPROM
- SRAM
- Target device
- JTAG
- CMOS
- TTL
- Propagation delay time
- Fan-out
- Unit load

FIXED-FUNCTION LOGIC DEVICES

(CMOS AND TTL SERIES)

74XX00	74XX02	74XX04
74XX08	74XX10	74XX11
74XX20	74XX21	74XX27
74XX30	74XX32	74XX86
74XX266		

WWW. VISIT THE COMPANION WEBSITE

Study aids for this chapter are available at
http://www.prenhall.com/floyd

8–1   THE INVERTER

The inverter (NOT circuit) performs the operation called *inversion* or *complementation.* The inverter changes one logic level to the opposite level. In terms of bits, it changes a 1 to a 0 and a 0 to a 1.

After completing this section, you should be able to

- Identify negation and polarity indicators
- Identify an inverter by either its distinctive shape symbol or its rectangular outline symbol
- Produce the truth table for an inverter
- Describe the logical operation of an inverter

Standard logic symbols for the **inverter** are shown in Figure 8–1. Part (a) shows the *distinctive shape* symbols, and part (b) shows the *rectangular outline* symbols. In this textbook, distinctive shape symbols are generally used; however, the rectangular outline symbols are found in many industry publications, and you should become familiar with them as well. (Logic symbols are in accordance with **ANSI/IEEE** Standard 91-1984.)

▷ **FIGURE 8–1**

Standard logic symbols for the inverter (ANSI/IEEE Std. 91-1984).

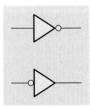

(a) Distinctive shape symbols with negation indicators

(b) Rectangular outline symbols with polarity indicators

The Negation and Polarity Indicators

The negation indicator is a "bubble" (○) that indicates **inversion** or *complementation* when it appears on the input or output of any logic element, as shown in Figure 8–1(a) for the inverter. Generally, inputs are on the left of a logic symbol and the output is on the right. When appearing on the input, the bubble means that a 0 is the active or *asserted* input state, and the input is called an active-LOW input. When appearing on the output, the bubble means that a 0 is the active or asserted output state, and the output is called an active-LOW output. The absence of a bubble on the input or output means that a 1 is the active or asserted state, and in this case, the input or output is called active-HIGH.

The polarity or level indicator is a "triangle" (◣) that indicates inversion when it appears on the input or output of a logic element, as shown in Figure 8–1(b). When appearing on the input, it means that a LOW level is the active or asserted input state. When appearing on the output, it means that a LOW level is the active or asserted output state.

Either indicator (bubble or triangle) can be used both on distinctive shape symbols and on rectangular outline symbols. Figure 8–1(a) indicates the principal inverter symbols used in this text. Note that a change in the placement of the negation or polarity indicator does not imply a change in the way an inverter operates.

Inverter Truth Table

When a HIGH level is applied to an inverter input, a LOW level will appear on its output. When a LOW level is applied to its input, a HIGH will appear on its output. This operation is summarized in Table 8–1, which shows the output for each possible input in terms of levels and corresponding bits. A table such as this is called a **truth table.**

Inverter Operation

Figure 8–2 shows the output of an inverter for a pulse input, where t_1 and t_2 indicate the corresponding points on the input and output pulse waveforms.

When the input is LOW, the output is HIGH; when the input is HIGH, the output is LOW, thereby producing an inverted output pulse.

▼ **TABLE 8–1**

Inverter truth table.

INPUT	OUTPUT
LOW (0)	HIGH (1)
HIGH (1)	LOW (0)

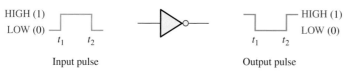

▲ **FIGURE 8–2**

Inverter operation with a pulse input.

Timing Diagrams

A **timing diagram** is basically a graph that accurately displays the relationship of two or more waveforms with respect to each other on a time basis. For example, the time relationship of the output pulse to the input pulse in Figure 8–2 can be shown with a simple timing diagram by aligning the two pulses so that the occurrences of the pulse edges appear in the proper time relationship. The rising edge of the input pulse and the falling edge of the output pulse occur at the same time (ideally). Similarly, the falling edge of the input pulse and the rising edge of the output pulse occur at the same time (ideally). This timing relationship is shown in Figure 8–3. Timing diagrams are especially useful for illustrating the time relationship of digital waveforms with multiple pulses.

A timing diagram shows how two or more waveforms relate in time.

▶ **FIGURE 8–3**

Timing diagram for the case in Figure 8–2.

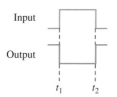

EXAMPLE 8–1

A waveform is applied to an inverter in Figure 8–4. Determine the output waveform corresponding to the input and show the timing diagram. According to the placement of the bubble, what is the active output state?

▶ **FIGURE 8–4**

Solution   The output waveform is exactly opposite to the input (inverted), as shown in Figure 8–5, which is the basic timing diagram. The active or asserted output state is **0.**

▶ FIGURE 8–5

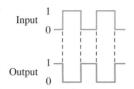

Related Problem If the inverter is shown with the negative indicator (bubble) on the input instead of the output, how is the timing diagram affected?

Logic Expression for an Inverter

Boolean algebra uses variables and operators to describe a logic circuit.

In **Boolean algebra,** which is the mathematics of logic circuits and will be covered thoroughly in Chapter 9, a variable is designated by a letter. The **complement** of a variable is designated by a bar over the letter. A variable can take on a value of either 1 or 0. If a given variable is 1, its complement is 0 and vice versa.

The operation of an inverter (NOT circuit) can be expressed as follows: If the input variable is called *A* and the output variable is called *X*, then

$$X = \bar{A}$$

This expression states that the output is the complement of the input, so if $A = 0$, then $X = 1$, and if $A = 1$, then $X = 0$. Figure 8–6 illustrates this. The complemented variable $\bar{A}$ can be read as "*A* bar" or "not *A*."

▶ FIGURE 8–6

The inverter complements an input variable.

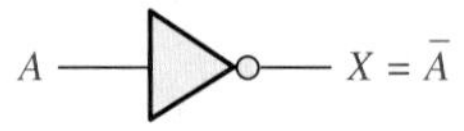

$$A \longrightarrow \!\!\!\!\!\triangleright\!\!\!\circ\!\!- X = \bar{A}$$

An Application

Figure 8–7 shows a circuit for producing the 1's complement of an 8-bit binary number. The bits of the binary number are applied to the inverter inputs and the 1's complement of the number appears on the outputs.

▶ FIGURE 8–7

Example of a 1's complement circuit using inverters.

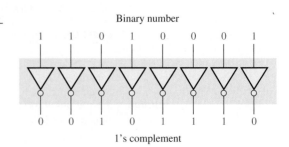

8-2 THE AND GATE

The AND gate is one of the basic gates that can be combined to form any logic function. An AND gate can have two or more inputs and performs what is known as logical multiplication.

After completing this section, you should be able to

- Identify an AND gate by its distinctive shape symbol or by its rectangular outline symbol

- Describe the operation of an AND gate

- Generate the truth table for an AND gate with any number of inputs

- Produce a timing diagram for an AND gate with any specified input waveforms

- Write the logic expression for an AND gate with any number of inputs

- Discuss examples of AND gate applications

The term *gate* is used to describe a circuit that performs a basic logic operation. The AND gate is composed of two or more inputs and a single output, as indicated by the standard logic symbols shown in Figure 8–8. Inputs are on the left, and the output is on the right in each symbol. Gates with two inputs are shown; however, an AND gate can have any number of inputs greater than one. Although examples of both distinctive shape symbols and rectangular outline symbols are shown, the distinctive shape symbol, shown in part (a), is used predominantly in this book.

COMPUTER NOTE

Logic gates are the building blocks of computers. Most of the functions in a computer, with the exception of certain types of memory, are implemented with logic gates used on a very large scale. For example, a microprocessor, which is the main part of a computer, is made up of hundreds of thousands or even millions of logic gates.

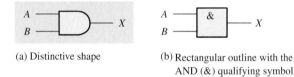

(a) Distinctive shape

(b) Rectangular outline with the AND (&) qualifying symbol

▲ **FIGURE 8-8**

Standard logic symbols for the AND gate showing two inputs (ANSI/IEEE Std. 91-1984).

Operation of an AND Gate

An **AND gate** produces a HIGH output *only* when *all* of the inputs are HIGH. When any of the inputs is LOW, the output is LOW. Therefore, the basic purpose of an AND gate is to determine when certain conditions are simultaneously true, as indicated by HIGH levels on all of its inputs, and to produce a HIGH on its output to indicate that all these conditions are true. The inputs of the 2-input AND gate in Figure 8–8 are labeled A and B, and the output is labeled X. The gate operation can be stated as follows:

An AND gate can have more than two inputs.

For a 2-input AND gate, output X is HIGH only when inputs A and B are HIGH; X is LOW when either A or B is LOW, or when both A and B are LOW.

Figure 8–9 illustrates a 2-input AND gate with all four possibilities of input combinations and the resulting output for each.

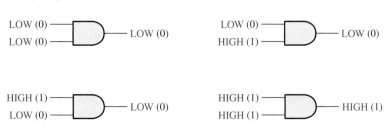

◀ **FIGURE 8-9**

All possible logic levels for a 2-input AND gate.

AND Gate Truth Table

For an AND gate, all HIGH inputs make a HIGH output.

The logical operation of a gate can be expressed with a truth table that lists all input combinations with the corresponding outputs, as illustrated in Table 8–2 for a 2-input AND gate. The truth table can be expanded to any number of inputs. Although the terms HIGH and LOW tend to give a "physical" sense to the input and output states, the truth table is shown with 1s and 0s; a HIGH is equivalent to a 1 and a LOW is equivalent to a 0 in positive logic. For any AND gate, regardless of the number of inputs, the output is HIGH *only* when *all* inputs are HIGH.

▶ TABLE 8–2

Truth table for a 2-input AND gate.

INPUTS		OUTPUT
A	B	X
0	0	0
0	1	0
1	0	0
1	1	1

1 = HIGH, 0 = LOW

The total number of possible combinations of binary inputs to a gate is determined by the following formula:

Equation 8–1

$$N = 2^n$$

where N is the number of possible input combinations and n is the number of input variables. To illustrate,

For two input variables: $N = 2^2 = 4$ combinations

For three input variables: $N = 2^3 = 8$ combinations

For four input variables: $N = 2^4 = 16$ combinations

You can determine the number of input bit combinations for gates with any number of inputs by using Equation 8–1.

EXAMPLE 8–2

(a) Develop the truth table for a 3-input AND gate.

(b) Determine the total number of possible input combinations for a 4-input AND gate.

Solution   (a) There are eight possible input combinations ($2^3 = 8$) for a 3-input AND gate. The input side of the truth table (Table 8–3) shows all eight combinations of three bits. The output side is all 0s except when all three input bits are 1s.

▶ **TABLE 8–3**

INPUTS			OUTPUT
A	B	C	X
0	0	0	0
0	0	1	0
0	1	0	0
0	1	1	0
1	0	0	0
1	0	1	0
1	1	0	0
1	1	1	1

(b) $N = 2^4 = 16$. There are 16 possible combinations of input bits for a 4-input AND gate.

Related Problem Develop the truth table for a 4-input AND gate.

Operation with Waveform Inputs

In most applications, the inputs to a gate are not stationary levels but are voltage waveforms that change frequently between HIGH and LOW logic levels. Now let's look at the operation of AND gates with pulse waveform inputs, keeping in mind that an AND gate obeys the truth table operation regardless of whether its inputs are constant levels or levels that change back and forth.

Let's examine the waveform operation of an AND gate by looking at the inputs with respect to each other in order to determine the output level at any given time. In Figure 8–10, inputs A and B are both HIGH (1) during the time interval, t_1, making output X HIGH (1) during this interval. During time interval t_2, input A is LOW (0) and input B is HIGH (1),

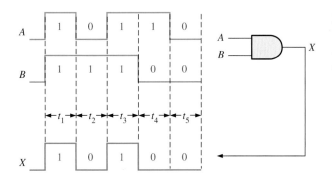

◀ **FIGURE 8–10**

Example of AND gate operation with a timing diagram showing input and output relationships.

so the output is LOW (0). During time interval $t3$, both inputs are HIGH (1) again, and therefore the output is HIGH (1). During time interval $t4$, input A is HIGH (1) and input B is LOW (0), resulting in a LOW (0) output. Finally, during time interval $t5$, input A is LOW (0), input B is LOW (0), and the output is therefore LOW (0). As you know, a diagram of input and output waveforms showing time relationships is called a *timing diagram*.

EXAMPLE 8–3

If two waveforms, *A* and *B*, are applied to the AND gate inputs as in Figure 8–11, what is the resulting output waveform?

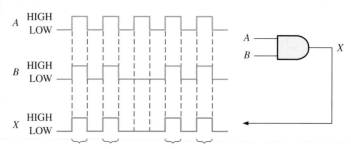

A and B are both HIGH during these four time intervals.
Therefore *X* is HIGH.

▲ **FIGURE 8–11**

Solution   The output waveform *X* is HIGH only when both *A* and *B* waveforms are HIGH as shown in the timing diagram in Figure 8–11.

Related Problem   Determine the output waveform and show a timing diagram if the second and fourth pulses in waveform *A* of Figure 8–11 are replaced by LOW levels.

Remember, when analyzing the waveform operation of logic gates, it is important to pay careful attention to the time relationships of all the inputs with respect to each other and to the output.

EXAMPLE 8–4

For the two input waveforms, *A* and *B*, in Figure 8–12, show the output waveform with its proper relation to the inputs.

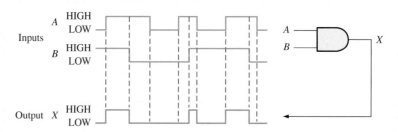

▲ **FIGURE 8–12**

Solution   The output waveform is HIGH only when both of the input waveforms are HIGH as shown in the timing diagram.

Related Problem   Show the output waveform if the *B* input to the AND gate in Figure 8–12 is always HIGH.

EXAMPLE 8–5

For the 3-input AND gate in Figure 8–13, determine the output waveform in relation to the inputs.

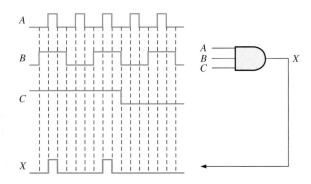

▲ **FIGURE 8–13**

Solution   The output waveform X of the 3-input AND gate is HIGH only when all three input waveforms A, B, and C are HIGH.

Related Problem   What is the output waveform of the AND gate in Figure 8-13 if the C input is always HIGH?

Logic Expressions for an AND Gate

The logical AND function of two variables is represented mathematically either by placing a dot between the two variables, as $A \cdot B$, or by simply writing the adjacent letters without the dot, as AB. We will normally use the latter notation because it is easier to write.

  Boolean multiplication follows the same basic rules governing binary multiplication, which were discussed in Chapter 7 and are as follows:

$$0 \cdot 0 = 0$$
$$0 \cdot 1 = 0$$
$$1 \cdot 0 = 0$$
$$1 \cdot 1 = 1$$

Boolean multiplication is the same as the AND function.

The operation of a 2-input AND gate can be expressed in equation form as follows: If one input variable is A, the other input variable is B, and the output variable is X, then the Boolean expression is

$$X = AB$$

COMPUTER NOTE

Computers can utilize all of the basic logic operations when it is necessary to selectively manipulate certain bits in one or more bytes of data. Selective bit manipulations are done with a *mask*. For example, to clear (make all 0s) the right four bits in a data byte but keep the left four bits, ANDing the data byte with 11110000 will do the job. Notice that any bit ANDed with zero will be 0 and any bit ANDed with 1 will remain the same. If 10101010 is ANDed with the mask 11110000, the result is 10100000.

Figure 8–14(a) shows the AND gate logic symbol with two input variables and the output variable indicated.

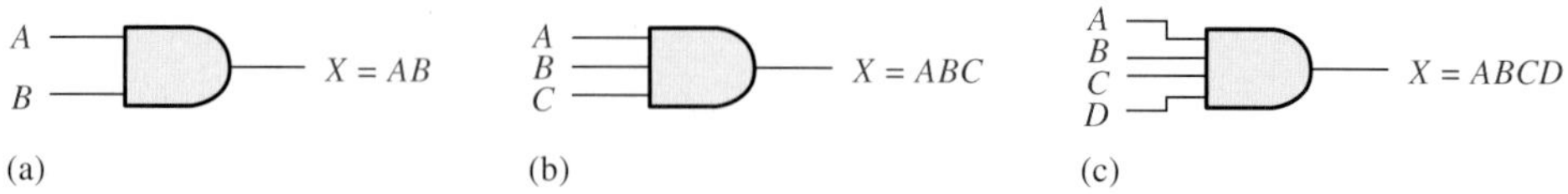

(a) $X = AB$ (b) $X = ABC$ (c) $X = ABCD$

FIGURE 8–14

Boolean expressions for AND gates with two, three, and four inputs.

When variables are shown together like *ABC*, they are ANDed.

To extend the AND expression to more than two input variables, simply use a new letter for each input variable. The function of a 3-input AND gate, for example, can be expressed as $X = ABC$, where A, B, and C are the input variables. The expression for a 4-input AND gate can be $X = ABCD$, and so on. Parts (b) and (c) of Figure 8–14 show AND gates with three and four input variables, respectively.

You can evaluate an AND gate operation by using the Boolean expressions for the output. For example, each variable on the inputs can be either a 1 or a 0; so for the 2-input AND gate, make substitutions in the equation for the output, $X = AB$, as shown in Table 8–4. This evaluation shows that the output X of an AND gate is a 1 (HIGH) only when both inputs are 1s (HIGHs). A similar analysis can be made for any number of input variables.

TABLE 8–4

A	B	AB = X
0	0	$0 \cdot 0 = 0$
0	1	$0 \cdot 1 = 0$
1	0	$1 \cdot 0 = 0$
1	1	$1 \cdot 1 = 1$

Applications

The AND Gate as an Enable/Inhibit Device   A common application of the AND gate is to **enable** (that is, to allow) the passage of a signal (pulse waveform) from one point to another at certain times and to inhibit (prevent) the passage at other times.

A simple example of this particular use of an AND gate is shown in Figure 8–15, where the AND gate controls the passage of a signal (waveform *A)* to a digital counter. The purpose of this circuit is to measure the frequency of waveform *A*. The enable pulse has a width of precisely 1 s. When the enable pulse is HIGH, waveform *A* passes through the gate to the counter; and when the enable pulse is LOW, the signal is prevented from passing through the gate (inhibited).

During the 1 second (1 s) interval of the enable pulse, pulses in waveform *A* pass through the AND gate to the counter. The number of pulses passing through during the 1 s interval is equal to the frequency of waveform *A*. For example, Figure 8–15 shows six pulses in one second, which is a frequency of 6 Hz. If 1000 pulses pass through the gate in the 1 s interval of the enable pulse, there are 1000 pulses/s, or a frequency of 1000 Hz.

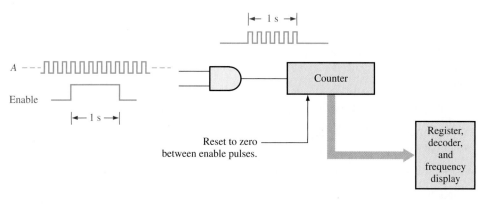

▲ **FIGURE 8–15**

An AND gate performing an enable/inhibit function for a frequency counter.

The counter counts the number of pulses per second and produces a binary output that goes to a decoding and display circuit to produce a readout of the frequency. The enable pulse repeats at certain intervals and a new updated count is made so that if the frequency changes, the new value will be displayed. Between enable pulses, the counter is reset so that it starts at zero each time an enable pulse occurs. The current frequency count is stored in a register so that the display is unaffected by the resetting of the counter.

A Seat Belt Alarm System   In Figure 8–16, an AND gate is used in a simple automobile seat belt alarm system to detect when the ignition switch is on *and* the seat belt is unbuckled. If the ignition switch is on, a HIGH is produced on input *A* of the AND gate. If the seat belt is not properly buckled, a HIGH is produced on input *B* of the AND gate. Also, when the ignition switch is turned on, a timer is started that produces a HIGH on input *C* for 30 s. If all three conditions exist—that is, if the ignition is on *and* the seat belt is unbuckled *and* the timer is running—the output of the AND gate is HIGH, and an audible alarm is energized to remind the driver.

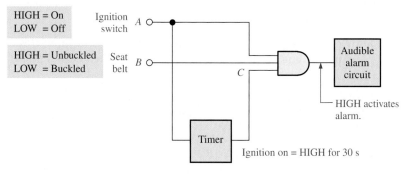

▲ **FIGURE 8–16**

A simple seat belt alarm circuit using an AND gate.

8–3 THE OR GATE

The OR gate is another of the basic gates from which all logic functions are constructed. An OR gate can have two or more inputs and performs what is known as logical addition.

After completing this section, you should be able to

- Identify an OR gate by its distinctive shape symbol or by its rectangular outline symbol
- Describe the operation of an OR gate
- Generate the truth table for an OR gate with any number of inputs
- Produce a timing diagram for an OR gate with any specified input waveforms
- Write the logic expression for an OR gate with any number of inputs
- Discuss examples of OR gate applications

An OR gate can have more than two inputs.

An **OR gate** has two or more inputs and one output, as indicated by the standard logic symbols in Figure 8–17, where OR gates with two inputs are illustrated. An OR gate can have any number of inputs greater than one. Although both distinctive shape and rectangular outline symbols are shown, the distinctive shape OR gate symbol is used in this textbook.

▶ **FIGURE 8–17**

Standard logic symbols for the OR gate showing two inputs (ANSI/IEEE Std. 91-1984).

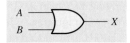

(a) Distinctive shape

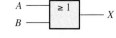

(b) Rectangular outline with the OR (≥ 1) qualifying symbol

Operation of an OR Gate

An OR gate produces a HIGH on the output when *any* of the inputs is HIGH. The output is LOW only when all of the inputs are LOW. Therefore, an OR gate determines when one or more of its inputs are HIGH and produces a HIGH on its output to indicate this condition. The inputs of the 2-input OR gate in Figure 8–17 are labeled A and B, and the output is labeled X. The operation of the gate can be stated as follows:

For a 2-input OR gate, output X is HIGH when either input A or input B is HIGH, or when both A and B are HIGH; X is LOW only when both A and B are LOW.

The HIGH level is the active or asserted output level for the OR gate. Figure 8–18 illustrates the operation for a 2-input OR gate for all four possible input combinations.

▶ **FIGURE 8–18**

All possible logic levels for a 2-input OR gate.

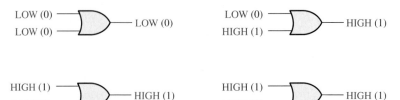

OR Gate Truth Table

The operation of a 2-input OR gate is described in Table 8–5. This truth table can be expanded for any number of inputs; but regardless of the number of inputs, the output is HIGH when one or more of the inputs are HIGH.

For an OR gate, at least one HIGH input makes a HIGH output.

▶ **TABLE 8–5**

Truth table for a 2-input OR gate.

INPUTS		OUTPUT
A	B	X
0	0	0
0	1	1
1	0	1
1	1	1

1 = HIGH, 0 = LOW

Operation with Waveform Inputs

Now let's look at the operation of an OR gate with pulse waveform inputs, keeping in mind its logical operation. Again, the important thing in the analysis of gate operation with pulse waveforms is the time relationship of all the waveforms involved. For example, in Figure 8–19, inputs A and B are both HIGH (1) during time interval t_1, making output X HIGH (1). During time interval t_2, input A is LOW (0), but because input B is HIGH (1), the output is HIGH (1). Both inputs are LOW(0) during time interval t_3, so there is a LOW (0) output during this time. During time interval t_4, the output is HIGH (1) because input A is HIGH (1).

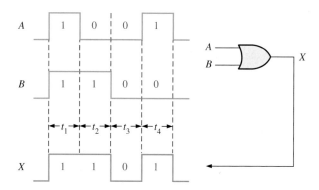

▲ **FIGURE 8–19**

Example of OR gate operation with a timing diagram showing input and output time relationships.

In this illustration, we have applied the truth table operation of the OR gate to each of the time intervals during which the levels are nonchanging. Examples 8–6 through 8–8 further illustrate OR gate operation with waveforms on the inputs.

EXAMPLE 8–6

If the two input waveforms, A and B, in Figure 8–20 are applied to the OR gate, what is the resulting output waveform?

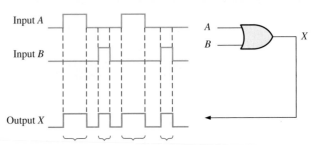

When either input or both inputs are HIGH, the output is HIGH.

▲ **FIGURE 8–20**

Solution The output waveform X of a 2-input OR gate is HIGH when either or both input waveforms are HIGH as shown in the timing diagram. In this case, both input waveforms are never HIGH at the same time.

Related Problem Determine the output waveform and show the timing diagram if input A is changed such that it is HIGH from the beginning of the existing first pulse to the end of the existing second pulse.

EXAMPLE 8–7

For the two input waveforms, A and B, in Figure 8–21, show the output waveform with its proper relation to the inputs.

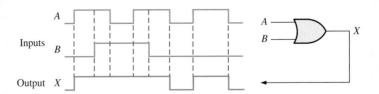

▲ **FIGURE 8–21**

Solution When either or both input waveforms are HIGH, the output is HIGH as shown by the output waveform X in the timing diagram.

Related Problem Determine the output waveform and show the timing diagram if the middle pulse of input A is replaced by a LOW level.

EXAMPLE 8-8

For the 3-input OR gate in Figure 8–22, determine the output waveform in proper time relation to the inputs.

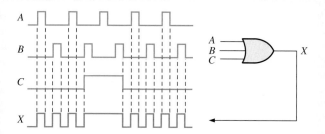

▲ FIGURE 8-22

Solution   The output is HIGH when one or more of the input waveforms are HIGH as indicated by the output waveform *X* in the timing diagram.

Related Problem   Determine the output waveform and show the timing diagram if input *C* is always LOW.

Logic Expressions for an OR Gate

The logical OR function of two variables is represented mathematically by a + between the two variables, for example, $A + B$.

When variables are separated by +, they are ORed.

Addition in Boolean algebra involves variables whose values are either binary 1 or binary 0. The basic rules for **Boolean addition** are as follows:

$$0 + 0 = 0$$
$$0 + 1 = 1$$
$$1 + 0 = 1$$
$$1 + 1 = 1$$

Boolean addition is the same as the OR function.

Notice that Boolean addition differs from binary addition in the case where two 1s are added. There is no carry in Boolean addition.

The operation of a 2-input OR gate can be expressed as follows: If one input variable is *A*, if the other input variable is *B*, and if the output variable is *X*, then the Boolean expression is

$$X = A + B$$

Figure 8–23(a) shows the OR gate logic symbol with two input variables and the output variable labeled.

(a) $X = A + B$	(b) $X = A + B + C$	(c) $X = A + B + C + D$

▲ FIGURE 8-23

Boolean expressions for OR gates with two, three, and four inputs.

COMPUTER NOTE

Another mask operation that is used in computer programming to selectively make certain bits in a data byte equal to 1 (called setting) while not affecting any other bit is done with the OR operation. A mask is used that contains a 1 in any position where a data bit is to be set. For example, if you want to force the most significant bit in a data byte to equal 1, but leave all other bits unchanged, you can OR the data byte with the mask 10000000.

To extend the OR expression to more than two input variables, a new letter is used for each additional variable. For instance, the function of a 3-input OR gate can be expressed as $X = A + B + C$. The expression for a 4-input OR gate can be written as $X = A + B + C + D$, and so on. Parts (b) and (c) of Figure 8–23 show OR gates with three and four input variables, respectively.

OR gate operation can be evaluated by using the Boolean expressions for the output X by substituting all possible combinations of 1 and 0 values for the input variables, as shown in Table 8–6 for a 2-input OR gate. This evaluation shows that the output X of an OR gate is a 1 (HIGH) when any one or more of the inputs are 1 (HIGH). A similar analysis can be extended to OR gates with any number of input variables.

▷ **TABLE 8–6**

A	B	A + B = X
0	0	0 + 0 = 0
0	1	0 + 1 = 1
1	0	1 + 0 = 1
1	1	1 + 1 = 1

An Application

A simplified portion of an intrusion detection and alarm system is shown in Figure 8–24. This system could be used for one room in a home—a room with two windows and a door. The sensors are magnetic switches that produce a HIGH output when open and a LOW output when closed. As long as the windows and the door are secured, the switches are closed and all three of the OR gate inputs are LOW. When one of the windows or the door is opened, a HIGH is produced on that input to the OR gate and the gate output goes HIGH. It then activates and latches an alarm circuit to warn of the intrusion.

▷ **FIGURE 8–24**

A simplified intrusion detection system using an OR gate.

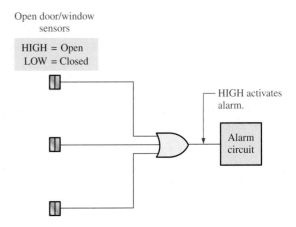

Open door/window sensors

HIGH = Open
LOW = Closed

HIGH activates alarm.

Alarm circuit

8-4   THE NAND GATE

The NAND gate is a popular logic element because it can be used as a universal gate; that is, NAND gates can be used in combination to perform the AND, OR, and inverter operations.

After completing this section, you should be able to

■ Identify a NAND gate by its distinctive shape symbol or by its rectangular outline symbol

■ Describe the operation of a NAND gate

■ Develop the truth table for a NAND gate with any number of inputs

■ Produce a timing diagram for a NAND gate with any specified input waveforms

■ Write the logic expression for a NAND gate with any number of inputs

■ Describe NAND gate operation in terms of its negative-OR equivalent

■ Discuss examples of NAND gate applications

The term *NAND* is a contraction of NOT-AND and implies an AND function with a complemented (inverted) output. The standard logic symbol for a 2-input NAND gate and its equivalency to an AND gate followed by an inverter are shown in Figure 8–25(a), where the symbol ≡ means equivalent to. A rectangular outline symbol is shown in part (b).

The NAND is the same as the AND except the output is inverted.

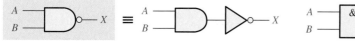

(a) Distinctive shape, 2-input NAND gate and its NOT/AND equivalent

(b) Rectangular outline, 2-input NAND gate with polarity indicator

▲ **FIGURE 8-25**

Standard NAND gate logic symbols (ANSI/IEEE Std. 91-1984).

Operation of a NAND Gate

A **NAND gate** produces a LOW output only when all the inputs are HIGH. When any of the inputs is LOW, the output will be HIGH. For the specific case of a 2-input NAND gate, as shown in Figure 8–25 with the inputs labeled *A* and *B* and the output labeled *X*, the operation can be stated as follows:

For a 2-input NAND gate, output *X* is LOW only when inputs *A* and *B* are HIGH; *X* is HIGH when either *A* or *B* is LOW, or when both *A* and *B* are LOW.

Note that this operation is opposite that of the AND in terms of the output level. In a NAND gate, the LOW level (0) is the active or asserted output level, as indicated by the bubble on the output. Figure 8–26 illustrates the operation of a 2-input NAND gate for all four input combinations, and Table 8–7 is the truth table summarizing the logical operation of the 2-input NAND gate.

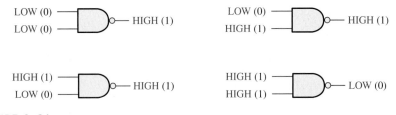

▲ FIGURE 8–26

Operation of a 2-input NAND gate.

▶ TABLE 8–7

Truth table for a 2-input NAND gate.

| INPUTS | | OUTPUT |
A	B	X
0	0	1
0	1	1
1	0	1
1	1	0

1 = HIGH, 0 = LOW.

Operation with Waveform Inputs

Now let's look at the pulse waveform operation of a NAND gate. Remember from the truth table that the only time a LOW output occurs is when all of the inputs are HIGH.

EXAMPLE 8–9

If the two waveforms A and B shown in Figure 8–27 are applied to the NAND gate inputs, determine the resulting output waveform.

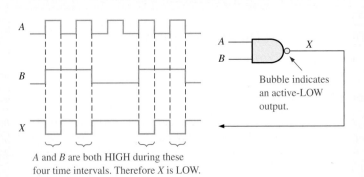

A and B are both HIGH during these four time intervals. Therefore X is LOW.

▲ FIGURE 8–27

Solution Output waveform X is LOW only during the four time intervals when both input waveforms A and B are HIGH as shown in the timing diagram.

Related Problem Determine the output waveform and show the timing diagram if input waveform B is inverted.

EXAMPLE 8-10

Show the output waveform for the 3-input NAND gate in Figure 8–28 with its proper time relationship to the inputs.

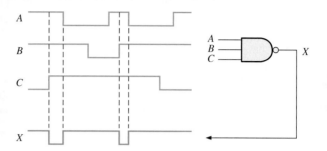

▲ FIGURE 8-28

Solution   The output waveform *X* is LOW only when all three input waveforms are HIGH as shown in the timing diagram.

Related Problem   Determine the output waveform and show the timing diagram if input waveform *A* is inverted.

Negative-OR Equivalent Operation of a NAND Gate   Inherent in a NAND gate's operation is the fact that one or more LOW inputs produce a HIGH output. Table 8–7 shows that output *X* is HIGH (1) when any of the inputs, *A* and *B,* is LOW (0). From this viewpoint, a NAND gate can be used for an OR operation that requires one or more LOW inputs to produce a HIGH output. This aspect of NAND operation is referred to as **negative-OR.** The term *negative* in this context means that the inputs are defined to be in the active or asserted state when LOW.

For a 2-input NAND gate performing a negative-OR operation, output *X* is HIGH when either input *A* or input *B* is LOW, or when both *A* and *B* are LOW.

When a NAND gate is used to detect one or more LOWs on its inputs rather than all HIGHs, it is performing the negative-OR operation and is represented by the standard logic symbol shown in Figure 8–29. Although the two symbols in Figure 8–29 represent the same physical gate, they serve to define its role or mode of operation in a particular application, as illustrated by Examples 8–11 through 8–13.

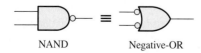

NAND   Negative-OR

◄ **FIGURE 8-29**

Standard symbols representing the two equivalent operations of a NAND gate.

EXAMPLE 8–11

A manufacturing plant uses two tanks to store certain liquid chemicals that are required in a manufacturing process. Each tank has a sensor that detects when the chemical level drops to 25% of full. The sensors produce a HIGH level of 5 V when the tanks are more than one-quarter full. When the volume of chemical in a tank drops to one-quarter full, the sensor puts out a LOW level of 0 V.

It is required that a single green light-emitting diode (LED) on an indicator panel show when both tanks are more than one-quarter full. Show how a NAND gate can be used to implement this function.

Solution Figure 8–30 shows a NAND gate with its two inputs connected to the tank level sensors and its output connected to the indicator panel. The operation can be stated as follows: If tank *A* and tank *B* are above one-quarter full, the LED is on.

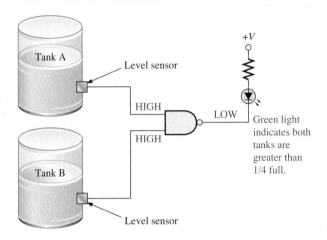

▲ **FIGURE 8–30**

As long as both sensor outputs are HIGH (5 V), indicating that both tanks are more than one-quarter full, the NAND gate output is LOW (0 V). The green LED circuit is arranged so that a LOW voltage turns it on.

Related Problem How can the circuit of Figure 8–30 be modified to monitor the levels in three tanks rather than two?

EXAMPLE 8–12

The supervisor of the manufacturing process described in Example 8–11 has decided that he would prefer to have a red LED display come on when at least one of the tanks falls to the quarter-full level rather than have the green LED display indicate when both are above one quarter. Show how this requirement can be implemented.

Solution Figure 8–31 shows a NAND gate operating as a negative-OR gate to detect the occurrence of at least one LOW on its inputs. A sensor puts out a LOW voltage if the volume in its tank goes to one-quarter full or less. When this happens, the gate output goes HIGH. The red LED circuit in the panel is arranged so that a HIGH voltage turns it on. The operation can be stated as follows: If tank *A* or tank *B* or both are below one-quarter full, the LED is on.

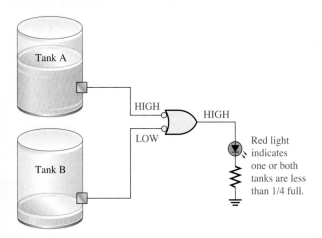

▲ FIGURE 8–31

Notice that, in this example and in Example 8–11, the same 2-input NAND gate is used, but a different gate symbol is used in the schematic, illustrating the different way in which the NAND and equivalent negative-OR operations are used.

Related Problem How can the circuit in Figure 8–31 be modified to monitor four tanks rather than two?

EXAMPLE 8–13

For the 4-input NAND gate in Figure 8–32, operating as a negative-OR, determine the output with respect to the inputs.

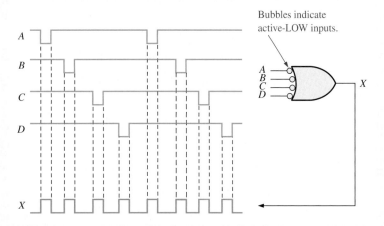

▲ FIGURE 8–32

Solution The output waveform *X* is HIGH any time an input waveform is LOW as shown in the timing diagram.

Related Problem Determine the output waveform if input waveform *A* is inverted before it is applied to the gate.

Logic Expressions for a NAND Gate

The Boolean expression for the output of a 2-input NAND gate is

$$X = \overline{AB}$$

This expression says that the two input variables, A and B, are first ANDed and then complemented, as indicated by the bar over the AND expression. This is a description in equation form of the operation of a NAND gate with two inputs. Evaluating this expression for all possible values of the two input variables, you get the results shown in Table 8–8.

▶ TABLE 8–8

A	B	$\overline{AB} = X$
0	0	$\overline{0 \cdot 0} = \overline{0} = 1$
0	1	$\overline{0 \cdot 1} = \overline{0} = 1$
1	0	$\overline{1 \cdot 0} = \overline{0} = 1$
1	1	$\overline{1 \cdot 1} = \overline{1} = 0$

Once an expression is determined for a given logic function, that function can be evaluated for all possible values of the variables. The evaluation tells you exactly what the output of the logic circuit is for each of the input conditions, and it therefore gives you a complete description of the circuit's logic operation. The NAND expression can be extended to more than two input variables by including additional letters to represent the other variables.

8–5   THE NOR GATE

The NOR gate, like the NAND gate, is a useful logic element because it can also be used as a universal gate; that is, NOR gates can be used in combination to perform the AND, OR, and inverter operations.

After completing this section, you should be able to

■ Identify a NOR gate by its distinctive shape symbol or by its rectangular outline symbol

■ Describe the operation of a NOR gate

■ Develop the truth table for a NOR gate with any number of inputs

■ Produce a timing diagram for a NOR gate with any specified input waveforms

■ Write the logic expression for a NOR gate with any number of inputs

■ Describe NOR gate operation in terms of its negative-AND equivalent

■ Discuss examples of NOR gate applications

The term *NOR* is a contraction of NOT-OR and implies an OR function with an inverted (complemented) output. The standard logic symbol for a 2-input NOR gate and its equivalent OR gate followed by an inverter are shown in Figure 8–33(a). A rectangular outline symbol is shown in part (b).

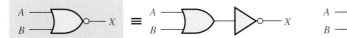

(a) Distinctive shape, 2-input NOR gate and its NOT/OR equivalent

(b) Rectangular outline, 2-input NOR gate with polarity indicator

▲ **FIGURE 8–33**

Standard NOR gate logic symbols (ANSI/IEEE Std. 91-1984).

Operation of a NOR Gate

A **NOR gate** produces a LOW output when *any* of its inputs is HIGH. Only when all of its inputs are LOW is the output HIGH. For the specific case of a 2-input NOR gate, as shown in Figure 8–33 with the inputs labeled A and B and the output labeled X, the operation can be stated as follows:

For a 2-input NOR gate, output X is LOW when either input A or input B is HIGH, or when both A and B are HIGH; X is HIGH only when both A and B are LOW.

This operation results in an output level opposite that of the OR gate. In a NOR gate, the LOW output is the active or asserted output level as indicated by the bubble on the output. Figure 8–34 illustrates the operation of a 2-input NOR gate for all four possible input combinations, and Table 8–9 is the truth table for a 2-input NOR gate.

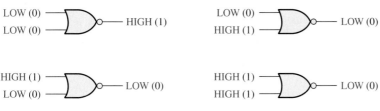

▲ **FIGURE 8–34**

Operation of a 2-input NOR gate.

▶ **TABLE 8–9**

Truth table for a 2-input NOR gate.

INPUTS		OUTPUT
A	B	X
0	0	1
0	1	0
1	0	0
1	1	0

1 = HIGH, 0 = LOW.

Operation with Waveform Inputs

The next two examples illustrate the operation of a NOR gate with pulse waveform inputs. Again, as with the other types of gates, we will simply follow the truth table operation to determine the output waveforms in the proper time relationship to the inputs.

EXAMPLE 8–14

If the two waveforms shown in Figure 8–35 are applied to a NOR gate, what is the resulting output waveform?

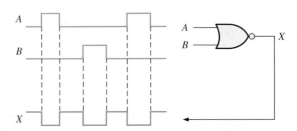

▲ **FIGURE 8–35**

Solution Whenever any input of the NOR gate is HIGH, the output is LOW as shown by the output waveform X in the timing diagram.

Related Problem Invert input B and determine the output waveform in relation to the inputs.

EXAMPLE 8–15

Show the output waveform for the 3-input NOR gate in Figure 8–36 with the proper time relation to the inputs.

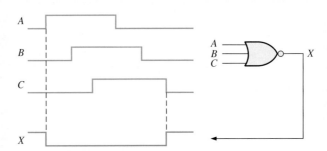

▲ **FIGURE 8–36**

Solution The output X is LOW when any input is HIGH as shown by the output waveform X in the timing diagram.

Related Problem With the B and C inputs inverted, determine the output and show the timing diagram.

Negative–AND Equivalent Operation of the NOR Gate   A NOR gate, like the NAND, has another aspect of its operation that is inherent in the way it logically functions. Table 8–9 shows that a HIGH is produced on the gate output only when all of the inputs are LOW. From this viewpoint, a NOR gate can be used for an AND operation that requires all LOW inputs to produce a HIGH output. This aspect of NOR operation is called **negative-AND.**

The term *negative* in this context means that the inputs are defined to be in the active or asserted state when LOW.

For a 2-input NOR gate performing a negative-AND operation, output *X* is HIGH only when both inputs *A* and *B* are LOW.

When a NOR gate is used to detect all LOWs on its inputs rather than one or more HIGHs, it is performing the negative-AND operation and is represented by the standard symbol in Figure 8–37. It is important to remember that the two symbols in Figure 8–37 represent the same physical gate and serve only to distinguish between the two modes of its operation. The following three examples illustrate this.

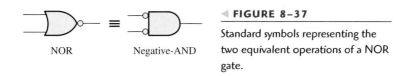

NOR   Negative-AND

◀ **FIGURE 8–37**

Standard symbols representing the two equivalent operations of a NOR gate.

EXAMPLE 8–16

A device is needed to indicate when two LOW levels occur simultaneously on its inputs and to produce a HIGH output as an indication. Specify the device.

Solution   A 2-input NOR gate operating as a negative-AND gate is required to produce a HIGH output when both inputs are LOW, as shown in Figure 8–38.

▷ **FIGURE 8–38**

LOW   ───   HIGH
LOW

Related Problem   A device is needed to indicate when one or two HIGH levels occur on its inputs and to produce a LOW output as an indication. Specify the device.

EXAMPLE 8–17

As part of an aircraft's functional monitoring system, a circuit is required to indicate the status of the landing gears prior to landing. A green LED display turns on if all three gears are properly extended when the "gear down" switch has been activated in preparation for landing. A red LED display turns on if any of the gears fail to extend properly prior to landing. When a landing gear is extended, its sensor produces a LOW voltage. When a landing gear is retracted, its sensor produces a HIGH voltage. Implement a circuit to meet this requirement.

Solution   Power is applied to the circuit only when the "gear down" switch is activated. Use a NOR gate for each of the two requirements as shown in Figure 8–39. One NOR gate operates as a negative-AND to detect a LOW from each of the three landing gear sensors. When all three of the gate inputs are LOW, the three landing gears are properly extended and the resulting HIGH output from the negative-AND gate turns on the green LED display. The other NOR gate operates as a NOR to detect if one or more of the landing gears remain retracted when the "gear down" switch is activated.

When one or more of the landing gears remain retracted, the resulting HIGH from the sensor is detected by the NOR gate, which produces a LOW output to turn on the red LED warning display.

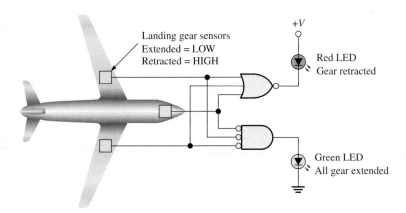

Landing gear sensors
Extended = LOW
Retracted = HIGH

+V

Red LED
Gear retracted

Green LED
All gear extended

▲ FIGURE 8–39

Related Problem What type of gate should be used to detect if all three landing gears are retracted after takeoff, assuming a LOW output is required to activate an LED display?

EXAMPLE 8–18

For the 4-input NOR gate operating as a negative-AND in Figure 8–40, determine the output relative to the inputs.

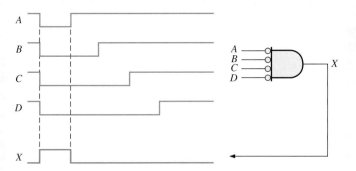

▲ FIGURE 8–40

Solution Any time all of the input waveforms are LOW, the output is HIGH as shown by output waveform X in the timing diagram.

Related Problem Determine the output with input D inverted and show the timing diagram.

Logic Expressions for a NOR Gate

The Boolean expression for the output of a 2-input NOR gate can be written as

$$X = \overline{A + B}$$

This equation says that the two input variables are first ORed and then complemented, as indicated by the bar over the OR expression. Evaluating this expression, you get the results shown in Table 8–10. The NOR expression can be extended to more than two input variables by including additional letters to represent the other variables.

▶ TABLE 8–10

A	B	$\overline{A+B}=X$
0	0	$\overline{0 + 0} = \overline{0} = 1$
0	1	$\overline{0 + 1} = \overline{1} = 0$
1	0	$\overline{1 + 0} = \overline{1} = 0$
1	1	$\overline{1 + 1} = \overline{1} = 0$

HANDS ON TIP

When driving a load such as an LED with a logic gate, consult the manufacturer's data sheet for maximum drive capabilities (output current). A regular IC logic gate may not be capable of handling the current required by certain loads such as some LEDs. Logic gates with a buffered output, such as an open-collector (OC) or open-drain (OD) output, are available in many types of IC logic gate configurations. The output current capability of typical IC logic gates is limited to the μA or relatively low mA range. For example, standard TTL can handle output currents up to 16 mA. Most LEDs require currents in the range of about 10 mA to 50 mA.

8–6   THE EXCLUSIVE-OR AND EXCLUSIVE-NOR GATES

Exclusive-OR and exclusive-NOR gates are formed by a combination of other gates already discussed, as you will see in Chapter 10. However, because of their fundamental importance in many applications, these gates are often treated as basic logic elements with their own unique symbols.

After completing this section, you should be able to

■ Identify the exclusive-OR and exclusive-NOR gates by their distinctive shape symbols or by their rectangular outline symbols

■ Describe the operations of exclusive-OR and exclusive-NOR gates

■ Show the truth tables for exclusive-OR and exclusive-NOR gates

■ Produce a timing diagram for an exclusive-OR or exclusive-NOR gate with any specified input waveforms

■ Discuss examples of exclusive-OR and exclusive-NOR gate applications

The Exclusive-OR Gate

Standard symbols for an exclusive-OR (XOR for short) gate are shown in Figure 8–41. The XOR gate has only two inputs.

COMPUTER NOTE

Exclusive-OR gates connected to form an adder circuit allow a computer to perform addition, subtraction, multiplication, and division in its Arithmetic Logic Unit (ALU). An exclusive-OR gate combines basic AND, OR, and NOT logic.

(a) Distinctive shape

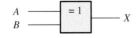

(b) Rectangular outline with the XOR

▲ FIGURE 8–41

Standard logic symbols for the exclusive-OR gate.

For an exclusive-OR gate, opposite inputs make the output HIGH.

The output of an **exclusive-OR gate** is HIGH *only* when the two inputs are at opposite logic levels. This operation can be stated as follows with reference to inputs A and B and output X:

For an exclusive-OR gate, output X is HIGH when input A is LOW and input B is HIGH, or when input A is HIGH and input B is LOW; X is LOW when A and B are both HIGH or both LOW.

The four possible input combinations and the resulting outputs for an XOR gate are illustrated in Figure 8–42. The HIGH level is the active or asserted output level and occurs only when the inputs are at opposite levels. The operation of an XOR gate is summarized in the truth table shown in Table 8–11.

▶ **FIGURE 8–42**

All possible logic levels for an exclusive-OR gate.

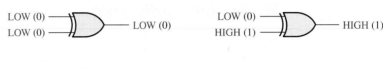

▶ **TABLE 8–11**

Truth table for an exclusive-OR gate.

INPUTS		OUTPUT
A	B	X
0	0	0
0	1	1
1	0	1
1	1	0

EXAMPLE 8–19

A certain system contains two identical circuits operating in parallel. As long as both are operating properly, the outputs of both circuits are always the same. If one of the circuits fails, the outputs will be at opposite levels at some time. Devise a way to detect that a failure has occurred in one of the circuits.

Solution   The outputs of the circuits are connected to the inputs of an XOR gate as shown in Figure 8–43. A failure in either one of the circuits produces differing outputs, which cause the XOR inputs to be at opposite levels. This condition produces a HIGH on the output of the XOR gate, indicating a failure in one of the circuits.

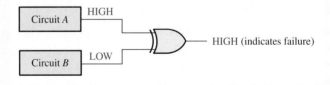

▲ **FIGURE 8–43**

Related Problem   Will the exclusive-OR gate always detect simultaneous failures in both circuits of Figure 8–43? If not, under what condition?

The Exclusive-NOR Gate

Standard symbols for an **exclusive-NOR** (XNOR) **gate** are shown in Figure 8–44. Like the XOR gate, an XNOR has only two inputs. The bubble on the output of the XNOR symbol indicates that its output is opposite that of the XOR gate. When the two input logic levels are opposite, the output of the exclusive-NOR gate is LOW. The operation can be stated as follows (*A* and *B* are inputs, *X* is the output):

For an exclusive-NOR gate, output *X* is LOW when input *A* is LOW and input *B* is HIGH, or when *A* is HIGH and *B* is LOW; *X* is HIGH when *A* and *B* are both HIGH or both LOW.

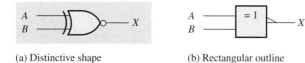

(a) Distinctive shape   (b) Rectangular outline

▲ FIGURE 8–44

Standard logic symbols for the exclusive-NOR gate.

The four possible input combinations and the resulting outputs for an XNOR gate are shown in Figure 8–45. The operation of an XNOR gate is summarized in Table 8–12. Notice that the output is HIGH when the same level is on both inputs.

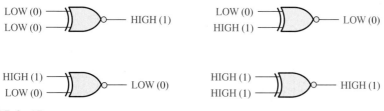

▲ FIGURE 8–45

All possible logic levels for an exclusive-NOR gate.

▶ TABLE 8–12

Truth table for an exclusive-NOR gate.

INPUTS		OUTPUT
A	B	X
0	0	1
0	1	0
1	0	0
1	1	1

Operation with Waveform Inputs

As we have done with the other gates, let's examine the operation of XOR and XNOR gates with pulse waveform inputs. As before, we apply the truth table operation during each distinct time interval of the pulse waveform inputs, as illustrated in Figure 8–46 for an XOR gate. You can see that the input waveforms A and B are at opposite levels during time intervals t_2 and t_4. Therefore, the output X is HIGH during these two times. Since both inputs are at the same level, either both HIGH or both LOW, during time intervals t_1 and t_3, the output is LOW during those times as shown in the timing diagram.

▶ **FIGURE 8–46**

Example of exclusive-OR gate operation with pulse waveform inputs.

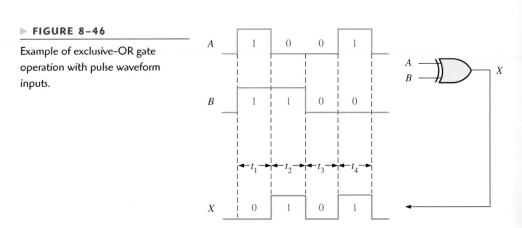

EXAMPLE 8–20

Determine the output waveforms for the XOR gate and for the XNOR gate, given the input waveforms, A and B, in Figure 8–47.

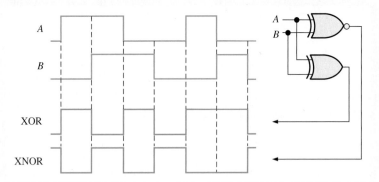

▲ **FIGURE 8–47**

Solution   The output waveforms are shown in Figure 8–47. Notice that the XOR output is HIGH only when both inputs are at opposite levels. Notice that the XNOR output is HIGH only when both inputs are the same.

Related Problem   Determine the output waveforms if the two input waveforms, A and B, are inverted.

An Application

An exclusive-OR gate can be used as a two-bit adder. Recall from Chapter 7 that the basic rules for binary addition are as follows: $0 + 0 = 0, 0 + 1 = 1, 1 + 0 = 1$, and $1 + 1 = 10$. An examination of the truth table for an XOR gate will show you that its output is the binary sum of the two input bits. In the case where the inputs are both 1s, the output is the sum 0, but you lose the carry of 1. Figure 8–48 illustrates an XOR gate used as a basic adder.

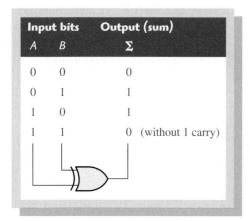

| Input bits | | Output (sum) |
A	B	Σ
0	0	0
0	1	1
1	0	1
1	1	0 (without 1 carry)

◄ **FIGURE 8–48**

An XOR gate used to add two bits.

8–7   FIXED-FUNCTION LOGIC

Two major digital integrated circuit (IC) technologies that are used to implement logic gates are CMOS and TTL. The logic operations of NOT, AND, OR, NAND, NOR, and exclusive-OR are the same regardless of the IC technology used; that is, an AND gate has the same logic function whether it is implemented with CMOS or TTL.

After completing this section, you should be able to

- Identify the most common CMOS and TTL series

- Compare CMOS and TTL in terms of device types and performance parameters

- Define *propagation delay time*

- Define *power dissipation*

- Define *fan-out*

- Define *speed-power product*

- Interpret basic data sheet information

CMOS stands for Complementary Metal-Oxide Semiconductor and is implemented with a type of field-effect transistor. **TTL** stands for Transistor-Transistor Logic and is implemented with bipolar junction transistors. Keep in mind that CMOS and TTL differ only in the type of circuit components and values of parameters and not in the basic logic operation. A CMOS AND gate has the same logic operation as a TTL AND gate. This is true for all the other basic logic functions. The difference in CMOS and TTL is in performance characteristics such as switching speed (propagation delay), power dissipation, noise immunity, and other parameters.

CMOS

There is little disagreement about which circuit technology, CMOS or TTL, is the most widely used. It appears that CMOS has become the dominant technology and may eventually replace TTL in small- and medium-scale ICs. Although TTL dominated for many years mainly because it had faster switching speeds and a greater selection of device types, CMOS always had the advantage of much lower power dissipation although that parameter is frequency dependent. The switching speeds of CMOS have been greatly improved and are now competitive with TTL, while low power dissipation and other desirable factors have been retained as the technology has progressed.

CMOS Series   The categories of CMOS in terms of the dc supply voltage are the 5 V CMOS, the 3.3 V CMOS, the 2.5 V CMOS, and the 1.8 V CMOS. The lower-voltage CMOS families are a more recent development and are the result of an effort to reduce the power dissipation. Since power dissipation is proportional to the square of the voltage, a reduction from 5 V to 3.3 V, for example, cuts the power by 34% with other factors remaining the same.

Within each supply voltage category, several series of CMOS logic gates are available. These series within the CMOS family differ in their performance characteristics and are designated by the prefix 74 or 54 followed by a letter or letters that indicate the series and then a number that indicates the type of logic device. The prefix 74 indicates commercial grade for general use, and the prefix 54 indicates military grade for more severe environments. We will refer only to the 74-prefixed devices in this textbook. The basic CMOS series for the 5 V category and their designations include

- 74HC and 74HCT—High-speed CMOS (the "T" indicates TTL compatibility)

- 74AC and 74ACT—Advanced CMOS

- 74AHC and 74AHCT—Advanced High-speed CMOS

The basic CMOS series for the 3.3 V category and their designations include

- 74LV—Low-voltage CMOS

- 74LVC—Low-voltage CMOS

- 74ALVC—Advanced Low-voltage CMOS

In addition to the 74 series there is a 4000 series, which is an older, low-speed CMOS technology that is still available, although in limited use. In addition to the "pure" CMOS, there is a series that combines both CMOS and TTL called BiCMOS. The basic BiCMOS series and their designations are as follows:

- 74BCT—BiCMOS

- 74ABT—Advanced BiCMOS

- 74LVT—Low-voltage BiCMOS

- 74ALB—Advanced Low-voltage BiCMOS

TTL

TTL has been a popular digital IC technology for many years. One advantage of TTL is that it is not sensitive to electrostatic discharge as CMOS is and, therefore, is more practical in most laboratory experimentation and prototyping because you do not have to worry about handling precautions.

TTL Series   Like CMOS, several series of TTL logic gates are available, all which operate from a 5 V dc supply. These series within the TTL family differ in their performance characteristics and are designated by the prefix 74 or 54 followed by a letter or letters that indicate the series and a number that indicates the type of logic device within the series. A TTL IC can be distinguished from CMOS by the letters that follow the 74 or 54 prefix.

The basic TTL series and their designations are as follows:

- 74—standard TTL (no letter)
- 74S—Schottky TTL
- 74AS—Advanced Schottky TTL
- 74LS—Low-power Schottky TTL
- 74ALS—Advanced Low-power Schottky TTL
- 74F—Fast TTL

Types of Fixed-Function Logic Gates

All of the basic logic operations, NOT, AND, OR, NAND, NOR, exclusive-OR (XOR), and exclusive-NOR (XNOR) are available in both CMOS and TTL. In addition to these, buffered output gates are also available for driving loads that require high currents. The types of gate configurations typically available in IC packages are identified by the last two or three digits in the series designation. For example, 74LS04 is a low-power **Schottky** hex inverter package. Some of the common logic gate configurations and their standard identifier digits are as follows:

- Quad 2-input NAND—**00**
- Quad 2-input NOR—**02**
- Hex inverter—**04**
- Quad 2-input AND—**08**
- Triple 3-input NAND—**10**
- Triple 3-input AND—**11**

- Dual 4-input NAND—**20**
- Dual 2-input AND—**21**
- Triple 3-input NOR—**27**
- Single 8-input NAND—**30**
- Quad 2-input OR—**32**
- Quad XOR—**86**
- Quad XNOR—**266**

IC Packages All of the 74 series CMOS are pin-compatible with the same types of devices in TTL. This means that a CMOS digital IC such as the 74HC00 (quad 2-input NAND), which contains four 2-input NAND gates in one IC package, has the identical package pin numbers for each input and output as does the corresponding TTL device. Typical IC gate packages, the dual in-line package (DIP) for plug-in or feedthrough mounting and the small-outline integrated circuit (SOIC) package for surface mounting, are shown in Figure 8–49. In some cases, other types of packages are also available. The SOIC package is significantly smaller than the DIP. The pin configuration diagrams for most of the fixed-function logic devices listed above are shown in Figure 8–50.

Single-Gate Logic A limited selection of CMOS gates is available in single-gate packages. With one gate to a package, this series comes in tiny 5-pin packages that are intended for use in last-minute modifications for squeezing logic into tight spots where available space is limited.

Logic Symbols The logic symbols for fixed-function integrated circuits use the standard gate symbols and show the number of gates in the IC package and the associated pin numbers for each gate as well as the pin numbers for V_{CC} and ground. An example is shown in Figure 8–51 for a hex inverter and for a quad 2-input NAND gate. Both the distinctive shape and the rectangular outline formats are shown. Regardless of the logic family, all devices with the same suffix are pin-compatible; in other words, they will have the same arrangement of pin numbers. For example, the 7400, 74S00, 74LS00, 74ALS00, 74F00, 74HC00, and 74AHC00 are all pin-compatible quad 2-input NAND gate packages.

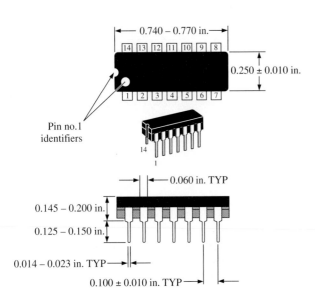

(a) 14-pin dual in-line package (DIP) for feedthrough mounting

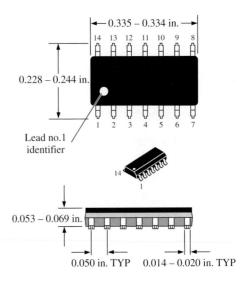

(b) 14-pin small outline package (SOIC) for surface mounting

▲ **FIGURE 8–49**

Typical dual in-line (DIP) and small-outline (SOIC) packages showing pin numbers and basic dimensions.

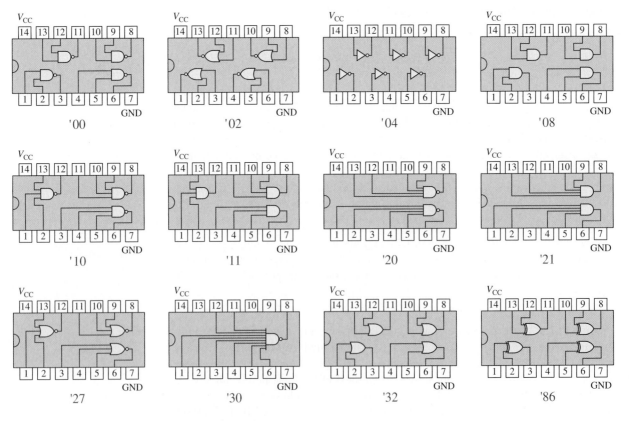

▲ **FIGURE 8–50**

Pin configuration diagrams for some common fixed-function IC gate configurations.

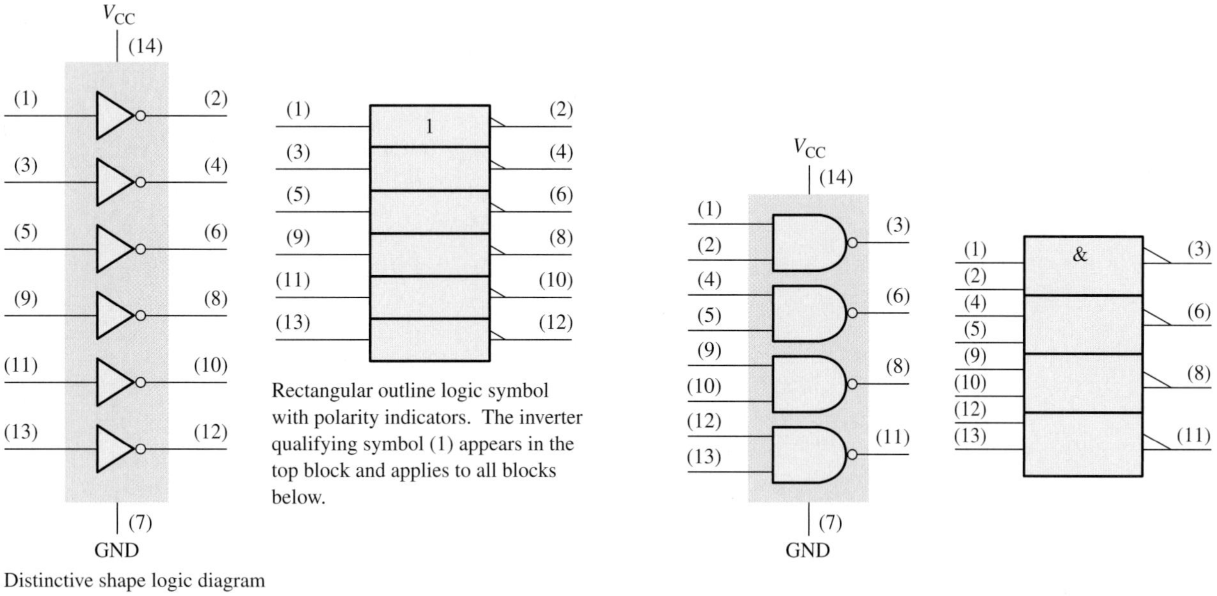

Rectangular outline logic symbol with polarity indicators. The inverter qualifying symbol (1) appears in the top block and applies to all blocks below.

Distinctive shape logic diagram

(a) Hex inverter

(b) Quad 2-input NAND

▲ **FIGURE 8–51**

Logic symbols for hex inverter (04 suffix) and quad 2-input NAND (00 suffix). The symbol applies to the same device in any CMOS or TTL series.

Performance Characteristics and Parameters

Several things define the performance of a logic circuit. These performance characteristics are the switching speed measured in terms of the propagation delay time, the power dissipation, the fan-out or drive capability, the speed-power product, the dc supply voltage, and the input/output logic levels.

High-speed logic has a short propagation delay time.

Propagation Delay Time   This parameter is a result of the limitation on switching speed or frequency at which a logic circuit can operate. The terms *low speed* and *high speed,* applied to logic circuits, refer to the propagation delay time. The shorter the propagation delay, the higher the speed of the circuit and the higher the frequency at which it can operate.

   Propagation delay time, *tp,* of a logic gate is the time interval between the application of an input pulse and the occurrence of the resulting output pulse. There are two different measurements of propagation delay time associated with a logic gate that apply to all the types of basic gates:

■ t_{PHL}: The time between a specified reference point on the input pulse and a corresponding reference point on the resulting output pulse, with the output changing from the HIGH level to the LOW level (HL).

■ t_{PLH}: The time between a specified reference point on the input pulse and a corresponding reference point on the resulting output pulse, with the output changing from the LOW level to the HIGH level (LH).

EXAMPLE 8–21

Show the propagation delay times of the inverter in Figure 8–52(a).

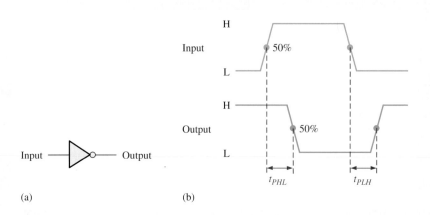

Input —▷o— Output

(a)   (b)

▲ **FIGURE 8–52**

Solution The propagation delay times, t_{PHL} and t_{PLH}, are indicated in part (b) of the figure. In this case, the delays are measured between the 50% points of the corresponding edges of the input and output pulses. The values of t_{PHL} and t_{PLH} are not necessarily equal but in many cases they are the same.

Related Problem One type of logic gate has a specified maximum t_{PLH} and t_{PHL} of 10 ns. For another type of gate the value is 4 ns. Which gate can operate at the highest frequency?

For standard-series TTL gates, the typical propagation delay is 11 ns and for F-series gates it is 3.3 ns. For HCT-series CMOS, the propagation delay is 7 ns, for the AC series it is 5 ns, and for the ALVC series it is 3 ns. All specified values are dependent on certain operating conditions as stated on a data sheet.

DC Supply Voltage (VCC) The typical dc supply voltage for CMOS is either 5 V, 3.3 V, 2.5 V, or 1.8 V, depending on the category. An advantage of CMOS is that the supply voltages can vary over a wider range than for TTL. The 5 V CMOS can tolerate supply variations from 2 V to 6 V and still operate properly although propagation delay time and power dissipation are significantly affected. The 3.3 V CMOS can operate with supply voltages from 2 V to 3.6 V. The typical dc supply voltage for TTL is 5.0 V with a minimum of 4.5 V and a maximum of 5.5 V.

Power Dissipation The **power dissipation,** *PD,* of a logic gate is the product of the dc supply voltage and the average supply current. Normally, the supply current when the gate output is LOW is greater than when the gate output is HIGH. The manufacturer's data sheet usually designates the supply current for the LOW output state as I_{CCL} and for the HIGH state as I_{CCH}. The average supply current is determined based on a 50% duty cycle (output LOW half the time and HIGH half the time), so the average power dissipation of a logic gate is

Equation 8–2

$$P_D = V_{CC}\left(\frac{I_{CCH} + I_{CCL}}{2}\right)$$

CMOS series gates have very low power dissipations compared to the TTL series. However, the power dissipation of CMOS is dependent on the frequency of operation. At zero frequency the quiescent power is typically in the microwatt/gate range, and at the maximum operating frequency it can be in the low milliwatt range; therefore, power is sometimes specified at a given frequency. The HC series, for example, has a power of 2.75 µW/gate at 0 Hz (quiescent) and 600 µW/gate at 1 MHz.

Power dissipation for TTL is independent of frequency. For example, the ALS series uses 1.4 µW/gate regardless of the frequency and the F series uses 6 µW/gate.

Input and Output Logic Levels V_{IL} is the LOW level input voltage for a logic gate, and V_{IH} is the HIGH level input voltage. The 5 V CMOS accepts a maximum voltage of 1.5 V as V_{IL} and a minimum voltage of 3.5 V as V_{IH}. TTL accepts a maximum voltage of 0.8 V as V_{IL} and a minimum voltage of 2 V as V_{IH}.

V_{OL} is the LOW level output voltage and V_{OH} is the HIGH level output voltage. For 5 V CMOS, the maximum V_{OL} is 0.33 V and the minimum V_{OH} is 4.4 V. For TTL, the maximum V_{OL} is 0.4 V and the minimum V_{OH} is 2.4 V. All values depend on operating conditions as specified on the data sheet.

Speed-Power Product (SPP) This parameter (**speed-power product**) can be used as a measure of the performance of a logic circuit taking into account the propagation delay time and the power dissipation. It is especially useful for comparing the various logic gate series within the CMOS or TTL family or for comparing a CMOS gate to a TTL gate.

The SPP of a logic circuit is the product of the propagation delay time and the power dissipation and is expressed in joules (J), which is the unit of energy. The formula is

$$SPP = t_P P_D$$

Equation 8-3

EXAMPLE 8-22

A certain gate has a propagation delay of 5 ns and $I_{CCH} = 1$ mA and $I_{CCL} = 2.5$ mA with a dc supply voltage of 5 V. Determine the speed-power product.

Solution $$P_D = V_{CC}\left(\frac{I_{CCH} + I_{CCL}}{2}\right) = 5\ V\left(\frac{1\ mA + 2.5\ mA}{2}\right) = 5\ V(1.75\ mA) = 8.75\ mW$$

$$SPP = (5\ ns)(8.75\ mW) = \textbf{43.75 pJ}$$

Related Problem If the propagation delay of a gate is 15 ns and its *SPP* is 150 pJ, what is its average power dissipation?

Fan-Out and Loading The **fan-out** of a logic gate is the maximum number of inputs of the same series in an IC family that can be connected to a gate's output and still maintain the output voltage levels within specified limits. Fan-out is a significant parameter only for TTL because of the type of circuit technology. Since very high impedances are associated with CMOS circuits, the fan-out is very high but depends on frequency because of capacitive effects.

Fan-out is specified in terms of **unit loads.** A unit load for a logic gate equals one input to a like circuit. For example, a unit load for a 74LS00 NAND gate equals *one* input to another logic gate in the 74LS series (not necessarily a NAND gate). Because the current from a LOW input (I_{IL}) of a 74LS00 gate is 0.4 mA and the current that a LOW output (*IOL*) can accept is 8.0 mA, the number of unit loads that a 74LS00 gate can drive in the LOW state is

A higher fan-out means that a gate output can be connected to more gate inputs.

$$\text{Unit loads} = \frac{I_{OL}}{I_{IL}} = \frac{8.0\ mA}{0.4\ mA} = 20$$

Figure 8–53 shows LS logic gates driving a number of other gates of the same circuit technology, where the number of gates depends on the particular circuit technology. For example, as you have seen, the maximum number of gate inputs (unit loads) that a 74LS series TTL gate can drive is 20.

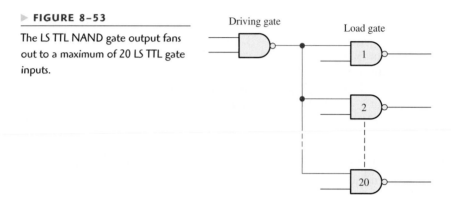

▶ **FIGURE 8–53**

The LS TTL NAND gate output fans out to a maximum of 20 LS TTL gate inputs.

Data Sheets

A typical data sheet consists of an information page that shows, among other things, the logic diagram and packages, the recommended operating conditions, the electrical characteristics, and the switching characteristics. Partial data sheets for a 74LS00 and a 74HC00A are shown in Figures 8–54 and 8–55, respectively. The length of data sheets vary and some have much more information than others. Additional data sheets are provided on the Texas Instruments CD-ROM accompanying this textbook.

HANDS ON TIP

Unused gate inputs for TTL and CMOS should be connected to the appropriate logic level (HIGH or LOW). For AND/NAND, it is recommended that unused inputs be connected to V_{CC} (through a 1.0 kΩ resistor with TTL) and for OR/NOR, unused inputs should be connected to ground.

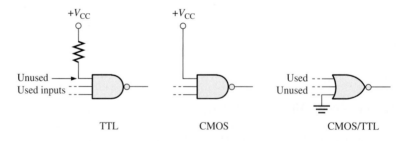

QUAD 2-INPUT NAND GATE

• ESD > 3500 Volts

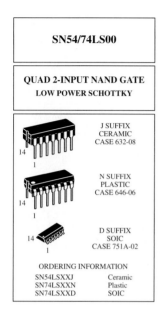

SN54/74LS00

QUAD 2-INPUT NAND GATE
LOW POWER SCHOTTKY

J SUFFIX
CERAMIC
CASE 632-08

14
1

N SUFFIX
PLASTIC
CASE 646-06

14
1

D SUFFIX
SOIC
CASE 751A-02

14
1

ORDERING INFORMATION

SN54LSXXJ   Ceramic
SN74LSXXN   Plastic
SN74LSXXD   SOIC

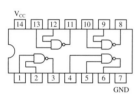

SN54/74LS00

DC CHARACTERISTICS OVER OPERATING TEMPERATURE RANGE (unless otherwise specified)

Symbol	Parameter		Limits			Unit	Test Conditions
			Min	Typ	Max		
V_{IH}	Input HIGH Voltage		2.0			V	Guaranteed Input HIGH Voltage for All Inputs
V_{IL}	Input LOW Voltage	54			0.7	V	Guaranteed Input LOW Voltage for All Inputs
		74			0.8		
V_{IK}	Input Clamp Diode Voltage			−0.65	−1.5	V	V_{CC} = MIN, I_{IN} = −18 mA
V_{OH}	Ouput HIGH Voltage	54	2.5	3.5		V	V_{CC} = MIN, I_{OH} = MAX, V_{IN} = V_{IH} or V_{IL} per Truth Table
		74	2.7	3.5		V	
V_{OL}	Ouput LOW Voltage	54, 74		0.25	0.4	V	I_{OL} = 4.0 mA · V_{CC} = V_{CC} MIN, V_{IN} = V_{IL}
		74		0.35	0.5	V	I_{OL} = 8.0 mA · or V_{IH} per Truth Table
I_{IH}	Input HIGH Current				20	μA	V_{CC} = MAX, V_{IN} = 2.7 V
					0.1	mA	V_{CC} = MAX, V_{IN} = 7.0 V
I_{IL}	Input LOW Current				−0.4	mA	V_{CC} = MAX, I_{N} = 0.4 V
I_{OS}	Short Circuit Current (Note 1)		−20		−100	mA	V_{CC} = MAX
I_{CC}	Power Supply Current Total, Output HIGH				1.6	mA	V_{CC} = MAX
	Total, Output LOW				4.4		

NOTE 1: Not more than one output should be shorted at a time, nor for more than 1 second.

AC CHARACTERISTICS (T_A = 25°C)

Symbol	Parameter		Limits		Unit	Test Conditions
		Min	Typ	Max		
t_{PLH}	Turn-Off Delay, Input to Output		9.0	15	ns	V_{CC} = 5.0 V
t_{PHL}	Turn-On Delay, Input to Output		10	15	ns	C_L = 15 pF

GUARANTEED OPERATING RANGES

Symbol	Parameter		Min	Typ	Max	Unit
V_{CC}	Supply Voltage	54	4.5	5.0	5.5	V
		74	4.75	5.0	5.25	
T_A	Operating Ambient Temperature Range	54	−55	25	125	°C
		74	0	25	70	
I_{OH}	Output Current — High	54, 74			−0.4	mA
I_{OL}	Output Current — Low	54			4.0	mA
		74			8.0	

▲ **FIGURE 8–54**

The partial data sheet for a 74LS00.

Quad 2-Input NAND Gate High-Performance Silicon–Gate CMOS

The MC54/74HC00A is identical in pinout to the LS00. The device inputs are compatible with Standard CMOS outputs; with pullup resistors, they are compatible with LSTTL outputs.

- Output Drive Capability: 10 LSTTL Loads
- Outputs Directly Interface to CMOS, NMOS and TTL
- Operating Voltage Range: 2 to 6 V
- Low Input Current: 1 μA
- High Noise Immunity Characteristic of CMOS Devices
- In Compliance With the JEDEC Standard No. 7A Requirements
- Chip Complexity: 32 FETs or 8 Equivalent Gates

LOGIC DIAGRAM

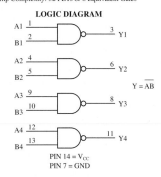

$$Y = \overline{AB}$$

PIN 14 = V_{CC}
PIN 7 = GND

Pinout: 14–Load Packages (Top View)

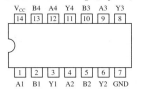

MC54/74HC00A

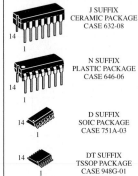

J SUFFIX
CERAMIC PACKAGE
CASE 632-08

N SUFFIX
PLASTIC PACKAGE
CASE 646-06

D SUFFIX
SOIC PACKAGE
CASE 751A-03

DT SUFFIX
TSSOP PACKAGE
CASE 948G-01

ORDERING INFORMATION

MC54HCXXAJ	Ceramic
MC74HCXXAN	Plastic
MC74HCXXAD	SOIC
MC74HCXXADT	TSSOP

FUNCTION TABLE

Inputs		Output
A	B	Y
L	L	H
L	H	H
H	L	H
H	H	L

MAXIMUM RATINGS*

Symbol	Parameter	Value	Unit
V_{CC}	DC Supply Voltage (Referenced to GND)	−0.5 to + 7.0	V
V_{in}	DC Input Voltage (Referenced to GND)	−0.5 to V_{CC} + 0.5	V
V_{out}	DC Output Voltage (Referenced to GND)	−0.5 to V_{CC} + 0.5	V
I_{in}	DC Input Current, per Pin	± 20	mA
I_{out}	DC Output Current, per Pin	± 25	mA
I_{CC}	DC Supply Current, V_{CC} and GND Pins	± 50	mA
P_D	Power Dissipation in Still Air, Plastic or Ceramic DIP†	750	mW
	SOIC Package†	500	
	TSSOP Package†	450	
T_{stg}	Storage Temperature	−65 to + 150	°C
T_L	Lead Temperature, 1 mm from Case for 10 Seconds		°C
	Plastic DIP, SOIC or TSSOP Package	260	
	Ceramic DIP	300	

* Maximum Ratings are those values beyond which damage to the device may occur.
  Functional operation should be restricted to the Recommended Operating Conditions.
† Derating — Plastic DIP: – 10 mW/°C from 65° to 125° C
  Ceramic DIP: – 10 mW/°C from 100° to 125° C
  SOIC Package: – 7 mW/°C from 65° to 125° C
  TSSOP Package: – 6.1 mW/°C from 65° to 125° C

RECOMMENDED OPERATING CONDITIONS

Symbol	Parameter		in	Max	Unit
V_{CC}	DC Supply Voltage (Referenced to GND)		2.0	6.0	V
V_{in}, V_{out}	DC Input Voltage, Output Voltage (Referenced to GND)		0	V_{CC}	V
T_A	Operating Temperature, All Package Types		−55	+125	°C
t_r, t_f	Input Rise and Fall Time	V_{CC} = 2.0 V	0	1000	ns
		V_{CC} = 4.5 V	0	500	
		V_{CC} = 6.0 V	0	400	

DC CHARACTERISTICS (Voltages Referenced to GND)

MC54/74HC00A

Symbol	Parameter	Condition	V_{CC} V	Guaranteed Limit −55 to 25°C	≤85°C	≤125°C	Unit
V_{IH}	Minimum High-Level Input Voltage	V_{out} = 0.1V or V_{CC} − 0.1V $\|I_{out}\| \leq 20\mu A$	2.0	1.50	1.50	1.50	V
			3.0	2.10	2.10	2.10	
			4.5	3.15	3.15	3.15	
			6.0	4.20	4.20	4.20	
V_{IL}	Maximum Low-Level Input Voltage	V_{out} = 0.1V or V_{CC} − 0.1V $\|I_{out}\| \leq 20\mu A$	2.0	0.50	0.50	0.50	V
			3.0	0.90	0.90	0.90	
			4.5	1.35	1.35	1.35	
			6.0	1.80	1.80	1.80	
V_{OH}	Minimum High-Level Output Voltage	V_{in} = V_{IH} or V_{IL} $\|I_{out}\| \leq 20\mu A$	2.0	1.9	1.9	1.9	V
			4.5	4.4	4.4	4.4	
			6.0	5.9	5.9	5.9	
		V_{in} = V_{IH} or V_{IL} $\|I_{out}\| \leq 2.4mA$	3.0	2.48	2.34	2.20	
		$\|I_{out}\| \leq 4.0mA$	4.5	3.98	3.84	3.70	
		$\|I_{out}\| \leq 5.2mA$	6.0	5.48	5.34	5.20	
V_{OL}	Maximum Low-Level Output Voltage	V_{in} = V_{IH} or V_{IL} $\|I_{out}\| \leq 20\mu A$	2.0	0.1	0.1	0.1	V
			4.5	0.1	0.1	0.1	
			6.0	0.1	0.1	0.1	
		V_{in} = V_{IH} or V_{IL} $\|I_{out}\| \leq 2.4mA$	3.0	0.26	0.33	0.40	
		$\|I_{out}\| \leq 4.0mA$	4.5	0.26	0.33	0.40	
		$\|I_{out}\| \leq 5.2mA$	6.0	0.26	0.33	0.40	
I_{in}	Maximum Input Leakage Current	V_{in} = V_{CC} or GND	6.0	±0.1	±1.0	±1.0	μA
I_{CC}	Maximum Quiescent Supply Current (per Package)	V_{in} = V_{CC} or GND I_{out} = 0μA	6.0	1.0	10	40	μA

AC CHARACTERISTICS (C_L = 50 pF, Input t_r = t_f = 6 ns)

Symbol	Parameter	V_{CC} V	Guaranteed Limit −55 to 25°C	≤85°C	≤125°C	Unit
t_{PLH}, t_{PHL}	Maximum Propagation Delay, Input A or B to Output Y	2.0	75	95	110	ns
		3.0	30	40	55	
		4.5	15	19	22	
		6.0	13	16	19	
t_{TLH}, t_{THL}	Maximum Output Transition Time, Any Output	2.0	75	95	110	ns
		3.0	27	32	36	
		4.5	15	19	22	
		6.0	13	16	19	
C_{in}	Maximum Input Capacitance		10	10	10	pF

		Typical @ 25°C, V_{CC} = 5.0 V, V_{EE} = 0 V	
C_{PD}	Power Dissipation Capacitance (Per Buffer)	22	pF

▲ **FIGURE 8–55**

The partial data sheet for a 74HC00A.

SUMMARY

- The inverter output is the complement of the input.
- The AND gate output is HIGH only when all the inputs are HIGH.
- The OR gate output is HIGH when any of the inputs is HIGH.
- The NAND gate output is LOW only when all the inputs are HIGH.
- The NAND can be viewed as a negative-OR whose output is HIGH when any input is LOW.
- The NOR gate output is LOW when any of the inputs is HIGH.
- The NOR can be viewed as a negative-AND whose output is HIGH only when all the inputs are LOW.
- The exclusive-OR gate output is HIGH when the inputs are not the same.
- The exclusive-NOR gate output is LOW when the inputs are not the same.
- Distinctive shape symbols and truth tables for various logic gates (limited to 2 inputs) are shown in Figure 8–56.

▶ FIGURE 8–56

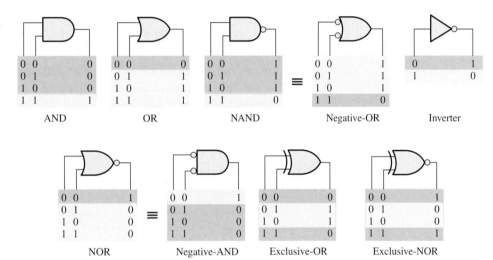

Note: Active states are shown in yellow.

KEY TERMS

AND array An array of AND gates consisting of a matrix of programmable interconnections.

AND gate A logic gate that produces a HIGH output only when all of the inputs are HIGH.

Boolean algebra The mathematics of logic circuits.

Complement The inverse or opposite of a number. LOW is the complement of HIGH, and 0 is the complement of 1.

Enable To activate or put into an operational mode; an input on a logic circuit that enables its operation.

Exclusive-OR (XOR) gate A logic gate that produces a HIGH output only when its two inputs are at opposite levels.

Exclusive-NOR gate A logic gate that produces a LOW only when the two inputs are at opposite levels.

Fan-out The number of equivalent gate inputs of the same family series that a logic gate can drive.

Inverter A logic circuit that inverts or complements its input.

NAND gate A logic gate that produces a LOW output only when all the inputs are HIGH.

NOR gate A logic gate in which the output is LOW when one or more of the inputs are HIGH.

OR gate A logic gate that produces a HIGH output when one or more inputs are HIGH.

Propagation delay time The time interval between the occurrence of an input transition and the occurrence of the corresponding output transition in a logic circuit.

Timing diagram A diagram of waveforms showing the proper timing relationship of all the waveforms.

Truth table A table showing the inputs and corresponding output(s) of a logic circuit.

Unit load A measure of fan-out. One gate input represents one unit load to the output of a gate within the same IC family.

SELF-TEST

Answers are at the end of the chapter.

1. When the input to an inverter is HIGH (1), the output is
   (a) HIGH or 1   (b) LOW or 1   (c) HIGH or 0   (d) LOW or 0

2. An inverter performs an operation known as
   (a) complementation   (b) assertion
   (c) inversion   (d) both answers (a) and (c)

3. The output of an AND gate with inputs A, B, and C is a 1 (HIGH) when
   (a) $A = 1, B = 1, C = 1$ (b) $A = 1, B = 0, C = 1$ (c) $A = 0, B = 0, C = 0$

4. The output of an OR gate with inputs A, B, and C is a 1 (HIGH) when
   (a) $A = 1, B = 1, C = 1$ (b) $A = 0, B = 0, C = 1$ (c) $A = 0, B = 0, C = 0$
   (d) answers (a), (b), and (c)   (e) only answers (a) and (b)

5. A pulse is applied to each input of a 2-input NAND gate. One pulse goes HIGH at $t = 0$ and goes back LOW at $t = 1$ ms. The other pulse goes HIGH at $t = 0.8$ ms and goes back LOW at $t = 3$ ms. The output pulse can be described as follows:
   (a) It goes LOW at $t = 0$ and back HIGH at $t = 3$ ms.
   (b) It goes LOW at $t = 0.8$ ms and back HIGH at $t = 3$ ms.
   (c) It goes LOW at $t = 0.8$ ms and back HIGH at $t = 1$ ms.
   (d) It goes LOW at $t = 0.8$ ms and back LOW at $t = 1$ ms.

6. A pulse is applied to each input of a 2-input NOR gate. One pulse goes HIGH at $t = 0$ and goes back LOW at $t = 1$ ms. The other pulse goes HIGH at $t = 0.8$ ms and goes back LOW at $t = 3$ ms. The output pulse can be described as follows:
   (a) It goes LOW at $t = 0$ and back HIGH at $t = 3$ ms.
   (b) It goes LOW at $t = 0.8$ ms and back HIGH at $t = 3$ ms.
   (c) It goes LOW at $t = 0.8$ ms and back HIGH at $t = 1$ ms.
   (d) It goes HIGH at $t = 0.8$ ms and back LOW at $t = 1$ ms.

7. A pulse is applied to each input of an exclusive-OR gate. One pulse goes HIGH at $t = 0$ and goes back LOW at $t = 1$ ms. The other pulse goes HIGH at $t = 0.8$ ms and goes back LOW at $t = 3$ ms. The output pulse can be described as follows:
   (a) It goes HIGH at $t = 0$ and back LOW at $t = 3$ ms.
   (b) It goes HIGH at $t = 0$ and back LOW at $t = 0.8$ ms.
   (c) It goes HIGH at $t = 1$ ms and back LOW at $t = 3$ ms.
   (d) both answers (b) and (c)

8. A positive-going pulse is applied to an inverter. The time interval from the leading edge of the input to the leading edge of the output is 7 ns. This parameter is
   (a) speed-power product   (b) propagation delay, t_{PHL}
   (c) propagation delay, t_{PLH} (d) pulse width

9. To measure the period of a pulse waveform, you must use
   (a) a DMM   (b) a logic probe
   (c) an oscilloscope   (d) a logic pulser

10. Once you measure the period of a pulse waveform, the frequency is found by
    (a) using another setting   (b) measuring the duty cycle
    (c) finding the reciprocal of the period   (d) using another type of instrument

PROBLEMS

SECTION 8–1 The Inverter

1. The input waveform shown in Figure 8–57 is applied to an inverter. Draw the timing diagram of the output waveform in proper relation to the input.

▷ **FIGURE 8–57**

V_{IN} HIGH LOW

2. A network of cascaded inverters is shown in Figure 8–58. If a HIGH is applied to point A, determine the logic levels at points B through F.

▷ **FIGURE 8–58**

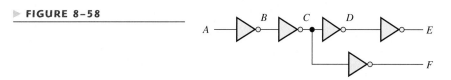

SECTION 8–2 The AND Gate

3. Determine the output, X, for a 2-input AND gate with the input waveforms shown in Figure 8–59. Show the proper relationship of output to inputs with a timing diagram.

▷ **FIGURE 8–59**

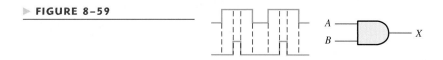

4. Repeat Problem 3 for the waveforms in Figure 8–60.

▷ **FIGURE 8–60**

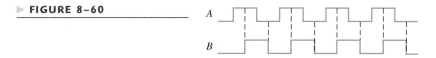

5. The input waveforms applied to a 3-input AND gate are as indicated in Figure 8–61. Show the output waveform in proper relation to the inputs with a timing diagram.

▷ **FIGURE 8–61**

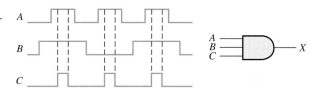

6. The input waveforms applied to a 4-input AND gate are as indicated in Figure 8–62. Show the output waveform in proper relation to the inputs with a timing diagram.

▷ **FIGURE 8–62**

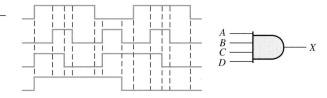

SECTION 8-3   The OR Gate

7. Determine the output for a 2-input OR gate when the input waveforms are as in Figure 8–60 and draw a timing diagram.

8. Repeat Problem 5 for a 3-input OR gate.

9. Repeat Problem 6 for a 4-input OR gate.

10. For the five input waveforms in Figure 8–63, determine the output for a 5-input AND gate and the output for a 5-input OR gate. Draw the timing diagram.

▷ FIGURE 8–63

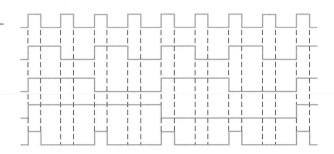

SECTION 8-4   The NAND Gate

11. For the set of input waveforms in Figure 8–64, determine the output for the gate shown and draw the timing diagram.

▷ FIGURE 8–64

12. Determine the gate output for the input waveforms in Figure 8–65 and draw the timing diagram.

▷ FIGURE 8–65

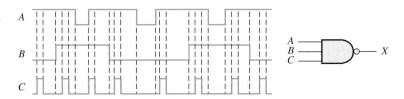

13. Determine the output waveform in Figure 8–66.

▷ FIGURE 8–66

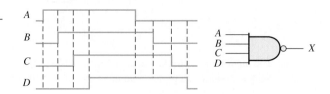

14. As you have learned, the two logic symbols shown in Figure 8–67 represent equivalent operations. The difference between the two is strictly from a functional viewpoint. For the NAND symbol, look for two HIGHs on the inputs to give a LOW output. For the negative-OR, look for at least one LOW on the inputs to give a HIGH on the output. Using these two functional viewpoints, show that each gate will produce the same output for the given inputs.

▷ **FIGURE 8–67**

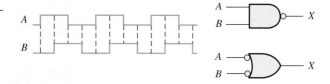

SECTION 8–5 The NOR Gate

15. Repeat Problem 11 for a 2-input NOR gate.

16. Determine the output waveform in Figure 8–68 and draw the timing diagram.

▷ **FIGURE 8–68**

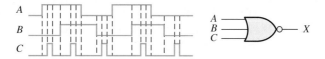

17. Repeat Problem 13 for a 4-input NOR gate.

18. The NAND and the negative-OR symbols represent equivalent operations, but they are functionally different. For the NOR symbol, look for at least one HIGH on the inputs to give a LOW on the output. For the negative-AND, look for two LOWs on the inputs to give a HIGH output. Using these two functional points of view, show that both gates in Figure 8–69 will produce the same output for the given inputs.

▷ **FIGURE 8–69**

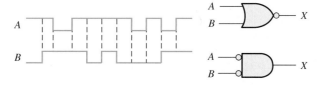

SECTION 8–6 The Exclusive-OR and Exclusive-NOR Gates

19. How does an exclusive-OR gate differ from an OR gate in its logical operation?

20. Repeat Problem 11 for an exclusive-OR gate.

21. Repeat Problem 11 for an exclusive-NOR gate.

22. Determine the output of an exclusive-OR gate for the inputs shown in Figure 8–69 and draw a timing diagram.

SECTION 8–7 Fixed-Function Logic

23. In the comparison of certain logic devices, it is noted that the power dissipation for one particular type increases as the frequency increases. Is the device TTL or CMOS?

24. Determine t_{PLH} and t_{PHL} from the oscilloscope display in Figure 8–70. The readings indicate V/div and sec/div for each channel.

 FIGURE 8–70

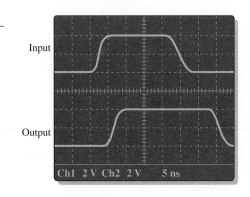

25. Gate A has $t_{PLH} = t_{PHL} = 6$ ns. Gate B has $t_{PLH} = t_{PHL} = 10$ ns. Which gate can be operated at a higher frequency?

26. If a logic gate operates on a dc supply voltage of $+5$ V and draws an average current of 4 mA, what is its power dissipation?

SELF-TEST

1. (d) 2. (d) 3. (a) 4. (e) 5. (c) 6. (a) 7. (d) 8. (b) 9. (c)
10. (c)

9

BOOLEAN ALGEBRA AND LOGIC SIMPLIFICATION

INTRODUCTION

In 1854, George Boole published a work titled *An Investigation of the Laws of Thought, on Which Are Founded the Mathematical Theories of Logic and Probabilities*. It was in this publication that a "logical algebra," known today as Boolean algebra, was formulated. Boolean algebra is a convenient and systematic way of expressing and analyzing the operation of logic circuits. Claude Shannon was the first to apply Boole's work to the analysis and design of logic circuits. In 1938, Shannon wrote a thesis at MIT titled *A Symbolic Analysis of Relay and Switching Circuits*.

This chapter covers the laws, rules, and theorems of Boolean algebra and their application to digital circuits. You will learn how to define a given circuit with a Boolean expression and then evaluate its operation.

CHAPTER OBJECTIVES

▨ Apply the basic laws and rules of Boolean algebra

▨ Apply DeMorgan's theorems to Boolean expressions

▨ Describe gate networks with Boolean expressions

▨ Evaluate Boolean expressions

▨ Simplify expressions by using the laws and rules of Boolean algebra

▨ Convert any Boolean expression into a sum-of-products (SOP) form

KEY TERMS

▨ Variable

▨ Complement

▨ Sum term

▨ Product term

▨ Sum-of-products (SOP)

WWW.   **VISIT THE COMPANION WEBSITE**
Study aids for this chapter are available at
http://www.prenhall.com/floyd

9–1 BOOLEAN OPERATIONS AND EXPRESSIONS

Boolean algebra is the mathematics of digital systems. A basic knowledge of Boolean algebra is indispensable to the study and analysis of logic circuits. In the last chapter, Boolean operations and expressions in terms of their relationship to NOT, AND, OR, NAND, and NOR gates were introduced.

After completing this section, you should be able to

- Define *variable*
- Define *literal*
- Identify a sum term
- Evaluate a sum term
- Identify a product term
- Evaluate a product term
- Explain Boolean addition
- Explain Boolean multiplication

COMPUTER NOTE

In a microprocessor, the arithmetic logic unit (ALU) performs arithmetic and Boolean logic operations on digital data as directed by program instructions. Logical operations are equivalent to the basic gate operations that you are familiar with but deal with a minimum of 8 bits at a time. Examples of Boolean logic instructions are AND, OR, NOT, and XOR, which are called *mnemonics*. An assembly language program uses the mnemonics to specify an operation. Another program called an *assembler* translates the mnemonics into a binary code that can be understood by the microprocessor.

Variable, complement, and *literal* are terms used in Boolean algebra. A **variable** is a symbol (usually an italic uppercase letter) used to represent a logical quantity. Any single variable can have a 1 or a 0 value. The **complement** is the inverse of a variable and is indicated by a bar over the variable (overbar). For example, the complement of the variable A is $\overline{A}$. If $A = 1$, then $\overline{A} = 0$. If $A = 0$, then $\overline{A} = 1$. The complement of the variable A is read as "not A" or "A bar." Sometimes a prime symbol rather than an overbar is used to denote the complement of a variable; for example, B' indicates the complement of B. In this book, only the overbar is used. A **literal** is a variable or the complement of a variable.

Boolean Addition

Recall from Chapter 8 that **Boolean addition** is equivalent to the OR operation and the basic rules are illustrated with their relation to the OR gate as follows:

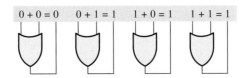

$$0 + 0 = 0 \qquad 0 + 1 = 1 \qquad 1 + 0 = 1 \qquad 1 + 1 = 1$$

In Boolean algebra, a **sum term** is a sum of literals. In logic circuits, a sum term is produced by an OR operation with no AND operations involved. Some examples of sum terms are $A + B$, $A + \overline{B}$, $A + B + \overline{C}$, and $\overline{A} + B + C + \overline{D}$.

A sum term is equal to 1 when one or more of the literals in the term are 1. A sum term is equal to 0 only if each of the literals is 0.

The OR gate is a Boolean adder.

EXAMPLE 9–1

Determine the values of $A, B, C,$ and D that make the sum term $A + \overline{B} + C + \overline{D}$ equal to 0.

Solution   For the sum term to be 0, each of the literals in the term must be 0. Therefore, A = 0, B = 1 so that $\overline{B} = 0$, C = **0**, and D = 1 so that $\overline{D} = 0$.

$$A + \bar{B} + C + \bar{D} = 0 + \bar{1} + 0 + \bar{1} = 0 + 0 + 0 + 0 = 0$$

Related Problem   Determine the values of A and B that make the sum term $\bar{A} + B$ equal to 0.

Boolean Multiplication

Also recall from Chapter 8 that **Boolean multiplication** is equivalent to the AND operation and the basic rules are illustrated with their relation to the AND gate as follows:

The AND gate is a Boolean multiplier.

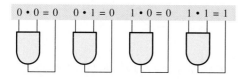

In Boolean algebra, a **product term** is the product of literals. In logic circuits, a product term is produced by an AND operation with no OR operations involved. Some examples of product terms are AB, $A\bar{B}$, ABC, and $A\bar{B}C\bar{D}$.

A product term is equal to 1 only if each of the literals in the term is 1. A product term is equal to 0 when one or more of the literals are 0.

EXAMPLE 9–2

Determine the values of A, B, C, and D that make the product term $A\bar{B}C\bar{D}$ equal to 1.

Solution   For the product term to be 1, each of the literals in the term must be 1. Therefore, $A = \mathbf{1}, B = \mathbf{0}$ so that $\bar{B} = 1$, $C = \mathbf{1}$, and $D = \mathbf{0}$ so that $\bar{D} = 1$.

$$A\bar{B}C\bar{D} = 1 \cdot \bar{0} \cdot 1 \cdot \bar{0} = 1 \cdot 1 \cdot 1 \cdot 1 = 1$$

Related Problem   Determine the values of A and B that make the product term $\bar{A}\bar{B}$ equal to 1.

9–2   LAWS AND RULES OF BOOLEAN ALGEBRA

As in other areas of mathematics, there are certain well-developed rules and laws that must be followed in order to properly apply Boolean algebra. The most important of these are presented in this section.

After completing this section, you should be able to

■ Apply the commutative laws of addition and multiplication

■ Apply the associative laws of addition and multiplication

■ Apply the distributive law

■ Apply twelve basic rules of Boolean algebra

Laws of Boolean Algebra

The basic laws of Boolean algebra—the **commutative laws** for addition and multiplication, the **associative laws** for addition and multiplication, and the **distributive law**—are the same as in ordinary algebra. Each of the laws is illustrated with two or three variables, but the number of variables is not limited to this.

Commutative Laws   The *commutative law of addition* for two variables is written as

Equation 9–1 $A + B = B + A$

This law states that the order in which the variables are ORed makes no difference. Remember, in Boolean algebra as applied to logic circuits, addition and the OR operation are the same. Figure 9–1 illustrates the commutative law as applied to the OR gate and shows that it doesn't matter to which input each variable is applied. (The symbol ≡ means "equivalent to.")

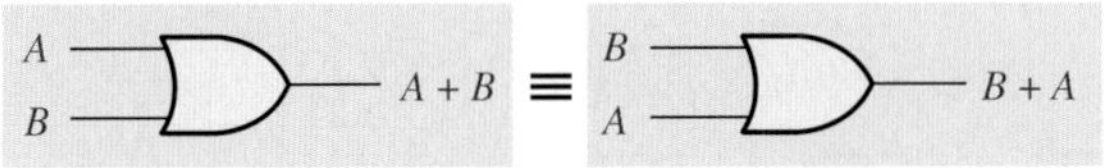

▶ **FIGURE 9–1**

Application of commutative law of addition.

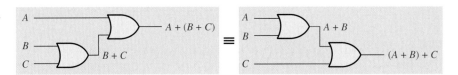

The *commutative law of multiplication* for two variables is

Equation 9–2 $AB = BA$

This law states that the order in which the variables are ANDed makes no difference. Figure 9–2 illustrates this law as applied to the AND gate.

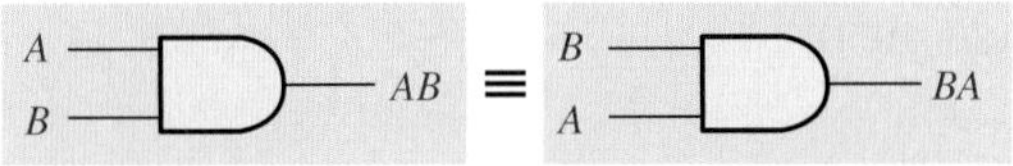

▶ **FIGURE 9–2**

Application of commutative law of multiplication.

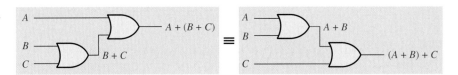

Associative Laws   The *associative law of addition* is written as follows for three variables:

Equation 9–3 $A + (B + C) = (A + B) + C$

Equation 9–3
This law states that when ORing more than two variables, the result is the same regardless of the grouping of the variables. Figure 9–3 illustrates this law as applied to 2-input OR gates.

▶ **FIGURE 9–3**

Application of associative law of addition.

The *associative law of multiplication* is written as follows for three variables:

Equation 9–4 $A(BC) = (AB)C$

This law states that it makes no difference in what order the variables are grouped when ANDing more than two variables. Figure 9–4 illustrates this law as applied to 2-input AND gates.

▶ **FIGURE 9–4**

Application of associative law of multiplication.

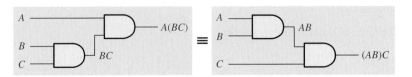

Distributive Law   The distributive law is written for three variables as follows:

Equation 9–5 $A(B + C) = AB + AC$

This law states that ORing two or more variables and then ANDing the result with a single variable is equivalent to ANDing the single variable with each of the two or more variables and then ORing the products. The distributive law also expresses the process of *factoring* in which the common variable A is factored out of the product terms, for example, $AB + AC = A(B + C)$. Figure 9–5 illustrates the distributive law in terms of gate implementation.

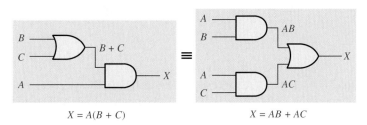

$$X = A(B + C)$$

$$X = AB + AC$$

◀ FIGURE 9–5

Application of distributive law.

Rules of Boolean Algebra

Table 9–1 lists 12 basic rules that are useful in manipulating and simplifying **Boolean expressions.** Rules 1 through 9 will be viewed in terms of their application to logic gates. Rules 10 through 12 will be derived in terms of the simpler rules and the laws previously discussed.

1. $A + 0 = A$	**7.** $A \cdot A = A$
2. $A + 1 = 1$	**8.** $A \cdot \overline{A} = 0$
3. $A \cdot 0 = 0$	**9.** $\overline{\overline{A}} = A$
4. $A \cdot 1 = A$	**10.** $A + AB = A$
5. $A + A = A$	**11.** $A + \overline{A}B = A + B$
6. $A + \overline{A} = 1$	**12.** $(A + B)(A + C) = A + BC$

A, B, or C can represent a single variable or a combination of variables.

◀ TABLE 9–1

Basic rules of Boolean algebra.

Rule 1. $A + 0 = A$ A variable ORed with 0 is always equal to the variable. If the input variable A is 1, the output variable X is 1, which is equal to A. If A is 0, the output is 0, which is also equal to A. This rule is illustrated in Figure 9–6, where the lower input is fixed at 0.

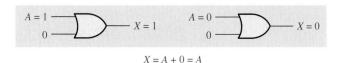

$$X = A + 0 = A$$

◀ FIGURE 9–6

Rule 2. $A + 1 = 1$ A variable ORed with 1 is always equal to 1. A 1 on an input to an OR gate produces a 1 on the output, regardless of the value of the variable on the other input. This rule is illustrated in Figure 9–7, where the lower input is fixed at 1.

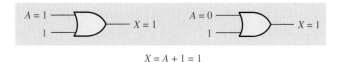

$$X = A + 1 = 1$$

◀ FIGURE 9–7

Rule 3. $A \cdot 0 = 0$ A variable ANDed with 0 is always equal to 0. Any time one input to an AND gate is 0, the output is 0, regardless of the value of the variable on the other input. This rule is illustrated in Figure 9–8, where the lower input is fixed at 0.

FIGURE 9–8

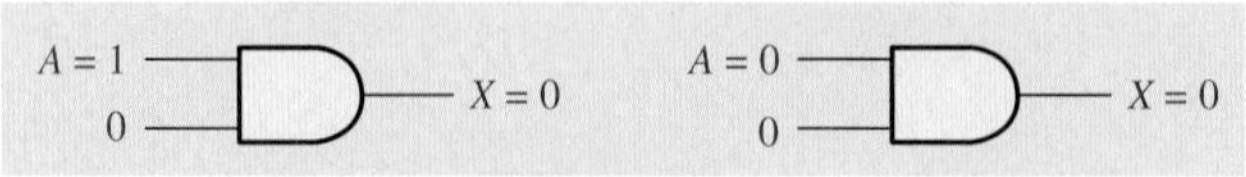

$X = A \bullet 0 = 0$

Rule 4. $A \cdot 1 = A$ A variable ANDed with 1 is always equal to the variable. If A is 0 the output of the AND gate is 0. If A is 1, the output of the AND gate is 1 because both inputs are now 1s. This rule is shown in Figure 9–9, where the lower input is fixed at 1.

FIGURE 9–9

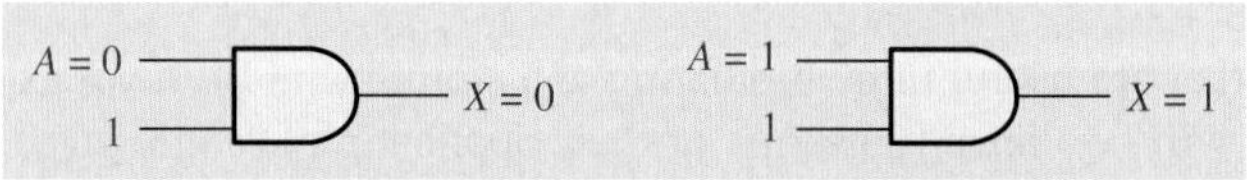

$X = A \bullet 1 = A$

Rule 5. $A + A = A$ A variable ORed with itself is always equal to the variable. If A is 0, then $0 + 0 = 0$; and if A is 1, then $1 + 1 = 1$. This is shown in Figure 9–10, where both inputs are the same variable.

FIGURE 9–10

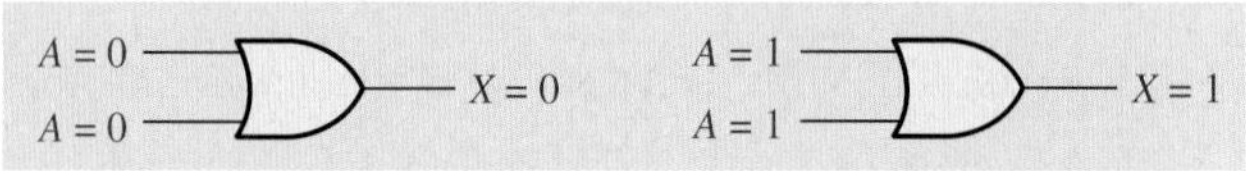

$X = A + A = A$

Rule 6. $A + \overline{A} = 1$ A variable ORed with its complement is always equal to 1. If A is 0, then $0 + \overline{0} = 0 + 1 = 1$. If A is 1, then $1 + \overline{1} = 1 + 0 = 1$. See Figure 9–11, where one input is the complement of the other.

FIGURE 9–11

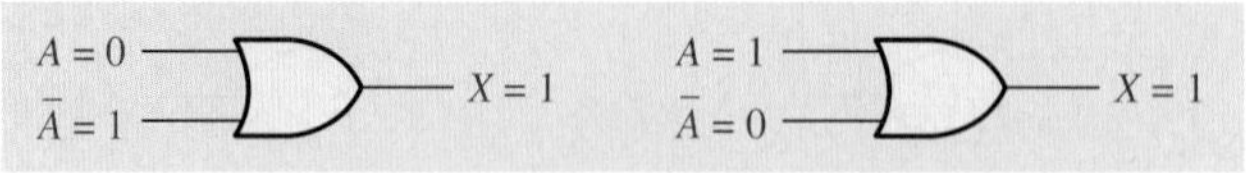

$X = A + \overline{A} = 1$

Rule 7. $A \cdot A = A$ A variable ANDed with itself is always equal to the variable. If $A = 0$, then $0 \cdot 0 = 0$; and if $A = 1$, then $1 \cdot 1 = 1$. Figure 9–12 illustrates this rule.

FIGURE 9–12

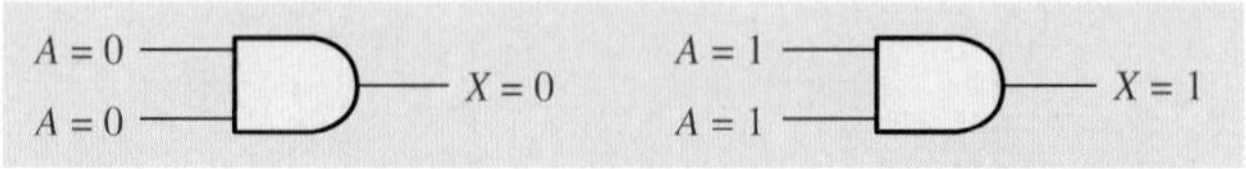

$X = A \bullet A = A$

Rule 8. $A \cdot \bar{A} = 0$ A variable ANDed with its complement is always equal to 0. Either A or $\bar{A}$ will always be 0; and when a 0 is applied to the input of an AND gate, the output will be 0 also. Figure 9–13 illustrates this rule.

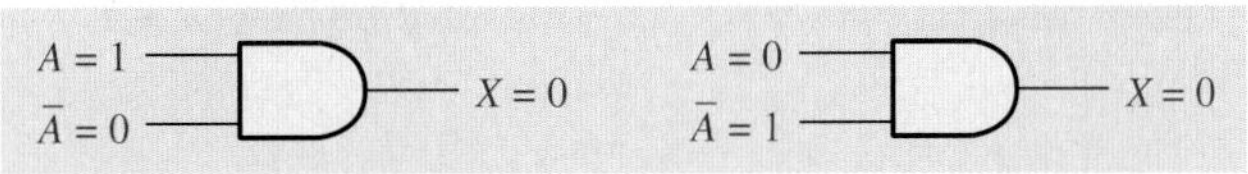

◀ FIGURE 9–13

$$X = A \cdot \bar{A} = 0$$

Rule 9. $\bar{\bar{A}} = A$ The double complement of a variable is always equal to the variable. If you start with the variable A and complement (invert) it once, you get $\bar{A}$. If you then take $\bar{A}$ and complement (invert) it, you get A, which is the original variable. This rule is shown in Figure 9–14 using inverters.

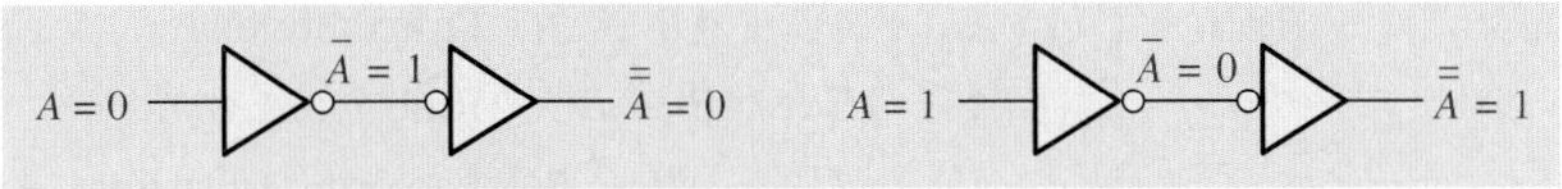

◀ FIGURE 9–14

$$\bar{\bar{A}} = A$$

Rule 10. $A + AB = A$ This rule can be proved by applying the distributive law, rule 2, and rule 4 as follows:

$$A + AB = A(1 + B) \quad \text{Factoring (distributive law)}$$
$$= A \cdot 1 \quad\quad \text{Rule 2: } (1 + B) = 1$$
$$= A \quad\quad\quad \text{Rule 4: } A \cdot 1 = A$$

The proof is shown in Table 9–2, which shows the truth table and the resulting logic circuit simplification.

◀ TABLE 9–2

Rule 10: $A + AB = A$.

A	B	AB	A + AB
0	0	0	0
0	1	0	0
1	0	0	1
1	1	1	1

equal

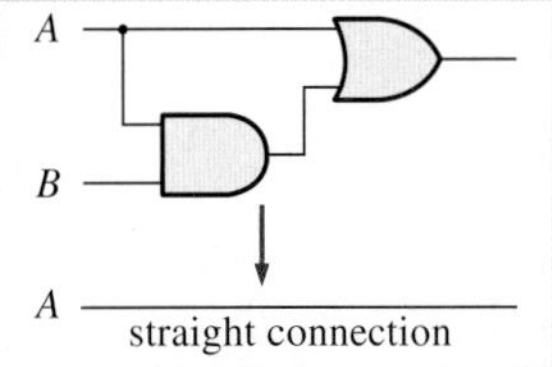

Rule 11. $A + \bar{A}B = A + B$ This rule can be proved as follows:

$$A + \bar{A}B = (A + AB) + \bar{A}B \quad\quad \text{Rule 10: } A = A + AB$$
$$= (AA + AB) + \bar{A}B \quad\quad \text{Rule 7: } A = AA$$
$$= AA + AB + A\bar{A} + \bar{A}B \quad \text{Rule 8: adding } A\bar{A} = 0$$
$$= (A + \bar{A})(A + B) \quad\quad \text{Factoring}$$
$$= 1 \cdot (A + B) \quad\quad\quad \text{Rule 6: } A + \bar{A} = 1$$
$$= A + B \quad\quad\quad\quad \text{Rule 4: drop the 1}$$

The proof is shown in Table 9–3, which shows the truth table and the resulting logic circuit simplification.

▶ **TABLE 9–3**

Rule 11: $A + \overline{A}B = A + B$.

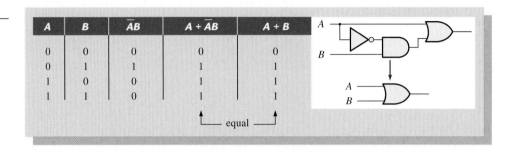

A	B	$\overline{A}B$	$A + \overline{A}B$	$A + B$
0	0	0	0	0
0	1	1	1	1
1	0	0	1	1
1	1	0	1	1

equal

Rule 12. $(A + B)(A + C) = A + BC$ This rule can be proved as follows:

$$
\begin{aligned}
(A + B)(A + C) &= AA + AC + AB + BC & \text{Distributive law} \\
&= A + AC + AB + BC & \text{Rule 7: } AA = A \\
&= A(1 + C) + AB + BC & \text{Factoring (distributive law)} \\
&= A \cdot 1 + AB + BC & \text{Rule 2: } 1 + C = 1 \\
&= A(1 + B) + BC & \text{Factoring (distributive law)} \\
&= A \cdot 1 + BC & \text{Rule 2: } 1 + B = 1 \\
&= A + BC & \text{Rule 4: } A \cdot 1 = A
\end{aligned}
$$

The proof is shown in Table 9–4, which shows the truth table and the resulting logic circuit simplification.

▽ **TABLE 9–4**

Rule 12: $(A + B)(A + C) = A + BC$.

A	B	C	A + B	A + C	(A + B)(A + C)	BC	A + BC
0	0	0	0	0	0	0	0
0	0	1	0	1	0	0	0
0	1	0	1	0	0	0	0
0	1	1	1	1	1	1	1
1	0	0	1	1	1	0	1
1	0	1	1	1	1	0	1
1	1	0	1	1	1	0	1
1	1	1	1	1	1	1	1

equal

9–3 DEMORGAN'S THEOREMS

DeMorgan, a mathematician who knew Boole, proposed two theorems that are an important part of Boolean algebra. In practical terms, DeMorgan's theorems provide mathematical verification of the equivalency of the NAND and negative-OR gates and the equivalency of the NOR and negative-AND gates, which were discussed in Chapter 8.

After completing this section, you should be able to

■ State DeMorgan's theorems

■ Relate DeMorgan's theorems to the equivalency of the NAND and negative-OR gates and to the equivalency of the NOR and negative-AND gates

■ Apply DeMorgan's theorems to the simplification of Boolean expressions

One of DeMorgan's theorems is stated as follows:

The complement of a product of variables is equal to the sum of the complements of the variables.

Stated another way,

The complement of two or more ANDed variables is equivalent to the OR of the complements of the individual variables.

The formula for expressing this theorem for two variables is

$$\overline{XY} = \overline{X} + \overline{Y}$$

Equation 9–6

DeMorgan's second theorem is stated as follows:

The complement of a sum of variables is equal to the product of the complements of the variables.

Stated another way,

The complement of two or more ORed variables is equivalent to the AND of the complements of the individual variables.

The formula for expressing this theorem for two variables is

$$\overline{X + Y} = \overline{X}\overline{Y}$$

Equation 9–7

Figure 9–15 shows the gate equivalencies and truth tables for Equations 9–6 and 9–7.

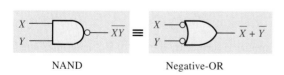

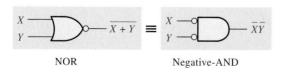

Inputs		Output	
X	Y	$\overline{XY}$	$\overline{X} + \overline{Y}$
0	0	1	1
0	1	1	1
1	0	1	1
1	1	0	0

Inputs		Output	
X	Y	$\overline{X + Y}$	$\overline{X}\overline{Y}$
0	0	1	1
0	1	0	0
1	0	0	0
1	1	0	0

◀ FIGURE 9–15

Gate equivalencies and the corresponding truth tables that illustrate DeMorgan's theorems. Notice the equality of the two output columns in each table. This shows that the equivalent gates perform the same logic function.

As stated, DeMorgan's theorems also apply to expressions in which there are more than two variables. The following examples illustrate the application of DeMorgan's theorems to 3-variable and 4-variable expressions.

EXAMPLE 9–3

Apply DeMorgan's theorems to the expressions $\overline{XYZ}$ and $\overline{X + Y + Z}$.

Solution

$$\overline{XYZ} = \overline{X} + \overline{Y} + \overline{Z}$$

$$\overline{X + Y + Z} = \overline{X}\,\overline{Y}\,\overline{Z}$$

Related Problem Apply DeMorgan's theorem to the expression $\overline{\overline{X} + \overline{Y} + \overline{Z}}$.

EXAMPLE 9–4

Apply DeMorgan's theorems to the expressions $\overline{WXYZ}$ and $\overline{W + X + Y + Z}$.

Solution

$$\overline{WXYZ} = \overline{W} + \overline{X} + \overline{Y} + \overline{Z}$$

$$\overline{W + X + Y + Z} = \overline{W}\,\overline{X}\,\overline{Y}\,\overline{Z}$$

Related Problem Apply DeMorgan's theorem to the expression $\overline{\overline{W}\,\overline{X}\,\overline{Y}\,\overline{Z}}$.

Each variable in DeMorgan's theorems as stated in Equations 9–6 and 9–7 can also represent a combination of other variables. For example, X can be equal to the term $AB + C$, and Y can be equal to the term $A + BC$. So if you can apply DeMorgan's theorem for two variables as stated by $\overline{XY} = \overline{X} + \overline{Y}$ to the expression $\overline{(AB + C)(A + BC)}$, you get the following result:

$$\overline{(AB + C)(A + BC)} = \overline{(AB + C)} + \overline{(A + BC)}$$

Notice that in the preceding result you have two terms, $\overline{AB + C}$ and $\overline{A + BC}$, to each of which you can again apply DeMorgan's theorem $\overline{X + Y} = \overline{X}\,\overline{Y}$ individually, as follows:

$$\overline{(AB + C)} + \overline{(A + BC)} = (\overline{AB})\overline{C} + \overline{A}(\overline{BC})$$

Notice that you still have two terms in the expression to which DeMorgan's theorem can again be applied. These terms are $\overline{AB}$ and $\overline{BC}$. A final application of DeMorgan's theorem gives the following result:

$$(\overline{AB})\overline{C} + \overline{A}(\overline{BC}) = (\overline{A} + \overline{B})\overline{C} + \overline{A}(\overline{B} + \overline{C})$$

Although this result can be simplified further by the use of Boolean rules and laws, DeMorgan's theorems cannot be used any more.

Applying DeMorgan's Theorems

The following procedure illustrates the application of DeMorgan's theorems and Boolean algebra to the specific expression

$$\overline{\overline{A + B\overline{C}} + D(\overline{E + \overline{F}})}$$

Step 1. Identify the terms to which you can apply DeMorgan's theorems, and think of each term as a single variable. Let $\overline{A + B\overline{C}} = X$ and $D(\overline{E + \overline{F}}) = Y$.

Step 2. Since $\overline{X + Y} = \overline{X}\,\overline{Y}$,

$$\overline{\overline{(A + B\overline{C})} + \overline{(D(E + \overline{F}))}} = \overline{\overline{(A + B\overline{C})}}\,\overline{\overline{(D(E + \overline{F}))}}$$

Step 3. Use rule 9 $(\overline{\overline{A}} = A)$ to cancel the double bars over the left term (this is not part of DeMorgan's theorem).

$$\overline{\overline{(A + B\overline{C})}}\,\overline{\overline{(D(E + \overline{F}))}} = (A + B\overline{C})\overline{\overline{(D(E + \overline{F}))}}$$

Step 4. Applying DeMorgan's theorem to the second term,

$$(A + B\overline{C})\overline{\overline{(D(E + \overline{F}))}} = (A + B\overline{C})(\overline{D} + \overline{\overline{(E + \overline{F})}})$$

Step 5. Use rule 9 $(\overline{\overline{A}} = A)$ to cancel the double bars over the $E + \overline{F}$ part of the term.

$$(A + B\overline{C})(\overline{D} + \overline{\overline{E + \overline{F}}}) = (A + B\overline{C})(\overline{D} + E + \overline{F})$$

The following three examples will further illustrate how to use DeMorgan's theorems.

EXAMPLE 9–5

Apply DeMorgan's theorems to each of the following expressions:

(a) $\overline{(A + B + C)D}$ **(b)** $\overline{ABC + DEF}$ **(c)** $\overline{A\overline{B} + \overline{C}D + EF}$

Solution   Let $A + B + C = X$ and $D = Y$. The expression $\overline{(A + B + C)D}$ is of the form $\overline{XY} = \overline{X} + \overline{Y}$ and can be rewritten as

$$\overline{(A + B + C)D} = \overline{A + B + C} + \overline{D}$$

Next, apply DeMorgan's theorem to the term $\overline{A + B + C}$.

$$\overline{A + B + C} + \overline{D} = \overline{A}\,\overline{B}\,\overline{C} + \overline{D}$$

(b) Let $ABC = X$ and $DEF = Y$. The expression $\overline{ABC + DEF}$ is of the form $\overline{X + Y} = \overline{X}\,\overline{Y}$ and can be rewritten as

$$\overline{ABC + DEF} = (\overline{ABC})(\overline{DEF})$$

Next, apply DeMorgan's theorem to each of the terms $\overline{ABC}$ and $\overline{DEF}$.

$$(\overline{ABC})(\overline{DEF}) = (\overline{A} + \overline{B} + \overline{C})(\overline{D} + \overline{E} + \overline{F})$$

(c) Let $A\overline{B} = X$, $\overline{C}D = Y$, and $EF = Z$. The expression $\overline{A\overline{B} + \overline{C}D + EF}$ is of the form $\overline{X + Y + Z} = \overline{X}\,\overline{Y}\,\overline{Z}$ and can be rewritten as

$$\overline{A\overline{B} + \overline{C}D + EF} = (\overline{A\overline{B}})(\overline{\overline{C}D})(\overline{EF})$$

Next, apply DeMorgan's theorem to each of the terms $\overline{A\overline{B}}$, $\overline{\overline{C}D}$, and $\overline{EF}$.

$$(\overline{A\overline{B}})(\overline{\overline{C}D})(\overline{EF}) = (\overline{A} + B)(C + \overline{D})(\overline{E} + \overline{F})$$

Related Problem   Apply DeMorgan's theorems to the expression $\overline{\overline{ABC} + D + E}$.

EXAMPLE 9–6

Apply DeMorgan's theorems to each expression:

(a) $\overline{\overline{(A + B) + \overline{C}}}$ (b) $\overline{\overline{(\overline{A} + B) + CD}}$ (c) $\overline{\overline{(A + B)\overline{C}D + E + \overline{F}}}$

Solution   (a) $\overline{\overline{(A + B) + \overline{C}}} = \overline{(A + B)}\overline{\overline{C}} = (A + B)C$

(b) $\overline{\overline{(\overline{A} + B) + CD}} = \overline{(\overline{A} + B)}\overline{CD} = (\overline{\overline{A}}B)(\overline{C} + \overline{D}) = A\overline{B}(\overline{C} + \overline{D})$

(c) $\overline{\overline{(A + B)\overline{C}D + E + \overline{F}}} = ((A + B)\overline{C}D)(\overline{E + \overline{F}}) = (\overline{A}\overline{B} + C + \overline{D})\overline{E}F$

Related Problem   Apply DeMorgan's theorems to the expression $\overline{\overline{AB(C + \overline{D})} + E}$.

EXAMPLE 9–7

The Boolean expression for an exclusive-OR gate is $A\overline{B} + \overline{A}B$. With this as a starting point, use DeMorgan's theorems and any other rules or laws that are applicable to develop an expression for the exclusive-NOR gate.

Solution   Start by complementing the exclusive-OR expression and then applying DeMorgan's theorems as follows:

$$\overline{A\overline{B} + \overline{A}B} = (\overline{A\overline{B}})(\overline{\overline{A}B}) = (\overline{A} + B)(\overline{\overline{A}} + \overline{B}) = (\overline{A} + B)(A + \overline{B})$$

Next, apply the distributive law and rule 8 ($A \cdot \overline{A} = 0$).

$$(\overline{A} + B)(A + \overline{B}) = \overline{A}A + \overline{A}\overline{B} + AB + B\overline{B} = \overline{A}\overline{B} + AB$$

The final expression for the XNOR is $\overline{A}\overline{B} + AB$. Note that this expression equals 1 any time both variables are 0s or both variables are 1s.

Related Problem   Starting with the expression for a 4-input NAND gate, use DeMorgan's theorems to develop an expression for a 4-input negative-OR gate.

9–4   BOOLEAN ANALYSIS OF LOGIC CIRCUITS

Boolean algebra provides a concise way to express the operation of a logic circuit formed by a combination of logic gates so that the output can be determined for various combinations of input values.

After completing this section, you should be able to

■ Determine the Boolean expression for a combination of gates

■ Evaluate the logic operation of a circuit from the Boolean expression

■ Construct a truth table

Boolean Expression for a Logic Circuit

To derive the Boolean expression for a given logic circuit, begin at the left-most inputs and work toward the final output, writing the expression for each gate. For the example circuit in Figure 9–16, the Boolean expression is determined as follows:

1. The expression for the left-most AND gate with inputs C and D is CD.

2. The output of the left-most AND gate is one of the inputs to the OR gate and B is the other input. Therefore, the expression for the OR gate is $B + CD$.

3. The output of the OR gate is one of the inputs to the right-most AND gate and A is the other input. Therefore, the expression for this AND gate is $A(B + CD)$, which is the final output expression for the entire circuit.

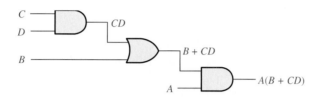

FIGURE 9–16

A logic circuit showing the development of the Boolean expression for the output.

Constructing a Truth Table for a Logic Circuit

Once the Boolean expression for a given logic circuit has been determined, a truth table that shows the output for all possible values of the input variables can be developed. The procedure requires that you evaluate the Boolean expression for all possible combinations of values for the input variables. In the case of the circuit in Figure 9–16, there are four input variables (A, B, C, and D) and therefore sixteen ($2^4 = 16$) combinations of values are possible.

A logic circuit can be described by a truth table.

Evaluating the Expression   To evaluate the expression $A(B + CD)$, first find the values of the variables that make the expression equal to 1, using the rules for Boolean addition and multiplication. In this case, the expression equals 1 only if $A = 1$ and $B + CD = 1$ because

$$A(B + CD) = 1 \cdot 1 = 1$$

Now determine when the $B + CD$ term equals 1. The term $B + CD = 1$ if either $B = 1$ or $CD = 1$ or if both B and CD equal 1 because

$$B + CD = 1 + 0 = 1$$
$$B + CD = 0 + 1 = 1$$
$$B + CD = 1 + 1 = 1$$

The term $CD = 1$ only if $C = 1$ and $D = 1$.

To summarize, the expression $A(B + CD) = 1$ when $A = 1$ and $B = 1$ regardless of the values of C and D or when $A = 1$ and $C = 1$ and $D = 1$ regardless of the value of B. The expression $A(B + CD) = 0$ for all other value combinations of the variables.

Putting the Results in Truth Table Format   The first step is to list the sixteen input variable combinations of 1s and 0s in a binary sequence as shown in Table 9–5. Next, place a 1 in the output column for each combination of input variables that was determined in the evaluation. Finally, place a 0 in the output column for all other combinations of input variables. These results are shown in the truth table in Table 9–5.

▶ **TABLE 9–5**

Truth table for the logic circuit in Figure 9–16.

INPUTS				OUTPUT
A	B	C	D	A(B + CD)
0	0	0	0	0
0	0	0	1	0
0	0	1	0	0
0	0	1	1	0
0	1	0	0	0
0	1	0	1	0
0	1	1	0	0
0	1	1	1	0
1	0	0	0	0
1	0	0	1	0
1	0	1	0	0
1	0	1	1	1
1	1	0	0	1
1	1	0	1	1
1	1	1	0	1
1	1	1	1	1

9–5   SIMPLIFICATION USING BOOLEAN ALGEBRA

Many times in the application of Boolean algebra, you have to reduce a particular expression to its simplest form or change its form to a more convenient one to implement the expression most efficiently. The approach taken in this section is to use the basic laws, rules, and theorems of Boolean algebra to manipulate and simplify an expression. This method depends on a thorough knowledge of Boolean algebra and considerable practice in its application, not to mention a little ingenuity and cleverness.

After completing this section, you should be able to

■ Apply the laws, rules, and theorems of Boolean algebra to simplify general expressions

A simplified Boolean expression uses the fewest gates possible to implement a given expression. Examples 9–8 through 9–11 illustrate Boolean simplification.

EXAMPLE 9–8

Using Boolean algebra techniques, simplify this expression:

$$AB + A(B + C) + B(B + C)$$

Solution The following is not necessarily the only approach.

Step 1: Apply the distributive law to the second and third terms in the expression, as follows:

$$AB + AB + AC + BB + BC$$

Step 2: Apply rule 7 ($BB = B$) to the fourth term.

$$AB + AB + AC + B + BC$$

Step 3: Apply rule 5 ($AB + AB = AB$) to the first two terms.

$$AB + AC + B + BC$$

Step 4: Apply rule 10 ($B + BC = B$) to the last two terms.

$$AB + AC + B$$

Step 5: Apply rule 10 ($AB + B = B$) to the first and third terms.

$$B + AC$$

At this point the expression is simplified as much as possible. Once you gain experience in applying Boolean algebra, you can often combine many individual steps.

Related Problem Simplify the Boolean expression $A\overline{B} + A(\overline{B + C}) + B(\overline{B + C})$.

Figure 9–17 shows that the simplification process in Example 9–8 has significantly reduced the number of logic gates required to implement the expression. Part (a) shows that five gates are required to implement the expression in its original form; however, only two gates are needed for the simplified expression, shown in part (b). It is important to realize that these two gate circuits are equivalent. That is, for any combination of levels on the *A, B,* and *C* inputs, you get the same output from either circuit.

Simplification means fewer gates for the same function.

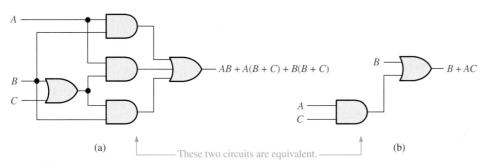

(a) ——— These two circuits are equivalent. ——— (b)

▲ **FIGURE 9–17**

Gate circuits for Example 9–8.

EXAMPLE 9–9

Simplify the following Boolean expression:

$$[A\overline{B}(C + BD) + \overline{A}\,\overline{B}]C$$

Note that brackets and parentheses mean the same thing: the term inside is multiplied (ANDed) with the term outside.

Solution   **Step 1:**   Apply the distributive law to the terms within the brackets.

$$(A\overline{B}C + A\overline{B}BD + \overline{A}\,\overline{B})C$$

Step 2:   Apply rule 8 $(\overline{B}B = 0)$ to the second term within the parentheses.

$$(A\overline{B}C + A \cdot 0 \cdot D + \overline{A}\,\overline{B})C$$

Step 3:   Apply rule 3 $(A \cdot 0 \cdot D = 0)$ to the second term within the parentheses.

$$(A\overline{B}C + 0 + \overline{A}\,\overline{B})C$$

Step 4: Apply rule 1 (drop the 0) within the parentheses.

$$(A\overline{B}C + \overline{A}\,\overline{B})C$$

Step 5: Apply the distributive law.

$$A\overline{B}CC + \overline{A}\,\overline{B}C$$

Step 6: Apply rule 7 $(CC = C)$ to the first term.

$$A\overline{B}C + \overline{A}\,\overline{B}C$$

Step 7: Factor out $\overline{B}C$.

$$\overline{B}C(A + \overline{A})$$

Step 8: Apply rule 6 $(A + \overline{A} = 1)$.

$$\overline{B}C \cdot 1$$

Step 9: Apply rule 4 (drop the 1).

$$\overline{B}C$$

Related Problem   Simplify the Boolean expression $[AB(C + \overline{BD}) + \overline{AB}]CD$.

EXAMPLE 9–10

Simplify the following Boolean expression:

$$\overline{A}BC + A\overline{B}\,\overline{C} + \overline{A}\,\overline{B}\,\overline{C} + A\overline{B}C + ABC$$

Solution   **Step 1:**   Factor BC out of the first and last terms.

$$BC(\overline{A} + A) + A\overline{B}\,\overline{C} + \overline{A}\,\overline{B}\,\overline{C} + A\overline{B}C$$

Step 2:   Apply rule 6 $(\overline{A} + A = 1)$ to the term in parentheses, and factor $A\overline{B}$ from the second and last terms.

$$BC \cdot 1 + A\overline{B}(\overline{C} + C) + \overline{A}\,\overline{B}\,\overline{C}$$

Step 3: Apply rule 4 (drop the 1) to the first term and rule 6 $(\overline{C} + C = 1)$ to the term in parentheses.

$$BC + A\overline{B} \cdot 1 + \overline{A}\,B\overline{C}$$

Step 4: Apply rule 4 (drop the 1) to the second term.

$$BC + A\overline{B} + \overline{A}\,B\overline{C}$$

Step 5: Factor $\overline{B}$ from the second and third terms.

$$BC + \overline{B}(A + \overline{A}\,\overline{C})$$

Step 6: Apply rule 11 $(A + \overline{A}\,\overline{C} = A + \overline{C})$ to the term in parentheses.

$$BC + \overline{B}(A + \overline{C})$$

Step 7: Use the distributive and commutative laws to get the following expression:

$$BC + A\overline{B} + \overline{B}\,\overline{C}$$

Related Problem   Simplify the Boolean expression $AB\overline{C} + \overline{A}\,BC + \overline{A}BC + \overline{A}\,\overline{B}\,\overline{C}$.

EXAMPLE 9–11

Simplify the following Boolean expression:

$$\overline{AB + AC} + \overline{A}\,BC$$

Solution   **Step 1:** Apply DeMorgan's theorem to the first term.

$$(\overline{AB})(\overline{AC}) + \overline{A}\,BC$$

Step 2: Apply DeMorgan's theorem to each term in parentheses.

$$(\overline{A} + \overline{B})(\overline{A} + \overline{C}) + \overline{A}\,BC$$

Step 3: Apply the distributive law to the two terms in parentheses.

$$\overline{A}\,\overline{A} + \overline{A}\,\overline{C} + \overline{A}\,\overline{B} + \overline{B}\,\overline{C} + \overline{A}\,BC$$

Step 4: Apply rule 7 $(\overline{A}\,\overline{A} = \overline{A})$ to the first term, and apply rule 10 $[\overline{A}\,\overline{B} + \overline{A}\,BC = \overline{A}\,\overline{B}(1 + C) = \overline{A}\,\overline{B}]$ to the third and last terms.

$$\overline{A} + \overline{A}\,\overline{C} + \overline{A}\,\overline{B} + \overline{B}\,\overline{C}$$

Step 5: Apply rule 10 $[\overline{A} + \overline{A}\,\overline{C} = \overline{A}(1 + \overline{C}) = \overline{A}]$ to the first and second terms.

$$\overline{A} + \overline{A}\,\overline{B} + \overline{B}\,\overline{C}$$

Step 6: Apply rule 10 $[\overline{A} + \overline{A}\,\overline{B} = \overline{A}(1 + \overline{B}) = \overline{A}]$ to the first and second terms.

$$\overline{A} + \overline{B}\,\overline{C}$$

Related Problem   Simplify the Boolean expression $\overline{AB + AC} + \overline{A}\,B\overline{C}$.

9–6   STANDARD FORMS OF BOOLEAN EXPRESSIONS

All Boolean expressions, regardless of their form, can be converted into either of two standard forms: the sum-of-products form or the product-of-sums form. Standardization makes the evaluation, simplification, and implementation of Boolean expressions much more systematic and easier.

After completing this section, you should be able to

- Identify a sum-of-products expression
- Determine the domain of a Boolean expression
- Convert any sum-of-products expression to a standard form
- Evaluate a standard sum-of-products expression in terms of binary values
- Identify a product-of-sums expression
- Convert any product-of-sums expression to a standard form
- Evaluate a standard product-of-sums expression in terms of binary values
- Convert from one standard form to the other

The Sum-of-Products (SOP) Form

An SOP expression can be implemented with one OR and two or more ANDs.

A product term is a term consisting of the product (Boolean multiplication) of literals (variables or their complements). When two or more product terms are summed by Boolean addition, the resulting expression is a **sum-of-products (SOP).** Some examples are

$$AB + ABC$$
$$ABC + CDE + \overline{B}C\overline{D}$$
$$\overline{A}B + \overline{A}B\overline{C} + AC$$

Also, an SOP expression can contain a single-variable term, as in $A + \overline{A}\overline{B}C + BC\overline{D}$. Refer to the simplification examples in the last section, and you will see that each of the final expressions was either a single product term or in SOP form. In an SOP expression, a single overbar cannot extend over more than one variable; however, more than one variable in a term can have an overbar. For example, an SOP expression can have the term $\overline{A}\,\overline{B}\,\overline{C}$ but not $\overline{ABC}$.

Domain of a Boolean Expression   The **domain** of a general Boolean expression is the set of variables contained in the expression in either complemented or uncomplemented form. For example, the domain of the expression $\overline{A}B + A\overline{B}C$ is the set of variables A, B, C and the domain of the expression $AB\overline{C} + C\overline{D}E + \overline{B}C\overline{D}$ is the set of variables A, B, C, D, E.

▶ **FIGURE 9–18**

Implementation of the SOP expression AB + BCD + AC.

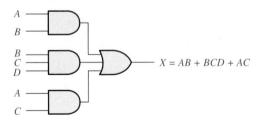

AND/OR Implementation of an SOP Expression Implementing an SOP expression simply requires ORing the outputs of two or more AND gates. A product term is produced by an AND operation, and the sum (addition) of two or more product terms is produced by an OR operation. Therefore, an SOP expression can be implemented by AND-OR logic in which the outputs of a number (equal to the number of product terms in the expression) of

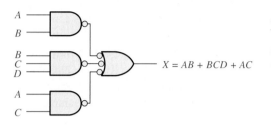

$X = AB + BCD + AC$

◄ **FIGURE 9–19**

This NAND/NAND implementation is equivalent to the AND/OR in Figure 9–18.

AND gates connect to the inputs of an OR gate, as shown in Figure 9–18 for the expression $AB + BCD + AC$. The output X of the OR gate equals the SOP expression.

NAND/NAND Implementation of an SOP Expression NAND gates can be used to implement an SOP expression. Using only NAND gates, an AND/OR function can be accomplished, as illustrated in Figure 9–19. The first level of NAND gates feed into a NAND gate that acts as a negative-OR gate. The NAND and negative-OR inversions cancel and the result is effectively an AND/OR circuit.

Conversion of a General Expression to SOP Form

Any logic expression can be changed into SOP form by applying Boolean algebra techniques. For example, the expression $A(B + CD)$ can be converted to SOP form by applying the distributive law:

$$A(B + CD) = AB + ACD$$

EXAMPLE 9–12

Convert each of the following Boolean expressions to SOP form:

(a) $AB + B(CD + EF)$ (b) $(A + B)(B + C + D)$ (c) $\overline{(\overline{A + B}) + C}$

Solution (a) $AB + B(CD + EF) = AB + BCD + BEF$

(b) $(A + B)(B + C + D) = AB + AC + AD + BB + BC + BD$

(c) $\overline{(\overline{A + B}) + C} = \overline{(\overline{A + B})}\,\overline{C} = (A + B)\overline{C} = A\overline{C} + B\overline{C}$

Related Problem Convert $\overline{A}B\overline{C} + (A + \overline{B})(B + \overline{C} + A\overline{B})$ to SOP form.

The Standard SOP Form

So far, you have seen SOP expressions in which some of the product terms do not contain all of the variables in the domain of the expression. For example, the expression $\overline{A}B\overline{C} + \overline{A}B\overline{D} + \overline{A}B\overline{C}D$ has a domain made up of the variables *A*, *B*, *C*, and *D*. However, notice that the complete set of variables in the domain is not represented in the first two terms of the expression; that is, D or $\overline{D}$ is missing from the first term and C or $\overline{C}$ is missing from the second term.

A *standard SOP expression* is one in which *all* the variables in the domain appear in each product term in the expression. For example, $A\overline{B}CD + \overline{A}\,\overline{B}C\overline{D} + AB\overline{C}D$ is a standard SOP expression. Standard SOP expressions are important in constructing truth tables, and in the Karnaugh map simplification method. Any nonstandard SOP expression (referred to simply as SOP) can be converted to the standard form using Boolean algebra.

Converting Product Terms to Standard SOP Each product term in an SOP expression that does not contain all the variables in the domain can be expanded to standard form to include all variables in the domain and their complements. As stated in the following steps, a nonstandard SOP expression is converted into standard form using Boolean algebra rule 6 ($A + \overline{A} = 1$) from Table 9–1: A variable added to its complement equals 1.

Step 1. Multiply each nonstandard product term by a term made up of the sum of a missing variable and its complement. This results in two product terms. As you know, you can multiply anything by 1 without changing its value.

Step 2. Repeat Step 1 until all resulting product terms contain all variables in the domain in either complemented or uncomplemented form. In converting a product term to standard form, the number of product terms is doubled for each missing variable, as Example 9–13 shows.

EXAMPLE 9–13

Convert the following Boolean expression into standard SOP form:

$$A\overline{B}C + \overline{A}\,\overline{B} + AB\overline{C}D$$

Solution The domain of this SOP expression is A, B, C, D. Take one term at a time. The first term, $A\overline{B}C$, is missing variable D or $\overline{D}$, so multiply the first term by $D + \overline{D}$ as follows:

$$A\overline{B}C = A\overline{B}C(D + \overline{D}) = A\overline{B}CD + A\overline{B}C\overline{D}$$

In this case, two standard product terms are the result.

The second term, $\overline{A}\,\overline{B}$, is missing variables C or $\overline{C}$ and D or $\overline{D}$, so first multiply the second term by $C + \overline{C}$ as follows:

$$\overline{A}\,\overline{B} = \overline{A}\,\overline{B}(C + \overline{C}) = \overline{A}\,\overline{B}C + \overline{A}\,\overline{B}\,\overline{C}$$

The two resulting terms are missing variable D or $\overline{D}$, so multiply both terms by $D + \overline{D}$ as follows:

$$\overline{A}\,\overline{B} = \overline{A}\,\overline{B}C + \overline{A}\,\overline{B}\,\overline{C} = \overline{A}\,\overline{B}C(D + \overline{D}) + \overline{A}\,\overline{B}\,\overline{C}(D + \overline{D})$$
$$= \overline{A}\,\overline{B}CD + \overline{A}\,\overline{B}C\overline{D} + \overline{A}\,\overline{B}\,\overline{C}D + \overline{A}\,\overline{B}\,\overline{C}\,\overline{D}$$

In this case, four standard product terms are the result.

The third term, $AB\overline{C}D$, is already in standard form. The complete standard SOP form of the original expression is as follows:

$$A\overline{B}C + \overline{A}\,\overline{B} + AB\overline{C}D = A\overline{B}CD + A\overline{B}C\overline{D} + \overline{A}\,\overline{B}CD + \overline{A}\,\overline{B}C\overline{D} + \overline{A}\,\overline{B}\,\overline{C}D + \overline{A}\,\overline{B}\,\overline{C}\,\overline{D} + AB\overline{C}D$$

Related Problem Convert the expression $W\overline{X}Y + \overline{X}Y\overline{Z} + WX\overline{Y}$ to standard SOP form.

Binary Representation of a Standard Product Term A standard product term is equal to 1 for only one combination of variable values. For example, the product term $A\overline{B}C\overline{D}$ is equal to 1 when $A = 1, B = 0, C = 1, D = 0$, as shown below, and is 0 for all other combinations of values for the variables.

$$A\overline{B}C\overline{D} = 1 \cdot \overline{0} \cdot 1 \cdot \overline{0} = 1 \cdot 1 \cdot 1 \cdot 1 = 1$$

In this case, the product term has a binary value of 1010 (decimal ten).

Remember, a product term is implemented with an AND gate whose output is 1 only if each of its inputs is 1. Inverters are used to produce the complements of the variables as required.

An SOP expression is equal to 1 only if one or more of the product terms in the expression is equal to 1.

EXAMPLE 9–14

Determine the binary values for which the following standard SOP expression is equal to 1:

$$ABCD + A\overline{B}\,\overline{C}D + \overline{A}\,\overline{B}\,\overline{C}\,\overline{D}$$

Solution The term $ABCD$ is equal to 1 when $A = 1, B = 1, C = 1,$ and $D = 1$.

$$ABCD = 1 \cdot 1 \cdot 1 \cdot 1 = 1$$

The term $A\overline{B}\,\overline{C}D$ is equal to 1 when $A = 1, B = 0, C = 0,$ and $D = 1$.

$$A\overline{B}\,\overline{C}D = 1 \cdot \overline{0} \cdot \overline{0} \cdot 1 = 1 \cdot 1 \cdot 1 \cdot 1 = 1$$

The term $\overline{A}\,\overline{B}\,\overline{C}\,\overline{D}$ is equal to 1 when $A = 0, B = 0, C = 0,$ and $D = 0$.

$$\overline{A}\,\overline{B}\,\overline{C}\,\overline{D} = \overline{0} \cdot \overline{0} \cdot \overline{0} \cdot \overline{0} = 1 \cdot 1 \cdot 1 \cdot 1 = 1$$

The SOP expression equals 1 when any or all of the three product terms is 1.

Related Problem Determine the binary values for which the following SOP expression is equal to 1:

$$\overline{X}YZ + X\overline{Y}Z + XY\overline{Z} + \overline{X}Y\overline{Z} + XYZ$$

Is this a standard SOP expression?

The Product-of-Sums (POS) Form

A sum term is a term consisting of the sum (Boolean addition) of literals (variables or their complements). When two or more sum terms are multiplied, the resulting expression is a **product-of-sums (POS)**. Some examples are

$$(\overline{A} + B)(A + \overline{B} + C)$$
$$(\overline{A} + \overline{B} + \overline{C})(C + \overline{D} + E)(\overline{B} + C + D)$$
$$(A + B)(A + \overline{B} + C)(\overline{A} + C)$$

A POS expression can contain a single-variable term, as in $\overline{A}(A + \overline{B} + C)(\overline{B} + \overline{C} + D)$. In a POS expression, a single overbar cannot extend over more than one variable; however, more than one variable in a term can have an overbar. For example, a POS expression can have the term $\overline{A} + \overline{B} + \overline{C}$ but not $\overline{A + B + C}$.

Implementation of a POS Expression Implementing a POS expression simply requires ANDing the outputs of two or more OR gates. A sum term is produced by an OR operation, and the product of two or more sum terms is produced by an AND operation. Therefore, a POS expression can be implemented by logic in which the outputs of a number (equal to the number of sum terms in the expression) of OR gates connect to the inputs of an AND gate, as Figure 9–20 shows for the expression $(A + B)(B + C + D)(A + C)$. The output X of the AND gate equals the POS expression.

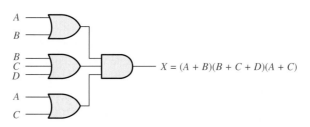

◄ FIGURE 9–20

Implementation of the POS expression $(A + B)(B + C + D)(A + C)$.

$X = (A + B)(B + C + D)(A + C)$

The Standard POS Form

So far, you have seen POS expressions in which some of the sum terms do not contain all of the variables in the domain of the expression. For example, the expression

$$(A + \overline{B} + C)(A + B + \overline{D})(A + \overline{B} + \overline{C} + D)$$

has a domain made up of the variables A, B, C, and D. Notice that the complete set of variables in the domain is not represented in the first two terms of the expression; that is, D or $\overline{D}$ is missing from the first term and C or $\overline{C}$ is missing from the second term. A standard POS expression is one in which *all* the variables in the domain appear in each sum term in the expression. For example,

$$(\overline{A} + \overline{B} + \overline{C} + \overline{D})(A + \overline{B} + C + D)(A + B + \overline{C} + D)$$

is a standard POS expression. Any nonstandard POS expression (referred to simply as POS) can be converted to the standard form using Boolean algebra.

Converting a Sum Term to Standard POS Each sum term in a POS expression that does not contain all the variables in the domain can be expanded to standard form to include all variables in the domain and their complements. As stated in the following steps, a nonstandard POS expression is converted into standard form using Boolean algebra rule 8 $(A \cdot \overline{A} = 0)$ from Table 9–1: A variable multiplied by its complement equals 0.

Step 1. Add to each nonstandard product term a term made up of the product of the missing variable and its complement. This results in two sum terms. As you know, you can add 0 to anything without changing its value.

Step 2. Apply rule 12 from Table 9–1: $A + BC = (A + B)(A + C)$

Step 3. Repeat Step 1 until all resulting sum terms contain all variables in the domain in either complemented or uncomplemented form.

EXAMPLE 9–15

Convert the following Boolean expression into standard POS form:

$$(A + \overline{B} + C)(\overline{B} + C + \overline{D})(A + \overline{B} + \overline{C} + D)$$

Solution The domain of this POS expression is A, B, C, D. Take one term at a time. The first term, $A + \overline{B} + C$, is missing variable D or $\overline{D}$, so add $D\overline{D}$ and apply rule 12 as follows:

$$A + \overline{B} + C = A + \overline{B} + C + D\overline{D} = (A + \overline{B} + C + D)(A + \overline{B} + C + \overline{D})$$

The second term, $\overline{B} + C + \overline{D}$, is missing variable A or $\overline{A}$, so add $A\overline{A}$ and apply rule 12 as follows:

$$\overline{B} + C + \overline{D} = \overline{B} + C + \overline{D} + A\overline{A} = (A + \overline{B} + C + \overline{D})(\overline{A} + \overline{B} + C + \overline{D})$$

The third term, $A + \overline{B} + \overline{C} + D$, is already in standard form. The standard POS form of the original expression is as follows:

$$(A + \overline{B} + C)(\overline{B} + C + \overline{D})(A + \overline{B} + \overline{C} + D) =$$
$$(A + \overline{B} + C + D)(A + \overline{B} + C + \overline{D})(A + \overline{B} + C + \overline{D})(\overline{A} + \overline{B} + C + \overline{D})(A + \overline{B} + \overline{C} + D)$$

Related Problem Convert the expression $(A + \overline{B})(B + C)$ to standard POS form.

Binary Representation of a Standard Sum Term A standard sum term is equal to 0 for only one combination of variable values. For example, the sum term $A + \overline{B} + C + \overline{D}$ is 0 when $A = 0$, $B = 1$, $C = 0$, *and* $D = 1$, as shown below, and is 1 for all other combinations of values for the variables.

$$A + \overline{B} + C + \overline{D} = 0 + \overline{1} + 0 + \overline{1} = 0 + 0 + 0 + 0 = 0$$

In this case, the sum term has a binary value of 0101 (decimal 5). Remember, a sum term is implemented with an OR gate whose output is 0 only if each of its inputs is 0. Inverters are used to produce the complements of the variables as required.

A POS expression is equal to 0 only if one or more of the sum terms in the expression is equal to 0.

EXAMPLE 9–16

Determine the binary values of the variables for which the following standard POS expression is equal to 0:

$$(A + B + C + D)(A + \overline{B} + \overline{C} + D)(\overline{A} + \overline{B} + \overline{C} + \overline{D})$$

Solution The term $A + B + C + D$ is equal to 0 when $A = 0, B = 0, C = 0,$ and $D = 0.$

$$A + B + C + D = 0 + 0 + 0 + 0 = 0$$

The term $A + \overline{B} + \overline{C} + D$ is equal to 0 when $A = 0, B = 1, C = 1,$ and $D = 0.$

$$A + \overline{B} + \overline{C} + D = 0 + \overline{1} + \overline{1} + 0 = 0 + 0 + 0 + 0 = 0$$

The term $\overline{A} + \overline{B} + \overline{C} + \overline{D}$ is equal to 0 when $A = 1, B = 1, C = 1,$ and $D = 1.$

$$\overline{A} + \overline{B} + \overline{C} + \overline{D} = \overline{1} + \overline{1} + \overline{1} + \overline{1} = 0 + 0 + 0 + 0 = 0$$

The POS expression equals 0 when any of the three sum terms equals 0.

Related Problem Determine the binary values for which the following POS expression is equal to 0:

$$(X + \overline{Y} + Z)(\overline{X} + Y + Z)(X + Y + \overline{Z})(\overline{X} + \overline{Y} + \overline{Z})(X + \overline{Y} + \overline{Z})$$

Is this a standard POS expression?

Converting Standard SOP to Standard POS

The binary values of the product terms in a given standard SOP expression are not present in the equivalent standard POS expression. Also, the binary values that are not represented in the SOP expression are present in the equivalent POS expression. Therefore, to convert from standard SOP to standard POS, the following steps are taken:

Step 1. Evaluate each product term in the SOP expression. That is, determine the binary numbers that represent the product terms.

Step 2. Determine all of the binary numbers not included in the evaluation in Step 1.

Step 3. Write the equivalent sum term for each binary number from Step 2 and express in POS form.

Using a similar procedure, you can go from POS to SOP.

EXAMPLE 9–17

Convert the following SOP expression to an equivalent POS expression:

$$\overline{A}\,\overline{B}\,\overline{C} + \overline{A}B\overline{C} + \overline{A}BC + A\overline{B}C + ABC$$

Solution The evaluation is as follows:

$$000 + 010 + 011 + 101 + 111$$

Since there are three variables in the domain of this expression, there are a total of eight (2^3) possible combinations. The SOP expression contains five of these combinations, so the POS must contain the other three which are 001, 100, and 110.

Remember, these are the binary values that make the sum term 0. The equivalent POS expression is

$$(A + B + \overline{C})(\overline{A} + B + C)(\overline{A} + \overline{B} + C)$$

Related Problem   Verify that the SOP and POS expressions in this example are equivalent by substituting binary values into each.

9–7   BOOLEAN EXPRESSIONS AND TRUTH TABLES

All standard Boolean expressions can be easily converted into truth table format using binary values for each term in the expression. The truth table is a common way of presenting, in a concise format, the logical operation of a circuit. Also, standard SOP or POS expressions can be determined from a truth table. You will find truth tables in data sheets and other literature related to the operation of digital circuits.

After completing this section, you should be able to

■ Convert a standard SOP expression into truth table format

■ Convert a standard POS expression into truth table format

■ Derive a standard expression from a truth table

■ Properly interpret truth table data

Converting SOP Expressions to Truth Table Format

Recall an SOP expression is equal to 1 only if at least one of the product terms is equal to 1. A truth table is simply a list of the possible combinations of input variable values and the corresponding output values (1 or 0). For an expression with a domain of two variables, there are four different combinations of those variables ($2^2 = 4$). For an expression with a domain of three variables, there are eight different combinations of those variables ($2^3 = 8$). For an expression with a domain of four variables, there are sixteen different combinations of those variables ($2^4 = 16$), and so on.

The first step in constructing a truth table is to list all possible combinations of binary values of the variables in the expression. Next, convert the SOP expression to standard form if it is not already. Finally, place a 1 in the output column (X) for each binary value that makes the standard SOP expression a 1 and place a 0 for all the remaining binary values. This procedure is illustrated in Example 9–18.

EXAMPLE 9–18

Develop a truth table for the standard SOP expression $\overline{A}\,\overline{B}C + A\overline{B}\,\overline{C} + ABC$.

Solution   There are three variables in the domain, so there are eight possible combinations of binary values of the variables as listed in the left three columns of Table 9–6. The binary values that make the product terms in the expressions equal to 1 are $\overline{A}\,\overline{B}C$: 001; $A\overline{B}\,\overline{C}$: 100; and ABC: 111. For each of these binary values, place a 1 in the output column as shown in the table. For each of the remaining binary combinations, place a 0 in the output column.

INPUTS			OUTPUT	
A	B	C	X	PRODUCT TERM
0	0	0	0	
0	0	1	1	$\overline{A}\,\overline{B}C$
0	1	0	0	
0	1	1	0	
1	0	0	1	$A\overline{B}\,\overline{C}$
1	0	1	0	
1	1	0	0	
1	1	1	1	ABC

Related Problem   Create a truth table for the standard SOP expression $\overline{A}B\overline{C} + A\overline{B}C$.

Converting POS Expressions to Truth Table Format

Recall that a POS expression is equal to 0 only if at least one of the sum terms is equal to 0. To construct a truth table from a POS expression, list all the possible combinations of binary values of the variables just as was done for the SOP expression. Next, convert the POS expression to standard form if it is not already. Finally, place a 0 in the output column (X) for each binary value that makes the expression a 0 and place a 1 for all the remaining binary values. This procedure is illustrated in Example 9–19.

EXAMPLE 9–19

Determine the truth table for the following standard POS expression:

$$(A + B + C)(A + \overline{B} + C)(A + \overline{B} + \overline{C})(\overline{A} + B + \overline{C})(\overline{A} + \overline{B} + C)$$

Solution   There are three variables in the domain and the eight possible binary values are listed in the left three columns of Table 9–7. The binary values that make the sum terms in the expression equal to 0 are $A + B + C$: 000; $A + \overline{B} + C$: 010; $A + \overline{B} + \overline{C}$: 011; $\overline{A} + B + \overline{C}$: 101; and $\overline{A} + \overline{B} + C$: 110. For each of these binary values, place a 0 in the output column as shown in the table. For each of the remaining binary combinations, place a 1 in the output column.

▶ TABLE 9–7

INPUTS			OUTPUT	
A	B	C	X	SUM TERM
0	0	0	0	$(A + B + C)$
0	0	1	1	
0	1	0	0	$(A + \overline{B} + C)$
0	1	1	0	$(A + \overline{B} + \overline{C})$
1	0	0	1	
1	0	1	0	$(\overline{A} + B + \overline{C})$
1	1	0	0	$(\overline{A} + \overline{B} + C)$
1	1	1	1	

Notice that the truth table in this example is the same as the one in Example 9–18. This means that the SOP expression in the previous example and the POS expression in this example are equivalent.

Related Problem   Develop a truth table for the following standard POS expression:

$$(A + \overline{B} + C)(A + B + \overline{C})(\overline{A} + \overline{B} + \overline{C})$$

Determining Standard Expressions from a Truth Table

To determine the standard SOP expression represented by a truth table, list the binary values of the input variables for which the output is 1. Convert each binary value to the corresponding product term by replacing each 1 with the corresponding variable and each 0 with the corresponding variable complement. For example, the binary value 1010 is converted to a product term as follows:

$$1010 \rightarrow A\overline{B}C\overline{D}$$

If you substitute, you can see that the product term is 1:

$$A\overline{B}C\overline{D} = 1 \cdot \overline{0} \cdot 1 \cdot \overline{0} = 1 \cdot 1 \cdot 1 \cdot 1 = 1$$

To determine the standard POS expression represented by a truth table, list the binary values for which the output is 0. Convert each binary value to the corresponding sum term by replacing each 1 with the corresponding variable complement and each 0 with the corresponding variable. For example, the binary value 1001 is converted to a sum term as follows:

$$1001 \rightarrow \overline{A} + B + C + \overline{D}$$

If you substitute, you can see that the sum term is 0:

$$\overline{A} + B + C + \overline{D} = \overline{1} + 0 + 0 + \overline{1} = 0 + 0 + 0 + 0 = 0$$

EXAMPLE 9–20

From the truth table in Table 9–8, determine the standard SOP expression and the equivalent standard POS expression.

▶ **TABLE 9–8**

INPUTS			OUTPUT
A	B	C	X
0	0	0	0
0	0	1	0
0	1	0	0
0	1	1	1
1	0	0	1
1	0	1	0
1	1	0	1
1	1	1	1

Solution There are four 1s in the output column and the corresponding binary values are 011, 100, 110, and 111. Convert these binary values to product terms as follows:

$$011 \rightarrow \overline{A}BC$$
$$100 \rightarrow A\overline{B}\,\overline{C}$$
$$110 \rightarrow AB\overline{C}$$
$$111 \rightarrow ABC$$

The resulting standard SOP expression for the output X is

$$X = \overline{A}BC + A\overline{B}\,\overline{C} + AB\overline{C} + ABC$$

For the POS expression, the output is 0 for binary values 000, 001, 010, and 101. Convert these binary values to sum terms as follows:

$$000 \rightarrow A + B + C$$
$$001 \rightarrow A + B + \overline{C}$$
$$010 \rightarrow A + \overline{B} + C$$
$$101 \rightarrow \overline{A} + B + \overline{C}$$

The resulting standard POS expression for the output X is

$$X = (A + B + C)(A + B + \overline{C})(A + \overline{B} + C)(\overline{A} + B + \overline{C})$$

Related Problem By substitution of binary values, show that the SOP and the POS expressions derived in this example are equivalent; that is, for any binary value they should either both be 1 or both be 0, depending on the binary value.

SUMMARY

- Gate symbols and Boolean expressions for the outputs of an inverter and 2-input gates are shown in Figure 9–21.

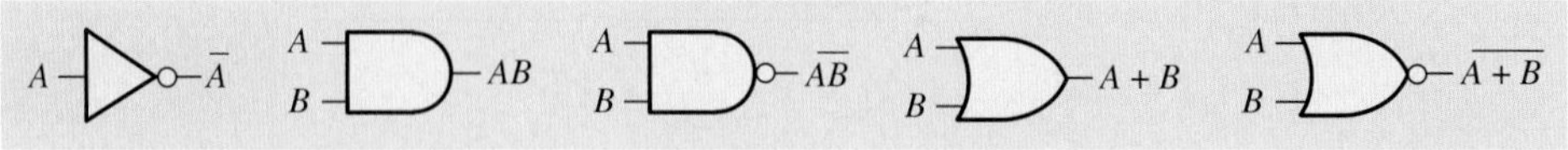

▲ **FIGURE 9–21**

- Commutative laws: $A + B = B + A$
  $$AB = BA$$

- Associative laws: $A + (B + C) = (A + B) + C$
  $$A(BC) = (AB)C$$

- Distributive law: $A(B + C) = AB + AC$

- Boolean rules:
1. $A + 0 = A$		**7.** $A \cdot A = A$
2. $A + 1 = 1$		**8.** $A \cdot \overline{A} = 0$
3. $A \cdot 0 = 0$		**9.** $\overline{\overline{A}} = A$
4. $A \cdot 1 = A$		**10.** $A + AB = A$
5. $A + A = A$		**11.** $A + \overline{A}B = A + B$
6. $A + \overline{A} = 1$		**12.** $(A + B)(A + C) = A + BC$

- DeMorgan's theorems:

  1. The complement of a product is equal to the sum of the complements of the terms in the product.

  $$\overline{XY} = \overline{X} + \overline{Y}$$

  2 The complement of a sum is equal to the product of the complements of the terms in the sum.

  $$\overline{X + Y} = \overline{X}\,\overline{Y}$$

KEY TERMS

Complement The inverse or opposite of a number. In Boolean algebra, the inverse function, expressed with a bar over a variable. The complement of a 1 is 0, and vice versa.

Product term The Boolean product of two or more literals equivalent to an AND operation.

Sum-of-products (SOP) A form of Boolean expression that is basically the ORing of ANDed terms.

Sum term The Boolean sum of two or more literals equivalent to an OR operation.

Variable A symbol used to represent a logical quantity that can have a value of 1 or 0, usually designated by an italic letter.

SELF-TEST

Answers are at the end of the chapter.

1. The complement of a variable is always

   (a) 0   (b) 1   (c) equal to the variable   (d) the inverse of the variable

2. The Boolean expression $A + \overline{B} + C$ is

   (a) a sum term   (b) a literal term   (c) a product term   (d) a complemented term

3. The Boolean expression $\overline{A}B\overline{C}\overline{D}$ is

   (a) a sum term   (b) a product term   (c) a literal term   (d) always 1

4. The domain of the expression $\overline{A}BCD + A\overline{B} + \overline{C}D + B$ is
   (a) A and D (b) B only   (c) A, B, C, and D (d) none of these

5. According to the commutative law of addition,
   (a) $AB = BA$ (b) $A = A + A$
   (c) $A + (B + C) = (A + B) + C$ (d) $A + B = B + A$

6. According to the associative law of multiplication,
   (a) $B = BB$ (b) $A(BC) = (AB)C$ (c) $A + B = B + A$ (d) $B + B(B + 0)$

7. According to the distributive law,
   (a) $A(B + C) = AB + AC$ (b) $A(BC) = ABC$ (c) $A(A + 1) = A$ (d) $A + AB = A$

8. Which one of the following is *not* a valid rule of Boolean algebra?
   (a) $A + 1 = 1$ (b) $A = \overline{A}$ (c) $AA = A$ (d) $A + 0 = A$

9. Which of the following rules states that if one input of an AND gate is always 1, the output is equal to the other input?
   (a) $A + 1 = 1$ (b) $A + A = A$ (c) $A \cdot A = A$ (d) $A \cdot 1 = A$

10. According to DeMorgan's theorems, the following equality(s) is (are) correct:
    (a) $\overline{AB} = \overline{A} + \overline{B}$ (b) $\overline{XYZ} = \overline{X} + \overline{Y} + \overline{Z}$
    (c) $\overline{A + B + C} = \overline{A}\,\overline{B}\,\overline{C}$ (d) all of these

11. The Boolean expression $X = AB + CD$ represents
    (a) two ORs ANDed together   (b) a 4-input AND gate
    (c) two ANDs ORed together   (d) an exclusive-OR

12. An example of a sum-of-products expression is
    (a) $A + B(C + D)$ (b) $\overline{A}B + A\overline{C} + A\overline{B}C$
    (c) $(\overline{A} + B + C)(A + \overline{B} + C)$ (d) both answers (a) and (b)

13. An example of a product-of-sums expression is
    (a) $A(B + C) + A\overline{C}$ (b) $(A + B)(\overline{A} + B + \overline{C})$
    (c) $\overline{A} + \overline{B} + BC$ (d) both answers (a) and (b)

14. An example of a standard SOP expression is
    (a) $\overline{A}B + A\overline{B}C + AB\overline{D}$ (b) $A\overline{B}C + A\overline{C}D$
    (c) $A\overline{B} + \overline{A}B + AB$ (d) $A\overline{B}C\overline{D} + \overline{A}B + \overline{A}$

PROBLEMS

SECTION 9–1   Boolean Operations and Expressions

1. Using Boolean notation, write an expression that is a 1 whenever one or more of its variables (A, B, C, and D) are 1s.

2. Write an expression that is a 1 only if all of its variables (A, B, C, D, and E) are 1s.

3. Write an expression that is a 1 when one or more of its variables (A, B, and C) are 0s.

4. Evaluate the following operations:
   (a) $0 + 0 + 1$ (b) $1 + 1 + 1$ (c) $1 \cdot 0 \cdot 0$
   (d) $1 \cdot 1 \cdot 1$ (e) $1 \cdot 0 \cdot 1$ (f) $1 \cdot 1 + 0 \cdot 1 \cdot 1$

5. Find the values of the variables that make each product term 1 and each sum term 0.
   (a) AB (b) $\overline{A}\overline{B}C$ (c) $A + \overline{B}$ (d) $\overline{A} + B + \overline{C}$
   (e) $\overline{A} + \overline{B} + C$ (f) $\overline{A} + B$ (g) $A\overline{B}\overline{C}$

6. Find the value of X for all possible values of the variables.
   (a) $X = (A + B)C + B$ (b) $X = (\overline{A + B})C$ (c) $X = A\overline{B}C + AB$
   (d) $X = (A + B)(\overline{A} + B)$ (e) $X = (A + BC)(\overline{B} + \overline{C})$

SECTION 9–2   **Laws and Rules of Boolean Algebra**

7. Identify the law of Boolean algebra upon which each of the following equalities is based:

(a) $A\overline{B} + CD + A\overline{C}D + B = B + A\overline{B} + A\overline{C}D + CD$

(b) $AB\overline{C}D + \overline{A}BC = D\overline{C}BA + \overline{C}B\overline{A}$

(c) $AB(CD + \overline{E}F + GH) = ABCD + AB\overline{E}F + ABGH$

8. Identify the Boolean rule(s) on which each of the following equalities is based:

(a) $\overline{AB + CD} + \overline{EF} = AB + CD + \overline{EF}$ (b) $A\overline{A}B + AB\overline{C} + AB\overline{B} = AB\overline{C}$

(c) $A(BC + \overline{B}C) + AC = A(BC) + AC$ (d) $AB(C + \overline{C}) + AC = AB + AC$

(e) $A\overline{B} + A\overline{B}C = A\overline{B}$ (f) $ABC + \overline{A}B + \overline{A}BCD = ABC + \overline{A}B + D$

SECTION 9–3   **DeMorgan's Theorems**

9. Apply DeMorgan's theorems to each expression:

(a) $\overline{\overline{A} + B}$ (b) $\overline{\overline{A}\overline{B}}$ (c) $\overline{A + B + C}$ (d) $\overline{ABC}$

(e) $\overline{A(B + C)}$ (f) $\overline{AB + CD}$ (g) $\overline{A\overline{B} + \overline{C}D}$ (h) $\overline{(A + \overline{B})(\overline{C} + D)}$

10. Apply DeMorgan's theorems to each expression:

(a) $\overline{A\overline{B}(C + \overline{D})}$ (b) $\overline{AB(CD + EF)}$

(c) $\overline{(A + \overline{B} + C + \overline{D}) + ABC\overline{D}}$ (d) $\overline{(\overline{\overline{A} + B + C + D})(\overline{AB}\,\overline{CD})}$

(e) $\overline{\overline{AB}(CD + \overline{E}F)(\overline{AB} + CD)}$

11. Apply DeMorgan's theorems to the following:

(a) $\overline{(\overline{\overline{ABC}})(\overline{EFG}) + (\overline{HIJ})(\overline{KLM})}$ (b) $\overline{(A + \overline{BC} + CD) + \overline{\overline{BC}}}$

(c) $\overline{(\overline{A + B})(\overline{C + D})(\overline{E + F})(\overline{G + H})}$

SECTION 9–4   **Boolean Analysis of Logic Circuits**

12. Write the Boolean expression for each of the logic gates in Figure 9–22.

▶ FIGURE 9–22

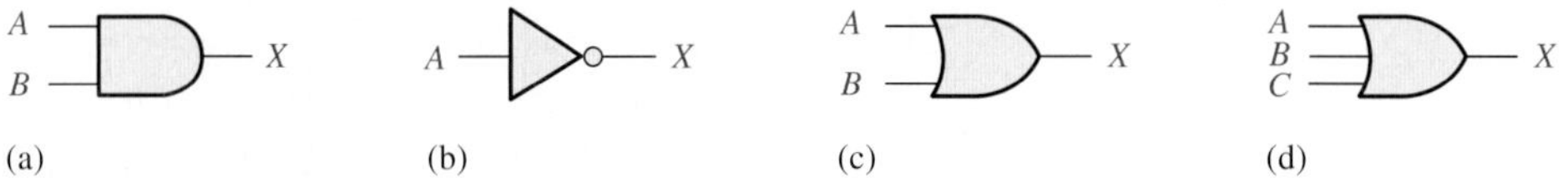

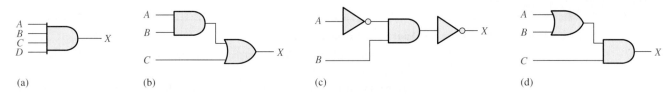

(a)   (b)   (c)   (d)

13. Write the Boolean expression for each of the logic circuits in Figure 9–23.

(a)   (b)   (c)   (d)

▲ FIGURE 9–23

14. Draw the logic circuit represented by each of the following expressions:

(a) $A + B + C$ (b) ABC (c) $AB + C$ (d) $AB + CD$

15. Draw the logic circuit represented by each expression:

(a) $A\overline{B} + \overline{A}B$ (b) $AB + \overline{A}\overline{B} + \overline{A}BC$

(c) $\overline{A}B(C + \overline{D})$ (d) $A + B[C + D(B + \overline{C})]$

16. Construct a truth table for each of the following Boolean expressions:

(a) $A + B$ (b) AB (c) $AB + BC$

(d) $(A + B)C$ (e) $(A + B)(\overline{B} + C)$

SECTION 9-5   Simplification Using Boolean Algebra

17. Using Boolean algebra techniques, simplify the following expressions as much as possible:

   (a) $A(A + B)$ **(b)** $A(\overline{A} + AB)$ **(c)** $BC + \overline{B}C$

   (d) $A(A + \overline{A}B)$ **(e)** $\overline{A}BC + A\overline{B}C + \overline{A}\overline{B}C$

18. Using Boolean algebra, simplify the following expressions:

   (a) $(A + \overline{B})(A + C)$ **(b)** $\overline{A}B + \overline{A}B\overline{C} + \overline{A}BCD + \overline{A}\overline{B}\overline{C}DE$

   (c) $AB + \overline{A}BC + A$ **(d)** $(A + \overline{A})(AB + AB\overline{C})$

   (e) $AB + (\overline{A} + \overline{B})C + AB$

19. Using Boolean algebra, simplify each expression:

   (a) $BD + B(D + E) + \overline{D}(D + F)$ **(b)** $\overline{A}\overline{B}C + \overline{(A + B + \overline{C})} + \overline{A}\overline{B}\overline{C}D$

   (c) $(B + BC)(B + \overline{B}C)(B + D)$ **(d)** $ABCD + AB(\overline{CD}) + (\overline{AB})CD$

   (e) $ABC[AB + \overline{C}(BC + AC)]$

20. Determine which of the logic circuits in Figure 9–24 are equivalent.

▷ **FIGURE 9-24**

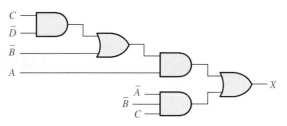

(a)

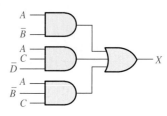

(b)

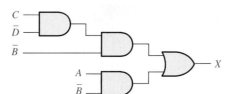

(c)

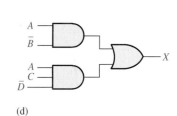

(d)

SECTION 9-6   Standard Forms of Boolean Expressions

21. Convert the following expressions to sum-of-product (SOP) forms:

   (a) $(A + B)(C + \overline{B})$ **(b)** $(A + \overline{B}C)C$ **(c)** $(A + C)(AB + AC)$

22. Convert the following expressions to sum-of-product (SOP) forms:

   (a) $AB + CD(A\overline{B} + CD)$ **(b)** $AB(\overline{B}\overline{C} + BD)$ **(c)** $A + B[AC + (B + \overline{C})D]$

23. Define the domain of each SOP expression in Problem 21 and convert the expression to standard SOP form.

24. Convert each SOP expression in Problem 22 to standard SOP form.

25. Determine the binary value of each term in the standard SOP expressions from Problem 23.

26. Determine the binary value of each term in the standard SOP expressions from Problem 24.

27. Convert each standard SOP expression in Problem 23 to standard POS form.

28. Convert each standard SOP expression in Problem 24 to standard POS form.

SECTION 9-7 **Boolean Expressions and Truth Tables**

29. Develop a truth table for each of the following standard SOP expressions:

    (a) $A\bar{B}C + \bar{A}B\bar{C} + ABC$ (b) $\overline{XYZ} + \bar{X}\bar{Y}Z + XY\bar{Z} + X\bar{Y}Z + \bar{X}YZ$

30. Develop a truth table for each of the following standard SOP expressions:

    (a) $\bar{A}B\bar{C}D + \bar{A}BCD + AB\bar{C}D + \bar{A}\,\bar{B}\,\bar{C}\,\bar{D}$

    (b) $WXYZ + WX\bar{Y}\bar{Z} + \bar{W}XYZ + W\bar{X}YZ + WX\bar{Y}Z$

31. Develop a truth table for each of the SOP expressions:

    (a) $\bar{A}B + AB\bar{C} + \bar{A}\,\bar{C} + A\bar{B}C$ (b) $\bar{X} + Y\bar{Z} + WZ + X\bar{Y}Z$

32. Develop a truth table for each of the standard POS expressions:

    (a) $(\bar{A} + \bar{B} + \bar{C})(A + B + C)(A + \bar{B} + C)$

    (b) $(\bar{A} + B + \bar{C} + D)(A + B + C + \bar{D})(A + \bar{B} + \bar{C} + D)(\bar{A} + B + C + \bar{D})$

33. Develop a truth table for each of the standard POS expressions:

    (a) $(A + B)(A + C)(A + B + C)$

    (b) $(A + \bar{B})(A + \bar{B} + \bar{C})(B + C + \bar{D})(\bar{A} + B + \bar{C} + D)$

34. For each truth table in Figure 9–25, derive a standard SOP and a standard POS expression.

ABC	X
0 0 0	0
0 0 1	1
0 1 0	0
0 1 1	0
1 0 0	1
1 0 1	1
1 1 0	0
1 1 1	1

(a)

ABC	X
0 0 0	0
0 0 1	0
0 1 0	0
0 1 1	0
1 0 0	0
1 0 1	1
1 1 0	1
1 1 1	1

(b)

ABCD	X
0 0 0 0	1
0 0 0 1	1
0 0 1 0	0
0 0 1 1	1
0 1 0 0	0
0 1 0 1	1
0 1 1 0	1
0 1 1 1	0
1 0 0 0	0
1 0 0 1	1
1 0 1 0	0
1 0 1 1	0
1 1 0 0	1
1 1 0 1	0
1 1 1 0	0
1 1 1 1	0

(c)

ABCD	X
0 0 0 0	0
0 0 0 1	0
0 0 1 0	1
0 0 1 1	0
0 1 0 0	1
0 1 0 1	1
0 1 1 0	0
0 1 1 1	1
1 0 0 0	0
1 0 0 1	0
1 0 1 0	0
1 0 1 1	1
1 1 0 0	1
1 1 0 1	0
1 1 1 0	0
1 1 1 1	1

(d)

▲ **FIGURE 9–25**

SELF-TEST

1. (d)   2. (a)   3. (b)   4. (c)   5. (d)   6. (b)   7. (a)   8. (b)   9. (d)

10. (d)   11. (c)   12. (b)   13. (b)   14. (c)

10

COMBINATIONAL LOGIC ANALYSIS

INTRODUCTION

In Chapters 8 and 9, logic gates were discussed on an individual basis and in simple combinations. You were introduced to SOP implementation which is a basic form of combinational logic. When logic gates are connected together to produce a specified output for certain specified combinations of input variables, with no storage involved, the resulting circuit is in the category of **combinational logic.** In combinational logic, the output level is at all times dependent on the combination of input levels. This chapter expands on the material introduced in earlier chapters with a coverage of the analysis and design of various combinational logic circuits.

CHAPTER OBJECTIVES

▪ Analyze basic combinational logic circuits, such as AND-OR, AND-OR-Invert, exclusive-OR, and exclusive-NOR

▪ Use AND-OR circuits to implement sum-of-products (SOP) expressions

▪ Write the Boolean output expression for any combinational logic circuit

▪ Develop a truth table from the output expression for a combinational logic circuit

▪ Design a combinational logic circuit for a given Boolean output expression

▪ Design a combinational logic circuit for a given truth table

▪ Apply combinational logic to a system application

CHAPTER OUTLINE

KEY TERMS

▪ Universal gate

▪ Negative-OR

▪ Negative-AND

▪ Node

WWW. VISIT THE COMPANION WEBSITE
Study aids for this chapter are available at
http://www.prenhall.com/floyd

10-1 BASIC COMBINATIONAL LOGIC CIRCUITS

In Chapter 9, you learned that SOP expressions are implemented with an AND gate for each product term and one OR gate for summing all of the product terms. As you know, this SOP implementation is called AND-OR logic and is the basic form for realizing standard Boolean functions. In this section, the AND-OR and the AND- OR-Invert are examined; the exclusive-OR and exclusive-NOR gates, which are actually a form of AND-OR logic, are also covered.

After completing this section, you should be able to

- Analyze and apply AND-OR circuits
- Analyze and apply AND-OR-Invert circuits
- Analyze and apply exclusive-OR gates
- Analyze and apply exclusive-NOR gates

AND-OR Logic

AND-OR logic produces an SOP expression.

Figure 10–1(a) shows an AND-OR circuit consisting of two 2-input AND gates and one 2-input OR gate; Figure 10–1(b) is the ANSI standard rectangular outline symbol. The Boolean expressions for the AND gate outputs and the resulting SOP expression for the output X are shown on the diagram. In general, an AND-OR circuit can have any number of AND gates each with any number of inputs.

▶ **FIGURE 10–1**

An example of AND-OR logic.

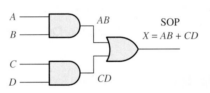

(a) Logic diagram (ANSI standard distinctive shape symbols)

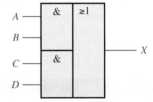

(b) ANSI standard rectangular outline symbol

▶ **TABLE 10–1**

Truth table for the AND-OR logic in Figure 10-1.

INPUTS						OUTPUT
A	B	C	D	AB	CD	X
0	0	0	0	0	0	0
0	0	0	1	0	0	0
0	0	1	0	0	0	0
0	0	1	1	0	1	1
0	1	0	0	0	0	0
0	1	0	1	0	0	0
0	1	1	0	0	0	0
0	1	1	1	0	1	1
1	0	0	0	0	0	0
1	0	0	1	0	0	0
1	0	1	0	0	0	0
1	0	1	1	0	1	1
1	1	0	0	1	0	1
1	1	0	1	1	0	1
1	1	1	0	1	0	1
1	1	1	1	1	1	1

The truth table for a 4-input AND-OR logic circuit is shown in Table 10–1. The intermediate AND gate outputs (the AB and CD columns) are also shown in the table. *An AND-OR circuit directly implements an SOP expression, assuming the complements (if any) of the variables are available.* The operation of the AND-OR circuit in Figure 10–1 is stated as follows:

For a 4-input AND-OR logic circuit, the output X is HIGH (1) if both input A and input B are HIGH (1) or both input C and input D are HIGH (1).

EXAMPLE 10–1

In a certain chemical-processing plant, a liquid chemical is used in a manufacturing process. The chemical is stored in three different tanks. A level sensor in each tank produces a HIGH voltage when the level of chemical in the tank drops below a specified point.

Design a circuit that monitors the chemical level in each tank and indicates when the level in any two of the tanks drops below the specified point.

Solution The AND-OR circuit in Figure 10–2 has inputs from the sensors on tanks A, B, and C as shown. The AND gate G_1 checks the levels in tanks A and B, gate G_2 checks tanks A and C, and gate G_3 checks tanks B and C. When the chemical level in any two of the tanks gets too low, one of the AND gates will have HIGHs on both of its inputs, causing its output to be HIGH; and so the final output X from the OR gate is HIGH. This HIGH input is then used to activate an indicator such as a lamp or audible alarm, as shown in the figure.

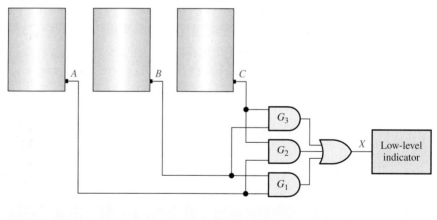

▲ **FIGURE 10–2**

Related Problem Write the Boolean SOP expression for the AND-OR logic in Figure 10–2.

AND-OR-Invert Logic

When the output of an AND-OR circuit is complemented (inverted), it results in an AND-OR-Invert circuit. Recall that AND-OR logic directly implements SOP expressions. POS expressions can be implemented with AND-OR-Invert logic. This is illustrated as follows, starting with a POS expression and developing the corresponding AND-OR-Invert expression.

$$X = (\overline{A} + \overline{B})(\overline{C} + \overline{D}) = (\overline{AB})(\overline{CD}) = \overline{(\overline{AB})(\overline{CD})} = \overline{\overline{AB} + \overline{CD}} = \overline{AB + CD}$$

The logic diagram in Figure 10–3(a) shows an AND-OR-Invert circuit and the development of the POS output expression. The ANSI standard rectangular outline symbol is shown in part (b). In general, an AND-OR-Invert circuit can have any number of AND gates each with any number of inputs.

▶ **FIGURE 10–3**

An AND-OR-Invert circuit produces a POS output.

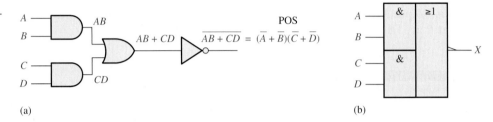

(a)   (b)

The operation of the AND-OR-Invert circuit in Figure 10–3 is stated as follows:

For a 4-input AND-OR-Invert logic circuit, the output *X* is LOW (0) if both input *A* and input *B* are HIGH (1) or both input *C* and input *D* are HIGH (1).

A truth table can be developed from the AND-OR truth table in Table 10–1 by simply changing all 1s to 0s and all 0s to 1s in the output column.

EXAMPLE 10–2

The sensors in the chemical tanks of Example 10–1 are being replaced by a new model that produces a LOW voltage instead of a HIGH voltage when the level of the chemical in the tank drops below a critical point.

Modify the circuit in Figure 10–2 to operate with the different input levels and still produce a HIGH output to activate the indicator when the level in any two of the tanks drops below the critical point. Show the logic diagram.

Solution   The AND-OR-Invert circuit in Figure 10–4 has inputs from the sensors on tanks *A*, *B*, and *C* as shown. The AND gate G_1 checks the levels in tanks *A* and *B*, gate G_2 checks tanks *A* and *C*, and gate G_3 checks tanks *B* and *C*. When the chemical level in any two of the tanks gets too low, each AND gate will have a LOW on at least one input causing its output to be LOW and, thus, the final output *X* from the inverter is HIGH. This HIGH output is then used to activate an indicator.

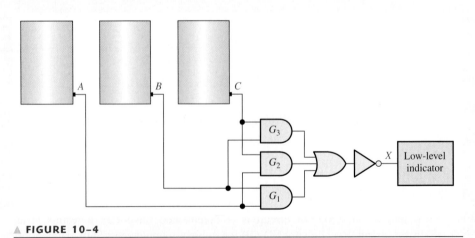

▲ **FIGURE 10–4**

Related Problem   Write the Boolean expression for the AND-OR-Invert logic in Figure 10–4 and show that the output is HIGH (1) when any two of the inputs *A*, *B*, and *C* are LOW (0).

Exclusive-OR Logic

The exclusive-OR gate was introduced in Chapter 8. Although, because of its importance, this circuit is considered a type of logic gate with its own unique symbol, it is actually a combination of two AND gates, one OR gate, and two inverters, as shown in Figure 10–5(a). The two ANSI standard logic symbols are shown in parts (b) and (c).

The XOR gate is actually a combination of other gates.

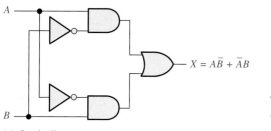

▶ FIGURE 10–5

Exclusive-OR logic diagram and symbols.

(a) Logic diagram

(b) ANSI distinctive shape symbol

(c) ANSI rectangular outline symbol

The output expression for the circuit in Figure 10–5 is

$$X = A\bar{B} + \bar{A}B$$

Evaluation of this expression results in the truth table in Table 10–2. Notice that the output is HIGH only when the two inputs are at opposite levels. A special exclusive-OR operator $\oplus$ is often used, so the expression $X = A\bar{B} + \bar{A}B$ can be stated as "X is equal to A exclusive-OR B" and can be written as

$$X = A \oplus B$$

▶ TABLE 10–2

Truth table for an exclusive-OR.

A	B	X
0	0	0
0	1	1
1	0	1
1	1	0

Exclusive-NOR Logic

As you know, the complement of the exclusive-OR function is the exclusive-NOR, which is derived as follows:

$$X = \overline{A\bar{B} + \bar{A}B} = (\overline{A\bar{B}})(\overline{\bar{A}B}) = (\bar{A} + B)(A + \bar{B}) = \bar{A}\bar{B} + AB$$

Notice that the output X is HIGH only when the two inputs, A and B, are at the same level.

The exclusive-NOR can be implemented by simply inverting the output of an exclusive-OR, as shown in Figure 10–6(a), or by directly implementing the expression $\bar{A}\bar{B} + AB$, as shown in part (b).

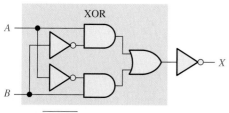

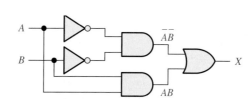

▶ FIGURE 10–6

Two equivalent ways of implementing the exclusive-NOR.

(a) $X = \overline{A\bar{B} + \bar{A}B}$

(b) $X = \bar{A}\bar{B} + AB$

10–2 IMPLEMENTING COMBINATIONAL LOGIC

In this section, examples are used to illustrate how to implement a logic circuit from a Boolean expression or a truth table. Minimization of a logic circuit using the methods covered in Chapter 9 is also included.

After completing this section, you should be able to

■ Implement a logic circuit from a Boolean expression

■ Implement a logic circuit from a truth table

■ Minimize a logic circuit

From a Boolean Expression to a Logic Circuit

For every Boolean expression there is a logic circuit, and for every logic circuit there is a Boolean expression.

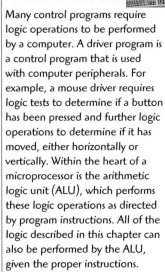

COMPUTER NOTE

Many control programs require logic operations to be performed by a computer. A driver program is a control program that is used with computer peripherals. For example, a mouse driver requires logic tests to determine if a button has been pressed and further logic operations to determine if it has moved, either horizontally or vertically. Within the heart of a microprocessor is the arithmetic logic unit (ALU), which performs these logic operations as directed by program instructions. All of the logic described in this chapter can also be performed by the ALU, given the proper instructions.

Let's examine the following Boolean expression:

$$X = AB + CDE$$

A brief inspection shows that this expression is composed of two terms, AB and CDE, with a domain of five variables. The first term is formed by ANDing A with B, and the second term is formed by ANDing C, D, and E. The two terms are then ORed to form the output X. These operations are indicated in the structure of the expression as follows:

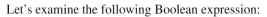

Note that in this particular expression, the AND operations forming the two individual terms, AB and CDE, must be performed *before* the terms can be ORed.

To implement this Boolean expression, a 2-input AND gate is required to form the term AB, and a 3-input AND gate is needed to form the term CDE. A 2-input OR gate is then required to combine the two AND terms. The resulting logic circuit is shown in Figure 10–7.

▶ **FIGURE 10–7**

Logic circuit for $X = AB + CDE$.

As another example, let's implement the following expression:

$$X = AB(\overline{CD} + EF)$$

A breakdown of this expression shows that the terms AB and $(\overline{CD} + EF)$ are ANDed. The term $\overline{CD} + EF$ is formed by first ANDing C and $\overline{D}$ and ANDing E and F, and then ORing these two terms. This structure is indicated in relation to the expression as follows:

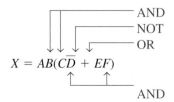

Before you can implement the final expression, you must create the sum term $\overline{CD} + EF$; but before you can get this term; you must create the product terms $\overline{CD}$ and EF; but before you can get the term $\overline{CD}$, you must create $\overline{D}$. So, as you can see, the logic operations must be done in the proper order.

The logic gates required to implement $X = AB(\overline{CD} + EF)$ are as follows:

1. One inverter to form $\overline{D}$

2. Two 2-input AND gates to form $C\overline{D}$ and EF

3. One 2-input OR gate to form $C\overline{D} + EF$

4. One 3-input AND gate to form X

The logic circuit for this expression is shown in Figure 10–8(a). Notice that there is a maximum of four gates and an inverter between an input and output in this circuit (from input D to output). Often the total propagation delay time through a logic circuit is a major consideration. Propagation delays are additive, so the more gates or inverters between input and output, the greater the propagation delay time.

Unless an intermediate term, such as $C\overline{D} + EF$ in Figure 10–8(a), is required as an output for some other purpose, it is usually best to reduce a circuit to its SOP form in order to reduce the overall propagation delay time. The expression is converted to SOP as follows, and the resulting circuit is shown in Figure 10–8(b).

$$AB(C\overline{D} + EF) = ABC\overline{D} + ABEF$$

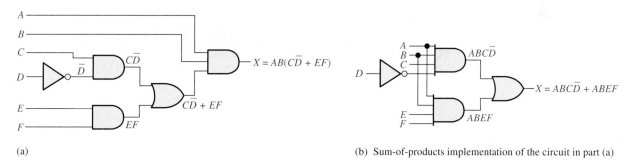

(a)

(b) Sum-of-products implementation of the circuit in part (a)

▲ FIGURE 10–8

Logic circuits for $X = AB(C\overline{D} + EF) = ABC\overline{D} + ABEF$.

From a Truth Table to a Logic Circuit

If you begin with a truth table instead of an expression, you can write the SOP expression from the truth table and then implement the logic circuit. Table 10–3 specifies a logic function.

The Boolean SOP expression obtained from the truth table by ORing the product terms for which $X = 1$ is

$$X = \overline{A}BC + A\overline{B}\,\overline{C}$$

◀ TABLE 10–3

INPUTS			OUTPUT	
A	B	C	X	PRODUCT TERM
0	0	0	0	
0	0	1	0	
0	1	0	0	
0	1	1	1	$\overline{A}BC$
1	0	0	1	$A\overline{B}\,\overline{C}$
1	0	1	0	
1	1	0	0	
1	1	1	0	

The first term in the expression is formed by ANDing the three variables $\overline{A}$, B, and C. The second term is formed by ANDing the three variables A, $\overline{B}$, and $\overline{C}$.

The logic gates required to implement this expression are as follows: three inverters to form the $\overline{A}$, $\overline{B}$, and $\overline{C}$ variables; two 3-input AND gates to form the terms $\overline{A}BC$ and $A\overline{B}\overline{C}$; and one 2-input OR gate to form the final output function, $\overline{A}BC + A\overline{B}\overline{C}$.

The implementation of this logic function is illustrated in Figure 10–9.

▶ FIGURE 10–9

Logic circuit for $X = \overline{A}BC + A\overline{B}\overline{C}$.

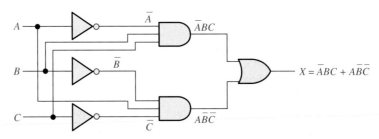

EXAMPLE 10–3

Design a logic circuit to implement the operation specified in the truth table of Table 10–4.

▼ TABLE 10–4

INPUTS			OUTPUT	
A	B	C	X	PRODUCT TERM
0	0	0	0	
0	0	1	0	
0	1	0	0	
0	1	1	1	$\overline{A}BC$
1	0	0	0	
1	0	1	1	$A\overline{B}C$
1	1	0	1	$AB\overline{C}$
1	1	1	0	

Solution Notice that $X = 1$ for only three of the input conditions. Therefore, the logic expression is

$$X = \overline{A}BC + A\overline{B}C + AB\overline{C}$$

The logic gates required are three inverters, three 3-input AND gates and one 3-input OR gate. The logic circuit is shown in Figure 10–10.

▶ FIGURE 10–10

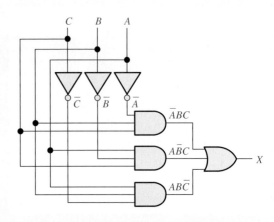

Related Problem Determine if the logic circuit of Figure 10–10 can be simplified.

EXAMPLE 10–4

Develop a logic circuit with four input variables that will only produce a 1 output when exactly three input variables are 1s.

Solution Out of sixteen possible combinations of four variables, the combinations in which there are exactly three 1s are listed in Table 10–5, along with the corresponding product term for each.

▶ TABLE 10–5

A	B	C	D	PRODUCT TERM
0	1	1	1	$\overline{A}BCD$
1	0	1	1	$A\overline{B}CD$
1	1	0	1	$AB\overline{C}D$
1	1	1	0	$ABC\overline{D}$

The product terms are ORed to get the following expression:

$$X = \overline{A}BCD + A\overline{B}CD + AB\overline{C}D + ABC\overline{D}$$

This expression is implemented in Figure 10–11 with AND-OR logic.

▶ FIGURE 10–11

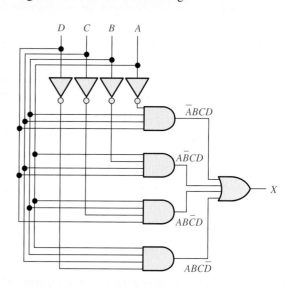

Related Problem Determine if the logic circuit of Figure 10–11 can be simplified.

EXAMPLE 10–5

Reduce the combinational logic circuit in Figure 10–12 to a minimum form.

▶ FIGURE 10–12

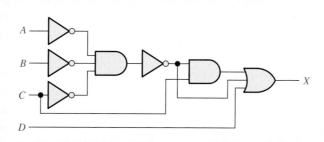

Solution   The expression for the output of the circuit is

$$X = (\overline{\overline{A}\,\overline{B}\,\overline{C}})C + \overline{\overline{\overline{A}\,\overline{B}\,\overline{C}}} + D$$

Applying DeMorgan's theorem and Boolean algebra,

$$X = (\overline{\overline{A}} + \overline{\overline{B}} + \overline{\overline{C}})C + \overline{\overline{A}} + \overline{\overline{B}} + \overline{\overline{C}} + D$$
$$= AC + BC + CC + A + B + C + D$$
$$= AC + BC + C + A + B + \mathcal{C} + D$$
$$= C(A + B + 1) + A + B + D$$
$$X = A + B + C + D$$

The simplified circuit is a 4-input OR gate as shown in Figure 10–13.

▶ **FIGURE 10–13**

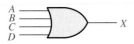

Related Problem   Verify the minimized expression $A + B + C + D$ using a Karnaugh map.

EXAMPLE 10–6

Minimize the combinational logic circuit in Figure 10–14. Inverters for the complemented variables are not shown.

▶ **FIGURE 10–14**

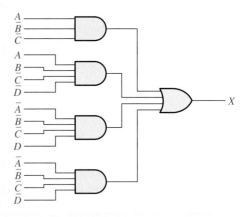

Solution   The output expression is

$$X = A\overline{B}\,\overline{C} + AB\overline{C}\overline{D} + \overline{A}\,\overline{B}\,C\overline{D} + \overline{A}\,\overline{B}\,\overline{C}\,\overline{D}$$

Expanding the first term to include the missing variables D and $\overline{D}$,

$$X = A\overline{B}\,\overline{C}(D + \overline{D}) + AB\overline{C}\overline{D} + \overline{A}\,\overline{B}\,C\overline{D} + \overline{A}\,\overline{B}\,\overline{C}\,\overline{D}$$
$$= A\overline{B}\,\overline{C}D + A\overline{B}\,\overline{C}\overline{D} + AB\overline{C}\overline{D} + \overline{A}\,\overline{B}\,C\overline{D} + \overline{A}\,\overline{B}\,\overline{C}\,\overline{D}$$

This expanded SOP expression is shown in Figure 10–15. Inverters are not shown.

▲ FIGURE 10–15

Related Problem   Develop the POS equivalent of the circuit in Figure 10–15.

10–3   THE UNIVERSAL PROPERTY OF NAND AND NOR GATES

Up to this point, you have studied combinational circuits implemented with AND gates, OR gates, and inverters. In this section, the universal property of the NAND gate and the NOR gate is discussed. The universality of the NAND gate means that it can be used as an inverter and that combinations of NAND gates can be used to implement the AND, OR, and NOR operations. Similarly, the NOR gate can be used to implement the inverter (NOT), AND, OR, and NAND operations.

After completing this section, you should be able to

■ Use NAND gates to implement the inverter, the AND gate, the OR gate, and the NOR gate

■ Use NOR gates to implement the inverter, the AND gate, the OR gate, and the NAND gate

The NAND Gate as a Universal Logic Element

The NAND gate is a **universal gate** because it can be used to produce the NOT, the AND, the OR, and the NOR functions. An inverter can be made from a NAND gate by connecting all of the inputs together and creating, in effect, a single input, as shown in Figure 10–16(a) for a 2-input gate. An AND function can be generated by the use of NAND gates alone, as shown in Figure 10–16(b). An OR function can be produced with only NAND gates, as illustrated in part (c). Finally, a NOR function is produced as shown in part (d).

NAND gates can be used to produce any logic function.

Universal application of NAND gates.

(a) One NAND gate used as an inverter

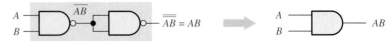

(b) Two NAND gates used as an AND gate

(c) Three NAND gates used as an OR gate

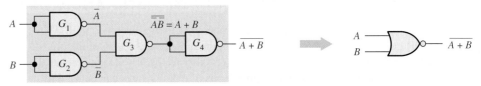

(d) Four NAND gates used as a NOR gate

In Figure 10–16(b), a NAND gate is used to invert (complement) a NAND output to form the AND function, as indicated in the following equation:

$$X = \overline{\overline{AB}} = AB$$

In Figure 10–16(c), NAND gates *G1* and *G2* are used to invert the two input variables before they are applied to NAND gate *G3*. The final OR output is derived as follows by application of DeMorgan's theorem:

$$X = \overline{\overline{A}\,\overline{B}} = A + B$$

In Figure 10–16(d), NAND gate *G4* is used as an inverter connected to the circuit of part (c) to produce the NOR operation $\overline{A + B}$.

The NOR Gate as a Universal Logic Element

NOR gates can be used to produce any logic function.

Like the NAND gate, the NOR gate can be used to produce the NOT, AND, OR, and NAND functions. A NOT circuit, or inverter, can be made from a NOR gate by connecting all of the inputs together to effectively create a single input, as shown in Figure 10–17(a) with a 2-input example. Also, an OR gate can be produced from NOR gates, as illustrated in Figure 10–17(b). An AND gate can be constructed by the use of NOR gates, as shown in Figure 10–17(c). In this case the NOR gates *G1* and *G2* are used as inverters, and the final output is derived by the use of DeMorgan's theorem as follows:

$$X = \overline{\overline{A} + \overline{B}} = AB$$

Figure 10–17(d) shows how NOR gates are used to form a NAND function.

(a) One NOR gate used as an inverter

(b) Two NOR gates used as an OR gate

(c) Three NOR gates used as an AND gate

(d) Four NOR gates used as a NAND gate

10-4 COMBINATIONAL LOGIC USING NAND AND NOR GATES

In this section, you will see how NAND and NOR gates can be used to implement a logic function. Recall from Chapter 8 that the NAND gate also exhibits an equivalent operation called the negative-OR and that the NOR gate exhibits an equivalent operation called the negative-AND. You will see how the use of the appropriate symbols to represent the equivalent operations makes "reading" a logic diagram easier.

After completing this section, you should be able to

■ Use NAND gates to implement a logic function

■ Use NOR gates to implement a logic function

■ Use the appropriate dual symbol in a logic diagram

NAND Logic

As you have learned, a NAND gate can function as either a NAND or a negative-OR because, by DeMorgan's theorem,

$$\overline{AB} = \overline{A} + \overline{B}$$

$$\text{NAND} \longrightarrow \qquad \longleftarrow \text{negative-OR}$$

Consider the NAND logic in Figure 10–18. The output expression is developed in the following steps:

$$X = \overline{(\overline{AB})(\overline{CD})}$$

$$= \overline{(\overline{A} + \overline{B})(\overline{C} + \overline{D})}$$

$$= \overline{(\overline{A} + \overline{B})} + \overline{(\overline{C} + \overline{D})}$$

$$= \overline{\overline{A}\overline{B}} + \overline{\overline{C}\overline{D}}$$

$$= AB + CD$$

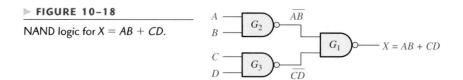

▶ **FIGURE 10–18**

NAND logic for $X = AB + CD$.

As you can see in Figure 10–18, the output expression, $AB + CD$, is in the form of two AND terms ORed together. This shows that gates G_2 and G_3 act as AND gates and that gate G_1 acts as an OR gate, as illustrated in Figure 10–19(a). This circuit is redrawn in part (b) with NAND symbols for gates G_2 and G_3 and a negative-OR symbol for gate G_1. Notice in Figure 10–19(b) the bubble-to-bubble connections between the outputs of gates G_2 and G_3 and the inputs of gate G_1. *Since a bubble represents an inversion, two connected bubbles represent a double inversion and therefore cancel each other.* This inversion cancellation can be seen in the previous development of the output expression $AB + CD$ and is indicated by the absence of barred terms in the output expression. Thus, the circuit in Figure 10–19(b) is *effectively* an AND-OR circuit, as shown in Figure 10–19(c).

▶ **FIGURE 10–19**

Development of the AND–OR equivalent of the circuit in Figure 10–18.

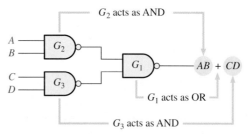

(a) Original NAND logic diagram showing effective gate operation relative to the output expression

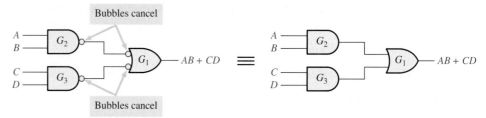

(b) Equivalent NAND/Negative-OR logic diagram (c) AND-OR equivalent

NAND Logic Diagrams Using Dual Symbols All logic diagrams using NAND gates should be drawn with each gate represented by either a NAND symbol or the equivalent negative-OR symbol to reflect the operation of the gate within the logic circuit. The NAND symbol and the **negative-OR** symbol are called *dual symbols.* When drawing a NAND logic diagram, always use the gate symbols in such a way that every connection between a gate output and a gate input is either bubble-to-bubble or nonbubble- to-nonbubble. A bubble output should not be connected to a nonbubble input or vice versa in a logic diagram.

Figure 10–20 shows an arrangement of gates to illustrate the procedure of using the appropriate dual symbols for a NAND circuit with several gate levels. Although using all NAND symbols as in Figure 10–20(a) is correct, the diagram in part (b) is much easier to "read" and is the preferred method. As shown in Figure 10–20(b), the output gate is represented with a negative-OR symbol. Then the NAND symbol is used for the level of gates right before the output gate and the symbols for successive levels of gates are alternated as you move away from the output.

The shape of the gate indicates the way its inputs will appear in the output expression and thus shows how the gate functions within the logic circuit. For a NAND symbol, the inputs appear ANDed in the output expression; and for a negative-OR symbol, the inputs appear ORed in the output expression, as Figure 10–20(b) illustrates. The dual-symbol diagram in part (b) makes it easier to determine the output expression directly from the logic diagram because each gate symbol indicates the relationship of its input variables as they appear in the output expression.

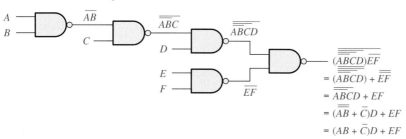

◄ **FIGURE 10–20**

Illustration of the use of the appropriate dual symbols in a NAND logic diagram.

(a) Several Boolean steps are required to arrive at final output expression.

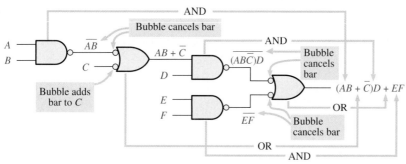

(b) Output expression can be obtained directly from the function of each gate symbol in the diagram.

EXAMPLE 10–7

Redraw the logic diagram and develop the output expression for the circuit in Figure 10–21 using the appropriate dual symbols.

▶ **FIGURE 10–21**

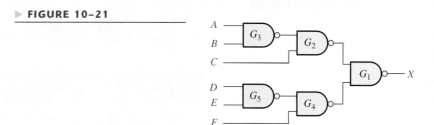

Solution   Redraw the logic diagram in Figure 10–21 with the use of equivalent negative-OR symbols as shown in Figure 10–22. Writing the expression for X directly from the indicated logic operation of each gate gives $X = (\overline{A} + \overline{B})C + (\overline{D} + \overline{E})F$.

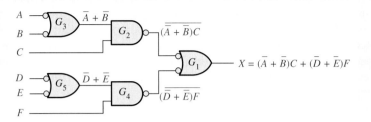

▲ FIGURE 10–22

Related Problem   Derive the output expression from Figure 10–21 and show it is equivalent to the expression in the solution.

EXAMPLE 10–8

Implement each expression with NAND logic using appropriate dual symbols:

(a) $ABC + DE$ **(b)** $ABC + \bar{D} + \bar{E}$

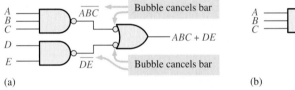

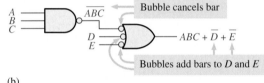

(a)   (b)

▲ FIGURE 10–23

Solution   See Figure 10–23.

Related Problem   Convert the NAND circuits in Figure 10–23(a) and (b) to equivalent AND-OR logic.

NOR Logic

 A NOR gate can function as either a NOR or a **negative-AND,** as shown by DeMorgan's theorem.

$$\overline{A + B} = \bar{A}\bar{B}$$

NOR ———↑   ↑——— negative-AND

Consider the NOR logic in Figure 10–24. The output expression is developed as follows:

$$X = \overline{\overline{A + B} + \overline{C + D}} = (\overline{\overline{A + B}})(\overline{\overline{C + D}}) = (A + B)(C + D)$$

▶ FIGURE 10–24

NOR logic for $X = (A + B)(C + D)$.

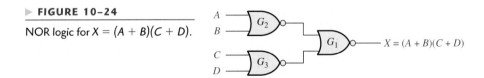

As you can see in Figure 10–24, the output expression $(A + B)(C + D)$ consists of two OR terms ANDed together. This shows that gates G_2 and G_3 act as OR gates and gate G_1 acts as an AND gate, as illustrated in Figure 10–25(a). This circuit is redrawn in part (b) with a negative-AND symbol for gate G_1.

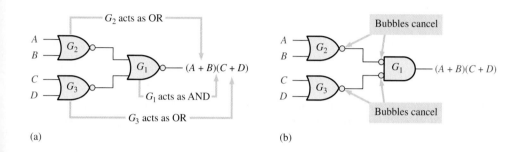

(a)

(b)

◀ FIGURE 10-25

NOR Logic Diagram Using Dual Symbols As with NAND logic, the purpose for using the dual symbols is to make the logic diagram easier to read and analyze, as illustrated in the NOR logic circuit in Figure 10–26. When the circuit in part (a) is redrawn with dual symbols in part (b), notice that all output-to-input connections between gates are bubble-to-bubble or nonbubble-to-nonbubble. Again, you can see that the shape of each gate symbol indicates the type of term (AND or OR) that it produces in the output expression, thus making the output expression easier to determine and the logic diagram easier to analyze.

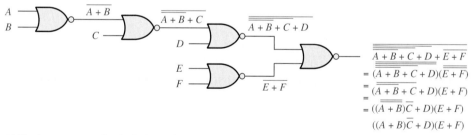

◀ FIGURE 10-26

Illustration of the use of the appropriate dual symbols in a NOR logic diagram.

(a) Final output expression is obtained after several Boolean steps.

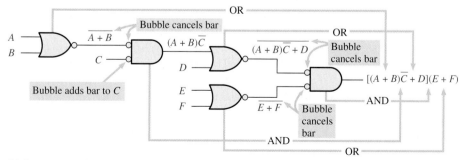

(b) Output expression can be obtained directly from the function of each gate symbol in the diagram.

EXAMPLE 10–9

Using appropriate dual symbols, redraw the logic diagram and develop the output expression for the circuit in Figure 10–27.

▶ **FIGURE 10–27**

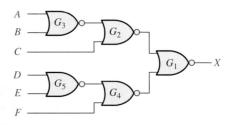

Solution Redraw the logic diagram with the equivalent negative-AND symbols as shown in Figure 10–28. Writing the expression for X directly from the indicated operation of each gate,

$$X = (\overline{A}\,\overline{B} + C)(\overline{D}\,\overline{E} + F)$$

▶ **FIGURE 10–28**

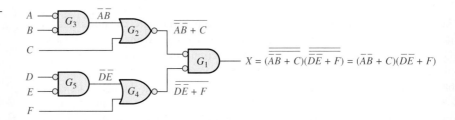

Related Problem Prove that the output of the NOR circuit in Figure 10–27 is the same as for the circuit in Figure 10–28.

SUMMARY

- AND-OR logic produces an output expression in SOP form.
- AND-OR-Invert logic produces a complemented SOP form, which is actually a POS form.
- The operational symbol for exclusive-OR is ⊕. An exclusive-OR expression can be stated in two equivalent ways:

  $$A\overline{B} + \overline{A}B = A \oplus B$$

- To do an analysis of a logic circuit, start with the logic circuit, and develop the Boolean output expression or the truth table or both.
- Implementation of a logic circuit is the process in which you start with the Boolean output expressions or the truth table and develop a logic circuit that produces the output function.
- All NAND or NOR logic diagrams should be drawn using appropriate dual symbols so that bubble outputs are connected to bubble inputs and nonbubble outputs are connected to nonbubble inputs.
- When two negation indicators (bubbles) are connected, they effectively cancel each other.

KEY TERMS

Negative-AND The dual operation of a NOR gate when the inputs are active-LOW. **Negative-OR** The dual operation of a NAND gate when the inputs are active-LOW.

Negative-OR The dual operation of a NAND gate when the inputs are active-LOW.

Node A common connection point in a circuit in which a gate output is connected to one or more gate inputs.

Universal gate Either a NAND gate or a NOR gate. The term *universal* refers to the property of a gate that permits any logic function to be implemented by that gate or by a combination of gates of that kind.

SELF-TEST

Answers are at the end of the chapter.

1. The output expression for an AND-OR circuit having one AND gate with inputs A, B, C, and D and one AND gate with inputs E and F is
   (a) $ABCDEF$ (b) $A + B + C + D + E + F$
   (c) $(A + B + C + D)(E + F)$ (d) $ABCD + EF$

2. A logic circuit with an output $X = A\overline{B}C + A\overline{C}$ consists of
   (a) two AND gates and one OR gate
   (b) two AND gates, one OR gate, and two inverters
   (c) two OR gates, one AND gate, and two inverters
   (d) two AND gates, one OR gate, and one inverter

3. To implement the expression $\overline{A}BCD + A\overline{B}CD + AB\overline{C}\overline{D}$, it takes one OR gate and
   (a) one AND gate
   (b) three AND gates
   (c) three AND gates and four inverters
   (d) three AND gates and three inverters

4. The expression $\overline{A}BCD + ABC\overline{D} + A\overline{B}\overline{C}D$
   (a) cannot be simplified
   (b) can be simplified to $\overline{A}BC + A\overline{B}$
   (c) can be simplified to $ABC\overline{D} + \overline{A}B\overline{C}$
   (d) None of these answers is correct.

5. The output expression for an AND-OR-Invert circuit having one AND gate with inputs, A, B, C, and D and one AND gate with inputs E and F is
   (a) $ABCD + EF$
   (b) $\overline{A} + \overline{B} + \overline{C} + \overline{D} + \overline{E} + \overline{F}$
   (c) $\overline{(A + B + C + D)(E + F)}$
   (d) $(\overline{A} + \overline{B} + \overline{C} + \overline{D})(\overline{E} + \overline{F})$

6. An exclusive-OR function is expressed as
   (a) $\overline{A}\overline{B} + AB$ (b) $\overline{A}B + A\overline{B}$
   (c) $(\overline{A} + B)(A + \overline{B})$ (d) $(\overline{A} + \overline{B}) + (A + B)$

7. The AND operation can be produced with
   (a) two NAND gates   (b) three NAND gates
   (c) one NOR gate   (d) three NOR gates

8. The OR operation can be produced with
   (a) two NOR gates   (b) three NAND gates
   (c) four NAND gates   (d) both answers (a) and (b)

9. When using dual symbols in a logic diagram,

    (a) bubble outputs are connected to bubble inputs

    (b) the NAND symbols produce the AND operations

    (c) the negative-OR symbols produce the OR operations

    (d) All of these answers are true.

    (e) None of these answers is true.

10. All Boolean expressions can be implemented with

    (a) NAND gates only

    (b) NOR gates only

    (c) combinations of NAND and NOR gates

    (d) combinations of AND gates, OR gates, and inverters

    (e) any of these

PROBLEMS

SECTION 10–1   Basic Combinational Logic Circuits

1. Draw the ANSI distinctive shape logic diagram for a 3-wide, 4-input AND-OR-Invert circuit. Also draw the ANSI standard rectangular outline symbol.

2. Write the output expression for each circuit in Figure 10–29.

3. Write the output expression for each circuit as it appears in Figure 10–30.

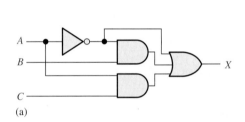

(a)

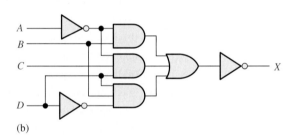

(b)

▲ FIGURE 10–29

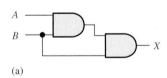

(a)

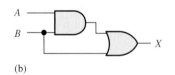

(b)

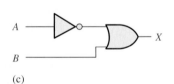

(c)

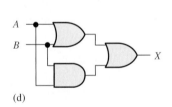

(d)

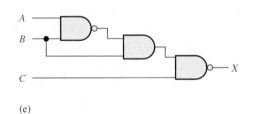

(e)

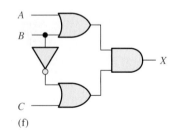

(f)

▲ FIGURE 10–30

4. Write the output expression for each circuit as it appears in Figure 10–31 and then change each circuit to an equivalent AND-OR configuration.

5. Develop the truth table for each circuit in Figure 10–30.

6. Develop the truth table for each circuit in Figure 10–31.

7. Show that an exclusive-NOR circuit produces a POS output.

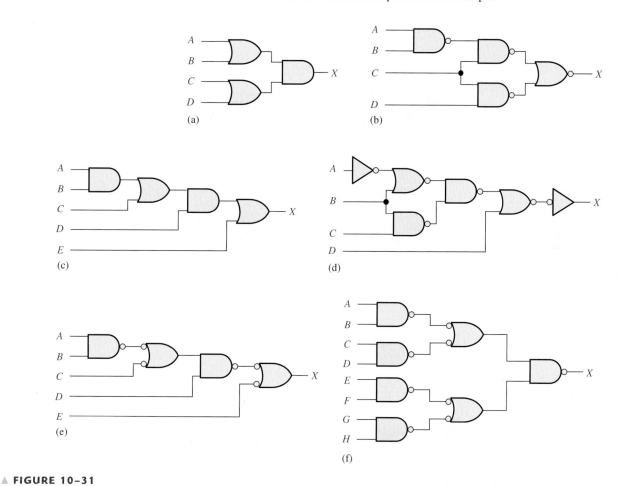

▲ FIGURE 10–31

SECTION 10–2   Implementing Combinational Logic

8. Use AND gates, OR gates, or combinations of both to implement the following logic expressions as stated:

   (a) $X = AB$

   (b) $X = A + B$

   (c) $X = AB + C$

   (d) $X = ABC + D$

   (e) $X = A + B + C$

   (f) $X = ABCD$

   (g) $X = A(CD + B)$

   (h) $X = AB(C + DEF) + CE(A + B + F)$

9. Use AND gates, OR gates, and inverters as needed to implement the following logic expressions as stated:

   (a) $X = AB + \overline{B}C$ (b) $X = A(B + \overline{C})$

   (c) $X = A\overline{B} + AB$ (d) $X = \overline{ABC} + B(EF + \overline{G})$

   (e) $X = A[BC(A + B + C + D)]$ (f) $X = B(\overline{CDE} + \overline{EFG})(\overline{AB} + C)$

10. Use NAND gates, NOR gates, or combinations of both to implement the following logic expressions as stated:

(a) $X = \overline{A}B + CD + (\overline{A + B})(ACD + \overline{BE})$

(b) $X = AB\overline{C}\overline{D} + D\overline{E}F + \overline{AF}$

(c) $X = \overline{A}[B + \overline{C}(D + E)]$

11. Implement a logic circuit for the truth table in Table 10–6.

▼ **TABLE 10–6**

INPUTS			OUTPUT
A	B	C	X
0	0	0	1
0	0	1	0
0	1	0	1
0	1	1	0
1	0	0	1
1	0	1	0
1	1	0	1
1	1	`1	1

12. Implement a logic circuit for the truth table in Table 10–7.

▼ **TABLE 10–7**

INPUTS				OUTPUT
A	B	C	D	X
0	0	0	0	0
0	0	0	1	0
0	0	1	0	1
0	0	1	1	1
0	1	0	0	1
0	1	0	1	0
0	1	1	0	0
0	1	1	1	0
1	0	0	0	1
1	0	0	1	1
1	0	1	0	1
1	0	1	1	1
1	1	0	0	0
1	1	0	1	0
1	1	1	0	0
1	1	1	1	1

13. Simplify the circuit in Figure 10–32 as much as possible, and verify that the simplified circuit is equivalent to the original by showing that the truth tables are identical.

14. Repeat Problem 13 for the circuit in Figure 10–33.

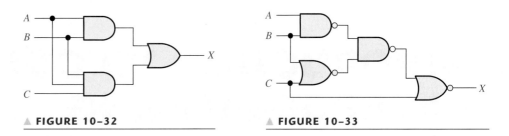

▲ **FIGURE 10–32**   ▲ **FIGURE 10–33**

15. Minimize the gates required to implement the functions in each part of Problem 9 in SOP form.

16. Minimize the gates required to implement the functions in each part of Problem 10 in SOP form.

17. Minimize the gates required to implement the function of the circuit in each part of Figure 10–31 in SOP form.

SECTION 10–3   The Universal Property of NAND and NOR Gates

18. Implement the logic circuits in Figure 10–29 using only NAND gates.

19. Implement the logic circuits in Figure 10–33 using only NAND gates.

20. Repeat Problem 18 using only NOR gates.

21. Repeat Problem 19 using only NOR gates.

SECTION 10–4   Combinational Logic Using NAND and NOR Gates

22. Show how the following expressions can be implemented as stated using only NOR gates:

    (a) $X = ABC$ **(b)** $X = \overline{ABC}$ **(c)** $X = A + B$

    (d) $X = A + B + \overline{C}$ **(e)** $X = \overline{AB} + \overline{CD}$ **(f)** $X = (A + B)(C + D)$

    (g) $X = AB[C(\overline{DE} + \overline{AB}) + \overline{BCE}]$

23. Repeat Problem 22 using only NAND gates.

24. Implement each function in Problem 8 by using only NAND gates.

25. Implement each function in Problem 9 by using only NAND gates.

SELF-TEST

1. (d)   **2.** (b)   **3.** (c)   **4.** (a)   **5.** (d)   **6.** (b)   **7.** (a)   **8.** (d)

9. (d)   **10.** (e)

11

INTRODUCTION TO COMPUTERS AND PROGRAMMING

WWW. VISIT THE COMPANION WEBSITE

Study aids for this chapter are available at
http://www.prenhall.com/floyd

11-1 INTRODUCTION

Think about some of the different ways that people use computers. In school, students use computers for tasks such as writing papers, searching for articles, sending email, and participating in online classes. At work, people use computers to analyze data, make presentations, conduct business transactions, communicate with customers and coworkers, control machines in manufacturing facilities, and many other things. At home, people use computers for tasks such as paying bills, shopping online, communicating with friends and family, and playing computer games. And don't forget that cell phones, iPods®, BlackBerries®, car navigation systems, and many other devices are computers too. The uses of computers are almost limitless in our everyday lives.

Computers can do such a wide variety of things because they can be programmed. This means that computers are not designed to do just one job, but to do any job that their programs tell them to do. A *program* is a set of instructions that a computer follows to perform a task. For example, Figure 11–1 shows screens from two commonly used programs: Microsoft Word and Adobe Photoshop. Microsoft Word is a word processing program that allows you to create, edit, and print documents with your computer. Adobe Photoshop is an image editing program that allows you to work with graphic images, such as photos taken with your digital camera.

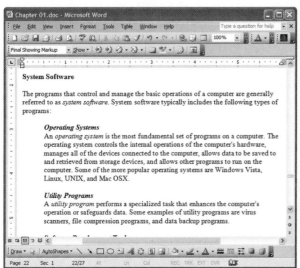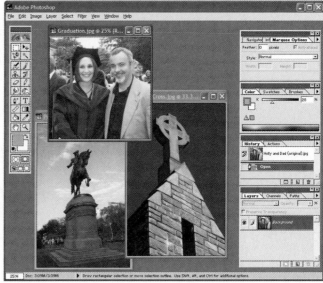

⚠ FIGURE 11–1

A word processing program and an image editing program.

Programs are commonly referred to as *software*. Software is essential to a computer because without software, a computer can do nothing. All of the software that we use to make our computers useful is created by individuals known as programmers or software developers. A *programmer*, or *software developer*, is a person with the training and skills necessary to design, create, and test computer programs. Computer programming is an exciting and rewarding career. Today, you will find programmers working in business, medicine, government, law enforcement, agriculture, academics, entertainment, and almost every other field.

This chapter will build a solid foundation of knowledge that you will continually rely on as you study computer science. First, we will discuss the physical components that computers are commonly made of. Next, we will look at how computers store data and execute programs. Finally, we will discuss the major types of software that computers use.

11-2 HARDWARE

CONCEPT: **The physical devices that a computer is made of are referred to as the computer's hardware. Most computer systems are made of similar hardware devices.**

The term *hardware* refers to all of the physical devices, or *components*, that a computer is made of. A computer is not one single device, but a system of devices that all work together. Like the different instruments in a symphony orchestra, each device in a computer plays its own part.

If you have ever shopped for a computer, you've probably seen sales literature listing components such as microprocessors, memory, disk drives, video displays, graphics cards, and so on. Unless you already know a lot about computers, or at least have a friend who does, understanding what these different components do can be confusing. As shown in Figure 11–2, a typical computer system consists of the following major components:

- The central processing unit (CPU)
- Main memory
- Secondary storage devices
- Input devices
- Output devices

Let's take a closer look at each of these components.

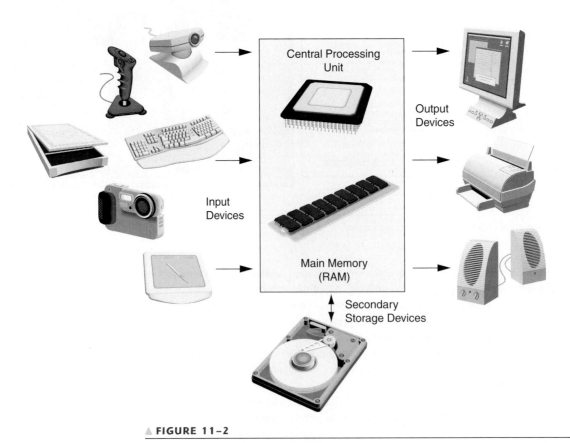

▲ FIGURE 11-2

Typical components of a computer system.

The CPU

When a computer is performing the tasks that a program tells it to do, we say that the computer is *running* or *executing* the program. The *central processing unit*, or *CPU*, is the part of a computer that actually runs programs. The CPU is the most important component in a computer because without it, the computer could not run software.

In the earliest computers, CPUs were huge devices made of electrical and mechanical components such as vacuum tubes and switches. Figure 11–3 shows such a device. The two women in the photo are working with the historic ENIAC computer. The *ENIAC* was the world's first programmable electronic computer, and was built in 1945 to calculate artillery ballistic tables for the U.S. Army. This machine, which was primarily one big CPU, was 8 feet tall, 100 feet long, and weighed 30 tons.

Today, CPUs are small chips known as *microprocessors*. Figure 11–4 shows a photo of a lab technician holding a modern-day microprocessor. In addition to being much smaller than the old electro-mechanical CPUs in early computers, microprocessors are also much more powerful.

◄ FIGURE 11–3

The ENIAC computer (courtesy of U.S. Army Historic Computer Images).

◄ FIGURE 11–4

A lab technician holds a modern microprocessor (photo courtesy of Intel Corporation).

Main Memory

You can think of *main memory* as the computer's work area. This is where the computer stores a program while the program is running, as well as the data that the program is working with. For example, suppose you are using a word processing program to write an essay for one of your classes. While you do this, both the word processing program and the essay are stored in main memory.

Main memory is commonly known as *random-access memory*, or *RAM*. It is called this because the CPU is able to quickly access data stored at any random location in RAM. RAM is usually a *volatile* type of memory that is used only for temporary storage while a program is running. When the computer is turned off, the contents of RAM are erased. Inside your computer, RAM is stored in chips, similar to the ones shown in Figure 11–5.

▶ **FIGURE 11–5**

Memory chips (photo courtesy of IBM Corporation).

Secondary Storage Devices

Secondary storage is a type of memory that can hold data for long periods of time, even when there is no power to the computer. Programs are normally stored in secondary memory and loaded into main memory as needed. Important data, such as word processing documents, payroll data, and inventory records, is saved to secondary storage as well.

The most common type of secondary storage device is the disk drive. A *disk drive* stores data by magnetically encoding it onto a circular disk. Most computers have a disk drive mounted inside their case. External disk drives, which connect to one of the computer's communication ports, are also available. External disk drives can be used to create backup copies of important data or to move data to another computer.

In addition to external disk drives, many types of devices have been created for copying data, and for moving it to other computers. For many years floppy disk drives were popular. A *floppy disk drive* records data onto a small floppy disk, which can be removed from the drive. Floppy disks have many disadvantages, however. They hold only a small amount of data, are slow to access data, and are notoriously unreliable. The use of floppy disk drives has declined dramatically in recent years, in favor of superior devices such as USB drives. *USB drives* are small devices that plug into the computer's USB (universal serial bus) port, and appear to the system as a disk drive. These drives do not actually contain a disk, however. They store data in a special type of memory known as *flash memory*. USB drives, which are also known as *memory sticks* and *flash drives*, are inexpensive, reliable, and small enough to be carried in your pocket.

Optical devices such as the *CD* (compact disc) and the *DVD* (digital versatile disc) are also popular for data storage. Data is not recorded magnetically on an optical disc, but is encoded as a series of pits on the disc surface. CD and DVD drives use a laser to detect the pits and thus read the encoded data. Optical discs hold large amounts of data, and because recordable CD and DVD drives are now commonplace, they are good mediums for creating backup copies of data.

Input Devices

Input is any data the computer collects from people and from other devices. The component that collects the data and sends it to the computer is called an *input device*. Common input devices are the keyboard, mouse, scanner, microphone, and digital camera. Disk drives and optical drives can also be considered input devices because programs and data are retrieved from them and loaded into the computer's memory.

Output Devices

Output is any data the computer produces for people or for other devices. It might be a sales report, a list of names, or a graphic image. The data is sent to an *output device*, which formats and presents it. Common output devices are video displays and printers. Disk drives and CD recorders can also be considered output devices because the system sends data to them in order to be saved.

11–3 HOW COMPUTERS STORE DATA

CONCEPT: **All data that is stored in a computer is converted to sequences of 0s and 1s.**

A computer's memory is divided into tiny storage locations known as *bytes*. One byte is only enough memory to store a letter of the alphabet or a small number. In order to do anything meaningful, a computer has to have lots of bytes. Most computers today have millions, or even billions, of bytes of memory.

Each byte is divided into eight smaller storage locations known as bits. The term *bit* stands for *binary digit*. Computer scientists usually think of bits as tiny switches that can be either on or off. Bits aren't actual "switches," however, at least not in the conventional sense. In most computer systems, bits are tiny electrical components that can hold either a positive or a negative charge. Computer scientists think of a positive charge as a switch in the *on* position, and a negative charge as a switch in the *off* position. Figure 11–6 shows the way that a computer scientist might think of a byte of memory: as a collection of switches that are each flipped to either the on or off position.

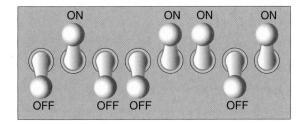

◄ FIGURE 11–6

Think of a byte as eight switches.

When a piece of data is stored in a byte, the computer sets the eight bits to an on/off pattern that represents the data. For example, the pattern shown on the left in Figure 11–7 shows how the number 77 would be stored in a byte, and the pattern on the right shows how the letter A would be stored in a byte as was discussed in Chapter 7.

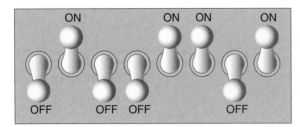

The number 77 stored in a byte.

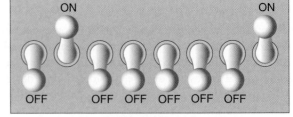

The letter A stored in a byte.

▲ **FIGURE 11–7**

Bit patterns for the number 77 and the letter A.

Other Types of Data

Computers are often referred to as digital devices. The term *digital* can be used to describe anything that uses binary numbers. *Digital data* is data that is stored in binary, and a *digital device* is any device that works with binary data. Computers work with many types of digital data.

For example, consider the pictures that you take with your digital camera. These images are composed of tiny dots of color known as *pixels*. (The term pixel stands for *picture element*.) As shown in Figure 11–8, each pixel in an image is converted to a numeric code that represents the pixel's color. The numeric code is stored in memory as a binary number.

▶ **FIGURE 11–8**

A digital image is stored in binary format.

The music that you play on your CD player, iPod or MP3 player is also digital. A digital song is broken into small pieces known as *samples*. Each sample is converted to a binary number, which can be stored in memory. The more samples that a song is divided into, the more it sounds like the original music when it is played back. A CD quality song is divided into more than 44,000 samples per second!

11–4   HOW A PROGRAM WORKS

CONCEPT: **A computer's CPU can only understand instructions that are written in machine language. Because people find it very difficult to write entire programs in machine language, other programming languages have been invented.**

Earlier, we stated that the CPU is the most important component in a computer because it is the part of the computer that runs programs. Sometimes the CPU is called the "computer's brain," and is described as being "smart." Although these are common metaphors, you should understand that the CPU is not a brain, and it is not smart. The CPU is an electronic device that is designed to do specific things. In particular, the CPU is designed to perform operations such as the following:

- Reading a piece of data from main memory

- Adding two numbers

- Subtracting one number from another number

- Multiplying two numbers

- Dividing one number by another number

- Moving a piece of data from one memory location to another

- Determining whether one value is equal to another value

- And so forth . . .

As you can see from this list, the CPU performs simple operations on pieces of data. The CPU does nothing on its own, however. It has to be told what to do, and that's the purpose of a program. A program is nothing more than a list of instructions that cause the CPU to perform operations.

Each instruction in a program is a command that tells the CPU to perform a specific operation. Here's an example of an instruction that might appear in a program:

```
10110000
```

To you and me, this is only a series of 0s and 1s. To a CPU, however, this is an instruction to perform an operation[1]. It is written in 0s and 1s because CPUs only understand instructions that are written in *machine language*, and machine language instructions are always written in binary.

A machine language instruction exists for each operation that a CPU is capable of performing. For example, there is an instruction for adding numbers; there is an instruction for subtracting one number from another; and so forth. The entire set of instructions that a CPU can execute is known as the CPU's *instruction set*.

The machine language instruction that was previously shown is an example of only one instruction. It takes a lot more than one instruction, however, for the computer to do anything meaningful. Because the operations that a CPU knows how to perform are so basic in nature, a meaningful task can be accomplished only if the CPU performs many operations. For example, if you want your computer to calculate the amount of interest that you will earn from your savings account this year, the CPU will have to perform a large number of instructions, carried out in the proper sequence. It is not unusual for a program to contain thousands, or even a million or more machine language instructions.

Programs are usually stored on a secondary storage device such as a disk drive. When you install a program on your computer, the program is typically copied to your computer's disk drive from a CD-ROM, or perhaps downloaded from a Web site.

Although a program can be stored on a secondary storage device such as a disk drive, it has to be copied into main memory, or RAM, each time the CPU executes it. For example, suppose you have a word processing program on your computer's disk. To execute the program you use the mouse to double-click the program's icon. This causes the program to be copied from the disk into main memory. Then, the computer's CPU executes the copy of the program that is in main memory. This process is illustrated in Figure 11–9.

COMPUTER NOTE

There are several microprocessor companies today that manufacture CPUs. Some of the more well-known microprocessor companies are Intel, AMD, and Freescale. If you look carefully at your computer, you might find a tag showing a logo for its microprocessor.

Each brand of microprocessor has its own unique instruction set, which is typically understood only by microprocessors of the same brand. For example, Intel microprocessors understand the same instructions, but they do not understand instructions for Freescale microprocessors.

---

[1] The example shown is an actual instruction for an Intel microprocessor. It tells the microprocessor to move a value into the CPU.

▶ FIGURE 11-9

A program is copied into main
memory and then executed.

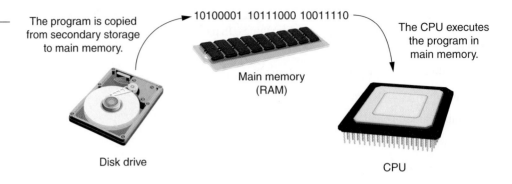

The program is copied
from secondary storage
to main memory.

10100001 10111000 10011110

Main memory
(RAM)

The CPU executes
the program in
main memory.

Disk drive

CPU

When a CPU executes the instructions in a program, it is engaged in a process that is known as the *fetch-decode-execute cycle*. This cycle, which consists of three steps, is repeated for each instruction in the program. The steps are:

1. **Fetch** A program is a long sequence of machine language instructions. The first step of the cycle is to fetch, or read, the next instruction from memory into the CPU.

2. **Decode** A machine language instruction is a binary number that represents a command that tells the CPU to perform an operation. In this step the CPU decodes the instruction that was just fetched from memory, to determine which operation it should perform.

3. **Execute** The last step in the cycle is to execute, or perform, the operation.

Figure 11–10 illustrates these steps.

▶ FIGURE 11-10

The fetch-decode-execute cycle.

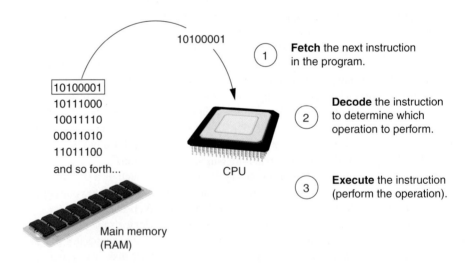

10100001

10100001
10111000
10011110
00011010
11011100
and so forth...

Main memory
(RAM)

CPU

(1) **Fetch** the next instruction
in the program.

(2) **Decode** the instruction
to determine which
operation to perform.

(3) **Execute** the instruction
(perform the operation).

From Machine Language to Assembly Language

Computers can only execute programs that are written in machine language. As previously mentioned, a program can have thousands, or even a million or more binary instructions, and writing such a program would be very tedious and time consuming. Programming in machine language would also be very difficult because putting a 0 or a 1 in the wrong place will cause an error.

Although a computer's CPU only understands machine language, it is impractical for people to write programs in machine language. For this reason, *assembly language* was created in the early days of computing[2] as an alternative to machine language. Instead of using binary numbers for instructions, assembly language uses short words that are known as *mnemonics*. For example, in assembly language, the mnemonic add typically means to add numbers, mul typically means to multiply numbers, and mov typically means to move a value to a location in memory. When a programmer uses assembly language to write a program, he or she can write short mnemonics instead of binary numbers.

Assembly language programs cannot be executed by the CPU, however. The CPU only understands machine language, so a special program known as an *assembler* is used to translate an assembly language program to a machine language program. This process is shown in Figure 11–11. The machine language program that is created by the assembler can then be executed by the CPU.

COMPUTER NOTE

There are many different versions of assembly language. It was mentioned earlier that each brand of CPU has its own machine language instruction set. Each brand of CPU typically has its own assembly language as well.

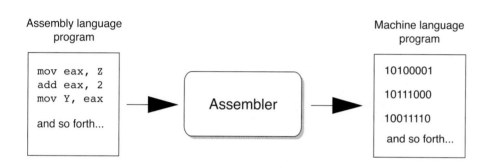

Assembly language program

```
mov eax, Z
add eax, 2
mov Y, eax

and so forth...
```

Assembler

Machine language program

```
10100001

10111000

10011110

and so forth...
```

◀ **FIGURE 11–11**

An assembler translates an assembly language program to a machine language program.

High-Level Languages

Although assembly language makes it unnecessary to write binary machine language instructions, it is not without difficulties. Assembly language is primarily a direct substitute for machine language, and like machine language, it requires that you know a lot about the CPU. Assembly language also requires that you write a large number of instructions for even the simplest program. Because assembly language is so close in nature to machine language, it is referred to as a *low-level language*.

In the 1950s, a new generation of programming languages known as *high-level languages* began to appear. A high-level language allows you to create powerful and complex programs without knowing how the CPU works, and without writing large numbers of low-level instructions. In addition, most high-level languages use words that are easy to understand. For example, if a programmer were using COBOL (which was one of the early high-level languages created in the 1950s), he or she would write the following instruction to display the message "Hello world" on the computer screen:

```
DISPLAY "Hello world"
```

Doing the same thing in assembly language would require several instructions, and an intimate knowledge of how the CPU interacts with the computer's video circuitry. As you can see from this example, high-level languages allow programmers to concentrate on the tasks they want to perform with their programs rather than the details of how the CPU will execute those programs.

Since the 1950s, thousands of high-level languages have been created. Table 11–1 lists several of the more well-known languages. If you are working toward a degree in computer science or a related field, you are likely to study one or more of these languages.

---

[2] The first assembly language was most likely developed in the 1940s at Cambridge University for use with an historical computer known as the EDSAC.

▶ **TABLE 11–1**

Programming languages.

LANGUAGE	DESCRIPTION
Ada	Ada was created in the 1970s, primarily for applications used by the U.S. Department of Defense. The language is named in honor of Countess Ada Lovelace, an influential and historical figure in the field of computing.
BASIC	**B**eginners **A**ll-purpose **S**ymbolic **I**nstruction **C**ode is a general-purpose language that was originally designed in the early 1960s to be simple enough for beginners to learn. Today, there are many different versions of BASIC.
FORTRAN	**FOR**mula **TRAN**slator was the first high-level programming language. It was designed in the 1950s for performing complex mathematical calculations.
COBOL	**C**ommon **B**usiness-**O**riented **L**anguage was created in the 1950s, and was designed for business applications.
Pascal	Pascal was created in 1970, and was originally designed for teaching programming. The language was named in honor of the mathematician, physicist, and philosopher Blaise Pascal.
C and C++	C and C++ (pronounced "c plus plus") are powerful, general-purpose languages developed at Bell Laboratories. The C language was created in 1972 and the C++ language was created in 1983.
C#	Pronounced "c sharp." This language was created by Microsoft around the year 2000 for developing applications based on the Microsoft .NET platform.
Java	Java was created by Sun Microsystems in the early 1990s. It can be used to develop programs that run on a single computer or over the Internet from a Web server.
JavaScript	JavaScript, created in the 1990s, can be used in Web pages. Despite its name, JavaScript is not related to Java.
Python	Python is a general purpose language created in the early 1990s. It has become popular in business and academic applications.
Ruby	Ruby is a general purpose language that was created in the 1990s. It is increasingly becoming a popular language for programs that run on Web servers.
Visual Basic	Visual Basic (commonly known as VB) is a Microsoft programming language and software development environment that allows programmers to create Windows-based applications quickly. VB was originally created in the early 1990s.

COMPUTER NOTE

Human languages also have syntax rules. Do you remember when you took your first English class, and you learned all those rules about commas, apostrophes, capitalization, and so forth? You were learning the syntax of the English language.

Although people commonly violate the syntax rules of their native language when speaking and writing, other people usually understand what they mean. Unfortunately, computers do not have this ability. If even a single syntax error appears in a program, the program cannot be executed.

Each high-level language has its own set of words that the programmer must learn in order to use the language. The words that make up a high-level programming language are known as *key words* or *reserved words*. Each key word has a specific meaning, and cannot be used for any other purpose. You previously saw an example of a COBOL statement that uses the key word DISPLAY to print a message on the screen. In the Python language the word print serves the same purpose.

In addition to key words, programming languages have *operators* that perform various operations on data. For example, all programming languages have math operators that perform arithmetic. In Java, as well as most other languages, the + sign is an operator that adds two numbers. The following adds 12 and 75:

```
12 + 75
```

In addition to key words and operators, each language also has it own *syntax*, which is a set of rules that must be strictly followed when writing a program. The syntax rules dictate how key words, operators, and various punctuation characters must be used in a program. When you are learning a programming language, you must learn the syntax rules for that particular language.

The individual instructions that you use to write a program in a high-level programming language are called *statements*. A programming statement can consist of key words, operators, punctuation, and other allowable programming elements, arranged in the proper sequence to perform an operation.

Compilers and Interpreters

Because the CPU understands only machine language instructions, programs that are written in a high-level language must be translated into machine language. Once a program has been written in a high-level language, the programmer will use a compiler or an interpreter to make the translation.

A *compiler* is a program that translates a high-level language program into a separate machine language program. The machine language program can then be executed any time it is needed. This is shown in Figure 11–12. As shown in the figure, compiling and executing are two different processes.

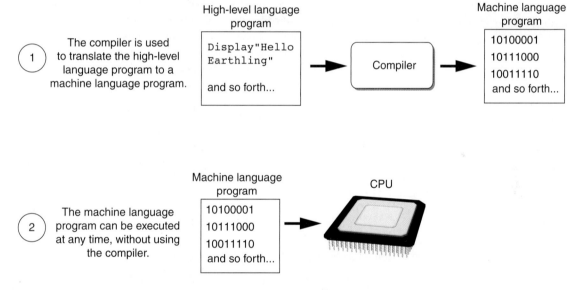

FIGURE 11–12

Compiling a high-level program and executing it.

An *interpreter* is a program that both translates and executes the instructions in a high-level language program. As the interpreter reads each individual instruction in the program, it converts it to a machine language instruction and then immediately executes it. This process repeats for every instruction in the program. This process is illustrated in Figure 11–13. Because interpreters combine translation and execution, they typically do not create separate machine language programs.

The statements that a programmer writes in a high-level language are called *source code*, or simply *code*. Typically, the programmer types a program's code into a text editor and then saves the code in a file on the computer's disk. Next, the programmer uses a compiler

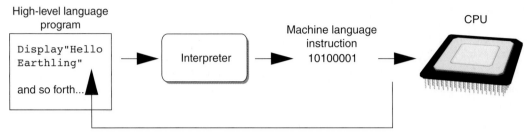

The interpreter translates each high-level instruction to
its equivalent machine language instructions and
immediately executes them.

This process is repeated for each high-level instruction.

▲ FIGURE 11–13

Executing a high-level program with an interpreter.

COMPUTER NOTE

Programs that are compiled
generally execute faster than
programs that are interpreted
because a compiled program is
already translated entirely to
machine language when it is
executed. A program that is
interpreted must be translated at
the time it is executed.

to translate the code into a machine language program, or an interpreter to translate and execute the code. If the code contains a syntax error, however, it cannot be translated. A *syntax error* is a mistake such as a misspelled key word, a missing punctuation character, or the incorrect use of an operator. When this happens the compiler or interpreter displays an error message indicating that the program contains a syntax error. The programmer corrects the error and then attempts once again to translate the program.

Integrated Development Environments

Although you can use a simple text editor such as Notepad (which is part of the Windows operating system) to write a program, most programmers use specialized software packages called *integrated development environments* or *IDEs*. Most IDEs combine the following programs into one software package:

- A text editor that has specialized features for writing statements in a high-level programming language

- A compiler or interpreter

- Useful tools for testing programs and locating errors

Figure 11–14 shows a screen from Microsoft Visual Studio, a popular IDE for developing programs in the C++, Visual Basic, and C# languages. Eclipse, NetBeans, Dev-C++, and jGRASP are a few other popular IDEs.

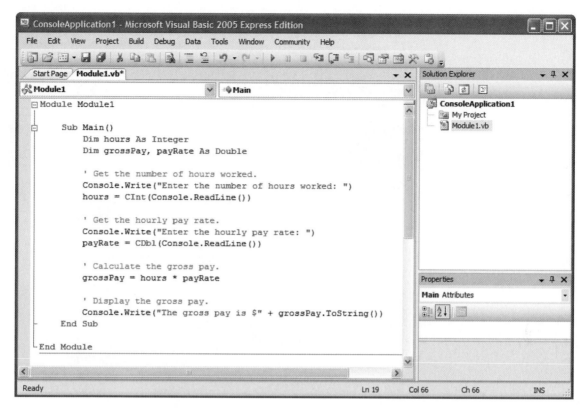

FIGURE 11-14

An integrated development environment.

11-5 TYPES OF SOFTWARE

CONCEPT: Programs generally fall into one of two categories: systems software or application software. System software is the set of programs that control or enhance the operation of a computer. Application software makes a computer useful for everyday tasks.

If a computer is to function, software is not optional. Everything that a computer does, from the time you turn the power switch on until you shut the system down, is under the control of software. There are two general categories of software: system software and application software. Most computer programs clearly fit into one of these two categories. Let's take a closer look at each.

System Software

The programs that control and manage the basic operations of a computer are generally referred to as *system software*. System software typically includes the following types of programs:

Operating Systems. An *operating system* is the most fundamental set of programs on a computer. The operating system controls the internal operations of the computer's hardware, manages all of the devices connected to the computer, allows data to be saved to and retrieved from storage devices, and allows other programs to run on the computer. Figure 11–15 shows screens from three popular operating systems: Windows Vista, Mac OS X, and Linux.

Screens from the Windows Vista, Mac OS X, and Fedora Linux operating systems.

Windows Vista

Mac OS X

Fedora Linux

Utility Programs. A *utility program* performs a specialized task that enhances the computer's operation or safeguards data. Examples of utility programs are virus scanners, file compression programs, and data backup programs.

Software Development Tools. *Software development tools* are the programs that programmers use to create, modify, and test software. Assemblers, compilers, and interpreters are examples of programs that fall into this category.

Application Software

Programs that make a computer useful for everyday tasks are known as *application software*. These are the programs that people normally spend most of their time running on their computers. Figure 11–1, at the beginning of this chapter, shows screens from two commonly used applications—Microsoft Word, a word processing program, and Adobe Photoshop, an image editing program. Some other examples of application software are spreadsheet programs, email programs, Web browsers, and game programs.

REVIEW QUESTIONS

Multiple Choice

1. A(n) _____ is a set of instructions that a computer follows to perform a task.
   (a) compiler
   (b) program
   (c) interpreter
   (d) programming language

2. The physical devices that a computer is made of are referred to as _____.
   (a) hardware
   (b) software
   (c) the operating system
   (d) tools

3. The part of a computer that runs programs is called _____.
   (a) RAM
   (b) secondary storage
   (c) main memory
   (d) the CPU

4. Today, CPUs are small chips known as _____.
   (a) ENIACs
   (b) microprocessors
   (c) memory chips
   (d) operating systems

5. The computer stores a program while the program is running, as well as the data that the program is working with, in _____.
   (a) secondary storage
   (b) the CPU
   (c) main memory
   (d) the microprocessor

6. This is a volatile type of memory that is used only for temporary storage while a program is running.
   (a) RAM
   (b) secondary storage

    (c) the disk drive

    (d) the USB drive

7. A type of memory that can hold data for long periods of time—even when there is no power to the computer is called _____.

    (a) RAM

    (b) main memory

    (c) secondary storage

    (d) CPU storage

8. A component that collects data from people or other devices and sends it to the computer is called _____.

    (a) an output device

    (b) an input device

    (c) a secondary storage device

    (d) main memory

9. A video display is a(n) _____ device.

    (a) output device

    (b) input device

    (c) secondary storage device

    (d) main memory

10. A _____ is enough memory to store a letter of the alphabet or a small number.

    (a) byte

    (b) bit

    (c) switch

    (d) transistor

11. A byte is made up of eight _____.

    (a) CPUs

    (b) instructions

    (c) variables

    (d) bits

12. In a(n) _____ numbering system, all numeric values are written as sequences of 0s and 1s.

    (a) hexadecimal

    (b) binary

    (c) octal

    (d) decimal

13. A bit that is turned off represents the following value: _____.

    (a) 1

    (b) −1

    (c) 0

    (d) "no"

14. The tiny dots of color that digital images are composed of are called _____.

    (a) bits

    (b) bytes

    (c) color packets

    (d) pixels

15. If you were to look at a machine language program, you would see _____.

    (a) Java code

    (b) a stream of binary numbers

(c) English words

(d) circuits

16. In the _____ part of the fetch-decode-execute cycle, the CPU determines which operation it should perform.

(a) fetch

(b) decode

(c) execute

(d) immediately after the instruction is executed

17. Computers can only execute programs that are written in _____.

(a) Java

(b) assembly language

(c) machine language

(d) C++

18. The _____ translates an assembly language program to a machine language program.

(a) assembler

(b) compiler

(c) translator

(d) interpreter

19. The words that make up a high-level programming language are called _____.

(a) binary instructions

(b) mnemonics

(c) commands

(d) key words

20. The rules that must be followed when writing a program are called _____.

(a) syntax

(b) punctuation

(c) key words

(d) operators

21. A(n) _____ program translates a high-level language program into a separate machine language program.

(a) assembler

(b) compiler

(c) translator

(d) utility

True or False

1. Today, CPUs are huge devices made of electrical and mechanical components such as vacuum tubes and switches.

2. Main memory is also known as RAM.

3. Any piece of data that is stored in a computer's memory must be stored as a binary number.

4. Images, like the ones you make with your digital camera, cannot be stored as binary numbers.

5. Machine language is the only language that a CPU understands.

6. Assembly language is considered a high-level language.

7. An interpreter is a program that both translates and executes the instructions in a high-level language program.

8. A syntax error does not prevent a program from being compiled and executed.

9. Windows Vista, Linux, UNIX, and Mac OSX are all examples of application software.

10. Word processing programs, spreadsheet programs, email programs, Web browsers, and games are all examples of utility programs.

Short Answer

1. Why is the CPU the most important component in a computer?
2. What number does a bit that is turned on represent? What number does a bit that is turned off represent?
3. What would you call a device that works with binary data?
4. What are the words that make up a high-level programming language called?
5. What are the short words that are used in assembly language called?
6. What is the difference between a compiler and an interpreter?
7. What type of software controls the internal operations of the computer's hardware?

Exercises

1. Use the Web to research the history of the BASIC, C++, Java, and Python programming languages, and answer the following questions:
   - Who was the creator of each of these languages?
   - When was each of these languages created?
   - Was there a specific motivation behind the creation of these languages? If so, what was it?

12

INPUT, PROCESSING, AND OUTPUT

WWW. **VISIT THE COMPANION WEBSITE**

Study aids for this chapter are available at
http://www.prenhall.com/floyd

12–1 DESIGNING A PROGRAM

CONCEPT: **Programs must be carefully designed before they are written. During the design process, programmers use tools such as pseudocode and flowcharts to create models of programs.**

In Chapter 11 you learned that programmers typically use high-level languages to write programs. However, all professional programmers will tell you that a program should be carefully designed before the code is actually written. When programmers begin a new project, they never jump right in and start writing code as the first step. They begin by creating a design of the program.

After designing the program, the programmer begins writing code in a high-level language. Recall from Chapter 11 that each language has its own rules, known as syntax, that must be followed when writing a program. A language's syntax rules dictate things such as how key words, operators, and punctuation characters can be used. A syntax error occurs if the programmer violates any of these rules.

If the program contains a syntax error, or even a simple mistake such as a misspelled key word, the compiler or interpreter will display an error message indicating what the error is. Virtually all code contains syntax errors when it is first written, so the programmer will typically spend some time correcting these. Once all of the syntax errors and simple typing mistakes have been corrected, the program can be compiled and translated into a machine language program (or executed by an interpreter, depending on the language being used).

Once the code is in an executable form, it is then tested to determine whether any logic errors exist. A *logic error* is a mistake that does not prevent the program from running, but causes it to produce incorrect results. (Mathematical mistakes are common causes of logic errors.)

If there are logic errors, the programmer *debugs* the code. This means that the programmer finds and corrects the code that is causing the error. Sometimes during this process, the programmer discovers that the original design must be changed. This entire process, which is known as the *program development cycle*, is repeated until no errors can be found in the program. Figure 12–1 shows the steps in the process.

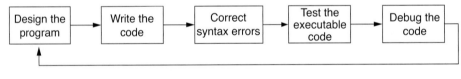

▲ FIGURE 12–1

The program development cycle.

This course focuses entirely on the first step of the program development cycle: designing the program. The process of designing a program is arguably the most important part of the cycle. You can think of a program's design as its foundation. If you build a house on a poorly constructed foundation, eventually you will find yourself doing a lot of work to fix the house! A program's design should be viewed no differently. If your program is designed poorly, eventually you will find yourself doing a lot of work to fix the program.

Designing a Program

The process of designing a program can be summarized in the following two steps:

1. Understand the task that the program is to perform.

2. Determine the steps that must be taken to perform the task.

Let's take a closer look at each of these steps.

Understand the Task That the Program Is to Perform It is essential that you understand what a program is supposed to do before you can determine the steps that the program will perform. Typically, a professional programmer gains this understanding by working directly with the customer. We use the term *customer* to describe the person, group, or organization that is asking you to write a program. This could be a customer in the traditional sense of the word, meaning someone who is paying you to write a program. It could also be your boss, or the manager of a department within your company. Regardless of whom it is, the customer will be relying on your program to perform an important task.

To get a sense of what a program is supposed to do, the programmer usually interviews the customer. During the interview, the customer will describe the task that the program should perform, and the programmer will ask questions to uncover as many details as possible about the task. A follow-up interview is usually needed because customers rarely mention everything they want during the initial meeting, and programmers often think of additional questions.

The programmer studies the information that was gathered from the customer during the interviews and creates a list of different software requirements. A *software requirement* is simply a single function that the program must perform in order to satisfy the customer. Once the customer agrees that the list of requirements is complete, the programmer can move to the next phase.

Determine the Steps That Must Be Taken to Perform the Task Once you understand the task that the program will perform, you begin by breaking down the task into a series of steps. This is similar to the way you would break down a task into a series of steps that another person can follow. For example, suppose your little sister asks you how to boil water. Assuming she is old enough to be trusted around the stove, you might break down that task into a series of steps as follows:

1. Pour the desired amount of water into a pot.

2. Put the pot on a stove burner.

3. Turn the burner to high.

4. Watch the water until you see large bubbles rapidly rising. When this happens, the water is boiling.

This is an example of an *algorithm*, which is a set of well-defined logical steps that must be taken to perform a task. Notice that the steps in this algorithm are sequentially ordered. Step 1 should be performed before Step 2, and so on. If your little sister follows these steps exactly as they appear, and in the correct order, she should be able to boil water successfully.

A programmer breaks down the task that a program must perform in a similar way. An algorithm is created, which lists all of the logical steps that must be taken. For example, suppose you have been asked to write a program to calculate and display the gross pay for an hourly paid employee. Here are the steps that you would take:

1. Get the number of hours worked.

2. Get the hourly pay rate.

3. Multiply the number of hours worked by the hourly pay rate.

4. Display the result of the calculation that was performed in Step 3.

Of course, this algorithm isn't ready to be executed on the computer. The steps in this list have to be translated into code. Programmers commonly use two tools to help them accomplish this: pseudocode and flowcharts. Let's look at each of these in more detail.

TIP

If you choose to become a professional software developer, your customer will be anyone who asks you to write programs as part of your job. As long as you are a student, however, your customer is your instructor! In every programming class that you will take, it's practically guaranteed that your instructor will assign programming problems for you to complete. For your academic success, make sure that you understand your instructor's requirements for those assignments and write your programs accordingly.

Pseudocode

Recall from Chapter 11 that each programming language has strict rules, known as syntax, that the programmer must follow when writing a program. If the programmer writes code that violates these rules, a syntax error will result and the program cannot be compiled or executed. When this happens, the programmer has to locate the error and correct it.

Because small mistakes like misspelled words and forgotten punctuation characters can cause syntax errors, programmers have to be mindful of such small details when writing code. For this reason, programmers find it helpful to write their programs in pseudocode (pronounced "sue doe code") before they write it in the actual code of a programming language.

The word "pseudo" means fake, so *pseudocode* is fake code. It is an informal language that has no syntax rules, and is not meant to be compiled or executed. Instead, programmers use pseudocode to create models, or "mock-ups" of programs. Because programmers don't have to worry about syntax errors while writing pseudocode, they can focus all of their attention on the program's design. Once a satisfactory design has been created with pseudocode, the pseudocode can be translated directly to actual code.

Here is an example of how you might write pseudocode for the pay calculating program that we discussed earlier:

```
Display "Enter the number of hours the employee worked."
Input hours
Display "Enter the employee's hourly pay rate."
Input payRate
Set grossPay = hours * payRate
Display "The employee's gross pay is $", grossPay
```

Each statement in the pseudocode represents an operation that can be performed in any high-level language. For example, all languages provide a way to display messages on the screen, read input that is typed on the keyboard, and perform mathematical calculations. For now, don't worry about the details of this particular pseudocode program. As you progress through this chapter you will learn more about each of the statements that you see here.

Flowcharts

Flowcharting is another tool that programmers use to design programs. A *flowchart* is a diagram that graphically depicts the steps that take place in a program. Figure 12–2 shows how you might create a flowchart for the pay calculating program.

Notice that there are three types of symbols in the flowchart: ovals, parallelograms, and rectangles. The ovals, which appear at the top and bottom of the flowchart, are called *terminal symbols*. The *Start* terminal symbol marks the program's starting point and the *End* terminal symbol marks the program's ending point.

Between the terminal symbols are parallelograms, which are used for both *input symbols* and *output symbols*, and rectangles, which are called *processing symbols*. Each of these symbols represents a step in the program. The symbols are connected by arrows that represent the "flow" of the program. To step through the symbols in the proper order, you begin at the *Start* terminal and follow the arrows until you reach the *End* terminal. Throughout this chapter we will look at each of these symbols in greater detail. For your reference, the appendix has a diagram that summarizes all of the flowchart symbols that we use in this course.

There are a number of different ways that you can draw flowcharts, and your instructor will most likely tell you the way that he or she prefers you to draw them in class. Perhaps the simplest and least expensive way is to simply sketch the flowchart by hand with pencil and paper. If you need to make your hand-drawn flowcharts look more professional you can visit your local office supply store (or possibly your campus bookstore) and purchase a flowchart template, which is a small plastic sheet that has the flowchart symbols cut into it. You can use the template to trace the symbols onto a piece of paper.

▼ **FIGURE 12–2**

Flowchart for the pay calculating program.

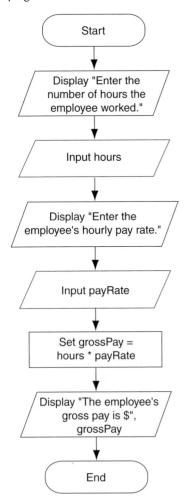

The disadvantage to drawing flowcharts by hand is that mistakes have to be manually erased, and in many cases, require that the entire page be redrawn. A more efficient and professional way to create flowcharts is to use software. There are several specialized software packages, such as Flowcode, available that allow you to create flowcharts.

12–2 OUTPUT, INPUT, AND VARIABLES

CONCEPT: **Output is data that is generated and displayed by the program. Input is data that the program receives. When a program receives data, it stores it in variables, which are named storage locations in memory.**

Computer programs typically perform the following three-step process:

1. Input is received.

2. Some process is performed on the input.

3. Output is produced.

Input is any data that the program receives while it is running. One common form of input is data that is typed on the keyboard. Once input is received, some process, such as a mathematical calculation, is usually performed on it. The results of the process are then sent out of the program as output.

Figure 12–3 illustrates these three steps in the pay calculating program that we discussed earlier. The number of hours worked and the hourly pay rate are provided as input. The program processes this data by multiplying the hours worked by the hourly pay rate. The results of the calculation are then displayed on the screen as output.

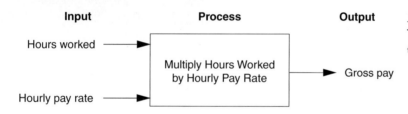

◄ FIGURE 12–3

The input, processing, and output of the pay calculating program.

In this section, you will look at some simple programs that perform two of these steps: output and input. In the next section, we will discuss how to process data.

Displaying Screen Output

Perhaps the most fundamental thing that you can do in a program is to display a message on the computer screen. As previously mentioned, all high-level languages provide a way to display screen output. In this book, we use the word `Display` to write pseudocode statements for displaying output on the screen. Here is an example:

```
Display "Hello world"
```

The purpose of this statement is to display the message *Hello world* on the screen. Notice that after the word `Display`, we have written `Hello world` inside quotation marks. The quotation marks are not to be displayed. They simply mark the beginning and the end of the text that we wish to display.

Suppose your instructor tells you to write a pseudocode program that displays your name and address on the computer screen. The pseudocode shown in Program 12–1 is an example of such a program.

PROGRAM 12–1

```
Display "Kate Austen"
Display "123 Dharma Lane"
Display "Asheville, NC 28899"
```

It is important for you to understand that the statements in this program execute in the order that they appear, from the top of the program to the bottom. This is shown in Figure 12–4. If you translated this pseudocode into an actual program and ran it, the first statement would execute, followed by the second statement, and followed by the third statement. If you try to visualize the way this program's output would appear on the screen, you should imagine something like that shown in Figure 12–5. Each `Display` statement produces a line of output.

▶ **FIGURE 12–4**

The statements execute in order.

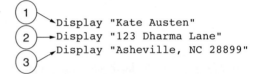

▶ **FIGURE 12–5**

Output of Program 12–1.

▼ **FIGURE 12–6**

Flowchart for Program 12–1.

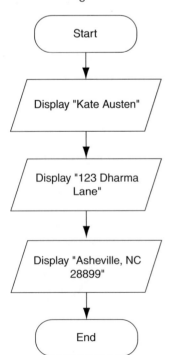

Figure 12–6 shows the way you would draw a flowchart for this program. Notice that between the *Start* and *End* terminal symbols there are three parallelograms. A parallelogram can be either an output symbol or an input symbol. In this program, all three parallelograms are output symbols. There is one for each of the `Display` statements.

Sequence Structures

It was mentioned earlier that the statements in Program 12–1 execute in the order that they appear, from the top of the program to the bottom. A set of statements that execute in the order that they appear is called a *sequence structure*. In fact, all of the programs that you will see in this chapter are sequence structures.

A *structure*, also called a *control structure*, is a logical design that controls the order in which a set of statements execute. In the 1960s, a group of mathematicians proved that only three program structures are needed to write any type of program. The simplest of these structures is the sequence structure. Later in this course, you will learn about the other two structures—decision structures and repetition structures.

Strings and String Literals

Programs almost always work with data of some type. For example, Program 12–1 uses the following three pieces of data:

```
"Kate Austen"
"123 Dharma Lane"
"Asheville, NC 28899"
```

These pieces of data are sequences of characters. In programming terms, a sequence of characters that is used as data is called a *string*. When a string appears in the actual code of a program it is called a *string literal*. In program code, or pseudocode, a string literal is usually enclosed in quotation marks. As mentioned earlier, the quotation marks simply mark where the string begins and ends.

In this book, we will always enclose string literals in double quote marks ("). Most programming languages use this same convention, but a few use single quote marks (').

Variables and Input

Quite often a program needs to store data in the computer's memory so it can perform operations on that data. For example, consider the typical online shopping experience: You browse a Web site and add the items that you want to purchase to the shopping cart. As you add items to the shopping cart, data about those items is stored in memory. Then, when you click the checkout button, a program running on the Web site's computer calculates the total of all the items you have in your shopping cart, applicable sales taxes, shipping costs, and the total of all these charges. When the program performs these calculations, it stores the results in the computer's memory.

Programs use variables to store data in memory. A *variable* is a storage location in memory that is represented by a name. For example, a program that calculates the sales tax on a purchase might use a variable named `tax` to hold that value in memory. And a program that calculates the distance from Earth to a distant star might use a variable named `distance` to hold that value in memory.

In this section, we will discuss a basic input operation: reading data that has been typed on the keyboard. When a program reads data from the keyboard, usually it stores that data in a variable so it can be used later by the program. In pseudocode we will read data from the keyboard with the `Input` statement. As an example, look at the following statement, which appeared earlier in the pay calculating program:

```
Input hours
```

The word `Input` is an instruction to read a piece of data from the keyboard. The word `hours` is the name of the variable in which the data will be stored. When this statement executes, two things happen:

- The program pauses and waits for the user to type something on the keyboard, and then press the (Enter) key.

- When the (Enter) key is pressed, the data that was typed is stored in the `hours` variable.

Program 12–2 is a simple pseudocode program that demonstrates the `Input` statement. Before we examine the program, we should mention a couple of things. First, you will notice that each line in the program is numbered. The line numbers are not part of the pseudocode. We will refer to the line numbers later to point out specific parts of the program. Second, the program's output is shown immediately following the pseudocode. From now on, all pseudocode programs will be shown this way.

PROGRAM 12–2

```
1  Display "What is your age?"
2  Input age
3  Display "Here is the value that you entered:"
4  Display age
```

Program Output (with Input Shown in Bold)

```
What is your age?
24 [Enter]
Here is the value that you entered:
24
```

▼ **FIGURE 12–7**

Flowchart for Program 12–2.

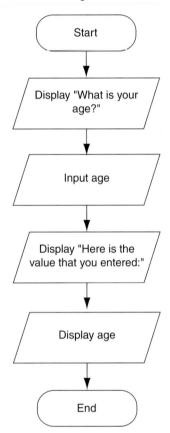

The statement in line 1 displays the string "What is your age?" Then, the statement in line 2 waits for the user to type a value on the keyboard and press ⓔ. The value that is typed will be stored in the age variable. In the example execution of the program, the user has entered 24. The statement in line 3 displays the string "Here is the value that you entered:", and the statement in line 4 displays the value that is stored in the age variable.

Notice that in line 4 there are no quotation marks around age. If quotation marks were placed around age, it would have indicated that we want to display the word "age" instead of the contents of the age variable. In other words, the following statement is an instruction to display the contents of the age variable:

```
Display age
```

This statement, however, is an instruction to display the word "age":

```
Display "age"
```

Figure 12–7 shows a flowchart for Program 12–2. Notice that the Input operation is also represented by a parallelogram.

Variable Names

All high-level programming languages allow you to make up your own names for the variables that you use in a program. You don't have complete freedom in naming variables, however. Every language has its own set of rules that you must abide by when creating variable names.

Although the rules for naming variables differ slightly from one language to another, there are some common restrictions:

■ Variable names must be one word. They cannot contain spaces.

■ In most languages, punctuation characters cannot be used in variable names. It is usually a good idea to use only alphabetic letters and numbers in variable names.

■ In most languages, the first character of a variable name cannot be a number.

In addition to following the programming language rules, you should always choose names for your variables that give an indication of what they are used for. For example, a variable that holds the temperature might be named temperature, and a variable that holds a car's speed might be named speed. You may be tempted to give variables names like x and b2, but names like these give no clue as to what the variable's purpose is.

Because a variable's name should reflect the variable's purpose, programmers often find themselves creating names that are made of multiple words. For example, consider the following variable names:

```
grosspay
payrate
hotdogssoldtoday
```

Unfortunately, these names are not easily read by the human eye because the words aren't separated. Because we can't have spaces in variable names, we need to find another way to separate the words in a multiword variable name, and make it more readable to the human eye.

One way to do this is to use the underscore character to represent a space. For example, the following variable names are easier to read than those previously shown:

```
gross_pay
pay_rate
hot_dogs_sold_today
```

Another way to address this problem is to use the *camelCase* naming convention. camelCase names are written in the following manner:

- You begin writing the variable name with lowercase letters.

- The first character of the second and subsequent words is written in uppercase.

For example, the following variable names are written in camelCase:

```
grossPay
payRate
hotDogsSoldToday
```

COMPUTER NOTE

This style of naming is called camelCase because the uppercase characters that appear in a name are sometimes reminiscent of a camel's humps.

Because the camelCase convention is very popular with programmers, we will use it from this point forward. In fact, you have already seen several programs in this chapter that use camelCase variable names. The pay calculating program shown at the beginning of the chapter uses the variable name `payRate`. In addition, Program 12–7 uses the variable names `originalPrice` and `salePrice`, and Program 12–9 uses the variable names `futureValue` and `presentValue`.

Displaying Multiple Items with One `Display` Statement

If you refer to Program 12–2 you will see that we used the following two `Display` statements in lines 3 and 4:

```
Display "Here is the value that you entered:"
Display age
```

We used two `Display` statements because we needed to display two pieces of data. Line 3 displays the string literal `"Here is the value that you entered:"`, and line 4 displays the contents of the `age` variable.

Most programming languages provide a way to display multiple pieces of data with one statement. Because this is a common feature of programming languages, frequently we will write `Display` statements in our pseudocode that display multiple items. We will simply separate the items with a comma, as shown in line 3 of Program 12–3.

PROGRAM 12-3

```
1  Display "What is your age?"
2  Input age
3  Display "Here is the value that you entered: ", age
```

Program Output (with Input Shown in Bold)

```
What is your age?
24 [Enter]
Here is the value that you entered: 24
```

String Input

The previous two programs read numbers from the keyboard, which were stored in variables by `Input` statements. Programs can also read string input. For example, the pseudocode in Program 12–4 uses two `Input` statements: one to read a string and one to read a number.

PROGRAM 12–4

```
1   Display "Enter your name."
2   Input age
3   Display "Enter your age."
4   Input age
5   Display "Hello ", name
6   Display "You are ", age, " years old."
```

Program Output (with Input Shown in Bold)

```
Enter your name.
Andrea [Enter]
Enter your age.
24 [Enter]
Hello Andrea
You are 24 years old.
```

The `Input` statement in line 2 reads input from the keyboard and stores it in the `name` variable. In the example execution of the program, the user entered Andrea. The `Input` statement in line 4 reads input from the keyboard and stores it in the `age` variable. In the example execution of the program, the user entered 24.

Prompting the User

Getting keyboard input from the user is normally a two-step process:

1. Display a prompt on the screen.

2. Read a value from the keyboard.

A *prompt* is a message that tells (or asks) the user to enter a specific value. For example, the pseudocode in Program 12–3 gets the user to enter his or her age with the following statements:

```
Display "What is your age?"
Input age
```

In most programming languages, the statement that reads keyboard input does not display instructions on the screen. It simply causes the program to pause and wait for the user to type something on the keyboard. For this reason, whenever you write a statement that reads keyboard input, you should also write a statement just before it that tells the user what to enter. Otherwise, the user will not know what they are expected to do. For example, suppose we remove line 1 from Program 12–3, as follows:

```
Input age
Display "Here is the value that you entered: ", age
```

If this were an actual program, can you see what would happen when it is executed? The screen would appear blank because the `Input` statement would cause the program to wait for something to be typed on the keyboard. The user would probably think the computer was malfunctioning.

The term *user-friendly* is commonly used in the software business to describe programs that are easy to use. Programs that do not display adequate or correct instructions are frustrating to use, and are not considered user-friendly. One of the simplest things that you can do to increase a program's user-friendliness is to make sure that it displays clear, understandable prompts prior to each statement that reads keyboard input.

TIP

Sometimes we computer science instructors jokingly tell our students to write programs as if "Uncle Joe" or "Aunt Sally" were the user. Of course, these are not real people, but imaginary users who are prone to making mistakes if not told exactly what to do. When you are designing a program, you should imagine that someone who knows nothing about the program's inner workings will be using it.

12-3 VARIABLE ASSIGNMENT AND CALCULATIONS

CONCEPT: You can store a value in a variable with an assignment statement. The value can be the result of a calculation, which is created with math operators.

Variable Assignment

In the previous section, you saw how the Input statement gets a value typed on the keyboard and stores it in a variable. You can also write statements that store specific values in variables. The following is an example, in pseudocode:

```
Set price = 20
```

This is called an assignment statement. An *assignment statement* sets a variable to a specified value. In this case, the variable price is set to the value 20. When we write an assignment statement in pseudocode, we will write the word Set, followed by the name of the variable, followed by an equal sign (=), followed by the value we want to store in the variable. The pseudocode in Program 12–5 shows another example.

PROGRAM 12-5

```
1   Set dollars = 2.75
2   Display "I have ", dollars, " in my account."
```

Program Output

```
I have 2.75 in my account.
```

In line 1, the value 2.75 is stored in the dollars variable. Line 2 displays the message "I have 2.75 in my account." Just to make sure you understand how the Display statement in line 2 is working, let's walk through it. The word Display is followed by three pieces of data, so that means it will display three things. The first thing it displays is the string literal "I have ". Next, it displays the contents of the dollars variable, which is 2.75. Last, it displays the string literal " in my account."

Variables are called "variable" because they can hold different values while a program is running. Once you set a variable to a value, that value will remain in the variable until you store a different value in the variable. For example, look at the pseudocode in Program 12–6.

PROGRAM 12-6

```
1   Set dollars = 2.75
2   Display "I have ", dollars, " in my account."
3   Set dollars = 99.95
4   Display "But now I have ", dollars, " in my account!"
```

Program Output

```
I have 2.75 in my account.
But now I have 99.95 in my account!
```

Line 1 sets the dollars variable to the 2.75, so when the statement in line 2 executes, it displays "I have 2.75 in my account." Then, the statement in line 3 sets the dollars variable to 99.95. As a result, the value 99.95 replaces the value 2.75 that was

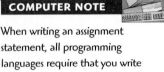

When writing an assignment statement, all programming languages require that you write the name of the variable that is receiving the value on the left side of the = operator. For example, the following statement is incorrect:

```
Set 99.95 = dollars
```
This is an error!

A statement such as this would be considered a syntax error.

In this book, we have chosen to start variable assignment statements with the word Set because it makes it clear that we are setting a variable to a value. In most programming languages, however, assignment statements do not start with the word Set. In most languages, an assignment statement looks similar to the following:

```
dollars = 99.95
```

If your instructor allows it, it is permissible to write assignment statements without the word Set in your pseudocode. Just be sure to write the name of the variable that is receiving the value on the left side of the equal sign.

previously stored in the variable. When line 4 executes, it displays "But now I have 99.95 in my account!" This program illustrates two important characteristics of variables:

■ A variable holds only one value at a time.

■ When you store a value in a variable, that value replaces the previous value that was in the variable.

In flowcharts, an assignment statement appears in a processing symbol, which is a rectangle. Figure 12–8 shows a flowchart for Program 12–6.

▶ **FIGURE 12–8**

Flowchart for Program 12–6.

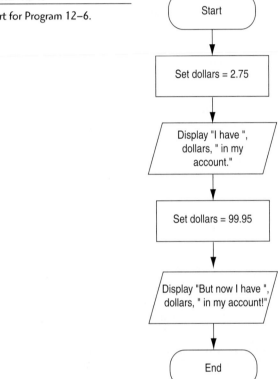

Performing Calculations

Most real-world algorithms require calculations to be performed. A programmer's tools for performing calculations are *math operators*. Programming languages commonly provide the operators shown in Table 12–1.

▶ **TABLE 12–1**

Common math operators

SYMBOL	OPERATOR	DESCRIPTION
+	Addition	Adds two numbers
−	Subtraction	Subtracts one number from another
*	Multiplication	Multiplies one number by another
/	Division	Divides one number by another and gives the quotient
MOD	Modulus	Divides one number by another and gives the remainder
^	Exponent	Raised a number to a power

Programmers use the operators shown in Table 12–1 to create math expressions. A *math expression* performs a calculation and gives a value. The following is an example of a simple math expression:

```
12 + 2
```

The values on the right and left of the + operator are called *operands*. These are values that the + operator adds together. The value that is given by this expression is 14.

Variables may also be used in a math expression. For example, suppose we have two variables named `hours` and `payRate`. The following math expression uses the * operator to multiply the value in the `hours` variable by the value in the `payRate` variable:

```
hours * payRate
```

When we use a math expression to calculate a value, normally we want to save that value in memory so we can use it again in the program. We do this with an assignment statement. Program 12–7 shows an example.

PROGRAM 12–7

```
1   Set price = 100
2   Set discount = 20
3   Set sale = price - discount
4   Display "The total cost is $" , sale
```

Program Output

```
The total cost is $80
```

Line 1 sets the `price` variable to 100, and line 2 sets the `discount` variable to 20. Line 3 sets the `sale` variable to the result of the expression `price - discount`. As you can see from the program output, the `sale` variable holds the value 80.

In the Spotlight:

Calculating a Percentage

Determining percentages is a common calculation in computer programming. In mathematics, the % symbol is used to indicate a percentage, but most programming languages don't use the % symbol for this purpose. In a program, you usually have to convert a percentage to a decimal number. For example, 50 percent would be written as 0.5 and 2 percent would be written as 0.02.

Let's step through the process of writing a program that calculates a percentage. Suppose a retail business is planning to have a storewide sale where the prices of all items will be 20 percent off. We have been asked to write a program to calculate the sale price of an item after the discount is subtracted. Here is the algorithm:

1. Get the original price of the item.

2. Calculate 20 percent of the original price. This is the amount of the discount.

3. Subtract the discount from the original price. This is the sale price.

4. Display the sale price.

In Step 1 we get the original price of the item. We will prompt the user to enter this data on the keyboard. Recall from the previous section that prompting the user is a two-step process: (1) display a message telling the user to enter the desired data, and (2) reading that data from the keyboard. We will use the following pseudocode statements to

Flowchart for Program 12–8.

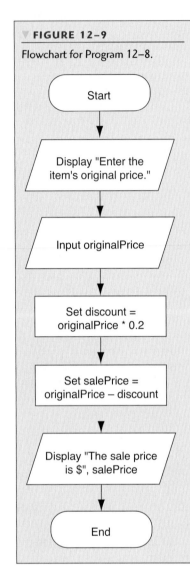

do this. Notice that the value entered by the user will be stored in a variable named `originalPrice`.

```
Display "Enter the item's original price: "
Input originalPrice
```

In Step 2, we calculate the amount of the discount. To do this we multiply the original price by 20 percent. The following statement performs this calculation and stores the result in the `discount` variable.

```
Set discount = originalPrice * 0.2
```

In Step 3, we subtract the discount from the original price. The following statement does this calculation and stores the result in the `salePrice` variable.

```
Set salePrice = originalPrice - discount
```

Last, in Step 4, we will use the following statement to display the sale price:

```
Display "The sale price is $", salePrice
```

Program 12–8 shows the entire pseudocode program, with example output. Figure 12–9 shows the flowchart for this program.

PROGRAM 12-8

```
1  Display "Enter the item's original price."
2  Input originalPrice
3  Set discount = originalPrice * 0.2
4  Set salePrice = originalPrice - discount
5  Display "The sale price is $", salePrice
```

Program Output (with Input Shown in Bold)

```
Enter the item's original price.
100 [Enter]
The sale price is $80
```

The Order of Operations

It is possible to build mathematical expressions with several operators. The following statement assigns the sum of 17, the variable x, 21, and the variable y to the variable `answer`.

```
Set answer = 17 + x + 21 + y
```

Some expressions are not that straightforward, however. Consider the following statement:

```
Set outcome = 12 + 6 / 3
```

What value will be stored in `outcome`? The number 6 is used as an operand for both the addition and division operators. The `outcome` variable could be assigned either 6 or 14, depending on when the division takes place. The answer is 14 because the *order of operations* dictates that the division operator works before the addition operator does.

In most programming languages, the order of operations can be summarized as follows:

The order of operations at work.

1. Perform any operations that are enclosed in parentheses.

2. Perform any operations that use the exponent operator to raise a number to a power.

3. Perform any multiplications, divisions, or modulus operations as they appear from left to right.

4. Perform any additions or subtractions as they appear from left to right.

Mathematical expressions are evaluated from left to right. When two operators share an operand, the order of operations determines which operator works first. Multiplication and division are always performed before addition and subtraction, so the statement

```
Set outcome = 12 + 6 / 3
```

works like this:

1. 6 is divided by 3, yielding a result of 2

2. 12 is added to 2, yielding a result of 14

It could be diagrammed as shown in Figure 12–10.

Table 12–2 shows some other sample expressions with their values.

```
Set outcome = 12 + 6 / 3

Set outcome = 12 +    2

Set outcome =     14
```

Some expressions

EXPRESSION	VALUE
5 + 2 * 4	13
10 / 2 - 3	2
8 + 12 * 2 - 4	28
6 - 3 * 2 + 7 - 1	6

Grouping with Parentheses

Parts of a mathematical expression may be grouped with parentheses to force some operations to be performed before others. In the following statement, the variables a and b are added together, and their sum is divided by 4:

```
Set result = (a + b) / 4
```

Without the parentheses, however, b would be divided by 4 and the result added to a. Table 12–3 shows more expressions and their values.

More expressions and their values

EXPRESSION	VALUE
(5 + 2) * 4	28
10 / (5 - 3)	5
8 + 12 * (6 - 2)	56
(6 - 3) * (2 + 7) / 3	9

In the Spotlight:

Calculating an Average

▼ FIGURE 12–11

Flowchart for Program 12–9.

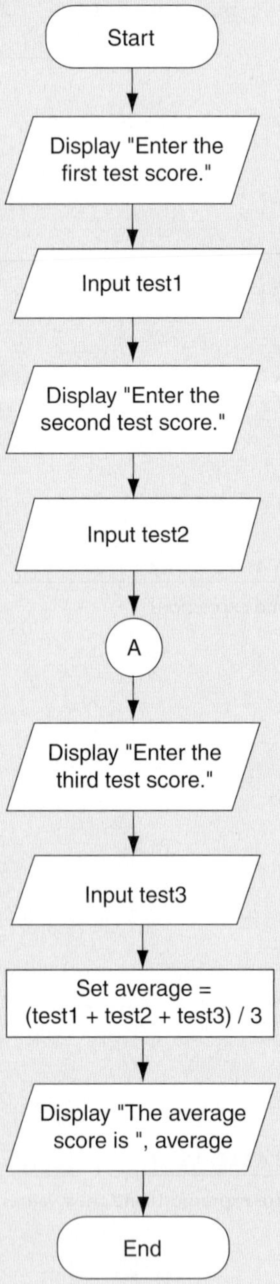

```
        ( Start )
           │
           ▼
  ╱ Display "Enter the ╱
  ╱ first test score." ╱
           │
           ▼
      ╱ Input test1 ╱
           │
           ▼
  ╱ Display "Enter the ╱
  ╱ second test score." ╱
           │
           ▼
      ╱ Input test2 ╱
           │
           ▼
         ( A )
           │
           ▼
  ╱ Display "Enter the ╱
  ╱ third test score." ╱
           │
           ▼
      ╱ Input test3 ╱
           │
           ▼
  ┌─────────────────────┐
  │  Set average =      │
  │ (test1 + test2 + test3) / 3 │
  └─────────────────────┘
           │
           ▼
  ╱ Display "The average ╱
  ╱ score is ", average  ╱
           │
           ▼
        ( End )
```

Determining the average of a group of values is a simple calculation: You add all of the values and then divide the sum by the number of values. Although this is a straightforward calculation, it is easy to make a mistake when writing a program that calculates an average. For example, let's assume that the variables a, b, and c each hold a value and we want to calculate the average of those values. If we are careless, we might write a statement such as the following to perform the calculation:

```
Set average = a + b + c / 3
```

Can you see the error in this statement? When it executes, the division will take place first. The value in c will be divided by 3, and then the result will be added to a + b. That is not the correct way to calculate an average. To correct this error we need to put parentheses around a + b + c, as shown here:

```
Set average = (a + b + c) / 3
```

Let's step through the process of writing a program that calculates an average. Suppose you have taken three tests in your computer science class, and you want to write a program that will display the average of the test scores. Here is the algorithm:

1. Get the first test score.

2. Get the second test score.

3. Get the third test score.

4. Calculate the average by adding the three test scores and dividing the sum by 3.

5. Display the average.

In steps 1, 2, and 3 we will prompt the user to enter the three test scores. We will store those test scores in the variables test1, test2, and test3. In Step 4 we will calculate the average of the three test scores. We will use the following statement to perform the calculation and store the result in the average variable:

```
Set average = (test1 + test2 + test3) / 3
```

Last, in Step 5, we display the average. Program 12–9 shows the pseudocode for this program, and Figure 12–11 shows the flowchart.

PROGRAM 12-9

```
1   Display "Enter the first test score."
2   Input test1
3   Display "Enter the second test score."
4   Input test2
5   Display "Enter the third test score."
6   Input test3
7   Set average = (test1 + test2 + test3) / 3
8   Display "The average score is ", average
```

Program Output (with Input Shown in Bold)

```
Enter the first test score.
90 [Enter]
Enter the second test score.
80 [Enter]
Enter the third test score.
100 [Enter]
The average score is 90
```

Notice that the flowchart uses a new symbol:

This is called a connector symbol and is used when a flowchart is broken into two or more smaller flowcharts. This is necessary when a flowchart does not fit on a single page, or must be divided into sections. A connector symbol, which is a small circle with a letter or number inside it, allows you to connect two flowcharts. In Figure 12–11 the A connector indicates that the second flowchart segment begins where the first flowchart segment ends.

Advanced Arithmetic Operators: Exponent and Modulus

In addition to the basic math operators for addition, subtraction, multiplication, and division, many languages provide an exponent operator and a modulus operator. The ^ symbol is commonly used as the exponent operator, and its purpose is to raise a number to a power. For example, the following pseudocode statement raises the length variable to the power of 2 and stores the result in the area variable:

```
Set area = length^2
```

The word MOD is used in many languages as the modulus operator. (Some languages use the % symbol for the same purpose.) The modulus operator performs division, but instead of returning the quotient, it returns the remainder. The following statement assigns 2 to leftover:

```
Set leftover = 17 MOD 3
```

This statement assigns 2 to leftover because 17 divided by 3 is 5 with a remainder of 2. You will not use the modulus operator frequently, but it is useful in some situations. It is commonly used in calculations that detect odd or even numbers, determine the day of the week, measure the passage of time, and other specialized operations.

Converting Math Formulas to Programming Statements

You probably remember from algebra class that the expression 2xy is understood to mean 2 times x times y. In math, you do not always use an operator for multiplication. Programming languages, however, require an operator for any mathematical operation. Table 12–4 shows some algebraic expressions that perform multiplication and the equivalent programming expressions.

◄ **TABLE 12-4**

Algebraic expressions

ALGEBRAIC EXPRESSION	OPERATION BEING PERFORMED	PROGRAMMING EXPRESSION
6B	6 times B	6 * B
(3)(12)	3 times 12	3 * 12
4xy	4 times x times y	4 * x * y

When converting some algebraic expressions to programming expressions, you may have to insert parentheses that do not appear in the algebraic expression. For example, look at the following formula:

$$x = \frac{a+b}{c}$$

To convert this to a programming statement, $a + b$ will have to be enclosed in parentheses:

```
Set x = (a + b) / c
```

Table 12–5 shows additional algebraic expressions and their pseudocode equivalents.

▶ **TABLE 12–5**

Algebraic and programming expressions

ALGEBRAIC EXPRESSION	PSEUDOCODE STATEMENT
$y = 3\dfrac{x}{2}$	Set y = x / 2 * 3
$z = 3bc + 4$	Set z = 3 * b * c + 4
$a = \dfrac{x+2}{a-1}$	Set a = (x + 2) / (a - 1)

In the Spotlight:

Converting a Math Formula to a Programming Statement

Suppose you want to deposit a certain amount of money into a savings account, and then leave it alone to draw interest for the next 10 years. At the end of 10 years you would like to have $10,000 in the account. How much do you need to deposit today to make that happen? You can use the following formula to find out.

$$P = \frac{F}{(1 + r)^n}$$

The terms in the formula are as follows:

▪ P is the present value, or the amount that you need to deposit today.

▪ F is the future value that you want in the account. (In this case, F is $10,000.)

▪ r is the annual interest rate.

▪ n is the number of years that you plan to let the money sit in the account.

It would be nice to write a computer program to perform the calculation, because then we can experiment with different values for the terms. Here is an algorithm that we can use:

1. Get the desired future value.

2. Get the annual interest rate.

3. Get the number of years that the money will sit in the account.

4. Calculate the amount that will have to be deposited.

5. Display the result of the calculation in Step 4.

In steps 1 through 3, we will prompt the user to enter the specified values. We will store the desired future value in a variable named futureValue, the annual interest rate in a variable named rate, and the number of years in a variable named years.

In Step 4, we calculate the present value, which is the amount of money that we will have to deposit. We will convert the formula previously shown to the following pseudocode statement. The statement stores the result of the calculation in the presentValue variable.

```
Set presentValue = futureValue / (1 + rate)^years
```

In Step 5, we display the value in the presentValue variable. Program 12–10 shows the pseudocode for this program, and Figure 12–12 shows the flowchart.

PROGRAM 12-10

```
1  Display "Enter the desired future value."
2  Input futureValue
3  Display "Enter the annual interest rate."
4  Input rate
5  Display "How many years will you let the money grow?"
6  Input years
7  Set presentValue = futureValue / (1 + rate)^years
8  Display "You will need to deposit $", presentValue
```

Program Output (with Input Shown in Bold)

```
Enter the desired future value.
10000 [Enter]
Enter the annual interest rate.
0.05 [Enter]
How many years will you let the money grow?
10 [Enter]
You need to deposit $6139
```

► FIGURE 12-12

Flowchart for Program 12–10.

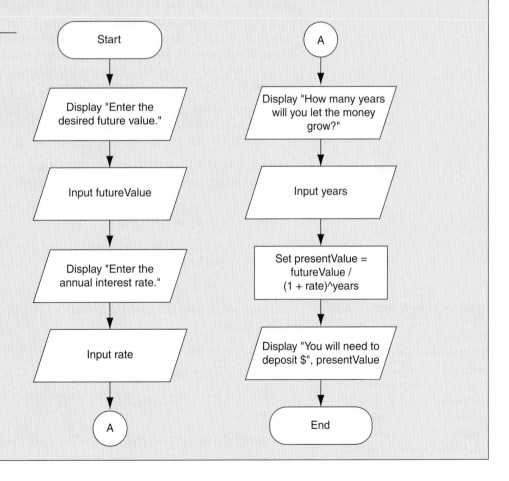

12-4 VARIABLE DECLARATIONS AND DATA TYPES

CONCEPT: **Most languages require that variables be declared before they are used in a program. When a variable is declared, it can optionally be initialized with a value. Using an uninitialized variable is the source of many errors in programming.**

Most programming languages require that you *declare* all of the variables that you intend to use in a program. A *variable declaration* is a statement that typically specifies two things about a variable:

- The variable's name

- The variable's data type

A variable's *data type* is simply the type of data that the variable will hold. Once you declare a variable, it can be used to store values of only the specified data type. In most languages, an error occurs if you try to store values of other types in the variable.

The data types that you are allowed to use depend on the programming language. For example, the Java language provides four data types for integer numbers, two data types for real numbers, one data type for strings, and others.

So far, we haven't declared any of the variables that we have used in our example pseudocode programs. We have simply used the variables without first declaring them. This is permissible with short pseudocode programs, but as programs grow in length and complexity, it makes sense to declare them. When you declare variables in a pseudocode program, it will make the job of translating the pseudocode to actual code easier.

In this book, we will use only three data types when we declare variables: Integer, Real, and String. Here is a summary of each:

- A variable of the Integer data type can hold whole numbers. For example, an Integer variable can hold values such as 42, 0, and –99. An Integer variable cannot hold numbers with a fractional part, such as 22.1 or –4.9.

- A variable of the Real data type can hold either whole numbers or numbers with a fractional part. For example, a Real variable can hold values such as 3.5, –87.95, and 3.0.

- A variable of the String data type can hold any string of characters, such as someone's name, address, password, and so on.

In this book, we will begin variable declarations with the word Declare, followed by a data type, followed by the variable's name. Here is an example:

```
Declare Integer length
```

COMPUTER NOTE

In addition to a String data type, many programming languages also provide a Character data type. The difference between a String variable and a Character variable is that a String variable can hold a sequence of characters of virtually any length, and a Character variable can hold only one character. In this book, we will keep things simple. We will use String variables to hold all character data.

This statement declares a variable named length, of the Integer data type. Here is another example:

```
Declare Real grossPay
```

This statement declares a variable named grossPay, of the Real data type. Here is one more example:

```
Declare String name
```

This statement declares a variable named name, of the String data type.

If we need to declare more than one variable of the same data type, we can use one declaration statement. For example, suppose we want to declare three variables, length, width, and height, all of the Integer data type. We can declare all three with one statement, as shown here:

```
Declare Integer length, width, height
```

Declaring Variables Before Using Them

The purpose of a variable declaration statement is to tell the compiler or interpreter that you plan to use a particular variable in the program. A variable declaration statement typically causes the variable to be created in memory. For this reason, you have to write a variable's declaration statement *before* any other statements in the program that use the variable. This makes perfect sense because you cannot store a value in a variable if the variable has not been created in memory.

For example, look at the following pseudocode. If this code were converted to actual code in a language like Java or C++, it would cause an error because the Input statement uses the age variable before the variable has been declared.

```
Display "What is your age?"
Input age                        This pseudocode has an error!
Declare Integer age
```

Program 12–11 shows the correct way to declare a variable. Notice that the declaration statement for the age variable appears before any other statements that use the variable.

PROGRAM 12–11

```
1   Declare Integer age
2   Display "What is your age?"
3   Input age
4   Display "Here is the value that you entered:"
5   Display age
```

Program Output (with Input Shown in Bold)

```
What is your age?
24 [Enter]
Here is the value that you entered:
24
```

Program 12–12 shows another example. This program declares a total of four variables: three to hold test scores and another to hold the average of those test scores.

PROGRAM 2–12

```
1    Declare Real test1
2    Declare Real test2
3    Declare Real test3
4    Declare Real average
5
6    Set test1 = 88.0
7    Set test2 = 92.5
8    Set test3 = 97.0
9    Set average = (test1 + test2 + test3) / 3
10   Display "Your average test score is ", average
```

Program Output (with Input Shown in Bold)

```
Your average test score is 92.5
```

This program shows a common technique for declaring variables: they are all declared at the beginning of the program, before any other statements. This is one way of making sure that all variables are declared before they are used.

Notice that line 5 in this program is blank. This blank line does *not* affect the way the program works because most compilers and interpreters ignore blank lines. For the human reader, however, this blank line visually separates the variable declarations from the other statements. This makes the program appear more organized and easier for people to read.

Programmers commonly use blank lines and indentations in their code to create a sense of organization visually. This is similar to the way that authors visually arrange the text on the pages of a book. Instead of writing each chapter as one long series of sentences, they break it into paragraphs. This does not change the information in the book; it only makes it easier to read.

Although you are generally free to place blank lines and indentations anywhere in your code, you should not do this haphazardly. Programmers follow certain conventions when it comes to this. For example, you have just learned that one convention is to use a blank line to separate a group of variable declaration statements from the rest of the statements in a program. These conventions are known as *programming style*. As you progress through this book you will see many other programming style conventions.

Variable Initialization

When you declare a variable, you can optionally assign a value to it in the declaration statement. This is known as *initialization*. For example, the following statement declares a variable named `price` and assigns the value 49.95 to it:

```
Declare Real price = 49.95
```

We would say that this statement *initializes* the `price` variable with the value 49.95. The following statement shows another example:

```
Declare Integer length = 2, width = 4, height = 8
```

This statement declares and initializes three variables. The `length` variable is initialized with the value 2, `width` is initialized with the value 4, and `height` is initialized with the value 8.

Uninitialized Variables

An *uninitialized variable* is a variable that has been declared, but has not been initialized or assigned a value. Uninitialized variables are a common cause of logic errors in programs. For example, look at the following pseudocode:

```
Declare Real dollars
Display "I have ", dollars, " in my account."
```

In this pseudocode, we have declared the `dollars` variable, but we have not initialized it or assigned a value to it. Therefore, we do not know what value the variable holds. Nevertheless, we have used the variable in a `Display` statement.

You're probably wondering what a program like this would display. An honest answer would be "I don't know." This is because each language has its own way of handling uninitialized variables. Some languages assign a default value such as 0 to uninitialized variables. In many languages, however, uninitialized variables hold unpredictable values. This is because those languages set aside a place in memory for the variable, but do not alter the contents of that place in memory. As a result, an uninitialized variable holds the value that happens to be stored in its memory location. Programmers typically refer to unpredictable values such as this as "garbage."

Uninitialized variables can cause logic errors that are hard to find in a program. This is especially true when an uninitialized variable is used in a calculation. For example, look at the following pseudocode, which is a modified version of Program 12–12. Can you spot the error?

```
1   Declare Real test1
2   Declare Real test2
3   Declare Real test3
4   Declare Real average
5
6   Set test1 = 88.0
7   Set test2 = 92.5
8   Set average = (test1 + test2 + test3) / 3
9   Display "Your average test score is ", average
```

This pseudocode
contains an error!

This program will not work properly because the test3 variable is never assigned a value. The test3 variable will contain garbage when it is used in the calculation in line 8. This means that the calculation will result in an unpredictable value, which will be assigned to the average variable. A beginning programmer might have trouble finding this error because he or she would initially assume that something is wrong with the math in line 8.

In the next section, we will discuss a debugging technique that will help uncover errors such as the one in Program 12–12. However, as a rule you should always make sure that your variables either (1) are initialized with the correct value when you declare them, or (2) receive the correct value from an assignment statement or an Input statement before they are used for any other purpose.

Numeric Literals and Data Type Compatibility

Many of the programs that you have seen so far have numbers written into their pseudocode. For example, the following statement, which appears in Program 12–6, has the number 2.75 written into it.

```
Set dollars = 2.75
```

And, the following statement, which appears in Program 12–7, has the number 100 written into it.

```
Set price = 100
```

A number that is written into a program's code is called a *numeric literal*. In most programming languages, if a numeric literal is written with a decimal point, such as 2.75, that numeric literal will be stored in the computer's memory as a Real and it will be treated as a Real when the program runs. If a numeric literal does not have a decimal point, such as 100, that numeric literal will be stored in the computer's memory as an Integer and it will be treated as an Integer when the program runs.

This is important to know when you are writing assignment statements or initializing variables. In many languages, an error will occur if you try to store a value of one data type in a variable of another data type. For example, look at the following pseudocode:

```
Declare Integer i
Set i = 3.7 ◄─── This is an error!
```

The assignment statement will cause an error because it attempts to assign a real number, 3.7, in an Integer variable. The following pseudocode will also cause an error.

```
Declare Integer i
Set i = 3.0 ◄─── This is an error!
```

Even though the numeric literal 3.0 does not have a fractional value (it is mathematically the same as the integer 3), it is still treated as a real number by the computer because it is written with a decimal point.

COMPUTER NOTE

Most languages do not allow you to assign real numbers to Integer variables because Integer variables cannot hold fractional amounts. In many languages, however, you are allowed to assign an integer value to a Real variable without causing an error. Here is an example:

```
Declare Real r
Set r = 77
```

Even though the numeric literal 77 is treated as an Integer, it can be assigned to a Real variable without the loss of data.

COMPUTER NOTE

In Java, C++, C, and Python, the / operator throws away the fractional part of the result when both operands are integers. In these languages the result of the expression 3 / 2 would be 1. In Visual Basic, the / operator does not throw away the fractional part of the answer. In Visual Basic the result of the expression 3 / 2 would be 1.5.

Integer Division

Be careful when dividing an integer by another integer. In many programming languages, when an integer is divided by an integer the result will also be an integer. This behavior is known as *integer division*. For example, look at the following pseudocode:

```
Set number = 3 / 2
```

This statement divides 3 by 2 and stores the result in the number variable. What will be stored in number? You would probably assume that 1.5 would be stored in number because that's the result your calculator shows when you divide 3 by 2. However, that's not what will happen in many programming languages. Because the numbers 3 and 2 are both treated as integers, the programming language that you are using might throw away the fractional part of the answer. (Throwing away the fractional part of a number is called *truncation*.) As a result, the statement will store 1 in the number variable, not 1.5.

If you are using a language that behaves this way and you want to make sure that a division operation yields a real number, at least one of the operands must be a real number or a Real variable.

12–5 NAMED CONSTANTS

CONCEPT: **A named constant is a name that represents a value that cannot be changed during the program's execution.**

Assume that the following statement appears in a banking program that calculates data pertaining to loans:

```
Set amount = balance * 0.069
```

In such a program, two potential problems arise. First, it is not clear to anyone other than the original programmer what 0.069 is. It appears to be an interest rate, but in some situations there are fees associated with loan payments. How can the purpose of this statement be determined without painstakingly checking the rest of the program?

The second problem occurs if this number is used in other calculations throughout the program and must be changed periodically. Assuming the number is an interest rate, what if the rate changes from 6.9 percent to 7.2 percent? The programmer would have to search through the source code for every occurrence of the number.

Both of these problems can be addressed by using named constants. A *named constant* is a name that represents a value that cannot be changed during the program's execution. The following is an example of how we will declare named constants in our pseudocode:

```
Constant Real INTEREST_RATE = 0.069
```

This creates a constant named INTEREST_RATE. The constant's value is the Real number 0.069. Notice that the declaration looks a lot like a variable declaration, except that we use the word Constant instead of Declare. Also, notice that the name of the constant is written in all uppercase letters. This is a standard practice in most programming languages because it makes named constants easily distinguishable from regular variable names. An initialization value must be given when declaring a named constant.

An advantage of using named constants is that they make programs more self-explanatory. The following statement:

```
Set amount = balance * 0.069
```

can be changed to read

```
Set amount = balance * INTEREST_RATE
```

A new programmer can read the second statement and know what is happening. It is evident that `balance` is being multiplied by the interest rate. Another advantage to this approach is that widespread changes can easily be made to the program. Let's say the interest rate appears in a dozen different statements throughout the program. When the rate changes, the initialization value in the declaration of the named constant is the only value that needs to be modified. If the rate increases to 7.2 percent, the declaration can be changed to the following:

```
Constant Real INTEREST_RATE = 0.072
```

The new value of 0.072 will then be used in each statement that uses the `INTEREST_RATE` constant.

COMPUTER NOTE

A named constant cannot be assigned a value with a `Set` statement. If a statement in a program attempts to change the value of a named constant, an error will occur.

12-6   HAND TRACING A PROGRAM

CONCEPT: Hand tracing is a simple debugging process for locating hard to find errors in a program.

Hand tracing is a debugging process where you imagine that you are the computer executing a program. (This process is also known as *desk checking*.) You step through each of the program's statements one by one. As you carefully look at a statement, you record the contents that each variable will have after the statement executes. This process is often helpful in finding mathematical mistakes and other logic errors.

To hand trace a program, you construct a chart that has a column for each variable, and a row for each line in the program. For example, Figure 12–13 shows how we would construct a hand trace chart for the program that you saw in the previous section. The chart has a column for each of the four variables: `test1`, `test2`, `test3`, and `average`. The chart also has nine rows, one for each line in the program.

```
1   Declare Real test1
2   Declare Real test2
3   Declare Real test3
4   Declare Real average
5
6   Set test1 = 88.0
7   Set test2 = 92.5
8   Set average = (test1 + test2 + test3) / 3
9   Display "Your average test score is ", average
```

	test1	test2	test3	average
1				
2				
3				
4				
5				
6				
7				
8				
9				

◄ **FIGURE 12–13**

A program with a hand trace chart.

To hand trace this program, you step through each statement, observing the operation that is taking place, and then record the value that each variable will hold *after* the statement executes. When the process is complete, the chart will appear as shown in Figure 12–14. We have written question marks in the chart to indicate that a variable is uninitialized.

```
1   Declare Real test1
2   Declare Real test2
3   Declare Real test3
4   Declare Real average
5
6   Set test1 = 88.0
7   Set test2 = 92.5
8   Set average = (test1 + test2 + test3) / 3
9   Display "Your average test score is ", average
```

	test1	test2	test3	average
1	?	?	?	?
2	?	?	?	?
3	?	?	?	?
4	?	?	?	?
5	?	?	?	?
6	88	?	?	?
7	88	92.5	?	?
8	88	92.2	?	undefined
9	88	92.5	?	undefined

◄ **FIGURE 12–14**

Program with the hand trace chart completed.

When we get to line 8 we will carefully do the math. This means we look at the values of each variable in the expression. At that point we discover that one of the variables, test3, is uninitialized. Because it is uninitialized, we have no way of knowing the value that it contains. Consequently, the result of the calculation will be undefined. After making this discovery, we can correct the problem by adding a line that assigns a value to test3.

Hand tracing is a simple process that focuses your attention on each statement in a program. Often this helps you locate errors that are not obvious.

12-7 DOCUMENTING A PROGRAM

CONCEPT: **A program's external documentation describes aspects of the program for the user. The internal documentation is for the programmer, and explains how parts of the program work.**

A program's documentation explains various things about the program. There are usually two types of program documentation: external and internal. *External documentation* is typically designed for the user. It consists of documents such as a reference guide that describes the program's features, and tutorials that teach the user how to operate the program.

Sometimes the programmer is responsible for writing all or part of a program's external documentation. This might be the case in a small organization, or in a company that has a relatively small programming staff. Some organizations, particularly large companies, will employ a staff of technical writers whose job is to produce external documentation. These documents might be in printed manuals, or in files that can be viewed on the computer. In recent years it has become common for software companies to provide all of a program's external documentation in PDF (Portable Document Format) files.

Internal documentation appears as *comments* in a program's code. Comments are short notes placed in different parts of a program, explaining how those parts of the program work. Although comments are a critical part of a program, they are ignored by the compiler or interpreter. Comments are intended for human readers of a program's code, not the computer.

Programming languages provide special symbols or words for writing comments. In several languages, including Java, C, and C++, you begin a comment with two forward slashes (//). Everything that you write on the same line, after the slashes, is ignored by the compiler. Here is an example of a comment in any of those languages:

```
// Get the number of hours worked.
```

Some languages use symbols other than the two forward slashes to indicate the beginning of a comment. For example, Visual Basic uses an apostrophe ('), and Python uses the # symbol. In this book, we will use two forward slashes (//) in pseudocode.

Block Comments and Line Comments

Programmers generally write two types of comments in a program: block comments and line comments. *Block comments* take up several lines and are used when lengthy explanations are required. For example, a block comment often appears at the beginning of a program, explaining what the program does, listing the name of the author, giving the date that the program was last modified, and any other necessary information. The following is an example of a block comment:

```
// This program calculates an employee's gross pay.
// Written by Matt Hoyle.
// Last modified on 12/7/08
```

COMPUTER NOTE

Some programming languages provide special symbols to mark the beginning and ending of a block comment.

Line comments are comments that occupy a single line, and explain a short section of the program. The following statements, which could be taken from a Java program, show an example:

```
// Calculate the interest.
Set interest = balance * interestRate;
// Add the interest to the balance.
Set balance = balance + interest;
```

A line comment does not have to occupy an entire line. Anything appearing after the `//` symbol, to the end of the line, is ignored, so a comment can appear after an executable statement. Here is an example:

```
Input age     // Get the user's age.
```

As a beginning programmer, you might be resistant to the idea of liberally writing comments in your programs. After all, it's a lot more fun to write code that actually does something! It is crucial that you take the extra time to write comments, however. They will almost certainly save you time in the future when you have to modify or debug the program. Even large and complex programs can be made easy to read and understand if they are properly commented.

In the Spotlight:

Using Named Constants, Style Conventions, and Comments

Suppose we have been given the following programming problem: Scientists have determined that the world's ocean levels are currently rising at about 1.5 millimeters per year. Write a program to display the following:

- The number of millimeters that the oceans will rise in five years

- The number of millimeters that the oceans will rise in seven years

- The number of millimeters that the oceans will rise in ten years

Here is the algorithm:

1. Calculate the amount that the oceans will rise in five years.

2. Display the result of the calculation in Step 1.

3. Calculate the amount that the oceans will rise in seven years.

4. Display the result of the calculation in Step 3.

5. Calculate the amount that the oceans will rise in ten years.

6. Display the result of the calculation in Step 5.

This program is straightforward. It performs three calculations and displays the results of each. The calculations should give the amount the oceans will rise in five, seven, and ten years. Each of these values can be calculated with the following formula:

Amount of yearly rise × Number of years

The amount of yearly rise is the same for each calculation, so we will create a constant to represent that value. Program 12–13 shows the pseudocode for the program.

PROGRAM 12-13

```
1   // Declare the variables
2   Declare Real fiveYears
3   Declare Real sevenYears
4   Declare Real tenYears
5
6   // Create a constant for the yearly rise
7   Constant Real YEARLY_RISE = 1.5
8
9   // Display the amount of rise in five years
10  Set fiveYears = YEARLY_RISE * 5
11  Display "The ocean levels will rise ", fiveYears,
12      " millimeters in five years."
13
14  // Display the amount of rise in seven years
15  Set sevenYears = YEARLY_RISE * 7
16  Display "The ocean levels will rise ", sevenYears,
17      " millimeters in seven years."
18
19  // Display the amount of rise in ten years
20  Set tenYears = YEARLY_RISE * 10
21  Display "The ocean levels will rise ", tenYears,
22      " millimeters in ten years."
```

Program Output (with Input Shown in Bold)

```
The ocean levels will rise 7.5 millimeters in five years.
The ocean levels will rise 10.5 millimeters in seven years.
The ocean levels will rise 15 millimeters in ten years.
```

Three variables `fiveYears`, `sevenYears`, and `tenYears` are declared in lines 2 through 4. These variables will hold the amount that the ocean levels will rise in five, seven, and ten years.

Line 7 creates a constant, `YEARLY_RISE`, which is set to the value 1.5. This is the amount that the oceans rise per year. This constant will be used in each of the program's calculations.

Lines 10 through 12 calculate and display the amount that the oceans will rise in five years. The same values for seven years and ten years is calculated and displayed in lines 15 through 17 and 20 through 22.

This program illustrates the following programming style conventions:

- Several blank lines appear throughout the program (see lines 5, 8, 13, and 18). These blank lines do not affect the way the program works, but make the pseudocode easier to read.

- Line comments are used in various places to explain what the program is doing.

- Notice that each of the `Display` statements are too long to fit on one line. (See lines 11 and 12, 16 and 17, 21 and 22.) Most programming languages allow you to write long statements across several lines. When we do this in pseudocode, we will indent the second and subsequent lines. This will give a visual indication that the statement spans more than one line.

Figure 12–15 shows a flowchart for the program.

▼ **FIGURE 12–15**

Flowchart for Program 12–13.

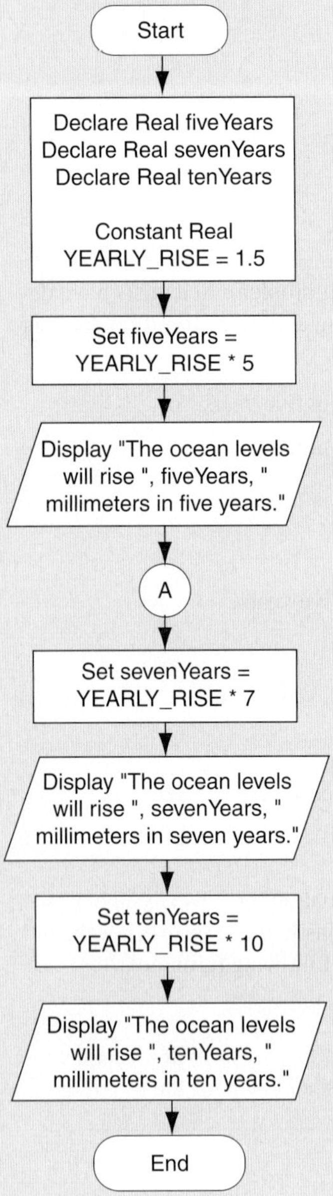

Multiple Choice

1. A _____ error does not prevent the program from running, but causes it to produce incorrect results.
   (a) syntax
   (b) hardware
   (c) logic
   (d) fatal

2. A _____ is a single function that the program must perform in order to satisfy the customer.
   (a) task
   (b) software requirement
   (c) prerequisite
   (d) predicate

3. A(n) _____ is a set of well-defined logical steps that must be taken to perform a task.
   (a) logarithm
   (b) plan of action
   (c) logic schedule
   (d) algorithm

4. An informal language that has no syntax rules, and is not meant to be compiled or executed is called _____.
   (a) faux code
   (b) pseudocode
   (c) Java
   (d) a flowchart

5. A _____ is a diagram that graphically depicts the steps that take place in a program.
   (a) flowchart
   (b) step chart
   (c) code graph
   (d) program graph

6. A(n) _____ is a set of statements that execute in the order that they appear.
   (a) serial program
   (b) sorted code
   (c) sequence structure
   (d) ordered structure

7. A _____ is a sequence of characters that is used as data.
   (a) sequence structure
   (b) character collection
   (c) string
   (d) text block

8. A _____ is a storage location in memory that is represented by a name.
   (a) variable
   (b) register
   (c) RAM slot
   (d) byte

9. A _____ is any hypothetical person that is using a program and providing input for it.

   (a) designer

   (b) user

   (c) guinea pig

   (d) test subject

10. A(n) _____ is a message that tells (or asks) the user to enter a specific value.

    (a) inquiry

    (b) input statement

    (c) directive

    (d) prompt

11. A(n) _____ sets a variable to a specified value.

    (a) variable declaration

    (b) assignment statement

    (c) math expression

    (d) string literal

12. In the expression 12 + 7, the values on the right and left of the + symbol are called _____.

    (a) operands

    (b) operators

    (c) arguments

    (d) math expressions

13. A(n) _____ operator raises a number to a power.

    (a) modulus

    (b) multiplication

    (c) exponent

    (d) operand

14. A(n) _____ operator performs division, but instead of returning the quotient it returns the remainder.

    (a) modulus

    (b) multiplication

    (c) exponent

    (d) operand

15. A(n) _____ specifies a variable's name and data type.

    (a) assignment

    (b) variable specification

    (c) variable certification

    (d) variable declaration

16. Assigning a value to a variable in a declaration statement is called _____.

    (a) allocation

    (b) initialization

    (c) certification

    (d) programming style

17. A(n) _____ variable is one that has been declared, but has not been initialized or assigned a value.

   (a) undefined

   (b) uninitialized

   (c) empty

   (d) default

18. A(n) _____ has a value that is read only and cannot be changed during the program's execution.

   (a) static variable

   (b) uninitialized variable

   (c) named constant

   (d) locked variable

19. A debugging process in which you imagine that you are the computer executing a program is called _____.

   (a) imaginative computing

   (b) role playing

   (c) mental simulation

   (d) hand tracing

20. Short notes placed in different parts of a program, explaining how those parts of the program work are called _____.

   (a) comments

   (b) reference manuals

   (c) tutorials

   (d) external documentation

True or False

1. Programmers must be careful not to make syntax errors when writing pseudocode programs.
2. In a math expression, multiplication and division takes place before addition and subtraction.
3. Variable names can have spaces in them.
4. In most languages, the first character of a variable name cannot be a number.
5. The name `gross_pay` is written in the camelCase convention.
6. In languages that require variable declarations, a variable's declaration must appear before any other statements that use the variable.
7. Uninitialized variables are a common cause of errors.
8. The value of a named constant cannot be changed during the program's execution.
9. Hand tracing is the process of translating a pseudocode program into machine language by hand.
10. Internal documentation refers to books and manuals that document a program, and are intended for use within a company's programming department.

Short Answer

1. What does a professional programmer usually do first to gain an understanding of a problem?
2. What is pseudocode?
3. Computer programs typically perform what three steps?
4. What does the term "user-friendly" mean?
5. What two things must you normally specify in a variable declaration?
6. What value is stored in uninitialized variables?

Algorithm Workbench

1. Design an algorithm that prompts the user to enter his or her height and stores the user's input in a variable named `height`.

2. Design an algorithm that prompts the user to enter his or her favorite color and stores the user's input in a variable named `color`.

3. Write assignment statements that perform the following operations with the variables a, b, and c.

   (a) Adds 2 to a and stores the result in b

   (b) Multiplies b times 4 and stores the result in a

   (c) Divides a by 3.14 and stores the result in b

   (d) Subtracts 8 from b and stores the result in a

4. Assume the variables `result`, w, x, y, and z are all integers, and that $w = 5$, $x = 4$, $y = 8$, and $z = 2$. What value will be stored in `result` in each of the following statements?

   (a) `Set result = x + y`

   (b) `Set result = z * 2`

   (c) `Set result = y / x`

   (d) `Set result = y - z`

5. Write a pseudocode statement that declares the variable `cost` so it can hold real numbers.

6. Write a pseudocode statement that declares the variable `total` so it can hold integers. Initialize the variable with the value 0.

7. Write a pseudocode statement that assigns the value 27 to the variable `count`.

8. Write a pseudocode statement that assigns the sum of 10 and 14 to the variable `total`.

9. Write a pseudocode statement that subtracts the variable `downPayment` from the variable `total` and assigns the result to the variable `due`.

10. Write a pseudocode statement that multiplies the variable `subtotal` by 0.15 and assigns the result to the variable `totalfee`.

11. If the following pseudocode were an actual program, what would it display?

```
Declare Integer a = 5
Declare Integer b = 2
Declare Integer c = 3
Declare Integer result


Set result = a + b * c
Display result
```

12. If the following pseudocode were an actual program, what would it display?

```
Declare Integer num = 99
Set num = 5
Display num
```

PROGRAMMING EXERCISES

1. Personal Information

   Design a program that displays the following information:

   • Your name

   • Your address, with city, state, and ZIP

   • Your telephone number

   • Your college major

2. **Sales Prediction**

   A company has determined that its annual profit is typically 23 percent of total sales. Design a program that asks the user to enter the projected amount of total sales, and then displays the profit that will be made from that amount.

   Hint: Use the value 0.23 to represent 23 percent.

3. **Land Calculation**

   One acre of land is equivalent to 43,560 square feet. Design a program that asks the user to enter the total square feet in a tract of land and calculates the number of acres in the tract.

   Hint: Divide the amount entered by 43,560 to get the number of acres.

4. **Total Purchase**

   A customer in a store is purchasing five items. Design a program that asks for the price of each item, and then displays the subtotal of the sale, the amount of sales tax, and the total. Assume the sales tax is 6 percent.

5. **Distance Traveled**

   Assuming there are no accidents or delays, the distance that a car travels down the interstate can be calculated with the following formula:

   $$Distance = Speed \times Time$$

   A car is traveling at 60 miles per hour. Design a program that displays the following:

   - The distance the car will travel in 5 hours
   - The distance the car will travel in 8 hours
   - The distance the car will travel in 12 hours

6. **Sales Tax**

   Design a program that will ask the user to enter the amount of a purchase. The program should then compute the state and county sales tax. Assume the state sales tax is 4 percent and the county sales tax is 2 percent. The program should display the amount of the purchase, the state sales tax, the county sales tax, the total sales tax, and the total of the sale (which is the sum of the amount of purchase plus the total sales tax).

   Hint: Use the value 0.02 to represent 2 percent, and 0.04 to represent 4 percent.

7. **Miles-per-Gallon**

   A car's miles-per-gallon (MPG) can be calculated with the following formula:

   $$MPG = Miles\ driven\ /\ Gallons\ of\ gas\ used$$

   Design a program that asks the user for the number of miles driven and the gallons of gas used. It should calculate the car's miles-per-gallon and display the result on the screen.

8. **Tip, Tax, and Total**

   Design a program that calculates the total amount of a meal purchased at a restaurant. The program should ask the user to enter the charge for the food, and then calculate the amount of a 15 percent tip and 7 percent sales tax. Display each of these amounts and the total.

9. **Celsius to Fahrenheit Temperature Converter**

   Design a program that converts Celsius temperatures to Fahrenheit temperatures. The formula is as follows:

   $$F = \frac{9}{5}C + 32$$

   The program should ask the user to enter a temperature in Celsius, and then display the temperature converted to Fahrenheit.

10. **Stock Transaction Program**

    Last month Joe purchased some stock in Acme Software, Inc. Here are the details of the purchase:

    - The number of shares that Joe purchased was 1,000.
    - When Joe purchased the stock, he paid $32.87 per share.
    - Joe paid his stockbroker a commission that amounted to 2 percent of the amount he paid for the stock.

Two weeks later Joe sold the stock. Here are the details of the sale:

- The number of shares that Joe sold was 1,000.
- He sold the stock for $33.92 per share.
- He paid his stockbroker another commission that amounted to 2 percent of the amount he received for the stock.

Design a program that displays the following information:

- The amount of money Joe paid for the stock.
- The amount of commission Joe paid his broker when he bought the stock.
- The amount that Joe sold the stock for.
- The amount of commission Joe paid his broker when he sold the stock.
- Did Joe make money or lose money? Display the amount of profit or loss after Joe sold the stock and paid his broker (both times).

13

MODULES

WWW. VISIT THE COMPANION WEBSITE

Study aids for this chapter are available at
http://www.prenhall.com/floyd

13-1 INTRODUCTION TO MODULES

CONCEPT: **A module is a group of statements that exist within a program for the purpose of performing a specific task.**

In Chapter 11 you learned that a program is a set of instructions that a computer follows to perform a task. Then, in Chapter 12 you saw a simple program that performs the task of calculating an employee's pay. Recall that the program multiplied the number of hours that the employee worked by the employee's hourly pay rate. A more realistic payroll program, however, would do much more than this. In a real-world application, the overall task of calculating an employee's pay would consist of several subtasks, such as the following:

- Getting the employee's hourly pay rate
- Getting the number of hours worked
- Calculating the employee's gross pay
- Calculating overtime pay
- Calculating withholdings for taxes and benefits
- Calculating the net pay
- Printing the paycheck

Most programs perform tasks that are large enough to be broken down into several subtasks. For this reason, programmers usually break down their programs into modules. A module is a group of statements that exist within a program for the purpose of performing a specific task. Instead of writing a large program as one long sequence of statements, it can be written as several small modules, each one performing a specific part of the task. These small modules can then be executed in the desired order to perform the overall task.

This approach is sometimes called *divide and conquer* because a large task is divided into several smaller tasks that are easily performed. Figure 13–1 illustrates this idea by comparing two programs: one that uses a long, complex sequence of statements to perform a task, and another that divides a task into smaller tasks, each of which are performed by a separate module.

When using modules in a program, you generally isolate each task within the program in its own module. For example, a realistic pay calculating program might have the following modules:

- A module that gets the employee's hourly pay rate
- A module that gets the number of hours worked
- A module that calculates the employee's gross pay
- A module that calculates the overtime pay
- A module that calculates the withholdings for taxes and benefits
- A module that calculates the net pay
- A module that prints the paycheck

Although every modern programming language allows you to create modules, they are not always referred to as modules. Modules are commonly called *procedures, subroutines, subprograms, methods,* and *functions.*

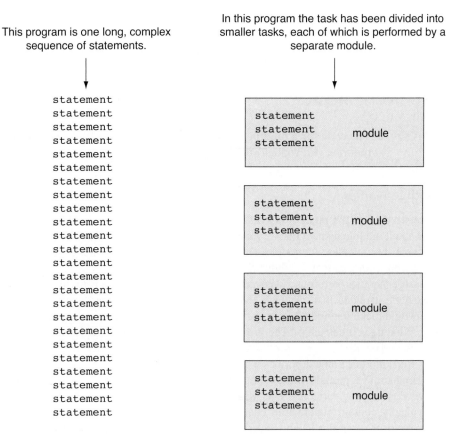

This program is one long, complex sequence of statements.

In this program the task has been divided into smaller tasks, each of which is performed by a separate module.

◄ FIGURE 13–1

Using modules to divide and conquer a large task.

Benefits of Using Modules

A program benefits in the following ways when it is modularized:

Simpler Code   A program's code tends to be simpler and easier to understand when it is modularized. Several small modules are much easier to read than one long sequence of statements.

Code Reuse   Modules also reduce the duplication of code within a program. If a specific operation is performed in several places in a program, a module can be written once to perform that operation, and then be executed any time it is needed. This benefit of using modules is known as *code reuse* because you are writing the code to perform a task once and then reusing it each time you need to perform the task.

Better Testing   When each task within a program is contained in its own module, testing and debugging becomes simpler. Programmers can test each module in a program individually, to determine whether it correctly performs its operation. This makes it easier to isolate and fix errors.

Faster Development   Suppose a programmer or a team of programmers is developing multiple programs. They discover that each of the programs perform several common tasks, such as asking for a username and a password, displaying the current time, and so on. It doesn't make sense to write the code for these tasks multiple times. Instead, modules can be written for the commonly needed tasks, and those modules can be incorporated into each program that needs them.

Easier Facilitation of Teamwork   Modules also make it easier for programmers to work in teams. When a program is developed as a set of modules that each performs an individual task, then different programmers can be assigned the job of writing different modules.

13-2   DEFINING AND CALLING A MODULE

CONCEPT: **The code for a module is known as a module definition. To execute the module, you write a statement that calls it.**

Module Names

Before we discuss the process of creating and using modules, we should mention a few things about module names. Just as you name the variables that you use in a program, you also name the modules. A module's name should be descriptive enough so that anyone reading your code can reasonably guess what the module does.

Because modules perform actions, most programmers prefer to use verbs in module names. For example, a module that calculates gross pay might be named `calculateGrossPay`. This name would make it evident to anyone reading the code that the module calculates something. What does it calculate? The gross pay, of course. Other examples of good module names would be `getHours`, `getPayRate`, `calculateOvertime`, `printCheck`, and so on. Each module name describes what the module does.

When naming a module, most languages require that you follow the same rules that you follow when naming variables. This means that module names cannot contain spaces, cannot typically contain punctuation characters, and usually cannot begin with a number. These are only general rules, however. The specific rules for naming a module will vary slightly with each programming language.

Defining and Calling a Module

To create a module you write its *definition*. In most languages, a module definition has two parts: a header and a body. The *header* indicates the starting point of the module, and the *body* is a list of statements that belong to the module. Here is the general format that we will follow when we write a module definition in pseudocode:

```
Module name()
   statement
   statement          These statements are the body of the module.
   etc.
End Module
```

The first line is the module header. In our pseudocode the header begins with the word `Module`, followed by the name of the module, followed by a set of parentheses. It is a common practice in most programming languages to put a set of parentheses after a module name. Later in this chapter, you will see the actual purpose of the parentheses, but for now, just remember that they come after the module name.

Beginning at the line after the module header, one or more statements will appear. These statements are the module's body, and are performed any time the module is executed. The last line of the definition, after the body, reads `End Module`. This line marks the end of the module definition.

Let's look at an example. Keep in mind that this is not a complete program. We will show the entire pseudocode program in a moment.

```
Module showMessage()
   Display "Hello world."
End Module
```

This pseudocode defines a module named showMessage. As its name implies, the purpose of this module is to show a message on the screen. The body of the showMessage module contains one statement: a Display statement that displays the message "Hello world."

Notice in the previous example that the statement in the body of the module is indented. Indenting the statements in the body of a module is not usually required,[1] but it makes your code much easier to read. By indenting the statements inside a module, you visually set them apart. As a result, you can tell at a glance which statements are inside the module. This practice is a programming style convention that virtually all programmers follow.

Calling a Module   A module definition specifies what a module does, but it does not cause the module to execute. To execute a module, we must call it. In pseudocode we will use the word Call to call a module. This is how we would call the showMessage module:

```
Call showMessage()
```

When a module is called, the computer jumps to that module and executes the statements in the module's body. Then, when the end of the module is reached, the computer jumps back to the part of the program that called the module, and the program resumes execution at that point.

To fully demonstrate how module calling works, we will look at Program 13–1.

PROGRAM 13–1

```
1  Module main()
2     Display "I have a message for you."
3     Call showMessage()
4     Display "That's all, folks!"
5  End Module
6
7  Module showMessage()
8     Display "Hello world"
9  End Module
```

Program Output

```
I have a message for you.
Hello world
That's all, folks!
```

First, notice that Program 13–1 has two modules: a module named main appears in lines 1 through 5, and the showMessage module appears in lines 7 through 9. Many programming languages require that programs have a *main module*. The main module is the program's starting point, and it generally calls other modules. When the end of the main module is reached, the program stops executing. In this book, any time you see a pseudocode program with a module named main, we are using that module as the program's starting point. Likewise, when the end of the main module is reached, the program will stop executing. This is shown in Figure 13–2.

---

[1] The Python language requires you to indent the statements inside a module.

▶ **FIGURE 13-2**

The main module.

The program begins
executing at the
`main` module.

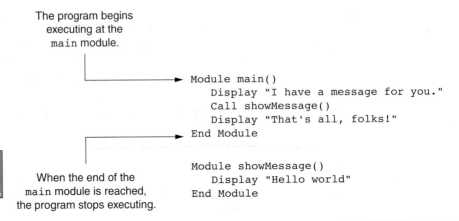

```
Module main()
    Display "I have a message for you."
    Call showMessage()
    Display "That's all, folks!"
End Module

Module showMessage()
    Display "Hello world"
End Module
```

When the end of the
`main` module is reached,
the program stops executing.

COMPUTER NOTE

Many languages, including Java, C, and C++, require that the main module actually be named main, as we have shown in Program 13-1. Some languages, most notably Visual Basic, allow the programmer to designate any module as the one that executes when the program starts.

Let's step through the program. When the program runs, the main module starts and the statement in line 2 displays "I have a message for you." Then, line 3 calls the `showMessage` module. As shown in Figure 13–3, the computer jumps to the `showMessage` module and executes the statements in its body. There is only one statement in the body of the `showMessage` module: the `Display` statement in line 8. This statement displays "Hello world" and then the module ends. As shown in Figure 13–4, the computer jumps back to the part of the program that called showMessage, and resumes execution from that point. In this case, the program resumes execution at line 4, which displays "That's all folks!" The main module ends at line 5, so the program stops executing.

▶ **FIGURE 13-3**

Calling the `showMessage` module.

The computer jumps to
the `showMessage` module
and executes the statements
in its body.

```
Module main()
    Display "I have a message for you."
    Call showMessage()
    Display "That's all, folks!"
End Module

Module showMessage()
    Display "Hello world"
End Module
```

▶ **FIGURE 13-4**

The `showMessage` module returns.

When the `showMessage` module
ends, the computer jumps back
to the part of the program that
called it, and resumes execution
from that point.

```
Module main()
    Display "I have a message for you."
    Call showMessage()
    Display "That's all, folks!"
End Module

Module showMessage()
    Display "Hello world"
End Module
```

COMPUTER NOTE

When a program calls a module, programmers commonly say that the *control* of the program transfers to that module. This simply means that the module takes control of the program's execution.

When the computer encounters a module call, such as the one in line 3 of Program 13–1, it has to perform some operations "behind the scenes" so it will know where to return after the module ends. First, the computer saves the memory address of the location that it should return to. This is typically the statement that appears immediately after the module call.

This memory location is known as the *return point.* Then, the computer jumps to the module and executes the statements in its body. When the module ends, the computer jumps back to the return point and resumes execution.

Flowcharting a Program with Modules

▲ FIGURE 13–5

Module call symbol.

In a flowchart, a module call is shown with a rectangle that has vertical bars at each side, as shown in Figure 13–5. The name of the module that is being called is written on the symbol. The example shown in Figure 13–5 shows how we would represent a call to the showMessage module.

Programmers typically draw a separate flowchart for each module in a program. For example, Figure 13–6 shows how Program 13–1 would be flowcharted. Notice that the figure shows two flowcharts: one for the main module and another for the showMessage module.

◀ FIGURE 13–6

Flowchart for Program 13-1.

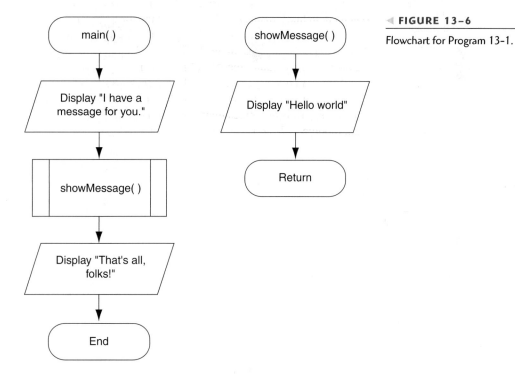

When drawing a flowchart for a module, the starting terminal symbol usually shows the name of the module. The ending terminal symbol in the main module reads End because it marks the end of the program's execution. The ending terminal symbol for all other modules reads Return because it marks the point where the computer returns to the part of the program that called the module.

Top-Down Design

In this section, we have discussed and demonstrated how modules work. You've seen how the computer jumps to a module when it is called, and returns to the part of the program that called the module when the module ends. It is important that you understand these mechanical aspects of modules.

COMPUTER NOTE

The top-down design process is sometimes called stepwise refinement.

Just as important as understanding how modules work is understanding how to design a modularized program. Programmers commonly use a technique known as *top-down design* to break down an algorithm into modules. The process of top-down design is performed in the following manner:

■ The overall task that the program is to perform is broken down into a series of subtasks.

■ Each of the subtasks is examined to determine whether it can be further broken down into more subtasks. This step is repeated until no more subtasks can be identified.

■ Once all of the subtasks have been identified, they are written in code.

This process is called top-down design because the programmer begins by looking at the topmost level of tasks that must be performed, and then breaks down those tasks into lower levels of subtasks.

Hierarchy Charts

Flowcharts are good tools for graphically depicting the flow of logic inside a module, but they do not give a visual representation of the relationships between modules. Programmers commonly use *hierarchy charts* for this purpose. A hierarchy chart, which is also known as a *structure chart,* shows boxes that represent each module in a program. The boxes are connected in a way that illustrates their relationship to one another. Figure 13–7 shows an example of a hierarchy chart for a pay calculating program.

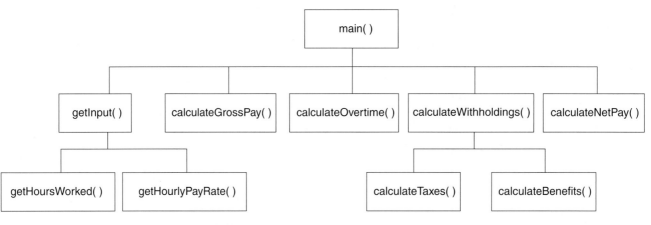

▲ **FIGURE 13-7**

A hierarchy chart.

The chart shown in Figure 13–7 shows the main module as the topmost module in the hierarchy. The main module calls five other modules: `getInput`, `calculateGrossPay`, `calculateOvertime`, `calculateWithholdings`, and `calculateNetPay`. The `getInput` module calls two additional modules: `getHoursWorked` and `getHourlyPayRate`. The `calculateWithholdings` module also calls two modules: `calculateTaxes` and `calculateBenefits`.

Notice that the hierarchy chart does not show the steps that are taken inside a module. Because they do not reveal any details about how modules work, they do not replace flowcharts or pseudocode.

In the Spotlight:

Defining and Calling Modules

Professional Appliance Service, Inc. offers maintenance and repair services for household appliances. The owner wants to give each of the company's service technicians a small handheld computer that displays step-by-step instructions for many of the repairs that they perform. To see how this might work, the owner has asked you to develop a program that displays the following instructions for disassembling an ACME laundry dyer:

Step 1: Unplug the dryer and move it away from the wall.

Step 2: Remove the six screws from the back of the dryer.

Step 3: Remove the dryer's back panel.

Step 4: Pull the top of the dryer straight up.

During your interview with the owner, you determine that that the program should display the steps one at a time. You decide that after each step is displayed, the user will be asked to press a key to see the next step. Here is the algorithm for the program:

1. Display a starting message, explaining what the program does.
2. Ask the user to press a key to see Step 1.
3. Display the instructions for Step 1.
4. Ask the user to press a key to see the next step.
5. Display the instructions for Step 2.
6. Ask the user to press a key to see the next step.
7. Display the instructions for Step 3.
8. Ask the user to press a key to see the next step.
9. Display the instructions for Step 4.

This algorithm lists the top level of tasks that the program needs to perform, and becomes the basis of the program's main module. Figure 13–8 shows the program's structure in a hierarchy chart.

▶ **FIGURE 13-8**

Hierarchy chart for the program.

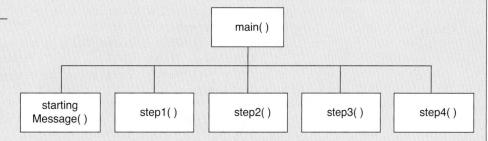

As you can see from the hierarchy chart, the main module will call several other modules. Here are summaries of those modules:

- startingMessage—This module will display the starting message that tells the technician what the program does.
- step1—This module will display the instructions for Step 1.
- step2—This module will display the instructions for Step 2.
- step3—This module will display the instructions for Step 3.
- step4—This module will display the instructions for Step 4.

Between calls to these modules, the main module will instruct the user to press a key to see the next step in the instructions. Program 13–2 shows the pseudocode for the program. Figure 13–9 shows the flowchart for the main module, and Figure 13–10 shows the flowcharts for the startingMessage, step1, step2, step3, and step4 modules.

PROGRAM 13-2

```
1   Module main()
2      // Display the starting message.
3      Call startingMessage()
4      Display "Press a key to see Step 1."
5      Input
6
7      // Display Step 1.
8      Call step1()
9      Display "Press a key to see Step 2."
10     Input
11
12     // Display Step 2.
13     Call step2()
14     Display "Press a key to see Step 3."
15     Input
16
17     // Display Step 3.
18     Call step3()
19     Display "Press a key to see Step 4."
20     Input
21
22     // Display Step 4.
23     Call step4()
24  End Module
25
26  // The startingMessage module displays
27  // the program's starting message.
28  Module startingMessage()
29     Display "This program tells you how to"
30     Display "disassemble an ACME laundry dryer."
31     Display "There are 4 steps in the process."
32  End Module
33
34     // The step1 module displays the instructions
35     // for Step 1.
36  Module step1()
37     Display "Step 1: Unplug the dryer and"
38     Display "move it away from the wall."
39  End Module
```

```
40
41   // The step2 module displays the instructions
42   // for Step 2.
43   Module step2()
44     Display "Step 2: Remove the six screws"
45     Display "from the back of the dryer."
46   End Module
47
48   // The step3 module displays the instructions
49   // for Step 3.
50   Module step3()
51     Display "Step 3: Remove the dryer's"
52     Display "back panel."
53   End Module
54
55   // The step4 module displays the instructions
56   // for Step 4.
57   Module step4()
58     Display "Step 4: Pull the top of the"
59     Display "dryer straight up."
60   End Module
```

Program Output

```
This program tells you how to
disassemble an ACME laundry dryer.
Display "There are 4 steps in the process."
Press a key to see Step 1.
[Enter]
Step 1: Unplug the dryer and
move it away from the wall.
Press a key to see Step 2.
[Enter]
Step 2: Remove the six screws
from the back of the dryer.
Press a key to see Step 3.
[Enter]
Step 3: Remove the dryer's
back panel.
Press a key to see Step 4.
[Enter]
Step 4: Pull the top of the
dryer straight up.
```

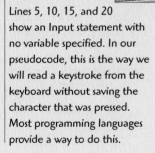

COMPUTER NOTE

Lines 5, 10, 15, and 20 show an Input statement with no variable specified. In our pseudocode, this is the way we will read a keystroke from the keyboard without saving the character that was pressed. Most programming languages provide a way to do this.

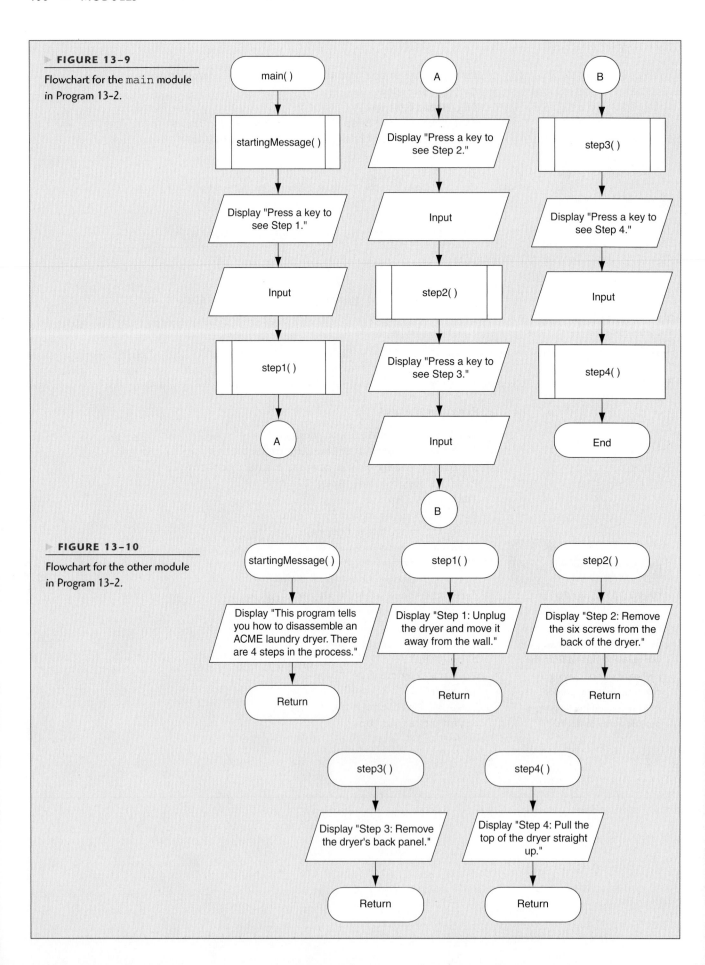

▶ FIGURE 13–9

Flowchart for the main module in Program 13-2.

▶ FIGURE 13–10

Flowchart for the other module in Program 13-2.

13-3 LOCAL VARIABLES

CONCEPT: A local variable is declared inside a module and cannot be accessed by statements that are outside the module. Different modules can have local variables with the same names because the modules cannot see each other's local variables.

In most programming languages, a variable that is declared inside a module is called *a local variable*. A local variable belongs to the module in which it is declared, and only statements inside that module can access the variable. (The term *local* is meant to indicate that the variable can be used only locally, within the module in which it is declared.)

An error will occur if a statement in one module tries to access a local variable that belongs to another module. For example, look at the pseudocode in Program 13–3.

PROGRAM 13-3

```
 1  Module main()
 2     Call getName()
 3     Display "Hello ", name        ◄──────── This will cause an error!
 4  End Module
 5
 6  Module getName()
 7     Declare String name    ◄──────── This is local variable.
 8     Display "Enter your name."
 9     Input name
10  End Module
```

The name variable is declared in line 7, inside the getName module. Because it is declared inside the getName module, it is a local variable belonging to that module. Line 8 prompts the user to enter his or her name, and the Input statement in line 9 stores the user's input in the name variable.

The main module calls the getName module in line 2. Then, the Display statement in line 3 tries to access the name variable. This results in an error because the name variable is local to the getName module, and statements in the main module cannot access it.

Scope and Local Variables

Programmers commonly use the term *scope* to describe the part of a program in which a variable may be accessed. A variable is visible only to statements inside the variable's scope.

A local variable's scope usually begins at the variable's declaration and ends at the end of the module in which the variable is declared. The variable cannot be accessed by statements that are outside this region. This means that a local variable cannot be accessed by code that is outside the module, or inside the module but before the variable's declaration. For example, look at the following code. It has an error because the Input statement tries to store a value in the name variable, but the statement is outside the variable's scope. Moving the variable declaration to a line before the Input statement will fix this error.

```
Module getName()
   Display "Enter your name."
   Input name    ◄──────────  This statement will cause an error because
   Declare String name        the name variable has not been declared yet.
End Module
```

Duplicate Variable Names

In most programming languages, you cannot have two variables with the same name in the same scope. For example, look at the following module:

```
Module getTwoAges()
    Declare Integer age
    Display "Enter your age."
    Input age

    Declare Integer age  ◄─────────────  This will cause an error!
    Display "Enter your pet's age."       A variable named age has
    Input age                             already been declared.
End Module
```

This module declares two local variables named age. The second variable declaration will cause an error because a variable named age has already been declared in the module. Renaming one of the variables will fix this error.

Although you cannot have two local variables with the same name in the same module, it is usually okay for a local variable in one module to have the same name as a local variable in a different module. For example, suppose a program has two modules: getPersonAge and getPetAge. It would be legal for both modules to have a local variable named age.

13-4 PASSING ARGUMENTS TO MODULES

CONCEPT: An argument is any piece of data that is passed into a module when the module is called. A parameter is a variable that receives an argument that is passed into a module.

Sometimes it is useful not only to call a module, but also to send one or more pieces of data into the module. Pieces of data that are sent into a module are known as *arguments*. The module can use its arguments in calculations or other operations.

If you want a module to receive arguments when it is called, you must equip the module with one or more parameter variables. A *parameter variable,* often simply called a *parameter,* is a special variable that receives an argument when a module is called. Here is an example of a pseudocode module that has a parameter variable:

```
Module doubleNumber(Integer value)
    Declare Integer result
    Set result = value * 2
    Display result
End Module
```

This module's name is doubleNumber. Its purpose is to accept an integer number as an argument and display the value of that number doubled. Look at the module header and notice the words Integer value that appear inside the parentheses. This is the declaration of a parameter variable. The parameter variable's name is value and its data type is Integer. The purpose of this variable is to receive an Integer argument when the module is called. Program 13–4 demonstrates the module in a complete program.

PROGRAM 13-4

```
1   Module main()
2      Call doubleNumber(4)
3   End Module
4
5   Module doubleNumber(Integer value)
6      Declare Integer result
7      Set result = value * 2
8      Display result
9   End Module
```

Program Output

```
8
```

When this program runs, the main module will begin executing. The statement in line 2 calls the `doubleNumber` module. Notice that the number 4 appears inside the parentheses. This is an argument that is being passed to the `doubleNumber` module. When this statement executes, the `doubleNumber` module will be called with the number 4 copied into the value parameter variable. This is shown in Figure 13–11.

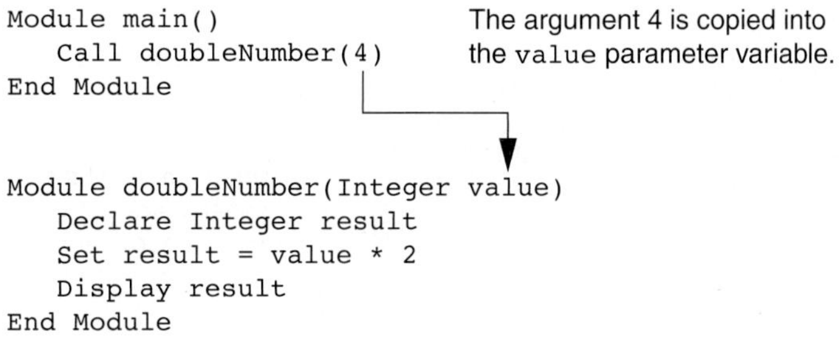

```
Module main()                              The argument 4 is copied into
   Call doubleNumber(4)                    the value parameter variable.
End Module
                          │
                          │
                          ▼
Module doubleNumber(Integer value)
   Declare Integer result
   Set result = value * 2
   Display result
End Module
```

◀ **FIGURE 13–11**

The argument 4 is copied into the value parameter variable.

Let's step through the `doubleNumber` module. As we do, remember that the value parameter variable will contain the number that was passed into it as an argument. In this program, that number is 4.

Line 6 declares a local `Integer` variable named `result`. Then, line 7 assigns the value of the expression `value * 2` to result. Because the `value` variable contains 4, this line assigns 8 to result. Line 8 displays the contents of the `result variable`. The module ends at line 9.

For example, if we had called the module as follows:

```
Call doubleNumber(5)
```

the module would have displayed 10.

We can also pass the contents of a variable as an argument. For example, look at Program 13–5. The `main` module declares an `Integer` variable named `number` in line 2. Lines 3 and 4 prompt the user to enter a number, and line 5 reads the user's input into the `number` variable. Notice that in line 6 `number` is passed as an argument to the `doubleNumber` module, which causes the `number` variable's contents to be copied into the `value` parameter variable. This is shown in Figure 13–12.

PROGRAM 13-5

```
1   Module main()
2       Declare Integer number
3       Display "Enter a number and I will display"
4       Display "that number doubled."
5       Input number
6       Call doubleNumber(number)
7   End Module
8
9   Module doubleNumber(Integer value)
10      Declare Integer result
11      Set result = value * 2
12      Display result
13  End Module
```

Program Output (with Input Shown in Bold)

```
Enter a number and I will display
that number doubled.
20 [Enter]
40
```

▶ **FIGURE 13-12**

The contents of the number variable passed as an argument.

```
Module main()
    Declare Integer number
    Display "Enter a number and I will display"
    Display "that number doubled."
    Input number
    Call doubleNumber(number)
End Module                              The contents of the number
                                    ┌──┐ variable are copied into the
                              └─────│20│─┐ value parameter variable.
                                    └──┘ │
                                         ▼
Module doubleNumber(Integer value)
    Declare Integer result
    Set result = value * 2
    Display result
End Module
```

Argument and Parameter Compatibility

When you pass an argument to a module, most programming languages require that the argument and the receiving parameter variable be of the same data type. If you try to pass an argument of one type into a parameter variable of another type, an error usually occurs. For example, Figure 13–13 shows that you cannot pass a real number or a Real variable into an Integer parameter.

▶ **FIGURE 13-13**

Arguments and parameter variables must be of the same type.

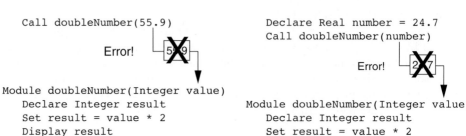

Parameter Variable Scope

Earlier in this chapter, you learned that a variable's scope is the part of the program in which the variable may be accessed. A variable is visible only to statements inside the variable's scope. A parameter variable's scope is usually the entire module in which the parameter is declared. No statement outside the module can access the parameter variable.

Passing Multiple Arguments

Most languages allow you to write modules that accept multiple arguments. Program 13–6 shows a pseudocode module named showSum, that accepts two Integer arguments. The module adds the two arguments and displays their sum.

PROGRAM 13-6

```
1   Module main()
2      Display "The sum of 12 and 45 is:"
3      Call showSum(12, 45)
4   End Module
5
6   Module showSum(Integer num1, Integer num2)
7      Declare Integer result
8      Set result = num1 + num2
9      Display result
10  End Module
```

Program Output

```
The sum of 12 and 45 is:
57
```

Notice that two parameter variables, num1 and num2, are declared inside the parentheses in the module header. This is often referred to as a *parameter list*. Also notice that a comma separates the declarations.

The statement in line 3 calls the showSum module and passes two arguments: 12 and 45. The arguments are passed into the parameter variables in the order that they appear in the method call. In other words, the first argument is passed into the first parameter variable, and the second argument is passed into the second parameter variable. So, this statement causes 12 to be passed into the num1 parameter and 45 to be passed into the num2 parameter, as shown in Figure 13–14.

```
Module main()
   Display "The sum of 12 and 45 is"
   Call showSum(12, 45)
End Module



Module showSum(Integer num1, Integer num2)
   Declare Integer result
   Set result = num1 + num2
   Display result
End Module
```

◄ **FIGURE 13-14**

Two arguments passed into two parameters.

Suppose we were to reverse the order in which the arguments are listed in the module call, as shown here:

```
Call showSum(45, 12)
```

This would cause 45 to be passed into the num1 parameter and 12 to be passed into the num2 parameter. The following pseudocode code shows one more example. This time we are passing variables as arguments.

```
Declare Integer value1 = 2
Declare Integer value2 = 3
Call showSum(value1, value2)
```

When the showSum methods executes as a result of this code, the num1 parameter will contain 2 and the num2 parameter will contain 3.

In the Spotlight:

Passing an Argument to a Module

Your friend Michael runs a catering company. Some of the ingredients that his recipes require are measured in cups. When he goes to the grocery store to buy those ingredients, however, they are sold only by the fluid ounce. He has asked you to write a simple program that converts cups to fluid ounces.

You design the following algorithm:

1. Display an introductory screen that explains what the program does.

2. Get the number of cups.

3. Convert the number of cups to fluid ounces and display the result.

This algorithm lists the top level of tasks that the program needs to perform, and becomes the basis of the program's main module. Figure 13–15 shows the program's structure in a hierarchy chart.

▶ **FIGURE 13–15**

Hierarchy chart for the program.

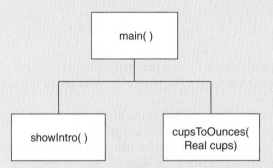

As shown in the hierarchy chart, the main module will call two other modules. Here are summaries of those modules:

■ showIntro—This module will display a message on the screen that explains what the program does.

■ cupsToOunces—This module will accept the number of cups as an argument and calculate and display the equivalent number of fluid ounces.

In addition to calling these modules, the main module will ask the user to enter the number of cups. This value will be passed to the cupsToOunces module. Program 13–7 shows the pseudocode for the program, and Figure 13–16 shows a flowchart.

PROGRAM 13-7

```
 1 Module main()
 2     // Declare a variable for the
 3     // number of cups needed.
 4     Declare Real cupsNeeded
 5
 6     // Display an intro message.
 7     Call showIntro()
 8
 9     // Get the number of cups.
10     Display "Enter the number of cups."
11     Input cupsNeeded
12
13     // Convert cups to ounces.
14     Call cupsToOunces(cupsNeeded)
15 End Module
16
17 // The showIntro module displays an
18 // introductory screen.
19 Module showIntro()
20     Display "This program converts measurements"
21     Display "in cups to fluid ounces. For your"
22     Display "reference the formula is:"
23     Display "    1 cup = 8 fluid ounces."
24 End Module
25
26 // The cupsToOunces module accepts a number
27 // of cups and displays the equivalent number
28 // of ounces.
29 Module cupsToOunces(Real cups)
30     // Declare variables.
31     Declare Real ounces
32
33     // Convert cups to ounces.
34     Set ounces = cups * 8
35
36     // Display the result.
37     Display "That converts to ",
38             ounces, " ounces."
39 End Module
```

Program Output (with Input Shown in Bold)

```
This program converts measurements
in cups to fluid ounces. For your
reference the formula is:
    1 cup = 8 fluid ounces.
Enter the number of cups.
```
2 [Enter]
```
That converts to 16 ounces.
```

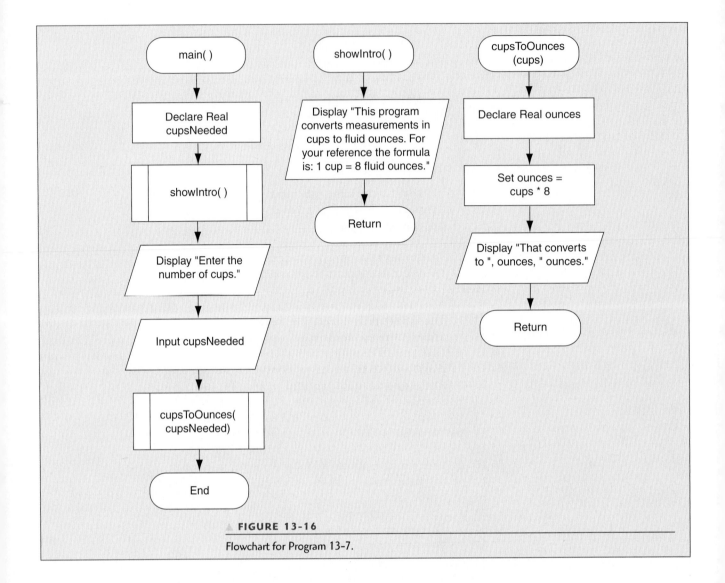

FIGURE 13-16

Flowchart for Program 13-7.

Passing Arguments by Value and by Reference

Many programming languages provide two different ways to pass arguments: by value and by reference. Before studying these techniques in detail, we should mention that different languages have their own way of doing each. In this chapter, we will teach you the fundamental concepts behind these techniques, and show you how to model them in pseudocode. When you begin to use these techniques in an actual language, you will need to learn the details of how they are carried out in that language.

Passing Arguments by Value

All of the example programs that we have looked at so far pass arguments by value. Arguments and parameter variables are separate items in memory. Passing an argument *by value* means that only a copy of the argument's value is passed into the parameter variable. If the contents of the parameter variable are changed inside the module, it has no effect on the argument in the calling part of the program. For example, look at Program 13–8.

The `main` module declares a local variable named `number` in line 2, and initializes it to the value 99. As a result, the `Display` statement in line 5 displays "The number is 99." The

PROGRAM 13-8

```
 1 Module main()
 2    Declare Integer number = 99
 3
 4    // Display the value stored in number.
 5    Display "The number is ", number
 6
 7    // Call the changeMe module, passing
 8    // the number variable as an argument.
 9    Call changeMe(number)
10
11    // Display the value of number again.
12    Display "The number is", number
13 End Module
14
15 Module changeMe(Integer myValue)
16    Display "I am changing the value."
17
18    // Set the myValue parameter variable
19    // to 0.
20    Set myValue = 0
21
22    // Display the value in myValue.
23    Display "Now the number is ", myValue
24 End Module
```

Program Output

```
The number is 99
I am changing the number.
Now the number is 0
The number is 99
```

number variable's value is then passed as an argument to the changeMe module in line 9. This means that in the changeMe module the value 99 will be copied into the myValue parameter variable.

Inside the changeMe module, in line 20, the myValue parameter variable is set to 0. As a result, the Display statement in line 23 displays "Now the number is 0". The module ends, and control of the program returns to the main module.

The next statement to execute is the Display statement in line 12. This statement displays "The number is 99". Even though the parameter variable myValue was changed in the changeMe method, the argument (the number variable in main) was not modified.

Passing an argument is a way that one module can communicate with another module. When the argument is passed by value, the communication channel works in only one direction: the calling module can communicate with the called module. The called module, however, cannot use the argument to communicate with the calling module.

Passing Arguments by Reference

Passing an argument *by reference* means that the argument is passed into a special type of parameter known as a *reference variable*. When a reference variable is used as a parameter in a module, it allows the module to modify the argument in the calling part of the program.

A reference variable acts as an alias for the variable that was passed into it as an argument. It is called a reference variable because it references the other variable. Anything that you do to the reference variable is actually done to the variable it references.

Reference variables are useful for establishing two-way communication between modules. When a module calls another module and passes a variable by reference, communication between the modules can take place in the following ways:

■ The calling module can communicate with the called module by passing an argument.

■ The called module can communicate with the calling module by modifying the value of the argument via the reference variable.

In pseudocode we will declare that a parameter is a reference variable by writing the word Ref before the parameter variable's name in the module header. For example, look at the following pseudocode module:

```
Module setToZero(Integer Ref value)
    Set value = 0
End Module
```

The word Ref indicates that value is a reference variable. The module stores 0 in the value parameter. Because value is a reference variable, this action is actually performed on the variable that was passed to the module as an argument. Program 13–9 demonstrates this module.

In the main module the variable x is initialized with 99, the variable y is initialized with

---

PROGRAM 13-9

```
 1 Module main()
 2     // Declare and initialize some variables.
 3     Declare Integer x = 99
 4     Declare Integer y = 100
 5     Declare Integer z = 101
 6
 7     // Display the values in those variables.
 8     Display "x is set to ", x
 9     Display "y is set to ", y
10     Display "z is set to ", z
11
12     // Pass each variable to setToZero.
13     Call setToZero(x)
14     Call setToZero(y)
15     Call setToZero(z)
16
17     // Display the values now.
18     Display "----------------"
19     Display "x is set to ", x
20     Display "y is set to ", y
21     Display "z is set to ", z
```

```
22 End Module
23
24 Module setToZero(Integer Ref value)
25     Set value = 0
26 End Module
```

Program Output

```
x is set to 99
y is set to 100
z is set to 101
----------------
x is set to 0
y is set to 0
z is set to 0
```

COMPUTER NOTE

In an actual program you should never use variable names like x, y, and z. This particular program is meant for demonstration purposes, however, and these simple names are adequate.

100, and the variable z is initialized with 101. Then, in lines 13 through 15 those variables are passed as arguments to the setToZero module. Each time setToZero is called, the variable that is passed as an argument is set to 0. This is shown when the values of the variables are displayed in lines 19 through 21.

COMPUTER NOTE

Normally, only variables may be passed by reference. If you attempt to pass a non-variable argument into a reference variable parameter, an error will result. Using the setToZero module as an example, the following statement will generate an error:

```
// This is an error!
setToZero(5);
```

In the Spotlight:

Passing an Argument by Reference

In the previous *In the Spotlight* case study, we developed a program that your friend Michael can use in his catering business. The program does exactly what Michael wants it to do: it converts cups to fluid ounces. After studying the program that we initially wrote, however, you believe that you can improve the design. As shown in the following pseudocode, the main module contains the code that reads the user's input. This code should really be treated as a separate subtask, and put in its own module. If this change is made, the program will be like the new hierarchy chart shown in Figure 13–17.

```
Module main()
    // Declare a variable for the
    // number of cups needed.
    Declare Real cupsNeeded

    // Display an intro message.
    showIntro()

    // Get the number of cups.
    Display "Enter the number of cups." ⎫ This code can be put
    Input cupsNeeded                    ⎬ in its own module.
                                        ⎭
    // Convert cups to ounces.
    cupsToOunces(cupsNeeded)
End Module
```

▶ **FIGURE 13–17**

Revised hierarchy chart.

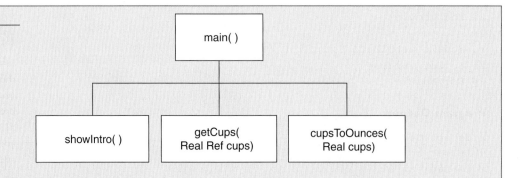

This version of the hierarchy chart shows a new module: getCups. Here is the pseudocode for the getCups module:

```
Module getCups(Real Ref cups)
    Display "Enter the number of cups."
    Input cups
End Module
```

The getCups module has a parameter, cups, which is a reference variable. The module prompts the user to enter the number of cups and then stores the user's input in the cups parameter. When the main module calls getCups, it will pass the local variable cupsNeed as an argument. Because it will be passed by reference, it will contain the user's input when the module returns. Program 13–10 shows the revised pseudocode for the program, and Figure 13–18 shows a flowchart.

COMPUTER NOTE

In this case study, we improved the design of an existing program without changing the behavior of the program. In a nutshell, we "cleaned up" the design. Programmers call this *refactoring*.

PROGRAM 13-10

```
 1 Module main()
 2     // Declare a variable for the
 3     // number of cups needed.
 4     Declare Real cupsNeeded
 5
 6     // Display an intro message.
 7     Call showIntro()
 8
 9     // Get the number of cups.
10     Call getCups(cupsNeeded)
11
12     // Convert cups to ounces.
13     Call cupsToOunces(cupsNeeded)
14 End Module
15
16 // The showIntro module displays an
17 // introductory screen.
18 Module showIntro()
19     Display "This program converts measurements"
20     Display "in cups to fluid ounces. For your"
21     Display "reference the formula is:"
22     Display "    1 cup = 8 fluid ounces."
23 End Module
24
25 // The getCups module gets the number of cups
26 // and stores it in the reference variable cups.
27 Module getCups(Real Ref cups)
28     Display "Enter the number of cups."
29     Input cups
30 End Module
```

```
31
32 // The cupsToOunces module accepts a number
33 // of cups and displays the equivalent number
34 // of ounces.
35 Module cupsToOunces(Real cups)
36    // Declare variables.
37    Declare Real ounces
38
39    // Convert cups to ounces.
40    Set ounces = cups * 8
41
42    // Display the result.
43    Display "That converts to ",
44             ounces, " ounces."
45 End Module
```

Program Output (with Input Shown in Bold)

```
This program converts measurements
in cups to fluid ounces. For your
reference the formula is:
    1 cup = 8 fluid ounces.
Enter the number of cups.
2 [Enter]
That converts to 16 ounces.
```

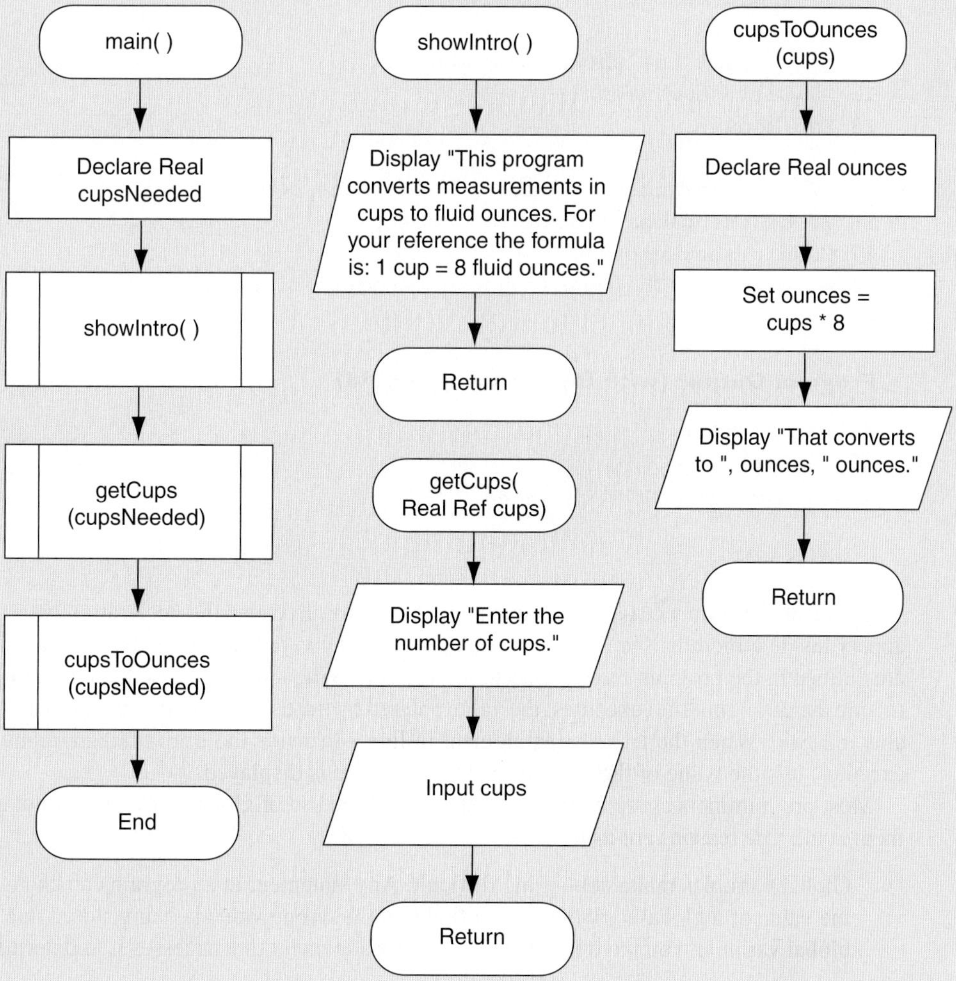

FIGURE 13-18

Flowchart for Program 13-10.

13-5 GLOBAL VARIABLES AND GLOBAL CONSTANTS

CONCEPT: **A global variable is accessible to all the modules in a program.**

Global Variables

A *global variable* is a variable that is visible to every module in the program. A global variable's scope is the entire program, so all of the modules in the program can access a global variable. In most programming languages, you create a global variable by writing its declaration statement outside of all the modules, usually at the top of the program. Program 13–11 shows how you can declare a global variable in pseudocode.

PROGRAM 13-11

```
 1 // The following declares a global Integer variable.
 2 Declare Integer number
 3
 4 // The main module
 5 Module main()
 6    // Get a number from the user and store it
 7    // in the global variable number.
 8    Display "Enter a number."
 9    Input number
10
11    // Call the showNumber module.
12    Call showNumber()
13 End Module
14
15 // The showNumber module displays the contents
16 // of the global variable number.
17 Module showNumber()
18    Display "The number you entered is ", number
19 End Module
```

Program Output (with Input Shown in Bold)

```
Enter a number.
22 [Enter]
The number you entered is 22
```

Line 2 declares an `Integer` variable named `number`. Because the declaration does not appear inside a module, the `number` variable is a global variable. All of the modules that are defined in the program have access to the variable. When the `Input` statement in line 9 (inside the `main` module) executes, the value entered by the user is stored in the global variable `number`. When the `Display` statement in line 18 (inside the `showNumber` module) executes, it is the value of the same global variable that is displayed.

Most programmers agree that you should restrict the use of global variables, or not use them at all. The reasons are as follows:

■ Global variables make debugging difficult. Any statement in a program can change the value of a global variable. If you find that the wrong value is being stored in a global variable, you have to track down every statement that accesses it to determine where the bad value is coming from. In a program with thousands of lines of code, this can be difficult.

- Modules that use global variables are usually dependent on those variables. If you want to use such a module in a different program, most likely you will have to redesign it so it does not rely on the global variable.

- Global variables make a program hard to understand. A global variable can be modified by any statement in the program. If you are to understand any part of the program that uses a global variable, you have to be aware of all the other parts of the program that access the global variable.

In most cases, you should declare variables locally and pass them as arguments to the modules that need to access them.

Global Constants

Although you should try to avoid the use of global variables, it is permissible to use global constants in a program. A *global constant* is a named constant that is available to every module in the program. Because a global constant's value cannot be changed during the program's execution, you do not have to worry about many of the potential hazards that are associated with the use of global variables.

Global constants are typically used to represent unchanging values that are needed throughout a program. For example, suppose a banking program uses a named constant to represent an interest rate. If the interest rate is used in several modules, it is easier to create a global constant, rather than a local named constant in each module. This also simplifies maintenance. If the interest rate changes, only the declaration of the global constant has to be changed, instead of several local declarations.

In the Spotlight:

Using Global Constants

Marilyn works for Integrated Systems, Inc., a software company that has a reputation for providing excellent fringe benefits. One of their benefits is a quarterly bonus that is paid to all employees. Another benefit is a retirement plan for each employee. The company contributes 5 percent of each employee's gross pay and bonuses to their retirement plans. Marilyn wants to design a program that will calculate the company's contribution to an employee's retirement account for a year. She wants the program to show the amount of contribution for the employee's gross pay and for the bonuses separately.

Here is an algorithm for the program:

1. Get the employee's annual gross pay.

2. Get the amount of bonuses paid to the employee.

3. Calculate and display the contribution for the gross pay.

4. Calculate and display the contribution for the bonuses.

Figure 13–19 shows a hierarchy chart for the program. The pseudocode for the program is shown in Program 13–12, and a set of flowcharts is shown in Figure 13–20.

Hierarchy chart.

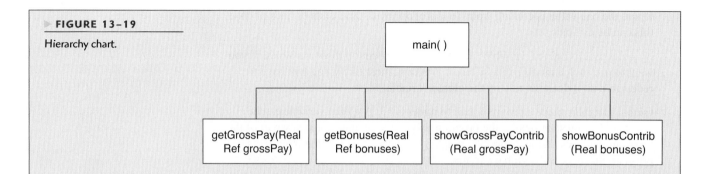

PROGRAM 13-12

```
1 // Global constant for the rate of contribution.
2 Constant Real CONTRIBUTION_RATE = 0.05
3
4 // main module
5 Module main()
6     // Local variables
7     Declare Real annualGrossPay
8     Declare Real totalBonuses
9
10     // Get the annual gross pay.
11     Call getGrossPay(annualGrossPay)
12
13     // Get the total of the bonuses.
14     Call getBonuses(totalBonuses)
15
16     // Display the contribution for
17     // the gross pay.
18     Call showGrossPayContrib(annualGrossPay)
19
20     // Display the contribution for
21     // the bonuses.
22     Call showBonusContrib(totalBonuses)
23 End Module
24
25 // The getGrossPay module gets the
26 // gross pay and stores it in the
27 // grossPay reference variable.
28 Module getGrossPay(Real Ref grossPay)
29     Display "Enter the total gross pay."
30     Input grossPay
31 End Module
32
33 // The getBonuses module gets the
34 // amount of bonuses and stores it
35 // in the bonuses reference variable.
36 Module getBonuses(Real Ref bonuses)
37     Display "Enter the amount of bonuses."
38     Input bonuses
39 End Module
40
```

```
41 // The showGrossPayContrib module
42 // accepts the gross pay as an argument
43 // and displays the retirement contribution
44 // for gross pay.
45 Module showGrossPayContrib(Real grossPay)
46     Declare Real contrib
47     Set contrib = grossPay * CONTRIBUTION_RATE
48     Display "The contribution for the gross pay"
49     Display "is $", contrib
50 End Module
51
52 // The showBonusContrib module accepts
53 // the bonus amount as an argument and
54 // displays the retirement contribution
55 // for bonuses.
56 Module showBonusContrib(Real bonuses)
57     Declare Real contrib
58     Set contrib = bonuses * CONTRIBUTION_RATE
59     Display "The contribution for the bonuses"
60     Display "is $", contrib
61 End Module
```

Program Output (with Input Shown in Bold)

```
Enter the total gross pay.
80000.00 [Enter]
Enter the amount of bonuses.
20000.00 [Enter]
The contribution for the gross pay
is $4000
The contribution for the bonuses
is $1000
```

A global constant named CONTRIBUTION_RATE is declared in line 2, and initialized with the value 0.05. The constant is used in the calculation in line 47 (in the showGrossPayContrib module) and again in line 58 (in the showBonusContrib module). Marilyn decided to use this global constant to represent the 5 percent contribution rate for two reasons:

▪ It makes the program easier to read. When you look at the calculations in lines 47 and 58 it is apparent what is happening.

▪ Occasionally the contribution rate changes. When this happens, it will be easy to update the program by changing the declaration statement in line 2.

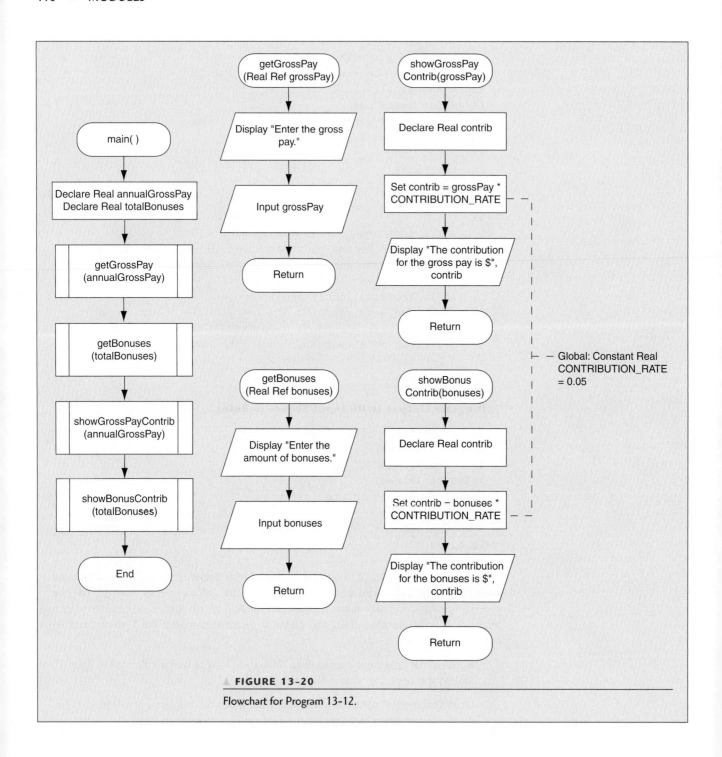

▲ FIGURE 13-20

Flowchart for Program 13-12.

Multiple Choice

1. A group of statements that exist within a program for the purpose of performing a specific task is a(n) _____.

   (a) block

   (b) parameter

   (c) module

   (d) expression

2. A benefit of using modules that helps to reduce the duplication of code within a program is _____.

   (a) code reuse

   (b) divide and conquer

   (c) debugging

   (d) facilitation of teamwork

3. The first line of a module definition is known as the _____.

   (a) body

   (b) introduction

   (c) initialization

   (d) header

4. You _____ the module to execute it.

   (a) define

   (b) call

   (c) import

   (d) export

5. A _____ point is the memory address of the location in the program that the computer will return to when a module ends.

   (a) termination

   (b) module definition

   (c) return

   (d) reference

6. A design technique that programmers use to break down an algorithm into modules is known as _____.

   (a) top-down design

   (b) code simplification

   (c) code refactoring

   (d) hierarchical subtasking

7. A _____ is a diagram that gives a visual representation of the relationships between modules in a program.

   (a) flowchart

   (b) module relationship chart

   (c) symbol chart

   (d) hierarchy chart

8. A _____ is a variable that is declared inside a module.
   (a) global variable
   (b) local variable
   (c) hidden variable
   (d) none of the above; you cannot declare a variable inside a module

9. A(n) _____ is the part of a program in which a variable may be accessed.
   (a) declaration space
   (b) area of visibility
   (c) scope
   (d) mode

10. A(n) _____ is a piece of data that is sent into a module.
    (a) argument
    (b) parameter
    (c) header
    (d) packet

11. A(n) _____ is a special variable that receives a piece of data when a module is called.
    (a) argument
    (b) parameter
    (c) header
    (d) packet

12. When _____, only a copy of the argument's value is passed into the parameter variable.
    (a) passing an argument by reference
    (b) passing an argument by name
    (c) passing an argument by value
    (d) passing an argument by data type

13. When _____, the module can modify the argument in the calling part of the program.
    (a) passing an argument by reference
    (b) passing an argument by name
    (c) passing an argument by value
    (d) passing an argument by data type

14. A variable that is visible to every module in the program is a _____.
    (a) local variable
    (b) universal variable
    (c) program-wide variable
    (d) global variable

15. When possible, you should avoid using _____ variables in a program.
    (a) local
    (b) global
    (c) reference
    (d) parameter

True or False

1. The phrase "divide and conquer" means that all of the programmers on a team should be divided and work in isolation.

2. Modules make it easier for programmers to work in teams.

3. Module names should be as short as possible.

4. Calling a module and defining a module mean the same thing.

5. A flowchart shows the hierarchical relationships between modules in a program.

6. A hierarchy chart does not show the steps that are taken inside a module.

7. A statement in one module can access a local variable in another module.

8. In most programming languages, you cannot have two variables with the same name in the same scope.

9. Programming languages typically require that arguments be of the same data type as the parameters that they are passed to.

10. Most languages do not allow you to write modules that accept multiple arguments.

11. When an argument is passed by reference, the module can modify the argument in the calling part of the program.

12. Passing an argument by value is a means of establishing two-way communication between modules.

Short Answer

1. How do modules help you to reuse code in a program?

2. Name and describe the two parts that a module definition has in most languages.

3. When a module is executing, what happens when the end of the module is reached?

4. What is a local variable? What statements are able to access a local variable?

5. In most languages, where does a local variable's scope begin and end?

6. What is the difference between passing an argument by value and passing it by reference?

7. Why do global variables make a program difficult to debug?

Algorithm Workbench

1. Design a module named `timesTen`. The module should accept an `Integer` argument. When the module is called, it should display the product of its argument multiplied times 10.

2. Examine the following pseudocode module header, and then write a statement that calls the module, passing 12 as an argument.

   ```
   Module showValue(Integer quantity)
   ```

3. Look at the following pseudocode module header:

   ```
   Module myModule(Integer a, Integer b, Integer c)
   ```

   Now look at the following call to myModule:

   ```
   Call myModule(3, 2, 1)
   ```

   When this call executes, what value will be stored in a? What value will be stored in b? What value will be stored in c?

4. Assume that a pseudocode program contains the following module:

   ```
   Module display(Integer arg1, Real arg2, String arg3)
       Display "Here are the values:"
       Display arg1, " ", arg2, " ", arg3
   End Module
   ```

Assume that the same program has a main module with the following variable declarations:

```
Declare Integer age
Declare Real income
Declare String name
```

Write a statement that calls the display module and passes these variables to it.

5. Design a module named getNumber, which uses a reference parameter variable to accept an Integer argument. The module should prompt the user to enter a number and then store the input in the reference parameter variable.

6. What will the following pseudocode program display?

```
Module main()
    Declare Integer x = 1
    Declare Real y = 3.4
    Display x, " ", y
    Call changeUs(x, y)
    Display x, " ", y
End Module

Module changeUs(Integer a, Real b)
{
    Set a = 0
    Set b = 0
    Display a, " ", b
}
```

7. What will the following pseudocode program display?

```
Module main()
    Declare Integer x = 1
    Declare Real y = 3.4
    Display x, " ", y
    Call changeUs(x, y)
    Display x, " ", y
End Module

Module changeUs(Integer Ref a, Real Ref b)
{
    Set a = 0
    Set b = 0.0
    Display a, " ", b
}
```

Programming Exercises

1. Kilometer Converter

Design a modular program that asks the user to enter a distance in kilometers, and then converts that distance to miles. The conversion formula is as follows:

$$Miles = Kilometers \times 0.6214$$

2. Sales Tax Program Refactoring

Programming Exercise 6 in Chapter 12 was the Sales Tax program. For that exercise you were asked to design a program that calculates and displays the county and state sales tax on a purchase. If you have already designed that program, refactor it so the subtasks are in modules. If you have not already designed that program, create a modular design for it.

3. How Much Insurance?

Many financial experts advise that property owners should insure their homes or buildings for at least 80 percent of the amount it would cost to replace the structure. Design a modular program that asks the user to enter the replacement cost of a building and then displays the minimum amount of insurance he or she should buy for the property.

4. Automobile Costs

Design a modular program that asks the user to enter the monthly costs for the following expenses incurred from operating his or her automobile: loan payment, insurance, gas, oil, tires, and maintenance. The program should then display the total monthly cost of these expenses, and the total annual cost of these expenses.

5. Property Tax

A county collects property taxes on the assessment value of property, which is 60 percent of the property's actual value. For example, if an acre of land is valued at $10,000, its assessment value is $6,000. The property tax is then 64¢ for each $100 of the assessment value. The tax for the acre assessed at $6,000 will be $38.40. Design a modular program that asks for the actual value of a piece of property and displays the assessment value and property tax.

6. Body Mass Index

Design a modular program that calculates and displays a person's body mass index (BMI). The BMI is often used to determine whether a person with a sedentary lifestyle is overweight or underweight for their height. A person's BMI is calculated with the following formula:

$$BMI = Weight \times 703/Height^2$$

7. Calories from Fat and Carbohydrates

A nutritionist who works for a fitness club helps members by evaluating their diets. As part of her evaluation, she asks members for the number of fat grams and carbohydrate grams that they consumed in a day. Then, she calculates the number of calories that result from the fat, using the following formula:

$$Calories\ from\ Fat = Fat\ Grams \times 9$$

Next, she calculates the number of calories that result from the carbohydrates, using the following formula:

$$Calories\ from\ Carbs = Carb\ Grams \times 4$$

The nutritionist asks you to design a modular program that will make these calculations.

8. Stadium Seating

There are three seating categories at a stadium. For a softball game, Class A seats cost $15, Class B seats cost $12, and Class C seats cost $9. Design a modular program that asks how many tickets for each class of seats were sold, and then displays the amount of income generated from ticket sales.

9. Paint Job Estimator

A painting company has determined that for every 115 square feet of wall space, one gallon of paint and eight hours of labor will be required. The company charges $20.00 per hour for labor. Design a modular program that asks the user to enter the square feet of wall space to be painted and the price of the paint per gallon. The program should display the following data:

- The number of gallons of paint required
- The hours of labor required
- The cost of the paint
- The labor charges
- The total cost of the paint job

10. **Monthly Sales Tax**

A retail company must file a monthly sales tax report listing the total sales for the month, and the amount of state and county sales tax collected. The state sales tax rate is 4 percent and the county sales tax rate is 2 percent. Design a modular program that asks the user to enter the total sales for the month. From this figure, the application should calculate and display the following:

- The amount of county sales tax
- The amount of state sales tax
- The total sales tax (county plus state)

In the pseudocode, represent the county tax rate (0.02) and the state tax rate (0.04) as named constants.

14

DECISION STRUCTURES AND BOOLEAN LOGIC

WWW. **VISIT THE COMPANION WEBSITE**

Study aids for this chapter are available at
http://www.prenhall.com/floyd

14-1 INTRODUCTION TO DECISION STRUCTURES

CONCEPT: **A decision structure allows a program to perform actions only under certain conditions.**

A control structure is a logical design that controls the order in which a set of statements execute. So far in this book we have used only the simplest type of control structure: the sequence structure. Recall from Chapter 12 that a sequence structure is a set of statements that execute in the order that they appear. For example, the following pseudocode is a sequence structure because the statements execute from top to bottom.

```
Declare Integer age
Display "What is your age?"
Input age
Display "Here is the value that you entered:"
Display age
```

Even in Chapter 13, where you learned about modules, each module was written as a sequence structure. For example, the following module is a sequence structure because the statements in it execute in the order that they appear, from the beginning of the module to the end.

```
Module doubleNumber(Integer value)
    Declare Integer result
    Set result = value * 2
    Display result
End Module
```

Although the sequence structure is heavily used in programming, it cannot handle every type of task. Some problems simply cannot be solved by performing a set of ordered steps, one after the other. For example, consider a pay calculating program that determines whether an employee has worked overtime. If the employee has worked more than 40 hours, he or she gets paid extra for all the hours over 40. Otherwise, the overtime calculation should be skipped. Programs like this require a different type of control structure: one that can execute a set of statements only under certain circumstances. This can be accomplished with a *decision structure*. (Decision structures are also known as *selection structures*.)

In a decision structure's simplest form, a specific action is performed only if a certain condition exists. If the condition does not exist, the action is not performed. The flowchart shown in Figure 14–1 shows how the logic of an everyday decision can be diagrammed as a decision structure. The diamond symbol represents a true/false condition. If the condition is true, we follow one path, which leads to an action being performed. If the condition is false, we follow another path, which skips the action.

▶ **FIGURE 14-1**

A simple decision structure.

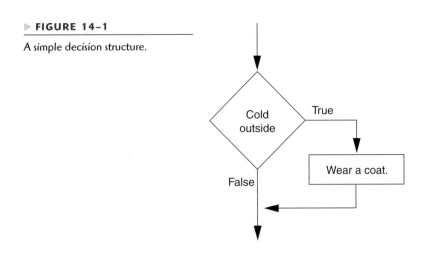

In the flowchart, the diamond symbol indicates some condition that must be tested. In this case, we are determining whether the condition *Cold outside* is true or false. If this condition is true, the action *Wear a coat* is performed. If the condition is false, the action is skipped. The action is *conditionally executed* because it is performed only when a certain condition is true.

Programmers call the type of decision structure shown in Figure 14–1 a *single alternative decision structure*. This is because it provides only one alternative path of execution. If the condition in the diamond symbol is true, we take the alternative path. Otherwise, we exit the structure.

Combining Structures

You cannot use decision structures alone to create a complete program. You use a decision structure to handle any part of a program that needs to test a condition and conditionally execute an action depending on the outcome of the condition. For other parts of a program you need to use other structures. For example, Figure 14–2 shows a complete flowchart that combines a decision structure with two sequence structures.

The flowchart in the figure starts with a sequence structure. Assuming you have an outdoor thermometer in your window, the first step is *Go to the window*, and the next step is *Read thermometer*. A decision structure appears next, testing the condition *Cold outside*. If this is true, the action *Wear a coat* is performed. Another sequence structure appears next. The step *Open the door* is performed, followed by *Go outside*.

Quite often, structures must be nested inside of other structures. For example, look at the partial flowchart in Figure 14–3. It shows a decision structure with a sequence structure nested inside it. The decision structure tests the condition *Cold outside*. If that condition is true, the steps in the sequence structure are executed.

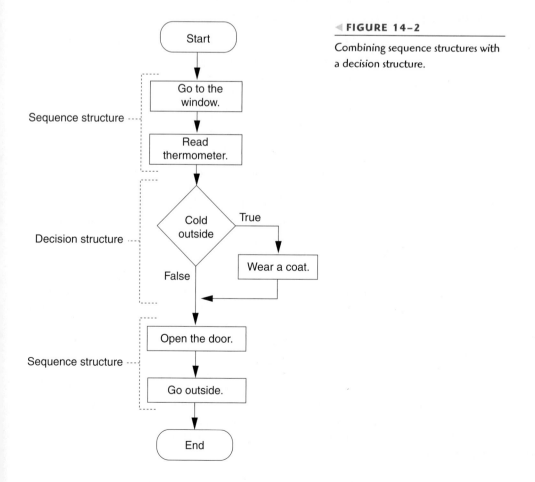

◄ **FIGURE 14–2**

Combining sequence structures with a decision structure.

A sequence structure nested inside a decision structure.

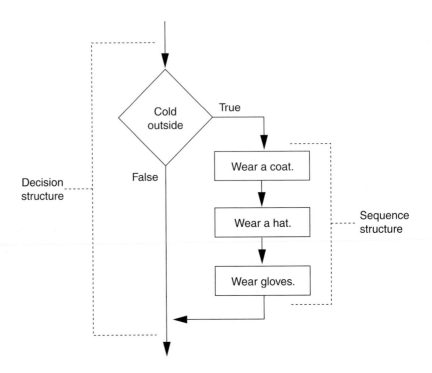

Writing a Decision Structure in Pseudocode

In pseudocode we use the If-Then statement to write a single alternative decision structure. Here is the general format of the If-Then statement:

```
If condition Then
    statement
    statement
    etc.
End If
```

These statements are conditionally executed

For simplicity, we will refer to the line that begins with the word If as the If *clause*, and we will refer to the line that reads End If as the End If *clause*. In the general format, the *condition* is any expression that can be evaluated as either true or false. When the If-Then statement executes, the *condition* is tested. If it is true, the statements that appear between the If clause and the End If are executed. The End If clause marks the end of the If-Then statement.

Boolean Expressions and Relational Operators   All programming languages allow you to create expressions that can be evaluated as either true or false. These are called *Boolean expressions*, named in honor of the English mathematician George Boole. In the 1800s Boole invented a system of mathematics in which the abstract concepts of true and false can be used in computations. The condition that is tested by an If-Then statement must be a Boolean expression.

Typically, the Boolean expression that is tested by an If-Then statement is formed with a relational operator. A *relational operator* determines whether a specific relationship exists between two values. For example, the greater than operator (>) determines whether one value is greater than another. The equal to operator (==) determines whether two values are equal. Table 14–1 lists the relational operators that are commonly available in most programming languages.

▼ TABLE 14-1

Relational operators.

OPERATOR	MEANING
>	Greater than
<	Less than
>=	Greater than or equal to
<=	Less than or equal to
==	Equal to
!=	Not equal to

The following is an example of an expression that uses the greater than (>) operator to compare two variables, length and width:

```
length > width
```

This expression determines whether the value of length is greater than the value of width. If length is greater than width, the value of the expression is true. Otherwise, the value of the expression is false. Because the expression can be only true or false, it is a Boolean expression. The following expression uses the less than operator to determine whether length is less than width:

```
length < width
```

Table 14–2 shows examples of several Boolean expressions that compare the variables x and y.

The >= and <= Operators   Two of the operators, >= and <=, test for more than one relationship. The >= operator determines whether the operand on its left is greater than *or* equal to the operand on its right. For example, assuming that a is 4, b is 6, and c is 4, both of the expressions b >= a and a >= c are true and a >= 5 is false.

The <= operator determines whether the operand on its left is less than or equal to the operand on its right. Once again, assuming that a is 4, b is 6, and c is 4, both a <= c and b <= 10 are true, but b <= a is false.

The == Operator   The == operator determines whether the operand on its left is equal to the operand on its right. If both operands have the same value, the expression is true. Assuming that a is 4, the expression a == 4 is true and the expression a == 2 is false.

In this book, we use two = characters as the equal to operator to avoid confusion with the assignment operator, which is one = character. Several programming languages, most notably Java, C, and C++, also follow this practice.

The != Operator   The != operator is the not equal to operator. It determines whether the operand on its left is not equal to the operand on its right, which is the opposite of the == operator. As before, assuming a is 4, b is 6, and c is 4, both a != b and b != c are true because a is not equal to b and b is not equal to c. However, a != c is false because a is equal to c.

Note that != is the same character sequence used by several languages for the not equal to operator, including Java, C, and C++. Some languages, such as Visual Basic, use <> as the not equal to operator.

Putting It All Together

Let's look at the following example of the If-Then statement in pseudocode:

```
If sales > 50000 Then
    Set bonus = 500.0
End If
```

This statement uses the > operator to determine whether sales is greater than 50,000. If the expression sales > 50000 is true, the variable bonus is assigned 500.0. If the expression is false, however, the assignment statement is skipped. Figure 14–4 shows a flowchart for this section of code.

The following example conditionally executes a set of statements. Figure 14–5 shows a flowchart for this section of code.

```
If sales > 50000 Then
    Set bonus = 500.0
    Set commissionRate = 0.12
    Display "You've met your sales quota!"
End If
```

▼ **TABLE 14–2**

Boolean expressions using relational operators.

EXPRESSION	MEANING
x > y	Is x greater than y?
x < y	Is x less than y?
x >= y	Is x greater than or equal to y?
x <= y	Is x less than or equal to y?
x == y	Is x equal to y?
x != y	Is x not equal to y?

WARNING

When programming in a language that uses == as the equal to operator, take care not to confuse this operator with the assignment operator, which is one = sign. In languages such as Java, C, and C++ the == operator determines whether a variable is equal to another value, but the = operator assigns the value to a variable.

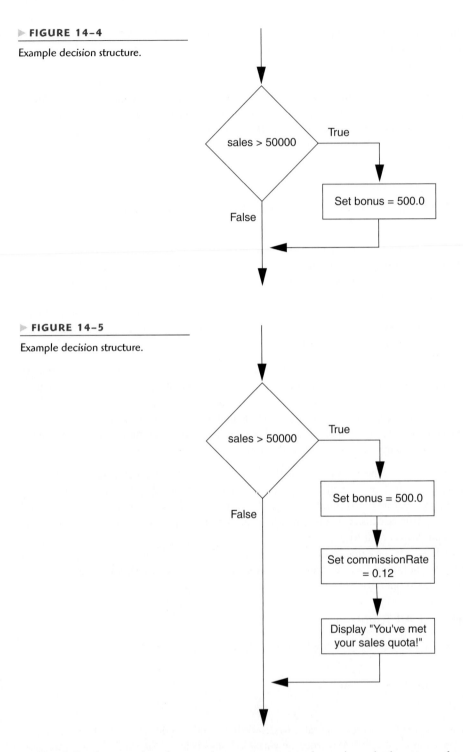

▶ **FIGURE 14–4**

Example decision structure.

▶ **FIGURE 14–5**

Example decision structure.

The following pseudocode uses the == operator to determine whether two values are equal. The expression balance == 0 will be true if the balance variable is set to 0. Otherwise the expression will be false.

```
If balance == 0 Then
    // Statements appearing here will
    // be executed only if balance is
    // equal to 0.
End If
```

The following pseudocode uses the != operator to determine whether two values are *not* equal. The expression choice != 5 will be true if the choice variable is not set to 5. Otherwise the expression will be false.

```
If choice != 5 Then
    // Statements appearing here will
    // be executed only if choice is
    // not equal to 5.
End If
```

Programming Style and the If-Then Statement

As shown in Figure 14–6, you should use the following conventions when you write an If-Then statement:

- Make sure the If clause and the End If clause are aligned.

- Indent the conditionally executed statements that appear between the If clause and the End If clause.

By indenting the conditionally executed statements you visually set them apart from the surrounding code. This makes your program easier to read and debug. Most programmers use this style of writing If-Then statements in both pseudocode and actual code.

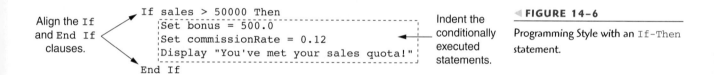

Align the If and End If clauses.

```
If sales > 50000 Then
    Set bonus = 500.0
    Set commissionRate = 0.12
    Display "You've met your sales quota!"
End If
```

Indent the conditionally executed statements.

◀ FIGURE 14–6

Programming Style with an If-Then statement.

In the Spotlight:

Using the If-Then Statement

Kathryn teaches a science class and her students are required to take three tests. She wants to write a program that her students can use to calculate their average test score. She also wants the program to congratulate the student enthusiastically if the average is greater than 95. Here is the algorithm:

1. Get the first test score.

2. Get the second test score.

3. Get the third test score.

4. Calculate the average.

5. Display the average.

6. If the average is greater than 95, congratulate the user.

Program 14–1 shows the pseudocode, and Figure 14–7 shows a flowchart for the program.

PROGRAM 14–1

```
 1 // Declare variables
 2 Declare Real test1, test2, test3, average
 3
 4 // Get test 1
 5 Display "Enter the score for test #1."
 6 Input test1
 7
 8 // Get test 2
 9 Display "Enter the score for test #2."
10 Input test2
11
12 // Get test 3
13 Display "Enter the score for test #3."
14 Input test3
15
16 // Calculate the average score.
17 Set average = (test1 + test2 + test3) / 3
18
19 // Display the average.
20 Display "The average is ", average
21
22 // If the average is greater than 95
23 // congratulate the user.
24 If average > 95 Then
25    Display "Congratulations! Great average!"
26 End If
```

Program Output (with Input Shown in Bold)

Enter the score for test #1.
82 [Enter]
Enter the score for test #2.
76 [Enter]
Enter the score for test #3.
91 [Enter]
The average is 83

Program Output (with Input Shown in Bold)

Enter the score for test #1.
93 [Enter]
Enter the score for test #2.
99 [Enter]
Enter the score for test #3.
96 [Enter]
The average is 96
Congratulations! Great average!

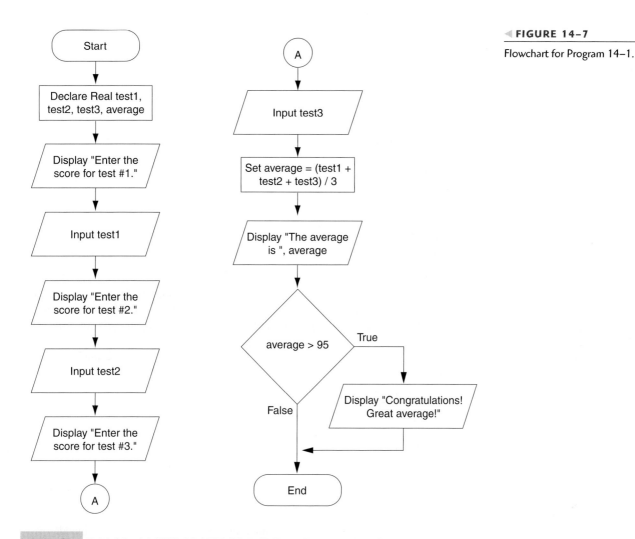

Flowchart for Program 14–1.

14-2 DUAL ALTERNATIVE DECISION STRUCTURES

CONCEPT: **A dual alternative decision structure will execute one group of statements if its Boolean expression is true, or another group if its Boolean expression is false.**

A *dual alternative decision structure* has two possible paths of execution—one path is taken if a condition is true, and the other path is taken if the condition is false. Figure 14–8 shows a flowchart for a dual alternative decision structure.

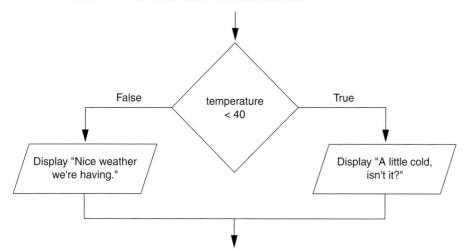

◀ FIGURE 14–8

A dual alternative decision structure.

The decision structure in the flowchart tests the condition temperature < 40. If this condition is true, the statement Display "A little cold, isn't it?" is performed. If the condition is false, the statement Display "Nice weather we're having." is performed.

In pseudocode we write a dual alternative decision structure as an If-Then-Else statement. Here is the general format of the If-Then-Else statement:

```
If condition Then
    statement
    statement       ⎫
    etc.            ⎬ These statements are executed if the condition is true.
Else                ⎭
    statement
    statement       ⎫
    etc.            ⎬ These statements are executed if the condition is false.
End If              ⎭
```

In the general format, the *condition* is any Boolean expression. If the expression is true, the statements that appear next are executed, up to the line that reads Else. If the expression is false, the statements that appear between Else and End If are executed. The line that reads End If marks the end of the If-Then-Else statement.

The following pseudocode shows an example of an If-Then-Else statement. This pseudocode matches the flowchart that was shown in Figure 14–8.

```
If temperature < 40 Then
    Display "A little cold, isn't it?"
Else
    Display "Nice weather we're having."
End If
```

We will refer to the line that reads Else as the Else *clause*. When you write an If-Then-Else statement, use the following style conventions:

■ Make sure the If clause, the Else clause, and the End If clause are aligned.

■ Indent the conditionally executed statements that appear between the If clause and the Else clause, and between the Else clause and the End If clause.

This is shown in Figure 14–9.

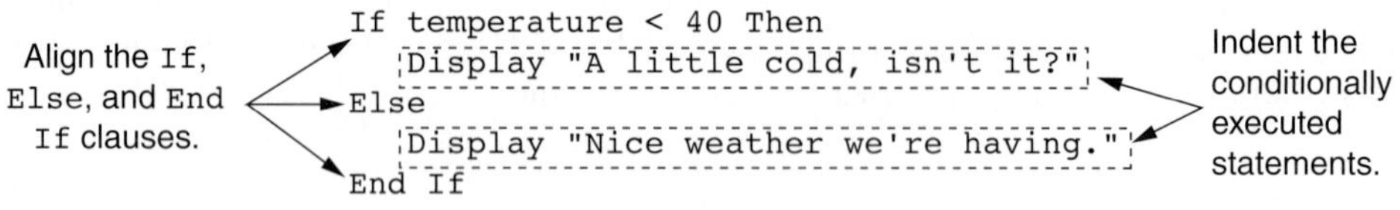

▶ **FIGURE 14–9**

Programming style with an If-Then-Else statement.

Align the If, Else, and End If clauses.

```
If temperature < 40 Then
    Display "A little cold, isn't it?"
Else
    Display "Nice weather we're having."
End If
```

Indent the conditionally executed statements.

In the Spotlight:

Using the If-Then-Else Statement

Chris owns an auto repair business and has several employees. If an employee works over 40 hours in a week, Chris pays that employee 1.5 times his or her regular hourly pay rate for all hours over 40. Chris has asked you to design a simple payroll program that calculates an employee's gross pay, including any overtime wages. You design the following algorithm:

1. Get the number of hours worked.

2. Get the hourly pay rate.

3. If the employee worked more than 40 hours, calculate the gross pay with overtime. Otherwise, calculate the gross pay as usual.

4. Display the gross pay.

You go through the top-down design process and create the hierarchy chart shown in Figure 14–10. As shown in the hierarchy chart, the main module will call four other modules. The following are summaries of those modules:

- getHoursWorked—This module will ask the user to enter the number of hours worked.

- getPayRate—This module will ask the user to enter the hourly pay rate.

- calcPayWithOT—This module will calculate an employee's pay with overtime.

- calcRegularPay—This module will calculate the gross pay for an employee with no overtime.

The main module, which executes when the program is run, will call these modules and then display the gross pay. The pseudocode for the program is shown in Program 14–2. Figures 4–11 and 4–12 show flowcharts for each of the modules.

▶ **FIGURE 14–10**

Hierarchy chart.

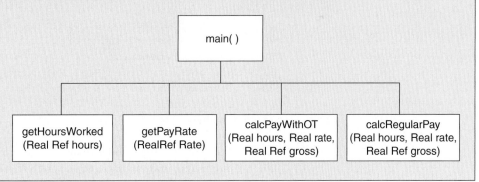

PROGRAM 14-2

```
 1 // Global constants
 2 Constant Integer BASE_HOURS = 40
 3 Constant Real OT_MULTIPLIER = 1.5
 4
 5 Module main()
 6     // Local variables
 7     Declare Real hoursWorked, payRate, grossPay
 8
 9     // Get the number of hours worked.
10     Call getHoursWorked(hoursWorked)
11
12     // Get the hourly pay rate.
13     Call getPayRate(payRate)
14
15     // Calculate the gross pay.
16     If hours > BASE_HOURS Then
17        Call calcPayWithOT(hoursWorked, payRate,
18                        grossPay)
19     Else
20        Call calcRegularPay(hoursWorked, payRate,
21                        grossPay)
22     End If
23
24     // Display the gross pay.
25     Display "The gross pay is $", grossPay
26 End Module
27
28 // The getHoursWorked module gets the number
29 // of hours worked and stores it in the
30 // hours parameter.
31 Module getHoursWorked(Real Ref hours)
32     Display "Enter the number of hours worked."
33     Input hours
34 End Module
35
36 // The getPayRate module gets the hourly
37 // pay rate and stores it in the rate
38 // parameter.
39 Module getPayRate(Real Ref rate)
40     Display "Enter the hourly pay rate."
41     Input rate
42 End Module
43
44 // The calcPayWithOT module calculates pay
45 // with overtime. The gross pay is stored
```

```
46 // in the gross parameter.
47 Module calcPayWithOT(Real hours, Real rate,
48                     Real Ref gross)
49    // Local variables
50    Declare Real overtimeHours, overtimePay
51
52    // Calculate the number of overtime hours.
53    Set overtimeHours = hours - BASE_HOURS
54
55    // Calculate the overtime pay
56    Set overtimePay = overtimeHours * rate *
57                    OT_MULTIPLIER
58
59    // Calculate the gross pay.
60    Set gross = BASE_HOURS * rate + overtimePay
61 End Module
62
63 // The calcRegularPay module calculates
64 // pay with no overtime and stores it in
65 // the gross parameter.
66 Module calcRegularPay(Real hours, Real rate,
67                     Real Ref gross)
68    Set gross = hours * rate
69 End Module
```

Program Output (with Input Shown in Bold)

```
Enter the number of hours worked.
40 [Enter]
Enter the hourly pay rate.
20 [Enter]
The gross pay is $800
```

Program Output (with Input Shown in Bold)

```
Enter the number of hours worked.
50 [Enter]
Enter the hourly pay rate.
20 [Enter]
The gross pay is $1100
```

Notice that two global constants are declared in lines 2 and 3. The BASE_HOURS constant is set to 40, which is the number of hours an employee can work in a week without getting paid overtime. The OT_MULTIPLIER constant is set to 1.5, which is the pay rate multiplier for overtime hours. This means that the employee's hourly pay rate is multiplied by 1.5 for all overtime hours.

Flowchart for the main module.

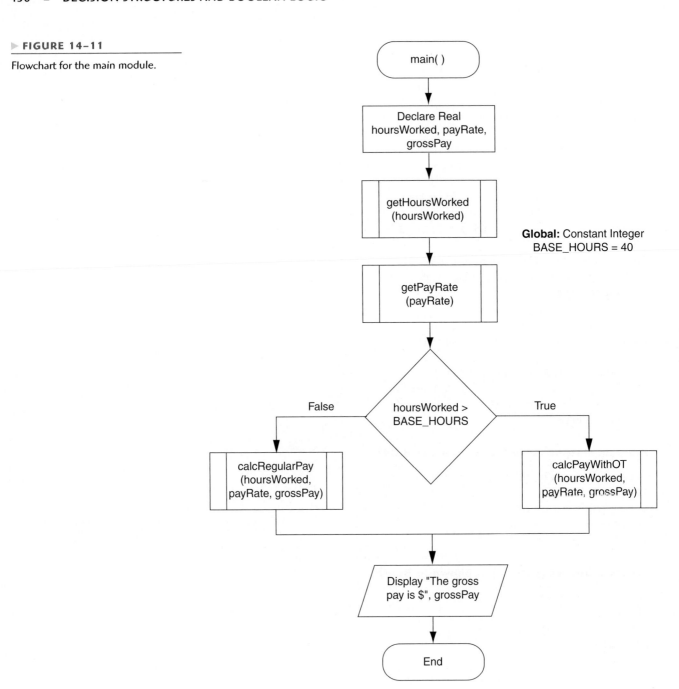

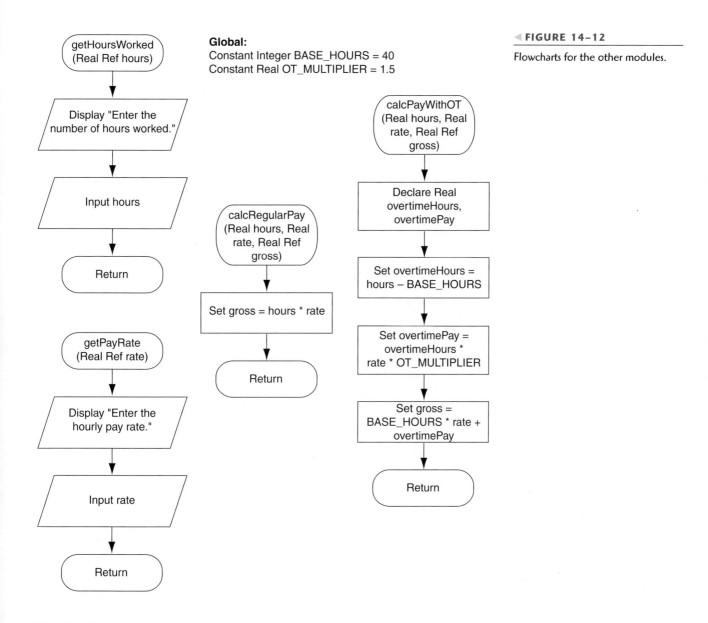

14–3 COMPARING STRINGS

CONCEPT: **Most programming languages allow you to compare strings. This allows you to create decision structures that test the value of a string.**

You saw in the preceding examples how numbers can be compared. Most programming languages also allow you to compare strings. For example, look at the following pseudocode:

```
Declare String name1 = "Mary"
Declare String name2 = "Mark"
If name1 == name2 Then
    Display "The names are the same"
Else
    Display "The names are NOT the same"
End If
```

The == operator tests name1 and name2 to determine whether they are equal. Since the strings "Mary" and "Mark" are not equal, the Else clause will display the message "The names are NOT the same".

You can compare String variables with string literals as well. Assume month is a String variable. The following pseudocode sample uses the != operator to determine whether month is not equal to "October."

```
If month != "October" Then
    statement
End If
```

The pseudocode in Program 14–3 demonstrates how two strings can be compared. The program prompts the user to enter a password and then determines whether the string entered is equal to "prospero".

PROGRAM 14–3

```
 1 // A variable to hold a password.
 2 Declare String password
 3
 4 // Prompt the user to enter the password.
 5 Display "Enter the password."
 6 Input password
 7
 8 // Determine whether the correct password
 9 // was entered.
10 If password == "prospero" Then
11     Display "Password accepted."
12 Else
13     Display "Sorry, that is not the correct password."
14 End If
```

Program Output (with Input Shown in Bold)

```
Enter the password.
ferdinand [Enter]
Sorry, that is not the correct password.
```

Program Output (with Input Shown in Bold)

```
Enter the password.
prospero [Enter]
Password accepted.
```

NOTE

In most languages, string comparisons are case sensitive. For example, the strings "saturday" and "Saturday" are not equal because the "s" is lowercase in the first string, but uppercase in the second string.

Other String Comparisons

In addition to determining whether strings are equal or not equal, many languages allow you to determine whether one string is greater than or less than another string. This is a useful capability because programmers commonly need to design programs that sort strings in some order.

Recall that computers do not actually store characters, such as A, B, C, and so on, in memory. Instead, they store numeric codes that represent the characters. ASCII (the American Standard Code for Information Interchange) is the most commonly used character coding system. Here are some facts about ASCII:

- The uppercase characters "A" through "Z" are represented by the numbers 65 through 90.

- The lowercase characters "a" through "z" are represented by the numbers 97 through 122.

- When the digits "0" through "9" are stored in memory as characters, they are represented by the numbers 48 through 57. (For example, the string "abc123" would be stored in memory as the codes 97, 98, 99, 49, 50, and 51.)

- A blank space is represented by the number 32.

In addition to establishing a set of numeric codes to represent characters in memory, ASCII also establishes an order for characters. The character "A" comes before the character "B", which comes before the character "C", and so on.

When a program compares characters, it actually compares the codes for the characters. For example, look at the following pseudocode:

```
If "a" < "b" Then
    Display "The letter a is less than the letter b."
End If
```

This If statement determines whether the ASCII code for the character "a" is less than the ASCII code for the character "b". The expression "a" < "b" is true because the code for "a" is less than the code for "b". So, if this were part of an actual program it would display the message "The letter a is less than the letter b."

Let's look at how strings containing more than one character are typically compared. Suppose we have the strings "Mary" and "Mark" stored in memory, as follows:

```
Declare String name1 = "Mary"
Declare String name2 = "Mark"
```

Figure 14–13 shows how the strings "Mary" and "Mark" would actually be stored in memory, using ASCII codes.

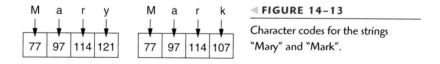

◄ FIGURE 14–13

Character codes for the strings "Mary" and "Mark".

When you use relational operators to compare these strings, they are compared character-by-character. For example, look at the following pseudocode:

```
Declare String name1 = "Mary"
Declare String name2 = "Mark"
If name1 > name2 Then
    Display "Mary is greater than Mark"
Else
    Display "Mary is not greater than Mark"
End If
```

The > operator compares each character in the strings "Mary" and "Mark," beginning with the first, or leftmost, characters. This is shown in Figure 14–14.

Comparing each character in a string.

Here is how the comparison typically takes place:

1. The "M" in "Mary" is compared with the "M" in "Mark." Since these are the same, the next characters are compared.

2. The "a" in "Mary" is compared with the "a" in "Mark." Since these are the same, the next characters are compared.

3. The "r" in "Mary" is compared with the "r" in "Mark." Since these are the same, the next characters are compared.

4. The "y" in "Mary" is compared with the "k" in "Mark." Since these are not the same, the two strings are not equal. The character "y" has a higher ASCII code (121) than "k" (107), so it is determined that the string "Mary" is greater than the string "Mark."

If one of the strings in a comparison is shorter than the other, many languages compare only the corresponding characters. If the corresponding characters are identical, then the shorter string is considered less than the longer string. For example, suppose the strings "High" and "Hi" were being compared. The string "Hi" would be considered less than "High" because it is shorter.

The pseudocode in Program 14–4 shows a simple demonstration of how two strings can be compared with the < operator. The user is prompted to enter two names and the program displays those two names in alphabetical order.

PROGRAM 14–4

```
 1 // Declare variables to hold two names.
 2 Declare String name1
 3 Declare String name2
 4
 5 // Prompt the user for two names.
 6 Display "Enter a name (last name first)."
 7 Input name1
 8 Display "Enter another name (last name first)."
 9 Input name2
10
11 // Display the names in alphabetical order.
12 Display "Here are the names, listed alphabetically:"
13 If name1 < name2 Then
14     Display name1
15     Display name2
16 Else
17     Display name2
18     Display name1
19 End If
```

Program Output

```
Enter a name (last name first).
Jones, Richard [Enter]
Enter another name (last name first).
Costa, Joan [Enter]
Here are the names, listed alphabetically:
Costa, Joan
Jones, Richard
```

14-4 NESTED DECISION STRUCTURES

CONCEPT: **To test more than one condition, a decision structure can be nested inside another decision structure.**

In Section 14.1, we mentioned that programs are usually designed as combinations of different control structures. In that section you saw an example of a sequence structure nested inside a decision structure (see Figure 14–3). You can also nest decision structures inside of other decision structures. In fact, this is a common requirement in programs that need to test more than one condition.

For example, consider a program that determines whether a bank customer qualifies for a loan. To qualify, two conditions must exist: (1) the customer must earn at least $30,000 per year, and (2) the customer must have been employed at his or her current job for at least two years. Figure 14–15 shows a flowchart for an algorithm that could be used in such a program. Assume that the `salary` variable contains the customer's annual salary, and the `yearsOnJob` variable contains the number of years that the customer has worked on his or her current job.

If we follow the flow of execution, we see that the condition `salary >= 30000` is tested. If this condition is false, there is no need to perform further tests; we know that the customer does not qualify for the loan. If the condition is true, however, we need to test the second condition. This is done with a nested decision structure that tests the condition `yearsOnJob >= 2`. If this condition is true, then the customer qualifies for the loan. If this condition is false, then the customer does not qualify. Program 14–5 shows the pseudocode for the complete program.

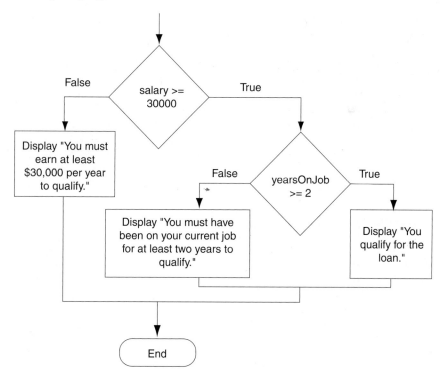

◄ **FIGURE 14-15**

A nested decision structure.

PROGRAM 14–5

```
 1 // Declare variables
 2 Declare Real salary, yearsOnJob
 3
 4 // Get the annual salary.
 5 Display "Enter your annual salary."
 6 Input salary
 7
 8 // Get the number of years on the current job.
 9 Display "Enter the number of years on your"
10 Display "current job."
11 Input yearsOnJob
12
13 // Determine whether the user qualifies.
14 If salary >= 30000 Then
15     If yearsOnJob >= 2 Then
16         Display "You qualify for the loan."
17     Else
18         Display "You must have been on your current"
19         Display "job for at least two years to qualify."
20     End If
21 Else
22     Display "You must earn at least $30,000"
23     Display "per year to qualify."
24 End If
```

Program Output (with Input Shown in Bold)

Enter your annual salary.
35000 [Enter]
Enter the number of years on your
current job.
1 [Enter]
You must have been on your current
job for at least two years to qualify.

Program Output (with Input Shown in Bold)

Enter your annual salary.
25000 [Enter]
Enter the number of years on your
current job.
5 [Enter]
You must earn at least $30,000
per year to qualify.

Program Output (with Input Shown in Bold)

Enter your annual salary.
35000 [Enter]
Enter the number of years on your
current job.
5 [Enter]
You qualify for the loan.

Look at the `If-Then-Else` statement that begins in line 14. It tests the condition `salary >= 30000`. If this condition is true, the `If-Then-Else` statement that begins in line 15 is executed. Otherwise the program jumps to the `Else` clause in line 21 and executes the two `Display` statements in lines 22 and 23. The program then leaves the decision structure and the program ends.

Programming Style and Nested Decision Structures

For debugging purposes, it's important to use proper alignment and indentation in a nested decision structure. This makes it easier to see which actions are performed by each part of the structure. For example, in most languages the following pseudocode is functionally equivalent to lines 14 through 24 in Program 14–5. Although this pseudocode is logically correct, it would be very difficult to debug because it is not properly indented.

```
If salary >= 30000 Then

If yearsOnJob >= 2 Then

Display "You qualify for the loan."          Don't write pseudocode
                                             like this!
Else

Display "You must have been on your current"

Display "job for at least two years to qualify."

End If

Else

Display "You must earn at least $30,000"

Display "per year to qualify.

End If
```

Proper indentation and alignment also makes it easier to see which `If`, `Else`, and `End If` clauses belong together, as shown in Figure 14–16.

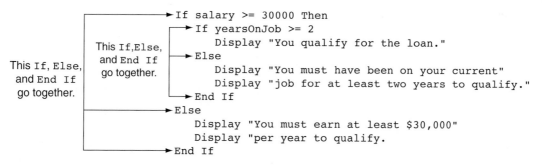

Alignment of **If**, **Else**, and **End If** clauses.

Testing a Series of Conditions

In the previous example you saw how a program can use nested decision structures to test more than one condition. It is not uncommon for a program to have a series of conditions to test, and then perform an action depending on which condition is true. One way to accomplish this is to have a decision structure with numerous other decision structures nested inside it. For example, consider the program presented in the following *In the Spotlight* section.

In the Spotlight:

Multiple Nested Decision Structures

Dr. Suarez teaches a literature class and uses the following 10 point grading scale for all of his exams:

Test Score	Grade
90 and above	A
80–89	B
70–79	C
60–69	D
Below 60	F

He has asked you to write a program that will allow a student to enter a test score and then display the grade for that score. Here is the algorithm that you will use:

1. Ask the user to enter a test score.

2. Determine the grade in the following manner:

> If the score is less than 60, then the grade is "F".
> Otherwise, if the score is less than 70, then the grade is "D".
> Otherwise, if the score is less than 80, then the grade is "C".
> Otherwise, if the score is less than 90, then the grade is "B".
> Otherwise, the grade is "A".

You decide that the process of determining the grade will require several nested decision structures, as shown in Figure 14–17. Program 14–6 shows the pseudocode for the complete program. The code for the nested decision structures is in lines 9 through 25.

▶ **FIGURE 14–17**

Nested decision structure to determine a grade.

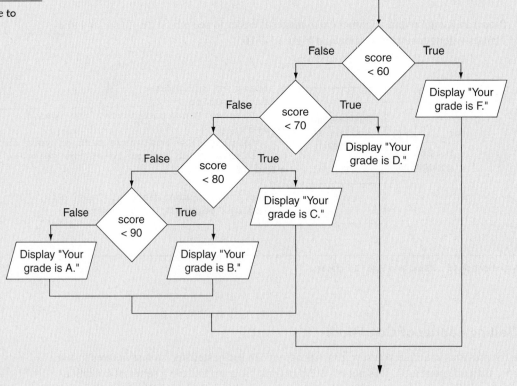

PROGRAM 14-6

```
 1 // Variable to hold the test score
 2 Declare Real score
 3
 4 // Get the test score.
 5 Display "Enter your test score."
 6 Input score
 7
 8 // Determine the grade.
 9 If score < 60 Then
10    Display "Your grade is F."
11 Else
12    If score < 70 Then
13        Display "Your grade is D."
14    Else
15        If score < 80 Then
16            Display "Your grade is C."
17        Else
18            If score < 90 Then
19                Display "Your grade is B."
20            Else
21                Display "Your grade is A."
22            End If
23        End If
24    End If
25 End If
```

Program Output (with Input Shown in Bold)

```
Enter your test score.
78 [Enter]
Your grade is C.
```

Program Output (with Input Shown in Bold)

```
Enter your test score.
84 [Enter]
Your grade is B.
```

The If-Then-Else If Statement

Even though Program 14–6 is a simple example, the logic of the nested decision structure is fairly complex. Most languages provide a special version of the decision structure known as the If-Then-Else If statement, which makes this type of logic simpler to write. In pseudocode we will write the If-Then-Else If statement using the following general format:

```
If condition_1 Then
    statement                    If condition_1 is true these statements are executed,
    statement                    and the rest of the structure is ignored.
    etc.
Else If condition_2 Then
    statement                    If condition_2 is true these statements are executed,
    statement                    and the rest of the structure is ignored.
    etc.
```

Insert as many `Else If` *clauses as necessary*

```
Else
    statement
    statement
    etc.
End If
```

These statements are executed if none of the conditions above are true.

When the statement executes, *condition_1* is tested. If *condition_1* is true, the statements that immediately follow are executed, up to the `Else If` clause. The rest of the structure is ignored. If *condition_1* is false, however, the program jumps to the very next `Else If` clause and tests *condition_2*. If it is true, the statements that immediately follow are executed, up to the next `Else If` clause. The rest of the structure is then ignored. This process continues until a condition is found to be true, or no more `Else If` clauses are left. If none of the conditions are true, the statements following the `Else` clause are executed.

The following is an example of the `If-Then-Else If` statement. This code works the same as the nested decision structure in lines 9 through 25 of Program 14–6.

```
If score < 60 Then
    Display "Your grade is F."
Else If score < 70 Then
    Display "Your grade is D."
Else If score < 80 Then
    Display "Your grade is C."
Else If score < 90 Then
    Display "Your grade is B."
Else
    Display "Your grade is A."
End If
```

Notice the alignment and indentation that is used with the `If-Then-Else If` statement: The `If`, `Else If`, `Else`, and `End If` clauses are all aligned, and the conditionally executed statements are indented.

You never have to use the `If-Then-Else If` statement because its logic can be coded with nested `If-Then-Else` statements. However, a long series of nested `If-Then-Else` statements has two particular disadvantages when you are debugging code:

■ The code can grow complex and become difficult to understand.

■ Because indenting is important in nested statements, a long series of nested `If-Then-Else` statements can become too long to be displayed on the computer screen without horizontal scrolling. Also, long statements tend to "wrap around" when printed on paper, making the code even more difficult to read.

The logic of an `If-Then-Else If` statement is usually easier to follow than a long series of nested `If-Then-Else` statements. And, because all of the clauses are aligned in an `If-Then-Else If` statement, the lengths of the lines in the statement tend to be shorter.

14–5 THE CASE STRUCTURE

CONCEPT: **The case structure lets the value of a variable or an expression determine which path of execution the program will take.**

The *case structure* is a *multiple alternative decision structure*. It allows you to test the value of a variable or an expression and then use that value to determine which statement or set of statements to execute. Figure 14–18 shows an example of how a case structure looks in a flowchart.

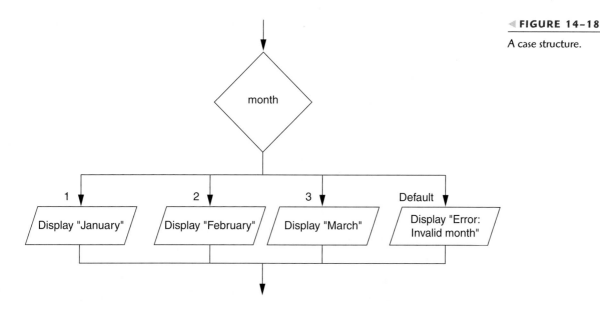

A case structure.

In the flowchart, the diamond symbol contains the name of a variable. If the variable contains the value 1, the statement Display "January" is executed. If the variable contains the value 2 the statement Display "February" is executed. If the variable contains the value 3 the statement Display "March" is executed. If the variable contains none of these values, the statement labeled Default is executed. In this case, the statement Display "Error: Invalid month" is executed.

To write a case structure in pseudocode we will use a Select Case statement. Here is the general format:

```
Select testExpression   ◄── This is a variable or an expression.
    Case value_1:
    statement           ⎫  These statements are executed if the
    statement           ⎬  testExpression is equal to value_1.
    etc.                ⎭
    Case value_2:
    statement           ⎫  These statements are executed if the
    statement           ⎬  testExpression is equal to value_2.
    etc.                ⎭
    Insert as many Case sections as necessary
    Case value_N:
    statement           ⎫  These statements are executed if the
    statement           ⎬  testExpression is equal to value_N.
    etc.                ⎭
     Default:           ⎫  These statements are executed if the testExpression
    statement           ⎬  is not equal to any of the values listed after the Case
    statement           ⎭  statements.
    etc.
End Select   ◄────────── This is the end of the structure.
```

The first line of the structure starts with the word Select, followed by a *testExpression*. The *testExpression* is usually a variable, but in many languages it can also be anything that gives a value (such as a math expression). Inside the structure there is one or more blocks of statements that begin with a Case statement. Notice that the word Case is followed by a value.

When the Select Case statement executes, it compares the value of the *testExpression* with the values that follow each of the Case statements (from top to bottom). When it finds a Case value that matches the *testExpression*'s value, the program branches to the Case statement. The statements that immediately follow the Case statement are executed, and then the program jumps out of the structure. If the *testExpression* does not match any of the Case values, the program branches to the Default statement and executes the statements that immediately follow it.

For example, the following pseudocode performs the same operation as the flowchart shown in Figure 14–18:

```
Select month
    Case 1:
        Display "January"
    Case 2:
        Display "February"
    Case 3:
        Display "March"
    Default:
        Display "Error: Invalid month"
End Select
```

In this example, the *testExpression* is the month variable. If the value in the month variable is 1, the program will branch to the Case 1: section and execute the Display "January" statement that immediately follows it. If the value in the month variable is 2, the program will branch to the Case 2: section and execute the Display "February" statement that immediately follows it. If the value in the month variable is 3, the program will branch to the Case 3: section and execute the Display "March" statement that immediately follows it. If the value in the month variable is not 1, 2, or 3, the program will branch to the Default: section and if the value in the month variable is 1, the program will branch to the Case 1: section and execute the Display "Error: Invalid month" statement that immediately follows it.

Case structures are never required because the same logic can be achieved with nested decision structures. For example, Figure 14–19 shows nested decision structures that are equivalent to the case structure in Figure 14–18. In situations where they can be used, however, case structures are more straightforward.

> **NOTE**
>
> In many languages the case structure is called a switch statement.

FIGURE 14–19

Nested decision structures.

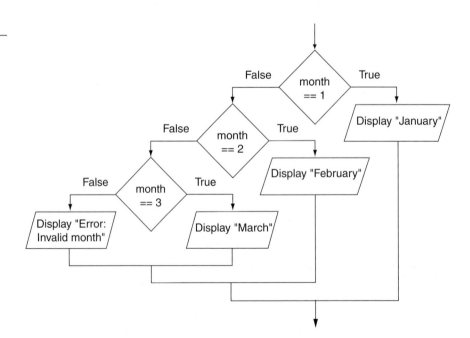

In the Spotlight:

Using a Case Structure

Lenny, who owns Lenny's Stereo and Television, has asked you to write a program that will let a customer pick one of three TV models and then displays the price and size of the selected model. Here is the algorithm:

1. Get the TV model number.

2. If the model is 100, then display the information for that model.

    Otherwise, if the model is 200, then display the information for that model.

    Otherwise, if the model is 300, then display the information for that model.

At first, you consider designing a nested decision structure to determine the model number and display the correct information. But you realize that a case structure will work just as well because a single value, the model number, will be used to determine the action that the program will perform. The model number can be stored in a variable, and that variable can be tested by the case structure. Assuming that the model number is stored in a variable named modelNumber, Figure 4–20 shows a flowchart for the case structure. Program 4–7 shows the pseudocode for the program.

▶ **FIGURE 14–20**

Flowchart for the case structure

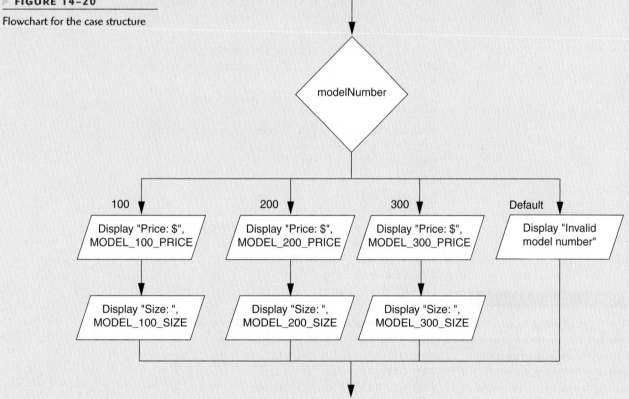

PROGRAM14–7

```
1 // Constants for the TV prices
2 Constant Real MODEL_100_PRICE = 199.99
3 Constant Real MODEL_200_PRICE = 269.99
4 Constant Real MODEL_300_PRICE = 349.99
5
```

```
 6 // Constants for the TV sizes
 7 Constant Integer MODEL_100_SIZE = 24
 8 Constant Integer MODEL_200_SIZE = 27
 9 Constant Integer MODEL_300_SIZE = 32
10
11 // Variable for the model number
12 Declare Integer modelNumber
13
14 // Get the model number.
15 Display "Which TV are you interested in?"
16 Display "The 100, 200, or 300?"
17 Input modelNumber
18
19 // Display the price and size.
20 Select modelNumber
21     Case 100:
22         Display "Price: $", MODEL_100_PRICE
23         Display "Size: ", MODEL_100_SIZE
24     Case 200:
25         Display "Price: $", MODEL_200_PRICE
26         Display "Size: ", MODEL_200_SIZE
27     Case 300:
28         Display "Price $", MODEL_300_PRICE
29         Display "Size: ", MODEL_300_SIZE
30     Default:
31         Display "Invalid model number"
32 End Select
```

Program Output (with Input Shown in Bold)
Which TV are you interested in?
The 100, 200, or 300?
100 [Enter]
Price: $199.99
Size: 24

Program Output (with Input Shown in Bold)
Which TV are you interested in?
The 100, 200, or 300?
200 [Enter]
Price: $269.99
Size: 27

Program Output (with Input Shown in Bold)
Which TV are you interested in?
The 100, 200, or 300?
300 [Enter]
Price: $349.99
Size: 32

Program Output (with Input Shown in Bold)
Which TV are you interested in?
The 100, 200, or 300?
500 [Enter]
Invalid model number

> **NOTE**
>
> The details of writing a case structure differ from one language to another. Because of the specific rules that each language uses for writing case structures, you might not be able to use the case structure for every multiple alternative decision. In such an event, you can use the If-Then-Else If statement or a nested decision structure.

14-6 LOGICAL OPERATORS

CONCEPT: The logical **AND** operator and the logical **OR** operator allow you to connect multiple Boolean expressions to create a compound expression. The logical **NOT** operator reverses the truth of a Boolean expression.

Programming languages provide a set of operators known as logical operators, which you can use to create complex Boolean expressions. Table 14–3 describes these operators.

◀ **TABLE 14–3**

Logical operators

OPERATOR	MEANING
AND	The AND operator connects two Boolean expressions into one compound expression. Both subexpressions must be true for the compound expression to be true.
OR	The OR operator connects two Boolean expressions into one compound expression. One or both subexpressions must be true for the compound expression to be true. It is only necessary for one of the subexpressions to be true, and it does not matter which.
NOT	The NOT operator is a unary operator, meaning it works with only one operand. The operand must be a Boolean expression. The NOT operator reverses the truth of its operand. If it is applied to an expression that is true, the operator returns false. If it is applied to an expression that is false, the operator returns true.

Table 14–4 shows examples of several compound Boolean expressions that use logical operators.

◀ **TABLE 14–4**

Compound Boolean expressions using logical operators.

EXPRESSION	MEANING
x > y AND a < b	Is x greater than y AND is a less than b?
x == y OR x == z	Is x equal to y OR is x equal to z?
NOT (x > y)	Is the expression x > y NOT true?

NOTE

In many languages, most notably C, C++, and Java, the AND operator is written as &&, the OR operator is written as | |, and the NOT operator is written as !.

The AND Operator

The AND operator takes two Boolean expressions as operands and creates a compound Boolean expression that is true only when both subexpressions are true. The following is an example of an If-Then statement that uses the AND operator:

```
If temperature < 20 AND minutes > 12 Then
    Display "The temperature is in the danger zone."
End If
```

In this statement, the two Boolean expressions temperature < 20 and minutes > 12 are combined into a compound expression. The Display statement will be executed only if temperature is less than 20 AND minutes is greater than 12. If either of the Boolean subexpressions is false, the compound expression is false and the message is not displayed.

Table 14–5 shows a truth table for the AND operator. The truth table lists expressions showing all the possible combinations of true and false connected with the AND operator. The resulting values of the expressions are also shown.

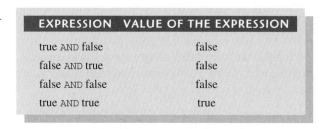

EXPRESSION	VALUE OF THE EXPRESSION
true AND false	false
false AND true	false
false AND false	false
true AND true	true

As the table shows, both sides of the AND operator must be true for the operator to return a true value.

The OR Operator

The OR operator takes two Boolean expressions as operands and creates a compound Boolean expression that is true when either of the subexpressions is true. The following is an example of an If-Then statement that uses the OR operator:

```
If temperature < 20 OR temperature > 100 Then
    Display "The temperature is in the danger zone."
End If
```

The Display statement will execute only if temperature is less than 20 OR temperature is greater than 100. If either subexpression is true, the compound expression is true. Table 14–6 shows a truth table for the OR operator.

▶ TABLE 14–6

Truth table for the OR operator.

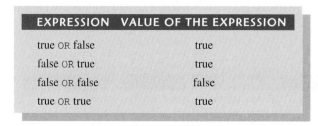

EXPRESSION	VALUE OF THE EXPRESSION
true OR false	true
false OR true	true
false OR false	false
true OR true	true

All it takes for an OR expression to be true is for one side of the OR operator to be true. It doesn't matter if the other side is false or true.

Short-Circuit Evaluation

In many languages both the AND and OR operators perform *short-circuit evaluation*. Here's how it works with the AND operator: If the expression on the left side of the AND operator is false, the expression on the right side will not be checked. Because the compound expression will be false if only one of the subexpressions is false, it would waste CPU time to check the remaining expression. So, when the AND operator finds that the expression on its left is false, it short-circuits and does not evaluate the expression on its right.

Here's how short-circuit evaluation works with the OR operator: If the expression on the left side of the OR operator is true, the expression on the right side will not be checked. Because it is only necessary for one of the expressions to be true, it would waste CPU time to check the remaining expression.

The NOT Operator

The NOT operator is a unary operator that takes a Boolean expression as its operand and reverses its logical value. In other words, if the expression is true, the NOT operator returns false, and if the expression is false, the NOT operator returns true. The following is an If-Then statement using the NOT operator:

```
If NOT(temperature > 100) Then
    Display "This is below the maximum temperature."
End If
```

First, the expression (temperature > 100) is tested and a value of either true or false is the result. Then the NOT operator is applied to that value. If the expression (temperature > 100) is true, the NOT operator returns false. If the expression (temperature > 100) is false, the NOT operator returns true. The previous code is equivalent to asking: "Is the temperature not greater than 100?"

Table 14–7 shows a truth table for the NOT operator.

EXPRESSION	VALUE OF THE EXPRESSION
NOT true	false
NOT false	true

Truth table for the NOT operator.

The Loan Qualifier Program Revisited

In some situations the AND operator can be used to simplify nested decision structures. For example, recall that the loan qualifier program in Program 14–5 uses the following nested If-Then-Else statements:

```
If salary >= 30000 Then
    If yearsOnJob >= 2 Then
        Display "You qualify for the loan."
    Else
        Display "You must have been on your current"
        Display "job for at least two years to qualify."
    End If
Else
    Display "You must earn at least $30,000"
    Display "per year to qualify."
End If
```

The purpose of this decision structure is to determine that a person's salary is at least $30,000 and that he or she has been at their current job for at least two years. Program 14–8 shows a way to perform a similar task with simpler code.

NOTE

In this example, we have put parentheses around the expression temperature > 100. The reason for this is that, in many languages, the NOT operator has higher precedence than the relational operators. Suppose we wrote the expression as follows:

NOT temperature > 100

In many languages this expression would not work correctly because the NOT operator would be applied to the temperature variable, not the expression temperature > 100. To make sure that the operator is applied to the expression, we enclose it in parentheses.

PROGRAM 14–8

```
 1 // Declare variables
 2 Declare Real salary, yearsOnJob
 3
 4 // Get the annual salary.
 5 Display "Enter your annual salary."
 6 Input salary
 7
 8 // Get the number of years on the current job.
 9 Display "Enter the number of years on your ",
10        "current job."
```

```
11 Input yearsOnJob
12
13 // Determine whether the user qualifies.
14 If salary >= 30000 AND yearsOnJob >= 2 Then
15    Display "You qualify for the loan."
16 Else
17    Display "You do not qualify for this loan."
18 End If
```

Program Output (with Input Shown in Bold)

```
Enter your annual salary.
35000 [Enter]
Enter the number of years on your current job.
1 [Enter]
You do not qualify for this loan.
```

Program Output (with Input Shown in Bold)

```
Enter your annual salary.
25000 [Enter]
Enter the number of years on your current job.
5 [Enter]
You do not qualify for this loan.
```

Program Output (with Input Shown in Bold)

```
Enter your annual salary.
35000 [Enter]
Enter the number of years on your current job.
5 [Enter]
You qualify for the loan.
```

NOTE

A careful observer will realize that Program 14–8 is similar to Program 14–5, but it is not equivalent. If the user does not qualify for the loan, Program 14–8 displays only the message "You do not qualify for this loan" whereas Program 14–5 displays one of two possible messages explaining why the user did not qualify.

The If-Then-Else statement in lines 14 through 18 tests the compound expression salary >= 30000 AND yearsOnJob >= 2. If both subexpressions are true, the compound expression is true and the message "You qualify for the loan" is displayed. If either of the subexpressions is false, the compound expression is false and the message "You do not qualify for this loan" is displayed.

Yet Another Loan Qualifier Program

Suppose the bank is losing customers to a competing bank that isn't as strict about whom it loans money to. In response, the bank decides to change its loan requirements. Now, customers have to meet only one of the previous conditions, not both. Program 14–9 shows the pseudocode for the new loan qualifier program. The compound expression that is tested by the If-Then-Else statement in line 14 now uses the OR operator.

PROGRAM 14–9

```
1 // Declare variables
2 Declare Real salary, yearsOnJob
3
4 // Get the annual salary.
5 Display "Enter your annual salary."
```

```
 6 Input salary
 7
 8 // Get the number of years on the current job.
 9 Display "Enter the number of years on your"
10 Display "current job."
11 Input yearsOnJob
12
13 // Determine whether the user qualifies.
14 If salary >= 30000 OR yearsOnJob >= 2 Then
15         Display "You qualify for the loan."
16 Else
17    Display "You do not qualify for this loan."
18 End If
```

Program Output (with Input Shown in Bold)

```
Enter your annual salary.
35000 [Enter]
Enter the number of years on your
current job.
1 [Enter]
You qualify for the loan.
```

Program Output (with Input Shown in Bold)

```
Enter your annual salary.
25000 [Enter]
Enter the number of years on your
current job.
5 [Enter]
You qualify for the loan.
```

Program Output (with Input Shown in Bold)

```
Enter your annual salary.
12000 [Enter]
Enter the number of years on your
current job.
1 [Enter]
You do not qualify for this loan.
```

Checking Numeric Ranges with Logical Operators

Sometimes you will need to design an algorithm that determines whether a numeric value is within a specific range of values or outside a specific range of values. When determining whether a number is inside a range, it is best to use the AND operator. For example, the following If-Then statement checks the value in x to determine whether it is in the range of 20 through 40:

```
If x >= 20 AND x <= 40 Then
    Display "The value is in the acceptable range."
End If
```

The compound Boolean expression being tested by this statement will be true only when x is greater than or equal to 20 AND less than or equal to 40. The value in x must be within the range of 20 through 40 for this compound expression to be true.

When determining whether a number is outside a range, it is best to use the OR operator. The following statement determines whether x is outside the range of 20 through 40:

```
If x < 20 OR x > 40 Then
    Display "The value is outside the acceptable range."
End If
```

It is important not to get the logic of the logical operators confused when testing for a range of numbers. For example, the compound Boolean expression in the following pseudocode would never test true:

```
// This is an error!
If x < 20 AND x > 40 Then
    Display "The value is outside the acceptable range."
End If
```

Obviously, x cannot be less than 20 and at the same time be greater than 40.

14-7 BOOLEAN VARIABLES

CONCEPT: A Boolean variable can hold one of two values: true or false. Boolean variables are commonly used as flags, which indicate whether specific conditions exist.

So far in this book we have worked with Integer, Real, and String variables. In addition to numeric and string data types, most programming languages provide a Boolean data type. The Boolean data type allows you to create variables that may hold one of two possible values: True or False. Here is an example of the way we declare Boolean variables in this book:

```
Declare Boolean isHungry
```

Most programming languages have key words such as True and False that can be assigned to Boolean variables. Here are examples of how we assign values to a Boolean variable:

```
Set isHungry = True
Set isHungry = False
```

Boolean variables are most commonly used as flags. A *flag* is a variable that signals when some condition exists in the program. When the flag variable is set to False, it indicates the condition does not exist. When the flag variable is set to True, it means the condition does exist.

For example, suppose a salesperson has a quota of $50,000. Assuming the sales variable holds the amount that the salesperson has sold, the following pseudocode determines whether the quota has been met:

```
If sales >= 50000 Then
    Set salesQuotaMet = True
Else
    Set salesQuotaMet = False
End If
```

As a result of this code, the salesQuotaMet variable can be used as a flag to indicate whether the sales quota has been met. Later in the program we might test the flag in the following way:

```
If salesQuotaMet Then
    Display "You have met your sales quota!"
End If
```

This code displays the message "You have met your sales quota!" if the `Boolean` variable `salesQuotaMet` equals `True`. Notice that we did not have to use the `==` operator to explicitly compare the `salesQuotaMet` variable with the value `True`. This code is equivalent to the following:

```
If salesQuotaMet == True Then
    Display "You have met your sales quota!"
End If
```

REVIEW QUESTIONS

Multiple Choice

1. A _____ structure can execute a set of statements only under certain circumstances.
   - (a) sequence
   - (b) circumstantial
   - (c) decision
   - (d) Boolean

2. A _____ structure provides one alternative path of execution.
   - (a) sequence
   - (b) single alternative decision
   - (c) one path alternative
   - (d) single execution decision

3. In pseudocode, the `If-Then` statement is an example of a _____.
   - (a) sequence structure
   - (b) decision structure
   - (c) pathway structure
   - (d) class structure

4. A(n) _____ expression has a value of either true or false.
   - (a) binary
   - (b) decision
   - (c) unconditional
   - (d) Boolean

5. The symbols >, <, and == are all _____ operators.
   - (a) relational
   - (b) logical
   - (c) conditional
   - (d) ternary

6. A(n) _____ structure tests a condition and then takes one path if the condition is true, or another path if the condition is false.
   - (a) `If-Then` statement
   - (b) single alternative decision
   - (c) dual alternative decision
   - (d) sequence

7. You use a(n) _____ statement in pseudocode to write a single alternative decision structure.

   (a) `Test-Jump`

   (b) `If-Then`

   (c) `If-Then-Else`

   (d) `If-Call`

8. You use a(n) _____ statement in pseudocode to write a dual alternative decision structure.

   (a) `Test-Jump`

   (b) `If-Then`

   (c) `If-Then-Else`

   (d) `If-Call`

9. A _____ structure allows you to test the value of a variable or an expression and then use that value to determine which statement or set of statements to execute.

   (a) variable test decision

   (b) single alternative decision

   (c) dual alternative decision

   (d) multiple alternative decision

10. A(n) _____ section of a `Select Case` statement is branched to if none of the case values match the expression listed after the `Select` statement.

    (a) `Else`

    (b) `Default`

    (c) `Case`

    (d) `Otherwise`

11. `AND`, `OR`, and `NOT` are _____ operators.

    (a) relational

    (b) logical

    (c) conditional

    (d) ternary

12. A compound Boolean expression created with the _____ operator is true only if both of its subexpressions are true.

    (a) `AND`

    (b) `OR`

    (c) `NOT`

    (d) `BOTH`

13. A compound Boolean expression created with the _____ operator is true if either of its subexpressions is true.

    (a) `AND`

    (b) `OR`

    (c) `NOT`

    (d) `EITHER`

14. The _____ operator takes a Boolean expression as its operand and reverses its logical value.

    (a) `AND`

    (b) `OR`

    (c) `NOT`

    (d) `EITHER`

15. A _____ is a Boolean variable that signals when some condition exists in the program.

    (a) flag

    (b) signal

    (c) sentinel

    (d) siren

True or False

1. You can write any program using only sequence structures.

2. A program can be made of only one type of control structure. You cannot combine structures.

3. A single alternative decision structure tests a condition and then takes one path if the condition is true, or another path if the condition is false.

4. A decision structure can be nested inside another decision structure.

5. A compound Boolean expression created with the AND operator is true only when both subexpressions are true.

Short Answer

1. Explain what is meant by the term "conditionally executed."

2. You need to test a condition and then execute one set of statements if the condition is true. If the condition is false, you need to execute a different set of statements. What structure will you use?

3. If you need to test the value of a variable and use that value to determine which statement or set of statements to execute, which structure would be the most straightforward to use?

4. Briefly describe how the AND operator works.

5. Briefly describe how the OR operator works.

6. When determining whether a number is inside a range, which logical operator is it best to use?

7. What is a flag and how does it work?

Algorithm Workbench

1. Design an If-Then statement (or a flowchart with a single alternative decision structure) that assigns 20 to the variable y and assigns 40 to the variable z if the variable x is greater than 100.

2. Design an If-Then statement (or a flowchart with a single alternative decision structure) that assigns 0 to the variable b and assigns 1 to the variable c if the variable a is less than 10.

3. Design an If-Then-Else statement (or a flowchart with a dual alternative decision structure) that assigns 0 to the variable b if the variable a is less than 10. Otherwise, it should assign 99 to the variable b.

4. The following pseudocode contains several nested If-Then-Else statements. Unfortunately, it was written without proper alignment and indentation. Rewrite the code and use the proper conventions of alignment and indentation.

```
If score < 60 Then
Display "Your grade is F."
Else
If score < 70 Then
Display "Your grade is D."
Else
If score < 80 Then
Display "Your grade is C."
Else
If score < 90 Then
```

```
Display "Your grade is B."
Else
Display "Your grade is A."
End If
End If
End If
End If
```

5. Design nested decision structures that perform the following: If amount1 is greater than 10 and amount2 is less than 100, display the greater of amount1 and amount2.

6. Rewrite the following If-Then-Else If statement as a Select Case statement.

```
If selection == 1 Then
    Display "You selected A."
Else If selection == 2 Then
    Display "You selected 2."
Else If selection == 3 Then
    Display "You selected 3."
Else If selection == 4 Then
    Display "You selected 4."
Else
    Display "Not good with numbers, eh?"
End If
```

7. Design an If-Then-Else statement (or a flowchart with a dual alternative decision structure) that displays "Speed is normal" if the speed variable is within the range of 24 to 56. If speed holds a value outside this range, display "Speed is abnormal."

8. Design an If-Then-Else statement (or a flowchart with a dual alternative decision structure) that determines whether the points variable is outside the range of 9 to 51. If the variable holds a value outside this range it should display "Invalid points." Otherwise, it should display "Valid points."

9. Design a case structure that tests the month variable and does the following:
   • If the month variable is set to 1, it displays "January has 31 days"
   • If the month variable is set to 2, it displays "February has 28 days"
   • If the month variable is set to 3, it displays "March has 31 days"
   • If the month variable is set to anything else, it displays "Invalid selection"

10. Write an If-Then statement that sets the variable hours to 10 when the flag variable minimum is set.

Programming Exercises

1. Roman Numerals

Design a program that prompts the user to enter a number within the range of 1 through 10. The program should display the Roman numeral version of that number. If the number is outside the range of 1 through 10, the program should display an error message.

2. Areas of Rectangles

The area of a rectangle is the rectangle's length times its width. Design a program that asks for the length and width of two rectangles. The program should tell the user which rectangle has the greater area, or if the areas are the same.

3. Mass and Weight

Scientists measure an object's mass in kilograms and its weight in Newtons. If you know the amount of mass of an object, you can calculate its weight, in Newtons, with the following formula:

$$Weight = Mass \times 9.8$$

Design a program that asks the user to enter an object's mass, and then calculates its weight. If the object weighs more than 1000 Newtons, display a message indicating that it is too heavy. If the object weighs less than 10 Newtons, display a message indicating that it is too light.

4. **Book Club Points**

Serendipity Booksellers has a book club that awards points to its customers based on the number of books purchased each month. The points are awarded as follows:

- If a customer purchases 0 books, he or she earns 0 points.
- If a customer purchases 1 book, he or she earns 5 points.
- If a customer purchases 2 books, he or she earns 15 points.
- If a customer purchases 3 books, he or she earns 30 points.
- If a customer purchases 4 or more books, he or she earns 60 points.

Design a program that asks the user to enter the number of books that he or she has purchased this month and displays the number of points awarded.

5. **Software Sales**

A software company sells a package that retails for $99. Quantity discounts are given according to the following table:

Quantity	Discount
10–19	20%
20–49	30%
50–99	40%
100 or more	50%

Design a program that asks the user to enter the number of packages purchased. The program should then display the amount of the discount (if any) and the total amount of the purchase after the discount.

6. **Shipping Charges**

The Fast Freight Shipping Company charges the following rates:

Weight of Package	Rate per Pound
2 pounds or less	$1.10
Over 2 pounds but not more than 6 pounds	$2.20
Over 6 pounds but not more than 10 pounds	$3.70
Over 10 pounds	$3.80

Design a program that asks the user to enter the weight of a package and then displays the shipping charges.

7. **Body Mass Index Program Enhancement**

In Programming Exercise 6 in Chapter 13 you were asked to design a program that calculates a person's body mass index (BMI). Recall from that exercise that the BMI is often used to determine whether a person with a sedentary lifestyle is overweight or underweight for their height. A person's BMI is calculated with the following formula:

$$BMI = Weight \times 703 / Height^2$$

Enhance the program so it displays a message indicating whether the person has optimal weight, is underweight, or is overweight. A sedentary person's weight is considered to be optimal if his or her BMI is between 18.5 and 25. If the BMI is less than 18.5, the person is considered to be underweight. If the BMI value is greater than 25, the person is considered to be overweight.

8. **Time Calculator**

Design a program that asks the user to enter a number of seconds, and works as follows:

- There are 60 seconds in a minute. If the number of seconds entered by the user is greater than or equal to 60, the program should display the number of minutes in that many seconds.

- There are 3,600 seconds in an hour. If the number of seconds entered by the user is greater than or equal to 3,600, the program should display the number of hours in that many seconds.

- There are 86,400 seconds in a day. If the number of seconds entered by the user is greater than or equal to 86,400, the program should display the number of days in that many seconds.

15

REPETITION STRUCTURES

WWW. VISIT THE COMPANION WEBSITE

Study aids for this chapter are available at
http://www.prenhall.com/floyd

15–1 INTRODUCTION TO REPETITION STRUCTURES

CONCEPT: **A repetition structure causes a statement or set of statements to execute repeatedly.**

Programmers commonly have to write code that performs the same task over and over. For example, suppose you have been asked to write a program that calculates a 10 percent sales commission for several salespeople. Although it would not be a good design, one approach would be to write the code to calculate one salesperson's commission, and then repeat that code for each salesperson. For example, look at the following pseudocode:

```
// Variables for sales and commission.
Declare Real sales, commission

// Constant for the commission rate.
Constant Real COMMISSION_RATE = 0.10

// Get the amount of sales.
Display "Enter the amount of sales."
Input sales

// Calculate the commission.
Set commission = sales * COMMISSION_RATE

// Display the commission
Display "The commission is $", commission
```

This calculates the first salesperson's commission.

```
// Get the amount of sales.
Display "Enter the amount of sales."
Input sales

// Calculate the commission.
Set commission = sales * COMMISSION_RATE

// Display the commission
Display "The commission is $", commission
```

This calculates the second salesperson's commission.

And this code goes on and on . . .

As you can see, this is one long sequence structure containing a lot of duplicated code. There are several disadvantages to this approach, including the following:

- The duplicated code makes the program large.

- Writing a long sequence of statements can be time consuming.

- If part of the duplicated code has to be corrected or changed then the correction or change has to be done many times.

Instead of writing the same sequence of statements over and over, a better way to repeatedly perform an operation is to write the code for the operation once, and then place that code in a structure that makes the computer repeat it as many times as necessary. This can be done with a *repetition structure*, which is more commonly known as a *loop*.

Condition-Controlled and Count-Controlled Loops

In this chapter, we will look at two broad categories of loops: condition-controlled and count-controlled. A *condition-controlled loop* uses a true/false condition to control the number of times that it repeats. A *count-controlled loop* repeats a specific number of times. We will also discuss the specific ways that most programming languages allow you to construct these types of loops.

15-2 CONDITION-CONTROLLED LOOPS: WHILE, DO-WHILE, AND DO-UNTIL

CONCEPT: Both the `While` and `Do-While` loops cause a statement or set of statements to repeat as long as a condition is true. The `Do-Until` loop causes a statement or set of statements to repeat until a condition is true.

The `While` Loop

The `While` loop gets its name from the way it works: *While a condition is true, do some task.* The loop has two parts: (1) a condition that is tested for a true or false value, and (2) a statement or set of statements that is repeated as long as the condition is true. Figure 15–1 shows the logic of a `While` loop.

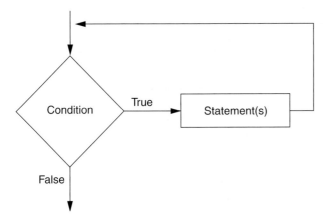

The diamond symbol represents the condition that is tested. Notice what happens if the condition is true: one or more statements are executed and the program's execution flows back to the point just above the diamond symbol. The condition is tested again, and if it is true, the process repeats. If the condition is false, the program exits the loop. In a flowchart, you will always recognize a loop when you see a flow line going back to a previous part of the flowchart.

Writing a `While` Loop in Pseudocode

In pseudocode, we will use the `While` statement to write a `While` loop. Here is the general format of the `While` statement:

```
While condition
    statement
    statement
    etc.
End While
```

These statements are the body of the loop. They are repeated while the condition is true.

In the general format, the *condition* is a Boolean expression, and the statements that appear on the lines between the `While` and the `End While` clauses are called the *body of the loop*. When the loop executes, the *condition* is tested. If it is true, the statements that appear in the body of the loop are executed, and then the loop starts over. If the *condition* is false, the program exits the loop.

As shown in the general format, you should use the following conventions when you write a While statement:

■ Make sure the While clause and the End While clause are aligned.

■ Indent the statements in the body of the loop.

By indenting the statements in the body of the loop you visually set them apart from the surrounding code. This makes your program easier to read and debug. Also, this is similar to the style that most programmers follow when writing loops in actual code.

Program 15–1 shows how we might use a While loop to write the commission calculating program that was described at the beginning of this chapter.

PROGRAM 15-1

```
 1 // Variable declarations
 2 Declare Real sales, commission
 3 Declare String keepGoing = "y"
 4
 5 // Constant for the commission rate
 6 Constant Real COMMISSION_RATE = 0.10
 7
 8 While keepGoing == "y"
 9     // Get the amount of sales.
10     Display "Enter the amount of sales."
11     Input sales
12
13     // Calculate the commission.
14     Set commission = sales * COMMISSION_RATE
15
16     // Display the commission
17     Display "The commission is $", commission
18
19     Display "Do you want to calculate another"
20     Display "commission? (Enter y for yes)."
21     Input keepGoing
22 End While
```

Program Output (with Input Shown in Bold)

```
Enter the amount of sales.
10000.00 [Enter]
The commission is $1000
Do you want to calculate another
commission? (Enter y for yes).
y [Enter]
Enter the amount of sales.
5000.00 [Enter]
The commission is $500
Do you want to calculate another
commission? (Enter y for yes).
y [Enter]
```

```
Enter the amount of sales.
12000.00 [Enter]
The commission is $1200
Do you want to calculate another
commission? (Enter y for yes).
n [Enter]
```

In line 2, we declare the `sales` variable, which will hold the amount of sales, and the `commission` variable, which will hold the amount of commission. Then, in line 3 we declare a `String` variable named `keepGoing`. Notice that the variable is initialized with the value "y". This initialization value is important, and in a moment you will see why. In line 6 we declare a constant, `COMMISSION_RATE`, which is initialized with the value 0.10. This is the commission rate that we will use in our calculation.

Line 8 is the beginning of a `While` loop, which starts like this:

```
While keepGoing == "y"
```

Notice the condition that is being tested: `keepGoing == "y"`. The loop tests this condition, and if it is true, the statements in the body of the loop (lines 9 through 21) are executed. Then, the loop starts over at line 8. It tests the expression `keepGoing == "y"`and if it is true, the statements in the body of the loop are executed again. This cycle repeats until the expression `keepGoing == "y"` is tested in line 8 and found to be false. When that happens, the program exits the loop. This is illustrated in Figure 15–2.

In order for this loop to stop executing, something has to happen inside the loop to make the expression `keepGoing == "y"` false. The statements in lines 19 through 21 take care of this. Lines 19 and 20 display a message asking "Do you want to calculate another commission (Enter y for yes)." Then, the `Input` statement in line 21 reads the user's input and stores it in the `keepGoing` variable. If the user enters y (and it must be a lowercase y), then the expression `keepGoing == "y"` will be true when the loop starts over. This will cause the statements in the body of the loop to execute again. But, if the user enters anything other than lowercase y, the expression will be false when the loop starts over, and the program will exit the loop.

This condition is tested.

```
While keepGoing == "y"

    // Get the amount of sales.
    Display "Enter the amount of sales."
    Input sales

    // Calculate the commission.
    Set commission = sales * COMMISSION_RATE

    // Display the commission
    Display "The commission is $", commission

    Display "Do you want to calculate another"
    Display "commission? (Enter y for yes)."
    Input keepGoing

End While
```

If the condition is true, these statements are executed, and then the loop starts over.

If the condition is false, these statements are skipped and the program exits the loop.

FIGURE 15–2

The `While` loop.

Now that you have examined the pseudocode, look at the program output in the sample run. First, the program prompted the user to enter the amount of sales. The user entered 10000.00, and then the program displayed the commission for that amount, which is $1000.00. Then, the user is prompted "Do you want to calculate another commission? (Enter y for yes)." The user entered y, and the loop started the steps over. In the sample run, the user went through this process three times. Each execution of the body of a loop is known as an *iteration*. In the sample run, the loop iterated three times.

Figure 15–3 shows a flowchart for Program 15–1. By looking at this flowchart you can see that we have a repetition structure (the While loop) with a sequence structure (the body of the loop) nested inside it. The fundamental structure of the While loop is still present, however. A condition is tested, and if it is true one or more statements are executed and the flow of execution returns to the point just above the conditional test.

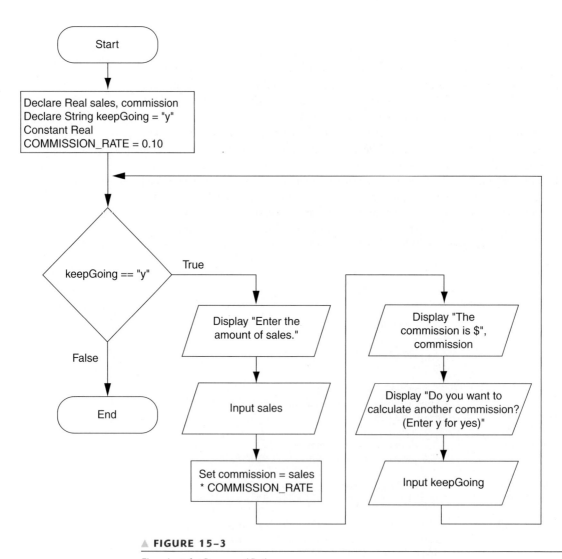

▲ FIGURE 15–3

Flowchart for Program 15–1.

The While Loop Is a Pretest Loop

The While loop is known as a *pretest* loop, which means it tests its condition *before* performing an iteration. Because the test is done at the beginning of the loop, you usually have to perform some steps prior to the loop to make sure that the loop executes at least once. For example, the loop in Program 15–1 starts like this:

```
While keepGoing == "y"
```

The loop will perform an iteration only if the expression keepGoing == "y" is true. To make sure the expression is true the first time that the loop executes, we declared and initialized the keepGoing variable in line 3 as follows:

```
Declare String keepGoing = "y"
```

If keepGoing had been initialized with any other value (or not initialized at all), the loop would never execute. This is an important characteristic of the While loop: it will never execute if its condition is false to start with. In some programs, this is exactly what you want. The following *In the Spotlight* section gives an example.

In the Spotlight:

Designing a While Loop

A project currently underway at Chemical Labs, Inc. requires that a substance be continually heated in a vat. A technician must check the substance's temperature every 15 minutes. If the substance's temperature does not exceed 102.5, then the technician does nothing. However, if the temperature is greater than 102.5, the technician must turn down the vat's thermostat, wait five minutes, and check the temperature again. The technician repeats these steps until the temperature does not exceed 102.5. The director of engineering has asked you to design a program that guides the technician through this process.

Here is the algorithm:

1. Get the substance's temperature.

2. Repeat the following steps as long as the temperature is greater than 102.5:
   a. Tell the technician to turn down the thermostat, wait five minutes, and check the temperature again.
   b. Get the substance's temperature.

3. After the loop finishes, tell the technician that the temperature is acceptable and to check it again in 15 minutes.

After reviewing this algorithm, you realize that steps 2(a) and 2(b) should not be performed if the test condition (temperature is greater than 102.5) is false to begin with. The While loop will work well in this situation, because it will not execute even once if its condition is false. Program 15–2 shows the pseudocode for the program, and Figure 15–4 shows a flowchart.

PROGRAM 15–2

```
1 // Variable to hold the temperature
2 Declare Real temperature
3
4 // Constant for the maximum temperature
5 Constant Real MAX_TEMP = 102.5
6
```

```
 7 // Get the substance's temperature.
 8 Display "Enter the substance's temperature."
 9 Input temperature
10
11 // If necessary, adjust the thermostat.
12 While temperature > MAX_TEMP
13     Display "The temperature is too high."
14     Display "Turn the thermostat down and wait"
15     Display "five minutes. Take the temperature"
16     Display "again and enter it here."
17     Input temperature.
18 End While
19
20 // Remind the user to check the temperature
21 // again in 15 minutes.
22 Display "The temperature is acceptable."
23 Display "Check it again in 15 minutes."
```

Program Output (with Input Shown in Bold)

```
Enter the water's temperature.
104.7 [Enter]
The temperature is too high.
Turn the thermostat down and wait
five minutes. Take the temperature
again and enter it here.
103.2 [Enter]
The temperature is too high.
Turn the thermostat down and wait
five minutes. Take the temperature
again and enter it here.
102.1 [Enter]
The temperature is acceptable.
Check it again in 15 minutes.
```

Program Output (with Input Shown in Bold)

```
Enter the water's temperature.
102.1 [Enter]
The temperature is acceptable.
Check it again in 15 minutes.
```

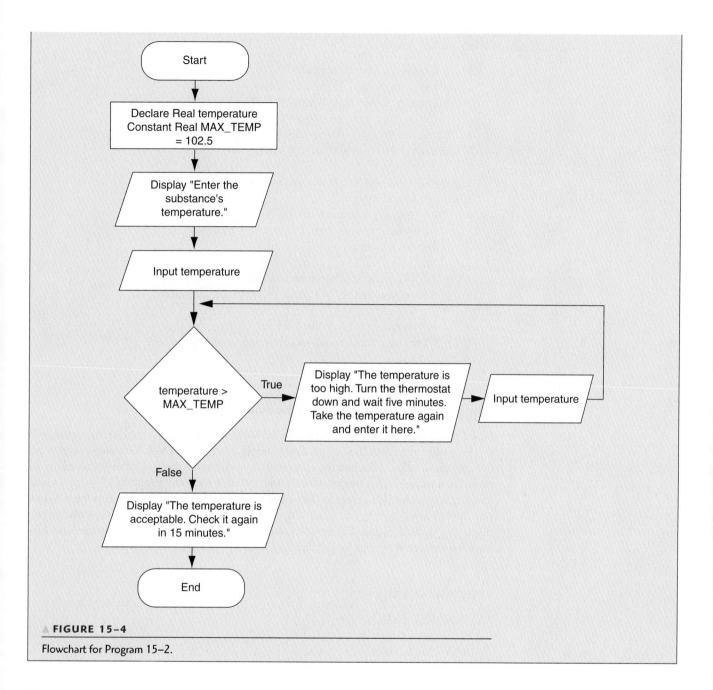

▲ **FIGURE 15-4**

Flowchart for Program 15-2.

Infinite Loops

In all but rare cases, loops must contain within themselves a way to terminate. This means that something inside the loop must eventually make the test condition false. The loop in Program 15–1 stops when the expression `keepGoing == "y"` is false. If a loop does not have a way of stopping, it is called an infinite loop. An *infinite loop* continues to repeat until the program is interrupted. Infinite loops usually occur when the programmer forgets to write code inside the loop that makes the test condition false. In most circumstances you should avoid writing infinite loops.

The pseudocode in Program 15–3 demonstrates an infinite loop. This is a modified version of the commission calculating program. In this version, we have removed the code that modifies the `keepGoing` variable in the body of the loop. Each time the expression `keepGoing == "y"` is tested in line 9, `keepGoing` will contain the string "y". As a consequence, the loop has no way of stopping.

PROGRAM 15–3

```
 1 // Variable declarations
 2 Declare Real sales, commission
 3 Declare String keepGoing = "y"
 4
 5 // Constant for the commission rate
 6 Constant Real COMMISSION_RATE = 0.10
 7
 8 // Warning! Infinite loop!
 9 While keepGoing == "y"
10    // Get the amount of sales.
11    Display "Enter the amount of sales."
12    Input sales
13
14    // Calculate the commission.
15    Set commission = sales * COMMISSION_RATE
16
17    // Display the commission
18    Display "The commission is $", commission
19 End While
```

Modularizing the Code in the Body of a Loop

Modules can be called from statements in the body of a loop. In fact, modularizing the code in a loop often improves the design. For example, in Program 15–3, the statements that get the amount of sales, calculate the commission, and display the commission can easily be placed in a module. That module can then be called in the loop. Program 15–4 shows how this might be done. This program has a main module, which executes when the program runs, and a showCommission module that handles all of the steps related to calculating and displaying a commission. Figure 15–5 shows a flowchart for the main module, and Figure 15–6 shows a flowchart for the showCommission module.

PROGRAM 15–4

```
 1 Module main()
 2    // Local variable
 3    Declare String keepGoing = "y"
 4
 5    // Calculate as many commissions
 6    // as needed.
 7    While keepGoing == "y"
 8       // Display a salesperson's commission.
 9       Call showCommission()
10
11       // Do it again?
12       Display "Do you want to calculate another?"
13       Display "commission? (Enter y for yes)."
14       Input keepGoing
15    End While
16 End Module
17
```

```
18  // The showCommission module gets the
19  // amount of sales and displays the
20  // commission.
21  Module showCommission()
22      // Local variables
23      Declare Real sales, commission
24
25      // Constant for the commission rate
26      Constant Real COMMISSION_RATE = 0.10
27
28      // Get the amount of sales.
29      Display "Enter the amount of sales."
30      Input sales
31
32      // Calculate the commission.
33      Set commission = sales * COMMISSION_RATE
34
35      // Display the commission
36      Display "The commission is $", commission
37  End Module
```

The output of this program is the same as that of Program 15–1

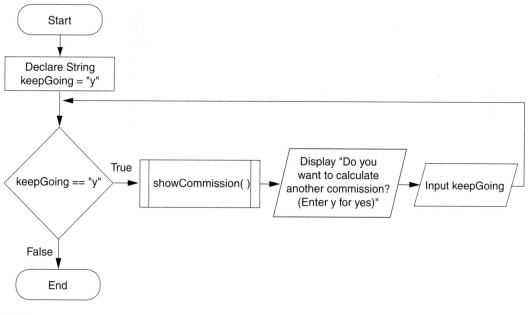

▲ **FIGURE 15–5**

The main module of Program 15–3.

▼ FIGURE 15–6

The showCommission module.

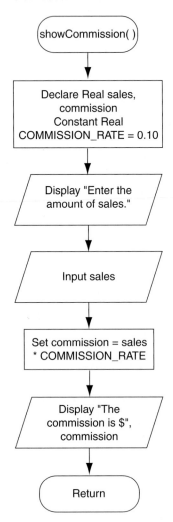

The Do-While Loop

You have learned that the While loop is a pretest loop, which means it tests its condition before performing an iteration. The Do-While loop is a *posttest* loop. This means it performs an iteration before testing its condition. As a result, the Do-While loop always performs at least one iteration, even if its condition is false to begin with. The logic of a Do-While loop is shown in Figure 15–7.

In the flowchart, one or more statements are executed, and then a condition is tested. If the condition is true, the program's execution flows back to the point just above the first statement in the body of the loop, and this process repeats. If the condition is false, the program exits the loop.

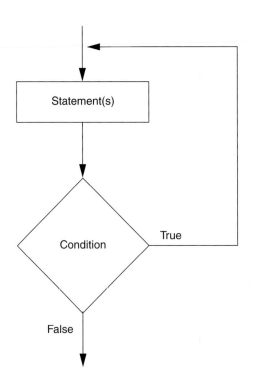

▲ FIGURE 15–7

The logic of a Do-While loop.

Writing a Do-While Loop in Pseudocode

In pseudocode, we will use the Do-While statement to write a Do-While loop. Here is the general format of the Do-While statement:

```
Do
    statement
    statement
    etc.
While condition
```

These statements are the body of the loop. They are always performed once, and then repeated while the condition is true.

In the general format, the statements that appear in the lines between the Do and the While clauses are the body of the loop. The *condition* that appears after the While clause is a Boolean expression. When the loop executes, the statements in the body of the loop are executed, and then the *condition* is tested. If the *condition* is true, the loop starts over and the statements in the body are executed again. If the *condition* is false, however, the program exits the loop.

As shown in the general format, you should use the following conventions when you write a Do-While statement:

■ Make sure the Do clause and the While clause are aligned.

■ Indent the statements in the body of the loop.

As shown in Program 15–5, the commission calculating program can be easily modified to use a Do-While loop instead of a While loop. Notice that in this version of the program, in line 3, we do not initialize the keepGoing variable with the string "y". It isn't necessary because the Do-While loop, in lines 7 through 15, will always execute at least once. This means that the Input statement in line 14 will read a value into the keepGoing variable before the condition is ever tested in line 15.

Figure 15–8 shows a flowchart for the main module.

PROGRAM 15–5

```
 1 Module main()
 2      // Local variable
 3      Declare String keepGoing
 4
 5      // Calculate commissions as many
 6      // times as needed.
 7      Do
 8          // Display a salesperson's commission.
 9          Call showCommission()
10
11          // Do it again?
12          Display "Do you want to calculate another"
13          Display "commission? (Enter y for yes)."
14          Input keepGoing
15      While keepGoing == "y"
16 End Module
17
18 // The showCommission module gets the
19 // amount of sales and displays the
20 // commission.
21 Module showCommission()
22      // Local variables
23      Declare Real sales, commission
24
25      // Constant for the commission rate
26      Constant Real COMMISSION_RATE = 0.10
27
28      // Get the amount of sales.
29      Display "Enter the amount of sales."
30      Input sales
31
32      // Calculate the commission.
33      Set commission = sales * COMMISSION_RATE
34
35      // Display the commission
36      Display "The commission is $", commission
37 End Module
```

The output of this program is the same as that of Program 15–1

▶ FIGURE 15–8

Flowchart for the main module in
Program 15–4.

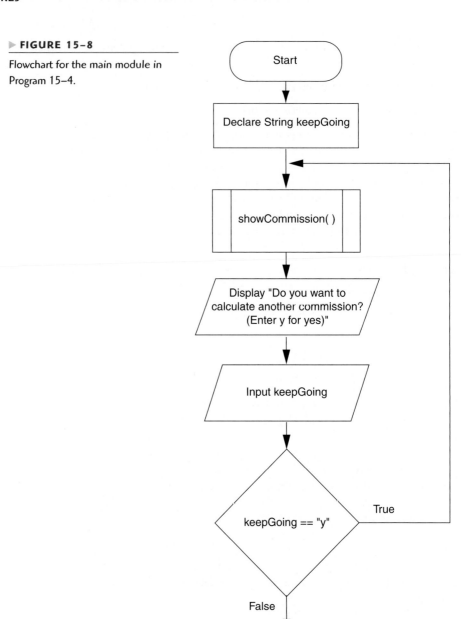

Although the Do-While loop is convenient to use in some circumstances, it is never re-quired. Any loop that can be written as a Do-While loop can also be written as a While loop. As previously mentioned, some circumstances require that you initialize data prior to executing a While loop, to ensure that it executes at least once.

In the Spotlight:

Designing a Do-While Loop

Samantha owns an import business and she calculates the retail prices of her products with the following formula:

Retail Price = Wholesale Cost × 2.5

She has asked you to design a program to do this calculation for each item that she receives in a shipment. You learn that each shipment contains various numbers of items, so you decide to use a loop that calculates the price for one item, and then asks her if she has another item. The loop will iterate as long as she indicates that she has another item. Program 15–6 shows the pseudocode for the program, and Figure 15–9 shows the flowchart.

PROGRAM 15–6

```
 1 Module main()
 2     // Local variable
 3     Declare String doAnother
 4
 5     Do
 6         // Calculate and display a retail price.
 7         Call showRetail()
 8
 9         // Do this again?
10         Display "Do you have another item? (Enter y for yes)"
11         Input doAnother
12     While doAnother == "y" OR doAnother == "Y"
13 End Module
14
15 // The showRetail module gets an item's wholesale cost
16 // from the user and displays its retail price.
17 Module showRetail()
18     // Local variables
19     Declare Real wholesale, retail
20
21     // Constant for the markup percentage
22     Constant Real MARKUP = 2.50
23
24     // Get the wholesale cost.
25     Display "Enter an item's wholesale cost."
26     Input wholesale
27
28     // Calculate the retail price.
29     Set retail = wholesale * MARKUP
30
31     // Display the retail price.
32     Display "The retail price is $", retail
33 End Module
```

Program Output (with Input Shown in Bold)

```
Enter an item's wholesale cost.
10.00 [Enter]
The retail price is $25
Do you have another item? (Enter y for yes)
y [Enter]
```

```
Enter an item's wholesale cost.
15.00 [Enter]
The retail price is $37.50
Do you have another item? (Enter y for yes)
y [Enter]
Enter an item's wholesale cost.
12.50 [Enter]
The retail price is $31.25
Do you have another item? (Enter y for yes)
n [Enter]
```

▶ **FIGURE 15–9**

Flowchart for Program 15–6.

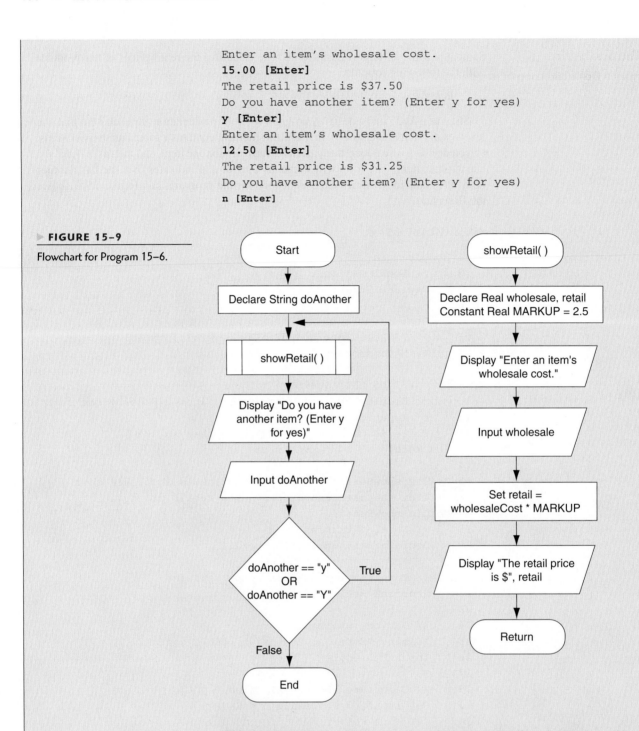

This program has two modules: main, which executes when the program runs, and showRetail, which calculates and displays an item's retail price. In the main module, a Do-While loop appears in lines 5 through 12. In line 7, the loop calls the showRetail module. Then, in line 10 the user is prompted "Do you have another item? (Enter y for yes)." In line 11, the user's input is stored in the doAnother variable. In line 12, the following statement is the end of the Do-While loop:

```
While doAnother == "y" OR doAnother == "Y"
```

Notice that we are using the logical OR operator to test a compound Boolean expression. The expression on the left side of the OR operator will be true if doAnother is equal to lowercase "y". The expression on the right side of the OR operator will be true if doAnother is equal to uppercase "Y". If either of these subexpressions is true, the loop will iterate. This is a simple way to make a case insensitive comparison, which means that it does not matter whether the user enters uppercase or lowercase letters.

The Do-Until Loop

Both the While and the Do-While loops iterate as long as a condition is true. Sometimes, however, it is more convenient to write a loop that iterates *until* a condition is true—that is, a loop that iterates as long as a condition is false, and then stops when the condition becomes true.

For example, consider a machine in an automobile factory that paints cars as they move down the assembly line. When there are no more cars to paint, the machine stops. If you were programming such a machine, you would want to design a loop that causes the machine to paint cars until there are no more cars on the assembly line.

A loop that iterates until a condition is true is known as a Do-Until loop. Figure 15–10 shows the general logic of a Do-Until loop.

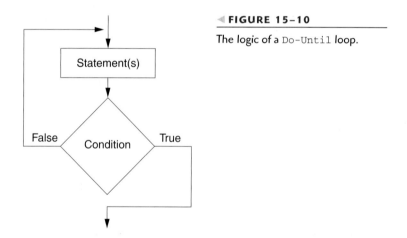

◀ FIGURE 15–10

The logic of a Do-Until loop.

Notice that the Do-Until loop is a posttesp loop. First, one or more statements are executed, and then a condition is tested. If the condition is false, the program's execution flows back to the point just above the first statement in the body of the loop, and this process repeats. If the condition is true, the program exits the loop.

Writing a Do-Until Loop in Pseudocode

In pseudocode, we will use the Do-Until statement to write a Do-Until loop. Here is the general format of the Do-Until statement:

```
Do
    statement
    statement
    etc.
Until condition
```

These statements are the body of the loop. They are always performed once, and then repeated until the condition is true.

In the general format, the statements that appear in the lines between the Do and the Until clauses are the body of the loop. The *condition* that appears after the While clause is a Boolean expression. When the loop executes, the statements in the body of the loop are executed, and then the *condition* is tested. If the *condition* is true, the program exits the loop. If the *condition* is false, the loop starts over and the statements in the body are executed again.

As shown in the general format, you should use the following conventions when you write a Do–Until statement:

■ Make sure the Do clause and the Until clause are aligned.

■ Indent the statements in the body of the loop.

The pseudocode in Program 15–7 shows an example of the Do-Until loop. The loop in lines 6 through 16 repeatedly asks the user to enter a password until the string "prospero" is entered. Figure 15–11 shows a flowchart for the program.

PROGRAM 15–7

```
 1 // Declare a variable to hold the password.
 2 Declare String password
 3
 4 // Repeatedly ask the user to enter a password
 5 // until the correct one is entered.
 6 Do
 7     // Prompt the user to enter the password.
 8     Display "Enter the password."
 9     Input password
10
11     // Display an error message if the wrong
12     // password was entered.
13     If password != "prospero" Then
14         Display "Sorry, try again."
15     End If
16 Until password == "prospero"
17
18 // Indicate that the password is confirmed.
19 Display "Password confirmed."
```

Program Output (with Input Shown in Bold)

```
Enter the password.
ariel [Enter]
Sorry, try again.
Enter the password.
caliban [Enter]
Sorry, try again.
Enter the password.
prospero [Enter]
Password confirmed.
```

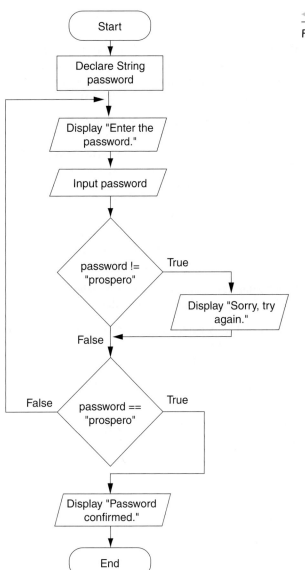

◄ FIGURE 15–11

Flowchart for Program 15–7.

Deciding Which Loop to Use

In this section, we have introduced three different types of condition-controlled loop: the While loop, the Do-While loop, and the Do-Until loop. When you write a program that requires a condition-controlled loop, you will have to decide which loop to use.

You want to use the While loop to repeat a task as long as a condition is true. The While loop is ideal in situations where the condition might be false to start with, and in such cases you do not want the loop to iterate at all. The pseudocode that you saw in Program 15–2 is a good example.

The Do-While loop is also a candidate in situations where a task must be repeated as long as a condition is true. It is the best choice, however, when you always want the task to be performed at least once, regardless of whether the condition is true or false to start with.

The Do-Until loop also performs a task at least once. It is the best choice, however, when you want to perform a task *until* a condition is true. The Do-Until loop will repeat as long as its condition is false. When the condition is true, the Do-Until loop stops.

COMPUTER NOTE

Not all programming languages provide a Do-Until loop because you can write a Do-While loop that *is* logically equivalent to any Do-Until loop.

15-3 COUNT-CONTROLLED LOOPS AND THE For STATEMENT

> **CONCEPT:** A count-controlled loop iterates a specific number of times. Although you can write the logic of a condition-controlled loop so it iterates a specific number of times, most languages provide a loop known as the For loop, which is specifically designed as a count-controlled loop.

As mentioned at the beginning of this chapter, a count-controlled loop iterates a specific number of times. Count-controlled loops are commonly used in programs. For example, suppose a business is open six days per week, and you are going to write a program that calculates the total sales for a week. You will need a loop that iterates exactly six times. Each time the loop iterates, it will prompt the user to enter the sales for one day.

The way that a count-controlled loop works is simple: the loop keeps a count of the number of times that it iterates, and when the count reaches a specified amount, the loop stops. A count-controlled loop uses a variable known as a *counter variable,* or simply *counter,* to store the number of iterations that it has performed. Using the counter variable, the loop typically performs the following three actions: *initialization, test,* and *increment:*

1. **Initialization**: Before the loop begins, the counter variable is initialized to a starting value. The starting value that is used will depend on the situation.

2. **Test**: The loop tests the counter variable by comparing it to a maximum value. If the counter variable is less than or equal to the maximum value, the loop iterates. If the counter is greater than the maximum value, the program exits the loop.

3. **Increment**: To *increment* a variable means to increase its value. During each iteration, the loop increments the counter variable by adding 1 to it.

Figure 5–12 shows the general logic of a count-controlled loop. The initialization, test, and increment operations are indicated with the ①, ②, and ③ callouts.

▶ **FIGURE 15–12**

Logic of a count-controlled loop.

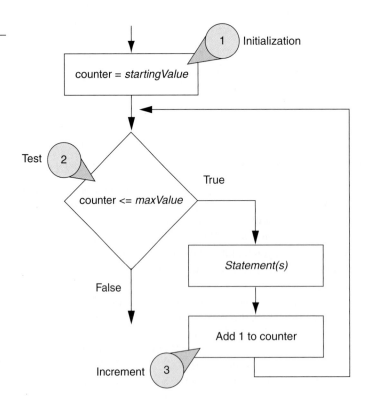

In the flowchart, assume that `counter` is an `Integer` variable. The first step is to set `counter` to the appropriate starting value. Then, determine whether `counter` is less than or equal to the maximum value. If this is true, the body of the loop executes. Otherwise, the program exits the loop. Notice that in the body of the loop one or more statements are executed, and then 1 is added to `counter`.

For example, look at the flowchart in Figure 15–13. First, an `Integer` variable named `counter` is declared and initialized with the starting value 1. Then, the expression `counter <= 5` is tested. If this expression is true the message "Hello world" is displayed and 1 is added to `counter`. Otherwise, the program exits the loop. If you follow the logic of this program you will see that the loop will iterate five times.

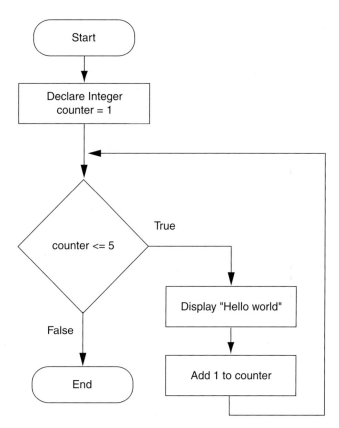

◀ FIGURE 15–13

A count-controlled loop.

The For Statement

Count-controlled loops are so common in programming that most languages provide a statement just for them. This is usually called the `For` statement. The `For` statement is specifically designed to initialize, test, and increment a counter variable. Here is the general format that we will use to write the `For` statement in pseudocode:

```
For counterVariable = startingValue To maxValue
    statement
    statement          These statements are the body of the loop.
    statement
    etc.
End For
```

In the general format, *counterVariable* is the name of a variable that is used as a counter, *startingValue* is the value that the counter will be initially set to, and *maxValue* is the maximum value that the counter can contain. When the loop executes, the following actions are performed:

1. The *counterVariable* is set to the *startingValue*.

2. The *counterVariable* is compared to the *maxValue*. If the *counterVariable* is greater than *maxValue*, the loop stops. Otherwise:
   a. The statements that appear in the body of the loop are executed.
   b. The *counterVariable* is incremented.
   c. The loop starts over again at Step 2.

An actual For loop is easy to understand, so let's look at one. The pseudocode in Program 15–8 uses a For loop to display "Hello world" five times. The flowchart in Figure 15–14 shows the logic of the program.

PROGRAM 15–8

```
1 Declare Integer counter
2 Constant Integer MAX_VALUE = 5
3
4 For counter = 1 To MAX_VALUE
5    Display "Hello world"
6 End For
```

Program Output

```
Hello world
Hello world
Hello world
Hello world
Hello world
```

Line 1 declares an Integer variable that will be used as the counter variable. You do not have to name the variable counter (you are free to name it anything you wish), but in many cases that is an appropriate name. Line 2 declares a constant named MAX_VALUE that will be used as the counter's maximum value. The For loop begins in line 4 with the statement For counter = 1 To MAX_VALUE. This specifies that the counter variable will start with the value 1 and will end with the value 5. At the end of each loop iteration, the counter variable will be incremented by 1, so this loop will iterate five times. Each time it iterates, it displays "Hello world."

Notice that the loop does not contain a statement to increment the counter variable. This happens automatically in a For loop, at the end of each iteration. For that reason, you should be careful not to place a statement that modifies the counter variable inside the body of a For loop. Doing so will usually disrupt the way the For loop works.

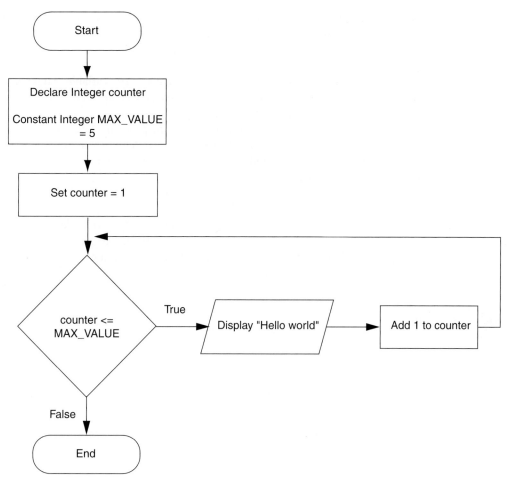

▲ **FIGURE 15–14**

Flowchart for Program 15–8.

Using the Counter Variable in the Body of the Loop

In a count-controlled loop, the primary purpose of the counter variable is to store the number of times that the loop has iterated. In some situations, it is also helpful to use the counter variable in a calculation or other task within the body of the loop. For example, suppose you need to write a program that displays the numbers 1 through 10 and their squares, in a table similar to the following:

Number	Square
1	1
2	4
3	9
4	16
5	25
6	36
7	49
8	64
9	81
10	100

This can be accomplished by writing a count-controlled loop that iterates 10 times. During the first iteration, the counter variable will be set to 1, during the second iteration it will be set to 2, and so forth. Because the counter variable will take on the values 1 through 10 during the loop's execution, you can use it in the calculation inside the loop.

TIP

Program 15–8 has a constant, MAX_VALUE, that represents the counter variable's maximum value. The first line of the loop could have been written as follows, to achieve the same result:

```
For counter = 1 To 5
```

Although creating the named constant is not necessary for this simple program, creating named constants to represent important values is a good habit. Recall from Chapter 12 that named constants make a program easier to read and easier to maintain.

The flowchart in Figure 15–15 shows the logic of such a program. Notice that in the body of the loop, the `counter` variable is used in the following calculation:

```
Set square = counter^2
```

This assigns the result of `counter^2` to the `square` variable. After performing this calculation, the contents of the `counter` variable and the `square` variable is displayed. Then, 1 is added to `counter` and the loop starts over again.

Program 15–9 shows the pseudocode for the program. Notice that the word `Tab` is used in the `Display` statements in lines 8 and 18. This is simply a way of indicating in pseudocode that we are indenting the screen output. For example, look at the following statement, which appears in line 18:

```
Display counter, Tab, square
```

This statement displays the contents of the `counter` variable, indents (or "tabs over"), and then displays the contents of the `square` variable. As a result, the numbers that are displayed will be aligned in two columns. Most programming languages provide a way to indent, or tab, screen output.

▶ FIGURE 15–15

Displaying the numbers 1 through 10 and their squares.

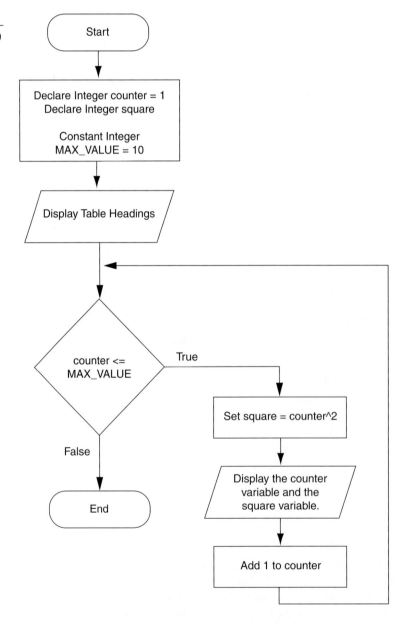

PROGRAM 15-9

```
 1 // Variables
 2 Declare Integer counter, square
 3
 4 // Constant for the maximum value
 5 Constant Integer MAX_VALUE = 10
 6
 7 // Display table headings.
 8 Display "Number", Tab, "Square"
 9 Display "----------------------"
10
11 // Display the numbers 1 through 10 and
12 // their squares.
13 For counter = 1 To MAX_VALUE
14    // Calculate number squared.
15    Set square = counter^2
16
17    // Display number and number squared.
18    Display counter, Tab, square
19 End For
```

Program Output

```
Number          Square
----------------------
1               1
2               4
3               9
4               16
5               25
6               36
7               49
8               64
9               81
10              100
```

Incrementing by Values Other Than 1

The amount by which the counter variable is incremented in a For loop is known as the *step amount*. By default, the step amount is 1. Most languages provide a way to change the step amount. This gives you the ability to increment the counter variable by any value you wish.

In pseudocode, we will use the Step clause to specify a step value in a For loop. For example, look at the following pseudocode:

```
For counter = 0 To 100 Step 10
    Display counter
End For
```

In this loop, the starting value of the counter variable is 0, and its ending value is 100. The Step clause specifies a step value of 10, which means that 10 is added to the counter variable at the end of each iteration. During the first iteration, counter is 0, during the second iteration, counter is 10, during the third iteration, counter is 20, and so forth.

The pseudocode in Program 15-10 gives another demonstration. The program displays all of the odd numbers from 1 through 11.

PROGRAM 15-10

```
 1 // Declare a counter variable
 2 Declare Integer counter
 3
 4 // Constant for the maximum value
 5 Constant Integer MAX_VALUE = 11
 6
 7 // Display the odd numbers from 1 through 11.
 8 For counter = 1 To MAX_VALUE Step 2
 9    Display counter
10 End While
```

Program Output

```
1
3
5
7
9
11
```

In the Spotlight:

Designing a
Count-Controlled
Loop with the For
Statement

Your friend Amanda just inherited a European sports car from her uncle. Amanda lives in the United States, and she is afraid she will get a speeding ticket because the car's speedometer works in kilometers per hour. She has asked you to write a program that displays a table of speeds in kilometers per hour with their values converted to miles per hour. The formula for converting kilometers per hour to miles per hour is:

$$MPH = KPH * 0.6214$$

In the formula, MPH is the speed in miles per hour and KPH is the speed in kilometers per hour.

The table that your program displays should show speeds from 60 kilometers per hour through 130 kilometers per hour, in increments of 10, along with their values converted to miles per hour. The table should look something like this:

KPH	MPH
60	37.284
70	43.498
80	49.712
etc. . . .	
130	80.782

After thinking about this table of values, you decide that you will write a For loop that uses a counter variable to hold the kilometer-per-hour speeds. The counter's starting value will be 60, its ending value will be 130, and a step value of 10 will be used. Inside the loop you will use the counter variable to calculate a speed in miles-per-hour. Program 15–11 shows the pseudocode for the program, and Figure 15–16 shows a flowchart.

PROGRAM 15–11

```
1 // Declare variables to hold speeds in MPH and KPH.
2 Declare Real mph
3 Declare Integer kph
4
5 // Display the table headings.
6 Display "KPH", Tab, "MPH"
7 Display "--------------------"
8
9 // Display the speeds.
10 For kph = 60 To 130 Step 10
11    // Calculate the miles-per-hour.
12    Set mph = kph * 0.6214
13
14    // Display KPH and MPH.
15    Display kph, Tab, mph
16 End For
```

Program Output

KPH	MPH
60	37.284
70	43.498
80	49.712
90	55.926
100	62.14
110	68.354
120	74.568
130	80.782

Notice that a variable named kph is used as the counter. Until now we have used the name counter for our counter variables. In this program, however, kph is a better name for the counter because it will hold speeds in kilometers-per-hour.

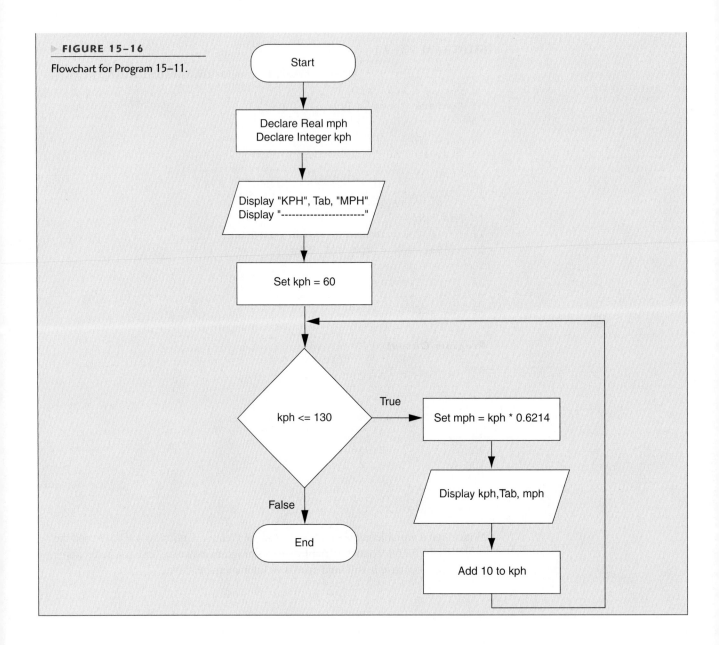

Counting Backward by Decrementing the Counter Variable

Although the counter variable is usually incremented in a count-controlled loop, you can alternatively decrement the counter variable. To *decrement* a variable means to decrease its value. In a For statement, you specify a negative step value to decrement the counter variable. For example, look at the following loop:

```
For counter = 10 To 1 Step -1
    Display counter
End For
```

In this loop, the starting value of the counter variable is 10, and its ending value is 1. The step value is –1, which means that 1 is subtracted from counter at the end of each iteration. During the first iteration, counter is 10; during the second iteration, counter is 9; and so forth. If this were an actual program, it would display the numbers 10, 9, 8, and so forth, down to 1.

Letting the User Control the Number of Iterations

In many cases, the programmer knows the exact number of iterations that a loop must perform. For example, recall Program 15–9, which displays a table showing the numbers 1 through 10 and their squares. When the pseudocode was written, the programmer knew that the loop had to iterate 10 times. A constant named MAX_VALUE was initialized with the value 10, and the loop was written as follows:

```
For counter = 1 To MAX_VALUE
```

As a result, the loop iterates exactly 10 times. Sometimes, however, the programmer needs to let the user decide the number of times that a loop should iterate. For example, what if you want Program 15–9 to be a bit more versatile by allowing the user to specify the maximum value displayed by the loop? The pseudocode in Program 15–12 shows how you can accomplish this.

PROGRAM 15–12

```
 1 // Variables
 2 Declare Integer counter, square, upperLimit
 3
 4 // Get the upper limit.
 5 Display "This program displays numbers, starting at 1,"
 6 Display "and their squares. How high should I go?"
 7 Input upperLimit
 8
 9 // Display table headings.
10 Display "Number", Tab, "Square"
11 Display "----------------------"
12
13 // Display the numbers and their squares.
14 For counter = 1 To upperLimit
15     // Calculate number squared.
16     Set square = counter^2
17
18     // Display number and number squared.
19     Display counter, Tab, square
20 End For
```

Program Output

```
This program displays numbers, starting at 1,
and their squares. How high should I go?
5 [Enter]
Number          Square
----------------------
1               1
2               4
3               9
4               16
5               25
```

Lines 5 and 6 ask the user how high the numbers in the table should go, and the statement in line 7 stores the user's input in the upperLimit variable. Then, the For loop uses the upperLimit variable as the counter's ending value:

```
For counter = 1 To upperLimit
```

As a result, the counter variable starts with 1, and ends with the value in upperLimit. In addition to specifying the counter's ending value, you can also specify its starting value. The pseudocode in Program 15–13 shows an example. In this program, the user specifies both the starting value and the ending value of the numbers displayed in the table. Notice that in line 20 the For loop uses variables to specify both the starting and ending values of the counter variable.

PROGRAM 15–13

```
1 // Variables
2 Declare Integer counter, square,
3       lowerLimit, upperLimit
4
5 // Get the lower limit.
6 Display "This program displays numbers and"
7 Display "their squares. What number should"
8 Display "I start with?"
9 Input lowerLimit
10
11 // Get the upper limit.
12 Display "What number should I end with?"
13 Input upperLimit
14
15 // Display table headings.
16 Display "Number", Tab, "Square"
17 Display "--------------------"
18
19 // Display the numbers and their squares.
20 For counter = lowerLimit To upperLimit
21    // Calculate number squared.
22    Set square = counter^2
23
24    // Display number and number squared.
25    Display counter, Tab, square
26 End For
```

Program Output

```
This program displays numbers and
their squares. What number should
I start with?
3 [Enter]
What number should I end with?
7 [Enter]
Number              Square
--------------------
3                   9
4                   16
5                   25
6                   36
7                   49
```

Designing a Count-Controlled While Loop

In most situations, it is best to use the For statement to write a count-controlled loop. Most languages, however, make it possible to use any looping mechanism to create a count-controlled loop. For example, you can create a count-controlled While loop, a count-controlled Do-While loop, or a count-controlled Do-Until loop. Regardless of the type of mechanism that you use, all count-controlled loops perform an initialization, test, and increment operation on a counter variable.

In pseudocode, you can use the following general format to write a count-controlled While loop:

① Declare Integer counter = *startingValue* ⟵——— Initialize a counter variable to the starting value.

② While counter <= *maxValue* ⟵——— Compare the counter to the maximum value.
        statement
        statement
        statement

③   Set counter = counter + 1 ⟵——— Add 1 to the counter variable during each iteration.
    End While

The ①, ②, and ③ callouts show where the initialization, test, and increment actions are performed.

① shows the declaration of an Integer variable that will be used as the counter. The variable is initialized with the appropriate starting value.

② shows where the While loop tests the expression counter <= *maxValue*. In this general format, *maxValue* is the maximum value that the counter variable can be set to.

③ shows where 1 is added to the counter variable. In a While loop, the counter variable will not automatically be incremented. You have to explicitly write a statement that performs this action. It's important that you understand how this statement works, so let's take a closer look at it:

        Set counter = counter + 1

This is how the statement would be executed by the computer: first, the computer would get the value of the expression on the right side of the = operator, which is counter + 1. Then, that value would be assigned to the counter variable. The effect of the statement is that 1 is added to the counter variable.

The pseudocode in Program 15–14 shows an example of a count-controlled While loop. This program follows the same logic that you previously saw in Figure 15–13, and displays "Hello world" five times. Figure 15–17 points out where the counter variable's initialization, test, and increment occur in the pseudocode.

> **WARNING**
>
> If you forget to increment the counter variable in a count-controlled While loop, the loop will iterate an infinite number of times.

PROGRAM 15–14

```
 1  // Declare and initialize a counter variable.
 2  Declare Integer counter = 1
 3
 4  // Constant for the maximum value
 5  Constant Integer MAX_VALUE = 5
 6
 7  While counter <= MAX_VALUE
 8      Display "Hello world"
 9      Set counter = counter + 1
10  End While
```

Program Output

```
Hello world
Hello world
Hello world
Hello world
Hello world
```

▶ **FIGURE 15–17**

The initialization, test, and increment of the counter variable.

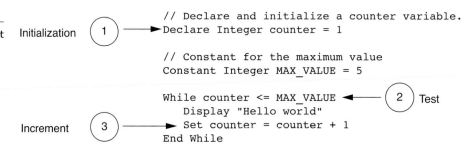

```
                            // Declare and initialize a counter variable.
Initialization    1  ────► Declare Integer counter = 1

                            // Constant for the maximum value
                            Constant Integer MAX_VALUE = 5

                            While counter <= MAX_VALUE  ◄────  2   Test
                                Display "Hello world"
Increment         3  ────►      Set counter = counter + 1
                            End While
```

The pseudocode in Program 15–15 shows another example. This program produces the same output that was produced by Program 15–9: the numbers 1 through 10 and their squares. The flowchart that you previously saw in Figure 15–15 shows the logic of this program.

PROGRAM 15–15

```
 1 // Variables
 2 Declare Integer counter = 1
 3 Declare Integer square
 4
 5 // Constant for the maximum value
 6 Constant Integer MAX_VALUE = 10
 7
 8 // Display table headings.
 9 Display "Number", Tab, "Square"
10 Display "---------------------"
11
12 // Display the numbers 1 through 10 and
13 // their squares.
14 While counter <= MAX_VALUE
15     // Calculate the square of a number.
16     Set square = counter^2
17
18     // Display the number and its square.
19     Display counter, Tab, square
20
21     // Increment counter.
22     Set counter = counter + 1
23 End While
```

Program Output

```
Number          Square
----------------------
1                 1
2                 4
3                 9
4                16
5                25
6                36
7                49
8                64
9                81
10              100
```

Incrementing by Values Other Than 1

In Programs 15–14 and 15–15 the counter variable is incremented by 1 during each loop iteration, with a statement such as this:

```
Set counter = counter + 1
```

This statement can be easily modified to increment the counter variable by values other than 1. For example, you could add 2 to the counter variable with the following statement:

```
Set counter = counter + 2
```

The pseudocode in Program 15–16 demonstrates how you can use this statement in a count-controlled While loop. The program displays all of the odd numbers from 1 through 11.

PROGRAM 15–16

```
 1 // Declare a counter variable
 2 Declare Integer counter = 1
 3
 4 // Constant for the maximum value
 5 Constant Integer MAX_VALUE = 11
 6
 7 // Display the odd numbers from 1
 8 // through 11.
 9 While counter <= MAX_VALUE
10    Display counter
11    Set counter = counter + 2
12 End While
```

Program Output

```
1
3
5
7
9
11
```

Counting Backward by Decrementing

Previously you saw how a negative step value can be used to decrement the counter variable in a For statement. In a count-controlled While loop, you decrement the counter variable with a statement such as the following:

```
Set counter = counter - 1
```

This statement subtracts one from the counter variable. If the counter variable is set to the value 5 before this statement executes, it will be set to 4 after the statement executes. The pseudocode in Program 15–17 demonstrates how you can use this statement in a While loop. The program counts backward from 10 down to 1.

PROGRAM 15–17

```
 1 // Declare a counter variable
 2 Declare Integer counter = 10
 3
 4 // Constant for the minimum value
 5 Constant Integer MIN_VALUE = 1
 6
 7 // Display a count-down.
 8 Display "And the countdown begins..."
 9 While counter >= MIN_VALUE
10     Display counter
11     Set counter = counter - 1
12 End While
13 Display "Blast off!"
```

Program Output

```
And the countdown begins...
10
9
8
7
6
5
4
3
2
1
Blast off!
```

Let's take a closer look at this program. Notice that line 11 subtracts 1 from the counter variable. Because we are counting backward, we have to reverse many parts of the logic. For example, in line 2 the counter variable must be initialized with the value 10 instead of 1. This is because 10 is the counter's starting value in this program. Also, in line 5 we create a constant to represent the counter's minimum value (which is 1) instead of the maximum value. Because we are counting down, we want the loop to stop when it reaches 1. Finally, notice that we are using the >= relational operator in line 9. In this program we want the loop to iterate as long as the counter is greater than or equal to 1. When the counter becomes less than 1, the loop should stop.

15–4 CALCULATING A RUNNING TOTAL

CONCEPT: A running total is a sum of numbers that accumulates with each iteration of a loop. The variable used to keep the running total is called an accumulator.

Many programming tasks require you to calculate the total of a series of numbers. For example, suppose you are writing a program that calculates a business's total sales for a week. The program would read the sales for each day as input and calculate the total of those numbers.

Programs that calculate the total of a series of numbers typically use two elements:

- A loop that reads each number in the series.

- A variable that accumulates the total of the numbers as they are read.

The variable that is used to accumulate the total of the numbers is called an accumulator. It is often said that the loop keeps a running total because it accumulates the total as it reads each number in the series. Figure 15–18 shows the general logic of a loop that calculates a running total.

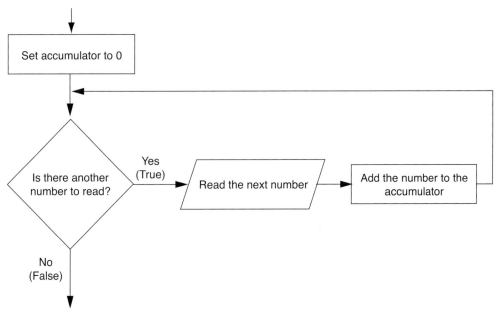

▲ **FIGURE 15–18**

Logic for calculating a running total.

When the loop finishes, the accumulator will contain the total of the numbers that were read by the loop. Notice that the first step in the flowchart is to set the accumulator variable to 0. This is a critical step. Each time the loop reads a number, it adds it to the accumulator. If the accumulator starts with any value other than 0, it will not contain the correct total when the loop finishes.

Let's look at the design of a program that calculates a running total. The pseudocode shown in Program 15–18 allows the user to enter five numbers, and it displays the total of the numbers entered.

PROGRAM 15–18

```
 1 // Declare a variable to hold each number
 2 // entered by the user.
 3 Declare Integer number
 4
 5 // Declare an accumulator variable,
 6 // initialized with 0.
 7 Declare Integer total = 0
 8
 9 // Declare a counter variable for the loop.
10 Declare Integer counter
11
12 // Explain what we are doing.
13 Display "This program calculates the"
14 Display "total of five numbers."
15
16 // Get five numbers and accumulate them.
17 For counter = 1 To 5
18    Display "Enter a number."
19    Input number
20    Set total = total + number
21 End For
22
23 // Display the total of the numbers.
24 Display "The total is ", total
```

Program Output (with Input Shown in Bold)

```
This program calculates the
total of five numbers.
Enter a number.
2 [Enter]
Enter a number.
4 [Enter]
Enter a number.
6 [Enter]
Enter a number.
8 [Enter]
Enter a number.
10 [Enter]
The total is 30
```

First, let's look at the variable declarations. The number variable, declared in line 3, will be used to hold a number entered by the user. The total variable, declared in line 7, is the accumulator. Notice that it is initialized with the value 0. The counter variable, declared in line 10, will be used as a counter by the loop.

The For loop, in lines 17 through 21, does the work of getting the numbers from the user and calculating their total. Line 18 prompts the user to enter a number, and line 19 gets the user's input and stores it in the number variable. Then, the following statement in line 20 adds number to total:

```
Set total = total + number
```

After this statement executes, the value in the number variable will be added to the value in the total variable. When the loop finishes, the total variable will hold the sum of all the numbers that were added to it. This value is displayed in line 24. Figure 15–19 shows a flowchart for the Program 15–18.

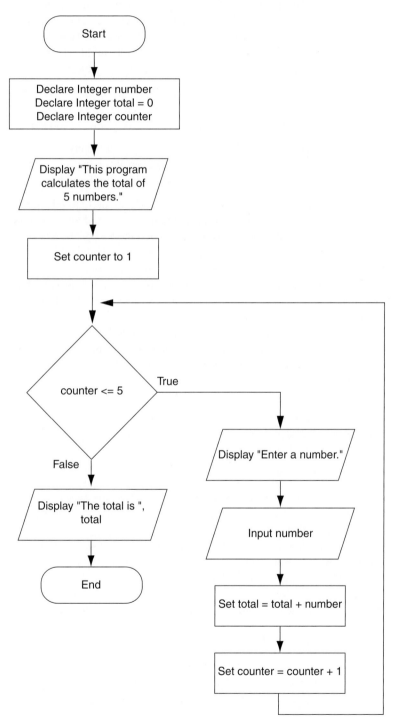

Flowchart for Program 15–18.

15-5 SENTINELS

CONCEPT: A sentinel is a special value that marks the end of a list of values.

Consider the following scenario: You are designing a program that will use a loop to process a long list of values. At the time you are designing the program, you do not know the number of values that will be in the list. In fact, the number of values in the list could be different each time the program is executed. What is the best way to design such a loop? Here are some techniques that you have seen already in this chapter, along with the disadvantages of using them when processing a long list of values:

- Simply ask the user, at the end of each loop iteration, if there is another value to process. If the list of values is long, however, asking this question at the end of each loop iteration might make the program cumbersome for the user.

- Ask the user at the beginning of the program how many items the list contains. This might also inconvenience the user, however. If the list is very long, and the user does not know the number of items in the list, it will require the user to count them.

When processing a long list of values with a loop, perhaps a better technique is to use a sentinel. A *sentinel* is a special value that marks the end of a list of items. When a program reads the sentinel value, it knows it has reached the end of the list, so the loop terminates. For example, suppose a doctor wants a program to calculate the average weight of all her patients. The program might work like this: A loop prompts the user to enter either a patient's weight, or 0 if are no more weights. When the program reads 0 as a weight, it interprets this as a signal that there are no more weights. The loop ends and the program displays the average weight.

A sentinel value must be unique enough that it will not be mistaken as a regular value in the list. In the example cited above, the doctor (or her medical assistant) enters 0 to signal the end of the list of weights. Because no patient's weight will be 0, this is a good value to use as a sentinel.

In the Spotlight:

Using a Sentinel

The county tax office calculates the annual taxes on property using the following formula:

$$Property\ Tax = Property\ Value \times 0.0065$$

Every day, a clerk in the tax office gets a list of properties and has to calculate the tax for each property on the list. You have been asked to design a program that the clerk can use to perform these calculations.

In your interview with the tax clerk, you learn that each property is assigned a lot number, and all lot numbers are 1 or greater. You decide to write a loop that uses the number 0 as a sentinel value. During each loop iteration, the program will ask the clerk to enter either a property's lot number, or 0 to end. Program 15–19 shows the pseudocode for the program, and Figure 15–20 shows a flowchart.

PROGRAM 15-19

```
1 Module main()
2     // Local variable for the lot number
3     Declare Integer lotNumber
4
5     // Get the first lot number.
6     Display "Enter the property's lot number"
7     Display "(or enter 0 to end)."
8     Input lotNumber
```

```
 9
10      // Continue processing as long as the user
11      // does not enter lot number 0.
12      While lotNumber != 0
13          // Show the tax for the property.
14          Call showTax()
15
16          // Get the next lot number.
17          Display "Enter the lot number for the"
18          Display "next property (or 0 to end)."
19          Input lotNumber
20      End While
21 End Module
22
23 // The showTax module gets a property's
24 // value and displays its tax.
25 Module showTax()
26      // Local variables
27      Declare Real propertyValue, tax
28
29      // Constant for the tax factor.
30      Constant Real TAX_FACTOR = 0.0065
31
32      // Get the property's value.
33      Display "Enter the property's value."
34      Input propertyValue
35
36      // Calculate the property's tax.
37      Set tax = propertyValue * TAX_FACTOR
38
39      // Display the tax.
40      Display "The property's tax is $", tax
41 End Module
```

Program Output (with Input Shown in Bold)

```
Enter the property's lot number
(or enter 0 to end).
417 [Enter]
Enter the property's value.
100000 [Enter]
The property's tax is $650
Enter the lot number for the
next property(or 0 to end).
692 [Enter]
Enter the property's value.
60000 [Enter]
The property's tax is $390
Enter the lot number for the
next property(or 0 to end).
0 [Enter]
```

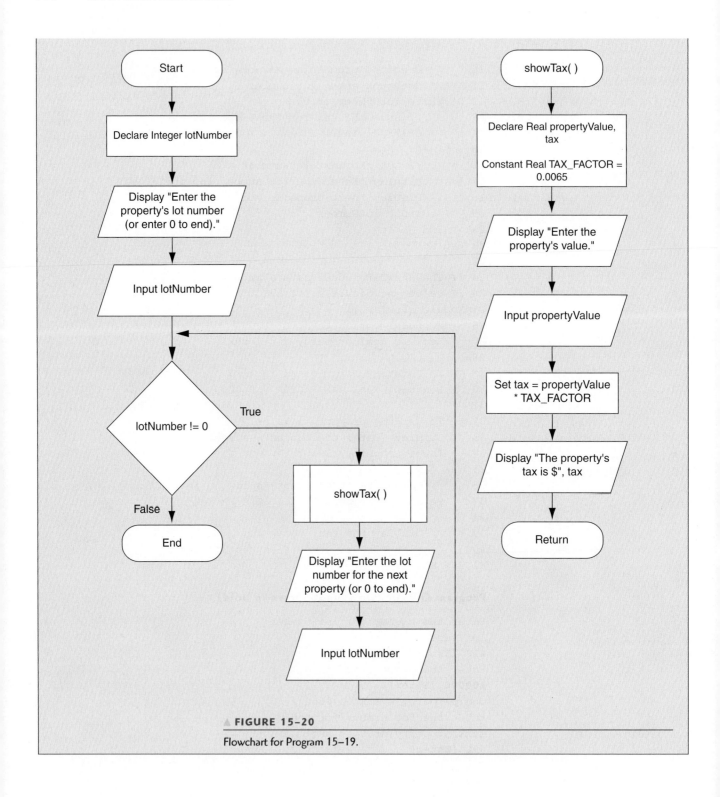

▲ FIGURE 15-20

Flowchart for Program 15–19.

15-6 NESTED LOOPS

CONCEPT: A loop that is inside another loop is called a nested loop.

A nested loop is a loop that is inside another loop. A clock is a good example of something that works like a nested loop. The second hand, minute hand, and hour hand all spin around the face of the clock. The hour hand, however, only makes 1 revolution for every 12 of the minute hand's revolutions. And it takes 60 revolutions of the second hand for the minute hand to make 1 revolution. This means that for every complete revolution of the hour hand, the second hand has revolved 720 times. Here is pseudocode with a loop that partially simulates a digital clock. It displays the seconds from 0 to 59:

```
Declare Integer seconds
For seconds = 0 To 59
    Display seconds
End For
```

We can add a `minutes` variable and nest the loop above inside another loop that cycles through 60 minutes:

```
Declare Integer minutes, seconds
For minutes = 0 To 59
    For seconds = 0 To 59
        Display minutes, ":", seconds
    End For
End For
```

To make the simulated clock complete, another variable and loop can be added to count the hours:

```
Declare Integer hours, minutes, seconds
For hours = 0 To 23
    For minutes = 0 To 59
        For seconds = 0 To 59
            Display hours, ":", minutes, ":", seconds
        End For
    End For
End For
```

If this were a real program, its output would be:

```
0:0:0
0:0:1
0:0:2
```

(The program will count through each second of 24 hours.)

```
23:59:59
```

The innermost loop will iterate 60 times for each iteration of the middle loop. The middle loop will iterate 60 times for each iteration of the outermost loop. When the outermost loop has iterated 24 times, the middle loop will have iterated 1,440 times and the innermost loop will have iterated 86,400 times! Figure 15–21 shows a flowchart for the complete clock simulation program previously shown.

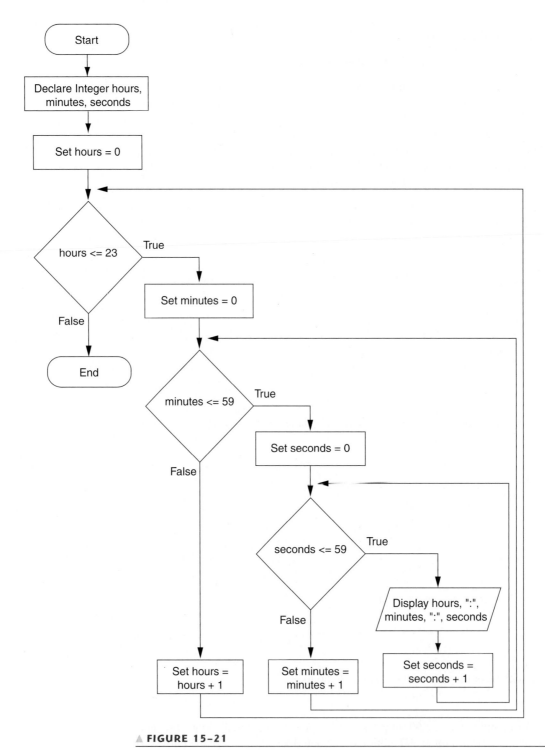

▲ FIGURE 15-21

Flowchart for a clock simulator.

The simulated clock example brings up a few points about nested loops:

■ An inner loop goes through all of its iterations for every single iteration of an outer loop.

■ Inner loops complete their iterations faster than outer loops.

■ To get the total number of iterations of a nested loop, multiply the number of iterations of all the loops.

REVIEW QUESTIONS

Multiple Choice

1. A _____-controlled loop uses a true/false condition to control the number of times that it repeats.

    (a) Boolean

    (b) condition

    (c) decision

    (d) count

2. A _____-controlled loop repeats a specific number of times.

    (a) Boolean

    (b) condition

    (c) decision

    (d) count

3. Each repetition of a loop is known as a(n) _____.

    (a) cycle

    (b) revolution

    (c) orbit

    (d) iteration

4. The While loop is a _____ type of loop.

    (a) pretest

    (b) posttest

    (c) prequalified

    (d) post iterative

5. The Do-While loop is a _____ type of loop.

    (a) pretest

    (b) posttest

    (c) prequalified

    (d) post iterative

6. The For loop is a _____ type of loop.

    (a) pretest

    (b) posttest

    (c) prequalified

    (d) post iterative

7. A(n) _____ loop has no way of ending and repeats until the program is interrupted.

    (a) indeterminate

    (b) interminable

    (c) infinite

    (d) timeless

8. A _____ loop always executes at least once.

    (a) pretest

    (b) posttest

    (c) condition-controlled

    (d) count-controlled

9. A(n) _____ variable keeps a running total.

    (a) sentinel

    (b) sum

    (c) total

    (d) accumulator

10. A(n) _____ is a special value that signals when there are no more items from a list of items to be processed. This value cannot be mistaken as an item from the list.

    (a) sentinel

    (b) flag

    (c) signal

    (d) accumulator

True or False

1. A condition-controlled loop always repeats a specific number of times.

2. The While loop is a pretest loop.

3. The Do-While loop is a pretest loop.

4. You should not write code that modifies the contents of the counter variable in the body of a For loop.

5. You cannot display the contents of the counter variable in the body of a loop.

6. It is not possible to increment a counter variable by any value other than 1.

7. The following statement decrements the variable x: Set x = x - 1.

8. It is not necessary to initialize accumulator variables.

9. In a nested loop, the inner loop goes through all of its iterations for every single iteration of the outer loop.

10. To calculate the total number of iterations of a nested loop, add the number of iterations of all the loops.

Short Answer

1. Why should you indent the statements in the body of a loop?

2. Describe the difference between pretest loops and posttest loops.

3. What is a condition-controlled loop?

4. What is a count-controlled loop?

5. What three actions do count-controlled loops typically perform using the counter variable?

6. What is an infinite loop? Write the code for an infinite loop.

7. A For loop looks like what other loop in a flowchart?

8. Why is it critical that accumulator variables are properly initialized?

9. What is the advantage of using a sentinel?

10. Why must the value chosen for use as a sentinel be carefully selected?

Algorithm Workbench

1. Design a While loop that lets the user enter a number. The number should be multiplied by 10, and the result stored in a variable named product. The loop should iterate as long as product contains a value less than 100.

2. Design a Do-While loop that asks the user to enter two numbers. The numbers should be added and the sum displayed. The loop should ask the user if he or she wishes to perform the operation again. If so, the loop should repeat, otherwise it should terminate.

3. Design a For loop that displays the following set of numbers:

    0, 10, 20, 30, 40, 50 . . . 1000

4. Design a loop that asks the user to enter a number. The loop should iterate 10 times and keep a running total of the numbers entered.

5. Design a `For` loop that calculates the total of the following series of numbers:

$$\frac{1}{30} + \frac{2}{29} + \frac{3}{28} + ...\frac{30}{1}$$

6. Design a nested loop that displays 10 rows of # characters. There should be 15 # characters in each row.

7. Convert the `While` loop in the following code to a `Do-While` loop:

```
Declare Integer x = 1
While x > 0
    Display "Enter a number."
    Input x
End While
```

8. Convert the `Do-While` loop in the following code to a `While` loop:

```
Declare String sure
Do
    Display "Are you sure you want to quit?"
    Input sure
While sure != "Y" AND sure != "y"
```

9. Convert the following `While` loop to a `For` loop:

```
Declare Integer count = 0
While count < 50
    Display "The count is ", count
    Set count = count + 1
End While
```

10. Convert the following `For` loop to a `While` loop:

```
Declare Integer count
For count = 1 To 50
    Display count
End For
```

Programming Exercises

1. **Bug Collector**

   A bug collector collects bugs every day for seven days. Design a program that keeps a running total of the number of bugs collected during the seven days. The loop should ask for the number of bugs collected for each day, and when the loop is finished, the program should display the total number of bugs collected.

2. **Calories Burned**

   Running on a particular treadmill you burn 3.9 calories per minute. Design a program that uses a loop to display the number of calories burned after 10, 15, 20, 25, and 30 minutes.

3. **Budget Analysis**

   Design a program that asks the user to enter the amount that he or she has budgeted for a month. A loop should then prompt the user to enter each of his or her expenses for the month, and keep a running total. When the loop finishes, the program should display the amount that the user is over or under budget.

4. **Distance Traveled**

The distance a vehicle travels can be calculated as follows:

$$Distance = Speed \times Time$$

For example, if a train travels 40 miles per hour for three hours, the distance traveled is 120 miles. Design a program that asks the user for the speed of a vehicle (in miles per hour) and how many hours it has traveled. It should then use a loop to display the distance the vehicle has traveled for each hour of that time period. Here is an example of the output:

```
What is the speed of the vehicle in mph? 40 [Enter]
How many hours has it traveled? 3 [Enter]
Hour    Distance Traveled
_____

1        40
2        80
3        120
```

5. **Average Rainfall**

Design a program that uses nested loops to collect data and calculate the average rainfall over a period of years. The program should first ask for the number of years. The outer loop will iterate once for each year. The inner loop will iterate twelve times, once for each month. Each iteration of the inner loop will ask the user for the inches of rainfall for that month. After all iterations, the program should display the number of months, the total inches of rainfall, and the average rainfall per month for the entire period.

6. **Centigrade to Fahrenheit Table**

Design a program that displays a table of the centigrade temperatures 0 through 20 and their Fahrenheit equivalents. The formula for converting a temperature from centigrade to Fahrenheit is

$$F = \frac{9}{5}C + 32$$

where F is the Fahrenheit temperature and C is the centigrade temperature. Your program must use a loop to display the table.

7. **Pennies for Pay**

Design a program that calculates the amount of money a person would earn over a period of time if his or her salary is one penny the first day, two pennies the second day, and continues to double each day. The program should ask the user for the number of days. Display a table showing what the salary was for each day, and then show the total pay at the end of the period. The output should be displayed in a dollar amount, not the number of pennies.

8. **Largest and Smallest**

Design a program with a loop that lets the user enter a series of numbers. The user should enter –99 to signal the end of the series. After all the numbers have been entered, the program should display the largest and smallest numbers entered.

Appendix: Conversions

DECIMAL	BCD(8421)	OCTAL	BINARY	DECIMAL	BCD(8421)	OCTAL	BINARY	DECIMAL	BCD(8421)	OCTAL	BINARY
0	0000	0	0	34	00110100	42	100010	68	01101000	104	1000100
1	0001	1	1	35	00110101	43	100011	69	01101001	105	1000101
2	0010	2	10	36	00110110	44	100100	70	01110000	106	1000110
3	0011	3	11	37	00110111	45	100101	71	01110001	107	1000111
4	0100	4	100	38	00111000	46	100110	72	01110010	110	1001000
5	0101	5	101	39	00111001	47	100111	73	01110011	111	1001001
6	0110	6	110	40	01000000	50	101000	74	01110100	112	1001010
7	0111	7	111	41	01000001	51	101001	75	01110101	113	1001011
8	1000	10	1000	42	01000010	52	101010	76	01110110	114	1001100
9	1001	11	1001	43	01000011	53	101011	77	01110111	115	1001101
10	00010000	12	1010	44	01000100	54	101100	78	01111000	116	1001110
11	00010001	13	1011	45	01000101	55	101101	79	01111001	117	1001111
12	00010010	14	1100	46	01000110	56	101110	80	10000000	120	1010000
13	00010011	15	1101	47	01000111	57	101111	81	10000001	121	1010001
14	00010100	16	1110	48	01001000	60	110000	82	10000010	122	1010010
15	00010101	17	1111	49	01001001	61	110001	83	10000011	123	1010011
16	00010110	20	10000	50	01010000	62	110010	84	10000100	124	1010100
17	00010111	21	10001	51	01010001	63	110011	85	10000101	125	1010101
18	00011000	22	10010	52	01010010	64	110100	86	10000110	126	1010110
19	00011001	23	10011	53	01010011	65	110101	87	10000111	127	1010111
20	00100000	24	10100	54	01010100	66	110110	88	10001000	130	1011000
21	00100001	25	10101	55	01010101	67	110111	89	10001001	131	1011001
22	00100010	26	10110	56	01010110	70	111000	90	10010000	132	1011010
23	00100011	27	10111	57	01010111	71	111001	91	10010001	133	1011011
24	00100100	30	11000	58	01011000	72	111010	92	10010010	134	1011100
25	00100101	31	11001	59	01011001	73	111011	93	10010011	135	1011101
26	00100110	32	11010	60	01100000	74	111100	94	10010100	136	1011110
27	00100111	33	11011	61	01100001	75	111101	95	10010101	137	1011111
28	00101000	34	11100	62	01100010	76	111110	96	10010110	140	1100000
29	00101001	35	11101	63	01100011	77	111111	97	10010111	141	1100001
30	00110000	36	11110	64	01100100	100	1000000	98	10011000	142	1100010
31	00110001	37	11111	65	01100101	101	1000001	99	10011001	143	1100011
32	00110010	40	100000	66	01100110	102	1000010				
33	00110011	41	100001	67	01100111	103	1000011				

Appendix: Powers of Two

2^n	n	2^{-n}
1	0	1.0
2	1	0.5
4	2	0.25
8	3	0.125
16	4	0.062 5
32	5	0.031 25
64	6	0.015 625
128	7	0.007 812 5
256	8	0.003 906 25
512	9	0.001 953 125
1 024	10	0.000 976 562 5
2 048	11	0.000 488 281 25
4 096	12	0.000 244 140 625
8 192	13	0.000 122 070 312 5
16 384	14	0.000 061 035 156 25
32 768	15	0.000 030 517 578 125
65 536	16	0.000 015 258 789 062 5
131 072	17	0.000 007 629 394 531 25
262 144	18	0.000 003 814 697 265 625
524 288	19	0.000 001 907 348 632 812 5
1 048 576	20	0.000 000 953 674 316 406 25
2 097 152	21	0.000 000 476 837 158 203 125
4 194 304	22	0.000 000 238 418 579 101 562 5
8 388 608	23	0.000 000 119 209 289 550 781 25
16 777 216	24	0.000 000 059 604 644 775 390 625
33 554 432	25	0.000 000 029 802 322 387 695 312 5
67 108 864	26	0.000 000 014 901 161 193 847 656 25
134 217 728	27	0.000 000 007 450 580 596 923 828 125
268 435 456	28	0.000 000 003 725 290 298 461 914 062 5
536 870 912	29	0.000 000 001 862 645 149 230 957 031 25
1 073 741 824	30	0.000 000 000 931 322 574 615 478 515 625
2 147 483 648	31	0.000 000 000 465 661 287 307 739 257 812 5
4 294 967 296	32	0.000 000 000 232 830 643 653 869 628 906 25
8 589 934 592	33	0.000 000 000 116 415 321 826 934 814 453 125
17 179 869 184	34	0.000 000 000 058 207 660 913 467 407 226 562 5
34 359 738 368	35	0.000 000 000 029 103 830 456 733 703 613 281 25
68 719 476 736	36	0.000 000 000 014 551 915 228 366 851 806 640 625
137 438 953 472	37	0.000 000 000 007 275 957 614 183 425 903 320 312 5
274 877 906 944	38	0.000 000 000 003 637 978 807 091 712 951 660 156 25
549 755 813 888	39	0.000 000 000 001 818 989 403 545 856 475 830 078 125
1 099 511 627 776	40	0.000 000 000 000 909 494 701 772 928 237 915 039 062 5
2 199 023 255 552	41	0.000 000 000 000 454 747 350 886 464 118 957 519 531 25
4 398 046 511 104	42	0.000 000 000 000 227 373 675 443 232 059 478 759 765 625
8 796 093 022 208	43	0.000 000 000 000 113 686 837 721 616 029 739 379 882 812 5
17 592 186 044 416	44	0.000 000 000 000 056 843 418 860 808 014 869 689 941 406 25
35 184 372 088 832	45	0.000 000 000 000 028 421 709 430 404 007 434 844 970 703 125
70 368 744 177 664	46	0.000 000 000 000 014 210 854 715 202 003 717 422 485 351 562 5
140 737 488 355 328	47	0.000 000 000 000 007 105 427 357 601 001 858 711 242 675 781 25
281 474 976 710 656	48	0.000 000 000 000 003 552 713 678 800 500 929 355 621 337 890 625
562 949 953 421 312	49	0.000 000 000 000 001 776 356 839 400 250 464 677 810 668 945 312 5
1 125 899 906 842 624	50	0.000 000 000 000 000 888 178 419 700 125 232 338 905 334 472 656 25
2 251 799 813 685 248	51	0.000 000 000 000 000 444 089 209 850 062 616 169 452 667 236 328 125
4 503 599 627 370 496	52	0.000 000 000 000 000 222 044 604 925 031 308 084 726 333 618 164 062 5
9 007 199 254 740 992	53	0.000 000 000 000 000 111 022 302 462 515 654 042 363 166 809 082 031 25
18 014 398 509 481 984	54	0.000 000 000 000 000 055 511 151 231 257 827 021 181 583 404 541 015 625
36 028 797 018 963 968	55	0.000 000 000 000 000 027 755 575 615 628 913 510 590 791 702 270 507 812 5
72 057 594 037 927 936	56	0.000 000 000 000 000 013 877 787 807 814 456 755 295 395 851 135 253 906 25
144 115 188 075 855 872	57	0.000 000 000 000 000 006 938 893 903 907 228 377 647 697 925 567 626 953 125
288 230 376 151 711 744	58	0.000 000 000 000 000 003 469 446 951 953 614 188 823 848 962 783 813 476 562 5
576 460 752 303 423 488	59	0.000 000 000 000 000 001 734 723 475 976 807 094 411 924 481 391 906 738 281 25
1 152 921 504 606 846 976	60	0.000 000 000 000 000 000 867 361 737 988 403 547 205 962 240 695 953 369 140 625
2 305 843 009 213 693 952	61	0.000 000 000 000 000 000 433 680 868 994 201 773 602 981 120 347 976 684 570 312 5
4 611 686 018 427 387 904	62	0.000 000 000 000 000 000 216 840 434 497 100 886 801 490 560 173 988 342 285 156 25
9 223 372 036 854 775 808	63	0.000 000 000 000 000 000 108 420 217 248 550 443 400 745 280 086 994 171 142 578 125
18 446 744 073 709 551 616	64	0.000 000 000 000 000 000 054 210 108 624 275 221 700 372 640 043 497 085 571 289 062 5
36 893 488 147 419 103 232	65	0.000 000 000 000 000 000 027 105 054 312 137 610 850 186 320 021 748 542 785 644 531 25
73 786 976 294 838 206 464	66	0.000 000 000 000 000 000 013 552 527 156 088 805 425 093 160 010 874 271 392 822 265 625
147 573 952 589 676 412 928	67	0.000 000 000 000 000 000 006 776 263 578 034 402 712 546 580 005 437 135 696 411 132 812 5
295 147 905 179 352 825 856	68	0.000 000 000 000 000 000 003 388 131 789 017 201 356 273 290 002 718 567 848 205 566 406 25
590 295 810 358 705 651 712	69	0.000 000 000 000 000 000 001 694 065 894 508 600 678 136 645 001 359 283 924 102 783 203 125
1 180 591 620 717 411 303 424	70	0.000 000 000 000 000 000 000 847 032 947 254 300 339 068 322 500 679 641 962 051 391 601 562 5
2 361 183 241 434 822 606 848	71	0.000 000 000 000 000 000 000 423 516 473 627 150 169 534 161 250 339 820 981 025 695 800 781 25
4 722 366 482 869 645 213 696	72	0.000 000 000 000 000 000 000 211 758 236 813 575 084 767 080 625 169 910 490 512 847 900 390 625

Appendix: Flowchart Symbols

This page shows the flowchart symbols that are used in this book.

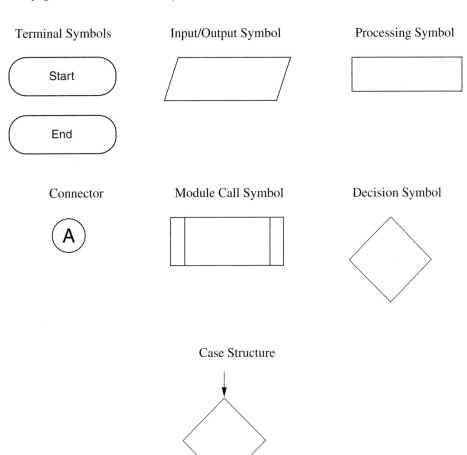

Terminal Symbols

Start

End

Input/Output Symbol

Processing Symbol

Connector

A

Module Call Symbol

Decision Symbol

Case Structure

1   2   3   Default

Index